OFFICE MAN

OFFICE MANAGEMENT

J. C. DENYER

ACIS, AHA, AMBIM, MIAM

Formerly Senior Lecturer in O & M at South-West London College
Formerly Examiner to Institute of Book-keepers and Related Data Processing

Fifth Edition

revised by

JOSEPHINE SHAW

MInstAM, MBIM, FBSC

Training Consultant for Management and Support Services
Part-time Moderator for the Business and Technician Education Council

Pitman

PITMAN PUBLISHING
128 Long Acre, London WC2E 9AN

A Division of Longman Group UK Limited

© Macdonald & Evans Ltd 1980

Fifth edition first published in Great Britain 1980
Reprinted 1983, 1986, 1989, 1990

ISBN 0 273 02589 9
ISE ISBN 0 273 02972 X

Text set in 10/11 pt Linotron 202 Bembo
Printed and bound in Singapore

Preface to previous editions

The ever-increasing size of business organisations has forced the development of new techniques in office management; the growth of mechanisation and the latest scientific methods of personnel selection and management are just two aspects of a subject growing rapidly more complex. One result of this has been that managing an office has become a specialist function; no longer can it be viewed as a side-line by any person occupying an administrative position.

This book is intended to be of value not only to students preparing for the various professional examinations, but also to those at present practising office management. To the latter class of readers, it may draw attention to those many aspects of office management which ought to receive attention but which often do not do so in practice.

The subject of office management remains as fascinating as ever, because of its breadth and constant development. With the continuing growth in office costs, it is hoped this revised edition will make some small contribution to greater efficiency in the office.

1959 and 1973   J. C. DENYER

Preface to the Fifth Edition

Since the first edition of *Office Management* was published in 1959 the face of office life has changed a great deal. Many of the items of equipment and procedures mentioned in that first edition as being "new" or "likely to become more popular in the future" are now standard features in many organisations. There is now a generation of young office workers who have no conception of an office without a copying machine, to whom ink duplicating is virtually unknown and to whom the idea of replying to a letter on the day it is received is novel and somewhat mystifying. Consequently there have been changes not only in the physical aspects of office life, but also in the conceptions and attitudes of office staff.

The office manager is more than ever a vital spoke in the wheel of administration. The function and role of office management is continually developing to take account of the vast growth in mechanisation, the changes mentioned above, the plethora of employment legislation and the growth and closer involvement of white-collar unions. Though the concept of the function has broadened, it is still essential that the office manager, perhaps more than any other specialist manager, should be aware of detail in procedures and systems. Consequently the detail in the fourth edition has been revised to bring it up to date. However, it should be pointed out that with the current speed of development in the field of electronic information and communications handling the student is bound to find that on-going research is essential if he or she is to keep up to date in this field.

Although the original edition of *Office Management* has been revised frequently it was felt that some rearrangement of the material was needed in this edition to reflect the change of emphasis in current office management practices. Mention is made of computer applications wherever appropriate. There is more emphasis on the management aspects, especially the management of staff, and on communications, which are the life-blood of administration. Some topics have been expanded, for example the section on print rooms which are now common in many organisations. Some of the detail of how machines work has been deleted because no book can adequately cover the vast range of machines available. The principles on which the various types of machines work are covered.

The case studies of previous editions have been deleted, the relevant content being incorporated in the text of the chapters. Questions have been brought together in an appendix. Many of the questions cover several aspects of office management and cannot be related to one specific chapter. For this reason the questions are grouped under section headings rather than chapter headings. The intention is to encourage students to think beyond the confines of one particular aspect of a topic. Some of the questions cannot be answered solely by reference to the text. Research may be needed and personal experience should be drawn upon.

The aims of the book are: (1) to provide a sound basis for the study of office management by students taking the various professional examinations; and (2) to provide a series of criteria by which practising administrative officers, office managers and office supervisors can assess their own performance.

Management of an office is, like any other type of management, essentially practical. No matter how hard and long a study of the subject is made the student will become a successful office manager only by practical application of the principles involved. Therefore study of material relevant to the examination syllabuses should be combined with practical experience or, at the very least, discussions with practising managers. They are the only people who can give real-life examples of the enormous variety of problems and situations that arise in any office, the innovative methods used to forestall and/or solve problems and the pitfalls in various types of organisation structure, systems, procedures and staff.

It has been a great responsibility to revise a well-known standard work by such an authority as Mr. Denyer was before his death in 1976. I have worked in the hope that he would have approved this revision and that students will gain as much from this edition as former students gained from earlier editions.

August 1980   J.S.

Contents

Acknowledgments

Many people have been involved in the revision of this book. I am grateful to them all for their interest, encouragement, realistic advice and practical help, without which the work could not have been completed. Many organisations, large and small, have contributed photographs, forms and diagrams. These are acknowledged in the captions. Professional institutes★ have allowed me to reproduce questions from examination papers (*see* Appendix I). The source of each question is indicated and I very much appreciate the co-operation of the institutes concerned.

I am especially grateful to the staff of the Post Office Telecommunications for much up to date information; to Iris Broom who took on the challenge of tracking down some of the most elusive information; to Margaret Holding, who nobly tackled endless typing and retyping; to Mr. R. H. Caldwell for much useful information on computers and their applications; and to my brother James Shaw for enlightening me on the niceties of job evaluation in practice and other management techniques. Finally I would like to record my deepest gratitude to my mother for "holding the fort" on all fronts during the two years the revision was in progress.

J.S.

★ Frequent reference is made in the book to the Institute of Administrative Management. The correct title is The Institute of Administrative Management.

x

PART ONE
THE OFFICE MANAGEMENT FUNCTION

1. The Purpose and Importance of Office Management

Introduction: definitions

The Offices, Shops and Railways Premises Act 1963 defines an office as "a building, or part of a building, the sole or principal use of which is as an office or for office purposes". The activities which may be included in the term "office purposes" include:

    (1) receiving and despatching mail;

    (2) sorting, storing and retrieving documents;

    (3) recording information by manual or machine processes (both statistical data and non-statistical information);

    (4) preparation of correspondence, reports, etc., in manuscript, by dictation, and/or on the typewriter;

    (5) production of correspondence, reports and other documents from manuscript and/or dictated material by typing or word processing;

    (6) reproduction of documents by duplicating or copying processes;

    (7) handling money;

    (8) telephone, telegram and telex operating;

    (9) extracting, collecting, analysing, collating and synthesising data and information;

    (10) storing and retrieving information by electronic processes.

The word "manage" means to "guide", and to have under command or control. The term "office management" implies therefore the guidance of the personnel who carry out the activities listed above, which must, of course, be controlled. It is important to realise that these various activities are carried on to a greater or lesser degree in all organisations regardless of the type of business,

1

structure of the organisation and its size. They may be related to the work of a company secretary, an accountant, a buyer, an engineer, or any other executive function in an organisation. The purpose and function of the office varies according to the size and nature of the business and the organisational structure, but it still has to be managed.

The role of the office

The office, any office, provides a service. If we consider the five main functions of an organisation, viz. finance, production, marketing, administration and data processing, and look back to the list of activities given above it will be realised that these activities can be related to the five functions. If the finance of a business is to be properly organised it is necessary to have staff to receive and check invoices for raw materials, equipment, etc. purchased, to carry out the procedures for payment, to raise invoices for goods sold, to pay the people working for the organisation, to obtain and produce data on which future plans can be drawn up by the board of directors, and to provide the financial information that managers need in order to make executive decisions. These are but a few of the activities which have to be performed by staff servicing the finance function.

In addition there are controlling activities which have to be carried out. When budgets have been drawn up and approved they must be adhered to, so the procedures involved in ensuring that expenditure is kept within the budget, i.e. budgetary control, are a part of the office service. Checking the credit rating of potential customers and ensuring that existing customers do not exceed their credit are other controlling activities.

Each of the other four main functions of an organisation has to be serviced and controlled in the same way. It follows that the office is complementary to the main purpose of the organisation whether that main purpose be the production of goods or of services, and whether on a profit-making or non-profit-making basis. It is important to realise that the office is subordinate to the main functions of the organisation for the following two reasons.

(1) The office must be organised and managed so as to ensure that the main functions can be fulfilled and corporate objectives can be met.

(2) The costs involved in running an office are non-productive and have a strong bearing on the economic viability of the organisation. Excessive non-productive costs can cause havoc in the market place!

The functions of the office

If we look again at the list of activities we can see that many of them are concerned with the handling of communications of various kinds. We have seen that the office complements and controls the main functions of an organisation. More precisely the office is the channel by which information flows into, out of and around the organisation. The various activities carried on in an office can be grouped into five main categories. These are receiving/retrieving, sorting/analysing, arranging, recording and transmitting information. If the work of any office, be it sales, purchasing, personnel or the office in the corner of a workshop, is analysed, it will be seen that some or all of these main functions are being carried on most of the time.

The management of the office

The basic principles of management apply to the management of an office in the same way as they apply to the management of a production line, sales, personnel or any other function of an organisation. Just as production management, personnel management, etc. are specialised applications of the principles of management, so has office management become a specialised application.

In the past the management of an office tended to involve little more than organisation of people to carry out fairly well-defined and universal procedures as accurately and quickly as possible. In the last few years office management has developed as a specialisation in its own right, partly because of the growth and development of trade and government services and partly because of the enormous increase in electronic machines, including computers, and their application to office procedures. Even in a small organisation, as yet hardly mechanised, electronic processing cannot be ignored. Inevitably the small concern will be dealing with larger organisations which are probably fully or partially computerised and the small concern's own systems must be geared to meet the demands of other organisations as well as internal demands. In any case, the most recent developments in word processors, mini-computers and programmed electronic calculators are bringing a certain amount of automation close to even the very small office.

As the function of the office and the various activities undertaken to fulfil it are studied in greater detail in the following chapters, the application of management principles will be discussed in the appropriate contexts. It is important to bear in mind that management of the office is essential whatever the size of the office, whatever the type of business, and whatever the structure of the organisation. The problems may vary to some extent, the techniques may be applied in different ways, the machines used may be larger or smaller models and more or less sophisticated, the number, type and calibre of staff may vary, but it is a question of difference in degree and approach and not a question of whether office management is necessary.

The development of the office as a vital part of the organisation

There is now in the United Kingdom a vast army of people who work in offices. Since the early 1950s the streamlining of systems and procedures by the practice of Organisation and Methods (commonly referred to as O & M, see Chapter 43) has not reduced the number, and even with the advent of electronic automation in the 1970s the numbers are still increasing. This has happened in spite of the fears of redundancy expressed even today by staff when the introduction of mechanisation and automation is mooted. There are several possible reasons for this situation, apart from the increase in government services and in legislation requiring additional staff to implement it. The following are two important factors.

(1) There is a greater need than ever before for tight control—of finance, of production, of security, of stock, to mention a few.

(2) The techniques of management have become more sophisticated and decisions made by senior managers are frequently far-reaching in their implications for the growth, and sometimes even the survival, of the organisation as a whole. Such decisions cannot be made without accurate, up-to-date, appropriate information. The senior manager is often not in a position to know what information he does need in order to consider all the implications of each possible course of action. He must rely on the office to produce all relevant information including both that which he asks for and that which he is unaware of but needs to consider in order to minimise the risks he must take in coming to conclusions and making decisions. The office therefore assumes a major role in the organisation as a producer of information relevant to various situations and circumstances.

Having made a decision and set in motion whatever tasks are involved, the senior manager relies on information to indicate progress. Planned progress must be monitored to ensure that it is adequate, in conjunction with other functions of the organisation, to meet the over-all objectives. Variations must be examined with the minimum delay to identify problems and enable adjustments to be made as quickly as possible so that planned progress can be resumed. This scrutinising of the information for variations is a vital procedure and has to be carried out quickly and remorselessly. A price increase of a halfpenny a unit on a bought-in item used in the production of some consumer product can completely upset the revenue forecasts for the year if it is not "picked up" until several batches of the item have been used. The breakdown of a machine in the plant resulting in loss of production of several thousand items can completely invalidate production forecasts and ruin the possibility of meeting sales forecasts. It is the business of the office to provide such information immediately and systems must be designed to meet this requirement.

The office is an all-invading entity in the organisation. It does not stand alone. It could be regarded as the heart of the organisation, pumping its life-blood throughout the system in the form of information. If the heart stops beating the organisation dies; if, as is more likely, it develops a murmur or a disease it slows the body down until it is no longer able to compete nationally or internationally with other bodies.

2. The Office Manager

The office manager is the pivot around which the office function revolves. Because of his importance in ensuring the efficiency of the service provided by the office we must examine his job and the qualities required to perform it in some detail.

Function

The office manager's function may be divided into two parts, namely ensuring that:

(1) the receipt/retrieval, sorting/analysing, recording, arranging and transmission of information is carried out efficiently so as to provide an accurate, comprehensive and up-to-date information service to senior management;

(2) the clerical procedures which form a necessary part of the organisation's functions in the process of meeting corporate objectives are carried out systematically with maximum accuracy and speed at minimum cost.

The scope of the office manager's job is very flexible, depending on, among other things, the size and structure of the organisation. His duties vary in different businesses, and even in different offices of the same organisation. The more office specialists there are in a business, the less onerous are the duties of any one office manager. For example, in an organisation where there is an O & M department constantly reviewing systems and the use of office machines, while the office manager is not relieved of the duty of controlling and understanding the new systems introduced, nevertheless his responsibilities are to some extent lightened.

It is also worth noting that an office manager's title may vary from one organisation to another. For example, in a large organisation an administrative officer may be fully responsible for certain major areas of office management. In a smaller organisation the administrative manager, responsible for the administration of the organisation as a whole, may well have the management of the office as a section of his responsibility. The office supervisor may well be an office manager, responsible for ensuring that his particular office plays its part efficiently in the over-all administration of the organisation.

Responsibilities

In order to fulfil his function the office manager has certain areas of responsibility. These include:

(1) the organisation of the office, i.e. planning how to achieve objectives, assessing and allocating resources;

(2) the systems and procedures of the office, i.e. designing the method by which objectives can be achieved—this includes determining the machines, equipment, supplies, etc. required;

(3) the personnel who carry out the procedures—determining the number, level, type, qualifications, personal qualities, and duties of the people required, and ensuring that they perform their job satisfactorily and cost-effectively;

(4) the environment of the office—the physical factors which affect the morale and performance of the personnel including such things as lighting, heating, ventilation, office layout, furniture suitable for the tasks to be performed, provision of adequate facilities such as cloakrooms, etc., tea and coffee service or vending machines.

All managerial responsibility revolves around the ability to get people to perform defined tasks to predetermined specification, i.e. to certain standards in accordance with a time schedule. The *human relations* aspect of an office manager's responsibilities is vital. Without people nothing can be achieved and without satisfactory job performance from all staff objectives cannot be met with maximum efficiency and cost-effectiveness. Managing people is, of course, the hardest part of any manager's job. It is relatively easy to organise systems, and indeed a system which looks beautiful on paper and in theory should work perfectly may well be a total failure because of poor staff management. Part Three of this book is devoted to this major area of office management.

Duties

As there is wide variation in the responsibilities of different office managers, so there is wide variation in the duties they are called upon to undertake. A list of duties which may be assigned to an office manager is given below. The list is divided into two groups, managerial duties and supervisory duties. Most office managers are likely to be required to undertake a selection from each group.

MANAGERIAL DUTIES
Duties in this category may include the following.

(1) To support and implement the policies of top management.

(2) To report problems which the office manager cannot solve alone, e.g. staffing difficulties which may need the assistance of the personnel department to solve.

(3) To review the systems and procedures to meet situations brought about by the implementation of policy decisions and other changes.

(4) To design and implement new systems and procedures including mail-handling and distribution procedures, telecommunications, and storage and retrieval of information.

(5) To implement/maintain work measurement as a means of ensuring that adequate staff are provided for the work-load; the redeployment of staff as a means of training and developing their potential, productivity and cost control.

(6) To interview staff for recruitment.

(7) To conduct staff appraisal interviews regularly and prepare reports making recommendations for promotions, salary increments, merit awards, etc.

(8) To consult union representatives/officials in relation to training, proposed changes in methods, productivity, etc.

(9) To deal with serious matters of indiscipline.

(10) To prepare estimates and ensure that budgets are adhered to.

(11) To purchase equipment when necessary.

(12) To organise/recommend appropriate training for subordinate staff.

SUPERVISORY DUTIES
The responsibility for supervision is likely to involve the following duties.

(13) To ensure that work is done to meet predetermined time-schedules and standards and that no delays occur because of sickness, annual holidays, etc.

(14) To exercise continuous control over quantity and quality of work, i.e. productivity and accuracy.

(15) To report arrears of work, acute work problems, staffing difficulties, unsatisfactory equipment, etc., so that even if the problems are solved they can be taken into consideration when

systems are monitored for possible changes aimed at improving efficiency.

(16) To ensure punctuality if office hours are fixed, or the observance of core time if flex time is established.

(17) To control the use of stationery and other supplies, the care and maintenance of equipment, and the use of the telephone.

(18) To recommend the purchase of equipment when required.

(19) To give on-the-job training to subordinate staff.

(20) To ensure that the office is in good order, i.e. clean, well organised and tidy.

The following specimen job specification illustrates the possible scope and variation in duties of an office manager.

JOB SPECIFICATION FOR AN OFFICE MANAGER

Taken from Appendix C(2) of *Training for Office Management*, published by the Department of Employment

Job title: Office Manager

Responsible to: Administrative Director

Job purpose: To ensure the effective and economical functioning of all the company's office services

Duties and responsibilities	Knowledge/skills required
(1) To ensure that adequate resources of personnel, equipment and facilities are available to meet the office requirements of the company.	Range and limits of personal responsibilities and authority—functional, financial and area.
(2) To ensure that the office resources of the company are used efficiently and as economically as possible.	Company policy and future plans, business organisation and functions.
(3) To advise company management on the office resources and methods needed to meet requirements, and how to employ these resources effectively.	Management principles and practices in relation to the office function, including sufficient knowledge of budgeting and costing to meet job needs.
	Methods of recording and analysing labour turnover; planning current and future requirements.
Activities	Recruitment and selection, recruitment sources, procedures, interviewing techniques, selection methods and criteria, use of selection tests.
(4) To carry out these duties and responsibilities, the Office Manager will need to be able to:	Industrial psychology, behaviour of individuals and groups of people at work, motivation, learning theory training methods, educational and training facilities.
(a) identify needs and priorities, and prepare forward estimates;	
(b) define methods and facilities to be used;	Communications: systems and methods, external and internal.
(c) estimate resources to meet needs, in terms of office space, personnel and equipment;	Employee remuneration, job descriptions, job analysis and job specifications, job evaluation, salary structures, appraisal schemes.
(d) prepare plans to meet requirements;	Terms of employment.
(e) prepare and submit proposals for expenditure;	Office organisation, legal requirements, layout, space allocation, furniture and equipment requirements, working conditions, reception arrangements, security including safeguarding
(f) prepare budget estimates and estimates for capital expenditure;	

Duties and responsibilities	Knowledge/skills required
(g) establish departmental budgets and office output targets;	office equipment and company information, office cleaning, machine maintenance. Systems
(h) establish office systems and procedures to meet company requirements for operational use, for control and management information;	and procedures, information processing theory, systems analysis, form design, information storage and retrieval, specific office functions.
(i) establish procedures to control expenditure against budgets, and output against targets;	Record keeping, statistical analysis, control of materials in use. Office machines and equipment including
(j) arrange recruitment and selection of suitable personnel to meet defined needs;	E.D.P. machinery and systems, P.O. facilities, computer bureaux, reprographic methods. Management services, organisation and
(k) arrange effective training and development procedures for office personnel, to meet present and future needs;	methods, operational research, clerical work measurement, work simplification. Output planning and control, inspection and quality control methods.
(l) establish effective two-way communication systems to meet the information requirements of the company, for both operational and personnel needs;	Planning, budgeting organising, co-ordinating, developing and controlling effectively. Setting objectives and priorities. Initiating, persuading, advising and deciding. Communicating at all levels with individuals and groups, verbally and in writing.
(m) establish and maintain formal and informal arrangements for staff consultation and for ensuring the safety, health and welfare of all office personnel;	Analysing and interpreting information and statistics. Advising on office methods and effectiveness.
(n) ensure a high state of efficiency and morale in the office function by clear directives to subordinates, defining responsibilities and co-ordination of duties, and effective co-operation between individuals and sections.	

Relationships

WITH TOP MANAGEMENT

The office manager is likely to be judged by top management on the basis of the efficiency with which he provides the information they need to make policy and executive decisions. His task of providing a service is complementary to their tasks of dealing with finance, producing products or services and marketing them. Without this information service and the administrative support which office management provides top managers would be lost. On the other hand, an inefficient service can be worse than no service at all. The frustrations and wrong decisions which result from inadequate, inaccurate or out-of-date information can be disastrous for the organisation's over-all performance. The office manager should therefore aim to achieve maximum understanding of the functions and objectives of top managers and to collaborate with them to ensure that the best possible service is provided.

WITH SUBORDINATES

The office manager is important because he *is* a part of management. He must see that the office work is done and that management policies are properly implemented. He is also important because, to his subordinates, he may be the only representative of management with whom they have daily contact. To a great extent the morale of the staff and their willingness to co-operate depend on him. He should help, advise and train subordinates and it may be true to say that the ultimate efficiency of the office depends very much on his efforts in these areas. He should recognise that his staff perform the work, and should take an interest in them and in the work they do. He should be the person to whom staff can turn for assistance, and he should encourage team spirit, and set a good example to staff.

The office manager has been called the "man in the middle". He has to face both ways—to represent the workers to management, and at the same time to represent management to the workers. His responsibility to provide the best possible service to management must not override his duty to his staff, or vice versa. A fine balance has to be established between these responsibilities.

WITH COLLEAGUES

Co-operation between colleagues should be standard practice. Unfortunately vested interests, empire building and lack of respect for another person's abilities are often the cause of personal friction which results in inefficiency. The office manager should be willing to co-operate with colleagues to the extent of transferring staff if it is of benefit to the organisation as a whole. He should ensure that there is good co-ordination at his own level, that office procedures follow common policies and that systems "dovetail" with one another.

QUALITIES REQUIRED

The office manager must have had the education, training and experience appropriate to the specialist nature of the job he is required to do. He must have the highest level of integrity and be honest and ethical in his dealings with everyone, both inside and outside the organisation. Because he is likely to be consulting and collaborating with people from all departments in the organisation he should have the ability to stand aside from "politics", to ignore interdepartmental friction and handle "situations" diplomatically.

The ability to delegate is fundamental to good management, i.e. the efficient running of the office, because this is only possible if the manager is able to get the best out of his staff. The *opportunity* to delegate depends on the manager's ability to recruit staff of the right calibre and to ensure that they are properly trained. It is indeed a derogation of his own managerial ability if he does not or is not able to delegate.

The qualities needed to manage people include professionalism, tact, kindliness, firmness, fairness, initiative, logical and objective thought processes, consideration for others, loyalty, integrity, honesty, poise, fluent verbal expression and precision (without being "finicky"), and the ability to inspire, guide and encourage. Perhaps the greatest managerial quality is "leadership", getting people to work as a team instead of as individuals. Teamwork is the key to departmental efficiency and is discussed in Chapter 16.

Techniques of office management

The way in which each of the office manager's responsibilities is fulfilled is likely to have a bearing on the efficiency with which the purpose of the office is achieved. Where a large staff is employed and where the business is very complicated, organisation may be the most vital factor. If the tasks are simple ones, installation of the best machines and provision of the most suitable environment may be of greatest value. If a proper balance is not maintained between these factors, i.e. if too much attention is given to one aspect, the other aspects will suffer. To give too much attention to machines and overlook the requirements of the human factors is as dangerous as to concentrate attention on the organisation of the office systems without due consideration of the best means by which they can be implemented.

Delegation has already been mentioned. Failure to delegate tasks may have serious repercussions, the most obvious of which is that the manager is so concerned with detail that he is unable to perform his proper function satisfactorily. Equally, failure to delegate the necessary authority to perform the tasks satisfactorily can only result in frustration and dissatisfaction on the part of subordinate staff. The manager can never delegate his responsibility but he can and must delegate tasks and adequate authority.

Paperwork has exploded to plague proportions in the last few years. This is partly because of the thirst for information for decision-making purposes and partly because of the ease with which documentation can now be produced. The production of paper for the sake of showing how much work the office can do, or the production of information for the sake of having it available in case it is needed, is bad management practice. O & M surveys have frequently revealed that much of the paper produced is not even

looked at by its recipients. It is often possible to reduce the number
of forms in a system by as much as two-thirds, after which the
work of the office has been performed more efficiently than
previously and also more effectively, because the right information
is given to the people who need it in the form in which they need it.

Systems and procedures should be as simple as possible. The
more complex a system becomes the more opportunities there are
usually for error, for misunderstanding and for delay, and the more
difficult it is to identify a problem and correct it.

Mechanisation and automation should be undertaken only after
the most careful investigations. The need for this change should be
firmly established before action is taken. Once a need for some
form of machine is established it is essential to spend time and effort
on finding the most suitable piece of equipment to meet the need
within the financial resources available. A decision to introduce
machines to handle work previously dealt with manually or to buy
more sophisticated machines invariably necessitates a review of
other factors. Systems and procedures may need to be revised; staff
may have to be retrained and/or redeployed; stocks of stationery
may become obsolete; and—vitally important—systems in other
offices/departments of the organisation may be affected.

The merits of centralisation and decentralisation may have to be
considered. There is no one set of arguments for or against
centralised or decentralised systems because the situation differs
completely from one organisation to another, and from one
department to another. The implications of centralisation and
decentralisation will be discussed in the context of individual
aspects of office management such as typewriting services, storage
and retrieval, in the appropriate chapters.

The office manager has at his disposal a wide range of techniques
with which to achieve his objectives. It is essential to realise,
however, that these techniques are developing rapidly and it is the
responsibility of the conscientious manager to keep up to date with
changes and the ways in which they can be utilised to improve the
efficiency of the office function.

PART TWO
OFFICE ORGANISATION

3. Organisation Structure

Introduction

In order to organise anything, whether it be an office, a task or a multinational company, it is necessary first to determine what the objectives are. What is the purpose of this particular office? Why is this task to be performed? What products/services is this multinational company to produce, for whom, in which market(s)? To meet the objectives certain work will have to be done involving a variety of activities. At this point organisation steps in.

Organisation is the arrangement of work by which the activities are divided among people or groups of people to whom *responsibilities, duties and authority* are allocated. This division of activities results in the creation of departments and sections which may be specialised, i.e. carrying out one particular type of activity, or may be concerned with a particular project or group of functional activities. The question of specialisation is discussed later in the chapter.

"Responsibilities" mean the area of work for which a person or group of people is accountable. For example, a departmental manager is responsible for co-ordinating the activities of the various sections in his department. "Duties" are the work requirements arising from the responsibilities. One of the duties of a typing-pool supervisor is to check the work of junior typists because the supervisor is responsible for the accuracy of the work even though it is typed by a subordinate. "Authority" means the right to make decisions and to take action. For example, a secretary may be given authority to sign orders up to a maximum of £550. She may also be given the authority to investigate anomalies on

15

orders or, on the other hand, she may have to refer such orders to her executive who will himself undertake the necessary investigation.

It often happens that activities are organised on a small scale, e.g. for an individual office or project, but there is a failure to co-ordinate the over-all activities of the many departments in the concern. This results in poor communications, duplication of effort, and frequent irritation and frustration for the people concerned. Each department tends to become an island unto itself. It is essential that the organisation is structured downwards, the starting-point being the corporate objectives (*see* Fig. 1). Every single person employed in the organisation, every single activity undertaken is, or should be, geared to the attainment of those objectives.

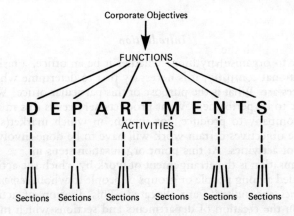

Fig. 1 *The development of an organisation structure.*

Individual managers must be given the responsibility and authority to organise their own departments but they should do it within the context of an over-all organisational policy. Though the need for over-all planning and the establishment of an organisational policy is greater in large concerns it should not be neglected in smaller ones because it is easier to adjust an existing organisation structure to cope with growth and change than it is to sort out the chaos of an organisation which has "just grown" like Topsy. If corporate objectives are to be the goal of everyone, the organisation structure must be cohesive, precise, yet flexible, i.e. capable of adaptation to meet changing needs resulting from growth and/or development.

Organising an office

The office manager is more likely to find himself reorganising than organising an office. There are occasions, though, when an office manager is asked to undertake the organisation of a new section/ department, e.g. a secretariat. The steps that have to be taken are as follows.

(1) Determine the objectives of the office to be established.

(2) Determine the functions arising from the objectives.

(3) Decide the activities involved in fulfilling the functions.

(4) Decide which activities are or can be dealt with by other offices already in existence, e.g. if there is a mail registry where incoming mail is opened this duty will not have to be undertaken for or in the new office.

(5) Estimate the volume/work-load of each activity.

(6) Estimate the number of man-hours required to perform each activity.

(7) Establish the interrelationship and sequence of activities.

(8) Determine the level of the various activities in terms of responsibility, qualifications and experience needed.

(9) Group the activities into reasonable work-loads (*see* Chapter 8).

(10) Prepare an organisation chart (*see* Chapter 4) based on the principles of organisation and techniques of organisation given below.

Principles of organisation

Since every organisation structure should be evolved to meet specific objectives there is no one set of principles which can be given as a blueprint for the office manager to follow. Nevertheless there are some basic principles which can be used as a guide-line even though they may not all be applicable to individual circumstances.

(1) Every person should be immediately responsible to *one person only*. Nothing is more confusing than for a person to receive conflicting instructions from more than one supervisor.

(2) Authority should be granted commensurate with responsibility. When this is not done the individual feels frustrated and loses his initiative.

(3) The span of control should be appropriate to the quality of staff, variety of work, and capabilities of the supervisor. "Span of control" means the number of subordinates responsible to a superior. This should normally be not more than five or six.

(4) The best use should be made of the specialist abilities of each individual.

(5) The number of levels of management should be kept to a minimum, otherwise communication (both upwards and downwards) suffers.

(6) There should be the right degree of centralisation, appropriate to work-flow requirements, staff specialist abilities, and other considerations discussed later in the chapter.

(7) There should be an even distribution of work.

(8) The maximum use should be made of the abilities of employees.

One modern view of organisation (the psychological or "human relations" approach) is that it is also concerned with the interrelationships of staff, referred to as the "informal organisation". Although the informal organisation is extremely difficult to assess or take into account it is an essential feature of successful organisation (*see also* page 21).

Techniques of organisation

After studying the objectives of the office and assessing the total volume of work, the proportions of different kinds of work and the staff required, the principles of organisation listed above can be applied in drawing up the organisation chart.

(1) Decide on the method of grouping (either homogeneous or heterogeneous—*see* page 21).

(2) Decide on the degree of specialisation to be used in the allocation of work.

(3) Decide on the size of groupings bearing in mind the span of control appropriate to the work, quality of subordinates and supervisor, and making allowances for holidays, sickness, etc.

(4) The number of section leaders and/or supervisors will arise from the decision on the size of groupings.

(5) Take account of human considerations (*see* above and page 21).

(6) Allocate responsibilities, duties and authority.

(7) Prepare a new organisation chart. Prepare job descriptions and job specifications.

After drawing up a chart of the formal organisation and assessing as far as possible the informal organisation contained within it, it should be checked against the principles of organisation listed above.

Reorganisation

The need for reorganisation should be established before it is undertaken. Nothing is more demoralising to staff than to be constantly "reorganised". It tends to happen in some organisations whenever a new head of department is appointed. The newly appointed office manger who takes the "new broom" attitude without first looking carefully at the existing structure is likely to alienate the staff.

On the other hand, reorganisation as a means of correcting faults should not be ignored. Bad organisation can be the root cause of inefficiency, the manifestations of that inefficiency being symptoms only. Some of the symptoms of bad organisation are:

(1) unacceptable delays;
(2) difficulty in locating documents;
(3) difficulty in retrieving information;
(4) lack of authority necessary to perform the duties of particular jobs;
(5) lack of co-ordination;
(6) duplication of procedures;
(7) inadequate or slow communications;
(8) low morale (may be due to other causes but is worth thinking about in terms of organisation);
(9) costs out of proportion to productivity;
(10) low productivity.

It should not be assumed that these faults are necessarily the result of bad organisation. One of the difficulties of improving organisation is that it is bound up with, and also may need consideration of, the procedures, machines used, and so on. All the elements of office efficiency are interrelated, and in fact the main problem is to distinguish whether it really is organisation which needs improving, or whether it is staffing or systems, or whether more appropriate machines should be installed.

Reorganisation may be necessary, not to correct faults, but to cope with changes brought about by growth and/or development. This situation may arise, for example, when a computer is to be installed. This means not only the organisation of the section or department which will operate the computer but also the complete reorganisation of the existing offices.

Steps to be taken when setting out to reorganise an office are listed below.

(1) Obtain an organisation chart of the former organisation as it exists. If a chart cannot be found, or it is out of date—and both these possibilities frequently occur—draw one up.

(2) Obtain the job descriptions of the workers. If these are not in existence it is necessary to ask each individual worker to list the tasks he undertakes.

(3) From the job descriptions summarise the duties which have to be performed in the office as a whole.

(4) Scrutinise the organisation chart and the job descriptions to diagnose faults, which may include one or more of the following:

    (a) inadequate delegation (particularly of authority);
    (b) bad distribution of work;
    (c) too much specialisation (or not enough);
    (d) inappropriate span of control (too narrow or too wide);
    (e) imprecise definition of responsibilities and authority;
    (f) too many levels of management.

(5) Review the objectives. Appraise the organisation chart, the work being done and the faults diagnosed in relation to those objectives. This appraisal should establish whether all the work being done is necessary, whether it is adequate, whether the systems and procedures are designed to meet the objectives, and whether the staff are adequate in number, type, level and ability.

(6) Consider alternative ways of organising the office, i.e. of distributing responsibilities, duties and authority (bearing in mind the purposes, the costs, and over-all control). At this point it is valuable to involve the subordinate staff. They are much more likely to co-operate in implementing the reorganisation finally decided upon if they have been consulted about it. Also, since they have been involved in the work, they may have good ideas as to how faults can be rectified.

(7) Assess whether and to what extent the proposed reorganisation will overcome the previous deficiencies or meet the demands of changes to be implemented.

(8) Prepare a new organisation chart and new job descriptions.

(9) Submit to top management for approval.

It is worth mentioning here that although wholesale reorganisation should not be the order of the day, the organisation is a living thing and needs to be reviewed regularly to ensure that it meets the changing needs and work requirements arising from changing objectives. Perhaps the situation which most often needs reorganisation in a fast growing concern is the span of control which can easily get out of hand if it is not constantly reviewed. The result of too large a span of control is that supervision becomes slack and inefficiency results.

Grouping of staff

HOMOGENEOUS AND HETEROGENEOUS GROUPINGS

There are two main types of staff grouping: homogeneous and heterogeneous.

Homogeneous grouping means that workers who are concerned with the same kind of activity, e.g. typists, are placed together in a pool or secretariat regardless of the section for which they work.

Heterogeneous grouping means that workers are placed together according to the function of their work, regardless of the kind of activity they undertake. For example, the handling of orders in a spares department might be dealt with by a group consisting of one or more mail clerks, correspondence clerks, typists and comptometer operators.

There are advantages to each type of grouping and the choice will depend upon the advantages required.

The advantages of homogeneous grouping are that it:

(1) facilitates the use of machines;
(2) reduces the effect of work fluctuations;
(3) enables better use to be made of specialisation;
(4) facilitates training;
(5) makes it easier to compare the work of different members of staff.

The advantages of heterogeneous grouping are that it:

(1) makes the exchange of staff easier;
(2) helps to develop a team spirit;
(3) makes it easier to fix responsibility;
(4) is better for customer relations;
(5) reduces the movement of paper;
(6) makes it easier to switch to new methods and systems;
(7) provides the workers with greater variety and interest (this last point is dealt with in some detail in Chapter 16).

HUMAN FACTORS

Apart from the organisational aspect of grouping staff there are other considerations which may be termed the human factors. The human aspects of the organisation are regarded by some people as the determining factor in the success or otherwise of any organisation. However good the formal organisation, it is unlikely that objectives will be achieved unless the staff are happy and work well together.

This informal aspect of the organisation includes such things as grouping by age, and putting together people who get on well with each other. It is not suggested that all staff should be placed in age groups, but if, for instance, a senior person is required to work alongside a large number of juniors it is unlikely that that person will be very happy.

It should not be necessary to keep people apart, but if there is a known clash of personalities it is advisable to bear this in mind when deciding on the groupings.

The generation of interest by allocating a variety of duties to each individual is obviously highly desirable, but people will not be happy if they are allocated tasks with which they are unable to cope. The more routine jobs should be allocated to people of limited capacity and more responsible jobs should be allocated to those people who can carry responsibility.

Types of organisation

There are four main types of organisation, viz. line, functional, line and staff, and committee. They are to some extent complementary and are most often used in that way, as is explained below.

LINE ORGANISATION

Line organisation (see Fig. 2) has been in use since earliest times and many concerns are still organised on this basis. It is characterised by direct lines of responsibility and authority from the top executive to the lowest subordinate. Thus, responsibility is greatest at the top and reduced at each successive level down the organisation scale.

Line organisation has the great advantage of being simple. It is readily understood by the personnel; there is no doubt about fixing responsibility for work at different levels; and it gives clear indication of lines of communication. Departmental heads are in sole charge of their particular sections of the concern. This may create a disadvantage in that unless there is first-class over-all planning there may be a lack of co-ordination of the work of the various departments. It may also tend to breed empire building.

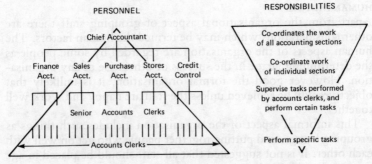

Fig. 2 *Line organisation: personnel and responsibilities.*

FUNCTIONAL ORGANISATION
In a functional organisation work is arranged according to the type
of activities, with experts placed in charge of the different aspects of
the concern. A simple example of this type of organisation is the
assignment of different experts to be in charge of the functions of
engineering, buying, selling, etc., regardless of whether the work
involved falls within the administrative province of another section
of the concern. This type of organisation makes the greatest use of
specialisation. A person's special skills are available "across the
board" and are not restricted by arbitrary departmental boundaries.
    It is virtually impossible to have a pure functional organisation:
there is always an element of line organisation with it. This is
inevitable because the people in charge of the functions must have
their subordinates to whom work can be delegated. The disadvantages of functional organisation tend to become most apparent in a
very large concern where there may be too many experts and too
many bosses. The workers become confused and the system may
become too elaborate and be uneconomic.

LINE AND STAFF ORGANISATION
Line organisation is normally executive. There are occasions when
line managers need expert advice in certain areas of their duties.
This advisory function is fulfilled either by other managers in the
organisation (*see* staff relationships, page 25) or by experts engaged
for the purpose. In the latter case this type of organisation is a
fusion of the line and functional and it is claimed that it has the
advantages of both. The principle of specialisation is retained and
responsibility is still fixed. Co-ordination is possible, yet discipline
can be maintained at the same time.
    The disadvantages centre around the people involved. Line
officers, who are the executives, may ignore the advice of the staff
officers, who are advisory. The staff officers may start issuing
orders countermanding those of the line officers. The worker,
caught between the two, becomes thoroughly confused and dissatisfied. In fact it is not always easy to be specific about executive
and advisory duties and this blurring of the organisational structure
can be confusing to management as well as to workers.

COMMITTEE ORGANISATION
Institutions may be governed by one or more committees. However, the collective action of the committee is normally taken in
respect of policy decisions and general management directives, but
there must be one or more executive officers to carry them out.
Committee organisation does exist in varying degrees in different

concerns, usually in addition to another type of organisation. Because it is an excellent medium of discussion and education, and of communication between management and workers, committee organisation helps to secure co-operation, and is a good source of collective advice, ideas and opinions.

The committee system has its disadvantages, which are that no single person is responsible for the committee's decisions, that decisions are usually made only after long and laborious discussion which can hold up executive activities, and that the decisions are usually weak because they are the result of compromise.

A major advantage of the committee system is that co-ordination should be easier and carried out more effectively as a result of the members pooling their knowledge and information. This has proved to be so in the case of the addition of a working committee to the organisation structure in the hospital service. Several hospital groups hold regular administrative officers conferences where the middle level of management meets under the chairmanship of the chief administrative officer. Frank exchange of opinions, requests for suggestions and ideas result in a keener appreciation of the "other fellow's job" leading to better co-operation and co-ordination.

Relationships

There are four main types of relationship between staff, viz. line, lateral, staff and functional. These relationships are related to the types of organisation.

LINE RELATIONSHIP

Each individual is in direct line relationship with his immediate superior and his immediate subordinate (see Fig. 3). He is expected to take instructions from his superior and to be responsible to that superior for the satisfactory performance of the work which has been delegated to him. He can give instructions and delegate work to his immediate subordinate and is responsible for seeing that the work is done satisfactorily.

LATERAL RELATIONSHIP

Two or more individuals who come within the span of control of the same superior are said to be in a lateral relationship. They are both directly responsible to the superior but may not be of the same status, or on the same salary, or have identical qualifications or experience. In the line relationship diagram (see Fig. 3) the four supervisors are in lateral relationship with each other. They may

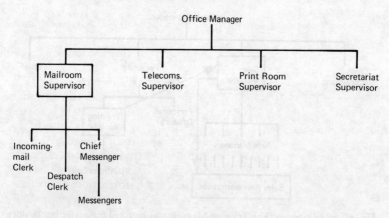

Fig. 3 *Line relationship.* The Mailroom Supervisor is directly responsible to the Office Manager for the efficiency of the mailroom. He gives instructions to the Incoming-mail Clerk, Despatch Clerk and Chief Messenger. He does not give instructions to the messengers—this must be done by the Chief Messenger.

not give instructions to one another or to the subordinates of another supervisor.

STAFF RELATIONSHIP

As mentioned above (*see* line and staff organisation) a manager may need the expert advice of another manager in order to perform his duties. For example, (*see* Fig. 4) the sales manager may need the advice of the training manager or training officer about suitable courses for his sales representatives. The sales manager is not obliged to follow that advice, though he would be foolish not to do so without good reason, and the training manager can do no more than give advice. Unfortunately many managers do not make sufficient use of staff relationships and consequently do not get the specialist advice they need to make decisions and/or run their departments satisfactorily. Alternatively, the manager gets the advice he needs from other sources at unnecessary cost of time, effort and sometimes money.

FUNCTIONAL RELATIONSHIP

A functional relationship is very similar to a staff relationship, and indeed it is sometimes difficult to differentiate between the two. The major difference is that where there is a functional relationship, the person called in for advice has the authority of his specialisation and can carry out his duties in another manager's domain. For example, a production manager might wish to dismiss a member of his staff but cannot do so without the authority of the personnel

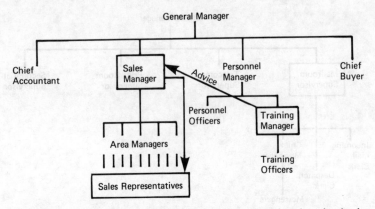

Fig. 4 *Staff relationship.* The Training Manager can be asked for advice but he does not give it unless requested. Neither can he instruct his training officers to carry out training unless the departmental managers agree. On the other hand, if the General Manager instructed the Personnel Manager to ensure that sales representatives were trained, then the Training Manager would have greater authority (*see* functional relationship).

manager. Though the production manager and the personnel manager, who will normally be in a lateral relationship, cannot give each other instructions, the personnel officer does have the authority to veto the dismissal if it contravenes company and/or legal regulations.

Specialisation

Specialisation is an important factor in establishing office procedures. In the clerical sphere, as in any other kind of work, it has the advantage of developing experts in particular fields of work. To take a mundane example, where one person is made responsible for all outgoing mail that person soon becomes an expert on the various rates of postage, and after a time can correctly stamp postal packages without reference to a guide. Other advantages of specialisation are listed below.

(1) It is useful when a service is to be centralised: typists working in a pool with no other duties than typing is an example.

(2) A greater volume of work is produced.

(3) Responsibility can be fixed. For example, one person may be authorised to write orders of a certain kind.

(4) It helps to establish routines, as there is only one particular person or section which performs a certain specialised function.

(5) The grading of jobs in an office is made easier. For example,

a person may be graded as a filing clerk, a shorthand typist or an audio typist.

(6) Operations can be made simpler, more accurate, faster and more efficient.

(7) Certain kinds of work can be performed more rhythmically by specialisation.

(8) It is easier to recruit and/or train people for specific jobs.

(9) Fraud is less likely. For example, one clerk may specialise in the preparation of the pay-roll while another pays out the wages, so that there is less likely to be collusion.

(10) Uniformity of practice is assured. For example, in granting credit a rigid code can be adhered to more easily.

Specialisation does also have disadvantages.

(1) Workers may know how to do their jobs but not why they are doing them unless they are given a very good induction training programme which enables them to see their job in the context of the whole organisation.

(2) It does not encourage the training of section leaders/supervisors/managers with all-round knowledge, which may result in poor management and lack of understanding of other departmental affairs at management level.

(3) Overspecialisation breeds monotony and boredom with the result that people lose their initiative.

(4) It can be difficult to deal with staff absences unless understudies have been trained.

(5) Peak loads may be more difficult to handle and work scheduling may sometimes be difficult because of the inflexibility of staff competence.

(6) Delays may be caused because each activity tends to become an end in itself and co-ordination is more difficult.

Inflexible specialisation is not to be encouraged. It is possible to achieve the advantages of specialisation and at the same time give the staff variety, which will increase interest and job satisfaction, by rotating people from one job to another. This can be done on a daily, weekly, monthly or even half-yearly basis. Over a period of time each employee becomes thoroughly competent in the performance of a number of activities. This goes a long way towards meeting the disadvantages listed above.

Centralisation

Many office services are centralised because they are common to the whole organisation and it would be uneconomic to provide the service for each department individually. For example, there is in most organisations one telephone switchboard which handles all the incoming calls for the whole organisation. There may be a need for a small switchboard in a particular department such as a parts department, however, where orders are pouring in non-stop. This may be a subsidiary to the main switchboard or a separate switchboard with its own lines.

There is usually one mailroom to handle all incoming mail. Except in a department where the incoming mail is exceptionally heavy it would not be realistic or necessary to have mailrooms located all over the organisation. On the other hand, part of the mail-handling operation may be, and frequently is, performed in the individual departments by a member of the secretarial staff who opens, sorts and distributes mail addressed to executives in the department, and prepares mail for despatch before sending it to the mailroom for franking and collection by the Post Office. Similarly, although clerical staff are normally allocated to one department, e.g. accounts, of a large organisation there may be a need for one or more accounts clerks to be assigned to and located in the stores.

It is not usually possible or desirable to centralise fully all office services. Equally, total decentralisation of services it not usually feasible nor would it be possible to provide the best administrative support to management at an economic cost. When deciding which services to centralise and which to locate in individual departments it is important to bear in mind the advantages and disadvantages of centralisation.

The main advantages are as follows.

(1) Better supervision of standards and productivity is possible.

(2) Work can be scheduled reasonably precisely and peak loads can be more easily handled.

(3) Greater flexibility in the use of staff is possible and job rotation is more easily arranged.

(4) The costs of services can be kept to a minimum;

(5) Machines can be used more economically.

(6) Comprehensive training programmes can be arranged.

(7) Staff absences can be handled more easily and have less effect on the work-load.

(8) Total integration of systems is more easily achieved.

(9) Consistency in procedures is easier to ensure.

(10) Expert management advice is more readily available for even the smallest unit in the system.

Rigid central control has its disadvantages, however. Some of them are listed below.

(1) Services may not be flexible enough to meet the special needs of individual departments.

(2) The work of the central services may tend to become an end in itself instead of being a complementary function providing a service to the rest of the organisation.

(3) The number of records necessary for control may have to be increased.

(4) Departmental managers tend to keep their own records in addition to the central records.

(5) The staff may tend to become frustrated because they are out of touch with corporate objectives and the work of the departments.

Usually the best arrangement is to have the main office services such as mail, telecommunications, correspondence and report production, and reprographic work organised centrally and supplemented in the departments where it is necessary for practical reasons. For example, all the duplicating and printing can be done in a central print room but copying machines can be provided in individual departments so that a few copies of a document can be reproduced quickly when required. The proportion of centralised services to services located in individual departments varies from one organisation to another depending on many factors. The arrangement will be influenced by the purpose and size of the organisation, the kind of work, physical factors such as location, accommodation available, and staff numbers and experience. Every effort should be made to get the best of both worlds by obtaining the advantages of centralisation without its disadvantages.

Developing the organisation structure

The structure of an organisation is influenced by many factors. These include the size and nature of the organisation, its objectives and functions, the complexity of the departments, the length of time the organisation has been in existence, its permanence or otherwise, the flow of business throughout the year (it may be steady or it may fluctuate, say, from season to season), the geographical location of the various units of the organisation, the autonomy given to divisions/departments/units of the organisation, the ratio of administrative staff to technical, specialist and professional staff, and the extent of mechanisation/automation.

The organisation structure which operates successfully in the offices of a medium-sized business located in one building in the main street of a town is unlikely to be successful in the offices of a group of companies with individual units located in various places around the country. Indeed the same structure may not be suitable for the various units.

One thing is certain: there is no one ideal organisation structure. There are many facets to organisation and many applications of the various aspects such as specialisation and centralisation. An office manager should know what is implied by good organisation, and he should always seek to evolve the best, that is, the one most suited to the work of his office. His task is to develop an organisation structure which will facilitate the flow of work, which will provide the information service required by management, which will give the best possible administrative support to the organisation as a whole, and thus make the most effective contribution possible to the fulfilment of corporate objectives.

After spending a lot of time and hard work on developing the most suitable structure within the context of the organisation concerned it is very tempting to lean back and consider the task completed. However, organisation is an on-going process and the structure must be flexible enough to change and develop alongside the growth and development of the organisation as a whole.

4. Function Analysis and Organisation Charts

It is difficult for anyone to understand and/or remember an organisation structure in its entirety unless it is presented on paper. A visual representation is most easily understood at a glance. An organisation chart is a diagrammatic illustration which may include some explanatory notes. The steps to be taken in preparing an organisation chart are, of course, the same as in developing an organisation structure.

Analysing the function

The *precise* function must be determined. The function must then be analysed to determine the duties involved (*see* the list of broad duties on page 1). The duties must then be analysed to establish what activities or tasks must be performed in order to carry out the duties. It may be useful at this point to prepare a chart of activities because it enables you to see whether similar activities are required in the performance of more than one duty and to estimate the volume of each activity. An activities chart is shown in Fig. 5.

The activities can now be grouped into jobs and the required manpower can be assessed for each type of job. Job grading can be carried out if required (*see* Chapter 9).

Working groups or sections can now be evolved. These may be homogeneous or heterogeneous (*see* page 21). The sections are then grouped into departments and the various levels of management are established, building upwards until the appropriate top level is reached.

The chart of activities shown in Fig. 5 might now look like the chart in Fig. 6.

31

FUNCTION: TO PROVIDE A COMPLETE MAIL SERVICE WITHIN THE ORGANISATION.

Duties	Activities
1. Receive and process incoming mail	1.1 Collect mail from Post Office
	1.2 Sign for registered letters and packets
	1.3 Sort mail into categories
	1.4 Open envelopes and packets
	1.5 Remove contents, check and date stamp
	1.6 Record registered mail
	1.7 Sort for delivery to departments
2. Distribute inwards mail to offices	2.1 Sort for delivery route
	2.2 Deliver to offices
	2.3 Obtain signatures for registered mail
3. Collect mail from offices	3.1 Collect mail from OUT trays
	3.2 Sort outgoing and internal mail
	3.3 Sort internal mail for delivery *en route* to post room
	3.4 Deliver internal mail to offices
	3.5 Deliver outgoing and remaining internal mail to post room
4. Despatch outgoing mail	4.1 Check outgoing letters
	4.2 Insert into window envelopes
	4.3 Address larger envelopes
	4.4 Seal envelopes
	4.5 Weigh and determine postage required
	4.6 Frank
	4.7 Deliver to Post Office (or Post Office van collection point)
	4.8 Obtain receipts for registered mail, etc.

Fig. 5 *Activities chart*. If this type of chart is prepared for a number of related functions, it is possible to group the activities into types of work.

Purposes of an organisation chart

An organisation chart serves several purposes.

(1) The whole organisation structure can be seen at a glance. This means that every member of the staff from the top to the bottom of the concern can be aware of how each section or department or the whole organisation is structured.

(2) It is easier to analyse and review the structure when it is represented graphically.

(3) Management relationships are visible.

Activities	Job	
(Refer to Activities Chart)	Personnel	Volume
1.1	Messenger	
1.2	Messenger	
1.3	Clerk	
1.4	Clerk	
1.5	Clerk	
1.6	Clerk	
1.7	Clerk	
2.1	Messenger	
2.2	Messenger	
2.3	Messenger	
3.1	Messenger	
3.2	Messenger	
3.3	Messenger	
3.4	Messenger	
3.5	Messenger	
4.1	Clerk	
4.2	Clerk	
4.3	Clerk	
4.4	Clerk	
4.5	Clerk	
4.6	Clerk	
4.7	Messenger	
4.8	Messenger	

Fig. 6 *Job chart*. The work-load indicated in the column headed "Volume" determines the number of personnel needed to fulfil the function. In a small organisation a clerk may also be the messenger. In an organisation with a large volume of mail but short delivery distances the messenger may undertake some clerical activities. In a large organisation several messengers and clerks may be needed.

(4) Spheres of responsibility and authority are defined.
(5) The span of control of each supervisor/manager can be seen.
(6) Lines of communication are visible.
(7) Weaknesses in organisation can be more easily diagnosed, e.g. weak lines of communication, unattached staff.

It should be noted that the levels, i.e. status, of each senior employee and groups of subordinate employees can be indicated but rarely are, because the chart would become too complicated to read at a glance. This point should always be made clear to staff because misunderstanding can give rise to feelings of unjustified superiority or inferiority.

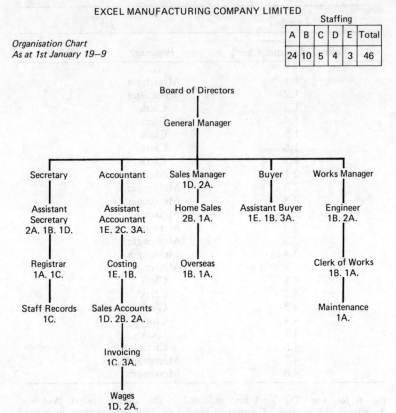

Fig. 7 *A typical organisation chart of a small business concern (line organisation)*. Shows job grades and number of staff in each grade for each function. The staffing information above the chart is a useful addition.

It is also important to realise that an organisation chart indicates only spheres of responsibility and authority, not *how much* responsibility and authority has been allocated to each individual. This information is obtained only from job descriptions.

No indication of informal or personal relationships is given. This aspect is particularly important in reviewing and revising organisation structures and is explained on page 20.

It should be mentioned that there is a school of thought which rejects the desirability of publicising organisation charts on the grounds that this leads to inflexibility. However, it is much easier to adapt and amend an organisation which is presented on paper

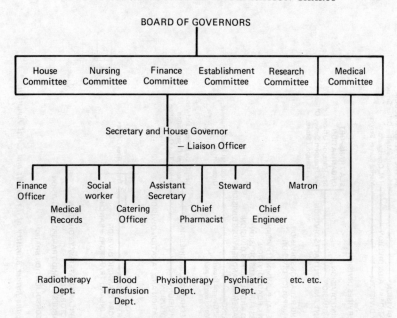

Fig. 8 *Organisation chart of departments of a large teaching hospital*, showing a committee and executive structure.

because the repercussions of the amendments can be more easily assessed.

Types of charts and methods of presentation

Organisation charts may indicate functions, departments and their sections, or posts. Names of people in the various positions should not be included because as individuals leave the organisation, are promoted or transferred to other jobs, the chart becomes out of date. Job gradings, however, can be indicated. Organisation charts may be presented in vertical or horizontal format. The former is most often used for the simple line organisation while the latter is frequently used to represent the functional organisation, but this is not necessarily so.

In the vertical format the straight vertical lines indicate the lines of responsibility and authority; the horizontal lines indicate lateral relationships. Dotted lines may be used to indicate functional relationships. Positions attached to a vertical line normally indicate a special function and/or relationship. These points are illustrated in the organisation charts shown in Figs. 7, 8, 9 and 10. It should be borne in mind that any organisation, except the very smallest,

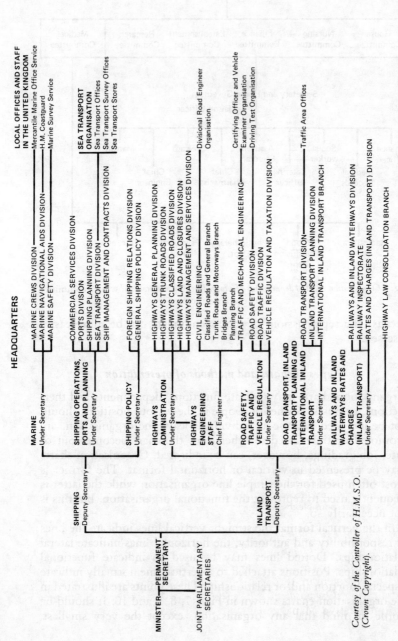

Fig. 9 *Specimen organisation chart (horizontal format) of a government department, the former Ministry of Transport and Civil Aviation.*

Courtesy of the Controller of H.M.S.O.
(Crown Copyright).

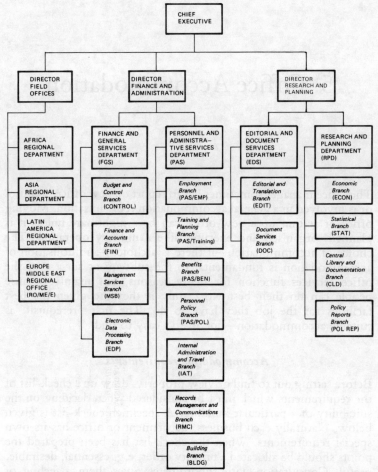

Fig. 10 *A specimen organisation chart format used in an international organisation.* The use of italics in some boxes indicates the relationship of each function to the over-all function of the department. In the case of the regional offices each office is directly responsible to the Director Field Services. In the other four departments the branches are responsible to the appropriate departmental heads who are responsible to their directors.

needs more than one chart to give a clear picture of the functions, working groups, people and activities involved.

More detailed information on the preparation of organisation charts is given in the Institute of Administrative Management publication *Organisation Charts* (available from the Institute of Administrative Management, 205 High Street, Beckenham, Kent BR3 1BA).

5. Office Accommodation

The office manager sometimes has to report on new office premises or is involved in a general accommodation reorganisation. Moving office or setting up a new office can be a nightmare unless it is planned, organised and executed like a military operation. The choice of accommodation—if there is a choice—and utilisation of accommodation is fundamental to the subsequent success of the office services function for many reasons, but mainly because people can do their best work only if they are given the best facilities for the job they have to do. The first prerequisite is suitable accommodation—not always easy to find.

Accommodation requirements

Before setting out to find or view property, draw up a check-list of the requirements which must be considered when deciding on the suitability of a particular building. A specimen check-list is given below. Naturally each business, department or office has its own special requirements. When the check-list has been prepared the points should be allocated a priority order, e.g. essential, desirable, useful. Consultation with subordinates gives them a feeling of involvement, is useful in determining priorities, and helps to ensure that existing inadequacies are prevented from recurring.

CHECK-LIST OF ACCOMMODATION REQUIREMENTS
  (1) *Location.*
      Proximity to bus/railway station.
      Proximity to car park.
      Convenience for customers/clients.
      Convenience for staff.
      Proximity to banks/post office.
      Availability of staff of the required type and level.

Type of environment (industrial, professional, prestige, etc.).

Freedom from hazards, e.g. chemicals causing pollution, fuel nearby creating a fire risk.

(2) *Site*.

Size.

Grounds/gardens.

Space for car park.

Access for goods deliveries.

Availability of services (water, electricity, gas, mains drainage, telephone lines).

(3) *Building*.

Size.

Number of staff to be accommodated (full-time, part-time, occasionally, e.g. sales representatives).

Likely expansion of business/staff over the next three/five years minimum.

Ground floor space required for heavy machinery, computers, etc.

Weight-carrying capacity of the floors if large quantities of records are to be kept or it is necessary to have machinery upstairs.

Projected office layout (individual offices or open-plan), entrance for customers/clients.

Outside appearance.

Adequate space and permission for outside signs.

Leasehold/freehold.

Space for canteen/restaurant facilities; adequate cloakrooms.

Adequate fire exits and other fire precautions set out in the Building Regulations 1976.

Security against burglary.

Security against intruders during office hours.

Planning permission to use the premises as offices.

(4) *Physical factors*.

Natural lighting required (e.g. for a drawing office).

Heating.

Ventilation.

Decoration.

Noise.

Type and condition of lifts.

Location of office buildings

It is possible that an office manager may be asked to report to the

Board on the merits and disadvantages of moving to a completely
new area and on the facilities and assistance that are available. From
about the mid-1960s to the mid-1970s there was a strong move
away from the large urban centres, particularly London, to new
towns and existing smaller towns. A large oil company moved its
headquarters near to Swindon, for example; a well-known insurance company moved to Bristol; a rapidly expanding publishing
house moved to Plymouth. (It is worth noting that all of these
towns are within easy reach of London by British Rail main lines
and by motorways.)

This trend of moving to the provinces was caused partly because
of escalating costs, particularly rents, in London and partly because
of the difficulty of recruiting clerical and secretarial staff, especially
the latter. Typists were at a premium in London, able to dictate
their own salaries, hours and conditions of service, and in many
cases were insufficiently qualified for the job they were asked to do.

The government encouraged this trend, in an endeavour to
overcome unemployment in the provinces, by establishing a special
department to give advice, arrange grants and so on. The smaller
towns themselves set out to attract industry and commerce by
advertising in professional journals and by offering many facilities
to organisations settling in their districts. These facilities vary from
one area of the country to another, and from one town to another.
The drift away from London has been slowing down for some time
now but the possibility of moving to the provinces or moving
within the provinces should not be ignored. In certain areas of high
unemployment very favourable facilities, e.g. rent-free or very low
rent office accommodation, are made available to employers moving into those areas, depending on the number of jobs to be created
within five years.

If such a move is under consideration the first step is to make
enquiries of the following.

(1) The Industrial Expansion Team of the Department of Industry (Millbank Tower, London SW1P 4QU, Tel. 01-211 5154)
which deals with new town and new industrial area development.

(2) The appropriate officer in the borough or district council of
the town which might be a suitable location: the planning officer or
the public relations officer are the most likely people to be in charge
of this aspect of a borough's affairs.

Enquiries should cover some or all of the following points.

(1) What financial assistance is available, for what period of
time, on what interest and repayment terms?

(2) What is the housing situation in the area? Can council
houses/flats be made available to staff who will transfer from the

existing offices, until they are able to find property to buy if they wish to do so?

(3) What local training facilities are there; both pre-service and in-service?

(4) If a new industrial estate is being developed what transport facilities will be provided by the council?

(5) What are the salary levels—will existing key staff be relatively highly paid? (Existing salaries cannot be reduced.)

(6) Can all the telecommunications facilities required be made available whenever necessary?

(7) If the location is out of town what services is the Post Office willing to provide in terms of collection and delivery of mail? What are the costs of these services likely to be?

Apart from the area, town or district in which the offices are to be situated, there is also the question of a suitable site. This depends entirely on the type of organisation. In some cases it may be essential that it should be in the centre of a town; a business which rarely has visitors can be perfectly well situated in a quiet back street or even out of the town; for prestige purposes an imposing corner site may be desirable.

Leasehold versus Freehold

When a building is bought freehold, it can be adapted and altered to meet the particular needs of the organisation, but this may not be possible if it is leasehold. A freehold building can be boldly decorated with the name of the concern, and even given a title incorporating the name of the company. This is not usually allowed within the terms of a lease. Although buying freehold means investing a large amount of capital, there may be a possibility of obtaining income by renting a portion of the building until extra space is needed. Leases very often restrict subletting.

If the office accommodation is to be permanent, buying outright might be preferable to leasing it, although it may be an advantage to be able to change the location if required, which is easier where the premises are leased. The outright purchase of a building is likely to provide a sound investment, but it does mean tying up a large amount of capital which may not be desirable.

The requirements of a small office may not be extensive or elaborate, in which case the most convenient arrangement may be to lease property. The management may then be free of maintenance worries, and the provision and maintenance of lighting and heating installations may be included in the arrangement.

When leasing a building it is essential to check in the greatest detail the facilities that are or will be made available, restrictions, and tenant's obligations. The organisation's legal adviser should be asked to scrutinise the lease to ensure that there are no "hidden" clauses which may later prove highly inconvenient, e.g. a guarantee to take on a further lease at an increased rental when the first lease expires. However, an option to negotiate a new lease must be included by law.

Choosing premises

Unless a building can be designed from scratch to meet the predetermined needs of the organisation it is certain that compromise will be necessary. The best facilities are likely to be available in purpose-built offices, though prestige blocks do not necessarily provide the ideal requirements for a particular company. Old buildings which have been or which can be converted for office use are rarely ideal and are often downright inconvenient, not to say costly to convert. On the other hand, the high cost of building may make conversion of an old building an economic proposition.

The best procedure is to:

(1) ensure that the check-list (*see* page 38) is comprehensive;

(2) check that all priority items are marked on the check-list;

(3) check that the priorities are met by the building(s) being considered;

(4) check how many of the desirable points on the check-list are covered;

(5) check the cost of alterations which may be necessary to meet priority requirements;

(6) determine the maintenance costs and check whether they are within the budget.

Finance is a critical factor. Expenditure guide-lines must be laid down before the hunt for premises begins. The guide-lines should cover capital expenditure (the cost of the building and/or the cost of necessary alterations, decorations, etc., plus the cost of the lease); recurrent expenditure (rent, rates, heating, etc.); the cost of installing the offices in the new premises; and the cost of training local staff.

When all aspects have been thoroughly investigated, the next step is to assess the relevant advantages and disadvantages of the various premises which have been examined—it is advisable to examine as many as possible in the area(s) which are suitable—and make a short list of those which most nearly meet the priorities and as many of the desirable aspects on the check-list as possible.

Unless the building is being built to specification or is a new purpose-built office block, it is vital to obtain a surveyor's report. When recommending property, reasons must be given for the choice, explaining advantages and disadvantages and how the latter can be overcome if this is possible.

Types of office layout

There are basically two ways in which offices can be arranged, viz. small offices which accommodate from one to, say, six or eight people, and open-plan offices which can be of any size to accommodate all the sections of a complete department or several departments. Open-plan offices have become more common in recent years primarily because the space can be used more effectively, i.e. more people can be accommodated in a given area of an open-plan office than would be the case if they were in small offices covering the same area. This is a very serious consideration because rents are charged per square foot.*

ADVANTAGES OF OPEN-PLAN OFFICES

(1) Approximately one-quarter of the space can be saved or 20 per cent more use made of it.

(2) Supervision is easier because the actions of everybody are obvious to all.

(3) Machines can be placed in the most suitable position.

(4) Rearrangement of the office to meet changing needs is very easy.

(5) Internal communications are quicker and easier because there are no doors or corridors to walk through.

(6) More economical use of services such as lighting and heating may be possible.

(7) Better work flow is possible.

DISADVANTAGES OF OPEN-PLAN OFFICES

(1) The old-fashioned type of open-plan office, i.e. not landscaped (see below), may look like a factory and create an impersonal atmosphere.

(2) Special steps must be taken to reduce noise, particularly telephone bells.

(3) The distraction of people moving around can be very frustrating for people whose work needs intense concentration.

* In 1979 the annual rent per square foot in a prestige office block in the City of London might be anything between £20 and £25. The average rental was £15 to £18 per square foot, though in the provinces it might be as little as £1.50/£2 per square foot.

(4) If adequate provision is not made for expansion of staff and/or equipment the area can easily become cramped.

(5) Because of the size of the room artificial lighting is generally necessary.

(6) Certain types of air conditioning can create draughts; and if the air conditioning is not fully efficient the atmosphere can become "stuffy".

(7) Infectious complaints can be more easily passed from one member of the staff to another.

OFFICE LANDSCAPING

Bürolandschaft or "office landscaping" originated in West Germany in the 1950s. It provided the answer to the "factory-like" atmosphere of the large open-plan office. New open-plan offices are almost invariably landscaped to some extent and there are consultants in office landscaping.

The special features of a landscaped office are:

(1) asymetrical layout of the furniture, usually in groups, facing in different directions;

(2) the judicious distribution of indoor plants to give a pleasant and relaxing atmosphere;

(3) a total concept including fitted carpets, soft lighting, air conditioning, integrated furniture, etc.;

(4) the arrangement of screens both for acoustic purposes and to give privacy;

(5) the provision of work space for all members of staff up to the most senior managers and in some firms including even the managing director.

These features are illustrated in Fig. 11.

The major disadvantage of noise in an open-plan office can be overcome to some extent in a landscaped office by the acoustic screens, acoustic ceiling tiles, carpets and curtains, all of which absorb sound. "Bleep" telephones are less disturbing than the conventional instrument with a bell. The non-regimented arrangement of the desks and provision of screens mitigates the impersonal feeling and gives an atmosphere of privacy.

Location of offices and office departments

Having obtained office premises and decided whether to have open-plan or individual offices, it is necessary to consider the allocation of space to the different departments in the accommodation available. The organisation fortunate enough to have offices built to its own requirements considers these aspects when the

[Courtesy Roche Products Ltd. and Organised Officer Designs Limited

Fig. 11 *A landscaped office.* This office in Roche Products Limited Building 40 won
the 1979 Office of the Year Award presented by the Institute of Administrative
Management. Note the spaciousness achieved by careful placing of furniture. The
"strutted" ceiling provides diffusion for the lighting.

building is being planned.

The first and most important factor is that departments that
work together should be allocated space near each other if constant
personal contact between the staff is necessary. It is worth re-
membering, though, that telephone communication may be just as
efficient as personal contact and is quicker.

Departments with a constant flow of visitors from outside the
organisation, such as personnel and purchasing, should be located
close to the reception area and have direct access from outside.
Important operating departments should be placed close to the
executive suite; perhaps the sales department is most important
here.

If access by staff of other departments is required in the service departments, such as the typing pool, mailroom and reprographic services, they should be sited centrally. However, with remote dictation, internal communication, and a properly organised mail distribution system this ought not to be a major factor.

Board rooms and conference and interview rooms should be as far from noise as possible; the back of the building away from the road is usually the most suitable situation. Heavy office machines are best sited on the lower floors to avoid annoying people on floors below and for convenience of installation.

When allocating areas it is essential to consider the future expansion of those departments which grow in size as the organisation develops. This is particularly relevant to the sales, records and typing departments. This does not mean that empty space should be left, but that less important space, e.g. storage rooms, should be located next to these departments so that expansion is possible without too much disturbance.

Drawing offices need maximum light and are best sited at the top of the building.

Toilets and cloakrooms should be distributed throughout the building and should be conveniently situated for most of those who have to use them, and not, as is so often the case, arranged to fit in with the plumbing.

If it has been decided to opt for small offices rather than open-plan, there is a wide variety of partition walls available which can easily be moved when changes are necessary.

Legal requirements

The Offices, Shops and Railway Premises Act 1963 lays down requirements concerning the size and standards of accommodation for office workers. These include an average minimum of 3.7 square metres (40 square feet) per employee (this includes space for machines, filing cabinets, etc.), and adequate lighting, ventilation, etc. (see also Chapter 7). Protection against fire hazards must be provided—the organisation's insurers and the chief fire officer of the district will be very glad to give advice. This is especially important in an office because of the vast quantities of paper, and wood if the furniture is mainly of this material. The fire hazard in new buildings, which are mainly of steel and concrete construction and decorated and furnished in fibre materials, is less than in old buildings with wooden floors and window frames, wooden ceiling joists, etc. Nevertheless proper precautions must always be taken. This may include fire doors in corridors, automatic fire alarm systems and automatic water sprinklers. Electrical wiring must of course be fully checked and if there is the slightest doubt about its safety the engineering department of the Regional Electricity Board should be consulted.

An office manager should be fully conversant with the 1963 Act but in the special circumstances of choosing and/or moving into new premises it is worth while checking the main points of the Act to ensure that they are complied with.

There is also the question of planning permission. Under the Town and Country Planning Acts planning permission must be obtained to use the premises as offices if they have not been so used continuously since 31st December 1963. If planning permission was obtained by a previous tenant it does not have to be renewed. It is also necessary to obtain approval under the Building Regulations 1976 if this has not been done.

An article entitled "Moving the Company 'House' " published in *Business Equipment Digest* and later published in the Members' Handbook of the Institute of Administrative Management gives valuable information and guidance on the physical aspects of moving office.

6. Office Furniture and Layout

There are four main criteria which form the basis of judgment as to the suitability of a piece of office furniture, viz. (i) is it functional; (ii) is it attractive; (iii) is it hard wearing; and (iv) is its cost within the budget? There is a very wide range of office furniture available and it is worth obtaining the catalogues of several manufacturers/suppliers from which to select two or three appropriate types to go and see.

Basic considerations

There are a number of basic factors which should be considered when buying office furniture.

(1) *Design:* size of top, height, number of drawers, suitability for the purpose, etc.

(2) *Capital outlay:* an obvious factor when buying any equipment.

(3) *Durability:* metal and fibreglass are virtually indestructible.

(4) *Saving in space:* some furniture is specially designed to save floor space (*see* modular or system furniture; *see also* page 51).

(5) *Fire risk:* metal and fibreglass are much less flammable than wood.

(6) *Weight:* if furniture has to be moved around, as it often does in a large office, lightweight is preferable and fibreglass is very suitable.

(7) *Hygiene:* can the piece of furniture be cleaned easily and is there plenty of space underneath for cleaning the floor?

(8) *Appearance:* attractive but workmanlike; prestige may be a factor if the furniture is to be in an area/office open to the public.

(9) *Comfort of the office worker:* a high level of comfort means that more work is likely to be performed with less distraction.

(10) *Safety:* rounded corners avoid the constant bruising caused

by square corners when space is limited: plate-glass tops may not
be safe in use.

(11) *Finish:* desk tops should be matt to avoid glare.

(12) *Labour-saving:* some furniture has built-in file units, which
can save walking about by the clerks and so save time.

Specifications

There are several British Standards which set out the essential
requirements of office furniture. The most important standard is
B.S. 3893: 1965 "Office desks, tables and seating", which gives
dimensions including heights for different types of desks used for
various purposes. It includes most of the recommendations in B.S.
3044: 1958 and B.S. 3079: 1959, both concerned with anthropometric design of chairs and tables, and B.S. 3404: 1961 "Office
chairs for machine operators". B.S. 5459 Part 1: 1977 and Part 2:
1977 are "specifications for performance requirements and tests for
office furniture". B.S. 5459 Part 1 may be important when heavy
machines are to be placed on desks.

Desks

MATERIALS

Desks are made in various types of material, each of which has its
advantages and disadvantages. The three most commonly used are
wood, metal and fibreglass.

(1) Wood is attractive but may be heavy, easily scratched, and
not fire resistant.

(2) Metal is hard wearing, fire resistant, but cold, and can get
chipped unless anodised metal is used.

(3) Laminated plastic/fibreglass is hard wearing, light in weight,
and fire resistant, but some types may scratch fairly easily.

Wooden desks may be built with tops of fibreglass or other hard
material which lengthens their life and does not detract from their
appearance.

TYPES

Office desks may be divided into five types, viz. executive, special,
built-in, general clerical, and modular.

(1) *Executive.* This type depends on the taste of the executive,
and is made with appearance very much in mind. Executive desks,
and other furniture, can be obtained in traditional styles such as
Regency and in very modern styles based on Swedish designs.

(2) *Special-purpose furniture.* Furniture designed for special use in

offices includes typists' desks, calculating-machine desks, collating desks, and so on.

The typist's desk most commonly found in offices is the single pedestal type. The pedestal contains drawers, in one of which there should be dividers for storing stationery, carbon paper, etc. A draught-proof skirting panel and hinged flap are useful additions to the standard desk. The flap provides the surface on which to place the copy if the pedestal is "on the wrong side" for an individual typist.

For the secretary or typist who has general/clerical work to do as well as typewriting, a desk giving surfaces of two heights should be provided. This can be an L-shaped desk with the smaller side at a slightly lower height than the longer side. Alternatively a normal desk may have a well to one side in which to stand the machine.

Yet another alternative is for the clerk/typist to have the typewriter on a small mobile desk. The two castors at the back allow the desk to be moved easily, the two legs at the front holding the table firmly in position when in use. Flaps are provided at each side and such desks can also be obtained with a side section for files.

(3) *Built-in furniture.* Maximum utilisation of floor space may be obtained by the use of built-in furniture. Materials are also saved in its construction. Furniture should be hygienic as well as functional: permanent fixtures can be tailored to fit in wall recesses so that there is no possibility of dirt lodging anywhere, and the flush fitting and outside surfaces can easily be cleaned and maintained. Hard-wearing materials such as fibreglass are ideal for surfaces which are likely to get rough usage, e.g. wrapping of parcels.

(4) *General clerical desks.* Ideally the size and design of a desk should be suitable for the work to be performed on it. Unfortunately this is not always possible as, to some extent, the space available dictates the size of the furniture. If a clerk is working for most of the time on small index cards, a very small desk would be sufficient. If another clerk needs to spread out ledgers and working papers, a desk 2 m by 1.5 m might be necessary and should be provided—regardless of prestige considerations. There is, however, an advantage in having all desks of a standard size. The appearance of the office is enhanced, it allows interchange of units, and better terms are usually obtained when buying. The two drawers usually provided in a clerical desk are adequate for normal purposes.

For some types of work it is useful to have a plate-glass topped desk, because of the hard writing surface and because schedules of standing information can be inserted under the glass for easy reference.

Cost is almost invariably a crucial factor. The standard two-drawer desk meets the average requirements at a reasonable cost. Simple wooden tables without drawers and topped with hard-wearing material are useful for sorting documents, for filing, or for occasional use in private and general offices.

The top of a desk is often cluttered up with blotter, telephones, ashtrays, lamps and other items. Provision for as much as possible of this equipment should be made in the desk. For example, telephones can be attached to wall brackets or to extending brackets fixed to the side of the desk. A shallow sliding tray in which office sundries such as paperclips can be kept should be provided above the top drawer of the pedestal.

(5) *Modular or system furniture.* Greater desk area using the minimum floor space can be obtained by using interlocking furniture known as "systems" or "modular" furniture. This provides up to 25 per cent more desk area, and saves up to 33 per cent

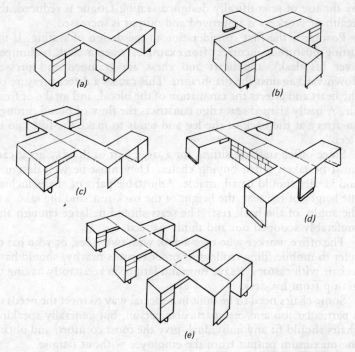

[*Courtesy The Shannon Ltd.*]

Fig. 12 *Various desk formations with system furniture: (a) a work station for two clerks; (b), (c) and (d) work stations for four clerks; (d) showing how records may be kept immediately to hand; and (e) accommodation for six clerks.*

in floor space. Diagrams of a variety of units are shown in Fig. 12. Desk units can be combined with storage units for files, record cards, etc. including automated storage and retrieval. The disadvantages of this type of furniture are that people can more easily talk together and concentration may be difficult because of the distraction caused by the movements of colleagues.

The importance of seating

At the end of the First World War, it was recognised that industrial fatigue was a problem which interfered with maximum production, and the Industrial Fatigue Research Board was appointed to investigate and advise on the question. "Ergonomics", a term first used in 1949, includes the study of the correct size and shape of furniture in order to avoid or reduce fatigue of the worker.*

Posture seating is now recognised as an industrial necessity, since by the use of scientifically designed seating fatigue is reduced, the health of workers is improved and output is increased.

Posture is the first consideration in the design of seating. If the sitting posture is incorrect (for example, when a clerk is slumped over his desk), the heart and chest are cramped and pressed downward against the diaphragm. This causes a direct pressure on the heart and affects the circulation of the blood, and intake of fresh air. A badly shaped seat edge constricts the flow of blood through an artery at the back of the leg and tends to make the feet "go to sleep".

Since office staff are sitting for a large part of the day great care must be taken when buying chairs. They must be well designed and ideally should be adjustable. Adjustable parts of chairs include the height of the seat, the height of the back rest, and the rake, i.e. the angle, of the back rest. The seats should be large enough and preferably scooped out and thinly padded.

The office worker who uses a desk with two sides, or who has to refer to mobile filing trolleys or other records nearby, should have a chair with castors to save time and fatigue in constantly having to get up from his desk.

Some chairs need to be built in a special way to meet the needs of a particular job and/or a particular person, but generally speaking chairs should fit any individual, give the most comfort, and obtain the maximum output from the employee without fatigue.

* A full definition of ergonomics, according to *Webster's Third International Dictionary*, is "the aspect of technology concerned with the application of biological and engineering data to problems relating to the mutual adjustment of man and the machines."

Office layout

Office furniture and equipment should be arranged in order to achieve the maximum output of work as well as the most attractive appearance. Though the final layout cannot be achieved until the precise dimensions of the furniture and equipment to be installed are known, it is useful to start the design of the layout before purchasing the furniture. This ensures that furniture that is too big is not purchased, that any new ideas arising out of looking at furniture may be incorporated, and that furniture requirements can be adapted as far as possible to the space available.

In order to design an office layout the office manager needs a knowledge of the flow of work, individual requirements, what work is to be done and the best way of doing it. Foresight of what might be required in the future is also necessary.

"Layout" is a very important aspect of office organisation because:

(1) a properly planned office helps to achieve efficiency in getting work done;

(2) the proper utilisation of floor space results in economies being made;

(3) supervision is easier;

(4) intercommunication is quicker;

(5) better use can be made of office equipment and machinery;

(6) from the workers' point of view, a well-planned office should be conducive to comfort and morale, whereas a cramped, badly planned layout can have the opposite effect.

The ideal office layout is rarely obtainable, as usually the furniture available has to be fitted into the space provided. However, there are certain principles which should be borne in mind.

(1) It is most important that the flow of work should be as regular as possible: a straight line, circle, or U-shape. This restricts the movement of people and of papers to the minimum, and gives maximum control.

(2) The floor space should be as free as possible from partitions, columns, or other impediments to free movement and observation.

(3) Desks should be arranged to avoid "uniformity" over a large area (see the points raised in discussing open-plan and landscaped offices on page 43). Ease of supervision must be borne in mind, however, and it may be advisable for small groups of desks to face the same way.

(4) Ideally, each clerk should have a minimum of working space for efficiency and health: about 4.6 square metres is common. The individual working requirements of each clerk should be studied, as

the space needed varies in different jobs. The legal requirements (*see* page 46) should also be borne in mind.

(5) All equipment, particularly reference files, should be within easy reach of those who have to use it and should be placed so that there is no interference with the movement or work of others when in use. Filing cabinets, for example, should be placed so that when the drawers are open they do not interfere with the free passage along the gangway.

(6) The number and location of gangways is important, the width usually being about 1 metre. Their arrangement depends on the work of the office and the number of desks and items of equipment.

(7) Lighting must be studied. Work requiring very good light should be sited close to the windows so as to get natural light, and the desks and other equipment should be positioned in such a way that the light from the windows is cast on the working plane.

(8) Ventilation must be considered if the office is not air-conditioned, particularly in an office of mixed staff. Men usually prefer to be close to the windows while the women prefer the warmer temperatures.

(9) The office layout should be balanced and attractive. Many business concerns are proud of their office decor which contributes to the corporate image by being a feature of public relations.

IMPROVING AN EXISTING LAYOUT

To improve the existing layout of an office the steps listed below should be followed.

(1) Obtain or prepare a floor plan. The standard scale is ¼ in. to the foot or 20 mm to the metre. Indicate ten-foot or three-metre sections along the walls.

(2) Indicate on the plan the movement of traffic via doors, staircases and lifts.

(3) Indicate electric plug points and telephone points on the plan; also lights and radiators if applicable.

(4) Make coloured cardboard templates of all the furniture and equipment units to be arranged in the various areas.

(5) Consult the heads of the working groups to give them an opportunity of making suggestions about their special requirements.

(6) Arrange the templates on the plan taking into account the flow of work, which can be indicated in pencil so that it can be erased easily.

(7) Discuss the proposals with the heads of working groups. They may well detect difficulties in the arrangement from the point

of view of work flow, movement of people, etc. This is the point at which compromise will have to be reached because it is rare indeed to be able to give everyone the ideal amount of space and/or arrangement within it.

(8) Outline the template on the plan. (A plastic template can be bought for drawing furniture, etc. to scale.)

An office layout before and after replanning is illustrated in Figs. 13(a) and 13(b).

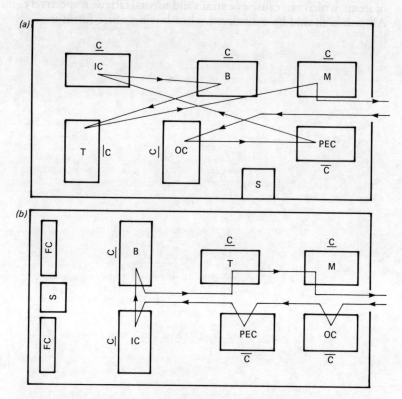

Fig. 13(a) *The original layout of an office.* KEY: FC = filing cabinet; T = typist; M = office manager; S = safe; B = book-keeper; PEC = prices and extension clerk; IC = invoice clerk; OC = order clerk.
Fig. 13(b) *The office layout after replanning (note the improved workflow).*

Legal requirements

The Health and Safety at Work etc. Act 1974 (H.A.S.A.W.A.) is concerned with employers' responsibilities for the health, safety and welfare of their employees. The fact that office staff are less at a risk from machinery than factory and other workers does not make it any less important to consider all possible ways in which they can be safeguarded from hazards of any kind. Eye strain, mental fatigue, physical discomfort and fatigue, irritation from unnecessary noise can all be avoided to some extent at least by the provision of the correct type of furniture. Writing surfaces that are too high or too low and chairs that scrape on the floor are just two examples of items which can cause eye strain and mental fatigue respectively. All points should be considered when buying office furniture.

7. Physical Conditions

In addition to obtaining suitable office accommodation, and seeing that the layout of furniture, etc. is properly planned, it is also necessary to ensure that appropriate physical conditions are provided and maintained. The most modern and expensive furniture can be spoiled by poor interior decorating. Clerical staff can be very unhappy if the ventilation is poor; work can be inaccurate if the lighting is bad or if there is excessive noise.

Clerical work requires more mental than physical effort, and it has been proved that mental work is more fatiguing than physical work. Concentration is needed even when the work is repetitive. A clear brain and physical conditions that do not cause distractions are prerequisites for efficient work. Adverse conditions cause mental strain which results in lower output, inaccurate work and low morale. It is the duty of the office manager to provide an environment which is pleasant, comfortable and conducive to good working habits.

Legal requirements

The Offices, Shops and Railway Premises Act 1963 was enacted to provide protection for office workers similar to that provided for industrial workers by the Factories Acts. The 1963 Act has been supplemented in certain respects by the Health and Safety at Work Act etc. 1974 and the Employment Protection Act 1975.

The Offices, Shops and Railway Premises Act covers all offices and office employees (*see* the definition in Chapter 1). Offices in which only near members of the family are engaged and dwellings of certain outworkers are excluded. Premises where the number of hours worked in each week does not exceed 21 are also exempt.*

* It should, however, be noted that the Health and Safety at Work etc. Act 1974 applies to all employers and employees except domestic servants in private households.

57

The physical conditions covered by the Act are cleanliness, overcrowding, temperature, ventilation, lighting, sanitary conveniences, washing facilities, drinking water, accommodation for clothing, building conditions, dangerous machinery, lifting excessive weights, first aid, fire precautions, accidents, and notification of accidents.

In general terms, the Act requires that lighting be sufficient and suitable; that sanitary conveniences be adequate and accessible; and that the supply of drinking water be adequate, etc.

There are a number of Regulations concerning sanitary conveniences, washing facilities, etc., although there are still no Regulations concerning other aspects such as lighting and reduction of noise. These points are covered to some extent by the Health and Safety at Work etc. Act 1974.

It is obviously difficult to lay down standards that would be equally applicable to all kinds of work in all offices, but the Act does prescribe the following.

(1) Prevention of overcrowding: to enforce a minimum standard of 11.3 cubic metres of space per person (ignoring ceiling height above 3 metres.) This standard is, however, calculated by reference to the total volume of a room compared with the number of people working in it, and is not an individual entitlement.

(2) Temperature: where workers are not engaged in efforts of severe physical motion, a minimum temperature of 15.5°C after the first working hour must be maintained.

(3) Washing facilities: a supply of clean running hot and cold water, and soap and towels (or other suitable means of cleaning or drying) must be provided. Communal arrangements may be made with other offices for this purpose. Fixed wash-basins (or other alternatives) must be provided in the following ratios.

(a) If the number of people employed on the premises does not normally exceed five, one wash-basin (or bowl) is sufficient.

(b) In all other cases, separate washing accommodation must be provided for each sex (if both are employed), and in the following numbers:

1 to 15   employees—1 wash-basin
16 to 30   employees—2 wash-basins
31 to 50   employees—3 wash-basins
51 to 75   employees—4 wash-basins
76 to 100 employees—5 wash-basins
over 100 employees—5 wash-basins plus 1 basin for every 25 people (or fraction thereof) in excess of 100.

(4) Fire prevention: where 20 or more workers are employed, or

where there are 10 or more persons employed at any time other than on the ground floor, it will be necessary to obtain from the Fire Authority a fire certificate to the effect that the premises are provided with reasonable means of escape.

(5) Cleaning: all office premises must be kept in a clean state, and floors and steps must be cleaned at least once a week by washing, or some other suitable method.

(6) First aid: a first-aid box must be provided for the use of employees in all office premises, and must be readily accessible. When more than 150 people are employed at a time, an additional box must be provided for each additional 150 people (or fraction thereof) employed.

Where more than 50 people are employed at any one time, one of the people in charge of the first-aid box must be trained in first aid.

(7) Sanitary conveniences: Regulations lay down the number of sanitary conveniences which must be provided, which are in the same ratios as for wash-basins (*see* above).

In addition to the exemptions already mentioned (family businesses), the Act allows certain exemptions regarding overcrowding, temperature, sanitary conveniences, and washing facilities by which the Regulations set out above may be varied in special cases.

The enforcement of regulations applicable to commercial offices is carried out by local authority inspectors appointed by local authorities as required under the Health and Safety at Work Act. Offices in factories are inspected by factory inspectors appointed by the Health and Safety Executive. All inspectors have authority to enter premises at any reasonable time, and, if obstructed, they may enlist the service of a police officer. They may ask questions of any employee and they may ask each employee to sign a declaration of the truth of his answers. There are prescribed penalties for obstructing an inspector and for other offences under the Act.

The importance of adequate and suitable lighting

Perhaps the most important of physical conditions in the office is lighting; bad handwriting, indistinct carbon copies and close figure-work all call for the provision of the best lighting possible. Bad lighting causes eye-strain and fatigue to workers, besides causing inferior quality work. It has been proved in a test experiment in the Bureau of Internal Revenue in Washington, U.S.A., that productivity in the office was increased by 5 per cent by the introduction of a brighter decorating scheme and improved lighting. It thus pays in terms of efficiency to have effective lighting in the office.

A list of ways to make optimum use of natural light published in a government report in 1952, *The Lighting of Office Buildings*, is still valid. The list includes:

(1) minor alterations to structure to increase effectiveness of existing windows;

(2) the use of external reflectors (i.e. outside the windows);

(3) diffusing glasses to redirect lighting in rooms where it is most wanted;

(4) better colour schemes;

(5) rearrangement of the furniture;

(6) supplementary lighting from artificial sources.

Typing and other machine work should be done near windows, and other less exacting work relegated to the darker areas of the office. Ideally, light should come from behind the left shoulder of an office worker who is right-handed, and over the right shoulder for the left-handed worker.

The aspect of an office building has an effect on the volume and quality of daylight received and where the building faces south, glaring sunlight might be troublesome. Remedies include the

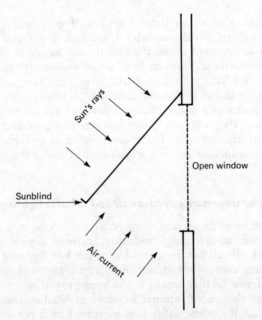

Fig. 14 *Protection afforded by external sunblind which gives ventilation at the same time.*

external veranda-type of sunblind (illustrated in Fig. 14) or vertical concrete or metal slats.

Interior sunblinds are not recommended unless the office is air-conditioned, as they interfere with the supply of fresh air.

In the government report mentioned above, quite detailed investigations were made into the necessity of cleaning windows. It was found that for a window facing east, the light transmission was reduced by 10 per cent in 50 days, and nearly 20 per cent in 100 days if the glass was left uncleaned. Ground-floor windows get dirty about twice as quickly as those on other floors, and in the winter upper-floor windows get dirty about 1.3 times as quickly as in summer. Generally speaking, therefore, it is desirable to clean windows on the ground floor twice as often as those on upper floors, and all windows should be cleaned more frequently in the winter.

ARTIFICIAL LIGHTING

There is usually little control over the amount of daylight in a room, but artificial light can be made to serve the exact requirements of work in an office. Table I examines the eight basic types of artificial lighting systems, each of which has advantages and disadvantages.

In most modern offices the cold cathode tube-light is found. The "shadowless soft" types of lighting, though pleasant, are not generally adequate for office work. Eyesight is a very precious attribute to every human being for personal life as well as work. Workers are entitled to lighting conditions which cause minimum strain to the eyes. It is suggested that the lighting should be checked with a light-meter by a service engineer at least three times a year to ensure that the required standards of lighting are constantly maintained.

There is no best kind of lighting suitable for all offices, as the lighting should be suited to the requirements of every individual office. The requirements vary according to the size of the office, the height of the ceiling, the type of work being performed there, the number of people in the office, and the positions of desks, machines, etc.

However, the following general principles are applicable to all offices.

(1) The light must be sufficient for the work but not too strong, otherwise glare will result.

(2) There should be no dark shadows cast (although some experts say that the presence of *some* shadow is desirable).

(3) The lighting system should be efficient, i.e. give the required

TABLE I. ADVANTAGES AND DISADVANTAGES OF DIFFERENT LIGHTING SYSTEMS.

Type of lighting	Advantages	Disadvantages
Direct*	Good intensity of light because directed downwards.	Rather hard. Casts dark shadows— bad for eyesight. Throws ceiling into relative darkness which psychologically is bad for office workers. Can cause glare.
Semi-direct*	Softer shadows. Ceiling partly illuminated.	
Indirect*	All light reflected— no glare. Soft light. Freedom from shadows. Well diffused.	Inadequate for clerical work unless supplemented by desk lamps.
Semi-indirect*	Most light is reflected. 10–35 per cent direct through the shade.	Shades accumulate dirt quickly. Inadequate for clerical work.
General*	Light falls equally above and below the light fitting as the light is completely surrounded by a translucent shade.	Difficult to get correct intensity of light on working surface. Shade may reduce light power by up to 33 per cent making it expensive. May cause glare.
Spot light	Well diffused. Soft light. No shadows. Dimmer switches can be installed to control intensity of light.	Inadequate for clerical work unless supplemented by desk lamps.
Fluorescent	Closer to daylight than any other type. Economic in use (gives at least twice as much light as incandescent light) for same consumption of current. Variety of colours including warm white, de luxe warm white, daylight and natural.	Installation costs higher than incandescent light. Causes glare but light diffusers can be used to overcome this. Flickering when light is switched on, but instant-start lamps are available.

* The direction of the light rays is illustrated in Fig. 15.

Type of lighting	Advantages	Disadvantages
Cold cathode	Long life (10,000–15,000 hours). Instant starting. Lengths or connected multiple lengths of 3 m. may be built up. Warmer light.	

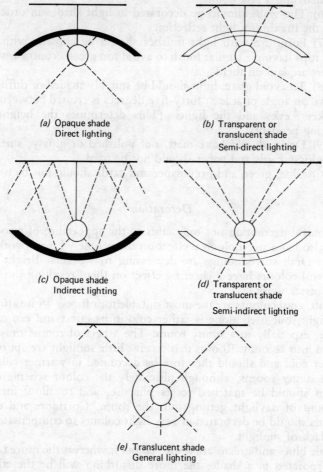

(a) Opaque shade
Direct lighting

(b) Transparent or
translucent shade
Semi-direct lighting

(c) Opaque shade
Indirect lighting

(d) Transparent or
translucent shade
Semi-indirect lighting

(e) Translucent shade
General lighting

Fig. 15 *Types of lighting.*

lighting at the minimum cost. (Running costs are usually more important than installation costs, although costs of maintenance should also be taken into account.)

(4) The light fittings should be sturdily made and of good appearance when both lit and unlit.

(5) It should be possible to vary the amount of light as required (for example, by suitable arrangement of switches, or by dimmer switches).

Various other points connected with lighting are mentioned in the appropriate sections of this and other chapters, but it is worth summarising a few points.

(6) The walls should be decorated in light shades in order to gain the maximum light reflection.

(7) Furniture with light finishes should be chosen, with the desk tops having a similar finish to avoid too great a contrast when papers are laid on them.

(8) To avoid glare, light should be suitably shaded or diffused, so that an angle of at least forty-five degrees is created between the workers' eyes and the lights. (This determines the height of hanging pendants).

(9) Desks should have matt, not polished or glossy, surfaces and glossy cards and paper should not be used.

(10) Blue, green and grey paper and cards should not be used.

Decoration

Colourful decoration not only adds to the appearance of a room, but also has a psychological effect on the people who are working in it. Drab surroundings are depressing to workers. Bright and cheerful colours have a cheering effect on them resulting in more and better work.

Soft, cool colours are the most suitable for offices. White attracts sunlight, but used alone is rather cold in its effect and can cause glare, especially in a sunny room. The aspect of rooms must be taken into account. Rooms that receive little sunlight are apt to be rather cold and should therefore be decorated in warmer colours than sunny rooms, although ultimately the colour scheme of a room should be matched to its purpose, and to allow for the amount of daylight getting into the room. Corridors and dark rooms should be decorated in very light colours to compensate for the lack of sunlight.

Pale blues and greens are restful colours, whereas the more red is incorporated in a shade, the more disturbing will be the effect. Colours of high reflective values help to get the maximum illumination from the artificial lighting. The effect of colour varies according to the quality and intensity of light it receives. For example, ordinary fluorescent-tube lighting accentuates yellow, green and blue, but depresses reds and browns. Reflective values of some common colours are set out in Table II.

TABLE II. REFLECTIVE VALUES OF COLOURS.

Colour	Percentage of reflection
White	88
Pale green	70
Portland stone	58
Lemon yellow	52
Sky blue	37
Silver grey	36
Salmon pink	36
Dark battleship grey	12
Middle brown	8
Dark brown	4
Chocolate	2

Colours can be combined to achieve a desired effect. If the end walls of a long room are decorated with dark colours and the other two walls in light tones, it has the effect of making the end walls seem nearer and so the room appears to be more square.

It used to be thought that a colour scheme should be harmonious so that, for example, primrose and green would be matched because they both share yellow as a common complement. Nowadays pinks are matched with grey, blues with mushroom, and so on; if pastel shades are used the effect can be very pleasant. Sharp contrasting colours should be avoided, as the effect is too dramatic. Matt or semi-gloss finishes are most suitable. Lastly, the cheerful effect of good decoration should not be marred by the indiscriminate hanging of calendars and notices. A neat notice board can be provided on one wall and some offices display one large calendar for all to see. The piling of office files and equipment on window sills is another despoiler of good order, and can be prevented by building sills on the slope.

Furnishings

FLOOR COVERING

There are many factors to be taken into account when buying floor covering for an office, and cost may be the deciding one. Safety is also very important. Highly polished parquet and terrazzo floors can be slippery and quite dangerous in the course of time. Other major points to be considered include ease of cleaning and wearing qualities.

Apart from adding warmth to a room both in appearance and use, some form of carpet acts as a sound absorber, thus reducing noise. Carpet-type floor covering can be conventional carpet laid over a foam rubber underlay or with a foam rubber backing. A mixture of wool and man-made fibre (e.g. nylon, Acrilan, polyester) is hard wearing, easy to clean, and does not flatten like a 100 per cent man-made fibre. All wool is not so easy to clean and in any case is now outrageously expensive.

The alternative to carpet is carpet tiles, normally made of very hard wearing man-made fibre on a composition backing. If this kind of tile is used it is essential to ensure that all the tiles are very firmly fixed to the floor. Sometimes the corners tend to curl: this is extremely dangerous.

There are other kinds of floor covering indicated in Table III, which shows the noise reduction given by each type. (The term "phons" is explained on page 67).

TABLE III. NOISE REDUCTION PROVIDED BY FLOOR COVERINGS.

Type of floor covering	Phons reduction
3 mm linoleum	5
Wood blocks	5–10
Thin rubber	5–10
3 mm carpet on 3 mm underfelt	10
6 mm cork composition	10
3 mm rubber on 6 mm sponge rubber	20

Various types of floating floor can also be installed; these use sound-absorbent packing between the concrete structure and the actual flooring. These floors are even more effective in reducing noise than the types listed in Table III.

CURTAINS

Curtains are provided in some offices, particularly in executive suites and offices and in typing pools. Apart from the pleasing atmosphere created by curtains they also provide a means of absorbing sound. Again ease of cleaning is important. Dry-cleaning is expensive so a man-made fibre makes cleaning costs more reasonable if washing is possible. The colours can either blend with the wall decoration or create a subdued contrast to add liveliness to the room.

MAINTENANCE

Both floor coverings and curtains should be cleaned regularly. There are specialist firms and cleaning contractors who use special shampooing machines which clean carpets so that they look new. In between the major cleans, the frequency of which depends on usage, spots and marks should be wiped off whenever possible. If floor tiles of any kind are used they should be checked regularly to ensure that there are no loose corners, which can be lethal.

Areas where the floor covering quickly becomes dirty, e.g. reception areas, below vending machines, and entrance/exit areas, can be kept cleaner with a non-slip dustmat which absorbs dust, dirt and moisture and can easily be cleaned regularly. A "collect dirty/deliver clean" service can be arranged.

There is a process of giving a high gloss to wood block floors so that no polishing is needed. The gloss does not chip and is ideal for use in entrance halls and corridors where the reduction of sound may not be so important.

Noise

The problem of noise in buildings is of fairly recent origin, and is caused partly by modern methods of building in steel and reinforced concrete. Compared with the heavy brick walls that buildings were once made of, these modern materials are apt to amplify and conduct noise.

Technically, there are two measurements of noise: the decibel, which might be described as the objective measurement of the intensity of sound, and the phon, which is directly related to what human beings find tolerable. The latter is the one in which noise-meters test sound, and a few examples of common sound measurements are as follows:

Sound levels	Phons
Threshold of painful sound	130
Pneumatic drills at 11 m	100
Typing pool	80
Busy London street	50–70
Normal conversation	up to 65
Quiet conversation	up to 45
Threshold of hearing	Zero

Noise affects the efficiency of the average office worker. Clerks may be unconscious of the noise, but they cannot get away from its effects. Experiments have shown that when noise has been deadened, errors in clerical work have been reduced, volume of work increased and its quality improved; the workers have also enjoyed better health.

Sharp unexpected or intermittent noises are much more disturbing than a continuous noise of one pitch. There can be no absolute levels of sound toleration, for it does to some extent depend on the individual.

With the clatter of modern machines and telephones, vying with outside traffic noises, the problem of reducing noise is not an easy one for office managers, but it should be given every attention. Many noises in the office are beyond control, but they can be investigated and attempts can be made to reduce them.

EXTERNAL NOISE

Careful siting of the office building is the first step in preventing noise. Preferably the building should be well set back from the road, and if possible separated from it by a row of trees. In towns this is rarely possible and, apart from offices dealing with the public, general offices should be placed at the top of office buildings.

Outside noises enter office buildings through windows and doors. Sound-baffles can be fitted inside windows; double glazing and/or double windows and double doors can also be fitted. Louvres fitted to window openings help to deaden external noise. There is no problem where air-conditioning is installed as windows are normally kept closed.

INTERNAL NOISE

The problems of internal noise are much more within the control of the office manager although the question of architectural design is of consequence. The building should be so planned that the noisy departments are sited away from those requiring peace and quiet.

In hospitals noise is a particular problem, and in the *Nuffield Provincial Hospitals Trust Report* it was reported that noise in wards comes chiefly from footsteps and voices in corridors, slamming of doors, wheeling of trolleys, operation of toilets and bed-pan washers, and at night-time from running machinery and water- or steam-pipes.

Noise, like light, is reflected from hard, polished surfaces, whereas it is absorbed and softened by the use of soft materials and matt surfaces. In an office noise is reverberated and amplified by hard, shiny surfaces of furniture and floors, and is usually a mixture of the ringing of telephones, the noise of office machines, conversation, footsteps and doors slamming.

PREVENTION OF INTERNAL NOISE

There are some steps which can be taken to prevent or reduce noise. The office manager should check that as many of these steps as possible are taken.

(1) First, there can be general absorption of sound by the use of sound-absorbent material on ceiling, walls and floor. Remarkable results can be obtained by either having a specially treated ceiling or fixing small sound-absorbent panels. At a hospital sound-absorbent panels of perforated gypsum plastic boards backed with glass silk were suspended from the ceiling, and were found to be very effective. Very attractive sound-absorbent screens can be obtained for open landscaped offices. Heavy curtains at windows also absorb sound (as well as providing warmth).

(2) Felt pads under typewriters and other noisy office machines help to reduce noise locally.

(3) Office machines that are extra noisy, e.g. telex machines, should be located in a separate room so that they do not disturb the work of others. If this is not possible an acoustic hood can be fitted to some machines such as telex.

(4) Telephone bells can be replaced by buzzers, light indicators or bleeps.

(5) Doors should be fitted with overhead automatic door-checks, and the door frames lined with rubber or felt. Where there is a constant stream of traffic through doorways, it is often preferable to have swing doors.

(6) A small private office should be made available for interviews (particularly confidential interviews) if at all possible. It does not help the success of an interview if it is frequently interrupted by telephone-ringing or by a buzz of conversation.

(7) The choice of floor covering (see page 65) dictates the amount by which noise made by people walking about can be reduced.

(8) A small but practical point is that the office manager must see that clerks do not talk unnecessarily loudly.

Ventilation

Ventilation is one of the more common of office problems; draughts can cause more strong feeling than any other aspect of the environment. Offices are often allowed to become too hot and stuffy, causing drowsiness resulting in slower and less accurate work. The requirements of good ventilation are that there shall be a constant flow of fresh air to remove staleness (at least 17 cubic metres per person per hour is the usual requirement) without causing draught.

Natural ventilation through windows can be increased by roof ventilators and internal tube ventilators which vent on the outside walls.

Artificial ventilation is achieved by electric fans; either propulsion or extraction systems are available, or a combination of both.

Air-conditioning is used in many modern office blocks. Warmed (or cooled), filtered and humidified fresh air is circulated into and out of the room, the temperature normally being thermostatically controlled. Some systems are more satisfactory than others and careful investigation of the various systems should be undertaken, preferably among users, before deciding on the installation of a particular system. It is expensive to install but is desirable in large open offices to ensure an even and acceptable temperature for more or less everyone.

To guard against draughts one or more of the following steps can be taken.

(1) Install air deflectors.

(2) Build wood, glass or metal screens around doors.

(3) Fit draught-prevention strips round door-jambs.

(4) Box in the lower parts of the office desks.

(5) Build a "lobby" around the outside door or install double doors to the street if space is available.

The problem of keeping an office warm and of introducing fresh air without causing draughts is a very difficult one. One point to watch is that people sometimes do not realise that they are sitting in a draught and get thoroughly chilled. If any employee complains about draughts all possible steps should be taken to rectify the matter.

Heating

For concentration, a clerk should not be conscious of either extreme heat or extreme cold. In Great Britain, office buildings need to be heated for a large part of the year, and it is quite important that an adequate and consistent temperature should be maintained throughout an office. There should also be uniform heat at the different levels of a room, so that the air is not warmer at head level than at floor level. The problems of heating are (i) how to generate warmth; and (ii) having done so, how to conserve it.

The following room temperatures are recommended by the Institute of Heating and Ventilation Engineers:

Offices	18°C
Hall, staircases and corridors	12°C
Store rooms	10°C

No organisation should spend money on heating unnecessarily, though it is useful to have some local control over heating systems. Temperatures can then be varied in different parts of the building according to their uses.

All heating systems warm partly by radiation, that is, by the direct rays of heat from the appliance, and partly by convection, that is, by setting up warm currents of air. The different methods of heating are listed in Table IV with some indication of their advantages and disadvantages.

TABLE IV. ADVANTAGES AND DISADVANTAGES OF DIFFERENT METHODS OF HEATING.

Method of heating	Advantages	Disadvantages
Radiation		
Gas fires.	Clean. Easily controlled. Warm the room quickly. Useful for supplementary heat.	Require an outlet flue. Risk of papers floating on to flames. Dry the atmosphere.
Electric fires.	Clean. Good auxiliary heating.	Unless fixed to a wall there are trailing wires. May be easily knocked over. Open elements, even if protected by bars, can be dangerous. Risk of papers floating on to elements.
Low-temperature panels recessed into walls and/or ceilings.	Clean. No open flame or element. People cannot be burnt by them.	Localised heating.
Convection		
Hot-water/steam radiators.	Choice of solid fuel, gas or oil-fired boiler. Thermostatic control either centrally and/or in individual rooms.	Walls may be marked. Need humidifiers to avoid drying the atmosphere. Take up wall space. Wooden furniture should not be placed too near as contraction caused by heat tends to loosen joints.

Method of heating	Advantages	Disadvantages
Hot-water/steam pipes in skirting.	Even distribution of warm air. Clean.	Difficult to place furniture and equipment against walls.
Hot-water/steam pipes with ducts in floor or skirting (known as duct-air heating).	Even distribution of warm air.	Necessity for grids needing cut-outs in carpet if ducts inserted in floor.
Electric convector heaters.	Clean.	Need humidifier to avoid drying the atmosphere. Slow to heat a room from cold. Unless fixed to a wall, wires may be trailing across the floor.
Electric tubular heaters.	Easily fixed to any wall where a plug point is available, in any position. Light in weight. Thermostatic control.	Cost of power. Walls may be marked.
Electric oil-filled radiators.	Large heating area.	Heavy in weight. Walls may be marked. Takes up wall space.
Night-storage heaters.*	Off-peak tariff.	Very heavy. Space-consuming. May not retain adequate heat for the whole day.
Electric under-floor heating.*	Off-peak tariff.	High capital expenditure. Causes people's feet to swell.
Gas heaters.	Efficient warming. Thermostatic control. Relatively cheap to run. Reasonable installation costs.	
Gas suspension heaters.	Warm an area of 14 to 19 square metres. Useful for large areas such as halls, hospital wards.	

* These systems take in heat during the night (off-peak) and gradually loose it into the atmosphere during the day.

It should be noted that Table IV is not comprehensive. Before installing a system the office manager would be well advised to consult gas and electricity authorities and air-conditioning consultants to get full information about the various systems available. In general, heating systems should not take up too much wall space, they should not accumulate dirt, they should be easy to keep clean, they should not cause discolouration of walls or ceilings, and of course they should give adequate warmth. At the same time everyone has a duty to conserve energy. Ways of doing this include double glazing, roof insulation and wall insulation. For example, an air-spaced lining of fibreboard to the walls of a building has been found to halve the loss of heat by transmission to the open air. Appropriate consultants should be called in to give advice as to the best means of retaining heat in the building.

Total concept

As mentioned previously, office landscaping involves the total concept of integrated colour schemes, etc. Although particularly applicable to the open-plan office, a harmonious impression is created in any room when thought is given to matching and contrasting colours, to the appearance of various kinds of floor covering in relation to curtain material and materials with which the office furniture is made. In other words the various colours, materials, type of lighting, heating and ventilation systems, the style of the furniture and equipment such as bookcases and cabinets, and the decorations, such as pictures and plants, should blend to create an impression and an atmosphere. That impression should also reflect the corporate image of the organisation. The chrome and steel office may look super modern but it also looks impersonal, an image most organisations would not wish to present.

To create an office which gives an impression of being a complete entity the rule is to prepare a check-list of the various items to be purchased and to find out what suitable materials, colours, patterns, styles, etc. are available in all of them before purchasing anything. If the decor has been planned in this way a pleasing effect can be achieved.

Cleanliness

It is little use obtaining ideal office accommodation, and fitting it out with the best furniture, if it is not kept clean and tidy. Not only is a dirty office unpleasant to work in, but it may affect the health of the workers in it. It is the office manager's task to see that the offices are kept clean, and to that end to see that the cleaners employed are properly supervised, and that they are provided with adequate equipment.

Dirt accumulates in less accessible places, such as the tops of cupboards and filing cabinets, and a programme should be laid down for when these and other more difficult places are given attention.

If cleaners are directly employed they should be given job descriptions setting out precisely what has to be done and the intervals at which each task should be performed, e.g. washing floors (*see* legal requirements), cleaning light fittings, washing walls, etc. Supervision for cleaning staff should be allocated specifically to one person.

If cleaning contractors are employed constant vigilance is needed to ensure that cleaning is done properly. At the first sign of slackness the matter should be reported to the management of the firm concerned.

One of the difficulties of supervising cleaning activities is that they are normally carried out before or after normal working hours. The person responsible for supervision should make it his/her business to look in occasionally while cleaning is going on, at least to show interest in the job and the people doing it if for no other reason.

Fire precautions

Offices contain a vast quantity of highly flammable material and there are serious fire risks which must be guarded against. The Chief Fire Officer of the local Fire Authority and the organisation's insurers can be asked for advice, and the following precautions should be taken.

(1) Mark fire exits clearly.

(2) Inform all members of staff individually how to find the nearest fire exit in the event of hearing the fire alarm.

(3) Test the fire alarm regularly. (Inform staff of the day and time at which the regular test takes place.)

(4) Install adequate fire extinguishing equipment.

(5) Train staff to use fire extinguishers.

(6) Inspect fire extinguishers regularly to ensure that they are in proper working order.

(7) Provide each member of staff individually with a carefully prepared procedure sheet explaining what to do in the event of a fire.

(8) Ensure that the telephone operator is aware of the procedure in case of fire.

(9) Hold fire drills regularly.

(10) Install an automatic fire alarm system.

(11) Provide ashtrays to avoid placing lighted cigarette stumps in waste-paper baskets.

(12) Where applicable the main electric switch in the building should be switched off when the offices are not occupied.

(13) Ensure that flammable materials are not left in the sun. (One serious fire was started by the action of the sun shining through an unshaded window on to the celluloid markers of a filing system.)

(14) Issue a fire prevention code to all staff incorporating such items as switching off all machines at night and *unplugging* them from the power points; ensuring that all heaters/fires are switched off.

(15) Exercise constant vigilance to ensure that staff do not create any fire risks and take action if any Regulations are contravened.

Benefits of good physical conditions

It was stated at the beginning of the chapter that the staff do better work in good conditions. Apart from any aesthetic considerations it is sheer good economics to provide the best working conditions possible within the limitations of finance and the type of accommodation. Since people spend almost a quarter of their lives in the office it is reasonable to expect them to want pleasing, as well as functional, surroundings. It has been said that if the working environment is made as nearly similar to home as possible people are much more willing to spend more time in it and to work harder. Pictures on the wall, for example, may seem a luxury, but they do break up vast areas of blank wall and add a touch of "homeliness".

People generally react well when given good conditions. They are likely to react even better if they are consulted whenever practicable. They will take a pride in keeping the place in good order, clean and tidy if they have been involved in choosing the colour scheme, have been asked for their opinion on different types of floor covering, curtains, etc., and if the benefits of various types of lighting, ventilation, heating, and/or air-conditioning have been explained to them. The result will be a group of people reasonably happy with their working environment, cheerful, able to concentrate and give of their best. The vast majority of people want to do just this.

The Health and Safety Executive's "Health and Safety at Work" booklets, published by Her Majesty's Stationery Office, may be useful sources of references on certain aspects of physical conditions. Relevant titles are as follows.

No. 5   *Cloakroom Accommodation and Washing Facilities*
No. 25 *Noise and the Worker*
No. 39 *Lighting in Offices, Shops and Railway Premises*
No. 40 *Means of Escape in case of Fire in Offices, Shops and Railway Premises*
No. 45 *Seats for Workers in Factories, Offices and Shops*
No. 48 *First Aid in Offices, Shops and Railway Premises*

PART THREE
STAFF MANAGEMENT

8. Defining the Job

Materials, machines, and even offices themselves can be replaced, and any risks involved can be insured against, but a good loyal team of workers cannot be replaced nearly so easily. Organisation and methods are of great importance but the success of the business depends ultimately on the performance of the staff, which is directly related to the standard of management.

It is amazing how much attention a manager will give to the buying of new equipment, but how little he will give to the selection and training of his staff. Fortunately this aspect of management is becoming widely recognised as crucial and training is given in a variety of ways to enable managers to develop the skills required to recruit and maintain a productive and contented staff.

The office manager's responsibility

In a large or medium-size organisation there is a personnel department which handles all the administrative details of recruitment, training, appraisal, welfare, etc. In a small organisation there may be a personnel officer who is responsible for all these activities or they may be the responsibility of the office manager. The extent of the personnel department's responsibility varies from one organisation to another but in any event each individual manager should know and practice the principles and skills of staff management.★

★ The term "staff management" is used to indicate the difference between carrying out various activities involved in handling staff, regardless of one's position in the organisation, and the highly specialised discipline of personnel management. There is an Institute of Personnel Management which has its own professional status and qualifications in the same way that the Institute of Administrative Management has its own status and qualifications in the administration field.

The management of human beings is a much more complex matter than the management of machines. It includes finding the right staff, training them, ensuring discipline and giving encouragement, and retaining their interest and loyalty while obtaining the maximum from them: a difficult task. It is achieved by the application of psychology, custom, law and science. It is an art, which often requires rule-of-thumb methods to be developed on the spot, according to the requirements of the situation. It calls for a knowledge of the work, and of the people who do the work. The engagement and control of shop-floor workers for a steel factory is not the same as the recruitment and control of people for office work. Yet both involve the same principles, and many of the same techniques can be used in both cases.

There is now a far greater awareness of the necessity for all managers to learn and use staff management techniques, but even so bad selection methods are still used, work output is still not measured, training is non-existent or cursory, and bad morale still exists in many organisations. Where there are bad supervision, indifferent staff reporting, poor salaries and no promotion policy, then frustration occurs and staff become listless and unenthusiastic.

Function analysis

Staff management has many processes. To begin at the beginning, it is essential first to decide precisely what work is required from a new employee and what kind of person is needed to fulfil the responsibilities and carry out the duties involved. It is necessary to go back to the function of the department, section or office in which the work is to be carried out. In Parts One and Two we looked at function analysis in terms of the whole organisation and at the office manager's role. When the structure of the organisation has been determined it is possible to establish operational areas, i.e. grouping of the tasks involved in fulfilling the various functions of the organisation. The next step is to decide how many people are needed to carry out the tasks and how the tasks shall be allocated to jobs. Questions of specialisation and centralisation arise (*see* Chapter 3). Considerations of cost, i.e. salary levels, availability of staff and their calibre, physical facilities and other resources must also be considered when deciding how the duties shall be allocated to jobs. In a very small organisation one person normally has to perform a very wide variety of duties because there is no need for more than one or two people to cover the total work-load. For example, in a one-man business a general clerk/typist may perform the duties of mail clerk, filing clerk, telephone operator, receptionist, book-keeper, typist, stores clerk, invoice clerk, etc. In a large organisation there could be anything from two to several hundred people performing each operation.

Job descriptions

When the duties required of an individual employee have been determined a job description must be written. It is used as a basis for recruitment, training, appraisal, promotion, job evaluation, job enlargement, job enrichment, and to some extent for restructuring the organisation. Time and care should be spent on preparing an accurate job description because it should form the basis of all future dealings with the person finally recruited in respect of all matters relating to the performance of duties, e.g. training, appraisal and promotion. It should be stressed that the job description produced at this stage is not a document for all time. It should be reviewed and revised at regular intervals (*see* page 115). At this stage it forms the basis on which to recruit the best person for the job.

A job description is a broad statement of what the job involves and should contain the following information.

(1) Function or aim: a statement of what the person is expected to achieve as a result of performing the duties listed.

(2) The person to whom the employee is responsible, i.e. the immediate superior.

(3) The person/people for whom the employee is responsible, i.e. the subordinates directly responsible to the employee and whose work he must supervise.

(4) Duties or activities: a broad statement of the duties which the employee will be required to undertake in order to fulfil the function.

(5) Special conditions, limitations or other specific information which the employee must be aware of, such as the scope of his activities within a department or organisation.

Some job descriptions set out the duties in general terms which may be referred to as "responsibilities" and then list specific tasks. In certain circumstances a job description can be developed out of the analysis of an individual's function. For example, a job description for a secretary to an individual manager should be very closely related to that manager's own job description and the means by which he performs his duties. If he has to hold meetings in order to carry out labour negotiations there are many aspects of this activity which can be carried out by a secretarial assistant, e.g. arranging the meeting, booking accommodation, arranging the room, preparing documents, taking notes at the meeting and drafting

Minutes, to mention a few. Therefore, when recruiting, one looks for a person who has had experience of these activities or who has the potential if trained to undertake them.

There are no hard and fast rules about the presentation of a job description. The following specimen is just one format.

JOB DESCRIPTION
Job: Personnel Records Clerk
Function: To ensure the availability of specific personnel information
Responsible to: Personnel Assistant
Responsible for: nil
Duties: (1) Prepare and process documentation for new employees
(2) Filing
(3) Send out documentation for and record salary and wage increases
(4) Prepare returns for Department of Employment
(5) Pass information about transfers
(6) Process holiday applications
(7) Maintain wage rates book

Job specification

Having decided what has to be done (the job description) the next step is to determine how it is to be done in the context of the function to be fulfilled, i.e. what knowledge and skills are needed to perform the duties to the standards laid down. Each duty is analysed so that the extent of knowledge and skills required for each activity can be established.

A clerk's job description may include the following duty: "to open and distribute mail". To perform this duty efficiently the employee needs to know:

(1) the procedures for opening, recording, sorting and distributing mail;

(2) the departments and personnel in the organisation and their respective functions.

Skills in handling mail and operating a letter-opening machine (if appropriate) are also necessary.

All office employees need to be able to use the telephone, for which communication skills are essential, and skill in handling people and situations may also be required, depending on the nature of the job and the people with whom the employee is in contact.

As with job descriptions there are various formats. It is not

JOB SPECIFICATION
Job: Personnel Records Clerk

Duties	Tasks	Knowledge requirements	Skill requirements (ability to:)
(1) Documentation for new employees	(1.1) Sends new employee advice forms to notify Time Officer.	Layout of employee advice forms.	
	(1.2) Makes out rate cards and computer cards.	Layout of computer and rate cards.	Write neatly.
	(1.3) Enters details of new employees in starters book and wage book.	Layout and use of starters book and wage book.	
	(1.4) If employee is disabled enters on registered disabled list.	Method of making entries in disabled list.	
	(1.5) Collects employee's personal documents (i.e. application form, letter of offer, etc,) for insertion in personal file.	Documents required. Personal Department filing system.	
	(1.6) Types out absence report form.	Layout and interpretation of forms.	Type acurately complete entries in printed forms.
	(1.7) Sends notification of starter's rate of pay for hourly-paid employees to Head of Department.	Organisation of Departments. Heads of Department. Location of Departments.	
	(1.8) Sends all relevant documents to Wages Department.	Documents required by Wages.	

Duties	Tasks	Knowledge requirements	Skill requirements (ability to:)
(2) Filing	(2.1) Maintains files for monthly, weekly and hourly-paid employees.	Filing system and indexing methods.	Maintain files securely.
(3) Salary and wage increases	(3.1) Sends out salary and wage increase slips to Heads of Department for all relevant employees. (3.2) On return of slips consolidates returns and passes to Personnel Officer for signature. (3.3) Makes revised entries in wage rates book.	Rates of pay and date of salary and wage increases.	
(4) Returns for Department of Employment	(4.1) Provides Department of Employment with statistics and information when required.	Statistical return form and procedure for indicating number of disabled employees on pay-roll.	Compile statistics.
(5) Transfers	(5.1) Notifies Time Office, Wages Department and Heads of Department of transfers.	Personnel records.	
(6) Holidays	(6.1) Receives holiday slips. (6.2) Transfers dates of holidays to absence sheets.	Interpretation of the forms.	Transcribe information accurately.

(6.3) Determines whether holiday is paid or not, refers to Assistant Personnel Officer, forwards holiday slips to Wages Department and notes for monthly statistics.	Company policy on holiday pay.
(7) Wage rates book (7.1) Keeps wage rates book up to date. (7.2) Issues new rate lists when necessary. (7.3) Sends quarterly return to Head Office on rates of pay.	Company policy on changes of rates of pay. Keep confidential information securely.

Reproduced in part from Booklet No. 8, *The Training of Clerks*, by courtesy of the Engineering Industry Training Board.

uncommon to prepare a job specification which combines the duties to be performed and the qualifications required for the job. This is probably adequate for the average specialised clerical post, e.g. filing clerk. When a wider variety of duties is included it may be advisable to go into greater detail.

The specimen job specification shown on pages 81–3 is an analysis of the job description on page 80.

Having prepared a job description and/or job specification, the job requirements have now been established on an individual basis. In large organisations it is impracticable to have a vast range of individual job descriptions. There must be some method of grouping or grading the multivarious activities carried on in offices. This aspect is dealt with in the next chapter.

9. Job Evaluation

Job evaluation has been practised in industry for some years and is now a specialised function of personnel management. Recently, largely as a result of pressure by white-collar unions, job evaluation has been introduced for clerical and secretarial occupations.

Purposes of job evaluation

The main purpose of job evaluation is to provide a basis for salary levels and differentials. It is a process of comparing jobs on the basis of common criteria with the aim of replacing subjective judgment by objective judgment when assessing jobs against each other. It is *not* a complete means for determining salary structures as will be shown later.

The result of a job evaluation exercise is a job-grading scheme within the organisation. The grading is used when compiling salary scales, selecting and engaging staff, transferring employees between departments, promoting staff, and setting up a training scheme, for pay-roll work, and for cost estimating and budgetary control.

Job evaluation must start from job analysis. A job description (or job definition) and a job specification must be prepared (*see* Chapter 8). The actual process of evaluating work done leads to job grading, which is followed by price fixing, or the determination of wage/salary levels and structure.

It must be stressed that job evaluation is concerned with the work done, and not the person doing it. It is the level of knowledge, skills, etc., required to perform a particular activity which are considered, and not the level of the person's qualifications.

Job grading

Job grading is the establishment of the relationship between jobs. For example, is the job of filing worth more than, less than or the same as display-typing★. After analysis the job can be grouped, classified or graded according to the requirements of the job. There are many methods of grading jobs, those most commonly used in offices being:

(1) the ranking method;
(2) the classification method;
(3) the points system.

RANKING OR PAIRED COMPARISONS

This is the most subjective, and therefore least accurate, of the methods. The variety of jobs are assessed as being less important than (score 0), the same value as (score 1) or more important than (score 2) the others. A grid is drawn up for comparison. In the example in Fig. 16 the office manager's job is compared with the

	Office manager	Executive secretary	Accountant	Switchboard operator	Stenographer	Typing-pool supervisor	Total
Office manager	X	2	1	2	2	2	9
Executive secretary	0	X	0	2	2	1	5
Accountant	1	2	X	2	2	2	9
Switchboard operator	0	0	0	X	1	0	1
Stenographer	0	0	0	1	X	0	1
Typing-pool supervisor	0	1	0	2	2	X	5

Fig. 16 *Job evaluation ranking matrix.*

★ The term "display-typing" is used instead of the more usual "copy-typing" because very few typists do in fact "copy". They are usually given manuscript material which must be accurately and appropriately displayed.

other jobs in turn. The process is repeated with each job down the vertical column. From the total number of points it can be seen that three grades emerge from the six jobs, viz. (i) office manager and accountant; (ii) executive secretary and typing-pool supervisor; and (iii) stenographer and switchboard operator.

The ranking method is suitable when only a small number of jobs are being graded, say up to a maximum of fifteen.

CLASSIFICATION
Many large organisations use this method of job grading. Some organisations work on the basis of standard designations, e.g. accounts clerk, section clerk, assistant accountant, etc. In the Civil Service the grades are clerical officer, executive officer, higher executive officer, and so on.

In other organisations jobs are slotted into predetermined groups which may be numbered or lettered. The grading scheme recommended for office work by the Institute of Administrative Management consists of eight grades listed from A to H. The grade definitions are as follows.

GRADE DEFINITIONS

A   Tasks which require no previous clerical experience; each individual task is allotted and is either very simple or is closely directed.

B   Tasks which, because of their simplicity, are carried out in accordance with a limited number of well-defined rules after a comparatively short period of training. These tasks are closely directed and checked, and are carried out in standard routine with short period control.

C   Tasks which are of a routine character and follow well-defined rules, but which require either some experience (several weeks) or a special aptitude for the task, and which are carried out according to a standard routine and are subject to short period control.

D   Tasks which require considerable experience, but a limited degree of initiative, and which are carried out according to a predetermined procedure. The tasks are carried out according to a standard routine which may vary, but will not vary enough to necessitate any considerable direction.

E   Tasks which may require one or more of the following:
     (a) a basic level of professional or specialised knowledge, for example Part I or II of the A.C.M.A. examinations;
     (b) performance or control of clerical or administrative work

requiring mostly routine decisions, but occasional use of discretion and initiative;

(c) work supervision of a range normally of two to six clerical staff. The number supervised may vary according to the complexity or level of the work.

F   Tasks which may require one or more of the following:

(a) professional or specialised knowledge equivalent to an intermediate level examination of an appropriate professional association, for example Part II or III of A.C.M.A. examinations;

(b) performance or control of complex clerical or routine administrative work requiring occasional decisions of a non-routine type, and some use of judgment or initiative on routine matters;

(c) supervision of a range, normally of five to twelve clerical staff, in a section compact enough to enable full personal control to be directly maintained. The numbers supervised may vary according to the complexity or level of the work, and may include E grade assistants.

G   Tasks which may require one or more of the following:

(a) professional or specialised knowledge equivalent to a university first degree or to an advanced but not necessarily final qualification of an appropriate professional association, for example, final years of A.C.A., the Institute's Diploma in Administrative Management, or Part III or IV of A.C.M.A.;

(b) performance or control of work of wide complexity or importance requiring regular non-routine decisions and a regular use of judgment and initiative in the execution of predetermined policies;

(c) supervision of a range normally of nine to twenty clerical staff. Control of clerical work may be exercised through two or more grade E or F supervisors; or supervision of a smaller number of grade E or F professional or specialist staff. The numbers supervised may vary according to the complexity or level of the work.

H   Tasks which may require one or more of the following:

(a) professional or specialised knowledge equivalent to a university first degree with some experience or a final qualification of an appropriate professional association such as A.C.A., the Institute's Diploma in Administrative Management, or A.C.M.A.;

(b) performance or control of work of significant complexity or importance requiring an extensive measure of judgment or initiative and responsibility for some contribution towards the development of departmental policies as well as for their execution;

(c) supervision of a range normally of twenty or more clerical staff. The numbers supervised may vary according to the complexity or level of the work, but control will normally require a deputy and two or more grade E or F supervisors; or supervision of a smaller number of grade E, F or G specialist staff.

NOTE: The above grade definitions are reproduced from *Office Job Evaluation*, by kind permission of the publishers, the Institute of Administrative Management.

Jobs are grouped into types of work, e.g. typing and secretarial, computing, accounting, and miscellaneous. In the computing section a stationery assistant is a grade A job, a data preparation operator and a computer operator is a grade D job, a systems project leader and a chief programmer are grade H jobs.

POINTS

The allocation of points for predetermined, precisely defined factors of a job is the most objective and, therefore, most accurate method used. There is still an element of subjectivity because it is impossible to be absolutely precise about certain factors, such as the level of decision-making. However, when a large number of jobs are being evaluated it is possible to compare such factors over a range of activities, which ensures a reasonable level of accuracy.

The processes of the points method of evaluation are as follows.

(1) First, the work is investigated, and job specifications are drafted for all jobs, if they are not already in existence.

(2) A standard list of all qualities required to do all the jobs is then prepared. Some qualities are listed in the example on page 90. Other qualities which might be considered include technical, specialist or professional knowledge, manual skills including dexterity, working conditions, judgment, intelligence, fatigue (mental and physical), accuracy, and contacts outside the department (letters, telephone calls, etc.).

(3) A scale of points is allocated to each item according to its estimated importance (*see* example on page 90).

(4) Each job is assessed in the light of these qualities, and is awarded a number of points for each quality required to do the job.

Quality	Points
Experience	3–20
Education	3–12
Complexity	3–10
Responsibility for information and/or cash	0–12
Supervision	0–10
Initiative	0–10
Alertness	1–10
Co-operation	0–6
Vision	1–5

(5) The points are then totalled for each job, and the job is graded in accordance with a predetermined pointing scale (*see* below).

Grade	Points
1	61 and over
2	51 to 60
3	42 to 50
4	34 to 41
5	27 to 33
6	21 to 26
7	Up to 20

Thus a job requiring the minimum of experience and education and of very little complexity, having no responsibility, supervision or initiative requirements and requiring moderate alertness, co-operation and vision might achieve a total of 20 points. This job would then be grade 7.

(6) Each job grade is then equated to the appropriate wage/salary scale.

Task analysis

For maximum accuracy a task analysis exercise should be conducted. This involves establishing the tasks involved in performing each duty given in a job description, and analysing each task into elements. The knowledge and skills required to perform each element are then determined. However, this is a very time-consuming task and ideally needs a team of analysts. A recent publication* of the International Labour Office provides a good foundation from which to work. The tasks normally carried out by clerical and secretarial staff are analysed, and the cognitive (mental), affective (attitudinal) and psychomotor (physical) skills are given. Knowledge required and variable factors in the tasks are also given. A specimen task analysis is given below.

TASK: RECEIVING AND CONNECTING A TELEPHONE CALL ON A MANUAL SWITCHBOARD
Task elements.
(1) Responds to external calling signal
(2) Greets
(3) Identifies
(4) Repeats name of person/extension wanted
(5) Checks extension number
(6) Obtains name of caller
(7) Repeats name of caller
(8) Determines nature of call
(9) Informs caller of appropriate person
(10) Requests caller to hold the line
(11) Checks that extension line is free
(12) Connects with extension
(13) Rings extension
(14) Informs extension user of caller's identification
(15) Informs caller that connection is being made when call accepted
(16) Connects caller

Skills required.
(1) Cognitive (mental):
    considering cost factors
    deciding nature of call
    deciding person able to assist caller
    eliciting information
    recognising calling signals
    recognising free and occupied extension lines
(2) Affective (social):
    being attentive

* *Modules of Employable Skill (MES), Analysis of Standard Clerical and Secretarial Tasks for the Development of Occupational Skills and Competence*, available from The International Labour Office, 87–91 New Bond Street, London W1Y 9LA.

    being aware of protocol
    being calm
    being considerate
    being co-operative
    being courteous
    being discreet
    being patient
    being pleasant
    being reliable
    being tactful
    being time-conscious
    being tolerant
    being trustworthy
    communicating effectively
    creating a good impression
    working under pressure
(3) Psychomotor (physical):
    operating switchboard
    recording data
    repeating spoken words
    speaking clearly
    speaking in a well-modulated voice

Determining job grades

As an organisation grows, it becomes increasingly necessary to evolve some form of job grading. No hard-and-fast rule can be given about the number of job grades established, but too many will be confusing and too few may be unfair to the workers. It may be impossible in the first round to bring the number of job grades down to the number required because of the wide range of salary levels in existence. There may also be a wide diversity of job titles for similar work. For example, in an American survey it was found that fifty-four titles were used for one type of job which was eventually designated "junior stock clerk". It is not usually possible to make this sort of change at one stroke. The ultimate aim should be to have the minimum number of job grades, and job titles within those grades, compatible with the range of duties to be performed to fulfil each individual function.

Advantages of job grading

The advantages of job grading can be summarised as follows.
(1) It provides a basis for salary, training and promotion schemes.

(2) It provides a useful blueprint when selecting staff to perform a certain job.

(3) It provides the data needed for collective bargaining.

(4) It reveals the work content of jobs and the differences between them, and indicates anomalies in wage/salary levels.

(5) It may improve relationships between management and workers.

(6) It may result in an improvement in morale leading to reduction in labour turnover, and increase in output.

Limitations of job grading

Job grading, though systematic, has its shortcomings. Some of these are given below.

(1) Salary scales cannot be fixed solely on the basis of job grading without reference to market conditions, trade union agreements, etc.

(2) Job grading takes no account of personal performance which must be assessed by merit rating (*see* Chapter 11).

(3) It depends on human assessments, which tend to be subjective, so that grading may not be uniform. This is particularly true if more than one assessor is used.

(4) Assessment may not be on the same basis throughout an organisation.

(5) Some clerical work, and particularly secretarial work, is difficult if not impossible to assess.

(6) The amount of responsibility may vary for different people doing similar jobs depending on the willingness and ability of their superiors to delegate.

(7) Jobs change and develop and regular re-evaluation is necessary to ensure that the work done is fairly rewarded.

(8) If the number of job grades is too limited many jobs of different character may be in the same grade which leads to a feeling of resentment on the part of the workers.

(9) There may be a tendency to view the worker as graded, whereas it is the job which is graded.

Undertaking a job evaluation exercise

For the newcomer to job evaluation there are many pitfalls to be avoided. *Office Job Evaluation*★ published by the Institute of Administrative Management provides a full description of the Institute

★ Available from Institute of Administrative Management, 205 High Street, Beckenham, Kent BR3 1EA.

grading system already explained, introduces the various methods of grading office work, and gives advice on how to introduce job evaluation in offices.

There must be interest and co-operation on the part of the staff and the unions must be informed and involved. All the members of the appraisal team must undergo suitable training, usually an appreciation course. It must be made absolutely clear at the beginning that no employee will lose as a result of the exercise. Clear explanations must be given as to the purpose(s) of the exercise, the method(s) to be used, and the ways in which the staff themselves will be asked to contribute.

There are three ways in which the information required for job evaluation can be obtained, viz. by questionnaires, by discussion with the worker and/or the supervisor, and by observation of the work being done. It is quite useful to start with a questionnaire, (i) because it starts the workers thinking about what they actually do, and (ii) because it provides a basis for discussion.

If the employees already have job descriptions these can form the basis for discussion, but most job descriptions do not normally contain sufficient detail for job evaluation purposes. A specimen job definition form prepared by Messrs. Binder, Hamlyn, Fry & Company, a firm of consultants, is shown in Fig. 17 together with guide-lines (below) for its completion.

Observation should be based on task analysis.

Guide-lines for completion of job definitions for job evaluation

MAIN PURPOSE AND JOB SUMMARY

(1) Summarise the purpose and content of the job in terms which will:
  (a) distinguish it from any other job;
  (b) highlight the most important activities;
  (c) account for most of the time and effort.

Do not try to list every detail since this may take attention away from the really important aspects, but where equipment is operated state size/make/speed where these are relevant.

PRINCIPAL SKILLS

(2) Identify which skills are required, how they are used, and the extent to which they are important. Take into account the previous experience or learning period which is necessary (where these are significant). State what specialist knowledge is necessary, e.g. of machinery, materials, working procedures.

PRINCIPAL RESPONSIBILITIES

(3) Describe the responsibilities where the consequence of errors is most significant; consider these under such headings as responsibility for:

JOB DEFINITION FOR JOB EVALUATION

JOB TITLE: REF No.

BRANCH: DEPT: Nos.

RESPONSIBLE TO:

MAIN PURPOSE & JOB SUMMARY (see guide-lines):

PRINCIPAL SKILLS (see guide-lines):

PRINCIPAL RESPONSIBILITIES (see guide-lines):

MENTAL REQUIREMENTS (see guide-lines)

MONOTONY (see guide-lines)

PHYSICAL EFFORT (see guide-lines)

DEXTERITY & CO-OPERATION (see guide-lines)

WORKING CONDITIONS INCLUDING HAZARDS (see guide-lines):

SIGNED: DATE: AGREED: DATE:

[*Courtesy Messrs. Binder, Hamlyn and Fry*

Fig. 17 *Specimen job definition form.* The form is completed by the employee in accordance with the guide-lines opposite as a basis for discussion leading to the evaluation of his/her job.

(*a*) quality and waste of material;
(*b*) effects on subsequent operations;
(*c*) teamwork, checking of other people's work and communications;
(*d*) working without direct and/or constant supervision.

Indicate the nature of the responsibility, the effect of errors, and the extent to which supervision and/or inspection limits the responsibility.

MENTAL REQUIREMENTS

(4) Describe any special needs for concentration, the analysis/understanding of written instructions and the level and type of decision-making which is required.

MONOTONY

(5) Consider monotony which could be caused by repetitive work with a very short time cycle and requiring little mental effort.

PHYSICAL EFFORT

(6) Only include anything which is exceptional in the physical effort required by the job and which is not implied by what has already been described, e.g.

(*a*) lifting: state weights and frequency;
(*b*) abnormal position: describe, e.g. working on ladders.

DEXTERITY AND CO-ORDINATION

(7) To what extent is it necessary to be agile in the use of hands neatly and quickly, or to co-ordinate the use of hands and feet and visual skills.

WORKING CONDITIONS INCLUDING HAZARDS

(8) Only include anything which is exceptional in the working conditions and which make the job requirements different from what would be expected elsewhere in the company, e.g. extreme noise, heat, dust, or risk of accidents.

GENERAL

(9) Under some headings a "Nil" entry may be appropriate or a general statement, e.g. "standard factory conditions".

Whatever method or combination of methods is used, the co-operation of the worker concerned is essential if the evaluation is to be as objective as possible. It is also essential to keep constantly in mind the necessity to eliminate subjective judgments as far as is humanly possible.

The grading scheme is normally finalised by a panel which includes a union representative who has been trained in job evaluation—assuming that there are union members in the organisation. The scheme is then made known to all employees.

There is a divergence of opinion as to whether employees should know how the final grading was arrived at. One school of thought says that public knowledge creates problems because some people will always compare themselves with other people and consider they have been under-graded. On the other hand, if the staff are not informed they may feel that the management has something to hide. Much depends on the state of management/worker relationships within the organisation.

There is also divergence of opinion as to whether employees should have the right of appeal against their own job gradings. This must be considered before the introduction of a scheme and machinery should be established for appeals procedures if it is decided to allow appeals to be made. Some organisations set a minimum period which must elapse before an appeal can be made.

Fixing salary scales

It has been stated that office workers will make do with soap boxes for furniture—provided the pay is high enough. This is only partially true, and would only be true of certain individuals and in certain circumstances. No doubt good remuneration helps to attract workers, but it is necessary that they should like the work, find the management agreeable, receive fair treatment and, above all, be treated as human beings.

Salaries are paid in the first place according to the work being performed, and secondly according to the way it is done. It must be recognised that in practice the two most potent factors in determining rates of pay are (i) what the firm can afford, and (ii) what market rates are payable for similar work.

Supposing the market rate was not the main determinant of salary scales, what factors should be taken into account in fixing different rates of pay? The most usual method is to assess the relative importance of the following factors: education, qualifications, experience, responsibility, complexity, i.e. judgment required as, for example, in referring to other organisations, and working conditions. Salary scales may be fixed according to work, according to a points classification, or entirely according to job grading.

When an organisation grows beyond, say, 50 employees, job grading is useful. Having graded the jobs, it is convenient to standardise rates of pay for the different kinds of work.

The advantages of having such scales are (i) the workers know that they are being paid the rate for the job; (ii) it is useful for them to know what salary they are likely to receive in successive years; (iii) it helps to build morale; (iv) workers know their own maximum salaries, and what the salaries are of grades above them, should they be promoted; and (v) secrecy with regard to salaries is eliminated; it is a firm contract.

The disadvantages are (i) lack of flexibility when a person reaches the limit of his potential, is doing a first-class job and has reached the top of the salary scale appropriate to that job; (ii) workers tend to resent any extension of their duties and/or responsibilities without extra pay, even in the interests of enhancing promotion prospects; (iii) there may be a status attitude towards jobs in certain types of work, e.g. accountancy staff may be regarded as more "professional" than certain other categories of office staff, resulting in salary anomalies for similar levels of work.

An important point with juniors is that they should receive regular advancement both in position and in salary. They are extremely sensitive of their positions, particularly when they come to a standstill because there are no suitable vacancies for them. Promises for the future will not hold them for long, and salary increases only for a short time. This is probably where the Civil Service and local government find it difficult to retain juniors whose salaries are fixed according to age. It might be advisable to give juniors increments every half-year and not every year as with other staff; a year seems a long time to a junior. He tends to live for the present, not for the future.

DRAFTING SALARY SCALES

When drafting salary scales, the following are some of the factors which should be borne in mind.

(1) Different scales should be compiled for different categories of work.

(2) Salaries should be sufficient to attract staff, but low enough to be an economic proposition; although this is a difficult thing to decide.

(3) The rates should preferably be a little above those paid by other concerns, if the best quality staff are required.

(4) Depending on the job, salaries would be less to a beginner than to an experienced person.

(5) To allow for flexibility in the rates of pay, minimum (beginner rates) and maximum (most experienced) rates should be fixed for the job.

(6) A number of intermediate rates should be allowed for, and this should depend on how long it takes to become proficient at a particular job, and on how often the salaries are reviewed. Thus, where salaries are reviewed (with merit gradings) every six

months, it is likely that a large number of increments would be advisable.

(7) It is usual to overlap salary scales for different grades. This is particularly convenient where a new employee works alongside a long-service employee of a lower grade.

(8) Where there are a large number of workers on a low rate of pay and there is little chance of their promotion, the granting of deferred increments (say every five or ten years) would be an advantage.

(9) For juniors (age 16 years upwards, sometimes to 21 years) it is usual to pay on a scale according to age, and while this may be inequitable there may be a large number of other inducements, such as welfare and pension schemes, which make it possible.

(10) Salary scales should be easy to understand.

(11) Salary scales should give scope for incentive payments and special merit awards where appropriate, (see Chapter 16).

(12) Salary scales should provide a career grade structure taking into account academic and work standards which must be achieved to justify progression.

10. Recruitment of Staff

Each stage in the recruiting process should be conducted with the utmost care. There is no guarantee of one hundred per cent success in recruiting exactly the right person for each job, but at least the unfortunate selections can be minimised by treating recruitment as an important aspect of managing the office.

Personnel specification

For recruitment purposes the job analysis is taken to a third stage, viz. the preparation of a personnel specification, or job profile as it is sometimes called. Having analysed the duties in the job description and assessed the knowledge and skills required to perform them, it is necessary to determine the following requirements:

(1) level of education;

(2) educational qualifications, e.g. C.S.E., G.C.E.;

(3) any particular subject and/or grades of educational qualifications required;

(4) vocational training, i.e. technical or professional—type and level;

(5) technical or professional qualifications;

(6) personal qualities;

(7) experience—general and/or specific essential/desirable;

(8) age range (dictated to some extent by the level of the vacant post, the qualities, qualifications and experience required, and the salary range).

The next step is to establish priorities. Is vocational training and experience more important than educational qualifications? Are personal qualities more important than skills? Is any particular personal quality, e.g. appearance, or the ability to communicate effectively, of paramount importance in this particular job? In other words, prepare a blueprint with which to compare the applicants.

The specimen personnel specification which follows is based on the job specification on page 81.

PERSONNEL SPECIFICATION
Job: Personnel Records Clerk
Education: General education to C.S.E. (good grades in English Language and Arithmetic essential) minimum
Qualifications: Typewriting—R.S.A. Stage I minimum, Stage II preferable, Pitman Intermediate
Office Practice—R.S.A. Stage I or Pitman Intermediate
BEC General Level with appropriate option modules
Experience: Office experience, including record keeping, desirable
Qualities: Attention to detail
Loyalty and integrity
Special attributes: Neat writing
Ability to copy accurately
Ability to communicate effectively
Liking for figures/statistics
NOTES: (1) It can be seen from the job specification on page 81 that most of the knowledge requirements would have to form the basis of an induction course as most of them relate to the organisation of the company and its procedures. (2) It should also be mentioned that many organisations produce a combined job/personnel specification rather than two separate documents. Nevertheless, the two processes both have to be carried out.

Sources of staff

Where can staff be found? There are many sources; some are more suitable for one kind of staff than for another; many are more suitable for one kind of business than for another. A brief outline of the main sources of recruitment is given below.

ADVERTISING
Advertisements can be inserted in national and local newspapers, and in trade and professional journals. Advertisements should give as much factual information as possible, stated in precise and accurate terms. Subjective or vague words and phrases should be avoided. Some firms prefer to advertise under box numbers, but it is now more common to give a person's name and/or designation with a telephone number. The identity of the advertiser is thus

concealed with the advantages of telephone contact. Some large firms have a direct line with an answer recording machine (*see* page 214) to take the names and addresses of applicants so that a job description and application form can be sent with the minimum of delay and staff time.

PRIVATE EMPLOYMENT BUREAUX

The use of employment bureaux saves the time and trouble of advertising, is useful when staff are wanted at short notice, and should ensure that the people attending interviews have the priority requirements. Under the Employment Agencies Act 1973 fees are payable by the employer, usually on the basis of a percentage of annual salary or the equivalent of the first month's salary.

FRIENDS, RELATIVES AND JOB–SEEKERS

Personal introductions, applications from job-seekers and "Situations Wanted" advertisers are all useful sources, though careful screening is essential.

EX–EMPLOYEES

People who have once worked in a concern are a known quantity, and if the parting was mutually acceptable and amicable such people may be a valuable source of contact.

OFFICE APPLIANCE COMPANIES

Many of the firms manufacturing calculating, accounting and other machines will supply trained staff, or alternatively will train staff in the firm's own office for them.

HOSPITALS AND EX–SERVICE ORGANISATIONS

Under the Disabled Persons (Employment) Act 1944, all businesses are under a legal obligation to employ one disabled person in every hundred employees; and hospital almoners and ex-Service organisations are useful contacts.

PROFESSIONAL ORGANISATIONS

Most of the appropriate professional organisations maintain employment registers of qualified professional people who wish to improve or change their positions, e.g. accountants, company secretaries, buyers.

SCHOOLS, COLLEGES AND UNIVERSITIES

Academic, commercial, engineering and technical colleges usually assist in placing their graduates. For office juniors, the appropriate source is the local authority's Careers Office.

CIRCULARS, POSTERS, ETC.

For staff in short supply, posters can be displayed outside the factory or office, advertisement slides shown at the local cinema and circulars distributed in suitable places.

CONSULTANTS

A number of management consultants have a special division for recruiting managerial staff. For very high level positions "head-hunting" agencies are becoming more common. A head-hunting agency contacts people thought to be suitable for the job available even though they are happily employed and not seeking a change. This is an American practice, not yet fully accepted in Britain. Recruiting through professional consultants is expensive but may be the only way to obtain the calibre of staff required.

Drafting advertisements

Advertisements must be brief, contain all relevant details stated concisely (including key duties; level/grade of the job; special working conditions; qualifications, experience, skills required), reflect the image of the organisation in its style, state the salary range, and indicate the method of application, e.g. telephone for details, write for details and application form or write giving curriculum vitae (c.v.). Under no circumstances should applicants be put to the trouble of writing their c.v. and then be asked to complete an application form.

A job should never be "glamourised" to attract staff. If the applicant discovers deception at the interview everyone's time has been wasted. If the deception continues to the stage of actual recruitment the employee will soon be dissatisfied and leave, and the whole process has to be repeated at a steadily increasing cost of time and money.

Choice of media for advertisements is important. You want to reach the largest possible reading audience of a particular type and/or level. Therefore choose the media with care and compose and present the advertisement to attract the readership you want.

Application forms

Most large organisations use printed application forms for employment. The advantages are that information is requested on the most vital aspects of the personal qualifications and none are omitted, and their use ensures that the information is in exactly the same order for all candidates. This saves time when comparing applications.

Application forms should be drafted and produced with the same care as any other business form. (Form design is dealt with in detail in Chapter 43.) The applicant should be able to identify easily the exact information required and have adequate space in which to give that information in handwriting. A specimen application form is shown in Fig. 18.

Short-listing

Short-listing should be a methodical exercise, selection of applicants for interview and testing being based on predetermined criteria. If a large number of applications are received the following steps may help to minimise the somewhat onerous chore of assessment.

(1) Remove the applications which do not meet the priority requirements (assuming these can be set down on paper, e.g. qualifications).

(2) Remove applications outside the desired age range (though there should be valid reasons for eliminating any age groups).

(3) Remove applications indicating present salary level higher than the salary range of the job or very much lower.

(4) Remove applications which do not give the information requested in the advertisement and those which are badly presented.

The remaining applications should have the essential and some of the desirable requirements. Further sifting can be done if necessary by matching applications as closely as possible with the job and personnel specifications, i.e. taking the applications with the greatest number of priorities. At this stage the "hopeless" applicants should be notified that they have not been selected for interview—a duplicated card or letter is adequate.

Interviewing

The purposes of the employment interview are:
(1) to assess the personality of the applicant;
(2) to check on factual data in the application;
(3) to give the applicant information about the job;
(4) to assess the applicant's suitability for the job—this may involve various types of tests (*see* page 107);
(5) to select the most suitable applicant for the job.

SERIAL NO:

Page One.

Pers. Form 2

CONFIDENTIAL
GEORGE PAYNE & CO. LTD.
APPLICATION FOR EMPLOYMENT: STAFF

POST APPLIED FOR:	PREVIOUS OCCUPATION

SURNAME: (block letters)	CHRISTIAN NAMES (in full & in block letters) MR./MISS./MRS.

ADDRESS: (block letters)

HOUSE OWNER: YES/NO	RENTED ACCOMMODATION: YES/NO	TELEPHONE NO:

SINGLE/MARRIED WIDOW-ER/DIVORCED	DATE OF BIRTH:	AGE:

NUMBER OF CHILDREN: AGE / SEX

PLACE OF BIRTH:

NATIONALITY:

EDUCATION: SECONDARY OR GRAMMAR SCHOOLS ATTENDED:	FROM	TO	EXAMINATIONS PASSED

UNIVERSITY OR COLLEGE:

OTHER TRAINING COURSES TAKEN (including languages spoken)

MEMBERSHIP OR PROFESSIONAL OR OTHER SIMILAR ASSOCIATIONS:

HOBBIES/SPORTS/OTHER INTERESTS:

DETAILS OF HEALTH

HAVE YOU ANY PHYSICAL DISABILITIES? YES/NO If yes state what they are and if permanent or temporary:

ARE YOU A REGISTERED DISABLED PERSON? YES/NO If Yes, state for what reason:

Registered Number
Date expires:

WHEN AVAILABLE TO TAKE UP POSITION IF OFFERED:

Date_____ Signature_____

Fig. 18 *Specimen application form.*

In some cases the contract of employment may be made at the interview, particularly for lower level posts.

PREPARATION
The success of an interview depends to a large extent on the care and attention to detail in preparation. To see people in their best light it is essential to provide the best conditions possible. The following guide-lines help to ensure that the applicant is free from tension and able to present his best image, and that the interviewer can give full attention to the applicant and assess his suitability for the vacant post.

(1) The waiting room should be attractive and well lit, and have interesting reading materials, ashtrays and comfortable chairs.

(2) Adequate time should be allowed for an interview so that if several applicants follow each other the later ones are not kept waiting beyond the time of the appointment.

(3) The interview should be conducted in a private room from which telephone calls and other staff are barred.

(4) The chairs should be arranged informally. The applicant's chair can be placed at the side of the interviewer's desk; a circular table is preferable to a rectangular one for a panel interview. Chairs should be comfortable and all of the same height.

(5) If the applicant is to be given an answer before leaving the organisation, but has to wait while the panel discuss the interview, it is pleasant if he can be shown to a room other than the waiting room. Applicants should always be conducted to other rooms where they are required, e.g. for testing.

(6) For panel interviews every member should have a copy of the completed application form, together with a brief summary of the applicant's age, education, qualifications and experience.

(7) An interview assessment form should be prepared for use as a check-list during the interview and for completion after the interview. This is known as "quality rating" and is discussed below.

(8) Questions should be framed before the interview with the aim of eliciting the required information. Brief notes of questions for individual applicants should be attached to the appropriate application.

(9) Panel interviewers should be allocated a specific area of the interview to deal with, e.g. past experience, technical expertise, ability to handle situations, i.e. personality traits, and so on.

THE INTERVIEW
It is perfectly in order to verify information given in an application form but the intelligent applicant is not likely to be impressed by

being asked to repeat it word for word. Questions aimed at expanding on the written information given will be much more productive. Questioning should be informal and friendly so that the applicant feels at ease and is encouraged to talk freely. Keep note-taking to a minimum as it can be distracting for both interviewer(s) and applicant.

Of course, the approach should be businesslike and questions can be searching and aimed at revealing important characteristics. Questions should never be framed in such a way as to require a "yes" or "no" answer. It is better to ask "how do you feel about that job?" rather than "did you like that job?" Questions should indicate clearly what information is required; leading questions and "trip" questions should be avoided.

No one can know everything about the technical aspects of the job, even in his own field. Therefore technical questions are best asked in the form of "what do you know about . . .?" or if the applicant is expected to outline the details of a procedure, for example, it is nice to ask first "have you done/do you do . . .?"

An interviewer should be neutral in attitude, but sympathetic; he should be interested in what the applicant is saying and encouraging. At the appropriate time, and this is not usually at the beginning of the interview, the duties of the job and any interesting background information which the applicant would want to know should be explained concisely and accurately. Most of the talking should be done by the applicant but the interviewer should be ready to answer questions however trivial they may seem.

Testing

Testing should be kept to the minimum necessary to reveal the particular abilities required for the job. Tests have the advantage of enabling competent people who show up badly in an interview to demonstrate their ability to do the job. For example, an applicant for the post of filing clerk may have a poor personality but a well-prepared test might reveal exceptional ability at filing. On the other hand, many people are so nervous when undergoing a test that they perform far below their normal standard.

A test must be well prepared and should be simple to administer and assess, be strictly related to the job for which it is designed and have specific objectives. All tests should be validated. They can be tried out on an employee of average ability. Average marks should be the result. Timing is important and this should be tried out beforehand. Extra time can be allowed when testing applicants to give them confidence.

There are a number of intelligence and aptitude tests available from various sources. Usually they need to be administered by a trained person. This can either be a consultant who specialises in this kind of testing or an employee, perhaps from the personnel department, who has been trained by the authors of the tests.

Occupational tests should always aim to evaluate the applicant's ability to do the job. "Subject" tests such as English and arithmetic do not indicate this. For example, a checker is required to detect errors. A test in the basic arithmetic principles will not reveal this ability, or lack of it. Verifying series of invoices, some of which contain errors, will.

A simple filing test would be to give the applicant about fifty cards bearing typed names and addresses and account numbers on them. The applicant would be asked to sort them alphabetically in order of name, in geographical order of address, and numerically in account number order. Speed and accuracy would be measured.

Some employers consider it unnecessary to test in specialist areas such as shorthand on the basis that applicants have passed public examinations. It is nevertheless always advisable to test, partly because the examinations have often been taken some time previously and partly because few examinations test the ability to work under office conditions, e.g. office-style dictation, typewriting when interrupted by telephone calls, conflicting instructions, etc.

Instructions for carrying out the tasks should be given clearly, concisely and fully, bearing in mind that the applicant does not know the organisation. All materials required should be provided and any limitations or constraints, e.g. time, should be indicated to the applicant.

Some people, especially at higher levels, may resent being asked to undergo a test. If the reason for the tests is explained, and if the applicant is asked if he is willing to take them, co-operation is likely to be forthcoming. If a person resents proving that he can do a job it is unlikely that he will have the right attitude in the job.

Quality rating

The main objective of the interviewing and testing processes is to compare applicants with the job and personnel specifications. This assessment is known as "quality rating". A grading structure is prepared by which a maximum number of points are allocated to each item on the assessment list which will consist of the experience, qualifications, qualities, etc., required. This can be done on the basis of a straight assessment of each item between, say, 1 and 5 points, depending on the standard at which the applicant is assessed. Alternatively each group of items—qualifications, personal qualities, etc.—can be allocated a number of points in accordance with its importance. Thus a job where personal qualities are a priority would have more points allocated for this than for skills, e.g. a receptionist. Another job might require first-class skills in preference to special personal qualities, e.g. an audio typist or an accounts clerk.

It must be understood that there is a limit to what can be assessed at an interview. In the specimen rating for a telephone operator (Fig. 19) no assessment can be made for "good temper" in the course of a 20–30 minute interview. Contact with a past or the present employer may reveal this but that is by no means certain. It is of course easier to give a quality rating for an existing employee than for an applicant because such qualities as reliability, reasoning power and loyalty are known.

The various qualities required to do a job should be grouped, e.g. technical, personal, intellectual and volitional. Provided it is logical the actual form of the grouping is of little importance. It is important that all the qualities necessary for the job are included.

Quality rating cannot be absolutely accurate, and should not be the sole basis for selection. It should be used as a valuable aid to judgment.

Quality rating cannot be totally objective in all areas; consequently it is regarded by some people as far from perfect. However, even though subjective to some extent it does serve several useful purposes. It is valuable for panel interviews because it ensures that all members assess the same qualities on the same basis. After the interview the marks awarded by the members of the panel can be compared. Quality rating ensures that a job is analysed to identify the qualities needed to perform it, and it is therefore useful for job grading as well. It helps to ensure that interviews and tests are structured to determine an applicant's ability to do the job. It helps to determine what development and training are needed by a new or existing employee to enhance job performance, record progress, indicate potential for job enlargement and/or promotion.

Because recruiting is an expensive process efforts have been made to make the selection of new employees less of a hit and miss affair. The National Institute of Industrial Psychology has a Seven Point Plan which contains headings relevant to the assessment of an applicant for any kind of job. These are:

(1) physique;
(2) attainments;
(3) general intelligence;

THE EXCEL PAINT CO. LTD.

Quality Rating

for the post of

TELEPHONE OPERATOR (P.B.X. 5/50)

Name of Applicant   Mr.
                     Mrs.
                     Miss_____ Date_____

	1	2	3	4	5
(1) Training (Post Office)					
" (other)					
Experience of T/O (business)					
" (......... years) P.B.X.					
Speech					
Hearing					
Pleasant personality					
Good temper					
Punctuality					
Tact					
(2) Good memory					
Co-operativeness					
Experience in the trade					
(3) Methodical					
Legibility					
Education					
Reliability					

Other Comments

KEY
1. Much above average.
2. Above average.
3. Average.
4. Below average.
5. Much below average.   Signed ....
                          (Interviewer)

Fig. 19 *Specimen quality rating for a telephone operator.*

(4) special aptitudes;
(5) interests;
(6) disposition;
(7) circumstances.
The required qualities of the job should be listed under the

various headings. It can then be decided which qualities can be assessed at an interview and which require testing.

Selection

Perhaps the most difficult aspect of management is the selection of new employees. So much depends on making the right choice. Occasionally the "natural" for the job stands out among the applicants. Sometimes the person who most nearly matches the personnel specification has one major defect which the employer must accept and "live with" if he recruits that person. More often it is difficult to make a choice between two or three applicants, either because they are all more or less of the same standard or because they each have different advantages. Yet another situation is that all the applicants are really unsuitable. In the latter case it is useful to review the recruitment procedures—was the advertising sufficiently accurate and was it undertaken in the right media? Was the interviewing and testing properly geared to the job?

In theory the person with the most points on the quality rating, including test results, should be the "winner". However, it is possible that excellent test results might give a person with lower personal qualities the edge over a more suitable person who "fluffed" the test through nervous tension. There is no golden rule for making this difficult decision but if the priorities for the job are taken as a guide, and the applicants compared individually with them, it is probably the best indication of suitability—providing of course the job has been adequately and accurately analysed in the first place.

Testimonials and references

Testimonials are general in character and usually begin "To whom it may concern". A testimonial is a permanent document given to an employee when he leaves an organisation so that he can produce it at any time in the future. Today it is more usual for an employer to ask applicants to quote names and addresses of "referees", who can be approached direct. Contact with a referee is normally in the form of a confidential letter and assurance is given that all information included in the reply will be treated in strict confidence.

Naturally no applicant will quote referees who will speak ill of him and when three or four references are requested an applicant will invariably include one or two names of friends. It may be useful to give guidance as to the kind of referees required, e.g. professional men whose integrity carries most weight, such as principals of colleges, doctors, solicitors, bank managers. Though the opinion of an employee's immediate superior may be valuable it should be borne in mind that no supervisor enjoys losing a good employee, and not everyone is fair-minded about other people's rights to improve themselves.

Some employers ask in a reference whether it is thought that the applicant would be able to perform the duties of the vacant post. In this case the copy of the job description must be enclosed with the enquiry.

A request for a reference should state specifically what information is required. A letter to a previous employer might ask the following.

(1) Between what dates was the applicant employed?
(2) What was his work?
(3) Was his work satisfactory?
(4) Why did he leave?
(5) What are his strengths and weaknesses?

An employer is not under any obligation (apart from any undertaking in a contract) to give a testimonial or reference. In cases where an employee has been unsatisfactory it is usual either not to give a reference at all or to give one which "damns with faint praise". At law, a reference is a privileged communication given on an occasion of qualified privilege because it is in the public interest that honest opinions should be available to prospective employers. The privilege would be lost if a bad reference was given out of spite, but provided the statements are true and can be proved to be true, an employer need have no fear of reporting adversely. It can be said that an employer has a moral obligation to warn prospective employers of an unsatisfactory employee.

When an employer does not wish to commit himself adversely on paper he may prefer to give a reference over the telephone, at least in part. Indeed a telephone conversation with a past employer often elicits more valuable information than a formal written reference.

Contract of employment

A contract of employment is made at the moment when an applicant for a job undertakes to work for the employer under the conditions laid down, i.e. salary, hours, type of work, etc. The contract may be made informally at the time of the interview, or by a written offer of employment accepted in writing.

It is normal procedure to issue a letter of appointment which may form the basis of the written statement of the main terms of employment required by law. A section of the Contracts of Employment Act 1972 (now incorporated in the Employment Protection (Consolidation) Act 1978) requires every employer to give each employee who works for more than sixteen hours a week a written statement about his main terms of employment within thirteen weeks of starting work. The Act requires the following details to be included in the statement.

(1) Identification of parties.

(2) Job title.

(3) Date of commencement of employment.

(4) Scale of pay or rate of remuneration.

(5) Intervals at which the wage or salary will be paid, e.g. monthly or weekly.

(6) Terms and conditions relating to hours of work, including normal hours of work and any guaranteed overtime.

(7) Terms and conditions relating to sickness and sick pay.

(8) Terms and conditions relating to pension and pension schemes.

(9) The length of notice to be given by either side to terminate the contract—minimum length of notice must be given in accordance with length of service (*see* page 151).

(10) Terms and conditions of service relating to holidays and holiday pay, including bank holidays.

(11) Disciplinary rules and procedures.

(12) Grievance procedures.

(13) Any special union arrangements such as a closed shop agreement.

A formal contract of service may be necessary in special circumstances, e.g. for overseas appointments, for an appointment of special importance such as a managing director, for a job involving secret processes or trade knowledge, or in cases where the employee is given the use of company property such as a house or car. In addition to the items listed above such a contract may include clauses relating to:

(1) prevention (after contract is terminated) from carrying on any similar profession or trade within a certain geographical area;

(2) restriction on using confidential information which comes to his knowledge while employed by the company;

(3) the method of arbitration in case of dispute.

For general employment, terms and conditions of service are usually set out in a staff handbook, a copy of which must be available for inspection by any employee at any time. It is normal practice to give a copy of the handbook to each new employee.

In the U.K., there are many legal obligations relating to the employment of staff, and employers should bear in mind the requirements of the numerous Acts of Parliament including the Truck Acts, Factories Acts, Shops Acts and more recently the Employment Protection Act 1975, the Trade Union and Labour Relations Act 1974*, and the Social Security Pensions Act 1975. Clauses relating to employment in the Sex Discrimination Act 1975 and the Race Relations Act 1976 are also relevant. When in doubt it is advisable to consult the local office of the Department of Employment. A series of useful booklets which give guidance on the main aspects of employment legislation has been issued by the Department.

Conditions of service

Today employees regard their conditions of service as equally important as salary levels. Fringe benefits such as luncheon vouchers, free or subsidised restaurant facilities, recreational facilities, standard of equipment and furniture for the job, bonus schemes, share allocation schemes, etc., are all useful means of attracting recruits and maintaining a happy and hard-working staff. People are usually keen to give of their best if they know (i) what is expected of them, (ii) what the rewards are, and (iii) the conditions under which they are to work. Therefore the conditions of service should be clearly set out in easily understood language. In the past employers have not always taken care to give all details to the respective employees, who have assumed that "everything would be alright", "didn't like to ask", or simply "did not think to ask". Consequently many misunderstandings arose and resulted in unnecessary arguments, termination of employment, etc.

If certain conditions are agreed at an interview they should be confirmed in the letter of appointment, e.g. if training is to be given or if a certain type of machine is to be provided. So often, agreements made glibly at an interview are not fulfilled and the employee becomes resentful, feeling that he has been employed under false pretences. Equally any specific negative conditions should be clearly stated, e.g. if there is no payment for overtime.

---

* Provisions of the Employment Protection Act 1975 and the Trade Union and Labour Relations Act 1974 relating to the individual rights of employees have now been incorporated into the Employment Protection (Consolidation) Act 1978.

11. Staff Appraisal and Reporting

Staff appraisal is a relatively new technique which has now been introduced into nearly all large organisations. In some cases pressure from union representatives has encouraged management to set up appraisal procedures following job evaluation exercises. It is also a development of the more open style of management which aims to develop the team approach.

Whatever the method or methods of appraisal used it should be carried out regularly. Formal appraisals should be conducted at least once a year: some organisations conduct half-yearly appraisals. Informal appraisals should take place as the need arises but certainly reviews of target achievements should be carried out on or near the target dates. Three or four times a year seems a reasonable frequency for an exchange of views on progress, development and problems.

Purposes of regular appraisals

The periodic interview (which may be complementary to merit grading, *see* below) has the following objectives:

(1) to review, and, if necessary, amend the details of the subordinate's work and job description;

(2) to discuss the subordinate's work problems and help him to find the solution to them;

(3) to discuss the subordinate's ambitions for the future;

(4) to identify the subordinate's deficiencies, or to help him to recognise them, and to discover to what extent training is needed and likely to improve performance;

(5) to assess the subordinate's potential, possibly for some other work and/or for promotion.

Appraisal methods

The two principal methods of appraisal are merit grading (or merit rating) and interviewing.

MERIT GRADING

Merit grading can be regarded as complementary to job grading (*see* Chapter 9). Job grading is an assessment of the work to be done and the "measurable" factors involved, i.e. the extent of responsibility, supervision, etc. Merit grading looks at the *subjective* factors involved in doing a job and is an attempt to assess the actual performance of each individual employee. The purpose of such an assessment is the determination of an employee's worth (within a job grade) to the organisation. It really forms the basis of staff appraisal and staff reporting, whether or not the employee is in a job-graded post.

The advantages of merit grading are as follows.

(1) It makes supervisors assess ability scientifically and put their judgments in writing, which is useful for comparisons and assessment of progress at a later date.

(2) From the employee's point of view, it provides a record of his progress in the organisation.

(3) It indicates weaknesses and may help to determine what training is needed.

(4) It highlights the strengths of an employee and exceptional ability in a particular area.

(5) It provides useful data when deciding transfers and promotion of staff.

(6) Knowing that a periodic review is made may motivate employees to give of their best.

Merit grading may be entirely the responsibility of an employee's supervisor or a joint committee may also be involved.

There is no precise measuring device for subjective factors, but the most common method of rating is to have grades, for example:

Type of assessment	Rating			
Descriptive	Excellent	Good	Fair	Poor
Numerical	1	2	3	4
Alphabetical	A	B	C	D
Percentile	100–90	80–70	60–50	40–30

Assessment is usually based on four basic qualities:

(1) quality of work;
(2) quantity of work;
(3) co-operativeness;
(4) dependability.

Many other qualities may be added to these, e.g.
    initiative;
    knowledge of work;
    judgment; and
    adaptability.

The qualities chosen depend on the type of work being performed and are normally those which are essential for the satisfactory performance of the job. The job and personnel specifications, and if necessary, task analyses, provide a useful basis on which to work.

The Institute of Administrative Management recommend five merit gradings for office staff:

(1) learners, and those who cannot reach normal;
(2) normal, representing satisfactory output;
(3) above normal—those who bring special skill to the work, and those who are fit for promotion;
(4) excellent;
(5) superlative.

Two specimen assessment forms are shown in Figs. 20 and 21.

Because of the subjective nature of merit grading it is very difficult to check the accuracy of the assessments. Supervisors should be given as much guidance as possible without inhibiting their personal judgment. Individual standards of supervisors vary greatly and will naturally influence their assessment. Although it is desirable to have assessment made by more than one person it is difficult for anyone other than the supervisor to know the personal attributes of each employee.

If a merit-rating plan is to be initiated or reviewed it is essential to involve the supervisors. Discussion among the raters, normally the supervisors, helps to ensure reasonable uniformity of rating. In any case, it is essential to have the whole-hearted support of supervisory staff if merit rating is to be manifestly fair.

In some organisations increments are tied to merit gradings. Standard increments are given for average ratings while additional increments are given for a certain number of points above average. In this case it is likely that the assessments of all supervisors would be scrutinised by a management panel to ensure reasonable uniformity of assessment. If one supervisor's assessments were all very high and another supervisor's assessments were all very low it would indicate a divergence of standards. When increments are tied to merit gradings each employee must have the right to discuss his or her merit grading with his head of department and it is the duty of the employee's supervisor to explain changes in grading.

OFFICE STAFF ASSESSMENT REPORT

NAME_____

DATE_____

AWARD Points_____
        Value_____

Maximum marks for grade	Bad —	Below Average 10	Average 25	Good 40	Exceptional 50
1. *Time-keeping* (Maximum 50 points). Arrival morning and afternoon.					
2. *Effectiveness* (Productivity) (maximum 50 points).					
3. *Reliability* (Maximum 50 points). Needs constant supervision to maintain effort. Needs more than average supervision to maintain effort. Average supervision. Works well without any supervision.					
4. *Initiative* (Maximum 50 points). Shows no interest in work. Shows little interest — a tendency to slackness. Shows average interest and tries to improve. Needs little prompting. Shows real interest and accepts responsibility. Exceptional interest and full acceptance of responsibility.					
5. *Attitude* (Maximum 50 points). Lacks team spirit. Inclined to be difficult and isolated. Does not enter into communal activities. Reasonably helpful and co-operative. Willing to help with the work of others and does work late if necessary. Will sacrifice personal convenience for Company's well-being. Happy to work as late as necessary.					

Comments of Panel.

Fig. 20 *Specimen merit rating form (for office staff).*

REPORT FOR ASSESSMENT

NAME _____ AGE _____
HOURLY RATE _____ DEPT. _____
  JOB _____

Using each grade as a guide and the dotted line below as the line along which the employee should be progressing, place a tick at the point you consider has been reached.

Qualities	BELOW AVERAGE		AVERAGE	ABOVE AVERAGE		Points
Production	Considerably less than expected. Many faults in quality.	Slightly less than expected. Some faults in quality.	Normal contribution. Acceptable quality. ✓	More than usually expected. Quality good.	Exceptionally quick workers. Highest possible quality.	22
Reliability	Time-keeping poor. Needs constant supervision.	Time-keeping fair. Needs more than average amount of supervision.	Generally reliable. Needs normal supervision.	Rarely loses time. Needs minimum amount of supervision.	Very punctual. Can be left without supervision. Completely reliable. ✓	17
Initiative	Shows no interest. Makes little effort	Not very interested. Tendency to slackness.	Tries and seeks to improve.	Industrious and suggests improvements. ✓	Very energetic and resourceful. Studies the job with good effect.	7
Attitude	Lacks team spirit. Uncooperative.	Inclined to be of difficult disposition. Not very helpful.	Reasonably helpful and considerate of others. ✓	Very co-operative. Does not mind being moved around. Considerate.	Exceptionally considerate. Will go out of way to be helpful.	5
Safety and economy	Careless and irresponsible.	Occasionally wasteful and inclined to take risks.	Careful within framework of job. Adheres to instructions regarding safety. ✓	Very careful. Waste-minded, orderly and tidy.	Exceptionally waste-minded and careful in every way.	11

Foreman's Signature	REMARKS	Total points: 62
B. Dayman		% Awarded: 16%
Date:		New Rate: £1.00 + 16p = £1.16
		Approved by: S.H.

[Courtesy Thermos (1925) Ltd.

Fig. 21 Specimen merit rating form used for indirect workers other than office staff.

INTERVIEWING

The points covered in interviewing for recruitment (*see* Chapter 10) are relevant. The appraisal interview should be properly structured and should be based on the objectives stated at the beginning of this chapter.

The interview should be a discussion between superior and subordinate and not a catechism from the superior. It is important to remember the main aims of staff appraisal during the interview. It is a means of involving the employee, of helping to solve his work problems, which may even be caused by the superior himself, unwittingly, also perhaps of helping to solve personal problems, and of developing his potential for the future good of the organisation, as well as for his own good.

Staff reporting

Annual staff reports have been a feature of the Civil Service since 1921 and in other official bodies for many years. The extension of staff appraisal, however informal, has led to written reports of employee's progress being kept in many organisations. Originally reports were used as one of the criteria in choosing people for promotion. They still serve this purpose but are also a component part of personnel records generally. The practice of not informing the employees of the contents of staff reports is changing with the extension of staff appraisal. In some organisations, both public and private, each officer has to sign his report and has the right to challenge anything with which he does not agree. With the growth of union interest in personnel matters such as job evaluation, and with the introduction of legislation to ensure protection for the employee, it is likely that the "open report" will become generally accepted. The fact that an employee's fault has been recorded is not fair and reasonable grounds for dismissal. If sufficient warning has been given and attempts have been made to help the employee overcome his deficiency, then the employee has only himself to blame if he makes no attempt to improve and does not get promotion, or is transferred to another job, or even dismissed. Thus the staff report should be an indication of attempts made to help the employee develop.

CONTENTS OF A REPORT

The qualities assessed in a staff report should be those relevant to the job, but there are differing views about which qualities should be included. It is difficult to generalise but inevitably the type of organisation has some bearing on those included. An example of

INDIVIDUAL ASSESSMENT FORM

NAME_____ SECTION_____ DATE_____

DURING PAST YEAR (OR PROBATIONARY PERIOD): TIMES LATE _____

NUMBER OF ABSENCES_____ TOTAL DAYS ABSENT_____

	HIGH			MID			LOW	
	+4	+3	+2	+1	0	−1	−2	−3	−4
1. Knowledge of job being done.									
2. Versatility.									
3. Ability to learn.									
4. Industry.									
5. Quality of work done.									
6. Quantity of work done.									
7. Dependability.									
8. Judgment.									
9. Initiative.									
10. Dealings with public, managers and sales representatives.									
11. Dealings with fellow members of staff									
12. Co-operation.									
13. Punctuality.									
14. Personal appearance.									
15. Leadership.									

16. Taking everything into consideration do you consider this individual:
VERY GOOD___GOOD___SATISFACTORY___UNSATISFACTORY___VERY UNSATISFACTORY___

17. Do you have any suggestions for improvement? YES_____ NO_____

18. Do you consider this individual's salary out of line in any way with other members of your staff? YES_____ NO_____

19. Is this individual's attitude towards the Company safisfactory? YES_____ NO_____

20. (To be answered only if individual is still on probation.) YES_____ NO_____
Do you recommend appointment to the permanent staff?

REMARKS:

_____ (Date) _____ (Signed)

Fig. 22 *Staff report form, with nine assessment columns.*

PRIVATE AND CONFIDENTIAL   **ANNUAL STAFF REPORT**

DATE:

                                           NAME:

DEPARTMENT: AGE:

                                           POST OCCUPIED:

DATE JOINED COMPANY:

PRESENT GRADE:

Professional/Technical Qualifications:

CHARACTER AND PERSONALITY:	OUT-STANDING	VERY GOOD	SATIS-FACTORY	UNSATIS-FACTORY	REMARKS
(a) Address and tact.					
(b) Force of character.					
(c) Initiative.					
CAPACITY					
(a) Judgment and common sense.					
(b) Power of supervision.					
(c) Zeal.					
(d) Punctuality.					
PERFORMANCE OF DUTIES:					
(a) Knowledge of post occupied.					
(b) Knowledge of department.					
(c) Knowledge of whole business.					
(d) Quality of output.					
(e) Quantity of output.					

Fig. 23 *Staff report form, with five assessment columns.*

the headings which might be included are:
Knowledge of the organisation/branch/department
Personality
Judgment
Acceptance of responsibility
Accuracy
Initiative
Ability to communicate
Ability to supervise
Creativity
Relations with colleagues/superiors/the public

In the Civil Service Report there is a section which incorporates questions directly bearing on the prospects of promotion for which the assessment is classed as:

(1) exceptionally well qualified;
(2) highly qualified;
(3) qualified;
(4) not yet qualified.

This is also common to local government reporting.

Assessment of each quality can vary from a simple "good, average, poor" to the nine-column assessment shown in Fig. 22. The five-column assessment in Fig. 23 seems a good compromise.

Staff reporting is a heavy responsibility on a supervisor because he may jeopardise a person's career for years to come by an unfavourable report. If the adverse comments are true it is fair, but not otherwise. On the other hand, a report which assesses an employee's qualities too highly is as bad because the person concerned is not made aware of his weaknesses. He also tends to become frustrated because he thinks he has greater abilities than is the case. It takes courage and honesty to give an accurate and fair report but every subordinate has a right to expect this.

Staff records

All organisations need to keep staff records, and the aim should be to record such information as is really required about each member of the staff. It is unnecessary and wasteful to maintain a particular item for, say, 5,000 employees when only 50 will have it recorded.

Staff records are important because reference may be wanted for one or other of the following reasons.

(1) Personal data (age, date of birth, address, etc.).
(2) Details of career in organisation (rates of pay, departments, etc.).
(3) National Insurance purposes.

(4) Income tax purposes.

(5) Sickness ⎫
              ⎬ (particularly where leave with pay is given).
(6) Holidays ⎭

(7) Pension   (particularly where a service qualification is required).

(8) Promotion (staff reports and details of qualifications).

(9) Disablement register.

(10) Space for giving references, should the employee leave (reason for leaving should be stated).

(11) Record of lateness (may also be connected with promotion).

In the design of the record, space should be allowed for the insertion of changes in the variable information such as clock number, address, department, rate of pay, marital status and number of children (required for National Insurance purposes).

FORMS OF STAFF RECORD

There are four main types of staff record:

(1) folder system;

(2) card index;

(3) envelopes;

(4) combined application form and staff record.

The folder type is probably the most popular as it is the simplest to operate. All documents relating to an employee, such as letters of application and of appointment, staff reports, etc., are inserted in a flat manilla folder. Unless sickness and lateness are recorded elsewhere, a special form is attached inside the front cover of the folder, although in some large organisations records of these items are not maintained regularly, special reports being inserted in the folder only in the event of exceptional periods of sickness or of serious lateness. The folders are usually filed vertically either in alphabetical or in pay-number order. If the latter, a separate card index is needed.

The second method makes use of a visible card index. Specimens of two facing cards from a card index are illustrated in Fig. 24. This system has three great advantages:

(1) the cards can be written on without withdrawing them from the system;

(2) any particular record may be referred to very quickly;

(3) coloured signals may be used to denote dates of increment, coming of age (18 for National Insurance purposes), a member of the pension fund and for many other purposes.

The only objection to keeping staff records in this way is that the

NAME		MARRIED		CHILDREN		CLOCK No.		
		SINGLE						
REASONS		SICKNESS PAY						
		WEEK ENDING	No. OF DAYS	N.H.I.	WEEK ENDING	No. OF DAYS	N.H.I.	WEEK ENDING	No. OF DAYS	N.H.I.

NAME				CLOCK NUMBER				
ADDRESS								
DATE OF BIRTH		MARRIED OR SINGLE			CHILDREN			
N.H.I. NUMBER			R.D.P. PARTS					
DATE OF EMPLOYMENT			INTRODUCED BY					
PARTICULARS OF EMPLOYMENT					DATE LEFT			
Date	Department	Wages	Date	Wages	Date	Wages		
							REASON	
							RE-ENGAGED	
							A	
							B	C	D	E
18 years of Age	Pensions Fund	Retirement Date						

Fig. 24 *Facing cards from a visible card index staff record system.* The upper card is backed by a record of time-keeping and absenteeism; sickness is recorded on the front.

letters of application and of appointment, as well as staff reports and other documents, still have to be kept separately. In some cases the record and the documents may need to be referred to together on some occasions.

A third method, which is more suited to some concerns than

others, is to have basic data and perhaps sickness records printed on the face of stout manilla envelopes, in which all the relevant correspondence and reports can be placed (*see* Fig. 25). The

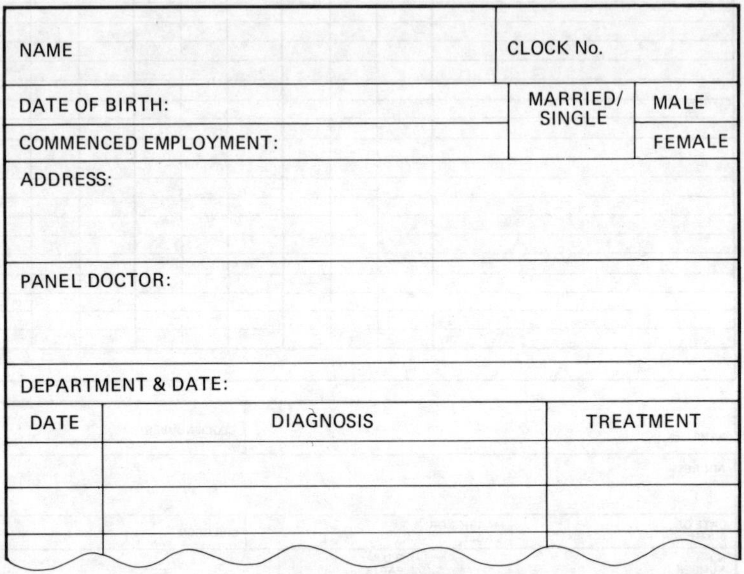

NAME		CLOCK No.	
DATE OF BIRTH:		MARRIED/SINGLE	MALE
COMMENCED EMPLOYMENT:			FEMALE
ADDRESS:			
PANEL DOCTOR:			
DEPARTMENT & DATE:			
DATE	DIAGNOSIS		TREATMENT

Fig. 25 *Typical layout of an individual staff record envelope.*

envelopes are filed vertically, and although it is not likely to be as speedy in reference as the visible card system, it has the advantages of being neat and compact, and all the information relating to each employee is in one place. The envelopes are usually stock size (say C4) and can be filed vertically in a filing cabinet.

The fourth method is a combined application for employment and staff record printed on thin card; the cards are filed vertically. It has the great advantage of being in the employee's own handwriting (saving work and transcription errors), as well as having his signature, which may be useful on occasions. Against this, however, the writing may be poor, the cards may be untidy in appearance and, as with visible card records, relevant correspondence and reports must be filed elsewhere.

In many large organisations personnel records are now stored on computer. The confidentiality of the records is maintained by limiting access to the information by means of special codes (*see* Chapter 39).

It is also possible to keep the records on microfilm but this is not usually found to be a very suitable method because fairly frequent updating is necessary. This involves reproducing a hard copy, updating, and filming the updated document. For an organisation with complete microfilming equipment and a vast number of employees, whose records are held centrally, this could solve a major storage space problem without too much difficulty. However, such an organisation could more easily use a computer storage and retrieval system.

12. Promoting Staff

Promotion involves a change of status and usually means appointment to a higher-grade post with greater responsibilities. It is an important aspect of staff management because it is in promotion that a worker obtains satisfaction, and it is in satisfying this desire to advance and develop that morale is kept at a high level. Staff condemned to routine clerical work without chance of promotion inevitably become frustrated, uninterested and lethargic resulting in the evils of high staff turnover, low productivity, and general dissatisfaction.

Promotion policy

Many large organisations have a policy of filling senior jobs by promotion from within, while others believe in having a quota of appointments from outside the organisation. Sometimes it happens that, although the former policy is adopted, none of the staff is suitable for promotion. This may be the result of selecting employees without the necessary potential for development or misjudging their potential, or it may be the result of inadequate development training. It is advisable for a large organisation to have a written policy on promotion. This might include a provision that no employee should be promoted until he has become duly qualified (either by experience or by examination, or by both), and that no employee should be promoted until he has trained a junior employee to perform his own job satisfactorily. (This infers that all superiors are involved in selecting their subordinates.)

A laid-down policy assists the management, and also encourages the staff, who know what is expected of them if they wish to be promoted. There are advantages both in promoting staff from within and in recruiting staff from outside the organisation. With promotion, there are less likely to be mistakes in selection, for the employees are known quantities. Really equitable promotions create a feeling of content among employees, and retain their interest in the company. Recruitment from outside can bring new ideas and avoid "staleness" in an organisation. It must be borne in mind that bad promotions or too many outside appointments can badly upset morale. The ultimate aim must be to appoint the person best able to do the job, whether it is from inside or outside the organisation.

CAREER STRUCTURES

When attending an interview most applicants will want to know what "prospects" there are. There should be clear structures for the progression of each type of staff. In addition it should be possible wherever practicable for staff to move "sideways" into another category of job. For example, if a secretary reaches the limit of promotion by reason of the nature of the organisation or some other cause it ought to be possible for her to move into administration, possibly personnel work, for which her secretarial experience will form a good basis. Clerical staff whose aptitudes are not appropriate to development in the department in which they work should be given an opportunity to move into another sphere of activity, when this becomes possible.

The requirements at each level of a career structure in any category should be laid down so that each individual knows what is required for promotion. This may be a number of years' experience, qualifications, or certain personal qualities, especially for supervisory posts. If people know what is required to obtain promotion to a higher-level job it is their own fault if they make no effort to attain the necessary standards.

DEVELOPMENT FOR PROMOTION

It is poor policy to wait until a vacancy arises before starting to look at existing employees for people who might meet the requirements. Even if a person does exist it is unfair to expect good performance if he has not been "groomed" for the job. He should have been encouraged to train a junior to take over from him. If he has not done this he may find himself doing both his old and the new job with catastrophic results.

Training to enable a likely employee to acquire the necessary attributes should be given in various ways. Opportunities to develop the *qualities* required for increased responsibilities should be given by arranging for him to "stand in" for one or more superiors during their absence on holiday or for sickness. The good office manager is constantly on the look out for people capable of development and this should be a routine component of all supervision.

Selection for promotion

Selection for promotion is usually based on a number of factors, which may vary depending on the type of job and the level of supervision/management. Similarly, more or less weight may be allocated to each factor in accordance with the requirements laid down in the job and personnel specifications. The most usual grounds for promotion are as follows.

(1) Length of service. (It should be made clear whether this means service in the company, or in the department.)

(2) Practical ability.

(3) General attitude and loyalty.

(4) Education and qualifications, either internal, e.g. as in the Civil Service, or external, e.g. professional examinations conducted by external bodies.

(5) Character and personality—this is particularly important for promotion to supervisory level or above but should not be given undue prominence.

Obviously promotion on the basis of personal likes and dislikes is guaranteed to produce trouble both for the management and for the person concerned.

ABILITY VERSUS SENIORITY

Promotion is often made on grounds of seniority, and it is useful to define what is meant by "seniority". It may mean seniority of age, of service in a particular department, or of service in the organisation; but the latter is the most usual meaning of the word. Promotion on grounds of seniority may be viewed as a reward for long service, and recognition of loyalty, or as a reward for experience; it tends to increase the feeling of security of existing staff. It may encourage all workers to see themselves as trainees for higher posts and avoid the friction which almost inevitably arises when junior staff are appointed to supervise longer-serving staff. On the other hand, "waiting for dead men's shoes" may not appeal to the younger staff who will move to other organisations to obtain promotion, resulting in high labour turnover.

Promotion by seniority alone is unlikely to be ideal. It should of course be taken into account, normally in conjunction with ability. It can be argued that promotion on the grounds of ability alone is the only way to obtain the utmost efficiency but it should also be remembered that a person's ability to do his existing job is not necessarily a guarantee that he will be able to meet the responsibilities of a higher-level job, particularly if he has to contend with resentment and jealousy from more senior colleagues. In practice, most people prefer to see recognition of ability and aptitude, with length of service carrying weight only when other factors are nearly equal.

SELECTION TECHNIQUES

Promotion is a variation of recruitment, starting with job analysis (*see* Chapters 8, 9 and 10). Various techniques may be used, such as the following.

(1) Interviews, mainly to assess character and personality.

(2) Merit rating and/or staff appraisal reports to assess ability.

(3) Internal examinations.

(4) Recommendations from the heads of departments.

(5) Advertising internally or otherwise informing existing staff of the vacancy so that interested employees can apply.

(6) Training programmes geared to promotion.

It is likely that a combination of techniques are used, especially when the short list is reached.

Difficulties of promotion

Promotion is a difficult aspect of staff management. Workers often do not realise that the best worker may not always be the best supervisor because special qualities are required for supervision in addition to technical abilities. Often staff reports contain an assessment of what an individual is doing and not what he is capable of doing.

A good promotion may seem unfair to the staff and this will almost certainly cause jealousy, lowering of morale, and high labour turnover.

It is also decidedly difficult to promote if none of the existing staff have the required ability to warrant their being promoted. On the other hand, there may be more than one suitable candidate for promotion and it may be almost impossible to choose one from among them.

The good office manager sets out to avoid promotion difficulties by:

(1) establishing a career structure for his staff;

(2) recruiting with the development of staff through the career structure in mind;

(3) developing staff potential both on the job and by training;

(4) establishing job grading, merit rating and regular staff appraisal;

(5) encouraging supervisors to undertake informal staff appraisals fairly frequently.

13. Training Staff

Legislation

Under the Industrial Training Act 1964 the U.K. Government established Industrial Training Boards (I.T.B.s) for the various types of industry—engineering, construction, distributive, etc.—to give advice and provide training facilities for employees in those industries. Although a Clerical Training Council was established it was not successful probably because clerical work is essential in all industries and each I.T.B. dealt with clerical training as it applied in its particular industry. Several of the Boards have done a great deal of research into the training needs of clerical staff and have produced some excellent programmes and publications in this field. The principal aim of the 1964 Act was to improve training nationally and to spread the cost of training so that it was not borne solely by those organisations which had good training policies and programmes.

Under the Act the government is empowered to make a training levy. Employers pay a percentage of their leviable emoluments, the amount being recommended annually by the individual I.T.B.s to the Secretary of State for Employment, who makes the Levy Order. Organisations which provide training for their employees, to the required standard in accordance with specific criteria, may claim exemption from the levy (*see* below).

MANPOWER SERVICES COMMISSION

Under the Employment and Training Act 1973 the Manpower Services Commission was established to run the public employment and training services. The main aims of the Commission which are relevant to training are:

(1) to assist manpower resources to be developed and contribute fully to economic well-being;

(2) to help secure for each worker the opportunities and services he or she needs in order to lead a satisfying working life;

(3) to improve the quality of decisions affecting manpower.

TRAINING SERVICES DIVISION

The Training Services Divsion (T.S.D.), an executive arm of the Manpower Services Commission, was originally established as the Training Services Agency (T.S.A.) under the 1973 Act, with responsibility for the co-ordination of training nationally. The T.S.A. developed the network of skillcentres (previously "Government Training Centres") for industrial training and retraining and centres for clerical and secretarial training. The Training Opportunities Scheme (TOPS) was established by the T.S.A., and TOPS courses continue under the aegis of the T.S.D. in many colleges and training institutions.

The relationship of organisations with Industrial Training Boards

Each major industry is covered by an I.T.B. Each organisation, or part of an organisation, i.e. establishment, is covered by the I.T.B. which is related to its activity, or *major* activity when it is involved in more than one. Only the Hotel and Catering Industries Training Board covers all kinds of organisations, i.e. wherever catering is carried on. There are, however, large areas of the public sector, nationalised industries and parts of the private sector, such as the professions, which are not covered by I.T.B.s.

Most of the Industrial Training Boards are structured on a regional basis with area training advisers. Each organisation is "under the wing" of a particular training adviser or, in the case of a very large organisation, a team of advisers. The services of each Board are related to the needs of the industry it serves. Some Boards' services are made up of three main elements, viz. review, advice and grants. Other Boards have a commitment to direct training activities, e.g. the Shipbuilding, Construction, Agricultural and Road Transport I.T.B.s have their own training centres in which industry-related courses are conducted. Some I.T.B.s conduct training courses for supervisors emphasising on-the-job training techniques.

REVIEW

The review element involves visits by Board staff to employers to determine the extent to which claims for exemption from the training levy are valid. Certain criteria must be met by the employer. The following information on these criteria is taken from the Food, Drink and Tobacco I.T.B. whose levy for 1979/80 was 0.7 per cent of total leviable emoluments. The reduction allowed for each stage of the criteria is indicated below. It is stressed that the criteria and levels of levy exemption differ substantially from one Board to another.

(1) *Commitment and responsibility.*
  (i) The employer agrees to and receives visits by Board training staff to discuss his training policy and practice.
  (ii) The employer has a written statement of training policy which has been published to employees.
  (iii) The employer has a senior manager with over-all responsibility for ensuring that the training policy is translated into practice.
  (iv) The senior managers at the headquarters of the organisation and elsewhere have sufficient knowledge and understanding of training to recognise the contribution effective training can make to business performance.
  (v) Each unit of an organisation under review has the assistance of staff able to take the responsibility (full- or part-time) for the practical details of translating policy into practice.

Compliance with these criteria reduces the levy liability to 0.63 per cent of emoluments.

(2) *Assessment and planning.*
  (vi) The employer is able to demonstrate that an over-all assessment of the company's training needs has been carried out.
  (vii) The employer has written training plans based on this assessment.

Compliance with these criteria reduces the levy liability to 0.33 per cent of emoluments.

(3) *Introductory training.*
  (viii) The employer provides introductory training to all new entrants and all employees taking on a new job with all training based on a written programme.

Compliance with this criterion reduces the levy liability to 0.23 per cent of emoluments.

(4) *Training of managers and supervisors.*
  (ix) The employer provides training for all managers and supervisors for whom needs are identified.

(5) *Training in other priority areas.*
  (x) The employer provides systematically planned training for the other areas of priority identified in the over-all training plans.

Compliance with criterion 4 or 5 reduces the levy liability to 0.13 per cent of emoluments: compliance with both criteria reduces the liability to 0.03 per cent of emoluments.

(6) *Evidence and evaluation.*

   (xi) Records are kept to show that the training plans are being applied.

   (xii) Provision should be made for reviewing the effectiveness of training and this review takes place on an on-going basis.

Compliance with all these criteria qualify for full exemption from the training levy. When the I.T.B. receives an application for levy exemption an inspection is carried out in the organisation by the Board staff and exemption of a portion or all of the levy is granted according to which of the criteria, stated above, are met.

ADVICE

The primary function of the I.T.B.s is to ensure that adequate training to the required standard is provided for those who need it. To this end the Board's training advisers are available to give advice wherever necessary and if they are unable to provide it they can call on other Board staff who have the necessary specialised knowledge, and firms outside the organisation.

GRANTS

I.T.B.s influence areas of special training needs and may allow additional grants to organisations which meet these needs. For example, in a certain area there may be a shortage of employees with a particular skill. Organisations which provide this training would gain some financial benefit to offset some of the cost.

Each of the I.T.B.s sets priorities according to the needs of the industry it covers. It is, however, fairly general that training in certain areas such as industrial relations, sandwich courses and courses for women over 30 for managerial and senior supervisory posts qualify for grants.

Safety is another important area of training which may, in some industries, qualify for a special grant. It should in any case be included in all introductory training. The emphasis for special grants changes with the needs of industry. In most cases the grant is a means of encouraging employers to undertake a particular type of training needed urgently and/or for a large number of employees.

The training function

The primary objective of training is to develop an efficient work-force at all levels to ensure that corporate objectives can be met. Normally this implies obtaining maximum efficiency at minimum cost but in certain kinds of work these two criteria might be mutually exclusive. For example, to ensure 100 per cent accuracy in invoices would involve enormous costs for verifying which could not be justified. Therefore the standard of accuracy required must be related to the economic aspect of the process. Even so training will help to ensure better, i.e. more cost-effective, performance.

Within that primary objective there are three basic reasons for training, viz.:

(1) to enable the employee to do his present job more efficiently, i.e. to a higher performance standard;

(2) to prepare a worker for a higher-level job; and

(3) to prepare a person to undertake a completely different job from that with which he is familiar—retraining.

Within the criteria listed above there are many subsidiary purposes, the most important of which are:

(1) the acquisition of a broader educational, technical and/or organisational background;

(2) the improvement of existing skills and/or the acquisition of new skills;

(3) the attainment of technical/professional qualifications;

(4) the opportunity to make contacts, exchange ideas and discuss problems with colleagues or people from other organisations;

(5) a fresh interest in work by virtue of greater understanding and perception of the organisation and its objectives;

(6) a greater feeling of involvement by being able to discuss various aspects of work with greater confidence;

(7) a better understanding of people, their reactions, aspirations and problems;

(8) a better understanding of himself and the impetus needed for self-development.

Levels of training

There are various levels of training. A brief summary of the main ones are given below.

INDUCTION TRAINING
Every new employee at any level should undergo an induction training programme, which should include information on the organisation, its structure, products/services, policies, information about suggestion schemes, etc. It should include visits to the plant(s), visits to other departments and discussions with people in

other departments if it would help the new employee to have a better understanding of his own role. It should be arranged at intervals over a period of perhaps three to six months with the most important topics being covered in the early stages. What might be considered "trivial" details such as cloakroom facilities, eating facilities and how to obtain stationery supplies are all important to the newcomer and should not be overlooked.

JOB TRAINING

This nearly always consists of a combination of skills and knowledge needed to perform the duties of the job to the standards required. A carefully integrated programme consisting of on-the-job and off-the-job training is often the best approach.

JUNIOR STAFF

Juniors should be regarded as the raw material of future supervisors or managers, and be given commensurate attention. So often juniors are shown the mechanics of the postbook, how to make a telephone call, how to check a voucher—and are then left to their own devices. The basic skills of arithmetic and English are necessary, but should a junior show a bent in any particular direction, he should be encouraged, and work should be given which will be of the greatest interest to him.

It is important to juniors, perhaps more than to others, that they should not only be told what they have to do, but why things are done in that way. A smart youngster will soon find out a great many things for himself when he is given a job to do. Juniors should be encouraged to extend their learning at evening and/or day-release classes available in colleges. Day release may be inconvenient in a small or medium-sized office where there may not be anyone else available to take their places when absent, but the organisation will benefit in the long run. It is useful also if juniors are switched from one department to another, so that they gain experience of different kinds of work in the different offices. Combined with off-the-job training this can form the basis of an apprenticeship training scheme for school-leavers.

SUPERVISORY TRAINING

The person who shows excellent capabilities at his work does not necessarily automatically become a good supervisor when promoted. The newly promoted supervisor is likely to find himself concerned for the first time with identifying and solving problems involving decision-making. He has to motivate and control staff. This requires leadership skills which must be developed. He must be able to assess the training needs of subordinate staff and carry out on-the-job training when necessary. The supervisor is on the management ladder and must learn the art of delegation. Until fairly recently office supervisors were left to acquire these skills by experience but it can be a long hard process and is made much easier by proper training.

In addition to training courses covering the various aspects of supervision, other significant methods of training include job rotation (*see* Chapter 16) and deputising for the office manager when necessary.

MANAGEMENT TRAINING

Practical training for management often consists of a definite policy whereby clerks are regularly transferred from one department to another, so that a broad experience is obtained of all sides of an organisation. This is an excellent plan provided it is accepted by the employees, and is definitely linked with a programme of training in line with a promotion policy.

Most office managers take their places in higher management in specialised positions, such as company secretaries, accountants, sales managers, personnel managers, and so on. For each of these and for other special vocations there are various professional qualifications, and much of management training consists of practical training together with study for one of these qualifications.

Training for management can be divided into three main groups:

(1) management courses leading to the Diploma in Management Studies conducted at colleges, regional management centres, business schools and universities;

(2) short residential courses;

(3) in-house management development programmes.

Types of training

Training may be given either on the job or off the job. Training programmes very often combine the two since each type is complementary to the other. As mentioned earlier, on-the-job training should be given by supervisors who have been trained in the necessary instruction techniques. Off-the-job training can be arranged in a number of ways, either on an in-house or in-company basis, or externally.

IN-HOUSE OR EXTERNAL TRAINING

In-house training means that courses, workshops, seminars, etc., are conducted either on the organisation's own premises, which may include a training centre, or on premises hired for the purpose, e.g. a hotel conference room. The organisation may employ its own training officers/instructors to conduct the training and/or they may employ outside consultants when necessary, particularly for specialist training. External training means arranging for employees to take full-time or part-time courses at local technical colleges, polytechnics, etc. or to attend short-term residential or non-residential workshops, seminars, etc. conducted by various training institutions and organisations.

There are advantages and disadvantages to both in-house and external training. When training is conducted in-house it is possible to ensure that the content is geared to meet the precise needs of the organisation. On the other hand, unless the trainees come from a wide area of the organisation's activities there may not be the same enthusiasm for discussion and exchange of ideas and there is sometimes a tendency for discussion to lead to "complaints" as distinct from problems. When designing training programmes for individual employees these points should be borne in mind. There are occasions when the extra expense involved in external courses is worth while because of the added benefit the trainee will gain.

It can happen that when a particular training need is identified for one employee it raises the question as to whether it is a common need for several employees. In this case an in-house programme is generally more economic.

Assessing training needs

Before training needs can be assessed each employee must have a job description with predetermined standards of performance. A simple formula for establishing the training needed by any individual is:

optimum performance − actual performance = training needed.

However, there are four aspects to training, viz. knowledge (about the organisation and the function of the job), skills (for carrying out all the physical and mental activities involved in performing the duties of the job), application of knowledge and skills to meet individual situations, problems, etc., and attitudes to the job. An assessment must start from the job analysis. This enables the employee's performance to be compared with the personnel specification.

There are various ways in which training needs can be established, as follows.

(1) Questionnaires to the employees and to their superiors.

(2) Observation of performance. In this case task analysis may be necessary as for job evaluation (*see* Chapter 9).

(3) A predetermined development programme for all employees at each grade from which can be deleted the items not required by the individual because of previous experience, qualifications, etc.

Preparing training programmes

When the training needs of an individual or a group of employees have been identified one must then consider the best way to provide the training. The following check-list, aimed at establishing the best training programme for each individual, may be useful.

(1) Does training needed consist primarily of knowledge, skills, co-ordination and application of knowledge and skills, or attitudes?

(2) Would the training be of greatest benefit if given on the job or off the job, or is a combination of the two required?

(3) Is training needed for improvement of existing performance, to undertake newly introduced procedures, etc., to prepare the individual for job rotation, job enrichment or job enlargement, or to provide a basis for promotion?

(4) Would most benefit be gained from full-time or part-time training, in one module or in several modules taken at intervals?

(5) What type of training could the individual undergo taking into account social factors such as domestic commitments, etc.?

(6) What training facilities exist to meet the needs:
   (a) within the organisation; and
   (b) outside the organisation?

(7) If the training needed is of a fairly mundane nature, e.g. correct telephone techniques, are there other people in the organisation (outside one's own department/section) who might need similar training which would make an in-house programme worth while?

Having established individual needs, it is then necessary to determine priorities. These may be the areas in which the greatest number of people need training, or it may be areas of specialist training where the numbers are few. It may be particular grades or types of employees, e.g. new recruits, women, supervisors.

Some organisations give each department a training budget which frequently sets constraints on the amount of training that can be done in any given period. In some organisations where a special effort is being made to train people in specific categories there may be a common budget or funds may be made available in addition to the departmental budgets. In any event it is important to establish priorities to ensure that the training given results in maximum improvement in the department.

It is the role of the training department or training section of the personnel department to provide information and training facilities and to help individual managers secure the training needed for their staff. In some organisations the manager is the last person to be told that his subordinates are to attend a training course. In other organisations nominations for training are in the hands of the individual managers so that employees with managers who are not "training-minded" get a raw deal.

The training process

Whatever the type, method and level of training the superior of the individual to be trained must be involved from the beginning. The manager must set specific objectives which the individual should be able to meet as a result of undergoing training. It may be that the aim is greater productivity, wider responsibilities, more authority, or a special project. If the training is long term, regular discussions should be held to make sure that the employee is on the right road and recognises the relevance of the training to his future development. If the training is short term the manager should discuss with the employee its relevance to the predetermined objectives, and targets should be set to meet those objectives over a suitable period of time.

If on-the-job and off-the-job training are combined there must be liaison between the instructors, whether the off the job instructor is on the staff of the organisation, an external consultant or a member of staff of a training institution. It may be that special practical projects should be designed to enable the trainee to put into practice certain knowledge and skills he has learned in the classroom.

If training is on the job the manager must ensure that the person giving instruction is competent to do so. The standard procedures are given below.

(1) Explain what the task is, broken down into sections if necessary.

(2) Find out how much the trainee already knows.

(3) Explain why the task is done.

(4) Explain how the task is done, section by section, if appropriate.

(5) Demonstrate how to do the task. Sometimes it is advisable to demonstrate at normal speed of operation, then slowly, then again at normal speed. Normally some explanation is necessary during demonstration.

(6) Allow the trainee to practise the task, or section of the task, asking questions if necessary.

(7) Correct the trainee if necessary by repeating explanations and/or demonstrations.

(8) Allow the trainee to practise under supervision until he is competent and confident to perform the task alone.

The essential requirements for good on-the-job training are that the instructor should prepare beforehand by analysing the task and deciding how he is going to explain and demonstrate it; that he should be able to demonstrate perfectly; that he should be able to communicate simply, clearly and fluently; that he should make the trainee feel at ease; and that he should never show impatience.

Evaluation and validation

All training should be evaluated to determine whether it meets the objectives which it was intended to meet. The success of on-the-job training can generally be validated almost immediately. It may not be possible to validate off-the-job training for several months, because it takes time for a trainee to put into practice what he has learned, develop confidence in his ability to perform more effectively and meet the objectives set by his manager.

Many organisations ask employees who attend training courses of any kind, whether in-house or external, either to write a report or to complete an evaluation form. A specimen evaluation form is illustrated in Fig. 26.

Training records

Training records must be kept to provide confirmation to the Industrial Training Boards of training carried out. They also serve to justify training budget requirements and are an integral part of each employee's personnel record. Some organisations include the training record on the personnel record. Other organisations keep training and personnel records separately, each department having to refer to the other for information when necessary—hardly an efficient system. Some organisations duplicate the training record so that the personnel department has a complete dossier on each individual while the training department has only the information needed for its purpose.

As with staff records, there are a variety of methods of storing the information. A visible card index is useful because the cards can be colour-coded indicating at a glance the training undergone by each individual. A few organisations have training records on computer and a number of others are moving towards a computerised system. Access to information has to be strictly controlled.

	Course appraisal	Part A

To be completed by the student at the start of the course

Your name   Your job title

Your organisation's name and address

Please state *your* aims in attending this course

Course code   Course start date

_____
_____   ◄ Your manager's name
_____   ◄ Your manager's address
_____

	Part B/1
To be completed at the end of the course	Please tick the appropriate box in each section

1. To what extent were the *course* objectives achieved?

Not at all [ ][ ][ ][ ][ ][ ][ ] completely

2. To what extent have *your* aims been achieved?

Not at all [ ][ ][ ][ ][ ][ ][ ] completely

If they have not been achieved, or only partly achieved

(a) to what do you attribute this?

(b) what post-course activity would help you to achieve them?

If your aims have been achieved, what post-course activity would help to consolidate the lessons you have. learned?

3. What specific action are you going to take as a result of attending this course?

4. Please indicate your over-all assessment of the course by ticking the appropriate box in each section. Please give brief reasons for assessments made to the left of arrow.

	Poor	↓	Very good	
Value to you				
Comprehensiveness				
Generation of new ideas				
Standard of lectures				
Value of practical work				
Standard of handouts/manuals				
Over-all course appraisal				

5. General comments on the course

   (a) Would you add any sessions/topics? Why?

   (b) Would you omit any sessions? Why?

   (c) High points

   (d) Low points

6. Any other comments you would like to make on the structure and presentation of the course?

Student's signature   Date   Thank you for your comments

Fig. 26 *Specimen evaluation form.* Part A is completed by the trainee at the beginning of the course, and Part B is completed after undergoing training.

A specimen training record for an individual employee is illustrated in Fig. 27. A check-list type of record for a group of employees (section or department) is illustrated in Fig. 28. This can be used to record both on-the-job and off-the-job training.

Training: an on-going process

Training is a process which should be happening all the time. Any explanation to an employee about something new is automatically training because it will be an additional item of experience, a new piece of knowledge or an additional application of a skill. Consultation with an employee on a proposal will help that person to exchange ideas, see other points of view, and generally develop his own powers of analysis.

Perhaps one of the best ways of training, and one of the least used or most misused, is *delegation*. The manager who delegates *correctly* is training his subordinates in a practical way which will be of the

TRAINING AND DEVELOPMENT RECORD

NAME_____ JOB TITLE_____

DIVISION_____

DATE OF BIRTH_____ REPORTING TO_____

DATE OF JOINING_____ APPRAISAL TIME   JANUARY/JULY

CAREER DEVELOPMENT PLAN

APPRAISAL DATE	PLAN	DATE COMPLETED

Special Assignments Undertaken:
_____
_____
_____

INTERNAL TRAINING

DATES	COURSE TITLE

EXTERNAL TRAINING

DATES	COURSE TITLE	COSTS

Fig. 27 *Specimen training record for an individual employee.*

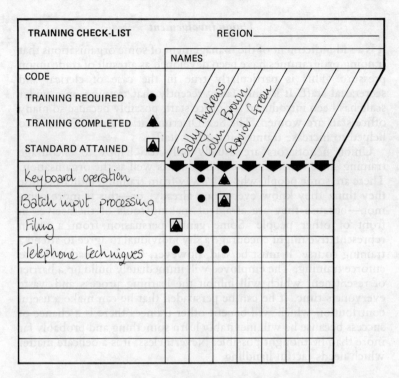

Fig. 28 *Specimen check-list training record*. Can be used to record on-the-job and/or off-the-job training given to a group of employees.

greatest benefit to them in the future. The process of delegation is not unlike the process of training. It is discussed in more detail in Chapter 17.

Another method of training is the presentation of well-prepared house manuals for different types of work. These can cover not only the way in which tasks are to be done, but also standards required. For example, a manual for secretaries would present the house style for the display of various documents produced and could include procedures for receiving visitors, answering the telephone, making telephone calls, etc.

Another aspect of training which is now of far greater significance since the introduction of the Health and Safety at Work etc. Act 1974 is safety and fire precautions. The safety hazards of particular types of work and the precautions which should be taken should be included in the appropriate manuals.

Union involvement

It is a sad indictment of the management of some organisations that
training programmes have been developed as a result of trade union
pressure. This is particularly true in the case of clerical and
secretarial staff. It is only fairly recently that training on a wider
scale has been introduced for office staff, possibly because so many
office staff are women. The Sex Discrimination Act 1975 has also
helped to increase training for office staff.

Union negotiators are usually only too happy to encourage
training since it benefits the individual as well as the organisation.
There are some people who shy away from training, either because
they think they know everything already, or—this is more common—because they are afraid of making fools of themselves in
front of other people. Some gentle persuasion from a union
representative might encourage a shy individual to agree to attend a
training course. It must be said, however, that it is inadvisable to
enforce training. The employee will immediately build up a barrier
of resentment which will inhibit the learning process and waste
everyone's time. If he can be persuaded that he can make a useful
contribution which will benefit other trainees there is a chance of
success because he will inevitably learn something and probably far
more than he thought possible. Nevertheless, it is a delicate matter
which needs tactful handling.

14. Dismissing Staff

Dismissing staff is never a pleasant duty but there are occasions when it is necessary. When staff can be dismissed, on what grounds, and when instant dismissal is justified are now constrained by legislation. Every office manager must be aware of the conditions under which dismissal is permissible.

Legislation affecting dismissal

In the U.K. protection against unfair dismissal of an employee is now covered in the Employment Protection (Consolidation) Act 1978, which brought together the relevant clauses of the Employment Protection Act 1975, the Contracts of Employment Act 1972 and the Trade Union and Labour Relations Act 1974. Dismissal from employment for reasons of sex or race is also covered in the Sex Discrimination Act 1975 and the Race Relations Act 1976. Every manager should be aware of the provisions against unfair dismissal in all these Acts of Parliament.

Disciplinary procedures

The Code of Practice No. 1, *Disciplinary Practice and Procedures in Employment*, published by the Advisory, Conciliation and Arbitration Service (ACAS), gives guidance to employers on how to draw up and operate the rules and procedures for disciplinary action. The aim of such rules and procedures is rather to encourage improvements in individual conduct than to "punish" employees. Disciplinary procedures should be set out in writing and agreed with the representatives of recognised trade unions. All employees must be informed of the regulations and should know the type of conduct which might incur dismissal, whether with notice or summarily. It is usual to include these rules and regulations in the conditions of service, reference to where they can be found being made in the statement of appointment.

The Code of Practice states that disciplinary procedures should:

(1) be in writing;

(2) specify to whom they apply;

(3) provide for matters to be dealt with quickly;

(4) indicate the disciplinary actions which may be taken;

(5) specify the levels of management which have the authority to take the various forms of disciplinary action, ensuring that immediate superiors do not normally have the power to dismiss without reference to senior managment;

(6) provide for individuals to be informed of the complaints against them and to be given an opportunity to state their case before decisions are reached;

(7) give individuals the right to be accompanied by a trade union representative or by a fellow employee of their choice;

(8) ensure that, except for gross misconduct, no employees are dismissed for a first breach of discipline;

(9) ensure that disciplinary action is not taken until the case has been carefully investigated;

(10) ensure that individuals are given an explanation for any penalty imposed;

(11) provide a right of appeal and specify the procedure to be followed.

These procedures apply to disciplinary action generally, e.g. suspension, loss of pay, etc., as well as to dismissal.

Grounds for dismissal

Under the Employment Protection Act 1975 it is stated that there must be "fair and reasonable grounds" for dismissal. Fair and reasonable grounds fall into four main categories, viz.:

(1) inability to do the job;

(2) misconduct, e.g. continual unpunctuality, deliberate refusal to carry out instructions;

(3) redundancy;

(4) statutory requirements (e.g. under the Official Secrets Act) or "some other substantial reason".

The aim of the Employment Protection Act is not to make it impossible to dismiss staff in reasonable circumstances, but to ensure that the employee is given a fair chance to prove his competence, rectify minor misconduct such as unpunctuality, and have adequate warning of redundancy and an opportunity to seek other employment before being "out of work". Where there are "fair and reasonable" grounds for dismissal, provided warnings have been given, and can be proved to have been given, and every effort has been made to help the employee to perform his duties satisfactorily, dismissal is fair.

Notice

Minimum periods of notice must be given to all employees who work more than sixteen hours a week or have worked more than eight hours a week for at least five years. The notice periods are tied to length of service, as follows:

1 week's notice for service of from 4 weeks to 2 years;
1 additional week's notice for each year of service from 2 to 12 years;
12 weeks' notice (maximum) for 12 years service or more.

If a formal contract includes a clause for a longer period of notice than the minimum required by law, the longer period is legally enforceable.

The only exception from the minimum notice requirement is in the case of gross misconduct, e.g. fighting and injuring a colleague.

Where employees are entitled to notice, pay in lieu may, of course, be given.

Unfair dismissal

Any employee who feels that his dismissal has been unfair may make a case to an Industrial Tribunal, provided he works for more than sixteen hours a week and has been in the service of the organisation for more than one year (or for more than eight hours a week with five years' service). If the reason for dismissal is associated with trade union membership or activity, racial discrimination, sex discrimination, or pregnancy in the case of a woman, no qualifying period of service is necessary. The onus of proving fair dismissal lies with the employer.

If the Industrial Tribunal finds that the dismissal was unfair four courses of action are possible. The employer may be ordered to:
(1) re-engage the employee;
(2) re-instate the employee;
(3) compensate the employee;
(4) give a Statement of Right.

Re-engagement means that the employee loses continuity of employment, i.e. there is a gap between the date when dismissal took effect and the date when he is re-engaged. Re-instatement means that continuity of employment is preserved—this may be important for pension rights, holiday pay, etc. Compensation may be payable to cover the period between dismissal and re-engagement or re-instatement.

If the employer refuses to re-engage or re-instate the employee a compensation award is made against the employer. This may range from one week's salary to a maximum fixed by the Government, and is based on length of service, salary level (up to a predetermined maximum) and the reason for dismissal. A Statement of Right is very occasionally awarded when a dismissed person has quickly found another job and seeks only to establish that the dismissal was unfair. If proved to be so the Statement of Right "clears the record".

Either the employee or the employer may appeal against the decision of an Industrial Tribunal to the Employment Appeal Tribunal on a point of law only.

It should be mentioned that where an employee makes a case for unfair dismissal to an Industrial Tribunal the employer and/or the employee can ask for an officer of the Advisory, Conciliation and Arbitration Service (ACAS) to attempt to settle the matter before the case is heard. If neither makes a request to ACAS an officer of that body can make the first approach if it is considered that a settlement might be reached without an official hearing. In fact well over 60 per cent of dismissal cases are settled before they reach the Industrial Tribunal.

Redundancy

Under the Employment Protection Act 1975 an employer must consult the trade union representative when redundancies are necessary if there is a recognised trade union for the group or category of employees to which the redundancy is applied. Consultation must begin a minimum of thirty days in advance if the number of redundances is between 10 and 99, or ninety days in advance if the number is more than 100. It is stressed that these periods are the minimum and it is advisable to start discussions as soon as possible.

An employee who is given dismissal notice because of redundancy is entitled to reasonable time off during the notice period to look for another job or to make arrangements for training for some other job.

ALTERNATIVE EMPLOYMENT
When a person's job ceases to exist, i.e. he becomes redundant, the employer should make every effort to offer alternative employ-

ment, which can be a different type of job. The employee has a right to a trial period of four weeks, which can be extended by agreement between employer and employee. If the new job is not suitable the employee retains his right to redundancy payment at the end of the trial period.

REDUNDANCY PAYMENT

Under the Employment Protection (Consolidation) Act 1978 (which incorporated provisions of the Redundancy Payments Acts 1965 and 1969) employers are liable to make redundancy payments based on the wage/salary and length of service of the redundant employee who works for more than sixteen hours a week. To meet these costs employers pay into a redundancy fund from which they may receive a grant when payments are made to redundant employees.

Instant dismissal

There are occasions when summary dismissal is necessary, but an office manager should be sure of his ground before he acts in such a way. Normally summary dismissal would only be carried out with the concurrence of the personnel manager. The following are some of the reasons which are valid:

(1) disobedience to reasonable orders given by responsible officials, provided the orders are lawful and not detrimental to the life or safety of employees;

(2) gross negligence; dishonesty; drunkenness such as to interfere with the performance of duties;

(3) wilful misconduct;

(4) disclosure of business secrets—where there are express terms about non-disclosure of business secrets or about carrying on a similar business within a radius of the existing business, the breaking of such a clause is sufficient for instant dismissal.

Dismissal on medical grounds

The question is often asked whether an employee can be dismissed while on sick leave. Providing the conditions of service regarding sickness are complied with the short answer is "yes". However, a good employer is not likely to do this. It is normal to be flexible in applying the rules for a genuinely sick person, especially in cases of long service.

People who are absent very frequently for medical reasons are difficult to deal with but if they are unable to attend work regularly through ill health this would normally be regarded as a fair reason for dismissal, provided adequate warning had been given so that the possible malingerer had an opportunity to improve. In such cases it is normal to seek a medical report from either the company doctor or an independent doctor.

Union involvement

If the employee to be dismissed is a member of a union it is prudent, not to say courteous, to explain the situation to the representative of the union concerned. Provided all the necessary warnings have been given, and can be proved to have been given, i.e. have been given in writing, and are on record in the appropriate personnel file, and the dismissal is fair and reasonable in terms of the reason and in conjunction with the treatment of other staff, there can be no objection. However, if one employee is being dismissed for continuous unpunctuality, for example, while another employee, perhaps a better worker, is not dismissed for the same or perhaps worse misconduct, the union representative, or even an Industrial Tribunal, may regard the dismissal as unfair.

Dismissal procedures

When a decision has been made to dismiss an employee the matter should be handled calmly and quickly. The person should be called into a private office, told of the decision and given the reason for the dismissal. He should be instructed what administrative procedures to follow, e.g. collection of income tax documents, and be given an opportunity to collect personal belongings. There is no point in making the interview more unpleasant than it inevitably is and it may be worth making a gesture by wishing the person well in his future employment. After all, incompatability can occur between the nicest people.

In conclusion it must be stressed that dismissal of staff now has to conform to the statutory principles. Every manager should take the trouble to study the various relevant Acts of Parliament. In the U.K., the Department of Employment booklets outlining the main points of the Employment Protection Act 1975 give useful guidance. A number of professional institutions and publishers have also produced guides. When confronted with the task or even the possibility of dismissing an employee it is advisable to seek the guidance of a colleague, probably a personnel manager, who is *au fait* with the many details of employment legislation. Alternatively, the local office of the Department of Employment or of ACAS should be able to give advice.

15. Working Hours and Time-keeping

Standard hours

Standard working hours for full-time employees vary between 35 and 37½ hours, with 40 hours in a few organisations. Working hours do not normally include lunch breaks which may vary from ½ an hour to 1½ hours, though the average is 1 hour. Morning and afternoon tea breaks are not usually deducted from the working hours. In some organisations the amount of time which may be taken is laid down—this is particularly so where employees have to go to a canteen or a restaurant for their coffee and tea. In other organisations employees are free to take their refreshment from the vending machine whenever they wish; in some cases "tea ladies" still visit offices at specific times of the day. The normal working day in London is likely to be from 9 a.m. to 5 p.m. with a 1-hour lunch break, i.e. 35 hours a week; in factory offices in the provinces it may be 8.30 a.m. to 5 p.m. or 5.30 p.m. with a 1 or 1½-hour lunch break, i.e. 37½ hours a week.

Overtime

In years gone by, overtime in the office was rarely paid for, but with the growth in the size of industries, and as a result of the action of Whitley Councils and trade unions, it is usual to pay overtime for office work in the same way as for overtime in the factory. Overtime is usually paid at the rate of time and a quarter or time and a half for evening work, time and a half for Saturday work and double time for Sunday. "Time" is the normal hourly rate, to which is added a quarter, half or double, as the case may be. Some organisations prefer a more elastic policy and overtime is expected when it is required, and in return time in lieu is given when it is convenient to allow it.

155

Continuous overtime by one or more workers is bad; it fatigues the workers and is a sign that either the staff have too much to do or that they are slow workers. It is generally accepted that some occasional overtime is nearly always necessary in every organisation, for example at financial year end, or for annual stocktaking. It is the responsibility of the office manager to ensure that there is a clear policy about overtime, its payment, time off in lieu, length of notice required, maximum overtime, and so on.

To gain the employees' co-operation when it comes to working overtime the employer should not be unduly harsh on other things such as time-keeping. Should it happen that a department or an individual works overtime continuously, an enquiry should be made, although the evening may be the only possible time for the performance of certain jobs requiring concentration and quiet conditions. Certain safeguards may then be necessary; for example, a clerk employed on cash records should not work overtime on his own, for obvious reasons. Slow working during the day should not be allowed so that employees can work paid overtime.

Flex time (or flexi time)

Under flex time staff can attend the office when they choose (within reason), as well as leaving off work at their own discretion, provided they are in the office during certain hours known as "core time" (usually about 9.30 or 10 a.m. to 12 noon and 2 p.m. to 4 or 4.30 p.m.). The required number of hours must be worked, e.g. an average of 35 hours per week. Usually the hours are accumulated until the end of the month (or every four weeks) when staff are allowed to carry forward a debit or credit of up to 10 hours. In some organisations up to two days' holiday may be taken in lieu of credit time worked.

ADVANTAGES OF FLEX TIME

(1) Participation of staff in deciding their own hours of work improves morale.

(2) It is particularly useful for married women who wish to start work late, for domestic reasons, and like to take long lunch times in order to go shopping.

(3) Overtime payments by the employer are reduced, sometimes almost completely.

(4) It reduces the need for supervision of hours of attendance.

(5) It may be useful for introducing a longer working day for manning the office, without extra cost to the employer.

(6) Provided the employee is in the office for core time it is

impossible to be unpunctual and feel guilty about it.

(7) It overcomes the difficulty of rush-hour travel.

(8) There is generally less absenteeism and sickness.

DISADVANTAGES OF FLEX TIME

(1) Unless office work is self-contained, it might mean that one section is unable to work because another section has not arrived at the office.

(2) If uncontrolled, it could mean that management could never rely on contacting members of staff when required.

(3) It might mean a way of introducing shift working without paying any extra for it.

(4) If employees attend extra early, or work extra late, it may mean paying for extra supervision to see the work is actually performed.

(5) Some employees object to the loss of dignity in having to "clock on" (however, this is usually soon forgotten in the enjoyment of the freedom given with flex time).

Time-recording methods

In some organisations staff are trusted to arrive and to depart on time, and while this is the ideal it may not be practicable in an establishment employing more than one or two dozen employees. It may be said that a supervisor can easily check on the time-keeping, but such checking can only be intermittent, and at best only casual. The simplest and possibly the most favoured method for office staff is the *signing-on book*. Each page of the book is headed with the date, and there are three columns; one for signature, and the other two for the times of arriving and departing. For recording later arrivals it is usual to draw a red line across the book at a certain time or to put out a separate "late book", or to ask all latecomers to report to a supervisor for signing-on. This method, however, is open to fraud and is well known to be inaccurate.

Some organisations do not use a signing-on book, but rely on the accuracy and honesty of a commissionaire, but again favouritism, fraud and collusion are almost unavoidable. To achieve an efficient time-recording system it must be simple, accurate and have automatic recording of time. Some systems and their advantages and disadvantages are discussed in the following pages.

AUTOGRAPHIC MACHINE

The autographic machine has a clock mechanism which controls a paper tape. When recording his time, an employee presses the handle at the side of the machine which automatically records the time on the tape, and at the same time releases a shutter over the tape, so that he can sign his name opposite the printed time. On releasing the handle, the shutter closes the aperture until the next entry.

This machine is ideal for a few dozen employees. It is automatic, fraud-proof and provides printed times for the use of the wages clerk. It reveals lateness and overtime, but takes time to operate and is no quicker than a signing-on book.

CARD TIME-RECORDERS (TIME CLOCKS)

The card time-recorder is based on an individual time record for each worker—the time card. The recording clock is flanked on each side by card racks, "IN" being on one side of it and "OUT" on the other. The cards are arranged so that the top edge of each, showing the pay number, is visible; an employee takes his card, drops it into a slot in the machine and, on a manually operated clock, presses a handle which operates the printing mechanism so that the time is printed in the appropriate space on the card. The advantages of using this machine are listed below.

(1) Lateness and overtime are usually printed in red (ordinary time in black or blue), and are easily picked out on the card when it comes to making up wages.

(2) An individual time record is created, and the attendances for a whole week are on the card; this is useful for wages purposes.

(3) A visual check on absentees can be made every morning; (if all employees are at work, the whole of the "OUT" rack should be empty at, say, one hour after starting time).

(4) An interesting and quite important use of the clock card is as an identification card for payment of wages. After wages have been calculated from them, the cards may be distributed to the workers, who then hand them back again (sometimes bearing their signatures) in exchange for their wages. The time card can also be used as a medium for the calculation of gross wages, or even of net wages.

(5) It is a suitable medium for the calculation of job costs. A specimen folded card, showing times and wage calculations on one side with allocation of labour costs to jobs on the reverse side, is shown in Fig. 29.

AUTOMATIC TIME-RECORDER

There is now a very compact electric digital recording clock where the employee has merely to drop his card in a slot. This type of

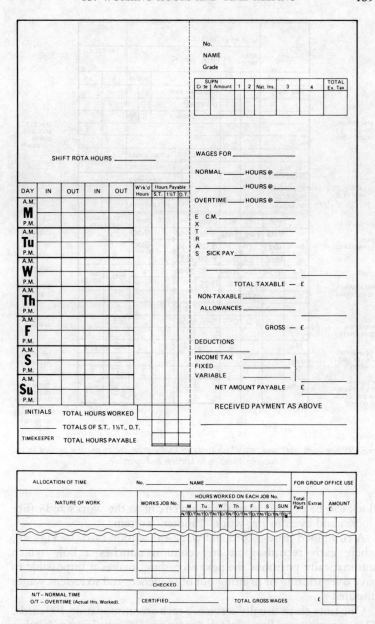

Fig. 29 *Both sides of a folded time card used by a large industrial concern.* Times, wages calculation and receipt are shown on one side, with costing details on the other. Both sides should agree in amount of gross wages payable.

No. 24	NAME W. JOHNSON			RATE	
	WEEK ENDING 9 JAN 19-5			TAX CODE	

DEDUCTIONS	£	p		HOURS	£	p
NAT. INS.			ORDINARY TIME	33		
			OVERTIME	10		
			O/T ALLOWANCE	5	2/3	

SPACES FOR OTHER DEDUCTIONS

SPACES FOR BONUS OR OTHER PAYMENTS

		GROSS WAGES	
INC. TAX		TOTAL DEDUCTIONS	
GROSS WAGES TO DATE		BALANCE	
TOTAL TAX DEDUCTED		INCOME TAX REFUND	
SIGNATURE		NET BALANCE	

LATE ARRIVALS

	MON.	TUES.	WED.	THURS.	FRI.	SAT.	SUN.	STANDARD WEEK HRS.
In	9.03	9.02	9.03	8.58	9.00		9.00	35
Out	12.29	12.30	12.30	8.05	12.30		12.00	
In	13.32	13.27	13.30	9.50	13.33			
Out	16.59	17.00	20.00	12.30	20.00			TOTAL / O/T ALLCE
In		17.30		13.25				
Out		18.30		17.00				
	.07	.02	.03	1.45	.03		2..	
	6.53	6.58	6.57	5.15	6.57		33	

CLASSIFIED OVERTIME RATES							TOTAL	O/T ALLCE
1 1/3	1	2		2			5	1 3/8
1 1/2		1		1			2	1
2						3	3	3
TOTAL HRS.							45	5 2/3

EARLY DEPARTURES

BREAK PRIOR TO OVERTIME

SPACE FOR OTHER RATES

SPACES FOR DAILY TOTAL OF HOURS WORKED IF REQUIRED

OVERTIME · SPECIAL LEAVE · OVERTIME · TOTAL LOST TIME · TOTAL ORDINARY TIME · OVERTIME ALLOWANCES · TOTAL OVERTIME ALLOWANCE · TOTAL HOURS WORKED IN WEEK

Fig. 30 *Specimen time card, on which times in heavy print are in practice printed in red, drawing attention to lateness and overtime.*

clock can be connected to the same circuit as the works and office clocks, and even to the works "hooter" system.

A combined time-record and wage-calculation card (*see* Fig. 30), where each recording in any column punches a hole which automatically positions the next recording, makes it impossible to have overprinting or printing out of sequence, and so lessens wages disputes.

One time clock usually services a rack accommodating 100 cards. This means providing a clock for every 100 employees. It takes about ten seconds for the employee to "clock-on" with the latest type of clock.

One disadvantage is that it is easy to clock-on for another employee, and the only precaution that can be taken is to supervise the clocking-on, even if only intermittently, as well as making it a serious offence for an employee to clock-on for another. Many firms make it an offence punishable by instant dismissal.

Flex time (*see* above) may be recorded in a signing-on book, by return of a weekly schedule of hours worked, completed by each employee, or by an electronic combined time clock/calculator. For the latter, the staff are issued with plastic embossed cards or keys which are inserted into the machine. The number of hours worked is automatically calculated and displayed on a counter. This machine is illustrated in Fig. 31.

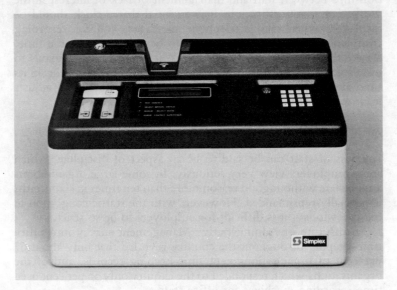

[*Courtesy Simplex Time Recorder Co. (U.K.) Ltd.*

Fig. 31 *The Simplex S.T.E.P. Model 99 attendance recorder.* This machine has an electronic memory and provides a printed record of each employee's arrival and departure times, distinguishing between normal time, normal overtime and special overtime. The daily and cumulative totals of each are recorded and any anomalies in attendance are printed in red. It can be programmed to record and calculate both flex time and fixed time.

WATCHMAN'S DETECTOR

There are various makes of time-recorder for recording times at which watchmen visit a number of fixed points on their patrol. The most usual type consists of portable recorders slung around the watchman's neck, and on which he clocks-on with special keys located at the various patrol points. Each key records its special station number and time of visit. The paper tape record is not only a check on the wakefulness of the watchman, but enables the security officer to vary the patrols to guard against intending burglars.

Clocks in the office

Some people say that if clocks are placed in conspicuous positions in an office it encourages "clock-watching". It is in fact much more likely that consciousness of time is the result of either bad relationships between staff and management or lack of interest in the work. For many office jobs it is essential that a clock should be displayed; when taking telephone messages, and for recording completion of work, it is essential to be able to check the time. Where there is a large suite of offices, it may be advantageous to install an electric synchronised system by which each unit checks its time automatically with a master clock every hour, and adjusts itself to the right time.

Time-keeping discipline

Lateness of staff can be said to be an aspect of discipline, which some employers view very seriously. In some large organisations anyone late without good reason more than ten times in six months is officially reprimanded. However, with the traffic congestion in big cities today, it is difficult for employers to be so strict.

An Institute of Administrative Management survey into office time-keeping throughout the country revealed that only about 57 per cent of organisations kept time-keeping records, and of the organisations which responded to the enquiry only 55 per cent used time-recording machines for office staff.

The modern tendency is to offer some incentive to arrive early, rather than to impose a penalty for arriving late. Some firms have abandoned time clocks, while other organisations offer such incentives as a half day off for a month of good time-keeping.

So far as time in the office is concerned, slackness in time-keeping may lead to slackness in other directions. Good time-keeping is usually reflected in the whole atmosphere of the office.

Cost of unpunctuality

It is an old business motto that "time is money", and it is truer today than ever before. All sides of a business work to a time schedule, and whether it is production, sales budgeting, accounting, or the general office, the office manager must ensure that proper use is made of working hours. It is essential that every person in an office should be aware of the value of his/her time, and that if, for example, gossiping takes place, it usually means the time wasted of two or three people, not just one person. To take an average wage of, say, £12 per day, if each member of a staff of 1,500 loses five minutes per day, the loss amounts to £54,000 per annum. A recent national survey produced the information that the average worker wastes three hours twenty minutes a week by arriving late, leaving early, taking longer breaks than the time allowed and "day dreaming". The cost in large organisations becomes astronomical.

During the last few decades there has grown up a greater need for precise measurement, as costing systems have become more elaborate. This is an added reason for accurate time-recording, apart from checking on punctuality.

16. Staff Morale

Introduction

The word "morale" was originally used in a military sense to denote the moral condition of the troops, but it has now taken on a broader meaning, and it may be defined as *the collective attitude of workers towards one another, their employer, the management, and their work.* Whether a man is happy in his work will be a matter of individual temperament, but it can greatly influence others, and it can in turn be greatly influenced by the personnel policy of an organisation. Morale is a collective term, and is meant to include the sum or average of all the individual attitudes. To improve morale it is necessary to examine the position of the individual in the work organisation.

Good morale means that staff are happy in their work. It is an established fact that the productive efficiency of workers increases with a rise in their interest and morale; they do more and better work when they are enthusiastic and have confidence in the jobs they do. A low level of morale can lead to inadequate output, absenteeism, waste of materials, and unnecessary disputes over discipline. The effect of expensive welfare schemes can be completely vitiated if morale is upset by some act of injustice, or even of only apparent injustice.

It is essential for morale to be kept at a high level, particularly where poor working conditions are beyond the control of management. If workers are convinced this is so, and if their morale is high, they will contend with all manner of discomforts in working conditions.

Labour turnover

Labour turnover (L.T.O.) is most usually expressed as the number of staff who leave the organisation over a set period of six or twelve months as a percentage of the average number of full-time workers. If 50 staff out of a total of 200 leave the organisation the L.T.O. is 25 per cent. Some of the 50 staff may have left compulsorily, owing to retirement, marriage or death, for example. In these cases it is usual to deduct the compulsory leavings from the turnover figure. In the above example, if 10 staff came under the compulsory category, 40 as a percentage of 200 would give an L.T.O. of 20 per cent.

Labour turnover may be taken as an index of the stability of the working force. A high L.T.O may not be a result of dissatisfaction on the part of the employees; it may be caused by bad recruitment or bad management, or by a state of full employment in the country which makes it easy for staff to move from job to job.

The index figure itself may be of no significance whatever, as a 50 per cent figure might be quite normal and acceptable for one industry but really disastrous for another. A high rate of L.T.O does mean that a great deal of time and money is spent on recruiting and on training staff. On that account alone it should be reduced to the very minimum. On the other hand, if L.T.O. is low, it may be because of stagnation, and not necessarily because of a high rate of efficiency. Many workers in large organisations are dissatisfied, but owing to the good salaries, pension rights and other excellent conditions of service they are loth to leave.

The average age and sex of employees in an organisation may be a factor in the stability of the L.T.O., as may be the state of the trade of the business concerned. In fact the *movement* of the L.T.O. rate may be of more significance than the rate itself.

REASONS FOR HIGH LABOUR TURNOVER

Although high labour turnover may be related to factors outside the control of management, the reasons listed below are commonly quoted and nearly all induce or are the result of poor morale in staff.

(1) Not having enough to do.

(2) Lax discipline.

(3) Irritation at bad planning of work, e.g. if one is idle during most of the day, then has a rush of work at 4 p.m.

(4) Poor equipment, e.g. old typewriters, making it impossible to produce good work.

(5) Fear that increasing mechanisation (particularly computers) will lead to an increase of boring jobs.

(6) Not knowing how one stands in the boss's opinion.

(7) Lack of knowledge of promotion prospects.

(8) Better staff amenities in other kinds of work.

(9) Dislike of sedentary work.

(10) Old-fashioned furniture.

(11) Not enough shorthand given to secretarial staff.

(12) Uncongenial colleagues and/or superiors.

(13) Desire for a job nearer home, probably owing to travelling difficulties.

(14) Job glamourised at the interview and then found not to live up to expectations.

(15) Unnecessary noise.

(16) Opportunity for higher pay and shorter hours working for agencies.

(17) Open-plan offices.

Contrary to the expectations of some people the rate of pay is rarely considered to be the most important factor. Environment and job satisfaction are frequently the most important factors in building staff morale (see below).

ATTITUDE SURVEYS

What can be done about an excessive L.T.O.? Employees usually leave an organisation for some reason, real or fancied, and it is useful to management to discover these reasons. Some employers offer good salaries and conditions of work, yet their L.T.O. remains high. This indicates that there are grievances and troubles which need very close investigation, with the aim of eradicating them. Many staff troubles are a result of nothing more than a lack of understanding between manager and subordinate, frequently caused by lack of "communication". Enlightened managers are attempting to make a scientific study of the causes of dissatisfaction among the employees, and one of the principal tools is the "attitude survey". There are four basic ways of checking on the reasons why employees leave an organisation: talking to employees on the job, issuing questionnaires whereby the staff can state their opinions anonymously, interviewing all staff when they leave and having a grievance committee.

Interviewing on the job needs to be done by an impartial member of the personnel department, i.e. not by any officers in the line organisation.

The value of a questionnaire is doubtful because although frankness is asked for, a most elaborate format must be used if the questionnaire is not to be abused. The questions must be drafted very carefully and it is advisable to have some expert advice on compiling the questionnaire. It is usual for a number of alternative answers to be allowed for each question. Analysing the result is time-consuming and the information obtained is necessarily limited.

Interviewing all employees when they leave is perhaps the easiest method, but it can only be of value if free answers are received. The interviews should therefore be conducted by a tactful person, and preferably one who is outside the employees' own departments, otherwise it is doubtful whether they would ever give true reasons for leaving.

Grievance committees are not very popular with trade unions, and although it is against the principle of their formation, joint consultative committees often develop into grievance committees. It is better to institute joint consultation than to have a platform specifically for grievances. This topic is discussed later in the chapter.

Job satisfaction

Most employees attach greater importance to job satisfaction than to the level of their salary. The fears that mechanisation in the office would mean boring and uninteresting jobs for clerical staff have not been justified. If properly handled, mechanisation should eliminate most of the drudgery so making it possible to give people more interesting work to do. It is an axiom of good management that employees should find interest in doing their jobs, and if they can identify themselves with their work morale is more likely to be high. Staff are likely to achieve job satisfaction if management engages the right people for the jobs, if there are adequate education and training schemes, and if there is full and free communication between management and workers. The various aspects of job design, including job enlargement, job enrichment and job rotation, should be carefully examined and implemented where appropriate and practicable.

Job design

The concept of job design originated in America and its ultimate objective is increased productivity. The various techniques used aim to eliminate or improve unsatisfactory elements which cause low productivity, e.g. lack of motivation, poor morale and job dissatisfaction. It also has positive subsidiary objectives such as improving the quality of work (by eliminating unnecessary equipment, processes or jobs), reducing the labour turnover and training costs, and introducing staff to new technology, i.e. training them in new skills, etc.

Three of the most commonly used job-design techniques are outlined briefly below.

JOB ENLARGEMENT

When a job is enlarged it covers a greater number of activities or tasks so that the employee is less specialised. The wider scope of duties is intended to decrease boredom and frustration from repetitiveness and to increase interest. For example, a mail clerk might be given responsibility for incoming and outgoing mail, and perhaps for obtaining the relevant files instead of just one of those tasks. This is sometimes referred to as horizontal job-building.

JOB ENRICHMENT

Job enrichment is a technique for involving subordinates in the planning, organising and controlling of work, i.e. to give them greater responsibility. The scope of activities may not be increased but the staff have greater responsibility for their own performance of the job. This implies the setting of performance targets by each individual in consultation with the superior. This may be referred to as vertical job-loading.

JOB ROTATION

Job rotation has two aims: (i) to give variety in work activity, and (ii) to enable each employee to acquire a wider range of knowledge and skills which will help him to develop his potential. Apprenticeship programmes have been based on job rotation for very many years. School-leavers and postgraduate recruits are often "trained" by job rotation. For the purpose of increasing work interest, any employees can be rotated within a section, department or even branches of an organisation. Rotation may be on a weekly, fortnightly, monthly or quarterly basis.

There may be some employees who prefer the security of one job which they know and feel happy doing. Nevertheless it is important to have one or more additional people trained to take over those duties in case of sickness, for holiday periods and for other eventualities.

GENERAL COMMENTS

These job-design techniques should be considered individually and in association with each other. It is vitally important to consider the staff to whom they may be applied because the success of job design is strongly dependent on the calibre of staff—both workers and supervisors. The reasons for introducing, say , job enlargement must be explained, otherwise the staff will think that they are being given more to do without additional payment. It is also important to involve the unions—for the same reason. The intention is not to save jobs, but to stretch people a little, to give them greater interest and pride in their work, and to provide a basis for the future development of each individual.

Incentives

An incentive is a generally accepted means of achieving greater productivity by stimulating workers either actually to do more work or to work with greater accuracy, thus reducing wasted work.

"Incentives" may include education, training and a good promotion policy, but it is more usual to apply the term to schemes by which extra payment to ordinary payment is made. The payment may have some fixed relationship to output, as with merit rating (*see* Chapter 11), or it may be a general distribution of cash and/or shares, frequently in proportion to salary, service, seniority of position, or a combination of these three criteria.

Co-partnership has had a chequered career; in fact in the gas industry (where it was founded) nationalisation has seen its disappearance. Perhaps the most successful venture of this kind is the John Lewis Partnership where all the employees are partners in the organisation. Basically, co-partnership is joint ownership and administration of an enterprise, but it may also include a bonus to workers in the form of employee shareholdings. It is somewhat doubtful whether employee shareholdings make for any direct incentive for workers to redouble their efforts, but, like suggestion schemes (*see* below), the benefits are the more intangible ones of harmonising the interests of shareholders, management and workers.

Cash bonuses are more direct incentives (though shares can be sold, of course), and many large business concerns distribute an annual cash bonus to every employee, the amount being related to the profits made during the year. Such an incentive really does give the workers added stimulus, and the fact that they are given as an addition to wages makes them seem like "windfalls", and therefore are a good morale booster.

Suggestion schemes

Another way to gain workers' interest (although of direct benefit to the firm also) is the institution of suggestion schemes, by which the management asks for suggestions from the workers about their work, very often with monetary rewards for those adopted. It has been proved that suggestion schemes are just as effective for the office as for the factory.

From the management point of view, there are benefits to be gained from suggestions that emanate from work level, and which are eminently practical, while from the workers view point, it gives an opportunity to the "quiet" worker to put forward his ideas— usually to his financial advantage. The usual method is to have a box in a prominent place, in which suggestion forms can be placed in a slot. Normally the suggestions are dealt with by a committee who sit periodically to consider them. A suggestion scheme must be supported from time to time by a publicity campaign to create interest in it. Well-designed posters, small "encouragement" prizes for near misses, essay competitions, weekly discussion groups, periodic suggestion weeks (for example, ladies' weeks), and special awards (perhaps for the best suggestion of the year) are all means of stimulating staff to make their contributions.

For suggestion schemes to be effective, not only must they be publicised, they must also be dealt with fairly, and any action taken on the suggestions must be prompt, for this is the only way to convince staff that the management is sincere in its desire to receive suggestions.

Joint consultation

The setting up of a workers' committee may be included as part of the programme for increasing employees' interest in their work. Some firms have "office committees" which are more or less welfare committees for approaching the management on questions affecting the working conditions of the office workers. However, some staff committees are much more than this; for example, they might be involved in framing salary scales, and encourage management to institute staff appraisal and reporting.

Probably the most useful arrangement is the joint consultative committee. This is a committee composed jointly of representatives of the management and of the employees, and its function is to promote a two-way flow of ideas and consultation. Most large organisations have now established joint consultative committees as a step towards "participation" and "industrial democracy". It is unfortunate that sometimes joint consultation committees have developed into grievance committees, and although this does provide a platform where grievances can be aired (from both sides), that is *not* its prime function, nor its greatest value.

The principle behind joint consultation is that the management consults the workers at committee meetings, even about the highest policy matters, and the workers are free to express their opinions without let or hindrance. This is not to say that policy and management problems are made the joint responsibility of management and employees, but rather that there is a sharing in that responsibility. It takes real effort to get rid of the fence that inevitably stands between the two sides.

Ideally, the committee should be a strictly non-partisan affair, and all members should be seated at a round table with nobody acting as the acknowledged head—or better still with a non-manager acting as chairman. The mechanics of setting up such a committee are quite simple, but the problems involved are those of being able to explain to the staff the real purpose of the committee, of overcoming the scepticism of the workers, and then of encouraging them to make use of the machinery.

Joint consultative committees have the immense value of providing a forum for discussion of work problems and providing a place where joint solutions can be made to difficulties which would be insurmountable without such a committee. It is useless to institute joint consultation unless both sides are wholly in favour of it; it will quickly wilt without proper support. It must be handled properly to ensure that it does not become a mere grievance committee, and the meetings nothing more than an afternoon's chatter between the management and some "bosses' men".

Welfare

Facilities provided by the employer which are in addition to wages or salaries may be grouped under the heading of "welfare". Some large organisations appoint welfare officers, the duties of whom are different from those of a staff or personnel officer in that they are concerned solely with the welfare and well-being of the employees. A staff officer is usually the liaison officer between the managing body and the workers, and is responsible for managing all affairs relating to staff, such as establishments, rates of pay and related subjects.

Welfare usually includes such provisions as medical services, sports and recreational facilities, staff magazines, protective clothing, education and technical libraries. A common welfare facility is the provision of low-cost or free meals at a subsidised staff canteen or restaurant, or the issue of luncheon vouchers which may be exchanged at specified restaurants towards the cost of a meal. Vouchers up to a maximum of 45p per day are not taxed.

Welfare facilities are provided to an increasing extent in order to attract and keep staff. Because these facilities are often used only by a small number of employees it is sometimes suggested that the provision of a sports field, squash courts or a swimming pool is an unnecessary and unjustifiable expense. Nevertheless, amateur athletics would be a great deal poorer were it not for the provision of such facilities by employers. Successful annual outings and dances help to build morale, but it is better if such events are arranged at the request of, and in consultation with, the employees concerned.

Hopkins in *Industrial Welfare* has suggested that welfare might be divided into the following.

(1) Economic welfare: facilities which can be valued in terms of cash, such as pension schemes, profit-sharing, mortgage loans at low rates of interest, luncheon vouchers, etc.

(2) Statutory welfare: that which is required by Act of Parliament, such as environmental standards laid down by the Offices, Shops and Railway Premises Act 1963 and the Health and Safety at Work Act etc. 1974.

(3) Social welfare: all the usual facilities included in welfare, such as recreational facilities, canteens, debating societies, etc.

Team-work: participation

Nearly all the methods of boosting morale mentioned above rely on team-work, or the participation of the staff, to a greater or lesser degree. A feeling of being involved, not only in the execution of a job, but also in the preparatory processes of planning, etc., does more to engender interest and keenness to work than a dozen pep talks. If people's views are sought they feel they are regarded as intelligent human beings, not just numbers on a pay-roll.

It may at first sight seem difficult to involve junior staff or staff doing repetitive work in the discussion stages of the job. It may be that the system is established, procedures laid down and the routine just carries on. It is likely that some thought will indicate ways to involve the staff. For example, if a visitor is to be shown around the department or have a system explained, one of the staff could be briefed to do this after the manager has had an introductory discussion. When any minor changes have to be made the member or members of staff whose work will be affected could be asked to work out the details. There are invariably at least minor modifications needed from time to time to meet the needs of changes and crises in other departments.

The very best system and procedures will fail if the staff who operate them do not work as a team. It is essential that they are aware of the objectives of the system and their own objectives within that system. It is important that each individual should realise that if he or she falls down on the job, umpteen other peoples' work will be affected with the possibility of a complete failure of the department to meet its objectives. Assuming that objectives are set at the highest management level, the staff in a department or section can be involved in the discussions on how to meet those objectives. It is unrealistic to expect to explain the situation or problem and receive an immediate answer. The staff must be given time to think things over, consider the implications of various courses of action and get any information needed. If the problem is particularly difficult, or courses of action are limited for various reasons, the possible courses of action should be explained and the reasons why other courses of action are not possible should be discussed. The staff can be asked to consider the practical alternatives and come up with the best solution.

LEADERSHIP

Good team-work depends on the quality of leadership. "There is no such thing as a bad crew, only a bad captain." If the team does not deliver the goods only the captain is to blame. He cannot blame his staff because presumably he chose or was involved in choosing them. He must look to the ways in which he motivates them, trains them and helps them to develop.

We all know of the soldiers who will follow a popular officer through hell-fire if necessary. We rarely hear of the manager whose subordinates will move heaven and earth not to let him down. Yet it happens. What are the qualities such leaders possess? The following list is far from exhaustive but may provide some guide for the self-analysis which every manager should practise from time to time.

(1) A genuine interest in achieving success for the department rather than for yourself.

(2) The ability to plan and organise.

(3) The ability to communicate simply and clearly.

(4) The ability to recognise individual people's strengths and weaknesses, and to maximise the former while helping them to overcome the latter.

(5) Firm but fair judgment of people's work performance and conduct.

(6) The ability to assess people's capabilities and show confidence in them.

(7) Professional expertise which commands respect.

(8) Open-minded approach: ready to discuss and, if suitable, accept other people's ideas.

(9) The ability to admit a mistake and to apologise when in the wrong.

(10) An even temper, pleasant manner and a "let's sit down and talk about it" attitude when people get themselves into difficulties with their work or seek guidance.

(11) A sense of humour, a calm manner in a crisis, the ability to "take the steam out of" a situation.

(12) The ability to create warmth or a happy atmosphere in the office.

(13) A willingness to "dig in" and help subordinates when necessary, never asking anyone to undertake a task you would not do yourself.

(14) The ability to inspire people with your own enthusiasm.

17. Managing the Staff

The most significant aspect of management, of any type and at any level, is the management of staff. If the staff do not, cannot, or will not produce work of a high enough standard or in great enough quantity the manager is to blame. Although the human relations aspect is often of paramount importance, there are several specific "tools" which the office manager can use to smooth his path in getting the staff to "deliver the goods".

Manpower planning

Every organisation as a whole should plan its manpower strategy, in however rudimentary a way. Even a small organisation can suddenly find itself without a management team because several managers have reached retirement age within a year or two of each other.

Basically, manpower planning is intended to ensure that the right number of staff are available at any time with the required training and expertise to do the work involved in meeting corporate objectives. A prerequisite of manpower planning is therefore long-range planning. Staff may expect to stay with the organisation for many years. They will certainly want to progress but the direction of their progress must be determined to some extent by the direction in which the organisation develops. Depending on the estimated products/services, turnover, market demand, etc., an attempt must be made to determine for each year over a period of up to twenty years:

(1) how many staff will be needed;

(2) what categories of staff will be needed;

(3) what types and levels of skills will be required to meet the demands of new technology;

(4) how many people in each category and with the various skills will be retiring;

(5) how many staff will have to be recruited;

(6) bearing in mind the training and development of existing staff, what types and levels of staff will be recruited.

Manpower planning is at best partly a "guestimate". Its success depends to a very great extent upon the policy-makers knowing what route they intend to tread. Inevitably, long-range and even medium-term plans get upset, for example by national monetary and fiscal policies, and national economic stress, thus throwing the most meticulous manpower planning out of gear. Nevertheless, every office manager should practise the basic concepts within his own department if he is not to find himself without suitable staff capable of fulfilling the objectives he sets.

Reviewing personnel policy

In organisations which have an established personnel department there should be a continuous review of personnel policy to ensure that the various methods of recruitment, training, etc. are adequate for and in line with the staff requirements. The office manager should undertake the same exercise perhaps on a yearly basis. As long as the staff are working satisfactorily and everyone seems cheerful one tends to take it for granted that all is well. Many a manager has been caught on the wrong foot through complacency. A regular review of all the aspects of staff management that have been dealt with in this part of the book is necessary to ensure that problems are foreseen and prevented from developing and that minor faults are corrected before they become major problems. The various aspects of personnel policy that should come under scrutiny are given below.

(1) *Budget comparison*. This is perhaps the commonest check, and is usually necessary because of the excessive overheads represented by labour costs. The real cost can only be measured against the output from the workers. Output and staffing numbers in different departments or sections should be compared, with the objective of increasing over-all productive efficiency.

(2) *Selection of staff*. Are the best staff recruited? If not, are the methods faulty? Perhaps some vocational testing might be advisable. Is quality rating used? Are there any square pegs in round holes?

(3) *Job grading*. Has job grading been established? If not, would it improve the staffing position? If it has been established, has it been done properly and uniformly? Is it related to the scales of pay?

(4) *Salary scales*. Are proper scales of pay in force? If so, are they adequate to attract and retain staff? Are they simple and fully understood, and do the staff know about them? (Some firms believe in keeping their scales secret.)

(5) *Conditions of work*. The various physical conditions mentioned earlier in this book should be checked to ensure that they are adequate for the work being done. Do they create a pleasant environment in which to work?

(6) *Labour turnover*. Is there an unduly high labour turnover? If so, would an attitude survey be advisable, or are the causes fairly obvious? If the latter, what must be done to cure them?

(7) *Training*. Is there a training programme? If so, is it adequate and properly supervised? Does it achieve its objectives? Is it related to the capacity to absorb the trainees and to the trainees' potential abilities?

(8) *Incentives*. Are there any incentives for workers to give of their best? If not, would it be better to have fewer staff with monetary incentives, perhaps coupled with a merit-rating scheme? Or could conditions, systems and staff structure be improved?

(9) *Promotion policy*. Is there a definite programme for promotion or is it haphazard? Is it linked with a clearly defined and executed system of staff appraisal and reporting so as to get the best from existing staff? Is it based on merit as well as other factors such as length of service? Are job descriptions updated regularly to ensure that each person is being paid for the work he does?

(10) *Discipline*. Are there any office rules and, if so, are they maintained? Is time-keeping good; smoking allowed; overtime and time-off administered fairly? What disciplinary and grievance procedures are there? Are the staff fully aware of them?

(11) *Morale*. Is morale high? If not, are salary scales and conditions of work the reasons—or are there other factors? If so, what are they and how can they be improved?

(12) *Welfare*. Are the rates of pay made more attractive by adequate facilities for staff? Are such facilities used? Women are particularly affected by welfare provisions, but it is wise to check any vast expenditure in this direction, and to ensure that money so spent meets a need.

(13) *Organisation*. Faulty organisation can give rise to internal strife, and an organisation chart should be drawn up and *kept up to date*. The possibility of improvement should not be overlooked. Is there a direct flow of authority and responsibilities, or is there a frustrating tussle between line and staff officers?

(14) *Unity of policy*. Is there a unity of policy on all these matters? For instance, the training scheme should be dovetailed with the

promotion policy, recruitment should be allied to training, salary schemes should be related to job grading, and so on.

(15) *Management policy.* Is the personnel policy being administered in accordance with the wishes of the management? A managing body usually makes personnel policy decisions from time to time which, if not checked, can lead to a piecemeal policy without cohesion rather than a comprehensive code. The same can happen at departmental level, and it is useful to summarise and assess the various factors from time to time.

Because every organisation is to some extent in competition with other organisations for good staff, it is useful to be aware of the salaries, conditions, morale, etc. outside one's own section or department. The office manager reviewing his own department may feel more confident if he discusses the various questions with the personnel manager and asks for an independent assessment by a member of the personnel staff. Such a person should be in a position to compare the various factors with those in other departments and in other organisations.

Causes of weakness in staff management

There is an almost unlimited number of causes of weakness in the management of staff from favouritism to rigid discipline, from lack of understanding of people and human relations to undue tolerance of the whims and idiosyncrasies of the individual. Most causes of weakness revolve around the personality, competence and leadership qualities of the manager. Some of the problems which the manager may have to rectify or alleviate in order to get the best out of his staff are listed below.

(1) A fear of infringing the statutory rights of workers.

(2) A fear of being unpopular.

(3) Lack of clearly defined objectives and of a clearly defined policy to meet those objectives, resulting in muddled thinking and lack of specific direction.

(4) Lack of adequate planning.

(5) Lack of involvement of staff in matters which affect them personally.

(6) Lack of interest in people as individuals, in their careers, work problems and achievements.

(7) Inability to communicate effectively.

(8) A feeling of insecurity resulting in an aggressive attitude.

(9) Failure to liaise with other managers.

(10) Lack of co-ordination between departments.

(11) Lack of direction from superiors.

(12) Lack of support from personnel staff.

(13) Inadequate resources—finance, space, equipment, supplies, etc.

(14) Consciousness of status.

(15) Inflexibility of ideas: unwillingness to exchange ideas, to consider and accept other people's ideas.

(16) Shirking of responsibility in solving problems that arise.

(17) Inadequate and/or unsatisfactory delegation.

(18) Inadequate and/or unsatisfactory guidance and supervision.

(19) Lack of confidence in other people to carry out tasks.

(20) Lack of adequate and suitable training.

(21) Inflexible rules and regulations.

(22) Lack of attention to safety.

(23) Lack of control of individual work-loads.

(24) Failure to train a subordinate as a deputy who will subsequently be able to take over when the manager moves on.

(25) Failure to cover for absence of staff so that certain tasks are not completed on time.

Each manager must assess his own performance against these criteria and decide which faults, if any, apply in his case. He must then determine which faults are within his power to rectify and which are outside his control. By eliminating those faults which are his concern he may well find that other faults outside his control are somewhat mitigated.

Handling people

The secret of handling people, i.e. getting the best out of them, is understanding them as individuals. It is time-consuming, exhausting, can be frustrating and irritating, but is eminently worth while for both personal and organisational satisfaction. How does one "handle people"?

First, one must examine oneself, one's own personal qualities, attitudes, strengths, weaknesses, methods of approach and achievements. The person who "believes in calling a spade a spade" may get results because he has other attributes which mitigate the effects of this blunt approach. On the other hand, it may cause resentment which will quickly become apparent in the deteriorating efficiency of the department if not in the hostile attitudes of individual staff. A few basic rules for getting the best out of people generally—not only staff—may be useful to the young manager who intends to "get along with people".

(1) Think of and talk to each person as an individual.

(2) Look for each person's strengths and weaknesses and make the best use of the strengths.

(3) Consider each individual's reaction to your approach and try to adapt your approach to get the best reaction.

(4) Discuss topics in such a way that ideas are produced or appear to be produced by the other person. They will take a far greater interest in making ideas work if they think they have produced them.

(5) Set out to create a happy atmosphere in the office, section or department. A stranger coming in should be able to feel it immediately.

(6) Encourage people to "stand on their own feet", i.e. to have confidence in their own abilities, but at the same time let them know that you are willing to discuss their problems.

(7) Guide people in overcoming their difficulties—do not solve their problems for them.

(8) Ensure that communications are complete, accurate, timed correctly, given in the right form and clearly understood.

(9) Ensure that each member of staff has a development programme, however simple.

(10) Show appreciation.

(11) Treat unsatisfactory work as a mutual problem to be solved together, i.e. by you and your subordinate.

(12) Never criticise anyone in front of other people.

(13) Give instructions in the form of a request, not an order.

(14) Always give deadlines for the completion of a task or part of a task, or the fulfilment of an instruction.

(15) Insist on deadlines being met or an explanation being given in good time if they cannot be met.

(16) "Stretch" people a little but do not thrust them "out of their depth".

(17) Fulfil *all* promises.

(18). Set standards and never criticise anyone for doing something you do yourself, e.g. arriving late at the office.

(19) Never ask anyone to do anything you have not done yourself or would not be prepared to do yourself.

(20) In times of stress be prepared to help with menial tasks if—and only if—this will help to achieve a desired result.

(21) When delegating duties delegate adequate authority to fulfil them and ensure that appropriate people know.

(22) Do not handle queries relating to duties that have been

delegated to other people; show your confidence in them by referring the queries to the subordinate concerned.

(23) Ensure that your own knowledge and skills are as good as you can make them, but do not be afraid to make the best possible use of other people's abilities to achieve your objectives—and to give credit to the people concerned.

(24) Encourage liaison with other departments.

(25) Insist on adequate induction training (including safety regulations and procedures) for all new staff and updating training for existing staff.

The value, or otherwise, of holding staff meetings has to be considered carefully. When a large number of people meet together for discussion little is achieved as a rule. On the other hand, such a meeting does give each member of the staff an opportunity to identify with the department. On the whole, smaller meetings of section staff, with section heads attending meetings with the office manager, are both more practicable and more worth while, provided there is a real reason for the meeting and it is not treated as an opportunity to air grievances. It might also be valuable for the office manager to attend the section meetings in rotation so that he gets to know staff with whom he is not normally in contact—and they get to know him. This also gives the manager an opportunity to assess individuals, knowledge which might be useful later in discussion with immediate subordinates.

Delegation

A good basic rule for delegation is "anything that can be done by anyone else should not be done by me". Far too many managers spend time doing things which their subordinates are paid to do. The ultimate result of this can only be that the manager has insufficient time to do what he is paid to do, viz. to think, make decisions, and foresee, prevent and solve problems.

A clear organisation structure, job descriptions for all staff, a cohesive policy for meeting objectives all make delegation easier. It must be made clear that responsibility can never be delegated. The top man is always responsible for the success—or otherwise—of his department. He can, and must, delegate authority. The root of successful delegation is, of course, a happy, well-trained, adequately skilled, interested and involved staff.

The process of delegation really starts at the stage of function analysis, and involves the following steps.

(1) Determine what activities are involved in fulfilling each of your responsibilities.

(2) Assess the approximate amount of time spent on each type of activity.

(3) Decide which activities only you have the knowledge and expertise to carry out.

(4) Decide which of the remaining activities subordinate staff are qualified to carry out and allocate them as duties to the appropriate people, depending on the volume and level.

(5) Decide who is best qualified to carry out remaining duties given appropriate training, and make arrangements. This can be approached either on the basis of those activities for which training can most easily be given or on the basis of the most time-consuming activities which will mean greater relief for you. It is important to set target dates for complete handover of activities and to review progress regularly.

The steps listed above may be regarded as the general principles of delegation. The day-to-day procedures are as follows.

(1) Decide who is the right person to carry out the task.

(2) Decide what preliminary investigation/organisation is necessary, if any.

(3) Decide what authority is needed by the person who is to carry out the task.

(4) Decide what controls for monitoring progress are needed.

(5) Decide what possible problems might be involved.

(6) Set a deadline for completion.

(7) Decide what explanation/instruction is necessary.

(8) Decide whether the instruction should be given face-to-face, on the telephone, or in written form.

(9) Allocate time for explanation and arrange with the subordinate.

(10) Give the necessary explanation/instruction clearly and concisely. Make sure all information is given. Ensure the person concerned knows exactly what is expected of him.

(11) Thereafter forget the task except to check the monitoring system.

(12) Keep the person informed of any changes which may affect the work in progress.

"A good department runs itself." This statement is not really true because situations are never static and crises occur which only the manager can handle. Nevertheless, one of the basic criteria for judging the efficiency of a department is whether the level of the department's competence is the same when the manager is away as when he is there. Properly conducted delegation at all times is the secret.

Safety

The welfare of staff must include consideration for their safety. This is legally enforced in the U.K. under the Health and Safety at Work etc. Act 1974 which provides for the establishment of safety committees when a request is made in writing by two safety representatives appointed under the Safety Representatives Regulations. The safety committees may be composed of safety representatives, union representatives or anyone else elected or appointed. Employers can, and do, establish safety committees without a request being made by the representatives.

Apart from complying with legal requirements, every office manager should ensure that staff work and behave in a manner which precludes accidents as far as is humanly possible. Laxity in removing hazards is unforgivable.

If the office manager has a safety representative in his department it would be worthwhile discussing with that person any possible ways of improving safety. The representative should be encouraged to seek the views of colleagues, apart from noting complaints. He or she should also be encouraged to report actions which might result in an accident, however slight, so that the careless employee can be given appropriate training.

The departmental "image"

As mentioned earlier, strangers get an impression of an office as soon as they walk into it. It is interesting to ask a visitor what his impression of the department is. An outsider can often unwittingly pinpoint faults which are overlooked because of familiarity on the part of the people involved. The atmosphere should be cheerful and people should get the impression that everyone works together as a team, willing to help anyone and everyone, interested in each individual as a person and keen to help satisfy his needs. This has to be supported by efficient action, of course. No one is taken in by smiles. Promises kept, messages delivered promptly, letters answered by return, pleasant telephone techniques, quiet dignified behaviour, someone always available during office hours to answer queries—all these go to make up the image of the department, and of the manager of that department.

It is principally a question of attitude, and although occasionally the right attitude may need the expenditure of a little more time it is time well spent if a customer or a colleague is satisfied and happy.

Industrial relations

"Industrial relations" is fundamentally the ability of the work-force and managers to co-operate to their mutual satisfaction for the good of the company and, ultimately, of themselves. Perhaps the first thing to be remembered is that employees are human and this applies equally to their representatives whether they are union officials or not.

Nowadays every manager must expect to spend quite a lot of his time in discussions with staff on matters of policy as well as day-to-day affairs. Indeed, involvement of employees in the decision-making process is simply a manifestation of the more "open" or participative style of management which is now becoming more generally accepted.

Most organisations have specific procedures for formal negotiation with union representatives about pay and major policy matters. The personnel manager or industrial relations manager is always involved in these negotiations. Line managers take a fairly active role in negotiating in some organisations while in others formal negotiations are largely out of the hands of line managers.

There are three main kinds of discussion between a manager and his subordinates.

(1) Discussions about matters which will be decided by agreement between the manager and subordinate.

(2) Discussions to obtain the views of subordinates before decisions are made by the manager which will take into account the views expressed.

(3) Discussions based on predetermined facts, or on opinions and views given by management for any purpose, and which cannot be altered, e.g. a board policy decision.

These may be regarded as the formal approaches to discussion, however informal the actual procedures. The legal obligations of the employer to the government, to the shareholders of the company, to the public and to the employees must always be borne in mind in the course of discussion.

Time and effort spent in developing good industrial relations are well repaid. Regard the staff, including their representatives, as team-mates wanting to do a good job—which they are in the vast majority of cases. Respect the views expressed by the staff, show them the courtesy of an explanation when their ideas cannot be accepted. If their views differ from yours, persuasion to your point of view is better than "steam-rollering". It comes back to the art of handling people.

Troublemakers should be spotted and dealt with firmly before they gain a hold over their colleagues. All too often, difficulties with the staff arise because situations have been allowed to develop instead of being "nipped in the bud". The manager who captains his ship with his hands firmly on the wheel can only gain respect. He is entitled to make it clear that he has no room for passengers and that co-operation all round is the order of the day.

PART FOUR
COMMUNICATIONS

18. Communication Systems

Establishing good communications

It is not an exaggeration to say that the standard of an organisation's corporate image and efficiency is directly related to the standard of its communication systems and their operation. Loss of business to the tune of millions of pounds, loss of customers and loss of prestige in the market can, and all too often do, result from poor communications.

All communications have to be originated, produced, transmitted, received and understood. Each communication is intended to provide information or evoke action. The main aspects of communications which need to be considered are therefore:

(1) the source of the communication, i.e. the sender;
(2) the content of the communication;
(3) the processes by which the communication is produced, e.g. dictation and typing;
(4) the method by which the communication is transmitted, e.g. letter, telephone, telex;
(5) procedures involved in receiving a communication, e.g. mail handling, distribution;
(6) the destination of the communication, i.e. the recipient;
(7) the understanding of the communication by the recipient.

Communications may be written, oral or visual, and systems must be designed to cater for a variety of each kind. Although communications is now a highly specialised field, involving a vast range of equipment and technology from the simple portable typewriter to computer terminals linked by satellite to computers thousands of miles away, the keynote of any system should be

187

simplicity in operation. The systems installed in any organisation should meet the specific needs of that organisation so as to give maximum effectiveness at minimum cost.

LINES OF COMMUNICATION

Communications can be grouped into two main types, viz. *internal,* i.e. within the organisation, even though it may be widely scattered all over the world, and *external,* i.e. with any person or organisation not employed by the organisation itself. Internal communications may be between employees, offices, departments, branches in different places including overseas, and companies within a group. External communications may be with customers/clients (including wholesalers, agents and distributors), suppliers, government departments and other official organisations, representative bodies such as trade unions and employers associations, professional institutions of all kinds, and consultants, to mention only a few. The success of a particular communication, i.e. the achievement of its objective, depends to a large extent on its being sent to the right person, at the right time, by the right method.

It is vitally important to ensure that a communication reaches the right person. This means deciding first of all who can best handle the query and give the information required, or who will react most favourably to the suggestion, understand new ideas and so on. There are times when it is best to communicate with the person "at the top" first; at other times it is advisable to gain the confidence of the person or people lower down the scale.

Another important consideration is who else needs to be informed or involved. How often does one hear the complaint "Nobody ever tells me anything!" This is especially true in a functional organisation (*see* page 23). In a line organisation (*see* page 22) it is most important that communications follow the correct "route". Each person should communicate directly with his superior and his subordinate. He should not "go over the head" of his superior or "by-pass" a subordinate to make a complaint or give instructions. Enormous trouble can be caused by carelessness in not communicating with people who should be involved in a particular matter. It causes resentment, inefficiency and frustration, and can lead to the breakdown of a department. Figure 32 shows a specimen communication chart which details the people who should be involved when a member of staff decides to leave the organisation.

IMPORTANCE OF FAST, ACCURATE COMMUNICATIONS

The criteria of a good communication system are that it should be

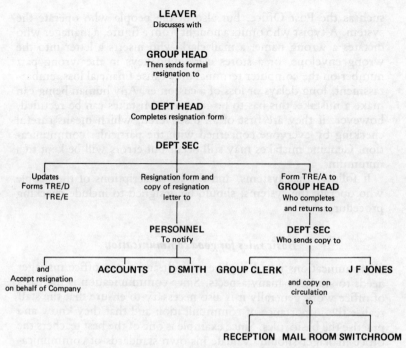

Fig. 32 *A specimen communication line chart* showing who should be informed at various stages in the administrative process for resignations.

fast (within its limitations and insofar as its speed can be controlled by the originator) and *accurate*. Very often the clinching of a contract, the acquisition of information to enable a tender date to be met or for a financial deal, or the replacement part for an aircraft grounded in the middle of Latin America depends on a communication being originated, produced, transmitted, received, **un**derstood and acted upon with minimum delay. Equally, the communication must be one hundred per cent accurate when it is received, understood and acted upon. It is of little use spending weeks preparing a tender if it arrives at its destination a day too late to be considered, or on the other hand, sending a request for a spare part so that it is received within an hour if the part number is incorrect resulting in the wrong part being sent for the grounded aircraft.

Communication systems must be designed to ensure maximum speed when required and complete accuracy at all times. Thus account must be taken not only of the machines, methods and various facilities available including those from outside sources such as the Post Office, but also of the people who operate the system. A typist who omits a nought from a figure, a manager who dictates a wrong name, a mail clerk who inserts a letter into the wrong envelope, or a stores clerk who keys in the wrong part number on the computer terminal may cause financial loss, embarrassment, long delays or loss of a customer. Any human being can make a mistake: this has to be accepted. Mistakes can be rectified, however, if they are first of all discovered, which means careful checking by everyone concerned with the particular communication. Genuine mistakes may still occur but errors will be kept to a minimum.

It follows that systems, and the job descriptions of the people who operate the systems, should be designed to include checking procedures.

Basic rules for good communication

Communications is a discipline in itself and every office manager needs to study its many aspects. Since communication is the basis of office work generally it is also necessary to ensure that the staff realise the importance of communication and that they know and practise the basic rules. Since example is one of the best teachers the office manager should evaluate his own standards of communication from time to time. The starting-point is never to blame anyone else if there has been a misunderstanding. Rather say, "It is my fault. I did not communicate adequately/clearly/effectively." In this way one gradually becomes self-critical and develops better communication habits.

The following basic rules, if followed carefully by everyone, should ensure fast, accurate communication in the office and with people outside the organisation.

(1) *Think* before communicating, i.e. prepare the communication. What is the objective of the communication? How can the objective best be achieved?

(2) *Consider the implications* of the communication, i.e. what result will it achieve?

(3) *Review* the proposed communication to ensure that it contains all the information required for the recipient to make a decision or take action, e.g. carry out an instruction, provide information.

(4) *Consider the reactions* of the person/people who will receive the communication—as regards both contents and tone.

(5) *Ensure* that the communication is *concise and clear*.

(6) *Consider the timing* of the communication. A few minutes

before staff leave to go home is not the best time to give an instruction for the next day.

(7) *Consider the place.* The middle of a busy office is not the place for a reprimand; nor is the corridor the place for a discussion leading to a policy decision.

(8) *Obtain feedback* to ensure that the recipient of the communication has heard and comprehended correctly.

(9) *Make a note of facts* which you may need for further action or information and insist that other people do the same—or give them a note.

If more thought were given to communications before the talking or writing started a lot of time would be saved. It is essential to "think through the content". How often does one hear: "If you had told me *that*, I would have known what you wanted."

Causes of poor communications

There are many reasons why communications fail to achieve their objectives. One main reason is probably sheer volume. There is far too much communication, but not nearly enough *effective* communication. If more time were spent on producing effective communications the results would be (i) that a lot of current communication would be unnecessary because much of it is caused by the fault of previous communications; and (ii) more time would be available to ensure the communications are effective and to act upon them. "Being too busy" to spend time on communicating properly is self-defeating. Poor communications create more and more poor communications.

A list of causes of poor communications is set out below. It contains but a few splashes of mud in the morass of causes, but it does indicate the necessity for care at every stage in the communication process.

FAULTS ON THE PART OF THE SPEAKER/WRITER
Content. Failure to:

(1) prepare adequately before starting to communicate;
(2) think clearly and logically;
(3) give adequate information;
(4) discern relevant and important information so as not to cloud the issue with too much information;
(5) discard irrelevant detail;
(6) include all critical/important details;
(7) realise that information is too technical for the person receiving it;

(8) update information/details given;

(9) check details, e.g. names, addresses, amounts;

(10) proof-read.

Delivery/presentation. Failure to:

(11) identify the right person/people to communicate with;

(12) explain facts clearly;

(13) present details in logical sequence;

(14) "come to the point";

(15) choose the most suitable time;

(16) take into account the age, education and cultural background of the person/people receiving the information;

(17) take sufficient time to explain;

(18) check what details are already known by the person/people receiving the information;

(19) avoid verbosity;

(20) avoid ambiguity;

(21) choose the most suitable words to express oneself to the particular person;

(22) use short simple sentences/phrases/words;

(23) speak clearly (enunciation);

(24) pronounce words correctly;

(25) write clearly;

(26) control a ponderous/pendantic/pompous/affected way of speaking/writing (which causes irritation);

(27) control distracting gestures/mannerisms;

(28) eradicate an aggressive/arrogant/supercilious manner;

(29) display written material for easy reading and comprehension;

(30) type/print name after signature;

(31) indicate telephone extension number on letters.

Management. Failure to:

(32) set deadlines;

(33) obtain feedback to check comprehension by the person receiving the information;

(34) follow up;

(35) delegate adequately;

(36) delegate in the proper manner;

(37) state clearly where information can be found;

(38) give adequate guidance/supervision;

(39) have confidence in other people's ability to carry out tasks;

(40) allow adequate time for the person receiving information to act on it;

(41) plan so as to avoid "panic" situations;

(42) exchange ideas;

(43) have confidence to prepare and transmit communications;

(44) recognise own and subordinates' weaknesses in communication and undergo suitable training;

(45) discuss communication problems with subordinate(s).

Use of media. Failure to:

(46) select/use the most suitable medium for the information being transmitted and the person receiving it;

(47) identify the person/department when answering the telephone;

(48) use correct telephone techniques;

(49) know/understand the requirements of the medium chosen, e.g. instructions needed for a telex message;

(50) dictate fluently;

(51) use accepted audio-dictation conventions;

(52) select/use appropriate machine/facilities to give suitable presentations, e.g. type-face and/or pitch.

FAULTS ON THE PART OF THE LISTENER/READER

Content. Failure to:

(53) take an interest in the communication;

(54) comprehend—as distinct from just listening;

(55) be aware of the importance of the communication;

(56) pass on messages exactly as given, i.e. without embellishment, omissions, or change of emphasis;

(57) ask when information not understood;

(58) check details when there is some doubt.

Reception. Failure to:

(59) concentrate (listen/read carefully);

(60) interpret correctly;

(61) hear correctly;

(62) take notes;

(63) use proper notepad (scraps of paper get lost);

(64) divert attention fully from other distractions to the communication;

(65) discount antipathy to the person giving information;

(66) correct poor hearing/eyesight.

Management. Failure to:

(67) determine the urgency/priority of each individual communication;

(68) plan so that pressure of work does not cause carelessness;

(69) have confidence in own ability to receive, understand and act on communications;

(70) recognise weakness in communication and undergo suitable training;

(71) discuss communication problems with superior.

FAULTS ON THE PART OF MEDIUM/MACHINE

(72) Breakdown of equipment before and/or during processing of communication.

(73) Faulty equipment—intermittent.

(74) Inadequate/unsatisfactory maintenance of equipment.

(75) Inadequate/unsuitable machinery to handle work-load, e.g. too small or wrong type of telephone switchboard for volume of traffic.

(76) Inadequate facilities for type of work, e.g. lack of appropriate symbols on typewriter for technical work.

DIFFICULTIES CAUSED BY CIRCUMSTANCES

(77) Clash of personalities.

(78) Lack of liaison between various levels of staff/departments.

(79) Insufficient knowledge of company/departments/duties of other staff/procedures.

(80) Lack of co-operation among staff.

(81) Inadequate staff to cope with work-load.

(82) Failure of individuals to notify movements, both temporary and permanent.

(83) Failure to maintain a daily/weekly staff movements list.

(84) Failure to prepare/update/ensure use of appropriate procedure manuals/reference lists, e.g. internal telephone directory.

(85) Failure to establish/use procedures for taking messages and delivering to appropriate staff for quick action.

(86) Inaccurate processing, e.g. wrong distribution of letters, telexes, etc., mail going astray.

(87) Loss of documents/files.

(88) Strikes by workers concerned with communications, both internally and externally.

Integrated systems

It is important to stress that communication systems comprise the people involved at the various stages through which communications have to pass, the machines used in their production and the methods used for their transmission. In addition to the integration of these three aspects of communications it is also necessary to integrate the individual systems into a total communication system within the organisation. This over-all system must include all the factors which are both directly and indirectly related to the efficiency with which communication is carried on. Some of these factors are listed below.

(1) Accommodation for interviews, meetings and conferences.

(2) Facilities for research, e.g. library, individual office (if most of the accommodation is open-plan).

(3) House styles for the production of correspondence, etc.

(4) Adequate and appropriate production facilities, e.g. typewriters, word-processing machines, computer terminals, telephone lines.

(5) The corporate image of the organisation.

(6) Training of operators, e.g. typists, telex and telephone operators, receptionists.

(7) Training of all staff in the various aspects of communications which their particular duties demand.

(8) Correct size and siting of direction and information notices for easy reading and comprehension.

(9) Guide-lines for use of facilities, i.e. criteria for choosing the method of transmission including cost, speed, suitability for the content, etc.

The efficiency of the components of an integrated system must be assessed both in relation to their individual aspects and in relation to the communication system as a whole. For example, a telex machine may be operating very satisfactorily, speeding up the processing of all orders or the acquisition of information, or achieving whatever other purpose it was installed to meet. Yet it may not have achieved a complementary objective of reducing telephone traffic and telephone costs. The reason for this could be quite simply that telex is being used in place of letters (with the results mentioned above), but not in place of telephone calls. The question then is whether the reduction in over-all correspondence costs provide the necessary cost-effectiveness. In any case, if the telex machine has spare capacity there is no reason why telephone costs should not be reduced by sending telex as often as possible if this is practicable. The volume of telephone traffic may also be a significant factor if the switchboard is overloaded. In this case the achievement of this particular objective, i.e. reduction of telephone traffic, is crucial.

Bearing in mind that the office manager's main responsibilities are the provision of information to top management and the maintenance of communications, it is his job to install, maintain, control and review a network of complementary systems which will meet the demands of the departments within the organisation and the demands of people outside including customers. In the smallest office the communications network will certainly include oral communication, correspondence, mail-handling, telephone switchboard and extension systems, typewriting and stationery. Additional components of the network may well be a teleprinter, telex, word processing, minute and report writing and visual presentations of various kinds.

The office manager must develop the ability to see the communications network as the arterial system of the organisation, and as a fundamental factor in the fulfilment of the office function and in the achievement of corporate objectives. He must be able to detect inadequacies and faults in any of its component parts. He must keep the integrated system constantly under review so as to ensure that it is capable of meeting increased and/or new demands made upon it. Any additions must be dovetailed into the whole system, not added on as an appendage. If changes are to be made the implications for every other aspect of the network and system must be carefully considered. Unless the communication system is "managed" in the fullest sense of the word, problems will inevitably arise and the efficiency of the organisation as a whole will suffer.

Choice of system

There are as many communication systems as there are organisations. Each system must be exclusive because it has to meet the particular and special demands made upon it by the people and circumstances of the organisation it serves. Choice of component systems and of the entire communication system will nevertheless be based on certain fundamental requirements and situations. These include:

(1) current volume of traffic/work-load;
(2) likely increase in volume of traffic/work-load;
(3) speed of transmission required;
(4) calibre of staff and cost of training;
(5) capital available for installation costs;
(6) maintenance and running costs;
(7) cost-effectiveness;
(8) area/distance to be covered;
(9) accommodation available;
(10) servicing facilities.

These factors will be discussed in relation to the component systems which are covered in the following chapters.

19. Face-to-face Communication

In an office a great deal of time is spent in communicating orally, both face-to-face and on the telephone. It is the office manager's responsibility to see (i) that the right facilities and environment needed for effective communication are provided, and (ii) that the staff are given encouragement and appropriate training to reduce the vast amount of time that is wasted by ineffective communication. This chapter looks at some of the important aspects of face-to-face communication, while telephone technique is examined in Chapter 21.

Facilities

The privacy and security aspects of face-to-face communication need consideration where offices are open-plan. This is particularly important in the case of interviews (*see* overleaf). In addition, accommodation for group discussions is needed by managers who have frequent meetings either with their staff or with visitors.

For larger groups one or more conference rooms should be provided. Depending on the type of meetings likely to be held, facilities for visual aids such as films and film slides may be needed. For meetings of not more than three or four people, meeting rooms provided with a writing table and chairs are adequate. It is desirable to have some means of indicating when the room is occupied, e.g. a sliding panel on the door, (*see* Fig. 33) or a light signal.

Fig. 33 *Sliding panel on the door can be moved to indicate when the room is occupied.*

Informal interviews

Consultations between two or more people and informal interviews for the giving and receiving of instructions are going on all the time. It is perhaps in these informal discussions that the faults in communication cause the greatest frustration. If the basic rules listed on page 190 are followed a lot less communication would be necessary and everyone would be happier.

CONSULTATION

All communication is a two-way exercise, but consultation involves the interaction of discussion, the exchange of ideas, the germination of new ideas from the seed planted by thoughts spoken aloud, etc. There should be an objective to the discussion and the people taking part should be aware of it. Consultation may be to obtain facts on which to base a decision—by one person or as a group; it may be to discuss progress made and future action; or it may be to produce ideas (brainstorming) which will eventually provide a basis for further discussion.

Consultation is a means of "getting people involved". If certain decisions are required from the discussion, very careful preparation is needed to ensure that those decisions are reached. Persuasion may be necessary. Clear thinking will be essential both before and during the discussions. Attempts at side-tracking must be (tactfully) frustrated. Above all, the discussion should not be a pretence. If the people participating feel that the decision has already been made and that their views, ideas, etc. will not be considered, not only is everyone's time wasted but co-operation is unlikely to be forthcoming later when it is needed to implement the decision.

INSTRUCTIONS

An instruction can have far-reaching effects. An incorrect or inadequate instruction can create chaos, lose an order, or cause resentment among staff, to mention but a few consequences. If the rules listed below are followed by everyone there should be fewer problems.

(1) Never "give an order". An instruction should be given in the form of a request.

(2) Give the essential background information which is needed to carry out an instruction intelligently. Background information includes such details as the reason for the instruction, what has been done so far, what is being done by other people, what the results of carrying out the instruction are likely to be, and what future action will be taken.

(3) Before giving an instruction consider whether the person knows how to carry it out. If not, additional explanation, demonstration and training will be necessary. It may be necessary to find out from the person concerned the extent of his knowledge. If he does know what to do, do not insult his intelligence by going into unnecessary detail.

(4) Ensure that all necessary documents, etc. are handed over when the instruction is given—or information is given as to where they can be obtained if required.

(5) Insist that all staff write down the action points of the instructions, e.g. dates, names, figures, etc.

(6) Obtain feedback which will indicate that the instruction has been correctly heard and understood.

(7) Set a deadline for completion of the work. This may be a matter for consultation.

(8) Indicate to the person concerned that you have full confidence in his ability to do the job but are around to be consulted if any problem arises which cannot be solved without consultation.

(9) Make a note of the deadline and then forget the task.

Formal interviews

There are many different types of formal interview, including interviews for:

(1) recruitment (*see* Chapter 10);
(2) disciplinary action;
(3) consultation/discussion;
(4) briefing;
(5) debriefing;
(6) research.

The keynote of a successful interview is preparation. This includes considering the objective or objectives of the interview; reserving/preparing proper accommodation; arranging for refreshments if appropriate; arranging for the reception of the person/ people to be interviewed; and being in attendance punctually. Many people can testify to the unprepared recruitment interview in which the person interviewed was given very little information of importance, was not given an opportunity to ask questions and felt the interviewer did not really know much about the vacant post anyway. In addition to the basic rules of communication (*see* page 190) which apply to all types of formal interview, there are certain special features applicable to each type.

DISCIPLINARY INTERVIEW

This may be for investigation into a fault that has been committed to establish where and/or with whom the fault lies, or it may be to reprimand and warn a person who has committed some breach of discipline, or whose work is inadequate, etc.

Be absolutely sure of the facts. This means thorough research beforehand. Consult with the personnel department and/or the office staff union representative if necessary before the interview. Arrange for a shorthand writer to be present if it is considered necessary to have a written record of the interview. Hold the interview as soon as possible after the fault has occurred, ensure absolute privacy, and stress the confidentiality of the interview to the shorthand writer.

At the beginning of the interview state the situation, or the case against the person, clearly and precisely. Give the person an opportunity to answer the case. State the action to be taken and confirm in writing if necessary.

CONSULTATION/DISCUSSION INTERVIEW

Consider carefully who should be consulted, and in what order. Consultation may be with more than one person, either in individual interviews or as a group. Consider the best way to achieve the objective of the consultation. During the interview note the main points raised. Ensure that all are considered and taken into account when a decision is made, whether at the interview or later. It is often useful to prepare an outline of the matter(s) to be discussed before the interview and send it to the person/people concerned so that they can be properly prepared. The interview is likely to be shorter and more constructive if this is done.

BRIEFING INTERVIEW

Decide precisely what the person/people being briefed will need to know. Obtain as much useful documentation as possible including background material. If possible send material for preparatory reading beforehand so that the interview time can be spent on discussing specific facts. Obtain or prepare supporting documents whenever possible, both because the person being briefed may find it difficult to take everything in at the interview, and because it avoids the necessity for note-taking. At the interview state the purpose of the briefing; give the information clearly and crisply, in logical sequence. Stop at pre-arranged points to give an opportunity for questions.

DEBRIEFING INTERVIEW

Decide what information you want or expect. It may be useful to draft some specific questions. If there is sufficient time the person to be debriefed should send background/basic information in writing beforehand so that the specially important areas for discussion, or points which need clarification, can be isolated.

RESEARCH INTERVIEW

A research interview may be a stage in a formal survey or research project or may be to obtain information for general purposes. In either case it is good practice to follow the basic principles—the end result will be of much greater value if this is done.

When preparing the interview decide what main areas the research is to cover. Prepare questions to elicit information which will meet the objectives. These questions will need careful thought if they are to achieve the desired result.

It is essential to state the purpose of the interview. The person being interviewed may appreciate receiving this in writing beforehand together with some background information so that he or she has an opportunity to prepare or obtain adequate and relevant information.

During the interview it is usually better to let the person talk, noting points for further discussion or questions which can be raised later. Quite often questions raised in the mind are answered later by further explanation.

THE ART OF INTERVIEWING

Perhaps one of the greatest assets an interviewer can have is the ability to listen objectively to what he is told. It is advisable to make brief notes immediately after the interview. Any misunderstandings or shortcomings in the interview may well be detected and cleared up before it is too late. Sometimes it is useful to send a copy of the notes to the other participant(s), particularly if certain action has been agreed upon.

Meetings

Meetings are always time-consuming and frequently time-wasting. By careful planning and proper control the time spent at a meeting can be kept to a minimum and time-wasting can be eliminated. There is then every possibility that the meeting will achieve its objectives.

PREPARATION

A meeting should be essential, i.e. it should have a specific objective or set of objectives and not be called "because we had better have a chat about it". That is not to say that meetings for general discussion should not be held, but the guide-lines for the discussion should be laid down beforehand. The participants in the meeting should be informed in advance about what is to be discussed.

There should always be an *agenda* (a list of the business to be discussed). If only one matter is under consideration it should be broken down into sections. This helps to ensure that discussion progresses in logical stages, that side-issues are kept to a minimum and that relevant decisions are reached. For a formal meeting the agenda should be distributed at least a week beforehand if this is possible.

Every participant in a meeting should prepare for it. It is not uncommon for a person to arrive at a meeting not even having looked at the agenda, never mind the supporting documents. A "meeting preparation sheet" on the lines of the specimen shown in Fig. 34 may be helpful. If this is used before a meeting, notes can be

MEETING PREPARATION SHEET

Meeting: Planning

Time: 10.30 hours   Date: 3.6.80   Place: Boardroom

Agenda item	Relevant documents	Notes
1. Minutes of previous meeting	Minutes Letter from Hetherington 12.5.80	
2. Land Registry - New site at Aston	Photocopy of deeds Surveyor's report	
3. Recruitment of Director	Photocopies of applications (six short-listed)	

Fig. 34 *Meeting preparation sheet.*

made of the points one wants to raise or questions to be asked. Participation in the meeting will be much more effective and constructive if this is done, and the pre-thinking which this involves usually enables one to express oneself better when the time comes to speak.

CONDUCT

There should be a Chairman of any discussion, however informal. To ensure that the discussion is effective the chairman should:

(1) state the matter to be discussed, giving any relevant information which should be borne in mind;

(2) state the aim of the meeting, e.g. "we have to discuss the proposed new product from the point of view of economic viability based on the figures which have been circulated, and decide whether or not to go ahead with production";

(3) ensure that each person at the meeting has an opportunity to state his views;

(4) check that action agreed upon at an earlier meeting has been taken, or is in progress, as the case may be;

(5) summarise the discussion at appropriate points during the meeting;

(6) summarise the points for and against proposed action, decisions, etc.;

(7) obtain at least a majority, but preferably a unanimous, agreement to a decision.

While discussion is going on, full attention should be given to each speaker. Most people are better able to express themselves if not interrupted whilst speaking. Questions can be asked or comments made when he has finished. Speakers who digress or "waffle" should be pulled back on course, and verbose speakers should be politely curtailed, perhaps by a question to another participant for his views. Criticism of a point raised should be constructive. Anyone disagreeing with a point should state why he disagrees. Negative reaction to a proposal should be followed by a positive alternative. Lines of thought must be followed through, e.g. a proposed action should be considered from the point of view of the people who will be involved, the reactions it will cause among other people, the effect it will have on other work, etc.

If discussion flags or deteriorates into acrimony or personal antagonism, all of which retard progress in coming to a conclusion, a provocative question which will inspire thought or a little light relief in the form of an anecdote can help to restore calm. Heated discussion is not necessarily a bad thing if it enables people to "get it off their chests", providing it does not go on for long and does ultimately lead towards a satisfactory conclusion or decision.

PROCEDURES

The office manager who is to chair or be secretary of a formal meeting should be aware of the correct terminology of procedures used. If he is the secretary he may have to prepare minutes of the business conducted (*see also* Chapter 25). Study of the subject is recommended. There are some useful publications which give good basic information on the various aspects of meetings, including the documents involved, procedures and pitfalls. Two useful publications are *Hours into Minutes* by P. J. C. Perry (British Association for Commercial and Industrial Education 1972) and *How to Take Minutes* by H. Graham-Helwig (Pitman 1974). A valuable training aid for anyone who has to attend meetings whether as Chairman, secretary or participant is a film entitled *Meetings Bloody Meetings* produced by Video Arts Limited (address: 205 Wardour Street, London W1V 3FA).

PERSONAL EVALUATION

Meetings are a special aspect of communications which should be given much greater thought than is usually the case. Everyone who has to attend meetings should be trained to understand their purpose and the procedures involved. Anyone who attends a meeting should evaluate (i) his own performance ("did I communicate my ideas, thoughts, questions effectively?"), (ii) the achievement of his own purpose in attending the meeting, and (iii) the achievement of the over-all objectives of the meeting. If the answer to any of these points is negative it is a useful exercise to try to determine why and how the meeting failed so as to avoid a recurrence of the faults.

Reception

Visitors to an organisation are impressionable—for better or for worse. Their first, and frequently most lasting impression, is created by the way in which they are received. It is therefore vitally important to ensure that every aspect of reception is given maximum attention.

ORGANISATION OF RECEPTION

The environment is fundamental in creating the right impression—"right" meaning appropriate to the image of the organisation and efficient without being too formal. The reception area does not have to be "plush", but it must be well laid out, clean and attractively furnished.

The time factor is important to every visitor. Most reasonable people do not mind waiting for a few minutes while a previous visitor is attended to. It is a different matter if the wait is a long one because the reception staff is inadequate to handle the volume of visitors. There may be peak periods, in which case arrangements should be made for additional staff to be on duty in reception at those times. This could be a clerk trained in reception duties. In most organisations it is not satisfactory to have a receptionist responsible for the telephone switchboard. Neither telephone callers nor visitors receive the attention they should have.

The reception area must be manned at all times. A relief receptionist should be available so that the full-time receptionist can have adequate breaks. It is not satisfactory for the receptionist to conduct visitors to the people they wish to see. The best arrangement is for the person concerned, or a member of the secretarial staff, to be informed by telephone that the visitor is waiting and come to the reception area to greet him/her.

Many large organisations find it convenient to have a general reception area at the main entrance with individual reception desks at each main department, or at the entrace to a group of departments located on one floor. Since most visitors will state their business at the main reception, it is impressive if the departmental reception can be notified of the visitor's arrival while he or she is on the way. This obviates the necessity for the visitor to restate his business.

SECURITY

Points raised above concerning organisation are relevant not only from the point of view of efficiency and saving of time for the visitor, but also from the point of view of security. Lack of adequate security can be a very real danger in the most unexpected places and can have unfortunate results ranging from the embarrassing to the disastrous. Chapter 49 discusses security procedures in greater detail. As far as communication is concerned, it is important that all staff realise that from the visitor's point of view security is a part of reception procedures. Therefore it is essential that all procedures be carried out with the corporate image in mind. Courtesy, pleasant but not over-familiar informality and a cheerful attitude will put any visitor into the best frame of mind for the forthcoming meeting.

PROCEDURES

Specific procedures should be laid down for the reception of visitors both in the reception area itself and by individuals. Every member of staff should be aware of the procedures and should abide by them. They should be carefully thought out to ensure that visitors are received and conducted to the person they wish to see as quickly as possible, with maximum courtesy. A specimen set of procedures is given below. This can be adapted to the individual needs and circumstances of the organisation, and should be incorporated in the house rules or manuals (*see* Chapter 13). The message form shown on page 241 is suitable for taking messages from casual visitors.

RECEPTION PROCEDURES

(1) Greet with a smile.

(2) Find out the visitor's requirements (if not stated).

(3) Check visitor's name and whether an appointment has been made or check appointments list. ("May I know your name please?" "Do you have an appointment with Mr. X?")

(4) Record name organisation, type of business, address, telephone number and extension number of new visitors.

(5) If an appointment has been made—

  (a) Offer seat; telephone the person concerned.

  (b) If the person is ready to see the visitor, escort, call messenger to escort or direct visitor to the correct office; knock office door, open, allow visitor to enter and announce visitor's name.

  (c) If the person wanted is not ready—apologise, indicate delay, offer refreshment if delay likely to be long, offer newspaper.

(6) If an appointment has not been made—

  (a) Offer seat; telephone the person wanted to find out if he is available.

  (b) If the person is available and ready—as 5b above.

  (c) If the person is available but not ready—as 5c above.

  (d) If the person is not available—offer alternatives:

    (i) see someone else;

    (ii) make an appointment, to be confirmed if necessary;

    (iii) leave a message;

    (iv) ask the person wanted to telephone.

(7) The interviewer should:

  (a) give full attention to the visitor;

  (b) greet with a smile; shake hands if this is customary;

  (c) ask the visitor to take a seat;

  (d) ask for telephone calls to be taken by someone else, or names and numbers to be taken so that callers can be telephoned as soon as the interviewer is free;

  (e) conduct the business pleasantly, helpfully and efficiently;

(f) apologise for any unavoidable interruptions.

(8) When visitors leave the interviewer should conduct them to an appropriate exit, e.g. office door or main entrance, and smile when wishing them goodbye.

RECEPTIONIST RECRUITMENT AND TRAINING

Because the reception function is of such enormous importance to the organisation, the recruitment of reception staff has additional significance as far as the corporate image is concerned. The various aspects of staff management discussed in Part Three are relevant. It should be added that appearance, speech and the ability to express oneself clearly are especially important attributes for a receptionist. These should be priority requirements when seeking new staff.

The ability to communicate with visitors of all types, at all levels, under all circumstances is essential. Manner, facial expression and gestures are all important. The ability to put people at ease, to be courteously firm with unwanted visitors and to give information quickly and accurately are the result of combining the right type of person with adequate training.

Information about the organisation, the people employed in it and their duties is an important part of induction training for any employee. It should be given special emphasis for reception staff. It is impossible for anyone to handle a visitor who is in a hurry, does not know the right person to see or has forgotten the name of the person with whom an appointment has been made, unless he or she has a thorough knowledge of the organisation and what goes on in it. This is the foundation stone of effective communication in the reception area.

20. Telephone Systems and Equipment

The telephone system installed in an organisation is, in most cases, the principal means of communication with the outside world. It is also the means by which the people in the various branches, departments, sections and offices of the organisation communicate with each other. A telephone system consists of:

(1) the equipment;
(2) the services for which the equipment is used;
(3) the personnel who use the equipment and services.

This chapter looks at some of the equipment available from British Telecom (in the U.K.) and from other manufacturers. However, the most up-to-date equipment providing all the services required in the organisation can seem thoroughly inefficient if all staff are not trained to use them as a fast, efficient means of communication. Chapter 21 therefore looks at the procedures which should be laid down for telephone systems and the training required for the people who use them.

Telephone equipment

There is a wide variety of telephone equipment available. British Telecom has a team of consultant engineers who are ready to advise subscribers on the best type of equipment and telecommunication system to meet the particular need of the individual organisation. The standard types of equipment are explained briefly below but there are many additional facilities available.

EXCHANGES

Two types of Private Branch Exchange (P.B.X.) can be rented from British Telecom.

The Private Manual Branch Exchange (P.M.B.X.) consists of either a cordless switchboard, which is operated by raising and depressing lever-type keys, or a cord switchboard, which is operated by plugging cords (really electric cables) into holes on the board to make the connections. The cordless type is supplied as a 2 + 6, i.e. with 2 exchange lines and 6 extensions, 3 + 12, 4 + 18 and 5 + 25. When more than five exchange lines are required the switchboards are supplied in units, depending on the volume of traffic. All incoming, outgoing and internal telephone calls must be routed through the operator, which means higher costs and slower service to and from the extensions.

The Private Automatic Branch Exchange (P.A.B.X.) may also be either cord or cordless. Cordless switchboards may be operated by keys (as the P.M.B.X. above) or by push-buttons (*see* Fig. 35).

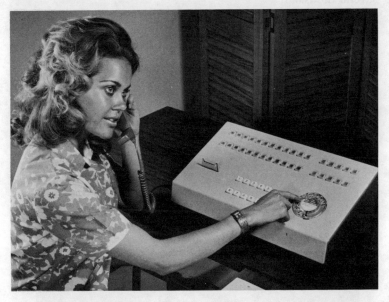

[*Courtesy British Telecom*

Fig. 35 *Cordless push-button automatic switchboard.*

The great advantage of the P.A.B.X. is that extension to extension calls and outgoing calls can be made by the extension users themselves, which greatly increases the speed of traffic. An external call is obtained by dialling first the digit 9, which gives the dialling tone if an exchange main line is free, followed by the number of the subscriber to be called. On some types of P.A.B.X. incoming calls are lost to the operator once they have been connected to an extension.

P.A.B.X. installations are manufactured as 4 + 15, 5 + 24, 7 + 35, 10 + 49 and 20 + 100. The switchboard with seven exchange lines is the largest that can be rented: larger switchboards, which must be approved by British Telecom, must be bought from the manufacturers. When more than 100 extensions are needed they are rented or purchased in blocks of 25.

It is also possible to purchase private internal automatic exchange systems for use in very large organisations where there is a large proportion of internal communications. The systems are available from 10 up to 600 exchange lines, and extensions may number several thousand.

For the smaller organisation which does not require the services of a telephone operator the Keymaster system may be adequate (*see* Fig. 36). This may consist of 1 exchange line with 5 extensions or 2

[*Courtesy British Telecom*

Fig. 36 *Telephone in the Keymaster (2 + 10) system.*

exchange lines with 10 extensions. Incoming calls may be taken on any of the instruments and connected to an extension by pressing the appropriate numbered key. External calls can be made by pressing an exchange line button to obtain an exchange line.

ELECTRONIC PROGRAMMED TELEPHONE SYSTEMS

It is now possible to purchase telephone systems which can be programmed by computer. An electronic system is fully automatic, only incoming calls being answered by the switchboard operator. When the call has been keyed to the extension the computer takes over. British Telecom, in collaboration with three British manufacturers of telephone equipment, plans to instal the first all-British electronic telephone exchange system in 1981. It is known at present as System X.

Electronic telephone systems provide a wide range of facilities, some of which are explained in the list on pages 228 to 230. Calls may be recorded on computer printout. This facility is normally used only for outgoing calls as a means of monitoring the volume and cost of calls made by staff.

An organisation which has a computer with spare capacity, or which can be extended, and has telecommunications problems caused by heavy traffic load and/or inadequate staff or equipment, is certain nowadays to at least consider the possibility of installing electronic telephone equipment when surveying the problems.

EXTENSION INSTRUMENTS

There is a variety of extension instruments available. When facilities for external dialling are not required, e.g. with an extension to a manual switchboard (although night extension facilities may be required—*see* page 229), or when it is not desirable that dialling facilities should be available to the extension user, instruments without a dial or push-buttons (called keyphones) can be installed. Alternatively it is possible for a certain number of extensions to be barred from outgoing external lines. Extensions to automatic switchboards may have facilities in addition to dialling, such as a call button to other extensions, or a transfer button to enable outside calls to be held and transferred to another extension without going through the switchboard. Up to 7 extensions can be installed to a direct line telephone (*see* below). There can be more than one instrument to one extension line though only one instrument can have the use of an external line at any one time.

An additional facility for an extension is known as Plan 107 (*see* Fig. 37). This consists of a main extension and a subsidiary extension. Incoming calls are normally received on the main

Fig. 37 *Plan 105/107 extension or direct line instrument, which allows calls to be "filtered" to a supplementary extension.*

extension. The call can then be held while the extension user buzzes and speaks to the subsidiary extension user before transferring the call to the subsidiary extension. If the main extension cannot be answered for any reason the instrument can be "switched through"

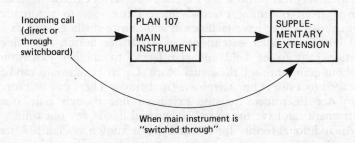

Fig. 38 *Plan 107 call routeing.*

so that calls can be received and made directly on the subsidiary extension (*see* Fig. 38). A variant of the Plan 107 extension system is the Plan 105 which has 2 subsidiary extensions.

The Plan 107 or 105 is ideal for a secretarial assistant handling telephone calls for one or two executives. The system can also be obtained as a direct line instrument (*see* below) which may be useful for the top executive and his secretary who do not always wish to make and/or receive calls through the switchboard.

DIRECT LINES

A direct line telephone is attached to a single British Telecom telephone line. Up to seven extensions (including Plan 105 or 107) can be attached to a direct line with facilities for receiving and making calls on each extension.

KEY AND LAMP UNITS

Each unit is connected to a number of main lines. Incoming calls are indicated by a flashing light. A steady light indicates a line in use. A call is received or made by switching a key. These units are particularly suitable in offices where all the staff handle calls from the public, e.g. an office dealing with sales orders. Any unit user who is free answers an incoming call. Suites of key and lamp units can be installed to by-pass the main switchboard. Alternatively they can be installed as extensions to the switchboard.

TYPES OF INSTRUMENT

There are many types of telephone instruments which provide facilities for a wide variety of circumstances and conditions, e.g. heavy-duty telephones for installation outside a building. Separate loud bells can be installed in a noisy workshop to indicate an incoming call on an instrument placed outside in a quieter place. Some telephones have buzzers instead of bells as they are less disturbing in open-plan offices.

Payphones or coinbox phones are often installed for the use of staff. The caller inserts money in the coinbox when the subscriber dialled has answered. Soundproof hoods or booths should be provided for public telephones, both for privacy and to eliminate noise as far as possible.

Ancillary equipment

There are many additional facilities available either on rental from British Telecom or by purchase from the manufacturers; in the latter case they must be usually approved by British Telecom. If the particular machine is not of an approved type the telephone line may be disconnected.

ANSWERING MACHINES

Telephone answering machines may be rented from British Telecom or purchased from manufacturers. The telephone subscriber records a message informing callers when and/or where he can be contacted. It is not possible for the caller to record a message on these "answer only" machines.

ANSWER-RECORDING MACHINES

Answer-recording machines allow the caller to record a message which the subscriber can play back later. Some machines now have highly sophisticated devices which allow the subscriber to call his own number from another telephone and, by dialling a code, play back the messages and reset the tape by remote control. The machine can also be used for recording telephone conversations and can "double" as a dictating machine (*see* Fig. 39).

[*Courtesy Robophone Ltd.*

Fig. 39 *Answer-recording machine attached to a telephone allows callers to record a message.* A more sophisticated version of this model has facilities for remote control play back and resetting of answer recording, and recording of two-way telephone conversions, and can be used as a dictation/transcription machine.

Banks of answer-recording machines have been installed in some organisations for taking orders from clients or sales representatives, for receiving urgent reports from consultants in the field and for receiving requests for sales literature or job application forms following an advertising campaign. They can also be used internally for recording progress reports, stationery orders, etc.

The use of answering machines provides a 24-hour service which enables routine calls such as those outlined above to be made after office hours at the cheapest rates. On the other hand, many callers are "nonplussed" when answered by a recording and tend to "freeze" into silence. For this reason British Telecom does not recommend them on the grounds that business can be lost.

LOUDSPEAKER SYSTEMS

There are various means by which the caller's voice can be amplified so that a conversation can be conducted on the telephone without the use of the handset. One method is to buy a simple amplifying instrument on which the telephone handset is placed. The amplifying instrument is switched on and the volume can be controlled.

British Telecom supplies a loudspeaker instrument, which is normally used without the handset, though this is provided for confidential conversations (*see* Fig. 40).

Also available from British Telecom is a speakerset which is linked to the telephone. By pressing a button the caller's voice is routed through the speakerset on which the volume can be adjusted. This is also useful when "holding the line" as one can be otherwise occupied while waiting. In addition, the hands are free for writing, turning papers, etc.

TELECOPIERS

It is often important for technical and professional people to be able to send formulae, drawings and other diagrammatic information quickly over a distance, for which a teleprinter or telex machine is not suitable.

A telecopier is a special copying machine which is linked to a telephone. The subscriber to whom the document is to be transmitted is dialled in the normal way and, providing he has a compatible telecopier attached to his telephone, the telephone is then switched to the telecopier into which the document is fed. An A4 size document can be transmitted in from one to six minutes depending on the type of machine.

A conversation can be held before and after the telecopying process. It is possible to send virtually any form of document or drawing, whether typed, printed or handwritten. The copy is always black on white.

The advantages are that no skilled operators are required; transmission can be over any distance, provided there is telephone

Fig. 40 *Loudspeaker instrument which can be rented from British Telecom.* A handset is
provided for confidential conversations.

communication; transmission can be selective from any part of the
document in the machine; transmission can be to two or more
receivers near or far; and the facsimile copies received are of good
quality and can be reproduced.

The only disadvantage is that not all types of machines are
compatible. While it is possible to standardise within an organisation, including offices, branches, etc. overseas, the scope of transmission may be limited between different organisations.

TELEWRITERS
A later development of the telecopier is the telewriter (*see* Fig. 41).
The machine is attached to a telephone and by pressing a switch,

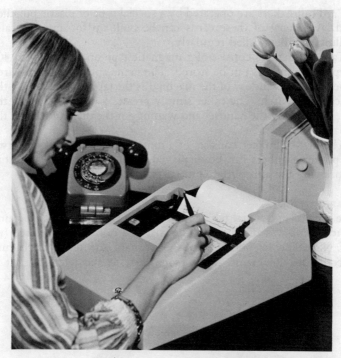

[*Courtesy Feedback Instruments Ltd.*

Fig. 41 *A telewriter which is connected to a telephone giving complete interchange of spoken and written communication over any distance.*

either of the people holding a conversation can stop talking and write with an electronic pencil on the paper in the machine. The writing or drawing is copied simultaneously on the telewriter of the other subscriber who can later amend or add to the written material. Constant interchange of speaking and writing is possible.

Examples of the use of this facility are technical discussions when sketches and diagrams are necessary to make the conversation meaningful, and for instant written confirmation of spoken agreements, discussions, etc.

AUTOMATIC DIALLING DEVICES

British Telecom is now supplying three automatic dialling devices, known generally as keycallers, repertory diallers, executive keycallers or auto diallers. The three British Telecom devices are card callmakers, tape callmakers and key callmakers.

Card callmakers are operated by a special type of plastic punched card. A battery of these cards can be built up for automatically dialling numbers called regularly.

Tape callmakers consist of a magnetic tape on which up to 400 telephone numbers can be stored. The name and number required appears in the window of the machine as the tape is revolved by the touch of a switch. The caller simply presses a button to make the call, after lifting the handset and waiting for the dialling tone in the usual way.

The key callmaker consists of a unit on which up to thirty-two telephone numbers can be displayed, each with a calling button. Depressing the appropriate button calls the number required.

CHARGE CLOCK

The cost of individual telephone calls can be monitored by a unit which computes and displays the cost of a call as it is metered (*see* Fig. 42). The telephone stands on top of the unit which runs directly off the mains and is connected to the telephone. It is

[*Courtesy Monitel Ltd.*

Fig. 42 *Telephone charge clock which indicates charges during calls.*

operated by a punched card which is programmed to take into account the day of the week, time of day, charge band tariffs and V.A.T. rate. This may be a good way of making employees aware of the cost of telephone calls and consequently more careful in following the rules for cutting costs (*see* Chapter 21).

VIDEOPHONE

Situations can arise where time (and money) would be saved if one person could talk to another face-to-face without having to make a journey; for example, if a medical consultant wants to discuss an X-ray with a doctor, or a manager wants to discuss certain parts of a report with a subordinate. Videophone has been developed to give the "face-to-face" situation as nearly as possible. It also has obvious applications for security, as a visitor could be asked to show his credentials at a videophone at the entrance to a building. Unfortuately this facility is very costly to provide because it requires a much higher quality transmission line than ordinary telephone lines. Consequently it is, as yet, not in common use.

LOGGING EQUIPMENT

It is possible to connect logging equipment to the P.A.B.X. switchboard to monitor outgoing telephone calls. The Telephone Traffic Data Analyser produces a report which gives details of calls made on each extension including the date, number called, town or country, time of the call, duration and cost (*see* Fig. 43). The Analyser can also indicate how long it takes to answer incoming calls.

Radio telephones

Radio telephones are particularly useful when contact between offices and a number of moving vehicles is required. In the U.K., application has to be made to British Telecom for the allocation of radio frequencies. The system is used by local authorities for calling ambulances, by private taxi services for directing their vehicles to a new fare, and for many services such as electricity service mechanics, and A.A. and R.A.C. road patrols. This saves time and expense of vehicles returning to headquarters to receive further instructions because they can finish one job and proceed immediately to the next one.

British Telecom has now provided a Radiophone service in certain areas by which a subscriber can make ordinary telephone calls from a moving vehicle. The telephone sets are not sold or maintained by British Telecom, but can be purchased privately.

IDENT.	EXTEN.	DATE D/M	TIME H.M	DURATION MIN.SEC	NO. DIALLED	COST £
224	223	15/02	9.53	6.39	098376055	1.20
224	223	17/02	10.05	3.34	0421263527	.66
239	240	14/02	11.17	5.04	0421263527	.93
239	240	17/02	12.30	16.10	039254300	2.91
239	240	20/02	10.02	6.38	073486584	1.29
240	241	23/02	8.59	1.00	01027118383471	1.05
240	241	23/02	9.45	10.08	01027118383471	10.65
240	241	24/02	9.04	3.51	0701881241	.72
245	246	12/02	12/02	2.53	2286400	.54
246	247	13/02	9.37	8.57	032152201	1.62
246	247	14/02	9.30	8.16	032152281	1.50
246	247	17/02	10.44	3.01	5801464	.57
246	247	18/02	12.23	9.47	0537236721	1.77
250	250	13/02	16.44	68.00	048084664	8.16
250	250	14/02	12.08	3.43	037444077	.69
250	250	14/02	12.38	4.19	0621816887	.87
273	273	17/02	11.17	37.18	0603611122	6.72
317	317	17/02	10.44	32.35	7238488	.51
331	331	17/02	17.23	49.51	5882471	.51
					TOTAL	42.69

Fig. 43. *Telephone Traffic Data Analysis*. The calls shown in this printout are in excess of a predetermined cost level which can be fixed for local, trunk (S.T.D.) and international (I.S.D.) calls.

Intercommunication systems

Apart from intercommunication provided by P.M.B.X. and P.A.B.X. systems (*see* above), internal telephone systems can be purchased or rented from British Telecom. These are sometimes referred to as multi-cord telephone systems, where no central exchange is involved. The different instruments in such a system are all interconnected by multi-cord cable, and contact can be made from any one station to another by the simple depression of a key, but none of the extensions are connected to the external telephone system. Conversations on these internal systems are often non-secret, that is, a conversation between two extensions can be "listened in to" by a third extension.

The instruments are made with a variety of extensions, viz. 5, 10, 20, or 30 stations, which is generally considered to be the maximum number of extensions for this type of system. These systems also incorporate full intercommunication between a maximum number of extensions simultaneously, for example up to 5 ways, whereby on pressing 5 levers simultaneously a communication can be given to 5 departments at the same time.

A development of the private intercommunication system is the executive system. A number of extensions radiate from a central instrument. There is usually "loud-to-loud" facility which operates by means of a highly sensitive microphone. This enables the executive to hear his caller's voice amplified, and speak into the instrument without having to lift a receiver, which leaves both hands free to refer to documents. (This is similar to the British Telecom loudspeaker telephone referred to above.) This system is very suitable for a small organisation; it has no exchange (connection is entirely automatic) and is usually used as a method of calling staff as well as providing means of intercommunication.

There are various additional facilities on these executive systems including a handset for private conversation, loudspeakers at each end of several lines so that a number of departments can be addressed simultaneously, and priority of the master instrument over all other calls, which can be interrupted if desired.

The extensions from the masterset may be one-way only, i.e. they cannot initiate calls but can only receive them from the masterset; they may be able to call the masterset but not other extensions; or they may be able to receive and make calls from and to the masterset and all other extensions as required.

Centralised dictation systems

Centralised dictation systems can be linked in to a P.A.B.X. telephone network. When an extension user wishes to dictate he picks up the handset, dials a code and the call is automatically routed to a free recording machine in the audio bank. This is explained in more detail in Chapter 27.

Paging systems

In large organisations it is often necessary to find a member of staff quickly. Managers in a factory, departmental chiefs in a store, or doctors in a hospital may all be wanted urgently. Many paging or staff-location systems are available, the suitability of each system depending on whether it is required for office, factory, hospital or store.

PUBLIC ADDRESS SYSTEM

The simplest, and in some circumstances the most effective, method is the loudspeaker system by which an appeal can be broadcast from a master station to all workshops or departments, requesting the attention of the person sought.

BELLS AND BUZZERS

A system of bells or buzzers can be installed. Each person on the "call list" has a code of so many long and so many short buzzes—rather similar to the Morse code.

The disadvantage of both the public address and the buzzer systems is that they are noisy and disturbing (particularly in a hospital), and are not a very accurate method of communication. With a coded buzzer, for example, everyone must stop and listen carefully to the signals to discover whether it is his particular call sign.

LIGHTED SIGNALS

To overcome the disturbance caused by sound signals, a system of lights may be used. There are three such methods. The first uses a code which is a combination of any of the numbers (which light up consecutively) on an indicator. Up to 80 coded signals can be transmitted on such a system. The second method is a clock on which the figures are illuminated either singly or in combination to indicate members of the staff called. The third system is a series of coloured lights only. Each member of staff who may be paged is allocated a combination of still and/or flashing colours, e.g. yellow still and red flashing.

The disadvantages of lighted signal systems are that they require coded signals, a large number of signal stations may be required to locate a person wherever he may be, and the signal is not so insistent as a bell or buzzer.

WIRELESS CALL SYSTEM

A wireless call system consists of a central transmitting station (usually at the telephone switchboard) and the allocation of a portable receiver to each member of the staff to be called (*see* Fig. 44). Each receiver picks up only its own particular frequency; thus when a member of the staff is wanted, a wireless signal is transmitted and is received by that member of staff *only*. The signal, usually a bleep, is unmistakable, it cannot be ignored, and the person receiving the call has to telephone the switchboard to see why he is wanted; it does not disturb any other person in the building, and the signal will reach the person called wherever he may be within a certain radius.

Call systems which allow two-way speech are also available but in most cases it may be advisable to use the bleep system so that the

[*Courtesy Cass Electronics Ltd.*

Fig. 44 *Wireless call system which enables a person within a fixed radius of a central calling point to be paged at any time.*

person called has to telephone for the message. The only disadvantage is that unco-operative members of staff do not always answer the call, but this applies equally to any other paging system.

Choice of system

The telephone system must be an integral part of the integrated communication system. It must complement the various other communication systems in the organisation. This is important because the capacity required must be considered and provided in relation to the volume of communications which must be dealt with by some form of telecommunication.

The basic criteria for choosing a telephone system are as follows.

(1) What is the volume of incoming calls, outgoing calls, internal calls?

(2) Who needs to use the telephone for incoming, outgoing and internal calls?

(3) What is the frequency of the various types of calls in each department/office?

(4) Where are telephone instruments required, and what type and number of instruments are required in each place?

(5) What is the cost of providing a telephone service to everyone who may need to use it, however infrequently, against the cost of providing the service to those who need it regularly but causing a certain amount of inconvenience and some waste of time to those who do not use it very frequently?

(6) What ancillary equipment or services would enable staff to be more efficient and/or enhance the corporate image of the organisation, e.g. auto-dialling facilities, loudspeaker facilities, or direct dialling for incoming calls whereby a caller can dial the extension direct if he knows the extension number?

(7) What facilities are required for paging, night service?

(8) What equipment is necessary to complement other facilities in the communication system? For example, is a record of conversations desirable or necessary; is a written record necessary; are many telephone conversations based on the contents of a document; is communication necessary with people who are moving around a great deal?

(9) What expansion may be required in the foreseeable future? Twelve extensions might be sufficient for immediate needs, but a switchboard for, say, twenty-four extensions might be advisable if more extensions are likely to be needed in the foreseeable future.

(10) What other transmission facilities will be linked into the telephone system, e.g. telecopier, datel, time-sharing access to a computer with duplex (a two-way teleprinter link)?

(11) What restrictions are required to control costs? Certain extensions can be barred from direct dialling out or from dialling S.T.D. and I.S.D. calls (*see* Chapter 21).

Costs

It is impossible to quote costs since this depends on the system, facilities and equipment installed in the individual organisation. Apart from installation costs there are the costs of maintenance, rental and units used (calls). There is also the cost of staff time wasted when a system is inadequate for the traffic or unsuitable for the needs of the users. Comparative costs of other forms of communication, e.g. telex, should also be investigated. The introduction of a paging system, answering machines or telecopiers will cost money but may well save more than it costs over not too long a period by increasing efficiency leading to more business.

Difficult though it often is to estimate and predict costs, it is an essential element in determining the system which meets the organisation's needs without running away with the profits. There are several factors to be considered when setting out to reduce the cost of the telephone system. There is the equipment itself, charges, supervision, human factors and time factors (*see also* Chapter 21). The check-list below of appropriate questions is reproduced by courtesy of Brian D. Simmons, Telecommunications Consultant, PACTEL. The questions are relevant whether the review is simply to achieve economies by reducing the cost of an existing system or to install new and/or additional equipment and facilities.

CHECK-LIST OF COST FACTORS
General.
(1) What is the importance of the telephone to the organisation? Are there other means that should be used?

(2) How rigidly are controls applied? Will these receive support from management, the staff committee, etc?

(3) Is everyone aware/convinced of the need for control and cost reduction?

(4) Can a spirit be engendered to make it work? How?

(5) What targets should be set?

System.
(6) Which telephone system is needed: ordinary telephone sets, Plan types, P.M.B.X., P.A.B.X., a mixed system?

(7) Which factors most affect the cost of the system?

(8) How many exchange lines, extensions, operators are needed? Can they be reduced? What can be done to help make a decision, e.g. traffic checks?

(9) Is the operator efficient, well-trained? Can she do other duties?

(10) Do all extensions need out-dialling access, e.g. canteen, conference rooms, etc.?

(11) Can equipment be simplified: cut out loudspeaker telephones, callmakers, etc.?

(12) Is there an accurate inventory of rented and purchased equipment?

(13) Is the relevant authority notified immediately when equipment is not to be used any longer?

(14) Are the correct procedures known for reporting faults, claiming rebates, contacting sales and special services representatives, registering service complaints?

(15) When was the last traffic check by British Telecom or an extension stroke count by users carried out?

(16) Would there be benefit in renting private wires or out-of-area exchange lines? (A stroke record or operator-call log would show.)

(17) If a British Telecom P.A.B.X. is rented, what measures are necessary to stay within the limits of size, e.g. shared extensions, direct lines for heavy users, etc.?

(18) On a purchased system, can extensions be kept below a multiple of 50 to reduce maintenance charges?

Charges.

(19) Are bills checked?

(20) How does the charge compare with the budget—and with the previous charge?

(21) Are other managers advised of communications costs?

(22) Is credit claimed for line outage, etc.?

(23) Are telephone expenses charged out?

(24) Is it worth metering heavy users?

(25) Are up-to-date British Telecom leaflets on facilities and cost of services available?

(26) How are telephone costs apportioned—flat-rate overhead, charging out on estimated usage, cost centering on measured usage?

(27) Will call-monitoring and data-recording equipment help?

(28) Changes of location, offices, etc. are costly—can they be reduced, can they be taken advantage of to simplify the system when changes come?

(29) Are credit cards used, reverse charge calls accepted, Freefone service used? Is this worth while in view of high costs?

Supervision.

(30) Is there a regular check with the telephonist/supervisor on telephone usage, people's habits, problems?

(31) Are line managers sufficiently involved in responsibility for communication by their staff?

(32) When was the last spot check on system use?

(33) What is company policy for private calls? Is this well communicated and observed?

(34) Is there a coinbox? Should one be installed for private calls by staff?

(35) Does management set a good example—foster self-accountability and good habits? Discuss with them.

(36) Are there adequate clocks or do staff have to dial the speaking clock?

Human factors.

(37) What staff habits must be recognised as reasonable/unreasonable in telephone use?

(38) Should a code of conduct be devised?

(39) Should temptation be taken away from staff, e.g. barr level 9 (i.e. barr the extensions to outgoing calls which are normally obtained by dialling the digit 9 to obtain an external line), issue dial locks or educate them into better habits?

(40) Would a seminar, campaign, suggestion scheme help to achieve economies?

(41) Publicity: has everything possible been done to bring awareness of the high cost of telephone services and calls? (Try notice boards, stickers, circulars, displays, etc.)

(42) Have staff been trained to take a pride in their telephone technique? (This aids accountability.)

Saving time.

(43) Telephone time saved reduces costs and can increase productivity. Have staff been instructed to observe the following points?

    (*a*) List the main points of your call before making it.

    (*b*) Know the number and dial or key correctly.

    (*c*) Avoid the peak charging period: 9 a.m. to 1 p.m.

    (*d*) Quickly exchange identities.

    (*e*) Be courteous, but brief.

    (*f*) Do not digress.

    (*g*) Do not hold on—call back or be called back.

    (*h*) Avoid busy hours if you can—mid/late mornings and afternoons.

    (*i*) Know when to stop talking and do so.

These check-list questions will also suggest others. Their application should result in reductions in the bill.

Summary.

Measure traffic and equipment needs.

Reduce lines, extensions and operators as appropriate.

Improve budgetary control.

Simplify the telephone system—have a purge.

Restrict outgoing calls.

Check all bills—challenge errors—claim rebates.

Introduce private wires/out-of-area lines.

Train and educate staff: run a campaign.

Foster accountability: managers must practise what they preach.

Look to achieve results across a broad front.

Some facilities available on telephone equipment

NOTE: The precise interpretation of this selection of terms depends upon the particular system. The brief explanations given below are general.

Abbreviated dialling. An exchange controlled by computer can be programmed to dial automatically up to a hundred telephone numbers when two or three digits only are dialled. This is particularly useful when overseas numbers, which can contain up to fifteen digits, are dialled frequently.

Absent extension answering. When a computer-controlled exchange connects a caller to an extension which is not answered the call is automatically transferred, after three, four or five rings, to another extension on a pre-arranged circuit. This process is repeated on all the extensions on the circuit (up to five) until the call reaches an extension which is answered.

Automatic call back. By lifting the receiver, dialling a code and replacing the receiver, the telephone instrument can be made to ring. Used by engineers for testing.

Automatic transfer. A call can be transferred from one extension to another by the extension user, i.e. the call does not have to be referred back to the switchboard.

Barred extensions. These are extensions on which external calls cannot be dialled directly; this can be applied selectively, e.g. to Subscriber Trunk Dialling (S.T.D.) and/or International Subscriber Dialling (I.S.D.). This facility is also referred to as *route restriction, level 9 busying,* or *level 9 access barred.*

Call overlapping/follow-on call trap. When an extension has received or made a call via the switchboard, that call must be cleared before a further call can be received or made by that extension.

Call waiting signal. A signal introduced into an existing call to inform the two people talking that another caller is waiting to speak to one of them.

Camp-on busy/ring when free. An extension user, on finding any extension engaged, can dial a code which will leave the call in. The caller can replace his receiver and his call will automatically be made when the extension called is free. This facility has now been developed so that the originator of the call is recalled first to ensure that he is available.

Conference call. Several people are able to speak to each other on one call.

Direct Dialling In (D.D.I.). Outside callers can dial directly to an extension, if they know the extension number, without being answered by the switchboard.

Extension metering. A series of meters is installed which records the number of units used by an extension on a P.A.B.X., usually installed in hotels where guests can dial their own calls and have them charged to their account.

Group calling/hunting. When incoming calls are connected by the operator to an extension the call is automatically re-routed to other extensions in turn on a programmed circuit. This facility is also available from internal extensions.

Hold for enquiry. The telephone operator can hold a call while enquiring of the extension user whether he wishes to take the call.

Inter-P.A.B.X. connection—private wires. When a private wire is connected into the P.A.B.X. system an extension user can use the private line, usually by dialling the digit 7 or 8 and the number of the private line.

Message waiting facility. Used mainly in hotels, a light on a panel is illuminated indicating that the operator should be contacted for a message.

Night busying. It is usual for night service (see below) to operate on selected extensions only. Where a switchboard has several lines on the same number with automatic transfer of incoming calls to second and subsequent lines on that number, it is possible to have an engaged signal on the lines not connected to night extensions.

Night service. There are three types of night service.

(1) A series of bells can be located throughout the premises. An incoming call will ring all the bells so that anyone who hears a bell goes to the nearest telephone, dials the digit 8 and receives the call. This is known as unattended night service.

(2) Exchange lines are plugged to specific extensions. In some cases the night service numbers are different from the daytime service numbers (known as "changed identity") though the calls are routed on the same lines. This enables senior managers to receive calls directly from people who know their night service numbers.

(3) Night service switchboard: calls are routed to a smaller switchboard which may be manned by a security officer. There is limited facility for connection of incoming calls.

Parking incoming calls. This facility is available to an operator when the extension required by an incoming caller is engaged. The operator can park the call in a store but can go back to the caller periodically.

Transfer and enquiry. A subscriber may hold a call, dial another number within the exchange area and later revert to the original call, or transfer the caller to the new number. This is similar to automatic transfer between extensions, applied to direct lines.

Trunk offering. When an operator wishes to interrupt a call, e.g. for an overseas call, she can press a button which creates a pipping tone over the call indicating to the extension users that the operator wishes to speak. This facility is also available between extensions on some systems.

Types of switchboard equipment. There are three types of switchboard equipment.

(1) Strouger, which consists of electrical mechanical moving parts.

(2) Crossbar, which has a combination of electronic and moving parts.

(3) Electronic, which has no moving parts.

21. Telephone Services

The telephone service within an organisation involves a great deal more than the equipment. The successful functioning of the system depends on the people who use it and the services which are available. This chapter looks at the most important ancillary aspects of the organisation's telephone system.

Types of call

All telephone users should be aware of the types of call available. Table V summarises those available in the U.K.

TABLE V. TYPES OF TELEPHONE CALL AVAILABLE IN THE U.K.

Type of call	*Facilities*
International Subscriber Dialling (I.S.D.).★	Direct dialling to most overseas countries (see telephone code directory).
Subscriber Trunk Dialling (S.T.D.).	Direct dialling to almost anywhere within the country (see telephone code directory).
International call through the telephone exchange operator.★	Pre-book (which may be necessary several days in advance for some countries).
Trunk call through the telephone exchange operator.†	Personal (person-to-person/particular person) call. Fixed time call. Transferred (reverse) charge call. Advice of duration and charge (A.D.C.) (to

★ Remember the time difference between countries.
† More expensive than direct dialling.

231

Type of call	Facilities
	be notified to operator before giving number required).
	Freefone call.
	Credit card call.
Local call.	Direct dialling (see telephone code directory for exchanges within the area but outside own exchange).
Local exchange operator services.	Fault reports.
	Number unobtainable enquiries.
	Alarm (morning) call.
	Freefone.
	International exchange.
	Phonogram.
Local direct dialling services.	Emergency service (999).
	Time.
	Weather conditions on roads.
	Principal events of the day in major cities (in English, French, German, Italian, Spanish).
	Test Match scores.
	Business News Summary.
	Recipes.
	Dial-a-disc.
	Bedtime story.

Telephone directories

There always seems to be a shortage of telephone directories in offices. It is not practicable to provide every extension user with a complete set of directories but everyone should have quick access to the directories he needs to use frequently. It may be that a complete set can be made available for each section or department.

EXTERNAL

British Telecom provides to all subscribers a directory for their area. The directory contains information including how to dial, services and charges. Subscribers are listed in alphabetical order of name in the white page section and by alphabetical order of type of business (and alphabetical order of names within the appropriate business section) in the yellow page section. The yellow pages are produced as a separate directory in some areas.

A telephone code directory is issued at regular intervals listing the codes to dial before the subscriber's number when making calls outside the local exchange area. International Subscriber Dialling (I.S.D.) codes are included.

Every subscriber is entitled to an entry in the white page section of the directory without charge, and a business subscriber is entitled to have his name printed in the yellow page section under the appropriate heading free of charge. In both sections, if entries are required in bold print, a small charge is made.

Additional copies of directories for the local area and other areas of the country are available at a small cost. The telephone directory contains a form on which to apply for the directories required.

INTERNAL

An internal directory is essential for any system where extension users have the facility for dialling other extensions directly. There are three aspects which need a great deal of thought and care, viz. the compilation of the directory, format and updating procedures.

In a small organisation it is adequate to compile the directory in alphabetical order of name. In a larger organisation it may be more suitable to have two sections. The first section lists the names of staff under departments; the second section lists the names alphabetically. The departmental section ought also to include the designation of each individual. This helps the person who forgets or does not know the name of the person but knows the department in which he works.

Each secretary should be listed in four ways:

(1) under her own name in the alphabetical order of names list;
(2) as "Secretary: Miss X" under the name of the person or people for whom she works in the alphabetical order of names list;
(3) under her own name in the appropriate departmental list;
(4) as "Secretary: Miss X" under the name of the person or people for whom she works in the departmental list.

Though this would appear to be a great deal of duplication it is not in fact, because "Secretary: Miss X" is a part of the entry for the manager.

When designing the format in which the internal directory is to be produced it is necessary to take into account the handling of it and ease of reading. A5 size is most suitable both for use and for storage. Some organisations produce the content on A4 and then reduce. This is not entirely satisfactory as the print can be difficult to read and mistakes can be made when one is in a hurry unless it is typed with one and a half line spacing.

Each entry should begin with the surname, preferably in capital

letters, followed by first name or initials. Miss, Mrs. or Ms. should
be included for female staff. (Note that some ladies are somewhat
"touchy" about their titles so it is advisable to find out how they
like to be addressed.)

It may be difficult to decide whether to issue the directory in
loose-leaf form or as a booklet. The advantage of loose leaf is that it
is easy to insert new sheets for updating. However, it is generally
necessary to update so many sheets that it is probably just as easy to
update the whole directory at, say, quarterly intervals and issue
updating sheets weekly so that extension users can amend their
own copies.

It is necessary to establish a procedure for notifying changes.
One person must be in charge of the internal directory. When an
employee changes his extension for whatever reason he should
inform the switchboard supervisor or operator who should then
pass this information weekly to the person in charge of the internal
directory updating. Alternatively all employees can be given a few
telephone updating forms. These are completed with name, previous extension number and new extension number and then sent
to a central point, e.g. the telephone exchange or the communications manager.

Switchboard operator

The telephone switchboard operator is the first link in the chain of
communication between people outside the organisation and those
inside. It is therefore vital that the operator should be technically
competent and have the personal attributes essential to the creation
of the right image. The "telephone voice" of the organisation is a
major contributor to the corporate image. It is therefore worth
taking time and trouble to select the right operator.

RECRUITMENT
The telephone operator is expected to be able to:
   (1) operate a switchboard quickly and accurately;
   (2) receive incoming calls and connect them to extensions;
   (3) direct calls to the correct extensions;
   (4) make calls to outside subscribers and connect to extensions;
   (5) use directories quickly and accurately;
   (6) keep records such as fault reports, and international and
trunk calls made by extension users.

In order to fulfil these duties the operator must know:
   (1) correct standard expressions ("Will you hold the line please?"
not "Hold on!");

(2) the telephone services available (types of call, etc.);

(3) the organisation's functions, departments and their functions, senior managers and their general responsibilities, and
sources of information within the organisation.

In order to create confidence in the callers the telephone operator
must:

(1) have a well-modulated and pleasant voice;

(2) have a genuine wish to help people;

(3) be patient;

(4) be tactful;

(5) be able to work calmly under extreme pressure.

Physical factors include good hearing and the ability to sit for
long periods without difficulty.

TRAINING

All telephone operators should be trained by British Telecom. If it
is not possible to recruit an operator with the appropriate training,
British Telecom conducts courses for new operators. Refresher
courses are also conducted which may be useful for a newly
recruited operator.

An induction training programme must be prepared to give a
steadily increasing knowledge of the organisation and its staff. As
the communications "entry point" of the organisation, the telephone operator must be able to direct callers without delay to the
person who can handle the call. Visits to the plant and offices are
beneficial because the operator will then be able to identify
departments and names more easily.

OPERATING PROCEDURES

Specific operating procedures should be drawn up and taught as
part of the induction training programme. A specimen set of
procedures for a manual switchboard is set out below. Procedures
must be prepared to enhance the technical efficiency of the telephone system in the organisation and meet the needs of the
extension users. This latter point is sometimes overlooked, yet if
extension users' time is wasted the organisation is wasting money.

TELEPHONE SWITCHBOARD PROCEDURES

(1) *Incoming calls.*

   (*a*) Greet pleasantly.

   (*b*) Identify the organisation correctly.

   (*c*) When the caller states whom he wishes to speak to,
         repeat the name of the person wanted.

   (*d*) Ask the name of the caller if he has not identified himself

("May I know your name please?").

(e) Ask him to hold the line ("Will you hold the line please Mr. X?").

(f) Ring the person wanted.

(g) When extension user answers inform him of the caller's name.

   (i) Call accepted: inform caller he is being connected ("Mr. X, I am putting you through to Mr. A.").

   (ii) Call not accepted: apologise to caller ("I am sorry Mr. X, Mr. A is not available at present"). Offer alternative—speak to someone else/Mr. A to ring back/Mr. X to leave a message. Note the name and number of Mr. X if Mr. A is to call back. Take down the message or pass to suitable person to take message. (Message should include name of person wanted, name of caller, organisation, telephone number, extension number, time and date, the message, initials of recipient.)

(h) Extension wanted engaged: inform caller ("I am sorry Mr. X, Mr. A is engaged. Will you wait?"). Keep in contact with caller about every thirty seconds. If the delay is likely to be long offer to call back and take the name and telephone number of the caller.

(2) *Calls from extensions.*

(a) First calls of the day—greet the extension user.

(b) "Number please."

(c) Write down and repeat the number or extension required.

(d) Ask for the extension number of the caller (automatic switchboards only).

(e) Ask the extension user to hold the line if a connection can be made immediately; if not say "you will be rung later".

(3) *Making calls.*

(a) Dial: when answered check the number and/or name of the organisation and ask for the person and extension number required.

(b) When answered by the extension user, greet, identify, explain who is calling.

(c) Connect to the originator of the call and inform him who is on the line.

(d) Cross the number off the list of calls to be made.

(e) If the number is engaged, or the person wanted is not available, inform the originator of the call. Try the engaged number again after three to five minutes.

(4) *Records.*
   (a) An alphabetical list of organisations called frequently, with telephone numbers, and, if possible, names of contacts and their extension numbers.
   (b) A list of trunk calls, overseas calls, etc., with date and time for checking against bills.
   (c) Fault book in which faults are recorded with the date and time when reported to the British Telecom Engineers and the date and time of follow-up reports.
(5) *Closing duties.*
   (a) Switch to night extension or connect answering machine.
   (b) Remove headset or handset and lock away.
   (c) Cover switchboard.
(6) *Opening duties.*
   (a) Disconnect answering machine or return switchboard to normal operation.
   (b) Connect headset or handset.
   (c) Dust switchboard.
   (d) Check for faults; record and report faults.

NOTES ON TELEPHONE SWITCHBOARD PROCEDURES

(1) (d) and (g) (i) These points may be omitted on automatic switchboards to save time.

(1) (g) (ii) Telephone operators on busy switchboards should not be expected to take messages other than brief ones. A typist or clerk can be designated to undertake this duty if there is no receptionist. A simple message form suitable for use by telephone operators is shown on page 241.

(2), (3) If the switchboard is automatic, extension users normally dial their own calls. *See* "extension users' procedures" below.

SUPERVISION

There should be strict supervision and monitoring of switchboard operation. This is not always easy but the occasional call from outside the organisation may indicate weaknesses which should be corrected. Any complaint should be dealt with immediately. It is difficult to prove lack of courtesy, unpleasant attitude, etc. in individual cases but a complaint should be discussed with the operator in an adult manner. Everyone is human and it is rare indeed for any single person to be perfect all the time. Nevertheless, this is the aim and every encouragement must be given to achieve it.

If there is more than one telephone operator on duty at the same time one of them should be "in charge". In the case of a large switchboard with a team of operators there must be a supervisor who is responsible to the office manager or communications manager as the case may be.

Extension user

TRAINING

Because a human being can speak it is often assumed that he can use a telephone correctly and efficiently. This is not true. There are special aspects of telephone communication which should be drawn to the attention of every extension user. The office manager should ensure that each person uses his telephone to increase his efficiency in the interests of the organisation. Training is essential. A short seminar or workshop of about four to six hours is usually adequate. Depending on the type and level of people being trained there are various approaches. Training aids include films, sound/slide sequences, short courses including special courses for telephone sales training, and role playing. It is advantageous to involve the switchboard supervisor (if there is one) or the telephone operator in the training of extension users because he or she can indicate ways in which co-operation ensures better service.

In the U.K. the Post Office Film Library has two films which can be borrowed free of charge. A tape of international signals can also be borrowed from the British Telecom Area office. British Telecom conduct in-house, two- to three-hour seminars on request. They provide the necessary teaching aids such as film, international signal tape and telephones for role playing.

PROCEDURES

The telephone operator cannot operate efficently unless the extension users work in accordance with procedures which complement the switchboard procedures. Specimen sets of procedures for extension users are set out below.

EXTENSION USERS' PROCEDURES—MANUAL SWITCHBOARD

(1) *Receiving calls.*
  (a) Identify yourself by name or section or department.
  (b) Accept call if announced by operator by saying "Thank you". If you are unable to accept a call ask the telephone operator to note the name and number of the caller so that you can ring back.
  (c) When the telephone operator connects a caller greet by name ("Good morning Mr. X.").

(d) Make a note of the main points of the telephone conversation for the file if it may be useful for reference later,
or note action required.
(e) If a colleague is wanted, ask the caller to hold the line
("Will you hold the line please Mr. X?").
(f) Inform the colleague of the call giving the name of the
caller.
(g) If there is any delay inform the caller and keep in contact.
(h) If the person wanted is not available offer to help or take
a message. Messages must be taken *accurately*. All details
including the main points of the message should be
repeated back to the caller to ensure that details are
correct and complete.
(2) *Making calls.*
(a) Prepare the call—the number required, the name and
extension number of the contact, notes of matters to be
discussed. Documents or files that might be needed
should be on the desk.
(b) Greet the operator (first call of the day). Give the name,
telephone number of the organisation wanted and the
name and extension number of the contact.
(c) Hold the line if the operator asks you to do so as this
means the number will be dialled immediately. If you do
not wish to hold, ask to be rung back.
(d) If you are connected to the organisation's switchboard
only give the name and extension number of the person
wanted.
(e) When connected to the person you want greet by name
and identify yourself.
(f) When the call is over, cross through the notes made and
if necessary make a brief record for the file.

NOTES ON EXTENSION USERS' PROCEDURES (*manual switchboard*)
(2)(a) Telephone operators should not be expected to find telephone numbers except when you are in difficulties. If possible have
a telephone directory and also keep a personal telephone directory
in which you note the names of organisations you call frequently
with their telephone numbers and the names and extension number
of contacts. The telephone number of an organisation and possibly
the extension numbers of your contacts are set out on the letterheads of correspondence with which you may be dealing.
(2)(c) Holding the line while the operator connects your call
saves time and is also a courtesy to the person you are calling.
(2)(d) It is advisable to give both the name and extension number

of the person wanted in case that person has changed his office or his extension number.

EXTENSION USERS' PROCEDURES—AUTOMATIC SWITCHBOARD

(1) *Receiving calls.*
   (a) Greet and identify yourself or identify, and then greet after the caller has identified himself.
(2) *Making calls.*
   (a) To extensions—dial the extension number.
   (b) To other subscribers.
      (i) Check the code and number of the organisation and extension number of the person wanted.
     (ii) Dial for a line (this may be the digit 9); await the dialling tone and then dial the number required. Dial correctly, allowing the dial to return freely by itself.
    (iii) When answered, wait for identification and then greet, identify yourself and ask for the name and extension number of the person wanted. If you get a wrong number apologise, replace the receiver and check the code and number. Repeat item (ii).
    (iv) If the person wanted is not available give your own name, number and extension number to be rung back; or ask for someone else; or leave a massage, e.g. with a secretary.

NOTES ON EXTENSION USERS' PROCEDURES (*automatic switchboard*)

(1) Though incoming calls are passed through the telephone operator it is normal for an automatic switchboard operator not to announce callers. This can be done if you wish, but one of the objectives of installing an automatic switchboard is to save time.

(2) The operator can be asked to make calls but again it saves time if you dial directly. However, in some countries telephone connections are not made easily and it may be rather time-consuming to dial your own calls.

When devising the procedures for extension users, costs should be borne in mind as well as the corporate image. Whatever type of telephone system is installed, the following points should always be incorporated and emphasised.

(1) Preparation of calls: list the main points to be discussed before dialling.

(2) Keep a personal telephone directory (a small alphabetical notebook is adequate) for numbers called frequently.

(3) Check the direct line and extension numbers before dialling and dial or key correctly.

```
┌─────────────────────────────────────────┐
│                                           │
│   Message For_____  │
│                                           │
│   Date_____ Time_____    │
│                                           │
│          WHILE YOU WERE OUT                │
│                                           │
│                                           │
│   Name _____   │
│                                           │
│   Organisation_____   │
│                                           │
│   Phone No_____   │
│                                           │
│   ┌──────────────────┬──┬───────────────┬──┐│
│   │ Telephoned       │  │ Please ring him│  ││
│   ├──────────────────┼──┼───────────────┼──┤│
│   │ Called to see you│  │ Will call again│  ││
│   ├──────────────────┼──┼───────────────┼──┤│
│   │ Wants to see you │  │ Urgent        │  ││
│   └──────────────────┴──┴───────────────┴──┘│
│                                           │
│   Message:                                │
│                                           │
│                                           │
│                                           │
│                                           │
│                  Signature_____  │
│                                           │
└───────────────────────────────────────────┘
```

Fig. 45(a) *Telephone message form suitable for use by anyone in the organisation, including the receptionist.*

(4) Avoid making calls during the peak charging period: 9.00 a.m. to 1.00 p.m.

(5) Avoid busy hours if possible—mid/late mornings and afternoons.

(6) Keep the conversation to the point and be as brief as possible, without being discourteous.

(7) Use telephone message forms. Two specimens are illustrated in Figs. 45 (*a*) and (*b*).

Co-operation between operator and extension user

It cannot be stressed too strongly that the efficiency of the organisation's telephone system depends on the people who use it.

```
┌──────────────────────────────────────────────────────────┐
│              PROVISIONAL BOOKING FORM                      │
│                                                            │
│   Booking Taken by:_____ Date of booking:_____ │
│                                                            │
│                                                            │
│   Course Title:_____│
│                                                            │
│   Course Dates:_____│
│                                                            │
│   Delegate Name:_____│
│                                                            │
│   Delegate Title:_____│
│                                                            │
│   Company Name:_____│
│                                                            │
│   Company Address:_____│
│   _____│
│                                                            │
│   Tel: No._____                     │
│                                                            │
│   Name of person making booking:_____ │
│                                                            │
│                                                            │
│      ADVISE CALLER TO CONFIRM IN WRITING AS SOON AS POSSIBLE│
│                                                            │
│                                                            │
│                ┌──────┬──────────┬──┬───────────┬──┐       │
│                │ SEND │ Brochure │  │ Programme │  │       │
│                └──────┴──────────┴──┴───────────┴──┘       │
│                                                            │
│   Special Notes                                            │
│   _____│
│   _____│
│                                                            │
│   _____│
│                                                            │
│   FROM WHAT SOURCE DID DELEGATE HEAR OF THIS COURSE?       │
│   _____│
└──────────────────────────────────────────────────────────┘
```

[*Courtesy Guardian Business Services*

Fig. 45(*b*) *Telephone message form for a specialist department.* This form is used by a training organisation for taking course reservations. The details included ensure that every member of the staff obtains all relevant information in the same format.

If there is lack of co-operation between the operator and extension user the system will falter and the caller (who may be a valuable customer) is forced to waste time and money, suffer frustration and will possibly take his orders elsewhere.

Unfortunately the operator is seldom seen by the staff in general. It might be helpful if each new operator could be introduced personally to heads of departments and their secretaries as a part of the induction programme. Similarly, new senior managers could meet the telephone operator as a part of their induction. It is very easy for an operator to feel "cut off" and not identify with the organisation as a whole unless some effort is made to overcome this.

A pleasant "good morning" to the operator at the first contact of the day and a word of thanks when some special service has been performed are particularly important to a person tucked away in a small room, often alone for long hours. Informing the operator when you will be out and, if possible, getting someone to take calls is helpful. In this connection a central communications point is invaluable. Whenever an extension is not answered or is engaged the caller should be able to speak to someone who can take a message. A suitable central communications point may be reception (if this is not already too busy) or a secretary who is not overloaded with work. With the electronic telephone systems which automatically transfer unanswered calls from one extension to another on a circuit there is no reason why the last extension on the circuit should not be a communications point. In a large organisation it would be appropriate to have a communications point for each department or perhaps for each floor. Of course, the communications point must be manned all the time.

Answering incoming calls promptly also helps the operator to handle incoming traffic efficiently.

Costs

ATTITUDES

Most employees have no idea of the amount of the telephone bill either for the calls they make or for the calls made in their department. A few organisations which have installed electronic telephone systems are now producing monthly figures on departmental telephone costs. This makes it possible to include telephone charges as an item in the budget and therefore makes people more aware of the cost of a call. The charge clock mentioned on page 218 may help in this respect.

Cost consciousness should be included in any training programme.

MONITORING

Telephone accounts should be carefully scrutinised. Charges for calls made through the operator should be compared with the international and trunk call record book. Computer printouts (for electronic systems) should be scrutinised not only for charges but also for the duration of calls and to check whether the same numbers are called on the same day. Calling the same numbers twice may be necessary, but on the other hand may indicate lack of preparation of calls. The reasons for very long duration calls should be investigated if they occur frequently.

Where telephone costs can be charged to individual departments, budget variances should be produced monthly and major variances should be investigated. Unusually heavy telephone traffic may be justified in certain circumstances but the number of calls made can increase for no valid reason if the staff do not exercise strict self-discipline.

Advisory services

It is in the interests of British Telecom that subscribers should be satisfied. Although sales are important, whether in terms of rental or calls, it is equally important that subscribers have an efficient economic service if business is to be maintained and developed. British Telecom provides certain advisory services free of charge and it is worth making use of these when economies are necessary, when the existing telephone system becomes inadequate or when training is needed.

Another source of advice is the Telecommunications Managers Association of the Institute of Administrative Management (address: 205 High Street, Beckenham, Kent BR3 1BA) whose members have a vast fund of experience from which to give guidance related to various circumstances.

22. Other Telecommunications Services

In addition to the telephone there are a number of other telecommunications services. These are explained briefly in this chapter.

Teleprinter

A teleprinter is a machine which resembles a large typewriter with a telephone dial. The operator dials the number of the organisation to be contacted and, when a signal is received to indicate that the connection is made, types the message which is simultaneously reproduced on the distant teleprinter. (The answer-back code is transmitted automatically provided the machine is free.) The message is printed on a roll of paper, normally in duplicate. The completed message is torn off the roll using the perspex guide as a cutting edge. If there is an operator at the receiving end it is possible to have a "conversation" if necessary. Provided a machine is switched on it can receive messages at any time of the day or night without an operator in attendance. This is one of the major advantages of teleprinters.

To attract the attention of an operator on a receiving machine the transmitting operator can press a key marked "Bell" which operates a bell or buzzer on the receiving machine. This might be done if a question is being transmitted which the receiving operator can answer immediately.

Many teleprinters now have a punched tape attachment. The message is typed and reproduced on punched tape without being transmitted (Fig. 46 shows a specimen punched tape). After checking the copy, which is produced in the normal way, the punched tape is "fed through" the machine for transmission. This ensures the accuracy of the message and is faster. Transmission speed from typing is approximately 35 words per minute; from punched tape the speed is approximately 66 words per minute. Machines are being developed which will be able to transmit about 260 words per minute when linked to a computer.

Private teleprinter networks are installed within organisations, e.g. between branches of a company. It is possible to have a receiving-only teleprinter installed to obtain information from a central point, e.g. stock prices. In the U.K., many stockbrokers have a teleprinter service from the Stock Exchange which gives constant updating of prices.

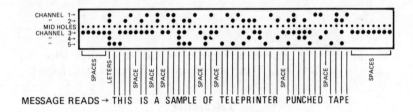

Fig. 46 *Specimen five-channel punched tape used in teleprinters.* The message is in the international punched tape code.

Apart from the time element and cost factor the teleprinter has the great advantage of providing a written copy and is used a great deal for orders between branches of an organisation, instructions, queries, etc.

Telex service

The telex services provided by British Telecom enable subscribers to rent one or more teleprinters so that they can contact other telex subscribers anywhere in the world (*see* Fig. 47). Direct dialling is possible to many countries. Transmission of messages is charged on a time basis—fast punched-tape transmission is therefore an advantage. The 24-hour service is especially useful when transmitting to countries with a wide time difference, e.g. the Far East. Telegrams can be sent by telex to British Telecom for onward transmission and can also be received on telex.

Telex users who have heavy traffice between two or more points can hire a private circuit from British Telecom. The telex system can also be linked to a computer for the transmission of data (*see* Chapter 40). The machine is then referred to as a "teleprinter terminal".

[*Courtesy British Telecom*

Fig. 47 *Telex machine available on rental from British Telecom.* The punched tape increases transmission speed from approximately 35 to 66 words per minute.

ADVANTAGES

Telex has the following advantages over the telephone.

(1) It is generally cheaper, though as tariffs change from time to time careful scrutiny of costs is necessary.

(2) The content is expressed in telegraphic style, saving the time of the originator and operator, as well as the cost of transmission.

(3) The written record can avoid costly mistakes which can occur orally.

(4) The distraction of a telephone call when one is in the middle of another task is avoided.

(5) When information is needed for an answer the caller does not have to "hold on" while it is being obtained.

(6) Messages cannot be extended into non-business discussions.

There are, however, times when discussion is necessary and the telephone is obviously the more suitable medium on these occasions.

TELEX LOCATION

The telex should not be located in the telephone exchange room. A teleprinter is noisy in operation and although noise can be reduced by enclosing the machine in a soundproof hood it still causes distraction for a telephone operator. If it is situated in a general office it must be enclosed in a soundproof hood, which can reduce operation noise by as much as 70 per cent.

The location must depend to a large extent on the arrangement which can be made for distribution of incoming messages and delivery of outgoing messages to the operator (*see* below). If a regular internal mail service is not available the telex must be situated as centrally as possible so that typists and secretaries are not obliged to waste expensive time walking to and from the telex room.

In a small organisation the telex may be operated by a secretary either in her own office or in a nearby telex room. In these circumstances it is usual for only very senior staff to be using the facility. In a large organisation this is unlikely to be the case and the location must be arranged for maximum efficiency in getting messages from and to the staff.

TELEX OPERATOR

The telex machine has a normal typewriting keyboard and any qualified typist can operate a telex after a few hours instruction (in the U.K. this can be provided by British Telecom's Telegraph Service). A high typewriting speed is not required—40 words per minute is adequate. However, accuracy is vital. If punched tape is used errors can be corrected but the operator *must* proof-read. Operators do not always take the trouble to query unintelligible messages with the originators—understandable when they are busy—but they must be encouraged to do so. Incidentally, it is important to stress here the need for very careful preparation of messages by the originator to avoid waste of the operator's time and confusion and frustration on the part of the recipient when the message does not make sense (*see also* below).

In a large organisation one or more full-time telex operators may be needed but in a small organisation it is normally a duty performed by a member of the secretarial staff. Under no circumstances should "anybody" be allowed to send messages. One person must be in charge both to collect incoming and to send outgoing messages. A trained relief operator must, of course, be available.

Essential qualities include a good standard of language, absolute discretion, patience, the ability to detect errors, and an alert mind. As for a telephone operator, a full induction programme is essential so that the telex operator can relate to departments and individuals when queries arise. The greater the operator's knowledge of the organisation the more likely it is that he or she will be able to pick up inaccuracies. A high standard must be insisted upon. Though relatively cheap, telex does still cost money. The accuracy and presentation of a telex message is just as important for the corporate image as a letter or telephone call. Faint printing ribbons and careless display are not acceptable.

In the U.K. British Telecom telegraph staff are very happy to give newly recruited telex operators the "once over" to ensure that they are operating correctly and producing texts in the correct format. This is a useful service to take advantage of even when the newly recruited operator has had previous training.

DISTRIBUTION OF INCOMING MESSAGES

It is essential to have a good back-up service with telephone/telex facilities. Incoming messages must be distributed as a matter of urgency. If there is a regular internal mail delivery service the messenger should include the telex room in his round. Incoming messages marked urgent should, however, receive special attention. The telex operator should telephone the addressee and either read the content or ask for collection of the message. If there is no internal mail delivery some means of delivering telex messages quickly must be devised.

Because telex is now being used a great deal more in place of telephone calls and letters there tends to be a lack of urgency in handling and processing the messages. Any message marked "urgent" should be dealt with immediately.

PREPARATION OF MESSAGES

Telex messages are composed in telegraphic style (*see* Chapter 24). The message should include the telex number to which it is to be transmitted (shown on the letterhead of the letter under reply or obtainable from the British Telecom Telex Directory for U.K. subscribers), the name of the organisation to be called and the name of the person or department to whom the message is addressed. It is important to ensure that the message is concise, but brevity should not take precedence over clarity. (A specimen telex message is shown in Fig. 48.)

Before the message is sent to the telex operator for transmission it should be checked for clarity (especially if handwritten) and accuracy (this applies especially to typewriting). Busy telex operators do not relish having to query illegible writing.

TRANSMISSION OF MESSAGES TO THE TELEX OPERATOR

There must be a system for transmission of messages to the operator. It must be decided whether any member of staff can originate a telex message or whether each message must be authorised. In view of the cost saving it seems unnecessary to insist on authorisation except for special reasons such as when the content deals with policy matters.

Messages should not be sent to the telex operator in batches, and peak traffic periods, particularly after 3.30 p.m., should be avoided. A special journey by a secretary to the telex room to deliver the message for transmission is costly. Unless there is great urgency the message should be delivered to the telex room by the internal mail service.

It is possible to have individual typewriters linked to the telex. When the typist produces the message on her typewriter the punched tape is produced by remote control on the telex. The telex operator then transmits the punched tape in the usual way. The linking of telex with word processors and computers is discussed in Chapters 28 and 40.

RECORDS OF MESSAGES

One copy of all incoming messages should be retained on a chronological master file in the telex room. If a duplicate copy is not produced on the telex machine a copy must be made.

A copy of each outgoing message should be sent to the originator and a copy should be filed on a chronological master file—separate from the incoming messages file.

```
MACKENZIE BIRMINGHAM
GREENIDGE BRISTOL


21-9-80        09.45 HRS      TLX 78632

ATTN MR PETER MAIN
------------------


FURTHER TO YOUR RECENT MEETING WITH OUR MR WRIGHT REGARDING
CARBURETTOR DELIVERIES THE FOLLOWING CARBURETTORS AND QUANTITIES
WILL BE REQUIRED BY END OF MONTH TO MAINTAIN AGREED SCHEDULE.

PART NO              QTY REQUIRED
-------              ------------

3451/1                   60

3451/3                   200

3451/6                   60

3453/2                   100

3453/4                   150


REGARDS
T E JOHNSON
CHIEF BUYER


HAS THE TELX COME THROUGH OK?
YES FINE THKS

OK BIBI

HANG ON SORI LAST LINE HAS DROPPED SHOULD IT BE AGREED SCHEDULE
YES THATS RIGHT
IS EVERYTHING ELSE CLEAR?

YES FINE I DIDNT SEE THAT AT FIRST
OK BIBI

GREENIDGE BRISTOL
MACKENZIE BIRMINGHAM
```

Fig. 48 *Specimen telex message*. Note the "conversation" at the end of the message.

Datel services

In the U.K. British Telecom provides a number of "datel" services
for the transmission of information into and out of computers
situated in computer centres.

A special input terminal is required for keying-in the information
to be processed by computer. The telephone, telex or telegraph line

must be of "suitable quality" to transmit the information from terminal to computer. The input is encoded for processing and decoded for retrieval/printout by a modem (modulator and demodulator).

Banks use the datel service for daily transmission of branch transactions to their computer centres where credits, debits, balances, etc. are stored till required. Sales organisations with a wide distribution network use datel services for information on stock.

Datel services are rented from British Telecom, the rental depending on the transmission speed required. The lowest speed by telephone is 200 bits per second. (A "bit" is a unit of information— see Chapter 39.) The fastest service is Datel 48K, i.e. 48,000 bits per second. Transmission by telex cannot exceed 50 bits per second, but a leased telegraph circuit can transmit at 110 bits per second.

Datel services are available throughout the U.K. and Europe, and, by satellite circuit, to Australia, Canada, Japan and Hong Kong.

Confravision

In certain large cities in the U.K. (London, Birmingham, Bristol, Glasgow and Manchester) it is possible to rent British Telecom television studios in which to hold meetings between groups of people in two or three different places. Each member of the groups sit in front of a microphone. Television screens are in view so that the speaker can see the people to whom he is talking (see Fig. 49). It is also possible to screen documents which may be important for technical meetings.

Although the cost of a confravision meeting is high, the cost of travel of one or two of the groups is saved, together with the cost of the people's time, which might be much more expensive than the studio rental charge. The meeting must be very well prepared to ensure maximum utilisation of studio time. Costs are based on distance.

Viewdata

Viewdata is operated by British Telecom in the U.K. under the registered name of "Prestel". It operates over a telephone line coupled to a television screen called a Prestel receiver. The subscriber "dials" for information by pressing a key on the keypad attached to the receiver. A wide range of information is held on the Prestel computer files, to which an index is held on the system

[*Courtesy British Telecom*

Fig. 49 *Confravision meeting.* A close-up of the T.V. screen showing the arrangement for a three-way "meeting".

itself. The information is provided by a large number of Information Providers (known as I.P.s) ranging from small specialist firms to large international organisations. Information, which is provided for local areas as well as nationally, includes news and weather, TV. and radio guide, sport, holidays, travel, hobbies, facts and figures, market place, buying advice, jobs and careers, Stock Exchange and Commodities, company and market information, manufacturing industry guide, service industry guide, reference information, government information, calculations and messages.

The cost of the Prestel service comprises the cost of the terminal, telephone calls at local charge rate, a very small British Telecom usage charge and an information charge, which depends on the type of information and/or the user involved.

Prestel may be connected to direct exchange lines, plans 1A, 4, 105, 107, P.A.B.X. with recall plan 4 and 1A.

Two other similar services, Ceefax and Oracle, are provided by the British Broadcasting Corporation and the Independent Television Companies' Association respectively. The information available on these teletext services is limited to a maximum of 800 pages per channel and is one-way, i.e. receiving, only. Prestel, however, has virtually unlimited information capacity and it is possible for users to send messages or respond to the computer.

Radio paging

British Telecom has developed a radio paging system which works on the same lines as the wireless call system explained on page 222. This extended paging service means that a telephone subscriber can be supplied with a pocket receiver which will be called from a Post Office telephone exchange. A person, e.g. a secretary, receiving an urgent message in the office can dial the paging code of her executive whose receiver will then "bleep". On receiving the "bleep" the subscriber would then call his own number for the message. It is also possible to have a coding system so that on hearing one bleep the subscriber calls, say, his office, and on hearing two bleeps his home. A doctor might have his surgery and the hospital as main contacts.

It is expected that this system will operate within two years in the south of England, as Solent Radio Paging. If this pilot scheme is successful it would be extended to other areas. Ultimately there could be a national paging, which would mean that contact could be made with people anywhere in the country.

23. Mail Handling Systems

Communications are generated in the industrial or works offices as well as in the administrative offices. The volume and type of communication varies from office to office and the times of highest output are likely to be different from one part of the organisation to another. The basic precept for developing a sound mail handling system is to collect the communication from the place of orgination and deliver it to its destination with minimum delay at minimum cost.

Collection and delivery

EXTERNAL

In the U.K. the Post Office offers the facility of a Post Office box or Private Bag. In this case the mail has to be collected from the Post Office. This is useful if mail is required early so that it can be sorted and distributed before or soon after opening time.

The normal mail delivery service is also available, of course, and large organisations may find it useful to have the mail pre-sorted into departments by the Post Office staff. Organisations which normally receive more than twenty letters a day have an individual postcode.

Similarly, outgoing stamped mail may be posted in a post-box, while franked mail may be taken to the Post Office or collected once or twice a day by Post Office mail-van. A docket is completed for each collection. Arrangements can be made for special collections of outgoing parcels as the need arises. Incidentally, it is helpful to the Post Office if they are warned of unusually large volumes of outgoing mail when these occur only occasionally.

INTERNAL

Large organisations usually have an internal messenger service, ranging from several employees employed exclusively on this work to a junior who incorporates collection and delivery of mail with other duties. A precise route and time schedule must be laid down based on postal times, volume of communications in the various offices and times of heavy output. Offices which generate little correspondence can be visited less frequently. Time schedules must be strictly adhered to and proper supervision is needed to ensure the smooth running of the service.

Messengers may be provided with satchels, baskets or skips for mail. Delivery time for internal communications can be reduced to a minimum by messengers sorting internal mail as they collect it and delivering at offices *en route*.

COLLECTION OF MAIL

Where there is central control of outgoing mail, mail should be collected as often as possible throughout the day so that congestion will be avoided at the end of the day. To ensure that correspondence is completed in time for the last collection of the day, a deadline, say 4.30 p.m., should be fixed after which post will not be accepted for posting that day. The time fixed should be related to the closing time of the office, and the latest time which will ensure post reaches the nearest Head Post Office by 7.00 p.m. to allow delivery of first-class mail at its destinations by 9.00 a.m. the next day (the delivery time which can normally be expected in large cities in the U.K.).

An alternative to a messenger service is for a member of the clerical or secretarial staff in each section or department to collect and deliver mail to a mailroom at intervals during the day. However, this can be time-consuming and frustrating when a particular item needing urgent attention is expected, as constant checking in the mailroom is then necessary.

INTERNAL MECHANICAL DELIVERY

Communications may have to be sent very frequently between certain offices or departments. There are various kinds of mechanical conveyances including internal lifts, overhead wires, gravity belts, conveyor belts and pneumatic tubes.

Mechanical systems are expensive but are particularly useful where documents have to be conveyed at frequent but irregular intervals, where messengers cannot be easily recruited, where space is limited for the passage of messengers, or where security demands limited access.

Incoming mail

Every office receives mail each day, and the method of dealing with it may have a great effect on the general efficiency of the office. Incoming mail should be properly supervised and not left to a junior member of staff.

The first thing to be decided is whether all incoming post for all departments should be opened, or whether it should be passed unopened to the various departments to be dealt with by them. The saving of departmental staff time if all mail is opened in the central registry may be offset by delay in distributing the mail. In some departments this may be a crucial factor. Consequently the system depends on the structure of the organisation, staff availability in appropriate locations and the time factor.

ARRANGEMENTS FOR OPENING THE MAIL

The morning mail is normally the heaviest. Arrangements should be made so that when the office opens for business the post, or the bulk of it, will already have been opened, sorted and distributed, ready for the attention of the staff concerned. It is usual for some of the office staff to come early each day (say half an hour to one hour), for which they receive either time in lieu or special payment. A senior person should also be present to supervise the opening (particularly where cash is received) and to deal with the "queries".

SORTING

The primary sorting may be done before the envelopes are opened. All envelopes marked personal or addressed to individuals or departmental heads, and classified mail (private, confidential or secret) are sorted into departments. Envelopes addressed to the company are placed in one pile for opening. The mail already sorted into departments is then placed ready for delivery to departmental secretaries. The general mail is then opened (*see* below) and sorted into departments for distribution.

Alternatively all mail, other than personal or classified material, may be opened before distribution, but as it is easier to sort envelopes than sheets of paper it is advisable to open the envelopes after the primary sorting.

Secondary sorting involves placing the documents in order of priority. Unopened personal mail is usually placed on top of the pile, followed by opened letters marked "urgent", unopened classified mail, other documents, and finally circulars and printed material at the bottom of the pile. This secondary sorting is normally done by departmental clerical staff or secretaries.

PRIVATE MAIL

Many firms do not allow incoming letters to be addressed to individuals as a prevention against fraud. This is a matter of policy which should be clearly laid down. From the correspondent's point of view it may be useful to know the name of the person who is dealing with a business matter, particularly in a large department, but a letter addressed personally may be held up for weeks if that person is absent from the office. A note on outgoing letters asking correspondents to quote a reference containing the originator's initials should enable the mail-receiving clerk to route incoming letters correctly. Another method is to ask for letters to be marked "For the attention of Mr. X".

OPENING THE MAIL

With a small post, letters will be opened by hand, but when a hundred or more letters are received a letter-opening machine can be installed; this will either halve or quarter the time spent on the job, according to whether a hand-operated or electrically operated machine is used. Both types of machine have a revolving knife edge which slices a very thin piece off the side of the envelope; it is advisable to shake the contents to the other side of the envelopes first!

REMOVING THE CONTENTS

When the contents of the envelopes are removed the envelopes should be checked to ensure that they are empty before throwing them away. Some organisations have a clerk specially detailed to check empty envelopes, while others keep the envelopes for a day or so before throwing them away. Another method is to have a lighted panel fixed in the centre of a table. The empty envelopes are passed over the panel to see that they are empty before being thrown away. In this way many postal orders and cheques un-attached to letters may be saved from the waste-paper basket!

Most correspondents indicate "Enclosures" or "Encs." at the bottom of their letters, and it is essential that this should be checked and ticked (e.g. with a coloured pencil) to ensure that the contents are in fact there and enclosures are attached. If enclosures are not attached, they should be fastened to the back of the letter. If the enclosure is missing a note to this effect should be made on the letter and initialled.

CASH MAIL

Registered mail should first be dealt with by the supervisor in charge and should always be recorded in a register kept for that purpose. Many businesses receive postal orders and cheques in the normal post and some clearly laid-down procedure should be adhered to, not only as a protection against theft, but also as a safeguard for the cashier's protection.

A simple method is to ensure that all remittance advices (or a special "cash received note") are ticked and initialled by the post opener, all the amounts either entered in a book, or listed on an adding machine, and the list passed to the firm's cashier with the amounts of money. A signature should be obtained from the cashier for the total.

As a further precaution, a copy of this list of remittances should be compared with the bank paying-in slip for the day. These remittance advice notes may be passed to another clerk to write out the receipt if a manual system is used.

RECORDING INCOMING MAIL

All letters should be rubber-stamped with the date and perhaps with the time of receipt. The time of receipt might be of importance where, for example, a letter was not received until late one afternoon and therefore not dealt with until the following morning.

Some organisations which have a central mail registry keep an inwards mail register (see Fig. 50). This is becoming less common

No.	Date	Name of Sender	Nature of contents	Dept. sent to	Date answered	Date ret'd to file
1	JAN 1	BROWN AND CO.	LETTER	ORDER D.	JAN. 2	
2	" 1	PEAK & JOHNSON	INVOICE	ACCOUNTS	—	
3	" 1	WRIGHT AND CO.	LETTER & CHEQUE	CASHIER	JAN. 2	

Fig. 50 *Specimen inwards mail register.*

because of the time factor but is sometimes retained by individual departments or secretaries as a means of keeping track of correspondence.

READING THE MAIL

An incoming letter can be directed quickly and easily to the right destination provided the reference on the letter under reply is quoted. Correspondents do not always quote these reference letters (which may also incorporate a file number), and some organisations prefer to use adhesive labels on their outgoing letters on which are entered the reference letters. The adhesive label is detached by the correspondent and affixed to his reply, thus aiding the subsequent sorting.

There are always letters about which there is some question as to who should deal with them, and a special box for such "queries" should be maintained for the supervisor's attention.

LETTERS FOR MORE THAN ONE PERSON

Every business receives letters which are the concern of more than one person or department, and some method should be adopted to ensure that they are seen by the people concerned. In a small office the names of the people or departments might be written at the top of the letter; in a larger office special rubber stamps, adhesive labels, or copying might be used.

A rubber stamp suitable for use in an office of a dozen or so staff and which could incorporate a date stamp is shown in Fig. 51.

19th March 19—7					
J. D. E. W. L. M. E. R. S. T. B. W. A. P.			P. R. T. E. G. T. W. D. F.		

Fig. 51 *Rubber stamp for letter circulation.*

Ticks are written in the first column against the initials of the people to see the letters, who should initial in the second column to signify that they have seen or dealt with the letter. Printed adhesive labels which can be attached to the top of the letter might be used in a similar way.

The disadvantage of all of these methods is that although they ensure that the letter is seen by the various people concerned, they do not avoid delay in those people dealing with the letter. To overcome this, such letters can be copied, a number of copies being distributed simultaneously to the office staff concerned.

ROUTINE

In an office of a large concern it is advisable if a routine is laid down for dealing with inwards mail. A specimen routine for dealing with 1,000–2,500 letters is given below.

POST OPENING AND HANDLING OF CASH

(1) All mail is opened three-quarters of an hour before the office opens, and a staff of six clerks and a junior with a supervisor will be designated from time to time.

(2) Unopened mail is sorted into four categories: General; Representatives; Specials; Works.

(3) All envelopes not marked Personal, Private, Confidential or Secret are opened by letter-opening machine.

(4) The contents are removed from all opened envelopes and empty envelopes are checked.

(5) The contents are checked for correct addressee and enclosures, which if loose are attached. Missing enclosures are noted.

(6) All contents are passed to the supervisor, who enters currency and other money in the book provided, initials book, and underlines amount on remittance paper in green pencil.

(7) All cheques, etc. are passed to "Marker" to endorse amount on letter, etc. and to rubber-stamp the cheques with firm's crossing stamp.

(8) All cheques, etc. are passed to cashier immediately his office opens.

(9) All mail is time- and date-stamped, preferably near the date, and sorted into sections.

(10) Juniors take mail to different departments by 15 minutes after office opens.

(11) Destinations of letters which are in doubt are decided by the supervisor.

Outgoing mail

Every organisation sends out post each day, and a good office system ensures that it is sent in the most economical and efficient manner. This aspect of communications needs as much attention as any other.

Even in small firms there is advantage in routeing all outgoing mail through one person or department: in larger concerns a post registry is set up for central control, which fixes responsibility. Expenditure on postage stamps is controlled and postal clerks gain proficiency in postage rates. The last point is of particular importance where foreign mail is involved. One particular economy is that letters from different offices addressed to the same addressee can be sent in one envelope instead of each letter being posted separately. Labels can be used for regular addressees. (Batches can be prepared on an addressing machine, word processor or computer.)

It is useful to divide outwards mail procedures into the various steps which are dealt with below.

FOLDING OF LETTERS

Typists should be supplied with the correct-sized envelopes (*see* Chapter 47) and they or the mail clerk should be taught to fold letters properly. The appearance of outgoing letters is improved by the absence of creases, so an envelope which requires the minimum folds in the letter should be used.

Where a large number of letters of identical size are to be folded, a folding machine can be used. This can automatically fold letters in one, two, or three parallel folds with additional numbers of cross-folds, at a speed of up to 15,000 sheets an hour.

PREPARATION OF ENVELOPES

It is usual for the envelopes to be typed at the same time as the letters. They are then sent with the letters when forwarded for signature, or are retained until the signed letters are returned to be prepared for despatch.

A great saving in time and prevention of letters being sent to wrong addresses can be achieved by the use of aperture or window envelopes. Where window envelopes are used, it is important that stationery should be carefully designed to fit them. There should be printed "box corners" to position the name and address of the recipient, and it is useful if there are fold marks printed down one edge of the paper.

Envelopes can be addressed by machine where communications are regularly sent to the same addressees, e.g. credit customers, committee members or shareholders (*see* Chapter 31 for addressing machines).

For quick delivery by the Post Office it is essential to ensure that the envelope has the *full* and *correct* address, *including the postcode*.

SORTING OF MAIL

All outgoing post is sorted according to the denomination of the stamping required. Time can be saved by placing mail ready for despatch in individual bags or boxes. This helps to avoid mistakes, makes it easier to calculate the postage and speeds up the stamping/franking process. In most organisations in the U.K., inland letters are sent by second-class mail unless "first class" is indicated on the envelope, or on the letter if mail is enveloped by the mail clerk.

Bearing in mind the cost of a letter (*see* page 280) it is worth considering whether the extra fee for first-class delivery may not be worth while to ensure quick delivery.

It is worth checking the frequency of flights to overseas countries and determining the days for posting. (In the U.K. there is not a daily flight service to every overseas country.) Letters for countries without daily flights can then be retained until the posting time to allow letters to the same addressee to be collated into one envelope.

Also important in saving airmail postal charges is the use of printed paper rate whenever practicable. Items within this category are listed in the *Post Office Guide* (*see* page 269). They include advertisements, illustrations, newspapers, periodicals, printed drawings, prospectuses, catalogues, maps, pamphlets, printed notices and books.

SEALING AND STAMPING

The sealing of a larger number of envelopes can be a very tedious job, and a sealing machine can be obtained where it is justified. Even for a small number it is useful to have a sponge and water bowl, and to overlap the gummed flaps so that a large number can be dampened at the same time.

Small offices without franking machines usually maintain a stamp folder, with sheets of stamps of different denominations in between manilla pages. The disadvantages of this are that loose stamps are easily lost, and it is a lengthy process to calculate the stamps in hand.

There is available a stamp folder which has perforated pages, so that the number of stamps can be seen at a glance through the perforations; in addition, the pages have printed on them the progressive values of different numbers of stamps in hand under each page. Alternatively, it is possible to use stamp-emitting machines in which rolls of stamps are inserted and the number used is recorded on a dial. It is necessary to have a separate machine for each denomination of stamp used.

POSTAL FRANKING

The manufacturers of franking machines claim that a minimum daily post of fifty is sufficient to warrant the use of a franking machine. A postal franker is a machine which prints on an envelope the design of a postage stamp and a date cancellation mark. A lever is set on the machine for the rate of postage required, and when letters are fed into it they are ejected suitably stamped and dated.

Larger packets and parcels are franked by means of adhesive tape which is inserted in the machine and franked for the required amount, torn off the reel, removed from the backing and stuck on to the envelope or parcel.

The makers of the machine obtain a licence in the buyer's name from the Post Office, and when the machine is delivered to the firm the meter has to be taken to the local post office, where payment is made in advance for an agreed total of postage. As the machine is used, it records on a dial the amount of money expended on franking (the machine adds the postage as it is used). The recording meter on the machine is set by the Post Office so that only the number of stamps paid for can be used, after which it locks itself and must be taken back to them with a further cheque as pre-payment.

Some types of franking machine operate on the basis of a kind of "credit card" which is bought at the Post Office. This obviates the need to take the meter for "recharging".

Advantages of postal franking.

(1) Speed is the main advantage; on a hand-operated machine, up to 2,000 letters an hour may be franked, while an electrical machine may deal with as many as 15,000 an hour.

(2) Security is of vital importance where many thousands of stamps would have to be used; a franking machine obviates the keeping of large stocks of stamps of all denominations.

(3) Expenditure on postage may be more easily controlled, and the total expenditure since the last payment to the Post Office can be read off the meter at any time.

(4) Convenience: for example, the need for repeated balancing of a post book is eliminated.

(5) Despatch of mail: because franked mail does not have to be date-stamped by the Post Office, it can be more quickly dealt with than ordinary mail put in the post-box.

(6) The cost of printing on envelopes may be saved, e.g. "Return to X Co. Ltd." can be incorporated in the franking.

Disadvantages of postal franking.

(1) Juniors may waste postage by franking the wrong amounts.

(2) If no post book is used, a franking machine may be more easily used for private mail.

(3) It may be viewed as a slight disadvantage that franked mail has to be taken to the Post Office every day, instead of being dropped in the public post-box (unless the volume is sufficient to warrant collection by Post Office van).

(4) It may be claimed that the need for keeping a post book as a record of outgoing mail is not eliminated.

(5) Even with a franking machine, it is still necessary to have loose stamps for "after hours" posting, receipt stamps, and for urgent letters.

ENTERING IN THE POST BOOK

Many offices keep a post book as a record of outgoing mail, as a check on postage expenditure, and as a check on the balance of stamps in hand. Post books with standard printing can be obtained from stationers. These have separate columns for names and addresses of addressees, but, in practice, the town only is inserted in the address column. A specimen ruling of a post book is shown in Fig. 52.

Date	Received	Date	Name	Address	Amount
Jan. 1	10.00	Jan. 1	Brown Co.	London	09
		" 1	46 Invoices at 7p		3.22

Fig. 52 *Specimen post book.*

The imprest system, the technique often used to keep a petty cash book, is the usual method of keeping the post book. A fixed sum of money (£10 in the example) is given to last, say, a week. At the end of the week an amount equivalent to the week's expenditure is given, which once again restores the fixed amount for the following week. It will be noticed that there are two sides to the post book, a receipt and an expenditure side, and the difference between the amounts entered on these two sides should always equal the balance of stamps in hand, or the amount of credit registered on the franking machine.

Postal services

There are many postal services available in the U.K. Full details are given in the *Post Office Guide* (*see* below). A few of the main facilities are listed in the table below, with an indication of the special use of each.

Inland mail.
First-class inland mail   When delivery is essential within 48 hours.

Second-class inland mail	Normal delivery—may take up to four days.

Security.

Recorded delivery	Proof of sending and delivery. Compensation for loss up to the value of £2 on letters and packets.
Registration	Proof of sending and delivery of any first-class letter. Compensation for loss up to a maximum of £600 depending on the fee paid.
Compensation fee (C.F.)	Compensation for loss of goods sent by parcel post up to a maximum of £200 depending on the fee paid.
Insurance	Available to countries to which mail cannot be registered. Compensation for loss up to a maximum of £600 depending on the fee paid.

Urgency.

Express delivery	Delivered by special messenger if the letter is received at the sorting office outside normal postal delivery hours.
Special messenger	Delivered by special messenger all the way.
Railway letter	Handed in at nearest railway station and sent by next passenger train, to be collected at the station by the addressee or posted in area of destination. First-class postage plus a railway fee.
Airway letter	Handed in at certain airports or air terminals to be sent by next direct flight, to be collected at the airport or air terminal or posted by the airline. First-class postage plus an airline fee.
Railex	Delivery of any unregistered packet by special messenger to the nearest railway station, collection by messenger from nearest railway station to destination and delivery either direct to addressee or to delivery office during normal working hours.

Nightrider

Overnight delivery of parcels in an area stretching from Egham in the west to Gravesend in the east, and from Croydon in the south to Enfield in the north is now available in the London Postal Region to organisations needing to send goods regularly. Charges are negotiated on the basis of operating costs, not solely on weight. (Details from Marketing and Customer Services Division, London Postal Region, 148–66 Old Street, London ECN 9HQ, tel. 01–278 9395.)

Datapost—inland

An overnight door-to-door delivery service within the United Kingdom for packages of any kind. A contract is negotiated with the Post Office for a regular service on a daily, weekly or monthly basis or for a schedule of dates.

Datapost "D"—inland

Available to senders with irregular demand for the service. Payment of an initial annual contract fee allows datapost packages to be handed in at a nominated posting centre at any time.

Datapost—overseas

Next-day delivery available to U.S.A. (by Concorde on Tuesdays and Fridays providing same day delivery for Central New York), Brazil, France, the Netherlands and Belgium.

Second day after collection delivery to Australia, Argentina, Kuwait.

Third day after collection delivery to Hong Kong, Japan, Singapore. (Delivery may be earlier for packages posted in London.)

Business papers may be sent to all the countries listed, merchandise may be sent to Australia, Hong Kong, the Netherlands and Singapore only.

Datapost "D"—overseas   A demand service for irregular data-post service. Not available to all countries.

NOTE: The datapost overseas service is gradually being extended so organisations requiring this service to a country not listed should check with the Post Office.

Bulk.

Parcel collection   Regular or special collection of parcels by the Post Office from the sender can be arranged. A minimum number of parcels is stipulated for free collection—20 for regular collection, 100 for special collection. A fee is charged for smaller quantities.

Second-class letters posted in bulk   When a minimum of 4,251 second-class letters of identical shape and size are posted at the same time by the same sender a special rebate on the postage is allowed. This does not apply to addresses in the Irish Republic, Channel Islands or Isle of Man.

Prepayment for Post Office franking   Letters requiring identical postage and prepared in bundles of 60 can be handed into the Post Office with the appropriate amount of postage. The Post Office will then frank the letters.

Licensed services.

Licences to use the services outlined below must be obtained from the Head Postmaster.

Business reply service   First- or second-class letters or cards may be received from senders without prepayment of postage. The envelopes or cards have to be printed in the style required by the Post Office and include the licence number. For each item a fee of ½p is charged to the licensee in addition to the postage.

Freepost   Similar to the business reply service but the sender uses a plain envelope or card and addresses it to FREEPOST plus a postcode. A fee of $\frac{1}{2}$p in addition to the postage is payable by the licensee.

Postage forward parcel service

The sender may despatch a parcel without paying postage, which is paid with an additional fee by the addressee.

There are two services which may be valuable to an organisation which has a large volume of outgoing mail. By arrangement with the Head Postmaster it is possible to have a Post Office sorter on the premises. This speeds up the processing at the Post Office sorting office.

Secondly, a Postal Services Representative is available for consultation at every Head Post Office. His advice can be sought on means to obtain the most suitable, efficient and economic postal service for the organisation.

Post Office directories

POST OFFICE GUIDE

The *Post Office Guide,* issued annually, contains full details of the facilities offered by the Post Office including postal services, telecommunications, giro, etc. It gives guidance as well as regulations and is a valuable reference book. By completing the post-paid card provided with the *Guide*, supplements can be received throughout the year. The *Guide* is available at main post offices for a small charge.

POSTCODE DIRECTORIES

Business organisations can obtain copies of the postcode directories covering the United Kingdom free of charge from the local Head Post Office. These directories are useful for ensuring that address lists include the postcodes.

DIRECTORY OF POSTAL ADDRESSES

The addresses for over 20,000 places in the United Kingdom are given in the Directory of Postal Addresses.

LONDON POST OFFICES AND STREETS

This is a directory giving the address of every Post Office in London and a list of streets.

Mailroom layout and equipment

The size and arrangement of the mailroom and equipment provided depends on the size and locations of sections of the organisation serviced and the volume of mail to be handled. In a small to medium organisation all incoming and outgoing mail including parcels may be handled. In a large organisation it is usual for parcels to be dealt with either in a special mailroom or by the despatch department.

LAYOUT
Space is needed for:
   (1) work surfaces for receiving mail and for machines;
   (2) bag racks, skips, trays or baskets for sorted outgoing mail;
   (3) pigeon-holes, trays, baskets or wire mesh systems for sorted mail for internal delivery;
   (4) a tray or basket for private, stamped mail;
   (5) movement of mailroom personnel.

All sorting stations, baskets, etc. must be properly labelled. The layout is determined by the flow of mail, internal and external, by the location of doors and windows, and by the number of staff and their area of responsibility. The flow of incoming and outgoing mail is illustrated in Figs. 53(a) and 53(b). A typical mailroom layout in a large organisation is shown in Fig. 53(c).

EQUIPMENT
Equipment can range from a paper knife and a sponge for damping envelopes and stamps, to a complete battery of machines that will handle every operation in the mailroom except sorting. Machines available include the following.

Weighscales—letter and parcel. These can be obtained with faces to show weights only or weights and charges (time-saving when a lot of overseas mail is involved).

Letter-opener: envelope slitters or guillotines are available.

Mail-sorter: sorts incoming mail into sizes at speeds up to 30,000 an hour; can also open mail.

Franking machine: with a meter or using a "credit card" (*see* page 264). Available for various thicknesses and sizes of envelope. Can also seal and stack franked letters.

Folding and inserting machines.

Lightbox (can be home-made) for checking that used envelopes are empty.

Self-adhesive labelling machine to stick computer-produced labels on envelopes.

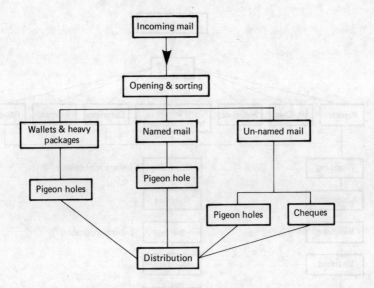

Fig. 53(a) *Typical incoming mail flow*.

Addressing machine: a wide variety are available from the small hand-operated spirit duplicating system to a fully computerised system which includes address selection and updating facilities (*see* Chapter 31).

Many of the machines can be "banked" to feed letters on from one operation to another. It must be stressed that most machines, apart from the franking and small addressing machines, are economically worth while only for large-volume mail.

Staff

The necessity for training mailroom staff should not be overlooked. Induction training aimed at steadily increasing the mail clerk's knowledge of the organisation and its functions, departments and staff is essential. The Post Office conducts local one-day mailroom courses which include information on the services available and how to use them and many aspects of day-to-day postal operations. The course includes a visit to a Post Office sorting office. Everyone can become stale, and services are constantly being improved/superseded/expanded, so it is useful for mailing staff to attend such a course perhaps every two or three years as a refresher.

The mailroom is also an excellent training ground for young new

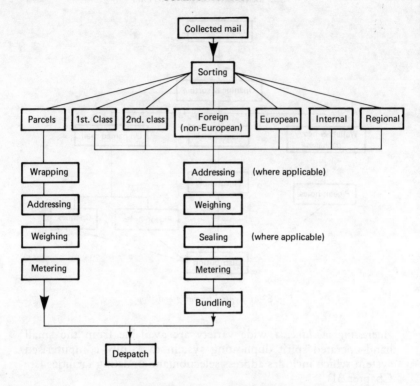

Fig. 53(b) *Typical outgoing mail flow.*

recruits. From that vantage point it is possible to obtain a "bird's eye view" of the organisation which will prove valuable to the employee wherever he may ultimately find his niche in the organisation. A short "stint" in the mailroom might usefully be included in all induction training programmes if this can be arranged without disruption of the mail service.

Costs

Mail costs money as does every other means of communication. Consequently, ways of minimising expenditure should be sought. There is no point in economising in ways which will lead to delays (unless tolerable) or time consumption of highly paid staff. Rather it is necessary to ensure that staff are aware of the ways in which they can co-operate with mailroom staff and minimise costs.

An additional thought on the question of costs is that while the Post Office has a monopoly of letter mail services (it is illegal to

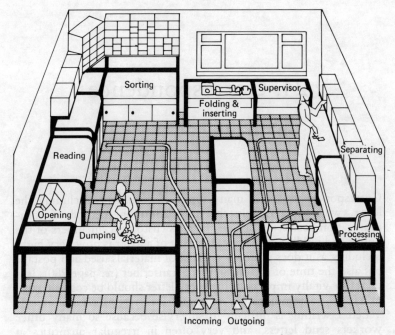

[*Courtesy Pitney Bowes Ltd.*]

Fig. 53(*c*) *Typical mailroom layout in a large organisation to ensure systematic physical progression of mail as it is processed.*

send letters by any other means for which payment has to be made)★ it does not have a monopoly of parcel services. It is worth investigating other carriers and comparing services and charges with similar areas available from the Post Office. It must be pointed out, however, that the Post Office has a very wide range of services to meet individual needs.

Internal mail, i.e. between companies, branches, etc., may be transmitted more cheaply, or more frequently at no greater cost, by the organisation's own transport. In organisations where staff are constantly travelling between locations there could be a regulation that itineraries should be notified to the mailroom so that mail can be sent at no cost at all.

★ The possible ending of this monopoly is under discussion.

24. Correspondence

Correspondence covers many types of document, including the letter, which is probably the most common method of communication between a business and its customers, members of the public and public authorities. The cost of a letter is now very high, including as it does not only the cost of materials used and postage but also the time of the dictater and transcriber (*see* page 280). It is therefore vitally important that every letter should be cost-effective in terms of communicating efficiently and creating a good image.

Letter writing is difficult to supervise because so many office workers send letters, and very often in irregular quantities at irregular intervals. Nevertheless, the task of the office manager is to get the necessary letters written well, and to prevent the writing of unnecessary ones.

Types of correspondence

Business letters may be formal or informal. The latter is becoming generally accepted and it is rare to see an "official" letter, which is likely to be used only in correspondence with a government department, for example, perhaps about a matter of policy or in connection with a contract.

Formal letters begin "Dear Sir" or "Dear Madam" and end "Yours faithfully".

The more personalised business letter begins "Dear Mr. Jones" and ends "Yours sincerely". In some types of business, notably insurance and shipping, "Yours truly" may still be used. Letters between professional offices, such as accountants and solicitors, and their clients may end "Kind regards, Yours sincerely".

Letters between managers of similar level in different organisations are often "semi-personal", i.e. begin "Dear Bob" and end "Yours sincerely" or "Yours ever".

INDIVIDUAL LETTER

A reply to a correspondent or a letter originating an enquiry or discussion must be prepared and presented so as to convey in precise and complete detail what the writer needs to say to enable the reader fully to understand the content. An individual letter is very susceptible to the pitfalls which create a bad impression because it is a "one off". Poor construction, spelling and typographical errors, verbosity, ambiguity, etc. soon dispel any illusions the reader may have had about the organisation's efficiency. On the other hand, a perfectly presented, easily understood letter can be an invaluable "aid to trade".

The main types of business letter include enquiries, replies to enquiries including estimates and quotations, orders for goods/services, acknowledgments, covering letters (enclosing a cheque for example), complaints, replies to complaints, confirmations of discussions or telegrams, letters asking for information and letters giving information.

STANDARD LETTERS

Where correspondence is concerned with standard situations, e.g. non-delivery of orders or enquiries for information about products, it is useful to have a set of standard or prepared paragraphs for reproduction. The typist and the dictater are supplied with a set of standard paragraphs which are numbered. The dictater then quotes the numbers of the paragraphs he wishes to use and dictates any additional details.

Standard letters are now frequently reproduced on automatic typewriters and word-processing machines (*see* Chapter 28).

FORM LETTER OR POSTCARD

A form letter is a pre-printed letter used to answer all correspondence of a similar and recurring nature, when the same information is required by a number of correspondents. A typical example of the use of form letters is in debt collection, where special letters are sent at fixed intervals. They are often numbered serially to denote the stage in the collection. Form letters are also used for acknowledging complaints, applications for employment, orders, and requests for prices or delivery dates. The details individual to each addressee, such as name and address, dates, amounts, etc., are the only typing required. There are many advantages in using form letters. The time of the dictater and the typist is saved; all letters of a similar nature are in the same style and form; correspondence is answered more quickly; and the cost of outgoing mail is reduced. On the other hand, form letters may be stilted and may not be sympathetic to individual cases, and because they lack the personal touch, their value may be discounted by their recipients.

When drafting form letters to suit a particular office, all outgoing letters should be studied over a period of, say, four weeks, after which the types of letter most frequently written can be analysed. The best reply can then be selected or drafted, standardised, and printed as a form letter. Form letters should follow the basic principles of good letter writing in the same way as individual letters. Construction, clarity and presentation should be faultless.

BLITZ REPLY

The answer is written on the original letter which is stamped to indicate that this method is being used to speed up the process of replying. The letter is photocopied, the original being returned to the sender and the photocopy being filed.

This method certainly speeds up the process but may tend to leave the recipient feeling "brushed off". It is not recommended except in cases of great urgency when a "proper" reply cannot possibly be prepared in time, or for internal use between branches/companies.

MEMORANDUM

A memorandum (or minute in government organisations) is used between offices within an organisation. It should conform to the basic principles of good letter writing (see below) and should be brief and "to the point". A memo can be "personalised" by signing it in full rather than initialling. There is no salutation or complimentary close.

RETURN MEMO SET

This is a set of three carbonised sheets on which messages can be typed or handwritten. The originator writes/types on the left-hand half of the sheet, retains the third copy and sends the top two sheets to the addressee. The reply is written/typed on the right-hand half of the sheet, the top copy is retained and the carbon copy returned to the originator. This is a very quick and easy method of getting answers to straightforward questions. The advantages over a telephone enquiry are that the addressee is not disturbed at an inappropriate moment and the originator does not have to "hold the line" while the addressee seeks the information required. In addition, when the originator receives the reply his original question is on the same sheet of paper.

MEMOGRAM

Used within an organisation, normally between offices or branches, a memogram is a memorandum written in telegraphic style. It could be regarded as a telex but is sent through the post (internal if available) when there is no necessity for it to be received immediately. It would normally be used where a straightforward memorandum would be rather long, thus saving the time of the dictater and the typist.

TELEGRAMS, TELEPRINTER AND TELEX MESSAGES

Brevity is the key note of messages sent by telegraph and telecommunications media, but it should not be at the expense of clarity. An additional word to ensure clarity will cost more, but an incomprehensible message is a total waste. Omission of a reference, for example, can make the missive totally meaningless.

The use of telegraphic addresses or telephone numbers in place of full addresses is a valuable economy in telegrams.

When sending telex messages avoid the peak period, which is normally between 3 p.m. and 4 p.m., and try to avoid sending "batches" of messages. They will be sent more quickly if the telex operator has only a small number to deal with.

Many organisations are now using telex messages in place of letters because there is relatively little difference in the cost, and delivery is immediate. A telex message is cheaper than a telephone call and has the advantage of giving a written copy to both the sender and the recipient.

Telegrams can be transmitted to and received from British Telecom by telephone and telex.

Good letter writing

A good letter is one which expresses clearly what has to be said, so that it is understood in a favourable way, i.e. so that favourable action is taken on it. A business letter should be *brief*, without being curt, *friendly*, without being familiar, *firm*, without being discourteous, and *positive*, by being helpful.

IMPROVING THE STANDARD OF LETTER WRITING

There are three ways in which the office manager may control letter writing in his department. He can:

(1) carry out a "spot check" on letters written by members of staff;

(2) hold regular conferences of the staff, in order to analyse the style of letters sent out and to suggest improvements;

(3) issue correspondence manuals setting out standard practices and instructions so as to ensure uniformity throughout the department/organisation. It is essential to explain to all members of staff the purpose of such a manual.

When checking letters written by staff the following check-list may be helpful.

(1) Does the letter have a beginning, a middle and an end? (The beginning is usually a reference to a letter, advertisement, etc. The end should point the way ahead, i.e. indicate what is to happen next.)

(2) Is the information accurate, up to date and complete?

(3) Does the tone give the right impression?

(4) Is it concise?

(5) Is it clear?

(6) Is it easy to read, i.e. are the sentences and words short and simple? Is jargon avoided (see below)?

(7) Does it conform to the house style?

REFERENCE BOOKS

There are many good reference books which can be used when one is in doubt about some detail of structure or usage in the English language.

A brief list is given below.

> *The Complete Plain Words*, Sir Ernest Gowers, Penguin Books 1970.
>
> *Thesaurus*, P. M. Roget, Penguin Books 1970.
>
> *Modern English Usage*, H. W. Fowler, Oxford University Press 1965.
>
> *An ABC of English Usage*, H. A. Treble and G. H. Vallins, Oxford University Press 1974.
>
> *Usage and Abusage,* Eric Partridge, Penguin Books 1970.

The Complete Plain Words by Sir Ernest Gowers gives excellent advice on how to avoid the use of commercial jargon, which is, or ought to be, now taboo, and other difficult aspects of letter writing, such as the composition of opening sentences.

PLANNING A LETTER

Successful letter writing is the result of careful planning. First of all, the writer should read through the letter to be answered and underline the main points in it; decide on the purpose of the letter to be sent in reply; note the main points to be included; obtain any information required; and check all relevant facts. Finally, before starting to draft or dictate, the writer should try to visualise the reader and assess his reaction to the letter. The reply should be prepared in an appropriate style and tone.

Methods of input for production

There are several methods by which the content of a letter can be transmitted from the originator to the typist. The method chosen depends to some extent on the facilities available and to some extent on the content of the letter.

(1) *Drafting in manuscript.* This method should be used only for very important or difficult letters, or letters containing a great deal of technical content, and not for routine correspondence. It is time-consuming, and poor handwriting can create difficulties for the typist.

(2) *Dictation to a shorthand writer.* This method requires the ability to speak "written" English. Some people are naturally more adept than others, but it is a skill which can be developed by practice based on straightforward rules and by experience. The beginner should start by dictating routine correspondence until he has gained sufficient confidence to tackle more difficult letters.

(3) *Audio dictation.* This is dealt with in detail in Chapter 27. It has the great advantage of not requiring the time of two people to be taken for dictation as with shorthand. It does require a very high standard of dictation expertise on the part of the dictater.

(4) *Direct (non-recorded) dictation.* In this case the typist actually produces the typewritten document simultaneously with dictation. It is the fastest method of transmission but requires superlative fluency on the part of the dictater and very high speed, accurate typewriting on the part of the typist.

(5) *Standard paragraphs.* This has already been mentioned above. The dictater chooses appropriate standard paragraphs and dictates any non-standard information.

(6) *Form letters.* The dictater indicates which form letter should be used and gives any variable details.

(7) *Verbal or written outline notes.* The framework of the main points of a letter are written or dictated in note form so that the secretary can compose the letter. It is essential that the secretary should have a good standard of English language.

(8) *Secretary to compose.* Provided the secretary can write a "good" letter, there are often many routine matters which she can deal with on her own initiative. Handing over a letter for her to answer or authorising her to deal with certain types of letter builds her confidence and lightens the manager's work-load.

Choosing the type of communication

The decision as to what type of communication is appropriate for each message is based on suitability for the content, speed of transmission required, and cost.

The office manager should review correspondence regularly to ensure that it is cost-effective, that all outgoing mail is necessary, and that the right kind of communications are being used to achieve the best results. Form letters do not give the best impression but if their use means the customers receive a reply in one day instead of in three days their use may be justified. If impression is of great importance, the use of automatic typewriters (*see* Chapter 28) should be considered.

Telex messages are received as soon as they are transmitted. It is also possible to have a "conversation" on the telex. This could be valuable where immediate replies to questions are needed and telephone lines are not clear or information is difficult to convey clearly over the telephone.

Cost of a letter

An average A4 three- to four-paragraph letter is estimated to cost between £5 and £8. The (minimum) cost is made up as follows:

Dictater's time for preparation, dictation, checking and signing: 20 minutes
(Assume a salary of £5,000 + 60 per cent standard additional cost = £8,000 per annum)　　　　　　　　　　　　　£1.60

Shorthand-typist's time for dictation research (references, addresses, etc.), transcription, proof-reading, envelope, preparation for mail: 40 minutes
(Assume a salary of £3,000 + 60 per cent = £4,800 per annum)　　　　　　　　　　　　　　　　　　　　　　　　1.92

Stationery: letterhead, envelope, copies　　　　　　　　　0.10

Postage, average depending on weight, class, etc.　　　　　0.15
　　　　　　　　　　　　　　　　　　　　　　　　　　　　―――
　　　　　　　　　　　　　　　　　　　　　　　　　　　　3.77

Overheads including capital cost of typewriter, franking machines, etc.; cost of filing clerks, mail clerks, messengers; office space—rent, rates; general costs—lighting, heating, insurance, etc. (add 35 per cent)　　　　　　1.32
　　　　　　　　　　　　　　　　　　　　　　　　　　　　―――
　　　　　　　　　　　　　　　　　　　　　　　　　　　　£5.09

The cost of a letter increases with the expertise and/or seniority of the dictater (higher salary), with the wasted output (retypes through inaccuracy or the dictater "changing his mind" when about to sign), and with the area and style of office premises (higher overheads).

Three questions are pertinent to ensure that correspondence costs are kept to a minimum.
(1) Is the communication necessary?
(2) If so, is there a cheaper way to communicate as effectively?
(3) If not, is the letter a fully effective communication?

Fluent dictation after adequate preparation, and accurate transcription are, of course, fundamental to cost-effectiveness.

Production procedures

Certain procedures must be followed to ensure that correspondence is produced quickly and accurately.

COPIES
If there is any deviation from the standard number of copies, the typist should be informed. Copies to be sent to people outside the organisation are normally typed on letterheads—typists may need to be reminded of this. Such copies may be indicated on the original (top copy) or may be sent as "blind" copies, i.e. not indicated on the original. Sometimes it is not desirable for the person to whom the letter is addressed to know that copies have been sent to other people.

DATES
All communications should be dated. Sometimes it is not possible for a letter to be signed on the day it is typed. Some organisations have only the month and year typed in, the day being inserted when the letter is signed. However, this does not create a good impression in a letter from a business organisation. It is common in modern styles of letter to omit the "st", "nd", "rd" and "th" from 1st, 2nd, 3rd, 4th, etc., in dates.

REFERENCES
The reference on the letter under reply, or in the advertisement or brochure referred to, should always be quoted as "your reference", and this, as a matter of courtesy and for the addressee's ease of reference, should be given first. "Our reference" should follow and normally consists of the dictater's initials followed by the typist's initials. In large organisations the reference may also contain a code

for the department and a file reference. The departmental code helps the mail clerk in sorting and distributing replies. A file number gives quick access to previous correspondence. Another alternative is for the dictater's and typist's initials to be located at the bottom left-hand corner of the letter, "our reference" containing only the file code. "Your" and "our references" normally appear at the top of a letter.

ADDRESSEES

Business letters may be addressed to the organisation, to a person by designation, e.g. sales manager, or to an individual by name. Note that "Messrs." is used before the name of a company only when it is not a limited liability company.

When a letter is addressed to an organisation but is to be dealt with by a particular individual, it is usual to include an "attention line" giving the name and/or designation of the person. In this case the salutation is "Dear Sirs", as shown in the example below.

> The Portman Carpet Co Ltd
> 6 Portman Street
> BIRMINGHAM B3 4QY
>
> Attention: J E Bates Esq
>
> Dear Sirs

SUBJECT HEADING

It is always helpful to a reader to be able to see at a glance what a letter is about. It also helps in identifying relevant correspondence. The subject heading is the key to the letter and should be brief and accurate.

ENCLOSURE NOTATIONS

Enclosures may be indicated by "Encs." typed a few lines below the signature, by a red flash attached to the letter, or by a line of dots in the left-hand margin against the line in which the enclosure is mentioned. It is important that some notation should be made to ensure that the enclosure is not forgotten when the letter is mailed and the addressee is made aware of its existence immediately upon opening the letter.

SIGNATURE

Some organisations include the name of the company immediately under the complimentary close to indicate that the letter is signed on behalf of the company. This is appropriate in formal letters but not really necessary for informal letters.

The name of the person who signs the letter should be typed with the designation. (Very few signatures are legible.)

If the typist is to sign the letter on behalf of the manager because of his absence it is usual to type "dictated by Mr. Smith and signed in his absence".

CHECKING

Before any document is signed it should be checked. It is the responsibility of the typist to proof-read but this does not give immunity against genuine errors resulting from misreading, mis-hearing or misunderstanding. No letter should be signed if it contains spelling errors, grammatical errors, typographical errors or an inaccuracy of any kind. Visible corrections should not be overlooked either. Retyping costs money but badly presented letters may lose business, which is even more expensive.

HOUSE STYLE

Many organisations have a "house style" which is followed by all typists. In other organisations each typist and secretary displays correspondence according to her own and/or her executive's whims. However, letter display forms an important part of the corporate image and a standard style should therefore be used throughout the organisation. For economy of time and neatness of appearance the modified full block style is recommended (illustrated in Fig. 54). All lines start at the left-hand margin except the date, which is typed on the right for ease of reference in files. If open punctuation (no commas or full stops above or below the body of the letter), no underscoring, no full stops after abbreviations and no brackets round item numbers are used, the appearance is clean and uncluttered, easy to ready and understand.

ENVELOPES

The name of the postal town should be typed in capital letters. The postcode should be the last line of the address, with one space between the two sections of the code and no full stops. No district should be addressed as "by" or "near" another town. Ideally, one and a half or double line spacing should be used if the address does not contain more than four lines.

Register of addresses

It is simple to maintain a loose-leaf or visible index file of addresses of customers or other correspondents. Difficulties sometimes arise

Flin Engineering Ltd

Flin House North Road Newcastle-upon-Tyne NC3 4AD

Telephone 0632 45789 Telex 57392 Cables FLINENGINE

Your ref	RT/ jn	12 February 1979
Our ref	JHT/DFS/1678	

J E Bloxham Esq
Microcopy Services Limited
16 Hatfield Road
MANCHESTER M2 6AB

Dear Mr Bloxham

MICROFILM DUPLICATING

Thank you for your letter of 9 February 1979. I note that you can
arrange to duplicate microfilm on customers' own premises. This
would be advantageous as it would be difficult for us to release
the film for more than a few hours.

Will you please let me know the additional cost that would be
charged for this service and what space and facilities you would
need? My previous estimate of 250,000 microfiches is somewhat low.
It is more likely to be of the order of 350,000. A minimum of ten
copies will be required of all microfiches with up to twenty copies
of selected batches.

Yours sincerely

Peter Wilson.

Administrative Officer

Registered in England 2284758 VAT Registration 009876

Fig. 54 *A letter in modified full block style (date on the right-hand side for easy reference) and
open punctuation.*

when changes in address are notified to the firm and are not
properly noted. A system must be devised and adhered to for
ensuring that the register is updated regularly. A simple method is
to maintain a "change of address register" and to allocate the duty

of entering notifications of change of address to a specific person. The register should then be checked daily and new entries transferred to the address register and notifications sent to other people and/or departments concerned, e.g. accounts, typing pool, etc.

Follow-up methods

It is often necessary to follow up outgoing letters when no reply has been received after a certain period. There are various methods of following up, some of which are explained below.

(1) One method is to maintain a diary, in which is entered in the appropriate day (i.e. the date by which a reply should have been received) a note that a follow-up letter should be sent. The efficiency of this system depends on having a good filing clerk or secretary.

(2) The sender may retain carbon copies of letters, mark them with a follow-up date, and insert them in a "bring forward" folder. Alternatively, the carbon copies may be inserted in a file (such as the concertina type) with divisions corresponding to days of the month. The appropriate division is referred to each day. However, both these methods keep carbon copies out of the filing system and make it difficult to locate them when they are required.

(3) Additional carbon copies may be made when follow up is required, and filed as explained in (2). This is probably the best system, even though it takes more stationery. It is possible to avoid making extra copies by having small preprinted slips of paper on which the details of the letter to be followed up are noted (date, file reference and addressee). The slips are then filed in a small box containing guide cards, one for each day.

25. Minutes of Meetings and Reports

Meetings

Attendance at meetings was discussed in Chapter 19. In addition to his responsibilities for preparing for and taking a constructive part in a meeting, the office manager may find himself responsible for producing an agenda (either as chairman or as secretary) and/or for preparing minutes of the meeting. These are tasks requiring great skill and much practice if the agenda and minutes are to fulfil their purpose.

Agendas

An agenda is a programme for the meeting (*see* Fig. 55). It is usually compiled by the secretary in consultation with the chairman of the meeting. The rules for the preparation and distribution of an agenda are as follows.

(1) It should contain:
   (*a*) the name of the group which is to meet;
   (*b*) the time, date and place of the meeting;
   (*c*) a list of the items to be discussed.

(2) Each item should be briefly stated and should indicate clearly what is expected of the members. For example, "Financial statement" is inadequate, but "To approve the financial statement for the half year to 30th June 1980" indicates precisely what members will have to consider.

(3) If there are papers or other references they should be indicated under the relevant item.

(4) Supplementary papers should be distributed with the agenda.

(5) The agenda and supplementary papers should be distributed not more than two weeks and not less than one week in advance of the meeting, assuming that the members have been notified of the

Tiddle & Flinders Limited

A meeting of the Communications Committee will be held at 10.30 hours on Thursday 20th March 1980 in the Conference Room.

AGENDA

(1) Minutes of meeting held on 21st February 1980.

(2) Reorganisation of mailroom.
    Diagrams of possible layout attached - Appendix I.

(3) Mail collection times.

(4) Installation of key and lamp units.

(5) Date of next meeting.

Donald Wilde

Secretary

Fig. 55 *Specimen agenda.*

time and date beforehand. If a lot of preparation is involved more time should be allowed to the members.

A chairman's agenda (*see* Fig. 56) is a useful aid to the chairman as it helps in the presentation of the points to be discussed. It must be prepared as late as possible so that all relevant details can be included. Most chairmen find this type of agenda of value because it saves time if they can give up-to-date information on an item and ensures that members are fully "in the picture".

Minutes

PURPOSE

Minutes are a legal record which can be produced in a court of law as evidence of the business transacted at a meeting. They are not a record of what was *said*—that is properly the purpose of a detailed report of the meeting. The minutes should provide a clear and concise indication of what actually happened, i.e. decisions taken

COMMUNICATIONS COMMITTEE - Chairman's Agenda		
Meeting at 10.30 hours on Thursday 20th March 1980 in the Conference Room		
Agenda Item	Remarks	Notes
(1) Minutes of meeting held on 21st February 1980.		
(2) Reorganisation of the mailroom.	Peter Fletcher has prepared diagrams of several layouts (distributed with agenda). Mailroom staff have been consulted. They prefer layout 3 - no specific reason could be discovered.	
(3) Mail collection times.	Secretarial staff have been complaining that mail collections are infrequent and irregular. At least three visits to mailroom are necessary each day to ensure that executives can deal with urgent matters.	
(4) Installation of key and lamp units.	Jacqueline Flint has been in touch with Post Office and will report to the meeting. No costs available yet.	
(5) Date of next meeting.	Pauline Needham on holiday 31st March to 11th April. Easter: 4th to 7th April.	

Fig. 56 *Specimen chairman's agenda.*

regarding policy, action to be taken, etc., agreements reached and resolutions passed.

CONTENTS OF MINUTES

Minutes must contain certain items of information.

(1) The name of the group which held the meeting (e.g. the Communications Committee).

(2) Date and place of the meeting (sometimes the time is also included).

(3) The names of the chairman and members present indicating office if any (e.g. secretary of the committee).

(4) Names, designations and organisations of people "in attendance", i.e. those who were not official members of the group but were invited to attend for some special reason, such as to give advice on a particular item to be discussed.

(5) Names of members who sent apologies for absence.

(6) The minutes.

STRUCTURE OF A MINUTE

There are two kinds of minute, viz. *a minute of narration* which includes the salient points of a discussion, and *a minute of resolution* which contains only the decision.

TITLE	REORGANISATION OF THE MAILROOM
SUBJECT MATTER	Following discussions at the previous meeting the layout of the mailroom had been investigated by John Farley. After discussions with the mailroom staff four possible layouts had been suggested and diagrams distributed with the agenda. The staff preferred diagram 3 but Mr. Farley recommended diagram 2 as being most economical for both equipment and staff.
OUTSIDE FACTORS	It had to be borne in mind that the maximum money available for new equipment would be £2,500.
THINKING	Discussion of the advantages and disadvantages of the various layouts revealed that the main problem appeared to stem from inadequate training of the staff as well as lack of equipment.
DECISION	IT WAS DECIDED: (i) to ask the Post Office to give training to the mailroom supervisor and her assistant; (ii) to ask the mailroom staff to suggest what equipment they regarded as priority; and (iii) to discuss the matter further at the next meeting when decisions (i) and (ii) should have been implemented.

Fig. 57 *Specimen minutes of narration indicating structure.* Not all minutes need all five parts.

A minute of narration (*see* Fig. 57) consists of five parts:

(1) the title;

(2) the subject matter, which the chairman should have stated at the beginning of the discussion of the relevant item on the agenda;

(3) outside factors, which should have been taken into account in discussing the matter and reaching a conclusion;

(4) the thinking which influenced the members in reaching an agreement/decision/resolution;

(5) the agreement/decision/resolution.

A minute of resolution consists of only two parts, viz. the title and the decision. This is adequate for routine items such as approval of minutes of the previous meeting, approval of monthly or quarterly financial statements, and any other items which have to be "rubber-stamped" by a committee and which need little or no discussion, unless there is some query or irregularity.

NOTE-TAKING AT A MEETING

It is extremely difficult to take part in a meeting and take adequate notes at the same time. Anyone who has to take notes for the purpose of preparing minutes is strongly recommended to learn a system of note-taking. This does not have to be a shorthand system. There are several easy and quick-to-learn alphabetical note-taking systems which can be mastered in a matter of a few hours. No great speed is needed.

The difficulty in taking notes is knowing what is important at the time it is said—a comment which seems a major factor in the discussion may turn out to be totally irrelevant, while some apparently unimportant remark may prove to be of crucial importance in reaching a decision. Consequently the note-taker has to mentally sift the points raised as the meeting progresses and note any facts which might be important in justifying a decision. At the same time, because he cannot make notes verbatim (neither can the average shorthand writer because verbatim reporting requires a speed of 180 words per minute) the note-taker has to mentally précis or summarise the points raised and note them down *in his own words*. This is the main reason why it is almost impossible both to take notes and to take part in the meeting effectively.

COMPOSITION OF MINUTES

Minutes are written in the third person and in the past tense. Names of contributors to the discussion should not be recorded unless there is a specific reason to do so, e.g. if a member wishes "to go on record" as having disagreed with the decision or a member has agreed to undertake a specific task. Bearing in mind the structure of a minute outlined above, the following points are important when writing minutes.

(1) The title of each minute should be brief but should convey the kernel of the subject. If the index of minutes is computerised the number of letters that can be used in the title may be limited. Some people use the agenda item as the title of the minute. This has the advantage of consistency but may not always be suitable. If a particular topic is discussed from one meeting to another the same title should be used throughout.

(2) The subject matter of the minute should contain the key factors mentioned by the chairman when he outlines the matter to be discussed. This would not include the contents of supplementary papers though reference should be made to them.

(3) Outside factors may have been stated by the chairman or possibly by a person in attendance who gave specialised advice. Again the key factors only should be included.

(4) The thinking which influenced the decision should set out the processes and precedents (if any) which led to a decision. The relevant facts must be included. If the chairman summarises the discussion (as a good chairman should) this summary is normally an adequate record. It may even be summarised further.

(5) The agreement/decision/resolution must be stated verbatim. An agreement may be reached as a result of a motion being voted upon. In this case the names of the proposer and seconder of the motion must be stated, the motion must be recorded verbatim and the voting must be recorded—unanimous, *nem con* or *nem dis* (without dissent), or actual numbers "for" and "against". The resolution should be a complete statement which indicates exactly what has been decided without reference to preceding sections of the minute.

(6) It is wise to compose the minutes as soon as possible after the meeting. Notes tend to lose their meaning after a time. A rough draft is adequate: it can be polished later. The important thing is to get down the key facts while they are still fresh in the mind.

PRESENTATION OF MINUTES

There are various methods of presenting minutes but it should be borne in mind that the style should be in line with the presentation of other documents. The presentation of any document should reflect the corporate image. There should be a house style for minutes as for letters so that presentation is consistent throughout the organisation. Whatever the style chosen it should be easy to read, understand and refer to. The specimen minutes shown in Fig. 58 are recommended as meeting these criteria.

Minutes should be numbered. It is recommended that this should be done either on a continuing basis from the birth of the group onwards, or annually. In either case it is useful to include the year in the number, e.g. 148/80.

An action column is helpful because each member can see immediately what he has to follow up. The name of each individual can be underlined in red on his copy. Minutes should normally be circulated immediately after the meeting. This is essential if members are to take specific action. Unless the minutes are purely "historical", in which case they can be circulated with the agenda for the next meeting, they should be distributed within a few days. In the case of action committees it is normal to distribute them within a day.

For the office manager who finds that meetings are an important part of his duties, the publications mentioned on page 204 may be

Tiddle & Flinders Limited

MINUTES OF THE COMMUNICATIONS COMMITTEE MEETING HELD AT 10.30 HOURS
ON THURSDAY 20th MARCH 1980 IN THE CONFERENCE ROOM

Present:

John Farley	Office Manager - Chairman
Peter Fletcher	DP Controller
Jacqueline Flint	Telephone Supervisor
Sheila Guthrie	Mailroom Supervisor
Pauline Needham	Secretariat Supervisor
Donald Wilde	Admin. Assistant - Secretary

15/80 MINUTES OF PREVIOUS MEETING

The minutes of the meeting held on 21st February 1980, having been circulated, were taken as read, approved as a true record of the proceedings and signed by the Chairman.

16/80 REORGANISATION OF MAILROOM

Following discussions at the previous meeting the layout of the mailroom had been investigated by John Farley. After discussions with the mailroom staff four possible layouts had been suggested and diagrams distributed with the agenda. The staff preferred diagram 3 but Mr. Farley recommended diagram 2 as being most economical both for equipment and staff.

It had to be borne in mind that the maximum money available for new equipment would be £2,500.

Discussion of the advantages and disadvantages of the various layouts revealed that the main problem appeared to stem from inadequate training of the staff as well as lack of equipment.

IT WAS DECIDED:

(i)   to ask the Post Office to give training to the mailroom supervisor and her assistant;

(ii) to ask the mailroom staff to suggest what equipment they regarded as priority; and

(iii) to discuss the matter further at the next meeting when decisions (i) and (ii) should have been implemented.

17/80 MAIL COLLECTION TIMES

Fig. 58 Specimen minutes of a meeting in block style.

helpful. Terms used in connection with meetings are explained in "How to Take Minutes" on page 204.

INDEXING MINUTES

One copy of each set of minutes should be pasted into a minute book or inserted in a special binder with a lock to prevent removal or alteration of pages.

For easy reference minutes should be indexed either in the minute book or in a separate strip index (*see* Fig. 59 and Chapter 34).

SUBJECT	No.	Date	No.	Date	No.	Date
Property maintenance	68	16.1.76	283	16.8.78		
	75	18.3.76	367	19.4.79		
	170	28.4.77				
Regional office	76	18.3.76	201	28.9.77		
	102	23.6.76				
	135	16.9.76				

Fig. 59 *Index of minutes.*

Reports

With the growth in size of business organisations, the increase in the number of professions, and the ever-widening activities of the State, there has arisen a growing need for written communication both within an organisation and with people concerned with the organisation from outside. Executives have become increasingly dependent on experts, and there has emerged the need for experts to report to the policy-making body. The Managing Director's report to the company board relies very often on reports from his departmental managers, who in turn rely on reports from supervisors. Reports are issued by government departments and public authorities, reports are made of company meetings, and newspapers print reports of various events every day.

PURPOSE

There are various types and styles of reports but every report has one basic function: it has to convey from the writer to the reader some conclusions and/or recommendations based on facts or circumstances which have been investigated. The facts investigated may be the result of experiment, inspection, experience or research, but the important thing is that they should be facts and not opinions. For example, if it is stated in a report that "the labour force is so diluted that the previous results could not now be obtained" this may be opinion, whereas "the diluted labour force contains 15 per cent untrained workers" expresses a fact.

The report may also have a complementary function, viz. to persuade the reader to take a decision or a course of action.

TYPES OF REPORT

Reports may be formal or informal, the latter being presented usually in the form of a memorandum or letter. It may even be on a pre-printed form, e.g. an insurance report. The same principles for the actual writing apply no matter what the type or subject of the report, but a lot more work is likely to be needed to produce a full-scale formal report.

CONTENTS AND STRUCTURE OF A REPORT

A report may have up to nine parts.

(1) *The title page* contains the title of the report, the author's name and position, the organisation by which it is authorised, the date and place of publication, classification (e.g. secret, confidential), and reference identification. A distribution list or indication of readership may also be included.

(2) *The contents list* gives titles of sections and subsections with page numbers.

(3) *The introduction* states the terms of reference and indicates the predetermined or self-imposed limitations on the scope of the report.

(4) *A summary of conclusions and recommendations* (if any) may follow the introduction to a long report to assist busy readers to identify the main points of interest.

(5) *The findings* giving the facts should be arranged in sections and subsections, with appropriate titles to indicate the content.

(6) *Conclusions* should match and summarise the findings.

(7) *Recommendations* follow the conclusions.

(8) *Appendixes*, sometimes called annexes, contain information which is not essential in the text and is of a type which is likely to distract from the main arguments, e.g. lists.

(9) *An index* may be helpful to the reader of a long report.

PREPARATION FOR WRITING A REPORT

The writing of a report is a great deal easier if it has been properly prepared first. The following steps may be a guide.

(1) Summarise the terms of reference in one sentence; summarise the aim of the report in one sentence; identify the readership.

(2) Write a random list of facts which must be given in the

report, including those facts which must be researched. If this can be done over a period of, say, two or three days it will be easier to make the list comprehensive, but this may not be possible. To make the next step easier it is useful to jot each fact on a small card or slip of paper.

(3) Arrange the items into main groups with a heading. (It is easier to move cards into sequence than it is to rearrange lists.)

(4) Do the research, which may be anything from checking a name or a figure to arranging and carrying out a programme of full-scale interviews. Bear in mind the readership—what will they need to know in order that the purpose of the report can be fulfilled?

(5) Review the items: add, amend, delete as necessary.

COMPOSITION

Having planned the report and done the necessary research, drafting can start.

(1) Arrange the groups of items into the required sequence. This sequence normally presents itself as it leads up to the conclusions and recommendations. Nevertheless there may, for example, be a choice between geographical and chronological arrangement. Consider the readers in this connection and decide which sequence will be easier for them to follow and understand.

(2) Draft, preferably by dictation, working quickly through the plan. Do not worry about structure, vocabulary, etc. at this stage. Get the "bones" of the material into a readable form. While drafting make a note of illustrations, diagrams, appendixes, etc. which will be needed. Talk in short sentences, using short words, phrases and paragraphs in preference to long ones, and bear in mind the readers' ages, backgrounds, education and experience.

(3) Obtain illustrations, prepare diagrams, etc., while waiting for the draft to be typed.

(4) Review the draft:

(a) for content, to ensure that facts are accurate, information is complete, sufficient supporting evidence is given;

(b) for readability, to ensure that:

   (i) structure is correct, vocabulary clear and easy to understand;

   (ii) technical terms used will be understood by the readers (if this is doubtful and the terms cannot be omitted they must be explained);

   (iii) punctuation is used only where essential;

   (iv) all unnecessary words and phrases are eliminated (if

necessary rewriting a sentence to obtain greater conciseness
and clarity);

   (v) the illustrations are adequate/necessary;

   (vi) the tone and style are appropriate to the readers.

(5) Number the sections and subsections and the paragraphs if
appropriate.

(6) If possible ask someone else to read the draft. You know
what you want to say and what you mean, the reader does not. A
second opinion may reveal lack of clarity in expression. If necessary
have a second draft typed but try to avoid this as it is time-
consuming and expensive.

(7) Compile the index including in it all major items which the
reader may wish to refer to later.

(8) Have the final copy/master typed.

(9) Check the final copy minutely to ensure that there is absolute
accuracy of typing including consistency of layout, correct sequence of illustrations, etc., and that numbering is correct.

(10) Sign the report if necessary.

PRESENTATION OF A REPORT

Reports, like minutes, should be presented in a similar style
throughout the organisation. There are a variety of styles, one of
the most "readable" being that with headings typed in block
capitals in the margin as shown in Fig. 60(a). A good typist should
be able to produce a variety of styles of headings for sections and
subsections so that they are easily identifiable.

Spacing should be used to aid comprehension. Some people have
reports typed in double line-spacing but on the whole it is easier to
read and understand if paragraphs are in single line-spacing with
double and treble line-spacing used between paragraphs and sections.

If unequal margins are used and the report is typed on both sides
of the paper the narrow margin must always be at the outside edge.
Similarly it is easier for reference purposes if the headings always
appear at the outside edge of the page (see Fig. 60(b)).

Pages should be numbered either in the centre at the bottom or
top of the page, or at the outside top corner.

REPRODUCTION OF A REPORT

A report may be reproduced by any of the reprographic methods
outlined in Chapter 29. The appearance of a thick report is
enhanced by having the cover page printed on card rather than on
paper. The method of fastening sheets should be such that it is easy
to open the pages. Stapling is suitable only for a few pages.

REPORT ON INSTALLATION OF WORD PROCESSING IN THE MANAGEMENT

SERVICES DEPARTMENT

by John D. Woods, Administrative Officer

INTRODUCTION	The typewriting work-load in the Management Services Department is very heavy and additional staff are constantly being recruited to ensure that a backlog is not allowed to build up. The situation is aggravated by the fact that staff turnover is high, largely because much of the work is retyping of reports and specifications which provides little job satisfaction. It was thought likely that the installation of word processing might solve both problems. The Administrative Officer was asked to conduct an investigation to establish whether word processing would be advantageous and, if so, to make recommendations regarding the processes and types of machine that might be suitable.
SURVEY	The survey was conducted over a period of two weeks from 3rd to 14th November 1980. All staff in the Management Services Department were interviewed. The purpose of the investigation was explained and full co-operation was given by each member of staff.
Type of Work	The bulk of the typewriting work consists of reports and specifications. Because of the nature of the work and the necessity for constant review and revision in the process of installing new procedures, systems and machines, reports frequently have to be retyped four and even five times. One report was being retyped for the seventh time during the survey. The amendments arise out of discussions with management which are necessary to establish and maintain maximum team effort.
Staff	The Management Services Department consists of a Head of Department (Management Services Director), Head of Work Study, Head of Organisation and Methods and Head of Systems Analysis.

Fig. 60(a) Specimen display for a report.

Methods of binding are outlined in Chapter 32.

Whatever the method chosen the report must create a good impression at first glance.

ACHIEVING THE AIM

It is worth emphasising that whatever the type, purpose, title,

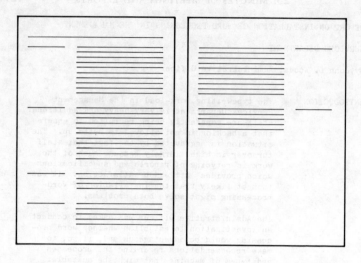

Fig. 60(b) *Display for double-sided printing.* Note that the margins and headings are reversed on the left- and right-hand pages.

content and style of the report, a short, concise, logical and easy-to-read report is much more likely to achieve the writer's aim.

A very important point to be remembered is the time schedule for the production of a report. A time schedule should be drawn up in consultation with the typist, secretary or secretariat supervisor to ensure that adequate time is allocated for every stage. A specimen list of items to be included in the schedule, which can be amended to suit individual needs, is given below. The times given are hypothetical and allow for routine work to be carried on; some of the tasks could be carried out simultaneously.

CHECK-LIST/TIME SCHEDULE FOR PRODUCTION OF A REPORT

Task	Number of days required
(1) Prepare outline.	2
(2) Check facts/research for information required.	5
(3) Review outline and arrange material into sequence.	1
(4) Draft report.	1
(5) Request and obtain illustrations.	15
(6) Type draft.	2
(7) Obtain information, etc. for appendixes.	5
(8) Draft appendixes.	2
(9) Type draft appendixes.	2
(10) Review draft.	2

(11) Obtain second opinion on draft.   3
(12) (a) Final corrections to draft.
     (b) Collation of draft.   2
(13) Type final copy/master.   2
(14) Design cover.   3
(15) Reproduce final copy.   2
(16) Reproduce cover.   2
(17) Collate and bind.   1
(18) Draft covering letter for distribution.   1
(19) Type and reproduce covering letter.   1
(20) Type envelopes.   1
(21) Prepare for distribution/despatch.   1

NOTE: The preparation of a network analysis (*see* Chapter 50) would identify the critical time factors and ensure that a report is started in time to complete it by the deadline.

There are some very good publications on report writing but for quick, clear and easy-to-follow instruction *Report Writing* published by the British Association for Commercial and Industrial Education is recommended. The British Institute of Management Checklist No. 2 is also a valuable aid to good report writing.

26. Visual Presentation

There are many occasions when purely verbal presentation (in the sense of using words only) is not adequate or suitable. In a learning situation, and that is what receiving and assimilating information is, 70 per cent of the impact is achieved visually. It follows that verbal information supported by visual impact will improve the chances of comprehension and therefore of appropriate follow-up, whether it be carrying out an instruction, being more highly motivated or having a better understanding of the reasons for doing a job.

Some methods of visual presentation are given below with an indication of their uses.

Visual aids

Visual aids, normally used in the teaching situation, may also be used for presenting information. Many companies now conduct seminars for their staff during which one or more films may be shown. Visual aids are also commonly used for sales presentations and for exhibitions.

Films are normally 16 mm, and can be hired, borrowed free of charge from certain organisations, or purchased. Some large companies sponsor the production of films relevant to business.

Closed circuit television (c.c.t.v.) is used mainly for training purposes and for security in public places.

Transparencies are shown on an overhead projector, easily prepared by hand or by more sophisticated means such as heat copiers or xerography.

Filmstrip or slide/tape sequence is a recorded tape (or cassette) synchronised with 35 mm filmstrip or filmslides. Such a sequence can be made in-company providing adequate equipment is available. It is commonly used for short sales presentations and for public relations activities.

Video cassettes are similar to films but are suitable for smaller groups of viewers as they are shown on a television screen. They can be replayed in sections which is an advantage for discussion purposes.

Boards may be chalkboard, feltboard, magnetic board or pinboard. The latter is most commonly used for posting notices in public areas and for displaying charts, etc. in offices. Magnetic boards (*see* Fig. 61) are particularly useful for planning, as the indicators,

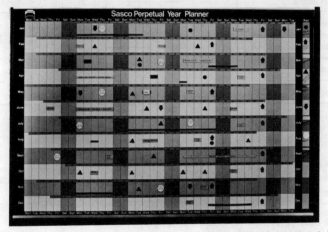

[*Courtesy Twinlock U.K. Ltd.*]

Fig. 61 *A magnetic board, used here for work planning.*

which are held on the board by magnetism, can be easily moved. However, this can also be a disadvantage if people knock against the board.

Charts

It is often desirable to illustrate an explanation with a chart. Statistical information which is to be distributed generally, e.g. about company profits, is better understood from an appropriate type of chart than from a table of figures. A chart of sales figures can indicate the trend or latest situation at a glance whereas it may take several minutes to determine these facts from a statistical table. There are many types of chart, the most common of which are explained briefly and illustrated below.

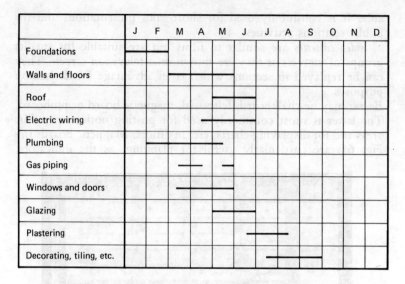

	J	F	M	A	M	J	J	A	S	O	N	D
Foundations												
Walls and floors												
Roof												
Electric wiring												
Plumbing												
Gas piping												
Windows and doors												
Glazing												
Plastering												
Decorating, tiling, etc.												

Fig. 62 *Bar chart: time schedule for building.*

BAR CHART (*sometimes called a horizontal bar chart*)
A bar chart (*see* Fig. 62) is used for comparison, for indicating time-scales, e.g. staff holidays, and for scheduling.

BAR GRAPH (*sometimes called a pillar graph*)
A bar graph (*see* Fig. 63) is used for comparison, for example of a moving total with a fixed total, or of changes over similar periods of time. It is also used to indicate increases/decreases from one period to another.

MULTIPLE BAR (OR PILLAR) GRAPH
A multiple bar graph has two or more component elements to be compared. For example, one could compare the levels of raw materials, the levels of bought-in parts and the levels of finished products from one month to the next all on the same chart. Colours or shadings can be used to differentiate the items represented. A key must be shown on the chart.

LINE GRAPH (*sometimes called a line chart*)
A single line graph (*see* Fig. 64) is normally used to indicate trends, but it may be used to compare progress with a target. Fixed and variable factors are represented on the horizontal and vertical axes respectively.

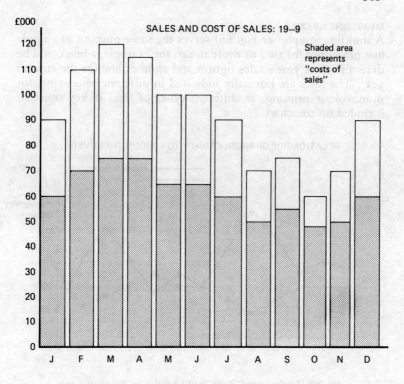

Fig. 63 *Bar graph.*

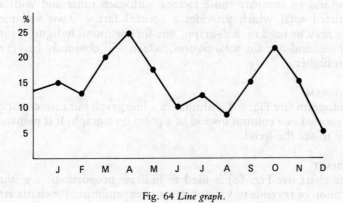

Fig. 64 *Line graph.*

MULTILINE GRAPH

A multiline graph (*see* Fig. 65) serves the same purpose as a single line graph but for two or more items; for example, a line could be drawn for last year's sales figures and another line for the current year. The lines are normally indicated in different colours or, for monocolour printing, in different types of line. A key must be included on the chart.

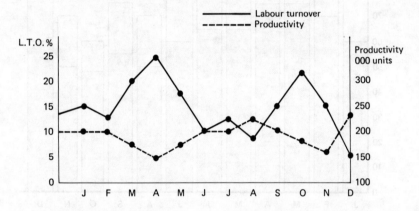

Fig. 65 *Multiline graph*. Note the two scales on the vertical axes.

Z-GRAPH

A Z-graph (*see* Fig. 66) is used to indicate trends of more than one factor and to compare those factors with each other and with a calculated total which provides a control factor. Two variable scales may be used on a Z-graph, one for the monthly figures, for example, and one for total figures, which will obviously be very much higher.

HISTOGRAM

A histogram (*see* Fig. 67) is similar to a line graph but each statistic is presented as a column instead of a point on a graph. It is perhaps easier to see the trend.

PIE CHART

A pie chart (*see* Fig. 68) is used to indicate proportions, e.g. the allocation of revenue to various items of expenditure. Pie charts are

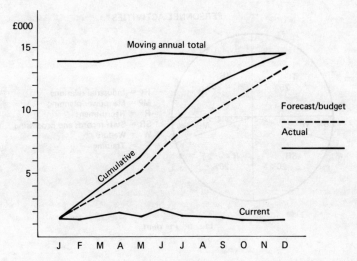

Fig. 66 *Z-graph showing current, cumulative and moving annual, i.e. year-on-year, total figures. This type of graph, which may have two scales, is particularly useful for management control.*

MANAGEMENT TRAINEES

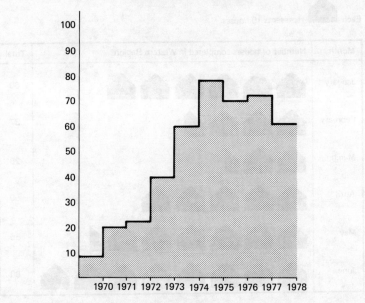

Fig. 67 *Histogram.*

PERSONNEL ACTIVITIES

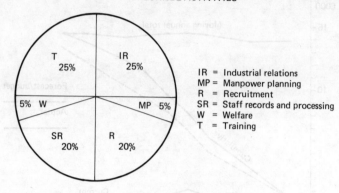

IR = Industrial relations
MP = Manpower planning
R = Recruitment
SR = Staff records and processing
W = Welfare
T   = Training

Fig. 68 *Pie chart.*

commonly used in annual reports, house journals and other media
for the distribution of information to employees and the public.

Each  represents 10 houses

Month	Number of houses completed in Western Region	Total
January	▲▲▲▲▲▲	60
February	▲▲▲▲	37
March	▲▲▲	25
April	▲▲▲▲▲	50
May	▲▲▲▲▲▲▲	65
June	▲▲▲▲▲▲▲▲	80

Fig. 69 *Pictogram.*

PICTOGRAM

A pictogram (*see* Fig. 69) is used to give a general comparison of one item over a variety of items. For example, the number of houses built in different areas can be indicated by representing ten houses by a picture of a house. A pictogram gives only a very rough comparison because it is impossible to indicate accurately a specific figure, e.g. 37.

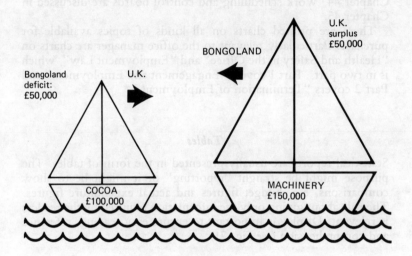

Fig. 70 *Picture chart.*

PICTURE CHART

A picture chart (*see* Fig. 70) is normally used to illustrate a list of facts; for example, a list of holidays giving the number of days and prices could each be shown in the appropriate width of ray in a sunray.

GENERAL POINTS

When preparing charts it is important to decide exactly what data has to be shown. The data should be kept to a minimum because the less "cluttered" a chart is the easier it is to understand. The scale is important too. Obviously this depends on where the chart is to be used, but if it is to be on public display, generally the bigger the better. It is important that figures should be represented accurately because even a relatively minor inaccuracy can give a completely distorted impression.

Equally important is the updating of charts. Whatever the time span between reporting—daily, weekly or monthly—the new information should be plotted on the chart at the correct time. Only in this way can a chart achieve its purpose of giving information.

All charts should have a title, a key and a few words of explanation if necessary.

Charts related to work-flow, processes, etc. are explained in Chapter 44. Work scheduling and control boards are discussed in Chapter 45.

There are printed charts on all kinds of topics available for purchase. Particularly relevant to the office manager are charts on "Health and Safety in the Office" and "Employment Law", which is in two parts. Part 1 covers "Engagement and Employment" and Part 2 covers "Termination of Employment".*

Tables

Statistical reports are usually presented in the form of tables. The purpose might be straight "reporting" or it might be to show comparisons, e.g. budget figures and actual expenditure figures. The rule about giving only the information required by the readers is relevant. Display is important to ensure easy reading, reference and comprehension (see Fig. 71).

Illustrations

DIAGRAMS

Many processes, etc. which are difficult to explain can be presented diagrammatically to convey the main points (see Fig. 72). However clear an explanation may be, it takes time to read or listen and assimilate. A diagram can often be understood at a glance.

LINE DRAWINGS

Line drawings are often used to add humour to a notice or some other informative publication. The humour of a cartoon, for example, often adds impact to the message.

* "Flow Chart Through Employment Law" and "Health and Safety in the Office" charts are available from Stewart Williams International Limited, Carlton Chambers, Station Road, Shortlands, Bromley, Kent BR2 0EY, telephone 01-464 5418. The employment charts can be updated. Discounts are given for quantities.

Department	Budget £000	Actual £000	Variance £000
Production	1,500	1,614	− 114
Sales	674	658	+ 16
Finance	385	387	− 2
Administration	210	205	+ 5
Personnel	86	82	+ 4
Data Processing	158	198	− 40
	£3,013	£3,144	− £131

Fig. 71 *Tabulated statistics*. Typed "frames" are less commonly used in modern presentations.

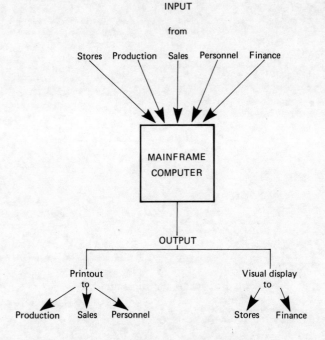

Fig. 72 *Diagrammatic illustration*.

PHOTOGRAPHS

Photographs may be half-tone or continuous tone, or in colour. There are reprographic processes (*see* Chapter 29), including copying machines, by which photographs can be reproduced.

Illustrations should not be used for the sake of including something different. An illustration should supplement the text in some way and be necessary for maximum comprehension, and should always complement it. A photograph should always be of the best possible quality—it is better not to have an illustration at all than to have a poor one.

27. Audio–Dictation Systems

The early wax cylinder dictating machine in use until 1939 was outmoded by the development of magnetic recording media. There is now a wide variety of dictating and transcribing machines and systems to cater for the needs of every situation in every type and size of organisation.

Recording media

Non-magnetic recording media (discs and belts), from which dictation cannot be erased, are used only when it is necessary to preserve the recording. Magnetic media are in general use in offices, usually in the form of discs (like miniature gramophone records) or cassettes (commonly mini size). Wire, plastic sheets and spools of tape are also found. Dictation capacity varies from ten minutes to two and a half hours, though automatic media–changing systems allow up to six hours of continuous dictation.

Equipment

Equipment falls into two main categories, viz. individual machines and centralised systems.

INDIVIDUAL MACHINES

Individual machines may be either single or dual-purpose. The latter is used for both dictation and transcription and has the obvious disadvantage of being available to only the dictater or the transcriber at any one time. Also it has to be moved from one to the other as required.

Single-purpose machines are made either for dictation or for transcription. Some manufacturers make a variety of dictating models all of which use the same size and type of recording

311

medium. Thus the varying needs of a number of dictaters can be met and serviced by one transcriber. This is very convenient if the dictation loads of individual dictaters are not heavy.

The operational facilities of standard types (i.e. desk dictating machines) are similar. These may include the following: record, playback, location of any part of recorded dictation, indication of length of each item of dictation and indication of special instructions on an index strip. "Cleaning" of old recorded dictation is normally automatic as new material is recorded. The additional facility for a telephone recording attachment to be fixed to the side of the telephone and plugged into the dictating machine may be useful. This allows both sides of a telephone conversation to be recorded.

Certain telephone answer-recording machines "double" as dual-purpose audio machines.

Transcription operation is usually by means of a foot pedal which controls playback, back-space (for rehearing) and reversing (for longer replaying). Some machines are also provided with hand controls. The typist normally uses a lightweight stethophone to listen to the dictation.

The "thought tank" which allows almost simultaneous dictation/transcription consists of a continuous recording "loop". Dictation in progress is indicated by a light and transcription can start within seconds of dictation beginning. There are two main systems. On one system the loop can hold up to twenty minutes dictation and is intended primarily for short items and note-making. A particularly useful application is during meetings when written notes of the discussion in progress are needed immediately.

A more recent system allows dictation up to three hours. There is an additional facility of linking the machine to a standard cassette transcriber so that dictation from a portable dictating machine, for example, can be transcribed. Dictation can be accepted from an outside telephone. The loop units can be built up into banks with a control console which indicates to the transcriber the amount of dictation held by each unit.

Some manufacturers now produce an attachment for their transcribing machines which accepts any cassettes, not only their own. This may be useful where a transcriber works for several dictaters who have different makes of dictating machines. Standardisation is desirable but the piecemeal introduction of dictation systems sometimes results in a variety of machines being used.

The portable or "pocket" dictating machine is particularly useful to a sales representative, site engineer, consultant or businessman who travels extensively. He can dictate correspondence and reports and post the recordings to base, so that the transcription can be ready when he returns. Draft reports can be typed ready for editing thus reducing the time required to produce the final copy. With the latest word-processing machines (*see* Chapter 28) major reports can be in their final form within two or three days of a manager's return to base.

Less formal uses include situations where "notes" rather than a report are required. When carrying out interviews, for example, the interviewer can dictate his impressions of each applicant in two or three minutes after each interview. These notes could be a valuable supplement to the formal information entered on the interview sheet.

Similarly an executive (particularly in the engineering world) might be examining a prototype of a new model, or a newly purchased machine; if he "thinks aloud" with the recorders running the recording gives the outline for a subsequent report.

A dictating machine can also be useful when stock-taking. Instead of having one clerk counting while another is writing down, one clerk can be equipped with a portable dictating machine with a small microphone worn in the coat lapel. The recorded stock-taking is then transcribed and typed direct on to the stock records.

Finally, a use often overlooked by managers who have secretaries is the dictation of non-urgent instructions. Many managers constantly call their secretaries to give an instruction while the thought is in their minds. Dictating the instruction saves the manager's time and enables the secretary to concentrate on her work so achieving higher productivity.

CENTRALISED SYSTEMS

There are two main types of central dictating installation obtainable.

(1) The multi-bank system: all the recording machines are banked together (*see* Fig. 73) in the audio-typing pool or secretariat and the supervisor controls the distribution of dictated material to the typists, each of whom has a machine for playing back the recordings.

(2) The tandem system: each typist has a "twin deck" machine on her desk, one for recording and one for playing back.

With the second system, the routeing of dictation to a free machine is usually automatic. The tandem machine (*see* Fig. 74) has a telephone dial so that the transcriber can contact the dictater when

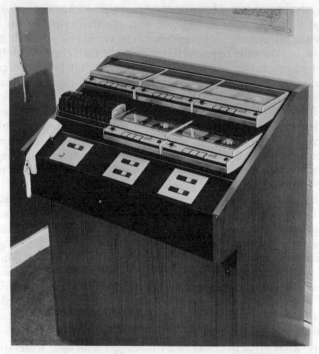

[*Courtesy Harford Dictation Systems Ltd.*

Fig. 73 *A bank of remotely controlled recording machines.*

necessary. This mitigates the impersonal atmosphere of centralised systems.

Dictation on a central system is recorded either by using a special internal telephone or microphone installed conveniently for each dictater, or on the normal PABX telephone extension. The dictater controls the recording either by dialling special codes (PABX) or by pressing control buttons. Depending on the average volume of dictation per day, one recording machine will serve up to six to eight dictaters.

Automatic recording media changers allow continuous dictation of up to six hours. A series of cassettes or discs are loaded into the machine and as the first cassette or disc is fully used the dictation is automatically recorded on the second one and so on. These systems have a locking device so that no other dictater can gain access to dictated material which may, of course, be confidential.

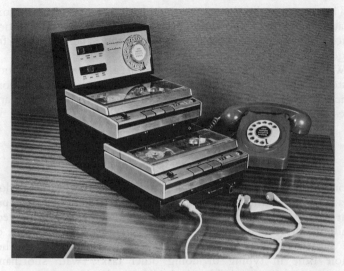

[*Courtesy Harford Dictation Systems Ltd.*

Fig. 74 *The Tandem audio-dictation system.* While one machine is recording dictation
the audio typist can transcribe from the other.

Choosing a machine or system

The choice of machine or system depends on a number of factors:
  (1) the volume of dictation:
    (*a*) in total;
    (*b*) from each individual dictater;
  (2) the average length of time spent dictating continuously;
  (3) the place or places where dictation is to be given;
  (4) the type of material to be dictated;
  (5) the number of people who can and should use the facility;
  (6) whether the recorded dictation should be preserved;
  (7) whether the recorded dictation has to be posted for
transcription;
  (8) the time permissible between dictation and transcription;
  (9) the proximity of the dictater and transcriber;
  (10) the additional facilities required, e.g. telephone attachment.
  A chart setting out these factors should be drawn up and the cost
of obtaining the equipment required to meet all needs should be
investigated. An alternative method is to decide which factors are
priorities, determine the capital available and find out how many of
the factors, priorities and others, can be met within the budget.

The cost of audio-dictation equipment can range from approximately £200 for a portable dictating machine, a transcription machine and a supply of cassettes, to many thousands of pounds for larger and more complex systems.

When considering the installation of a centralised dictation system it is useful to talk to office managers in other organisations where such a system is in use. There are pitfalls to be avoided and one can learn from other people's experience.

Advantages and disadvantages of audio-dictation systems

Shorthand typists are difficult to obtain, particularly in the London area, and it is claimed that by using dictating machines up to 50 per cent saving can be made in the number of typists employed. Undoubtedly economy is the chief advantage as only the time of the dictater is taken for dictation. The transcriber can spend her whole time in typing or doing other tasks. With shorthand dictation there are inevitably telephone and other interruptions, and in fact a letter that takes about half an hour to dictate can often be typed in ten minutes.

The second great advantage is the added convenience. A dictating machine does not tie the dictater to a schedule: he may dictate at any time (e.g. late in the evening), and at any place (e.g. at home or in the car). When transcription machines are installed in a typing pool (*see* Chapter 28) the work can be shared among the typists. It can also be measured. Thus supervision of work-flow, productivity and quality can be properly supervised.

A frequently quoted disadvantage is loss of personal contact between dictater and transcriber with a centralised system, unless tandem machines are used. This can be overcome to some extent by allocating the work of certain dictaters to a particular transcriber as far as practicable. The transcriber can also take the completed work to the dictater and contact him when queries arise.

Many shorthand typists dislike the audio system because they are afraid that they will lose their shorthand speed and because they say dictation is often very poor. Bearing in mind the time taken to master shorthand, this is very understandable. Dictaters who are used to dictating to a shorthand writer fail to realise that they have to be much more precise when using a machine. Consequently the transcriber has great difficulty in understanding the audio dictation and resorts to taking it down in shorthand before transcribing!

Today there are many trained audio typists who do not write shorthand. This does not ameliorate the transcription problems of bad dictation but it is overcoming the dislike of machines by secretarial staff. Few clerical staff are competent to use dictating machines, and training in the techniques of dictation is essential.

The training of audio typists aims to achieve simultaneous listening and typing but this depends to a great degree on the quality of the dictation.

Dictation techniques

When using a dictating machine it is essential that the typist be borne in mind. Before starting to dictate, the dictater should glance at the machine to ensure that the correct controls are switched on for recording. In the early days it is advisable for the dictater to make a few test recordings to find the best position and distance from the microphone (if this type of machine is being used) to suit his particular delivery. It is important to speak clearly and not to smoke while dictating.

Accurate transcription depends on fluent dictation. The dictater should follow the basic techniques listed below.

(1) Prepare an outline of the content of the dictation; this does *not* mean writing the communication out in full.

(2) Use an index slip (when using an individual machine) to indicate the number of items, their length, special instructions and any corrections which have been made.

(3) If amendments or insertions are made mark them on the index slip and record them at the end of the dictation.

(4) Switch off the machine when not actually dictating.

(5) Prefix all instructions with "typist" so that the instruction is not typed as part of the communication.

(6) Give the name of the dictater, department and number of the recording.

(7) At the *beginning* of each communication, say what type of document is to be dictated, and give instructions about priority requirements, the number of carbon copies (if different from routine), enclosures, postal directions, and special layout requirements.

(8) Dictate references, name and address of the addressee including postcode or zip code, attention line if there is one, salutation and subject heading.

(9) Dictate all punctuation which may not be obvious from voice inflections, particularly paragraph endings.

(10) Spell all unusual words and names which might have different spellings but the same sounds, e.g. Davis and Davies.

(11) If two words could quite logically be typed as one word,

e.g. Corn Hill (Cornhill), dictate as follows: "capital letter 'C'—Corn, capital letter 'H'—Hill".

(12) Use analogies for letters which are likely to be confused, e.g. F and S (F for Freddie, S for Samuel). Standard analogies are recommended by audio equipment manufacturers and consultants, but any analogy is in order provided it is clear to the listener.

(13) Dictate amounts of money with the £ sign first, e.g. "pound sign 1037".

(14) Figures to be typed in words should be prefixed with the instruction "typist: in words please—forty-eight".

(15) Indicate whether initial capital letters only are required or all capital letters, e.g. "initial capital P Peter"; "capital letters N A L G O".

(16) Indicate layout, e.g. centred heading, side heading.

Training dictaters

Good dictation techniques are the result of practice, but training makes the going a lot easier. When an audio system is installed it is essential to train the dictaters in the operation of their equipment and in the rules and conventions of dictation. It is useful to point out the problems of the transcribers if the rules are not followed.

Training audio transcribers

Audio transcription is now included in many secretarial training courses. Competence depends to a great extent on the transcriber having a very good linguistic knowledge and fluency. With this basic qualification a typist can become a proficient audio transcriber by undergoing a "conversion" course of about ten to twelve hours. Training is essential. The techniques are difficult and specialised. If a new system is installed a thorough induction training should be given to the transcribers as well as to the dictaters.

Future developments

There have for many years been experiments in processing dictation electronically, eliminating the typist. Great advances have been made in the research, but the English language does not lend itself readily to this treatment. At present and for the foreseeable future, even with word processing (see Chapter 28), the transcriber is an integral part of the system.

One problem which does arise with the introduction of word processing is that dictaters tend to become "sloppy" because they think that it is easy to make alterations to the text. Though this is true it is still time-consuming and it should be stressed that all dictation should be well prepared so that it is correct the first time whenever possible.

28. Word Output

Chapter 24 looked at the various methods of input, or transmission of words, from the originator to the typist. In Chapter 27 one of these methods, viz. audio–dictation systems, was discussed in detail. With all these methods, the final process in the actual production of words on to paper is still achieved by typewriting or operation of a keyboard.

Secretarial pools

Word production is a secretarial service which is normally provided by secretarial staff from junior typists to executive secretaries, working in individual offices or in "pools". When typists (the word is used in the general sense of anyone who types) are employed to work for individual managers there are always times when some of them are over-employed while others are idle. It is now common in medium and large-scale organisations to have "pools" or "secretariats" in which several secretarial staff work. The work-load can be distributed among the staff so that all are productive.

In addition to the more even distribution of work, other advantages of pools include the minimising of distraction to other employees caused by noise; better training for junior staff; provision of ideal working conditions; improved supervision; and higher productivity.

Not all secretarial staff prefer to work in pools and there are some disadvantages. Typists tend to lose personal contact with executives and they may lose their continuity of interest in the business when not engaged on a personal basis. Disadvantages from the management viewpoint are that the work may not be of high quality (different typists dealing with the same manager's work), there may be delays in getting work done, and the pool may encourage gossiping.

The choice is not necessarily between a personal service and a typing pool. A compromise usually works well whereby all staff are in a pool, but they work on a personal basis except when it is necessary to share the work out because one typist has a particularly heavy volume of work, or to cover for absences. This form of secretarial organisation can also work with small groups of personal secretaries.

In the early days typing pools were not popular with either typists or managers. Now that the main disadvantages have been overcome it is more generally accepted that pools are an economical, and therefore desirable, arrangement.

The lack of personal contact between secretarial staff and executives can be overcome by allocating each typist to one or more executives, depending on average work-load. The typist does not work exclusively for "her" executive as she will help other typists when she has no work. She may also undertake other duties such as filing, copying, etc. This also overcomes the problems which arise when certain executives have highly specialised or technical work to be typed as individual typists become accustomed to the terminology, thus ensuring that production is of a consistently high standard.

Another means of giving personal contact is to allow the staff to go to the mangers when there is particularly difficult work which needs to be explained. In addition, finished work can be taken by the typist to the executive.

Typewriters

The first practical typewriter was introduced in 1873. It caused a revolution in the office much as George Stephenson's steam engine changed the face of transport in the early nineteenth century. Among other things, it created the position of typist, which has contributed to the mass employment of women in the office. Today the typewriter keyboard forms the basic input medium for many highly sophisticated electronic machines.

The most important features of typewriters are outlined below.

TYPES OF MACHINE

There are three main types of machine, viz. portable, standard manual and standard electric.

Portable typewriters, standing only 70 or 80 mm high, are light and compact. Many of them incorporate all the main features of a standard machine, though in some cases there is no facility for tabulating, i.e. moving the carriage several spaces in one movement to a predetermined stop by pressing a key.

There are also machines known as semi-portable, which are a scaled-down version of a standard machine, usually having all the same facilities.

Electrical models of standard and semi-portable typewriters are now produced. An electric typewriter has some important advantages.

(1) There is an enormous reduction in fatigue for the typist. Striking a key on a manual machine absorbs about four times the amount of energy absorbed by a similar action on an electric machine.

(2) The electrically motivated keys produce an even density which enhances the appearance of the work.

(3) By adjusting the pressure control and using light-weight paper and carbons, up to twenty legible copies can be obtained on some machines.

The only disadvantage is the weight of the standard electric machine, but as anyone who has duties in addition to typing should be provided with a suitable desk giving space for both typing and writing, this should not be a problem.

KEYBOARDS

The standard keyboard used in Britain and America is known as the QWERTY keyboard, which has 45 keys giving 90 characters. Continental keyboards vary slightly.

The Dvořák keyboard, devised in 1932, has the letters arranged to minimise finger movement by having the most commonly used keys on the "home" row, i.e. the row over which the fingers hover. It has never become popular because of the enormous cost involved in changing over from QWERTY machines.

A recent development is the Maltron keyboard, devised by Lilian Malt. Although this can be used with a standard electric typewriter it is more appropriate to word processing and will be discussed in that context later in the chapter.

CARRIAGES

On many typewriters the carriage is removable so that carriages of different lengths can be interchanged for different types of work. The standard carriage for general use is 330 mm (13 in.).★ Carriages ranging up to 650 mm (26 in.) can be obtained for accounts, legal, shipping, insurance and other special documents and returns.

★ Carriage lengths are still often quoted in inches.

TYPE PITCH

There are three standard type sizes or pitches, viz. 2.54 mm (standard pica), 2.34 mm (usually known as continental), and 2.12 mm (standard élite). The pitch is the width of each letter. Smaller and larger pitches can be obtained for special purposes.

Many machines now have a half-space bar so that if a letter is omitted it can be inserted by rearranging the surrounding letters by half a space.

PROPORTIONAL SPACING

A feature on some electric typewriters is proportional spacing, i.e. the amount of space for each letter varies according to the width of the letter, enabling the typist to "justify" the right-hand margin. This means making it straight like the left-hand margin (*see* page 326). Proportional spacing gives a more professional appearance to the printed copy.

TYPE STYLES

There are many type styles available, some of which give the appearance of print (suitable for prestige work), some shaded (not suitable for preparing duplicating masters), and some for special work, e.g. italics. All typewriter manufacturers offer a choice of styles, including different alphabets.

TYPE FOUNTS

Some electric typewriters have type founts, commonly called "golfballs", in place of type-bars (*see* Fig. 75). As each key is struck the fount revolves to the correct typing position before coming into contact with the paper. In fact some of the oldest typewriters had this style of printing device. The fount moves along the carriage, which is fixed, unlike the carriage used with typebars. The fount is very easily interchangeable and a wide variety of type styles are available. On some "golfball" machines, pica and élite sizes are also interchangeable.

LINE-SPACING

The standard vertical line-spacing is six lines to the inch, though occasionally slightly different measurements are found. (The inch measurement is used internationally for typewriter line-spacing.) A line-space regulator enables the typist to adjust the line-spacing to give 1 (single), 1½, 2 (double), 2½ and 3 (treble) spaces. Not all machines have 1½, 2½ and 3 regulation but the majority do.

[*Courtesy I.B.M. (U.K.) Ltd.*

Fig. 75 *Type fount (a) (commonly called a "golfball") used on (b) a fixed-carriage electric typewriter.*

TABULATORS

Invoices, statistics, balance sheets and many forms involve the setting out of figures in columns. A tabulator mechanism allows the carriage to be automatically moved, or tabulated, to the correct typing position, by the operation of a single key or bar. Some typewriters have decimal tabulator keys by which the typist can tabulate to a position from one to six spaces before the actual stop. This is particularly useful when typing columns of figures varying from units to millions.

RIBBONS

Though many machines still have the standard ribbon spools with a cotton, nylon or silk ribbon threaded through the ribbon carrier at the print point, there are now other types of ribbon devices. Several machines which have ribbon spools have a dual-ribbon device. This means that a carbon ribbon or a correcting ribbon can be fixed to the machine in addition to the fabric ribbon. To change from one ribbon to the other requires only the movement of a lever on the front of the machine.

Ribbon cartridges or cassettes are used on some electric typewriters. It takes only a few seconds to change a cartridge so it is easy to use a variety of types and colours of ribbon.

Fairly recently carbon ribbons for standard spools have become available. The advantage of carbon (or plastic) ribbons is that a sharper impression is obtained, although nylon and silk ribbons used with a clear-cut type fount such as roman pica or élite also give a clear outline. A carbon ribbon should always be used for reproduction work (*see* Chapter 29).

CORRECTION FACILITIES

A dual-ribbon device allows for a correcting ribbon to be permanently on the typewriter. At the press of a switch the typist can retype her error which will be covered in a white deposit and then type in the correction. The cartridge system enables the typist to change to a correcting ribbon in a few seconds.

So-called "self-correcting" typewriters normally have this white ribbon facility. One machine does, however, have the facility for actually "lifting off" the incorrect letters, leaving the space blank in which to insert the correction.

CONTINUOUS STATIONERY ATTACHMENTS

When typing consists of repetitive work, such as typing forms, e.g. invoices, the stationery can be purchased in "continuous form", i.e. sets of pre-collated forms perforated and folded into concertina packs. An attachment can be fitted to the typewriter to hold the completed forms, refolding them into a concertina pack after typing. The pack is later separated into sets, and the sheets and carbons are decollated.

VARIABLE TYPE STYLES, SIZES AND CHARACTERS

When preparing offset plates for reproduction, masters for copy-duplicating, or captions, etc. for diagrams and visual aids, it is desirable that the finished result should have the appearance of professional printing. There are facilities for producing virtually any material in any format on a typewriter.

(1) There are several manufacturers who produce typewriters with type founts (golf-balls) which are interchangeable for both style and size (pitch). These machines usually have interchangeable pica and elite pitch, as do word processors. Some word processors can produce in smaller type such as 15 characters to the inch. The daisywheels which are commonly used on word processor printers are available in a wide range of styles also.

(a) When preparing offset plates for reproduction, masters for copy-duplicating, captions etc for diagrams and visual aids, it is desirable that the finished result should have the appearance of professional printing. There are facilities for producing virtually any material in any format on a typewriter.

(b) When preparing offset plates for reproduction, masters for copy-duplicating, captions etc for diagrams and visual aids, it is desirable that the finished result should have the appearance of professional printing. There are facilities for producing virtually any material in any format on a typewriter.

Fig. 76 *Proportional spacing gives a more professional appearance to typed material.* Compare (a) standard élite pitch (12 characters to the inch) with (b) proportional spacing. In (a), all characters are of equal width; in (b), each character is given a width proportional to its size.

(2) Certain kinds of work require special characters and symbols—scientific and mathematical formulae are examples. If a certain symbol is required frequently, an infrequently used key, e.g. a fraction, should be replaced by the symbol. Symbols and characters used only occasionaly can be catered for by using special attachments called *Typits. Alphamods, betamods* and *deltamods* are available for use with I.B.M. electric machines.

RIGHT–HAND MARGIN JUSTIFICATION

The appearance of printed material is enhanced by a "justified", i.e. even, right-hand margin. There are several methods of achieving this.

(1) A justification lever and reading scale is provided on certain manual and electric typewriters. The length of a printed line required is decided. A draft is typed, a reading being taken from the scale at the end of each line. A final copy is then prepared using the justification lever in conjunction with the readings. This automatically justifies the right-hand margin.

(2) Proportional spacing, explained on page 323, can be used to justify the right-hand margin. Slightly more or less space is left

between words as required to spread the material across the page to a predetermined right-hand margin.

(3) The Varityper and the Justowriter (still found in some offices) have a facility for margin justification. On the Justowriter this is done by the production of punched paper tape as well as a hard copy for checking at the first typing: the variation of spacing needed to justify each line is recorded at the same time. The paper tape is then fed through the typewriter for the production of justified copy.

Automatic typewriters

The basis of an automatic typewriter is that the letter (or paragraphs of it), having been coded by means of punched tape, edge-punched cards or tabulating cards, or recorded on magnetic tape, sheet or disk, is "played back" on the automatic typewriter which automatically produces the hard copy at between 135 words per minute (punched tape) and 180 words per minute (magnetic media). The typist inserts manually the variable material, such as

[*Courtesy British Olivetti Ltd.*

Fig. 77 *Electronic typewriter with daisy-wheel printer which uses magnetic tape as a recording medium.*

name and address, amounts and dates. It is claimed that the output on an automatic typewriter equals that of three to four high-speed typists, and that 160 to 180 business letters per machine can be produced in a day. An automatic typewriter which uses magnetic tape as a recording medium is illustrated in Fig. 77.

The great value of the automatic typewriter is its ability to reproduce identical copies of letters (with individually typed names and addresses and other data) at great speed, thus saving type-writing manpower and slashing the cost of production. There are many occasions when it is desirable to send letters which appear to be individually typed, e.g. for sales work, letters to shareholders, invitations to tender, credit letters, accounts collection letters, Christmas greetings and so on.

"Automatic" typewriters are now more usually referred to as "electronic" and "memory" machines. The original term has been retained here to distinguish clearly between the limited facility explained above and word processing.

Composing machines

As many organisations have established their own print rooms, the need has arisen for cold-type composing machines on which professionally displayed material can be prepared for offset plate-making by photographic processes. Both a hard copy and recorded tape is produced by typing. Typing errors are corrected by back-spacing and overtyping. After checking and editing, changes in the text can be made by producing a second tape incorporating the first tape and amendments to the text. The typist does not have to prepare the final copy which is automatically displayed when the plate is produced from the tape.

The I.B.M. Selectric Composer (*see* Fig. 78) has a wide variety of printing founts, very high quality and appearance of print and automatically justified right-hand margin facility.

Choosing a typewriting machine

There is a wide variety of typewriters available. The choice depends to a great extent on the type of work it is required to do. For example, a fixed-carriage machine cannot be used for accounts documents. Questions to be answered include the following.

(1) What type of documents have to be typed?
(2) What size are the documents?
(3) What type pitch is most suitable?

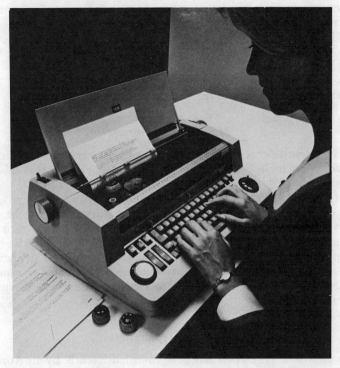

[Courtesy I.B.M. (U.K.) Ltd.

Fig. 78 *I.B.M. Selectric Composer on which material is prepared for offset plate-making.*

(4) What type style is most suitable?

(5) Are special characters or symbols used occasionally? Frequently?

(6) If statistical material is involved would a decimal tabulator be useful?

(7) Is easy interchange of ribbons needed?

(8) Is quick interchange of type style needed?

(9) What repetitive work is there?

(10) What reprographic masters have to be prepared?

(11) What correction facilities are needed?

(12) How many copies are usually needed from one typing?

Many organisations now have only electric typewriters and indeed many typists are unwilling to operate manual machines. Bearing in mind the fatigue factor and quality of production, who can blame them?

Practical points which may tip the balance in favour of one make of machine against another are:

(1) cost;
(2) period of guarantee;
(3) delivery date;
(4) maintenance contract price;
(5) distance of service technicians from the organisation.

Maintenance contracts

It is essential that all machines should be serviced regularly, typewriters included. A maintenance contract ensures that this is not overlooked.

There are two types of contract. A simple service contract covers regular visits by a mechanic to clean and adjust the machine. A service and spares contract includes the provision of spare parts as required at no cost. (The average cost is of course covered by the higher service charge.) Contracts are normally made on an annual basis. One point to watch is the inclusion of additional transport charges for service visits if the technicians are based some distance away.

"Pocket" typewriters

An electronic typewriter has been invented recently by an American. It is about the size of a large pocket calculator (*see* Fig. 79) and uses advanced computer technology involving the microprocessor "chip".

The electronic typewriter has five keys only. Each letter of the alphabet is "typed" by a "code" made up of a combination of keys. The letters appear on the display register in the same way as figures are indicated on a calculator. The twenty-six codes for the alphabet can be mastered in about half an hour. The input is retained in the typewriter memory.

To print the text a wire is attached from the electronic typewriter to an automatic typewriter and the hard copy is produced.

The amount of typescript which can be stored in the memory is limited as yet but it is hoped to develop a system for retaining the contents of a large book.

Word processors

Not so long ago any sophisticated means of producing typewritten material, i.e. any machine involving the use of a "memory" or

[*Courtesy the* Daily Telegraph

Fig. 79 *The electronic "pocket" typewriter based on the microprocessor "chip". Printout is obtained on an automatic typewriter.*

other recording device, was called a "word processor". Now the term has settled down to mean a combination of keyboard and visual display unit (a terminal), electronic memory and printer. The memory may be individual to the word-processing system or it may be the storage of a mainframe computer to which the word-processing system is linked.

There is a wide range of word-processing systems, the differences being in their capabilities as to the type of work that can be handled by the system, the speed of printout, the storage capacity, the potential for extensions to the system, the number of work-stations which can be linked to storage and printing resources, and, last but not least, cost.

SYSTEMS
There are three basic systems for word processing as follows.

[*Courtesy Siemens Ltd.*

Fig. 80 *Siemens Word Bank Model 580 consisting of keyboard, visual display unit and printer.* The line printer shown can be replaced by a bi-directional daisywheel printer if required.

(1) Stand-alone systems in which the keyboard, visual display unit, memory and printer are self-contained in one work-station. Figure 80 illustrates this type of word processor.

(2) Shared-facility systems in which a number of terminals feed text into a memory "bank" which is serviced by one or more printers.

(3) Shared-logic systems, similar to shared facility systems, but using a mainframe computer for storage of text, and also for additional facilities such as "intercommunication" between distant work-stations, telex printout, etc. (*see* Fig. 81). The work-stations are either terminals or printers.

OPERATION

As the operator keys in the text it is displayed on a screen so that the material can be checked and corrected as necessary. "Instructions" for margins, line ends, tabulation, line-spacing, indentions, etc. are given by means of keys. Once the material has been finalised it can be printed when required.

The writer can check the hard-copy draft and make amendments. When the amended draft is received by the operator she retrieves the text on the visual screen and inserts corrections, deletes and adds words, sentences or paragraphs. The position of

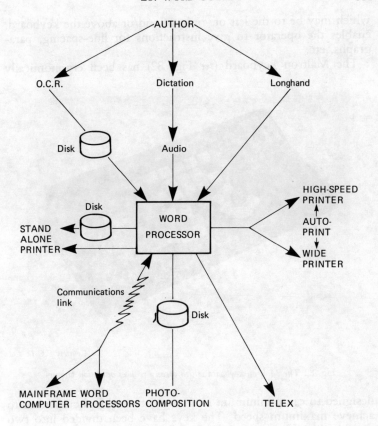

Fig. 81 *Word-processing system configuration*, showing how the word processor can be the focal point of a communications input/output system, including two-way links with a mainframe computer and other word processors via a telephone network.

the text which follows the amended material is automatically adjusted to follow on.

The editing process can be repeated as many times as necessary until the text is exactly right and ready for final printing.

The text is stored in the memory, which may be in the form of punched tape, disk, floppy disk, twin mini-floppy disk or mainframe computer storage. The text can then be produced on the printer whenever required.

KEYBOARDS

The standard keyboard consists of "typing" keys arranged like a QWERTY keyboard on a typewriter. An additional panel of keys, which may be to the left of, right of and/or above the keyboard, enables the operator to give instructions for line-spacing, paragraphs, etc.

The Maltron keyboard (*see* Fig. 82) has been ergonomically

[*Courtesy P.C.D. Ltd.*

Fig. 82 *The Maltron keyboard which greatly reduces operation fatigue.*

designed to cause minimum fatigue and to enable the operator to achieve maximum speed. The keys have been divided into two panels which are a comfortable distance apart for left and right hands. The keys are at different levels to allow for the variation in finger lengths. Keys which demand least finger movement represent most commonly used letters.

Typists can "convert" to operating the Maltron keyboard in a few hours and find that they can revert to the standard QWERTY keyboard at any time without difficulty.

It has three uses:

(1) it can be linked to a standard electric typewriter as a means of enabling a typist to produce more work with less fatigue;

(2) it can be linked to an automatic typewriter for quicker input of text;

(3) it can be linked to the input unit of a word-processing system.

Because it is so much easier to become a competent operator on a Maltron keyboard it can be used by a manager wishing to compose highly confidential material. Only he would know the code for retrieval from the word-processing memory.

The word-processing system in which the Maltron keyboard is used is portable. This gives a major facility in that it can be moved easily into the manager's office enabling him to give non-recorded dictation. The keyboard is quiet in operation so there is no distraction. The dictater can read his text on the visual display unit and amend it immediately. In this way a final copy of even difficult text could be produced within minutes of the dictation being completed.

Word-processing facilities

The facilities of the many systems available vary greatly. A few of the most important variations are listed below.

Work-stations using shared facilities vary in number from 2 to 16.

Visual display units screens range from approximately half a line script, to a full line, to a whole page or more. The screen width can accommodate as few as 80 or as many as 102 characters.

Storage of text (memory) may be on punched tape, floppy disk, or twin mini-floppy disk.

Storage capacity may be quoted in characters or in pages and ranges from 30 pages to 40,000 pages, from 65,000 characters to 400 million characters. It is worth checking the storage quantity because different manufacturers use different relationships between the number of characters and the number of pages.

Printers are usually either Diablo or Qume. Both have interchangeable print styles and sizes which are quoted either in points, e.g. 8 to 14 points, or in characters to the inch which may range, for example, from 10 to 17. The size of paper which can be produced ranges through A4 (210 mm wide), 380 mm and 750 mm; speeds range from 35 characters per second (540 words per minute) to 175 characters per second (2,100 words per minute). The printing mechanism is normally a bi-directional daisywheel (*see* Fig. 80) which means that printing is from left to right and "backwards" from right to left. It is interesting that the daisywheel was used as the printing mechanism on some very early typewriters. A justified right-hand margin can be achieved on bi-directional printers.

Printers take normal continuous stationery (*see* Chapter 47) with punched ratchet holes at each edge. Letterheads, forms, envelopes, etc. can be attached to continuous stationery with a fine line of adhesive so that the paper can be removed easily from the fanfold after printing. Continuous stationery is fed into the printer by traction feed. Individual sheets can be fed in manually one by one, as in a typewriter, or by hopper feed which holds a stack of paper and feeds in each sheet automatically for printing. Complementary facilities include:

(a) filing on floppy disks with retrieval by the word processor;

(b) glossary and indexing;

(c) collation of information intended for British Telecom's Viewdata/Prestel system (*see* Chapter 22);

(d) conversion via a mainframe computer of information for use on Viewdata/Prestel;

(e) simultaneous word and data processing;

(f) inter-communication between workstations and printers via telephone lines so that material keyed in one location can be printed in another, thousands of miles distant if necessary.

There is one system which at least can print out complicated drawings, (charts and diagrams), graphs and scientific formulae, while another can plot a line on a graph.

Word-processing applications

Word processing is an economic proposition for large volume work. It is not suitable for short letters and short "one-off" documents. It has three main applications—repetitive work, text editing, and updating, which is an extension of text editing.

REPETITIVE WORK

The main advantage over automatic typewriters is the greater speed of printout. Where large quantities of material are involved this is important. Answering mail order enquiries, production of direct mail letters are examples. The merging of names and addresses from mailing lists with standard material, e.g. letters, legal documents, and insertion of appropriate variables, is a facility which gives even greater speed of output.

TEXT EDITING

Especially valuable for technical, scientific, and accounting and other professional work, the text-editing facility obviates the need for umpteen "retypes" of drafts which are invariably thought to be the "final copy". It takes time to amend the text on a word processor but a great deal less time, frustration and boredom than retyping whole documents.

UPDATING

Material which is constantly changing, such as indexes, price lists, catalogues, stores lists, parts lists, directories, etc., can be updated quickly and easily by amending the text and reprinting. Lists can also be sorted into alphabetical, numeric or chronological sequence in ascending order on some machines.

INVOICING AND ANALYSES

Word processors which combine typewriting and calculating functions are available. All variable data such as invoice number, dates, methods of despatch and terms of payment are printed automatically by the machine. There are many standard programs available to meet the needs of most organisations but programs can be devised to meet specific needs.

FUTURE APPLICATIONS

Word processing is still relatively young. New applications are being devised with mesmerising rapidity. The extent to which communications systems will include word processing can only be surmised at present but it is a major "growth" area in the office and will undoubtedly have a great impact on word output.

Installing a word-processing system

As with any other new system, the value, in terms of cost-effectiveness, to the individual organisation must be carefully investigated. Questions of staff—training, numbers, redundancies, redeployment, acceptance of new technology—have to be discussed, planned and organised. Some organisations have installed a "pilot project" using, in some cases, more than one system so as to judge the benefits and disadvantages of various facilities.

In some organisations a word processor has been installed on a trial basis for use by any member of the secretarial staff with a suitable task to complete. A regular operator for non-individual work is usually employed. The results have been far from successful. The machine has been "a new toy" for the secretaries who have held back work in order to do it themselves rather than send to the regular operator. It is, of course, highly desirable that all staff should know the capabilities of word processing, but proper organisation is essential. It should be regarded as a facility available to the whole organisation in the same way as mailing facilities or any other common service.

There may be a case for installing word processing in or near the department where it is used most, but this should not preclude its use by other departments which have appropriate work which could be more economically produced by word processing.

If the facility is to be a central service to the whole organisation a careful survey of word output (types and quantity) must be mounted in all departments/branches and even companies within the organisation. Datapost (*see* Chapter 23) ensures very quick delivery of printout. A group consisting of a number of small companies might well benefit by the installation of a word-processing system in one location.

As with every other new type of technology, adequate training of both operators and users is essential. This should include advantages (if any) to the individual and the organisation, costs (investment and savings), facilities and performance capabilities, operation and input requirements. It is just as important to get dictation as accurate as possible the first time with word processing as it is with conventional typing.

There are over fifty manufactures of word processing systems. Choosing the right machine for particular needs is a formidable task. The first step is to prepare a list of the work which would be less time-consuming if produced by word processing instead of by typing. Accuracy should also be taken into consideration. Then obtain information from eight to twelve manufacturers and identify the facilities provided by each. See a demonstration of the machines with facilities which meet your anticipated needs. For example, horizontal transposition is essential for the production of current final accounts from the previous year's documents. Involve the secretarial staff at this stage.

Check on details such as service time, which can vary from 3+ hours to 24 hours; costs of disks—ranges from approximately £6 to £30 and over (1980); type of printer—supplies for Diablo printers are currently more expensive than those for Qume printers.

Word-processing costs

The main objective is obviously increased productivity by reduction in the unit cost of producing a document, taking into account all cost factors. The sort of figure that is quoted is an increased productivity rate of 148 per cent from 500 typists in one organisation. Where documents are produced in great quantity and each series is relatively similar, the cost of individual typing can be reduced to a little under a twentieth by word processing. In such operations as text editing and text retrieval a typist's productivity can be increased by up to 1,000 per cent, though this is rare.

The capital cost is high, ranging from approximately £6,000 (in 1980) for a sophisticated automatic typewriter-style word processor without a visual display unit (available as an optional extra) but with better performance capabilities, to £45,000 for a shared logic system comprising four work-stations (three terminals and one printer) with capacity for expansion to sixteen work-stations.

Ancillary equipment for typists

There are various items of equipment which can help to take the strain from the constant concentration needed for accurate word output.

COPYHOLDER
Copyholders are available ranging from a "lip" or groove on the front of a typewriter to hold a shorthand notebook to an electrically operated copyholder with cursor for statistical work (*see* Fig. 83).

[*Courtesy Data Presentation Co.*

Fig. 83 *Electric Dataliner Copyholder with magnifying reading bar which reduces eyestrain and fatigue for the keyboard operator.*

The cursor can be in the form of a magnifying reading bar, particularly useful for small print or "squiggly" manuscript corrections, or a draft.

Copyholders hold the copy at a slight angle from vertical which reduces eyestrain and consequently helps to improve accurate keyboard operation.

VISUAL DISPLAY UNIT TROLLEY STAND

A trolley stand designed for keyboard and visual display unit enables the terminal to be moved easily from place to place. Two of the four wheels have brakes so that the stand can be locked into position. Fixed and/or swivel shelves can be fitted.

PART FIVE

REPRODUCTION, STORAGE AND RETRIEVAL OF DOCUMENTS

29. Reprographic Methods and Applications

Possibly the first step towards mechanisation in the office was the endeavour to get rid of laborious hand-copying. Office work has always required copying to be done, even if it is only to keep a record of what has been said in outgoing correspondence.

James Watt is credited with having invented a duplicating machine in 1780, but it is said to have taken about six minutes to obtain a single copy, and for very many years the only way of obtaining a copy of a document was by hand-copying. In fact there was a lowly specialist vocation known as a "copy clerk". Then came the typewriter, which was eagerly sought after when it was found that a carbon copy of the outgoing letter could be made on the machine at the same time as the original was typed.

Carbon copying (manifolding)

The typing of an original with carbon copies is often the cheapest and quickest method of obtaining a limited number of copies. The number of clear copies obtainable depends on the weight and type of paper (a thin, hard-surfaced "bank" is suitable for producing many copies) and carbon paper (lightweight film carbon gives clear reproduction on more copies); on the type of ribbon (cotton gives the poorest results as the thickness of the materials tends to blur the impression of the letters); on the touch of the typist; and on the type of machine (up to twenty clear copies can be obtained on an electric typewriter using lightweight paper and carbons, up to twelve on a standard machine and up to about five on a portable machine). (*See also* Chapter 47 for different types of carbon paper.)

Duplicating methods

The development of office systems and the vast increase in paperwork have given added prominence to duplicators. With the increase in the number of duplicating methods there is a need to know which one to use for each job.

"Duplicating" may be defined as a process for obtaining multiple copies of a document from one master. It is different from copying which is a process by which, with a few exceptions, copies are made from the original (*see* Chapter 30).

There are three basic methods of duplicating, some of which can give as good a result as professional printing. They are: (i) spirit duplicating; (ii) stencil (or ink) duplicating; and (iii) offset lithography. These are discussed in detail below.

Spirit duplicating

This very simple process is sometimes known as the hectograph method. It is cheap, quick and can be carried out with relatively little training.

MASTERS

The master is prepared by typing or writing on a sheet of art paper (glossy surface) backed with a hectographic carbon or transfer sheet so that a reverse image is obtained on the back of the master. Alternatively a special attachment can be fitted to a typewriter to carry a hectograph ribbon behind the master. Spirit masters can also be prepared on a thermal copier (*see* page 361).

RUNNING OFF

Spirit duplicators are normally of the rotary type. The master is affixed to the drum on the machine, so that the carbon image is on the outside. As the copy paper is fed into the machine it is dampened with spirit (fed from a reservoir on the machine), and when the drum is rotated it is pressed against the master copy. The spirit on the paper dissolves a little of the carbon on the master which leaves a deposit, i.e. the impression on the copy paper. The small amount of spirit on the paper dries in a matter of seconds, leaving the image on the paper. Special glazed paper can be bought for running off but ordinary good quality typewriting paper is equally suitable. Manual and electric machines are available, most of them having automatic spirit control and paper feed.

COLOUR REPRODUCTION

Spirit duplicating is the only method by which up to seven colours can be reproduced simultaneously. This is achieved by changing the hectograph or transfer sheets before preparing each part of the master required in a different colour. It is ideal for charts, graphs, diagrams, maps, etc.

LINE SELECTION AND MASKING

Spirit duplicating is applied to production control and shipping documentation by means of a line selection machine (*see* Fig. 84). A

[*Courtesy Ozalid (U.K.) Ltd.*

Fig. 84 *A line selection spirit duplicator used to reproduce from one master all the documents involved in a transaction.* Push-button control allows reproduction of individual lines, groups of lines or items from the master.

master copy is prepared containing all the information needed for the entire transaction. Lines are then selected as required for reproduction on specific documents such as invoices and other customer documents, bills of lading and shipping documents, job cards, labels, etc.

An alternative method is to use masks. The mask for each type of document has cut-out areas or zones to allow only the relevant information to be reproduced on the appropriate form.

Stencil duplicating

In 1881 a flat-bed wax stencil duplicator was invented. The master was placed on a frame with copy paper underneath, and when the frame was shut down an inked roller was run over it. It was not until 1899 that this flat-bed machine was developed into a rotary duplicator.

STENCILS

Although the process started as "wax stencil" the master used now is a thin fibrous sheet covered on one side with a plastic coating through which ink will not pass. The stencil is then impressed (or cut): on a typewriter, with a hand stylus, on a thermal copier or on an electronic scanner (see below). "Universal" stencils are available which fit any make of duplicator, are tear-resistant and withstand rough handling.

RUNNING OFF

The cut stencil (master) is placed on a perforated and padded inked drum or on a screen stretched over two cylinders (depending on the type of machine). As the drum is rotated the copy paper is fed between it and an impression roller, and the ink is forced through the stencil on to the paper, producing the image required. The paper must be semi-absorbent, although modern "hard-sized" duplicating paper is available on which it is possible to write in pen and ink.

COLOUR REPRODUCTION

To produce multichromatic copies it is necessary to prepare a stencil for each different coloured section of the document and to put the copy paper through the machine once for each colour, using a different stencil for each. The drums and ink must also be changed. Although it may seem inconvenient to keep changing the inked drums, one British machine claims a 25-second drum change.

MACHINE FACILITIES

The modern manual or electric stencil duplicator has an automatic

[*Courtesy Roneo Vickers Ltd.*

Fig. 85 *Fully automatic ink duplicator controlled by operating push-button keys.*

inking device, automatic paper feed, and switches off the print lever automatically when the pre-set number of copies has been printed. One fully automatic machine is controlled by a panel of push-buttons (*see* Fig. 85). Machines are available to take stencils up to A3 size (420 mm wide).

Special attachments can be obtained for running off very small documents, e.g. labels, or thicker copy material such as card, and for interleaving copies made on non-absorbent paper to avoid "offsetting" by the wet ink on the copy underneath.

It is claimed that as many as 7,000 copies can be obtained from a high-quality stencil, although the average stencil gives about 2,000 good copies. The actual number of copies which can be obtained from a stencil varies with the quality of the stencil used, the skill of the typist when typing the master and the skill of the duplicator operator.

Used stencils can be stored and used again: they should be stored either flat in folders with a sheet of absorbent paper between each or hung on suspension rails.

PHOTOGRAPHIC FILM

This is a method of making a stencil from a film by a photographic process. The original must be in dense black ink on a transparent or semi-transparent paper which is then exposed to a strong light. After the developing, washing and drying processes, the film is then used as a stencil on a standard duplicating machine for rolling off copies in the normal way. Reduced or enlarged copies of the original can be made, and this is a distinct advantage of this method. This process is recommended for the reproduction of line drawings or technical data (which may be difficult work for a typist) where the number of copies required is not very large and no photocopying apparatus is to hand.

ELECTRONIC STENCIL

A facsimile copy of any document, whether on thick or thin paper, can be cut in a few minutes on an electronic scanner or stencil-cutting machine. The original, whether it be photograph, line drawing, printed document or a pencil sketch, can then be repro-duced in thousands.

The document to be copied is fixed on a drum beside which a second drum holds the electronic stencil, which may be either paper or plastic. The document is then electronically scanned and 500 perforations to the inch give a faithful reproduction on the stencil of every mark on the original.

Some scanners now have a colour selection facility. This means that each colour on a colour printed document can be cut on individual stencils. The stencils are then run off in turn on the same copy paper, thus reproducing coloured copies of the original.

Electronic scanning is particularly useful for the reproduction of forms, diagrams and documents "mocked up" from cuttings, typewriting, etc. Manufacturers' agents and typing bureaux offer a stencil-cutting service which is useful to organisations where the amount of such stencils required does not justify the purchase of a machine.

Offset lithography

THE OFFSET PROCESS

In 1796, Senefelder discovered that if a reverse image was drawn on a flat, smooth stone with a greasy crayon, and if the rest of the stone was kept damp, the application of an inking roller would apply ink to the image only, and copies could be made from it. Lithography has thus been in existence for very many years, but the modern process known as "offset lithography" was not developed until 1880, when zinc masters were used instead of stone.

The modern process is the same in principle and still depends on the antipathy of grease and water. A greasy image is produced on the master by typing, handwriting, photography or certain copying processes, and this is then fixed to the outside of a cylinder. The roller comes in contact with inked cylinders and water, and the image is then offset on to another roller (known as a blanket) on which it produces a negative impression. Paper is then fed between the blanket and an impression roller and receives a positive imprint.

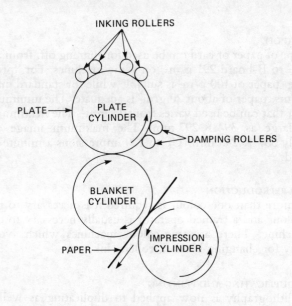

Fig. 86 *The offset process.*

OFFSET PLATES

One of the latest developments is the use of plastic pre-sensitised plates which can be prepared on a tranfer diffusion copier (*see* Chapter 30). As many as 10,000 copies are claimed from a plastic plate costing only a few pence. Offset plates can also be produced on electrostatic copiers, both xerographic and direct (*see* Chapter 30).

A wide variety of plates are available, the choice depending on the process by which the plate is to be prepared and the number of copies required. The different types of plate are listed below.

(1) *Copper plates* (comparatively expensive) prepared photographically give almost unlimited copies (40,000 to 50,000 easily).

(2) *Aluminium plates* prepared photographically give up to 25,000 copies. Many suppliers provide a plate-making service which is useful if they are needed infrequently.

(3) *Plastic plates* prepared on copying machines give up to 10,000 copies.

(4) *Paper plates* prepared by hand with a special pencil or on the typewriter give up to 5,000 copies, though some heavy duty plates will give up to 10,000 copies.

(5) *Parchment plates* prepared on the typewriter give at least 1,000 copies.

RUNNING OFF

Any type of paper or card can be used for running off, from airmail 45 g/m² to B-board 291 g/m², on some machines. For "prestige" printing, paper of 100 g/m² is suitable while for standard material, e.g. forms, paper of about 70 g/m² is adequate. The minimum size of paper that can be used varies from 75 mm². The maximum may be as large as 394 × 297 mm. The maximum image area is normally 337 × 248 mm. Up to 120 impressions a minute can be obtained.

COLOUR REPRODUCTION

When more than one colour is required it is necessary to run for each colour and a trained operator is usually necessary to operate the machine. There are two-colour machines which avoid the necessity for changing blanket, rollers, ink, etc.

OFFSET DUPLICATING AND PRINTING

Offset lithography is now applied to duplicating as well as to printing. A trained operator is required for the printing process. Offset duplicating can be undertaken by anyone in the office with no more training, and in some cases less, than is necessary for stencil duplicating. Fully automatic offset duplicators are available. These accept and affix the plate, run off the required number of copies, and release and remove the plate without any assistance other than the depression of a button. Most offset duplicators are table models no bigger than an ink duplicating machine (*see* Fig. 87).

[*Courtesy Gestetner Ltd.*

Fig. 87 *Gestetner Model 319 automatic offset duplicator.*

A numbering, signature and overprinting attachment can be obtained for an offset duplicator. Forms are normally required to be numbered sequentially, as are also tickets and official documents of various kinds. Direct mail letters can be "signed" by inserting a signature plate in the attachment. Overprinting may be required for special sales prices, trade marks, etc.

Collating units can be attached to an offset duplicator making the production of the finished document a quicker process.

The economy arising from using an offset-litho machine has become more and more apparent as normal printing costs have risen. The saving over normal outside printing costs is reckoned to be at least 30–40 per cent, and many local authorities and large business organisations have installed their own printing departments. The offset-litho process is recommended where long runs of thousands are required (and where a machine is already installed it is cheap for short runs if parchment masters are used), for line drawings or halftone illustrations, for reproducing on any kind of paper, and where permanence of the master and of the copies is required.

Typesetting

There are several methods of setting up the content of material to be duplicated. Most of them involve the use of a typewriter or a keyboard.

DIRECT TYPING

The master is prepared on the typewriter. This applies to spirit masters, ink duplicating stencils and offset plates (paper and parchment).

COLD-TYPE COMPOSING

The preparation of a master from which an offset plate may be produced by a photographic process is known as cold-type composing. This can be done on any electric typewriter, a Varityper or a composer (*see* Chapter 28).

PHOTO-TYPESETTING (OR PHOTO-COMPOSITION)

The text is "keyed into" a photographic machine. Different sizes and styles of print are "selected" by pressing an appropriate key. The text is seen on a small display.

"HOT METAL" TYPESETTING

The printer sets individual metal blocks for each letter or line into a block. It is a very slow process requiring great skill.

COMPUTER TYPESETTING

The text is "keyed into" the computer via a terminal which may be a word processor with a visual display unit. The operator instructs the computer as to the display required but does not have to produce displayed content. The material to be duplicated is produced on a printer, the hard copy then being used to prepare an offset plate.

COPYING PROCESSES

Spirit and ink duplicating stencils can be produced on a thermal copier (*see* page 361). The content of the original must have been prepared with a lead-base material, such as pencil, or carbon typewriting ribbon. Offset plates can be produced by several copying processes (*see* Chapter 30).

Choice of method

It is not possible to lay down which method is most suitable for certain purposes, as there are so many variable factors. A particular process which may seem expensive to run may prove to be economical if it is installed for more than one purpose and if the maximum use is made of the machine.

Many of the special features of the various processes have been mentioned. A summary is given below of the factors which should be considered when deciding on the appropriate duplicating process for a particular task.

(1) Number of copies required.

(2) Frequency of demand (how often the machine will be used).

(3) Speed of reproduction (sometimes speed is most important).

(4) Type of copy paper—perhaps a good writing surface is needed.

(5) Whether halftone illustrations, line drawings, and/or text is to be reproduced.

(6) Economy of operation (cost of materials and of operator).

(7) Whether it is wished to enlarge or reduce the size of originals.

(8) Whether variable details on pre-cut forms are needed.

(9) Number of colours required.

(10) Durability of image, and of master.

(11) Whether typewritten appearance is desired.

(12) Whether printed typeset appearance is preferred.

Summary of methods

A summary of the reprographic methods, including automatic typewriters, appears on pages 352 to 355, giving details of equipment and supplies needed, preparation of masters, applications, advantages and disadvantages.

PROCESS Types of equipment	Supplies	Master Method of preparation	Number of copies
CARBON PAPER Typewriter if material is type-written	Carbon sheets Coloured carbons available in a variety of colours, weights and sizes One-time carbons Film carbons (sharper image and longer life) Plastic backed carbons	 Handwriting Typewriting	Up to 4 Up to 20 (electric type-writer) depending on weight of paper and carbon
CARBON FREE AND CARBON PROCESSED PAPER Typewriter if material is type-written	Pre-collated sets of document forms, each sheet a different colour	 Handwriting Typewriting	Up to 6
AUTOMATIC TYPEWRITING Programming typewriter with attachment for magnetic tape or card, or punched tape, or with connection to computer with or without visual display unit	Tapes or cards Typewriting paper	Magnetic tape or card Punched tape Computer storage Typewriting	Unlimited
SPIRIT DUPLICATING Portable machine Standard manual machine Standard electric machine Line selection electric machines of several sizes with a variety of facilities for reproducing sets of documents from one master Addressing machine (a wide variety are available from miniature hand-operated to fully automatic)	Master sheets/transfer sheets (various colours) or hectograph carbon typewriter ribbon (various colours) Pre-collated master sets Correcting fluid or eraser Running-off paper (glossy surface or good quality typewriting paper) Spirit Address plates and storage box	Spirit master sheet with hectograph carbon/trans-fer sheet Thermal master Handwriting Typewriting Drawing Thermal copying machine	Up to 500
INK DUPLICATING Single drum or two cylinder machines can be obtained Portable machines Standard manual machine Standard electric machine Brief-size machine to take double width stencils Push-button electrical machine (single drum only) Colour change equipment Interleaving cradle and inter-leaves (for use with non-absorbent paper)	Stencils (a wide variety for different purposes are available including one with a stencil head to fit any duplicating machine) Plastic back plate (to give better impression) Transparent plastic film sheet or typewriter ribbon (to avoid clogging typewriting keys with wax from stencil) Styli (many different heads available for different purposes)	Wax stencil sheet Handwriting Typewriting Drawing	Up to 7,000

Uses	Advantages	Disadvantages
Correspondence, reports, business documents (including continuous stationery)	No master required	Limited number of copies Collating and decollating of carbon packs takes time Error correction on carbon copies is time-consuming
Memo sets Business documents	No master required Time saved by not collating and decollating carbon packs	Copies fade quite quickly
Standard letters Invitation to tender Quotations Communications with shareholders Reports	Speed of reproduction approx. 150 words a minute Automatic reproduction can be combined with individual typing of addresses, dates, amounts, etc. Accuracy assured Correction of errors on master easy The master can be amended easily at any time Every document appears to have been individually typed	Capital outlay is high
Internal circulars and notices Business documents Export documents Lesson notes Coloured charts, diagrams, maps Addressing	Quick and cheap to produce No special pens or tools required Simultaneous colour reproduction Master can be stored for further use up to 500 copies Complete set of documents can be prepared from one master by using masks or line selection Masters can be amended after use	Error correction on masters not easy Limited number of good copies Quality of reproduction is not very high Printed copy fades quickly in the light
Circulars for external distribution Reports Training materials	Excellent quality reproduction can be obtained from well-prepared stencils Any size of material can be reproduced from postcard size to brief/A3 size (depending on size of duplicating machine) Many different types of lines, drawings, etc. can be drawn Errors on stencils can be corrected easily before use Master can be stored for further use up to maximum number of copies	Expensive when few copies are required from one master Interleaving is necessary if copies are required on non-absorbent paper Separate runs have to be made for each colour necessitating changing parts of the machine

	Supplies	Master	Number of copies
		Method of preparation	
...aring sten-...ing) ...printing cards	Wheelpens (various "wheels" available for producing different types of dotted lines)	Electronic stencil (plastic or paper)	Up to 10,000
	Burnisher and burnishing block (for shading)	Electronic scanner (stencil-cutting machine)	
	Plate for signature writing Correction fluid (red or white)	Thermal stencil	Up to 7,000
	Running-off paper (semi-absorbent) Stencil storage folders Ink (many colours available) Cleaning spirit	Thermal copying machine	
Addressing machine	Address plates and storage box		
OFFSET LITHOGRAPHY	Metal plates* Paper plates Lithocarbon typewriting	Metal plate: copper aluminium	Up to 50,000 Up to 25,000
Photographic equipment (for preparing metal plates*)	ribbon Plate eraser Printing paper and card	Photography Photographic typesetting Computer typesetting	
* Metal plates are prepared by photographing a document typed with a carbon ribbon on good quality typewriting paper. An electric typewriter must be used.	Ink (many colours available) Blanket cleaner Cleaning spirit	Paper plate Parchment plate	Up to 10,000 Up to 1,000
		Typewriting with carbon or litho ribbon	
		Plastic plate	Up to 10,000
		Copying	
Mono-colour machine Bi-colour machine (a separate run for each colour is necessary, but equipment does not have to be changed) Fully automatic machine (when plate is fed into the machine it is attached to the fixing head, run off and detached automatically) Word processor, composer, Varityper, Flexowriter, Justowriter, or electric typewriter with proportional spacing if justified, i.e. straight, right-hand margin is required			

Uses	Advantages	Disadvantages
Printed materials Letterheads and forms Photographs and drawings Complicated diagrams Printed material Letterheads and forms Diagrams	Copy paper (absorbent and semi-absorbent) is relatively cheap and is available in a variety of weights and colours Individual colours on an original can be cut individually on separate stencils on certain types of electronic scanner	
Addressing		
Letterheads and forms Books and journals Advertising material	Fully professional reproduction Reproduction of photographs Up to 10,000 impressions an hour on some machines Cheap reproduction for large quantities and/or large volume of work Any type of paper can be used Plate can be stored for further use up to maximum number of copies	Trained operator required for some machines Capital outlay is high Separate runs have to be made for each colour including bi-colour machines Correction of errors on type-written plates is not easy

30. Copying Processes

Copying is a term which covers a number of processes, some of which have been used in offices for a great many years, while some have become common more recently. The term "photocopying" has been, and still is, commonly used but most of the processes are not photographic at all, being dependent on the use of heat or a combination of heat and light and requiring only the simplest of chemical processes. The result is the same whichever method is used. The basic concept of copying is that a facsimile of the original document is reproduced by using a special machine which obviates the need for copying on a typewriter. The quality of reproduction and also the cost vary according to the process used.

Advantages and disadvantages

Not only can exact copies of documents be obtained when required, and at short notice, but copies of complicated and detailed documents take no longer than those which are simpler. When a facsimile copy is obtained, every detail on the original document is faithfully reproduced. There is no need to check the copy. Thus the labour cost for typing and checking is eliminated.

Against this, however, photocopies have been known to fade and tend not to last as long as some other duplicated material. Some copying paper is coated with chemical emulsion, as a result of which it has a tendency to curl up instead of lying flat.

Processes

Basically, there are eight different methods of photocopying:
  (1) reflex;
  (2) diffusion transfer;
  (3) gelatine transfer;

(4) direct positive;
(5) dye-line;
(6) electrostatic;
(7) thermal;
(8) dual spectrum.

These are described below. Although there are several other processes, they are in the main variations of the above and have therefore not been included. (Microcopying is discussed in Chapter 36 as it is closely connected with the keeping of records.)

REFLEX

This method very closely resembles that used in conventional photographic dark-room procedures. Any kind of document can be used, whether opaque or translucent, or with an image on both sides. The first exposure gives, after processing, a laterally reversed negative from which any number of positive prints can be made by further exposure and processing.

Usually two successive baths for development and stabilisation are required. While the process can be carried out under a certain amount of artificial light, direct daylight must be excluded. The sensitised material provides a higher quality copy than any of the non-optical group of copiers.

DIFFUSION TRANSFER

This is perhaps the cheapest type of machine on the market. The first exposure is made on to a negative but, unlike the reflex process, the negative is processed in the machine together with a sheet of non-light-sensitive positive paper to produce an immediate readable positive copy. In practice, both negative and positive are fed into the machine together, with the original sandwiched in between, and after exposure and the removal of the original, the negative and positive are peeled apart to reveal a readable positive print.

It is possible, though not very practicable, to obtain further copies (as many as fifteen) from the same negative, using Multi-copy negative paper. Again, direct daylight must be excluded but, where only single copies are required, this machine processes automatically, and all that is necessary is to feed negative and positive with the original in one slot, and the positive copy is delivered from another slot in the machine.

The process is fairly quick (about one minute for one copy), and it can be used to create a negative and offset-litho plates directly from a positive original, which offers great benefits both in time and economy for offset-litho users. It is also possible to create a translucent master which can be used in conjunction with the dye-line process (*see* below).

GELATINE TRANSFER

This process enables copies to be made from both opaque and translucent originals. It can be operated in normal office lighting, but the quality of reproduction is not as high as in either of the two previous processes.

A gelatine-coated matrix is exposed to light with the original and is then put in an activating solution. The gelatine then becomes soft and subsequently transfers an image on to the copy paper, which is uncoated non-light-sensitive, making the process very cheap. It is normally used to make not less than six copies, but as many as fifteen can be obtained from the same original. It is also possible to make a translucent master for use on a dye-line copier. The matrix can also be used to transfer an image on to a paper plate for use with offset-litho duplicators.

DIRECT POSITIVE

The sensitised materials used with this process are much less sensitive than any of the previous processes mentioned, and therefore can be operated under a certain amount of daylight.

The first exposure by this method yields a black image on a white ground, from which further copies can be made in readable positive form by subsequent exposure and processing. Special translucent paper is available which, with the aid of a suitable light filter, can produce a right-way reading positive image, although the quality is slightly lower in this case.

The direct positive method gives very high quality copies and the materials are capable of giving good results from all coloured images. One of the virtues of the process (apart from requiring less critical light conditions) is that it is possible to provide a mirror copy on translucent material, ideally suited for subsequent use by the dye-line process.

DYE-LINE (DIAZO)

Originals which are to be reproduced by the dye-line (or Diazo) process need to be on transparent or translucent paper, which is placed in contact with special dye-line paper and subjected to light. The chemical coating on the copy paper is bleached white, leaving the image outlined on the paper, which has then to be developed, either by exposure to ammonia fumes or by the use of developing fluid, by which the image is dyed black. This process is suitable where the image appears only on one side of the paper and where the paper is transparent or translucent. Within these limitations, the process is simple, quick and cheap—for a limited number of copies.

The major use of this method is in systems application, where a great deal of repetitive work is involved; for example, it may prove cheaper to have office forms printed on transparent paper and to produce further copies as required by the dye-line process.

A variation of both reflex and dye-line processes is the use of a paper faced with perforated metal foil. This foil can be handled like any other translucent original.

The dye-line process can be operated in daylight, and in any amount of artificial light. Copies can also be produced on card, linen or manilla.

ELECTROSTATIC PROCESS

Although both reflex and dye-line processes constitute improvements on previous copying methods, it is still necessary to have both developing and fixing—even if it is "semi-dry".

The electrostatic process, developed in America but now available all over the world, is completely dry. There are two basic processes, viz. xerography (derived from Xerox, the original manufacturers) and electrofax. The main difference between the processes is that xerographic machines produce copies on plain paper while the electrofax process requires specially coated paper.

The xerographic machine contains a selenium-coated plate or drum which is given a positive charge of static electricity on its surface, then an illuminated image is exposed to it through a camera system. The light parts of the image make the corresponding areas on the plate lose their charge: thus an electrostatic pattern of the original is left on the plate.

On to this positively charged image is cascaded a negatively charged powder, which adheres to it, giving a powder image of the original; this is then transferred on to paper (or on to a printing master) and made permanent by heat or vapour fusing. The quality of reproduction is excellent; it is difficult to distinguish a copy from the original and a first-class copy can often be obtained from a fairly poor original. There is no feeding of the copy paper, no peeling apart, and no wet chemicals to corrode the machine.

The electrofax process is similar but usually a roll of the coated paper is inserted into the machine, the copy being automatically cut to the appropriate size before emission.

Electrostatic copiers are normally flat-bed type, i.e. copies can be made of pages from bound books. Any original, handwritten, typed, drawn, printed, coloured, can be copied but is reproduced in back and white (but *see* page 361).

Electrostatic copiers can be used to create masters for offset-litho machines and translucencies and for dye-line copiers.

High-speed machines have also been developed for reproducing documents and engineering drawings, and for recording the output of computers. The Registrar General in London uses this process for copying birth certificates, its outstanding virtues here being that the copies can be made on the specially water-marked paper designed to prevent fraud, and that the image is permanent.

Xerographic machines may be bought or rented from Rank Xerox. There are various models ranging from the simple copier which will produce up to ten copies at one setting of the pre-selector control to the "Concorde" of copiers, the Xerox 9200 (*see* Fig. 88), which will slightly enlarge originals to 102 per cent,

[*Courtesy Rank Xerox Ltd.*

Fig. 88 *Xerox 9200 copying machine has push-button control for every operation including enlargement, reduction double-sided (or reverse) copying and collation.*

reduce originals down to 61 per cent, allow movement of the image by up to 125 mm to centre it on the page, copy both sides of double-sided documents simultaneously, reproduce up to 999 copies at one setting, produce 7,200 copies per hour and collate a limitless number of copies in multiples of forty depending on the number of sets of bins linked to the copier. The "copier duplicator", as this high-speed reproduction machine is called, is now frequently used for low-volume copying, e.g. up to fifty copies. Thereafter the stencil or offset duplicating processes are cheaper.

The cost of copies for low-volume work is more than offset by the reduction in typing time.

The reduction facility can be used for producing a reduced size copy from which any duplicating master can be prepared, providing the facilities are available.

Many plain paper copiers print on paper of various weights from about 65 g/m² to about 130 g/m². On some machines the paper is inserted in cassettes for ease of handling. Regulation of image density is another feature of this type of copier.

A major development which has just been placed on the U.K. market is a machine which actually reproduces in colour, instead of reproducing colours in black and white. Another exciting development is the Xerox 9700 which can read magnetic tape and print text from it. Thus it is now possible to link a copier-duplicator into an electronic system to complement an automatic typewriter (magnetic tape), memory typewriter or word processor.

THERMAL PROCESS

The thermal process involves feeding the original to be copied and a piece of special heat-sensitive paper into a machine about the size of a typewriter. The copy is produced by thermal reaction on the copying paper, and in contrast to the light-sensitive methods, the black or image-bearing areas on the original set up a reaction on the paper.

The machine will reproduce any typed, printed or written material that has a graphite or metallic content. It will not copy ballpoint-pen inks, some coloured inks, and spirit-duplicated copy. The copy paper is relatively expensive, but the method is quick when only a few copies, say three or four, are required. Each copy takes only about four seconds to produce excluding time to collate the original and copy paper.

One outstanding advantage of the thermal process is that it is possible to make a spirit master in four seconds from which a hundred or more copies can be obtained on a normal spirit duplicator. Stencil duplicating masters can be made in the same way. However, the desirability mentioned above, of only copying originals with ink having a carbon content, still applies (but *see* dual spectrum).

Overhead projector transparencies can be made on a thermal copier and it is possible to make a transparency which can also be used for spirit duplicating. This is useful for training small groups or "off-the-cuff" presentations.

Some thermal copiers also provide the facility for laminating copies, which is useful when copies are to be displayed as the lamination gives longer life. Thermal copiers normally allow copies to be made from single sheets.

DUAL SPECTRUM

As mentioned above, thermal copiers do not usually copy coloured inks, because most colours have a vegetable dye base instead of a metallic base. To overcome this difficulty, one company produces a dual-spectrum machine, so called because it performs the exposure by light but the processing is by heat and the use of special paper.

This method is completely dry, and, since it is a flat-bed machine, it enables copies to be made from books. It can produce spirit masters and overhead projector transparencies from coloured originals as well.

Choice of process

Which copying process to use is a difficult question to answer, and can only be decided with full knowledge of all the facts. The following are some of the relevant factors which must be considered.

(1) The size and nature of the original; whether it is on opaque or transparent paper.

(2) The density of the image, and the nature of the ink used.

(3) Whether information has to be typed before duplication.

(4) Whether the documents are single or double-sided.

(5) The number of copies required.

(6) The cost of the expendable materials, such as copy paper, and of developing and fixing solutions.

(7) The relative cost of labour compared with other copying methods.

(8) What maximum convenience is offered, for example in the way of space required or special light conditions.

(9) Permanency of image required.

(10) Whether the original is in colour.

(11) Whether wet chemicals are used, and if so to what extent they corrode the machine and lose their properties.

(12) Whether reproduction of offset-litho, spirit, stencil or dyeline masters is required.

It must be remembered that it is the labour cost which is often the most expensive factor in office systems, and in copying the cost of typist labour is eliminated altogether.

Uses of copying

The application of one or other of the different processes is being continually extended, but the following are brief details of some of the uses.

(1) Copying of incoming letters for attention of different departments.

(2) Copying of contract and insurance policies (originals placed in safe deposit).

(3) Purchase orders and sales invoice systems.

(4) Obtaining monthly statements for customers (photocopies of ledger accounts).

(5) In share registrar work, copies may be made of marriage certificates, death certificates, etc. of shareholders.

(6) Documentation for batch manufacture, with variable information added by hand.

(7) Accounts department statistics—the copying of complicated statistics can be performed very quickly.

(8) Diagrams and drawings required for training purposes.

Costs

Considerations of the day-to-day copying requirements have to be weighed alongside considerations of cost. When large quantities of individual documents are required it is true to say that the capital outlay is more than offset by the reducing cost per copy.

Consideration must also be given to the merits of outright purchase as against renting or leasing. Maintenance costs are normally included in the rental whereas they have to be budgeted for when the machine is bought or leased. Yet another consideration is that machines are constantly being modified and updated, and new models come on the market fairly frequently. There is greater freedom to keep pace with the organisation's developing needs when a machine is rented. It is difficult to assess copying requirements several years ahead. For one thing, once a machine with certain facilities is installed it tends to generate a need.

Although costs are obviously of great importance, the real consideration is what type of material is to be copied and what standard of copies is required. A cheap machine and cheap copies are expensive if they do not produce what is wanted.

COST-CONSCIOUSNESS

To an office clerk 0.25p per copy seems an inconsiderable sum to "make a fuss about". Because of the low cost of copying and the ease with which copies can be made, there tends to be a lack of cost–consciousness where copying is concerned. Making a few extra copies of nearly every document "in case they are needed" may mean only a penny or two but if several hundred staff do it several times a day the total waste can be astronomical over a year. Sometimes extra copies are made because the location of the copying machine involves several minutes' walk. Also there may be a queue at the machine. If machines are provided on every floor several may be out of order—the penalty for allowing all "hands" to use them—which means time is needed to locate one that is functioning. These frustrations cost money, of course—perhaps more than the cost of a few extra copies.

It is essential therefore that the *organisation* of copying should be well thought out so that the service fulfils its purpose without creating problems of time consumption and cost. Volume copying should normally be the province of the reprographics section or print room. Many organisations have a rule that when more than a

| PROCESS | | Master | Number of copies |
Types of equipment	Supplies	Method of preparation	
COPYING	Diazo master sheets Developer/fixer	Negative	One
Silver halide (a) Diffusion transfer	Negative paper Positive paper (light sensitive) Offset-litho plates	Original exposed to light; negative and positive passed through combined developer/fixer	
Diffusion transfer copying machine			
(b) Gelatine transfer	Negative paper Positive paper (non-light sensitive) Offset-litho plates Development/fixer	Matrix (negative)	Up to 15
Gelatine transfer copying machine Positive paper (non-light sensitive) Offset-litho plates Developer/fixer		Original exposed to light; negative and positive passed through combined developer/fixer	
(c) Reflex	Negative paper Positive paper (light sensitive) Developer Fixer	Negative	Unlimited
Reflex copying machine		Original exposed to light; negative exposed with fresh positive paper, which is passed through developing and fixing chemicals	
(d) Direct positive		Original	One
Direct positive copying machine		Original exposed to light with positive paper, which is passed through developing and fixing chemicals	

certain number of copies, usually ten, is required the job must be sent to the printing department. Copiers are provided in various locations for individual small-volume copying. The problem that most frequently arises is the delay in obtaining work from the printing department. Consequently if twenty copies are required a secretary will go to the machine twice rather than pass out the job! One important factor is print-room organisation, which is dealt with in Chapter 32.

If the problems can be eliminated staff are more likely to be considerate about costs. "Extra copies" are a nuisance in an office and if it is easy to make a copy when it is needed exact numbers required can be produced.

Summary of methods

A summary of the copying processes including the most important details is given on pages 364 to 367.

Uses	Advantages	Disadvantages
Offset-litho plates Translucent masters for dye-line copying	Good quality reproduction Any colours can be copied in black and white Cheap reproduction	Wet chemicals Negative can be used more than once but not easily Sensitive to direct daylight
Ordinary copies Offset-litho plates	Very cheap for several copies Any colour can be copied in black and white	Quality of reproduction not very good Matrices cannot be stored Chemicals need to be at certain temperature for good results
Copy any type of document in black and white (half tones and colours)	High quality reproduction Negative can be stored for future use Unlimited number of copies	Wet chemicals Expensive Sensitive to direct daylight
Dye-line masters	Copies any document in any colour No negative required unless ordinary copy to be reproduced	Translucent copies not always acceptable

Types of equipment	Supplies	Master Method of preparation	Number of copies
Dye-line (Diazo) Diazo copying machine	Yellow dye-line paper Fixer	Original — Original and dyeline (yellow) paper exposed light; image fixed with chemical fumes or wet chemicals	One
Thermal (a) Infra-red Infra-red copying machine	Copy paper (heat sensitive)	Original — Original and heat-sensitive paper exposed to heat	One
(b) Infra-red transfer Infra-red transfer copying machine	Transfer sheets Copy paper (heat sensitive) Spirit master sets Overhead projector transparency sets Laminating sheets	Transfer sheet — Original and transfer sheet and ordinary copy paper exposed to heat	One
(c) Dual spectrum (3M) Dual-spectrum copying machine	Intermediate sheets (light sensitive) Copy paper (heat sensitive) Overhead projector transparency sets	Intermediate sheet — Exposure of original with intermediate sheet: then intermediate sheet with special copy paper	One
Electrostatic (a) Xerographic (Indirect electrostatic) Indirect electrostatic copying machine Machine with image reduction/enlargement facility Collating attachment Machine for reading and printing text on magnetic tape	Good quality paper Offset plates Overhead projector transparency sheets	Original — Original fed into machine; projected on to a selenium-coated plate charged with electricity	Unlimited
(b) Electrofax (Direct) Direct electrostatic copying machine Machine with paper-cutting device Copier-duplicating machine	Rolls of copy paper Offset plates Overhead projector transparency sheets	Original — Original fed into machine; paper coated with zinc oxide supplied in a roll cut automatically by machine	Unlimited

Uses	Advantages	Disadvantages
Office systems applications, e.g. sales documents Plans and drawings	Cheapest method of copying Can be used in ordinary daylight Originals can be stored for further use	Originals must be on translucent or transparent paper, single-sided Not very good reproduction Copies tend to fade if exposed to light for any length of time
Ordinary copies	No chemicals Fast and simple	Some colours will not copy (red, green) Ink on original must have carbon content
Spirit masters Thermal stencils Overhead projector transparencies Laminating		Not very good reproduction Only one copy at a time obtainable Slow process Up to about 9 or 10 copies only can be reproduced at one copying session (machine cuts out to avoid overheating)
Ordinary copies Overhead projector transparencies	Will copy ballpoint-pen ink	
Paper and metal offset-litho plates Anything written, typed, printed or drawn from originals in any colour Reduction of originals for reproduction in a smaller size	No wet chemicals Uses ordinary paper Good quality reproduction	Repeated maintenance may be required Will not copy all colours equally well Expensive for small-volume work
Paper and metal offset-litho plates Overhead projector transparencies	Colour reproduction Suitable for large-volume work	

31. Addressing Machines

The first addressing machines were sold commercially in 1893. The name "addressing" comes, of course, from the function for which the machine was first designed—the reproduction of names and addresses on newspaper wrappers. The machine is in reality an office duplicating machine, but instead of producing many copies of one master only, it prints one copy or a few copies as required of each of a series of masters.

Its use as an addressing medium is still the most popular, but it is also used for a much wider range of activities including the preparation of invoices and the printing of job cards and wages sheets, and in any job where information is repetitive, say from week to week, month to month, or even year to year (e.g. dividend lists).

Types of "plates"

There are five kinds of addressing machine "plates" or printing media: metal, stencil, spirit master, foil/plastic and card.

METAL PLATE

The metal plate (usually zinc or aluminium) is embossed with the name, address or other information to be duplicated. The plates can be either sent to the manufacturers for embossing or produced on the firm's own plate embossing machine, which is electrically operated.

The plates are of several sizes, carrying from five to nine lines of type, and the largest of them has a capacity of up to 414 characters. They may be mounted with an index card bearing the information on the plate as an aid to quick reference; or the plates can themselves be mounted on a report card, thus forming a complete card index and addressing medium combined. The metal plates are stronger than addressing stencils, and because they last longer, are preferable when several copies are required at one printing or when carbon copies of each impression are needed.

STENCIL PLATE

This type of machine uses a stencil mounted in a cardboard or plastic frame. The frame carries a label giving the same information as the stencil below it, for ease of reference. The stencil plate has the advantage of being prepared on the typewriter instead of on a special machine. They are also cheaper than metal plates but are not generally as durable though one manufacturer claims that 10,000 copies can be made from one plate.

SPIRIT MASTER PLATE

The spirit master plates are cheap and are easy to prepare on the typewriter without any special apparatus being fitted. In general, the machines using these plates have the same advantages as spirit duplicators, being neat, compact and inexpensive. Even though the number of copies obtainable from any single master is limited, their replacement is so cheap that it is easy to create another master copy when necessary. The spirit masters are pieces of art paper, and are typed with hectographic carbon at the back, after which they are mounted in cardboard or plastic frames.

FOIL AND PLASTIC PLATES

This type of plate is most commonly used by the general public for buying goods on credit and for identification when making payment by cheque or cashing a cheque at a different branch of the bank from the one which holds the drawer's account. For credit sales the card and a credit document are affixed in a hand-operated machine to reproduce the necessary details in a few seconds.

CARD PLATES

A card on which the information to be duplicated is typed is another kind of "plate". In one system the cards can be "programmed" to print a predetermined number of times at one printing, and also to eject themselves from the system when their life is ended. The cards can be coded so that, with the use of a master programme card, all similarly coded cards in the stack can be automatically "recognised" and printed at 300 per minute, bypassing the cards not required.

Types of machine

There is a wide range of machines from miniature hand-operated models using spirit master plates, suitable for small-volume work, to the fully automatic electric machines (*see* Fig. 89). The various

[*Courtesy Roneo Vickers Ltd.*

Fig. 89 *The Roneo Neopost Stielow 5400 electrically operated addressing machine.* Accepts cassettes of master stencil cards and automatically prints up to 7,500 addresses an hour on to envelopes or labels. Selective addressing can also be done.

types of machine have different features according to their size, the jobs they are intended to do and the individual manufacturers. Machines are now available with cut-out device, automatic selection, and other refinements. The following list of the operational features of various machines may be useful in determining the machine most suitable for particular needs.

(1) Automatic feed and ejection of plates and document (or envelopes).

(2) Dating device for entering date with every printing (this is useful in invoicing work).

(3) Numbering device—either for numbering each impression with the same number, or for sequential numbering of documents.

(4) Attachment for continuous stationery (invoices, cheques, etc.).

(5) Attachment for facsimile writing for signatures.

(6) "Cut-out device" for use when only part of the information on the plates is required to be printed.

(7) A special machine can print chronologically down a sheet of paper instead of on separate forms.

(8) A machine (known as "Duplex Lister") will print automatically from left to right in two columns down a sheet of paper (for example, pay number and name, and then gross pay).

(9) Automatic selection, by the use of signals on the plates, and a selection device on the machine. Thus printing can be obtained of selected plates, without having to disturb their order in the tray.

(10) Variable information, additional to that on the plates; for example, for a special printing it might be wished to mark every envelope "Personal", or "If undelivered return to X Company Ltd.".

(11) A repeating device, by which each plate can be repeated as often as necessary, perhaps for repeat printing on letter and on envelope, or for side-by-side printing.

(12) A "skip mechanism", by which plates that are not wanted for one particular batch can be passed through the machine without printing.

A combined addressing-printing machine can be used for either purpose, or for both combined. This machine can, for example, simultaneously print the letterheadings on the invoice and insert the customer's name and address and the amount charged (where there are standard charges within a limited range). It is said that this combined machine can perform in three days an invoice task which previously took one month to perform. Although the capital cost is high it is money well invested for a large organisation.

Uses of addressing machines

Although the primary use is still the repeat printing of names and addresses, other information can be incorporated in the printing media. Addressing machines can be used for:

(1) form letters for sales campaigns;

(2) preparation of statements and invoices;

(3) preparation of dividend warrants;

(4) notices of meetings;

(5) reports of meetings;

(6) proxy forms for meetings;

(7) preparation of pay sheets, pay slips, pay envelopes, and time and job cards;

(8) heading of ledger sheets;

(9) index and record cards;

(10) commission and credit lists.

The principle behind the use of the machine is that once the plates or stencils are checked the machine can be relied on to reproduce facsimile copies on future occasions, and as often as is desired; virtually no checking is required.

Advantages and disadvantages

The principal advantage is a saving in time. To reproduce 1,000 names and addresses, it would take:

by hand	12 hours
by typewriter	10 hours
by manually-operated addressing machine	2 hours
by electrically operated addressing machine	8 minutes

In addition to saving time, addressing machines obviate a great deal of checking and eliminate mistakes owing to inaccurate typing. Most machines are also simple to work, so that they can be operated by a junior with very little training, producing a great saving in overhead expenditure.

The disadvantages are few, but perhaps the most prominent one with the metal plate machine is the delay when new plates are required. Although embossing machines can be bought, they are rather expensive, and manufacturers usually provide a three-day service for the supply of new plates. Again, unless some stringent control is kept over alterations to the plate list, it can easily become out of date.

The duty of noting changes in an "alteration book", updating the list and amending or renewing plates should be allocated to individuals for whom procedures and time schedules should be clearly laid down. Adequate supervision to ensure proper implementation is essential.

32. Printing

Printing is an expensive item in the budget whether it is carried out by outside printers or in-house. All organisations have facilities for one or more of the reprographic methods discussed in the foregoing chapters. There comes a point in many organisations where a decision has to be made as to whether it would be cost-effective to establish an in-house printing department to do some or all of the printing work required. There are a number of questions to be answered to establish the justification for a decision in favour of in-house printing. First we should look at the main aspects of printing which concern the user, whether outside or in-house.

Ensuring cost-effective printing

PREPARATION OF COPY
Corrections of printed copy are expensive. Therefore the first copy submitted to the printer should be as accurate as possible. The layout of the copy should be clearly indicated and if necessary discussed with the printer. It is helpful to know the most commonly used sizes of print and to be familiar with print styles. These are illustrated in Figs. 90 and 91. The comprehension of the document depends to a large extent on the layout. This is especially true of forms. All forms should be validated before printing—duplicated copies can be used during validation.

TYPES OF PRINTING
There are three main types of printing, viz. plain ink printing, die stamping and thermographic printing. All three types of printing can be in various colours. Die stamping is the most expensive and is normally used for prestige work such as letterheads, brochures for professional purposes, and business cards. Thermographic printing has a similar appearance to die stamping but is less expensive.

EGYPTIENNE ROMAN
ABCDEFGHIJKL
abcdefghijklmno
1234567890&

METEOR MEDIUM
ABCDEFGHIJKLMN
abcdefghijklmnopqr
1234567890&

BEDFORD MONOSPACE
ABCDEFGHIJKL
abcdefghijkl
1234567890&

GOTHIC 13
ABCDEFGHIJKLMNO
abcdefghijklmnopq
1234567890&

BELMONT LIGHT
ABCDEFGHIJKLMNOPQR
abcdefghijklmnopqrstu
1234567890&

TIMES BOLD ITALIC
ABCDEFGHIJK
abcdefghijklmno
1234567890&

Fig. 90 *Examples of some commonly used print styles.*

INSTRUCTIONS TO THE PRINTER
When giving work to the printer the following instructions must be given.

(1) Layout required, including position of illustrations.
(2) Print style.
(3) Print size.
(4) Colour(s) of printing.
(5) Weight of paper and/or card (*see* Chapter 47).
(6) Colour of paper and/or card.
(7) Single or double-sided printing (i.e. printing on one side of the sheet only or on both sides).
(8) Number of copies.
(9) Time schedule—dates when proof is to be submitted by the printer; corrected proof to be returned to the printer; final copy to be delivered by the printer.
(10) Address where final copies are to be delivered.

When dealing with a new job it is worth discussing the details with the printer beforehand. He will be happy to advise on the

16 POINT

ABCDEFGHIJKLM
abcdefghijklmnop

14 POINT

ABCDEFGHIJKLMNO
abcdefghijklmnopqr

13 POINT

ABCDEFGHIJKLMNO
abcdefghijklmnopqrstu

12 POINT

ABCDEFGHIJKLMNOPQR
abcdefghijklmnopqrstuvwxy

11 POINT

ABCDEFGHIJKLMNOPQRS
abcdefghijklmnopqrstuvwxy

10 POINT

ABCDEFGHIJKLMNOPQRST
abcdefghijklmnopqrstuvwxyzfi

9 POINT

ABCDEFGHIJKLMNOPQRSTUVWX
abcdefghijklmnopqrstuvwxyzfiflfffffifflæ

8 POINT

ABCDEFGHIJKLMNOPQRSTUV
abcdefghijklmnopqrstuvwxyzfiflff

7 POINT

ABCDEFGHIJKLMNOPQRSTUVWXYZ
abcdefghijklmnopqrstuvwxyzfiflffffifflæœ

6 POINT

ABCDEFGHIJKLMNOPQRSTUVWXYZ&
abcdefghijklmnopqrstuvwxyzfiflfffffifflæœ

Fig. 91 Commonly used print sizes.

various aspects of paper grammages, styles, etc., and show some specimens of similar types of work. This avoids having to have two proof copies which wastes time and money.

The cost of each job should be agreed beforehand. It may be beneficial to get more than one quotation for a new job. Some printers specialise in certain types of work and are therefore cheaper for that type of job.

PROOF–READING

Proofs must be very carefully checked to ensure one hundred per cent accuracy. Printing errors create a bad impression in the reader's mind. Special care must be taken to correct errors in punctuation and spelling. The most common signs used in correcting printers' proofs are given below. Full details on the correction of proofs can be found in British Standard B.S. 5261: Part 2 1976 "Specification for typographic requirements, marks for copy preparation and proof correction, proofing procedure".

Marginal sign	Meaning
≡	Change letters underlined three times to large capitals
=	Change letters underlined twice to small capitals
⎵⎿	Change letters underlined once to italics
⊙	Insert a full stop
ʹ	Insert a comma
;/	Insert a semi-colon
⊙	Insert a colon
?/	Insert a question mark
⁗	Insert inverted commas
ʹ	Insert an apostrophe
/—/	Insert a hyphen
/——/	Insert a dash
✳/	Insert a superior character as indicated, in this case an asterisk
⅄	Equalise the spacing
Spell out	Spell out in full the abbreviations marked
X	Damaged letter (circled in text). Replace with a good letter
⊗	Wrong fount
∩	Letter "upside down". Turn right way up
⊥	Push down a space
‖	Straighten margin — type edge ragged
⸗	Straighten lines — type unevenly set
⊐	Indent

COSTS

There are ways in which printing costs can be kept to a minimum. These are summarised below.

(1) Prepare the copy as accurately as possible.

(2) Proof-read very carefully.

(3) Order in large quantities in preference to several batches of small quantities. Long runs are very much cheaper.

(4) Use thermographic printing instead of die stamping unless maximum prestige is required.

(5) Give full instructions to the printer.

Outside printing

It is worth establishing a good relationship with the printer to ensure that the problems that inevitably arise are minimised. Major difficulties are cost and time. Printers are renowned for not meeting deadlines. In addition, good printers are usually very busy and it may be several weeks before a particular job can be undertaken. The time schedule must take this into account. A steady flow of work with a reasonable assurance as to requirements over a period of, say, a year, will help printers to plan their work-load and to be more accommodating on deadlines. The main point, however, is that all printing work must be prepared well in advance.

In-house printing

A survey of printing requirements must be carried out to ensure that in-house printing would be beneficial financially and/or to cut the time factor. The survey should be wide ranging, covering the following points.

(1) Type of documents to be printed.

(2) Quantities of each type of document required annually.

(3) Present cost of outside printing for each type of document.

(4) Where each document is sent, i.e. outside the organisation or within it.

(5) Methods by which each document could be printed, bearing in mind the answer to item (4).

(6) The capital cost of establishing a print room within the organisation, bearing in mind the answer to item (1) which dictates the items of printing and ancillary equipment needed.

(7) The running costs for alternative arrangements, e.g. all forms such as invoices and materials for use within the organisation printed in-house and prestige material such as letterheads printed outside; all printing done in-house.

(8) The availability of operators—offset-litho printing requires trained operators.

(9) The space that would be required for an in-house printing unit.

(10) The desirability or otherwise of having all reprographic facilities in the print room. (It is usual and generally necessary to have some copying machines at other points in the organisation.)

PREPARATION OF MASTERS

Various methods of typesetting were discussed in Chapter 29. For professional printing it is essential to have trained composers, i.e. people who have learned printing display. For "run of the mill" printing it is normal for the secretarial staff to produce fair copy (typed on an electric typewriter with a carbon ribbon) from which a photographic plate is made. This eliminates the necessity of producing a proof copy thus saving time.

Production of masters on special machines such as Varitypers and Selectric composers, or by computer terminal, requires special training.

PRINT-ROOM EQUIPMENT

The equipment needed for offset printing depends on the type of work to be done and the method(s) by which the plates are to be produced. The advice of manufacturers should be sought and costs, both capital and running, should be compared.

ANCILLARY EQUIPMENT

Depending on the types of documents to be produced and their readership distribution, various items of ancillary equipment may be necessary for finishing the documents professionally.

(1) Joggers: used for aligning papers into a stack after they have been removed from the printing machine.

(2) Collating machine, which may be linked to a copying or printing machine: various sizes of machine are available for collating pages into sequence.

(3) Paper cutters: a paper cutter is needed for trimming small quantities of sheets.

(4) Guillotines: a guillotine is needed for cutting stacks of paper. A guillotine should be operated only by a person trained to use it.

(5) Stapling machines: long-arm staplers are used for fastening sheets into leaflet form, and heavy duty staplers are used for fastening thick stacks of pages.

(6) Punches: heavy duty punches are used for making holes in thick stacks of pages; variable punches are available for punching different numbers of holes with different distances between them.

(7) Drills: used for punching stacks of pages normally more than 10 mm deep.

(8) Plastic comb binding machine: a cheap and quick method of binding reports and documents up to 25 mm thick.

(9) Thermal binding machine: cheap and easy to use and gives a professional appearance to reports, etc.

(10) Stitching machine for professional bookbinding: needs a trained operator.

Staff

It is essential to have first-class supervision in a print room. Not only should the person in charge be able to "manage" the department, including costing, time scheduling and staff training; technical expertise is also essential. If a professional printing service is to be achieved a professional printer should be recruited to establish it. It is important to bear in mind that the production of photographic offset-litho plates requires a skilled operator as does the operation of offset printing machines and guillotines. Typesetters, whether employed in the print room or working in secretarial positions, must be given guidance on display for printing. Unless fully qualified staff can be recruited at the beginning it is better to allow the print room to develop, starting with relatively straightforward duplicating machines. Prestige printing should be sent out until adequate facilities are available to cope with it. Fast, accurate turn-round of work is required of a print room, but is difficult to achieve because of the nature of the work. This is one area where dedicated staff are worth their weight in gold.

33. Organisation of Records

In a modern community we all depend on records; whether for business, for government or for social club activities, records are vital. In the office records consist of contracts, invoices, letters, reports, cheques, vouchers, statistics, costings, personnel reports, tax records, price lists, catalogues, etc. Each type of record should be stored in the most suitable way for easy location and rapid retrieval when required.

Importance of filing

Filing, once an "odd job" allocated to the office junior, has developed into a major area of administration now generally regarded as an integral part of *information storage and retrieval*. Although modern methods of electronic information storage and retrieval are now common in many large organisations, such as banks, airlines and advertising agencies, the bulk of commercial, industrial and government records are still kept on paper filing systems. With the vast increase in the volume and complexity of information a misfiled document, a lost file or an inadequate index can cause havoc, not only in the office but in the whole organisation.

Records management covers many aspects including location, type of equipment, classifications, indexing, procedures, control of file movements, access and supervision, follow-up, retention periods, storage of non-active records and microcopying.

Essentials of a good filing system

Filing may be described as a process of arranging and storing records so that they can be located when required. There is no universal *best* system of filing. The requirements of each office/

section/department must be analysed and a system must be tailor-made to meet those requirements. The following aspects should be considered.

(1) Space is at a premium: modern filing equipment (*see* Chapter 35) is designed for space economy. The whole filing system must be designed in such a way that it uses the minimum of space consistent with easy location and retrieval of information.

(2) Accessibility: records must be readily accessible to the people who use them, and particular convenience is required where they are to be written on.

(3) Simplicity: the system must be easy to understand and simple to operate.

(4) Cost-effectiveness: a filing system must be cost-effective. Installation costs and operation costs have both to be taken into account. The acceptable cost level may well vary with the type of record depending on the speed of retrieval required.

(5) Flexibility: the system must be flexible in its capacity so that it can be expanded or contracted as needs change.

Location of records

It must be possible to locate records with the minimum delay acceptable. Records are not always required immediately and this aspect should be borne in mind when devising the system because economies are sometimes possible if a certain amount of delay is acceptable.

Records may be located at some central point within the organisation, or they may be placed at some point within a department, or they may be filed in an individual office. The choice of location depends on the type of record, who is to use the records and in what way, and the physical distances involved.

Where several departments need access to the same records it is advisable to have a centralised storage and retrieval system. Records which are generally of interest to one department only should be available within that department. There are advantages and disadvantages to locating records centrally and departmentally. The advantages of central filing include the following:

(1) uniformity of filing procedures;

(2) all correspondence about the same subject is filed together even though it may emanate from various departments;

(3) full-time filing staff can be properly trained;

(4) supervision is easier and should be more effective;

(5) access to files can be limited to filing staff so that greater control of file movements is possible;

(6) the condition of files can be monitored;

(7) the provision of equipment is usually more economical.

The disadvantages of central filing include the following:

(1) lack of specialised trade knowledge by the filing staff can result in misfiling;

(2) there may be delay in making files available;

(3) clerical and secretarial staff have only a very limited knowledge of the filing system and therefore have to depend on the filing staff to locate and retrieve documents.

The advantages and disadvantages of departmental filing are similar in respect of the department concerned but supervision tends to be more haphazard and it is more difficult to control access to the files with the result that very often file movements are not properly controlled. This in turn leads to files being mislaid and difficulty in locating files quickly.

Files should be located in an individual office for the use of an individual executive only when records are confidential and must be kept under lock and key, or are of such a specialised nature that only very few people are using them.

Equipment

The type of equipment is an integral part of any filing system. Factors to be considered when choosing equipment include the space available, cost, the type of record to be accommodated, the access required, the likely expansion over the next five to ten years and the weight that the floors can stand. This aspect of filing is covered more fully in Chapter 35.

Classification

Documents may be stored and retrieved by either direct or indirect methods. Direct filing means that the documents can be stored or retrieved without reference to an index. Documents and files are arranged in alphabetical order by name, by subject or by geographical location. Indirect filing means that reference has to be made to an index before a document or a file can be located. Each file is allocated a number and is then placed in numerical order. Index cards are filed in alphabetical order. Alternatively a combination of letters and numbers may be used and this is known as alpha-numeric. Again the arrangement may be by name or by subject. Some examples of the various classifications are shown below. There are many variations, of course, but it is wise to use the simplest classification compatible with the type of material.

Chronological filing, i.e. the arrangement of documents in date order, is often combined with some other arrangement.

The chart on page 387 shows some of the uses for which each classification is useful together with its advantages and disadvantages.

(1) ALPHABETICAL CLASSIFICATION BY NAME

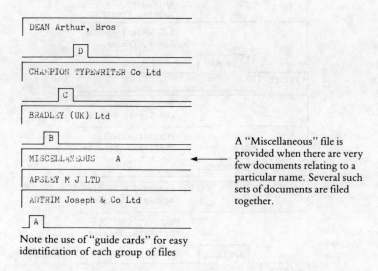

A "Miscellaneous" file is provided when there are very few documents relating to a particular name. Several such sets of documents are filed together.

Note the use of "guide cards" for easy identification of each group of files

(2) ALPHABETICAL CLASSIFICATION BY SUBJECT

WELFARE	SOCIAL CLUB
WELFARE	RESTAURANTS
WELFARE	MEDICAL SERVICES
WELFARE	
TRAINING	MANAGEMENT COURSES
TRAINING	ENGINEERING COURSES
TRAINING	CLERICAL COURSES
TRAINING	

Colour coding can be used, each "tab" being in a different colour and the folders for all topics filed under that subject heading in a similar colour.

(3) ALPHABETICAL CLASSIFICATION BY GEOGRAPHICAL LOCATION

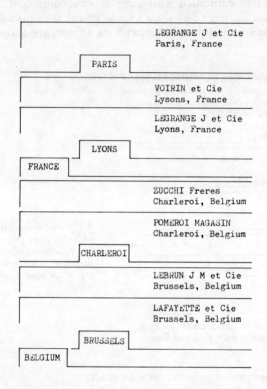

Again colour coding can be used, e.g. a different colour for each country or coloured strips representing countries and towns. This makes the replacement of files in the correct position easier.

(4) NUMERICAL—SEQUENTIAL CLASSIFICATION

Files		Index Cards	
ADEPT EMPLOYMENT AGENCY	4	GENERAL STORES LTD	1
ALBERT TRENT ESTATES Ltd	3	CHAMPION ESCALATORS Ltd	2
CHAMPION ESCALATORS Ltd	2	ALBERT TRENT ESTATES Ltd.	3
GENERAL STORES Ltd.	1	ADEPT EMPLOYMENT AGENCY	4

(5) NUMERICAL—SUBJECT CLASSIFICATION

File list (or Accession Register)
(Files would be arranged in numerical
order.)

				Index Cards	
TRAINING	16			VISUAL AIDS	16.1.1
MATERIALS	16.1		*	TRAINING	16
				SUPPLIES	16.1.2
Visual Aids	16.1.1		I	MATERIALS	16.1
Supplies	16.1.2			MANAGEMENT COURSES	16.2.2
COURSES	16.2			ENGINEERING COURSES	16.2.3
Clerical	16.2.1			COURSES	16.2
Management	16.2.2			CLERICAL .COURSES	16.2.1
Engineering	16.2.3				

*The main subdivisions should be listed on the index card.

I The topics within the subdivisions should be listed on the index card.

(6) ALPHA–NUMERIC—SEQUENTIAL CLASSIFICATION

Files		Index Cards	
LINDEN HOTELS GROUP	L3	LONDON TRADING Co Ltd	L1
LAWSON N M & Co	L2	LINDEN HOTELS GROUP	L3
LONDON TRADING Co Ltd	L1	LAWSON N M & CO	L2
KASTELER WINESHOPS Ltd	K2	KINGSWAY CHEMISTS Ltd	K1
KINGSWAY CHEMISTS Ltd	K1	KASTELER WINESHOPS Ltd	K2

(7) ALPHA–NUMERIC—SUBJECT CLASSIFICATION

The topics are arranged alphabetically before numbers are allocated.

61 SALES
    61.1 Export
    62.2 Home
62 SOCIAL WELFARE
    62.1 Medical Services
    62.2 Social Club
    62.3 Sports Club

(8) TERMINAL DIGIT

File numbers are in groups of two or three read from *right to left*, each group representing a particular location or some other coding.

Examples:

Number 123 456 089 could mean the document will be found in . . . . . file 089 behind guide card . . . . . 456 in drawer 123

Number 06 78 19 Document . . . . . 19 will be found in file 78 in drawer 06

Number 076 018 397 could mean: Policy document number 397 in All Risks . . . . . 018 First taken out in 076 (1976)

Indexing

There are many methods of indexing which are discussed in detail in Chapter 34. Here it should be stressed that any numerical filing classification must be accompanied by an alphabetical index.

Procedures

The ultimate aim of any filing system is the quick and accurate retrieval of documents. This can be achieved only when specific procedures for the operation of the system are established and adhered to. Procedures should be worked out in consultation with both operators and users of the system and should cover:

(1) storing documents;
(2) borrowing files (by the user);
(3) retrieving and lending files (including access);
(4) passing on files from one office to another;
(5) opening new files;
(6) closing full files and opening continuation files;
(7) segregating active, semi-active and non-active files;
(8) transfer of non-active files;
(9) destruction of unwanted documents and/or files;
(10) movement of and access to confidential files.

Filing clerks should be adequately trained in the procedures and given the authority to enforce them. The users of files should be informed of the procedures and their co-operation in following procedures laid down should be insisted upon.

Classification	Examples of application	Advantages	Disadvantages
(1) Alphabetical by name Note: British Standard BS 1749:1969 "Specification for Alphabetical Arrangement and the filing order of numerals and symbols" sets out the rules for placing alphabetical files in sequence	Clients/customers Students Personnel/staff Index cards for numerical files and cross-reference	Direct filing Simple to operate Maximum flexibility for insertion and extraction of files	Subdivision possibilities limited: if files are grouped, e.g. customers, staff, there is a danger of misfiling unless some form of coding, e.g. colour, is strictly observed Cross-reference may be necessary
(2) Alphabetical by subject	Products Supplies/Purchases Services Projects, contracts, etc. Index cards for numerical—subject files and subject cross-reference	Direct filing Subjects can be subdivided	Care must be taken that subdivisions do not overlap other subject areas Not suitable for a large number of files Cross-references may be necessary
(3) Alphabetical by geographical location	Sales territories Import/export Survey areas Provision of services Mail order Insurance	It is not necessary to remember the names of individual firms No cross-references likely to be needed	File list necessary when there are a large number of files
(4) Numerical—sequential	Customers, etc. Subjects—where no subdivision is required	Provides a file reference A block of numbers can be allocated to a particular department	No subdivision possible Files cannot be grouped in any way Index essential File list or Accession Register necessary if volume of files is large
(5) Numerical—subject	Products Supplies Services Functions of an organisation	Flexibility—easy to subdivide and add topics Can be combined with alphabetical or numerical coding for departments/sections of the organisation	Index essential File list or Accession Register necessary when contents of a document are not understood by filing clerk
(6) Alpha-numeric—sequential	Names—clients, trainees, etc. Single topics, i.e. subjects which require no subdivision	Provides a file reference	Index essential File list or Accession Register necessary Time consuming unless number of files is very small
(7) Alpha-numeric—subject	Technical material	File groups are preconceived to meet specific needs	Index essential Flexibility very limited Training filing clerk essential
(8) Terminal digit	Customers' accounts and mortgages Case records Insurance policy numbers Contract numbers	Easy to add new files Easy to identify a misplaced file	Index essential

CONTROL OF FILE MOVEMENTS

When a file is removed from its place for reference the fact must be recorded either in a register or, and this is to be preferred, on an OUT card. In a system in which the number of files are not great and suspension pockets are used the small OUT cards can be placed in each pocket. When the file is removed a note is made on the OUT card of the date and person to whom the file has been loaned. When the file is returned this note is crossed out.

OUT CARDS

In larger systems it is more practicable to have a supply of OUT cards such as that illustrated in Fig. 92. When a file is removed the

OUT				
File Identification	Date borrowed	By whom	Clerk's Initials	Date Returned
Johnson & Co	29.9.80	CA	～	30.8.80
Chipmunk Eng	2.10.80	DCA	～	6.10.80
Simple Dress Co.	15.10.80	Prodn. Mgr.	～	

Fig. 92 *An OUT card should be completed and inserted in the place of any file out on loan.*

OUT card is completed with the file name or number, the date and the person who has borrowed it. When the file is returned the OUT card is removed.

The advantage of using OUT cards is that when a file is required its whereabouts are known immediately. If file movements are recorded in a register it is easier to check every few days that files out on loan are still needed, but it takes longer to trace the whereabouts of any particular file.

PASSING SLIPS

It does happen in certain types of organisation that files are frequently passed from one officer to another, which makes it difficult to locate a file at any given time, even though the loan has been recorded. A solution to this problem is a "passing slip" which is completed by the person who passes on the file. This slip is sent to the filing clerk who can amend the record. An example of a passing slip is shown in Fig. 93.

```
┌─────────────────────────────────────────┐
│                                         │
│  FILE PASSING SLIP                      │
│                                         │
│  To: File Clerk                         │
│                                         │
│  Please note that File  16/7A           │
│                                         │
│  has been passed to  Sales Mgr.         │
│                                         │
│  at 3 am/pm on  31.8.80                 │
│                                         │
│  Signed  P.R. Jones                     │
│                                         │
└─────────────────────────────────────────┘
```

Fig. 93 *A passing slip.* Should be completed by any member of staff who passes a file on loan to any other member of staff. The slip is then sent to the filing clerk so that the OUT card can be amended.

ACCESS TO FILES

One of the most important aspects of controlling the movement of files is to limit the access of the staff to the files. Ideally no one but the filing clerk or clerks or person responsible for the files should be allowed to retrieve files or store documents in the system. Although this is not always practicable there should be strict limitation of who may actually retrieve files. If a number of people must have access to the files their co-operation in completing OUT cards should be insisted upon.

Follow-up

An efficient follow-up system is an essential aspect of records management. "Diarying" can be carried out in a book, on cards or in file folders. There are various methods of indicating when a document or file will be needed at a later date. A note can be written on the document in which case the filing clerk should record the note in a diary or on a card. Alternatively extra copies of documents to be brought up can be made and placed in diary files. The disadvantage of this system is that it means photocopying incoming letters that are to be brought up at a later date or making a separate note of the file required.

An excellent system is for the person requiring the file to complete a small diary slip (*see* Fig. 94). The slips are passed to the filing clerk who files them in chronological order of bring-forward

```
┌─────────────────────────────────────┐
│                                     │
│   Please bring forward              │
│                                     │
│   file no._____  │
│                                     │
│   on _____   │
│                                     │
│   Signed:_____   │
│                                     │
└─────────────────────────────────────┘
```

Fig. 94 *A diary slip ensures that a file is brought forward for attention when required.*

date. Each day the filing clerk removes the slips for that day and obtains the files required, attaches the slips to the relevant files and sends them to the people who had requested them.

Records retention

It is a fundamental of a good filing system that when records become inactive they should be separated from the active material. There are a number of ways of dealing with non-active material including:

(1) destruction of the documents;
(2) transfer of documents and/or files to archives;
(3) microcopying and destruction of the documents;
(4) microcopying and transfer of the documents to archives.

It is essential that a specific policy be established concerning the retention of records. A list of suggested retention periods is set out in the publication *Filing* by Oliver Standingford, published by the Institute of Administrative Management. Many company statutory records and records of the registrar should be retained permanently. Deeds of title, patent and trade mark records, account books and auditors' reports, instructions to banks, tax returns, labour agreements, pension scheme records, and certificates and documents concerning investments should also be preserved.

Certain documents may now be preserved on permanent microfilm but it would be wise to seek legal guidance before destroying the original document.

Most businesses keep a vast volume of records unnecessarily in case they are wanted. It is essential, of course, to ensure that records are not destroyed if it is likely that they may be required at some future date. Microcopying is one solution to the problem of storage and this is dealt with in detail in Chapter 36.

TRANSFER AND STORAGE OF NON–ACTIVE RECORDS
Once it has been decided what length of time documents should be
retained there is the question of separating non-active material from
active and semi-active material. This should be done at regular
intervals, at least once a year but preferably twice yearly. The
documents must, of course, be arranged systematically in transfer
or storage cases clearly labelled with dates and names or numbers of
files.

34. Indexing

An *index* is anything that "indicates" or "points out", and while modern indexes serve many other purposes, their prime function is to act as a guide to a body of data or to a collection of records. Sometimes there is confusion between the meanings of "classification" and "indexing", but whereas classification refers to the arrangements of files, indexing is basically the method used for making reference to the matter filed.

Indexes give not only individual selection, but also group classification and other information with the minimum of reference to the records themselves. This ensures economy in operation and speed of reference. Direct filing systems, for example files arranged in alphabetical sequence, do not need an index since individual files can be located and identified immediately.

There are five main types of index, viz. page index, loose or vertical card index, visible card index, strip index and rotary index.

Page index

A page index consists of a page or pages for each letter of the alphabet, fitted with a tab showing the letter. On each page are written the names beginning with that letter and quoting the relevant reference, usually a number. This is the type of index commonly used for such things as minutes and is comparable to the index at the back of this book. It can be seen that with minutes, the date or minute number might not be known, but by turning to the subject-matter in the index the minute number can be ascertained immediately. Such a page index may take the form of a separate book, or an index in the front or at the back of a book, or it may be a series of loose sheets inserted in front of each section of a file.

The disadvantages of a page index may be that:

(1) The names are entered on each page in the order in which they occur;

(2) names need to be deleted as they cease to be of interest;

(3) there may not be sufficient space to add all new names, which may mean the constant rewriting of the index.

Loose or vertical card index

The loose or vertical card index overcomes the disadvantages of the page index. Small cards (usually A6: 105 × 148 mm, or A7: 74 × 105 mm) containing the relevant data, usually with identification reference data along the top, are filed vertically.

The advantages of this system are that index cards for "dead" files can be removed easily when necessary; additional cards can be inserted in correct sequence at any place; and the cards can be easily taken from the drawers or trays in which they are stored for the purpose of writing on them.

On the other hand, the system is "blind", i.e. it takes longer to locate a particular index card than when using a visible reference system. Also the cards are loose and can be mislaid, and through constant handling they can become worn and "dog-eared".

Guide cards are used to indicate broad classifications such as letters (A to Z) or numerical sections. It is a cheap, flexible, and simple system, used in libraries and hospitals and in offices for credit records, staff records, etc.

Visible card index

The principle of all kinds of visible card index is that the cards overlap, so that one line of entry on each card projects and is visible, thus forming a one-line index (*see* Fig. 95).

This principle has been applied to card indexes and to loose-leaf ledgers. When a required card is located, it can be referred to quickly, and it can be written on without removal from the file, or easily removed and replaced, perhaps for quick ledger posting.

In some types of visible records, the cards are suspended in frames. Alternatively, they may be housed in pockets inside the frame. Visible card indexes are used for innumerable business records, but they are of outstanding use for pricing, credit control, stock records, and staff records.

Visible loose-leaf binders

When the visible system is used in conjunction with a loose-leaf binder, it gives speed in reference, speed in posting, and is not so

[Courtesy Twinlock U.K. Ltd.

Fig. 95 A visible card index tray.

expensive as the ordinary visible record cards in steel cabinets. The binder is used in the same way, and for the same purposes as visible record cards, but is cheaper and therefore preferred by some businesses.

Strip index

In every type of office, whatever the organisation, lists of names or numbers are needed, for the provision of simple one-line data—such as telephone numbers, accounts numbers and addresses. The strip index is specially designed for this purpose.

Although the forms of strip index vary, the principle is always the same. The record consists of one line entered on a strip of card which can easily be placed into or removed from a frame which may consist of a series of leaves on a free-standing base, or be attached to a wall (see Fig. 96), or form pages of a book.

Rotary index

The rotary or wheel index is a fairly recent development aimed primarily at saving space. The "wheel" may be vertical or horizon-

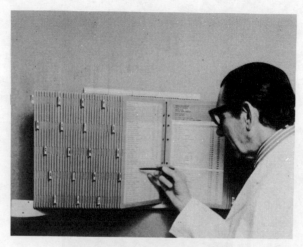

[Courtesy Twinlock U.K. Ltd.

Fig. 96 *Strip index—wall unit*. These indexes are also available in book form or as desk stand units.

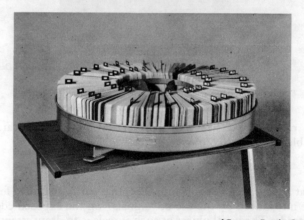

[Courtesy Rotader Systems Ltd.

Fig. 97 *Wheel card index*.

tal (*see* Fig. 97). Entries can be made on the cards without removing them from the vertical wheel. Reference is quick and insertion of new cards and removal of unwanted cards are very easy.

The rotary index may also be in the form of a drum (*see* Fig. 98). Cards are placed in slots which lie in vertical rows all around the drum. Drums are made in three sizes which take 1,000, 1,500 or

[*Courtesy System Designs Ltd.*

Fig. 98 *A rotary drum with index cards slotted in vertical rows.*

2,000 cards. Two sizes of plain or ruled T-shaped cards are available in various colours.

Signalling

A great advantage of visible indexes is that various control features can be introduced by the use of "signals" on the exposed edges of the records. The usual object of such signals is to draw attention to certain facts recorded on the cards. For example, on staff records a red signal may indicate membership of the staff pension scheme, or a blue one membership of the sports fund; by having a specially printed data "field" on the card's edge, incremental dates for salary purposes can also be indicated. Early types of signals used in conjunction with a blind vertical card index consisted of coloured projecting metal tabs which clipped on the top of the vertical edges of the cards. With the extended use of visible index records, other more flexible and suitable signals came into use.

Coloured transparent wafers are available which can be slid along the edges of a visible index card, or on a strip index. The use of these wafers may be extended by having punched holes of different geometrical shapes. Telescopic plastic signals are moved from behind a cut in the card edge over a pre-printed scale appropriate to the record. Such signals are useful for indicating stock positions, for production controls, and for credit control. Signals indicate information on the cards either by virtue of their colour or by their position on the edge of the card.

Application

While the general principles of indexing can be stated, the most suitable system for any particular records can only be decided by considering the requirements of the individual filing or record system. Some of the questions to be asked are as follows.

(1) How much information is wanted on the index?
(2) Will it be added to and subtracted from very frequently?
(3) Is it necessary to make entries on the index without extracting the relevant card?
(4) How much space is available?
(5) Can a signalling system be used?
(6) How much money is available?

35. Filing Equipment

The choice of filing equipment will certainly have an effect on the efficiency of a filing system, but a bad filing system will be just as bad whether it is housed in an expensive steel cabinet, or in a cardboard box. Equipment by itself cannot make a good filing system, although when suitable equipment is provided it can contribute substantially to over-all efficiency. Bad filing, complicated systems and bad supervisors can ruin any filing system. A wide selection of filing equipment is available, and an office manager must choose that which most nearly meets all the needs of the organisation.

Choice of equipment

Before deciding on the type of equipment to be used, the following are points for consideration:

(1) the number and size of the records involved;

(2) the frequency of reference (this will be related to speed of reference);

(3) the speed with which documents have to be retrieved;

(4) the degree of protection required, i.e. from dust, fire, and/or water (this will depend on the importance of the records);

(5) prevention of theft or fraud;

(6) whether signals will need to be used with the system;

(7) appearance of the equipment as a piece of furniture;

(8) quality of workmanship, which will ensure the long life and trouble-free use of the equipment.

Methods of filing

There are three basic methods of storing files, viz. vertical, lateral and horizontal.

VERTICAL

The files are placed one behind the other in drawers or boxes so that the identification is seen clearly from the front. Guide cards indicating letters of the alphabet, numerical sections, main subjects or geographical areas are placed in front of the relevant files.

LATERAL

The files are placed side by side. The identification is written/painted on the spines of ring binders, and lever arch and box files. Folders cannot be identified so easily unless in suspension pockets (*see* page 403). Guide cards with protruding identification tabs are placed between groups of files.

HORIZONTAL

The documents or files lie flat in a drawer, on a shelf or in a pigeon-hole. It is rarely used except for filing maps, plans and drawings as it can be both time-consuming and tiring to extract files from a pile and insert them in correct sequence. The horizontal system is used when current invoices (pending payment) are kept in alphabetical order in a cabinet of shallow trays or drawers, each tray or drawer being indexed on the front.

Filing cabinets

VERTICAL CABINETS

For general office use, vertical filing cabinets are fitted with drawers, which can be obtained to accommodate foolscap, A4 or A5 size documents. The drawers may also be shallow and contain dividers to take cards or microfilm. The cabinets are made of steel or wood.

Steel cabinets are often declared by the makers to be "flameproof", but where important documents such as sales accounts are stored in them, it is advisable to buy cabinets which are certified as fireproof and which have a solid lining of asbestos. For security purposes cabinets are also made with special locking devices including combination locks.

LATERAL CABINETS

The standard vertical filing cabinet requires a floor area of approximately a square metre including space to open drawers and for the operator to stand. Four drawers is generally the maximum height because the operator must be able to see into and extract files from inside.

Lateral filing, whereby the files are stored on a shelf or in pockets suspended side by side from frames, achieves a substantial saving in space because a greater height can be utilised. It is also possible to use existing shelving, cupboards and any awkward spaces to advantage. Files may be more easily identified and retrieved when stored laterally because the pockets have index strips on the visible ends of the files.

MULTI-PURPOSE CABINETS

Cabinets can be obtained to provide various kinds of file storage in one cabinet, e.g. lateral suspension filing (*see* below), card trays, suspension rails for stencils/plans/computer printout, shelves for ring binders/lever arch and/or box files.

ROUNDABOUT SHELVES

A great saving of space is achieved by storing lever arch files on circular revolving shelves which can take up to 100 files in five tiers.

PLAN CABINETS

Maps, plans and drawings may be filed flat in cabinets containing shallow drawers. There are also vertical cabinets in which the documents are inserted between corrugated dividers which keep them standing firmly. This vertical method gives easier access to documents and refiling is quicker.

ROTARY CABINETS

Electrically operated rotary filing cabinets consist of trays containing cards or brackets holding files suspended round a drum (*see* Fig. 99). The operator sits in front of a console which contains a panel of push-buttons. Depression of a key or keys brings the required tray of cards or frame of files into the operator's range. Some of the rotary cabinets used for file storage can be built up through two floors of a building.

Used in organisations where access to hundreds of thousands of files is essential, electrically operated filing reduces fatigue because the operator is seated, and gives very quick reference to documents. Although expensive it saves a great deal of space and labour and gives far more efficient service than is normally possible with manual systems.

MOBILE CABINETS

Another innovation giving maximum utilisation of space is the mobile cabinet. A series of lateral filing cabinets set on wheels stand

[*Courtesy Kardex Systems (U.K.) Ltd.*]

Fig. 99 *Electrically operated filing cabinet for record cards.*

on metal tracks. The cabinets are double-sided, as if two cabinets were standing back to back. The tracks are long enough to accommodate the cabinets plus the width of an aisle. The cabinets can be moved along the tracks by either mechanical or electrical operation, thus providing space to move between the cabinets from which files are required.

Types of file folders

MANILLA FOLDERS

Various types of folders are available including square-cut (both sides of equal size), edge-cut (the front side slightly narrower than the back leaving an edge on which to insert the identification) and tabbed (with protruding tabs "stepped" across a series of five folders). Square-cut, edge-cut and thumb-cut (with a semi-circular cut-out for separating front and back) plastic folders, usually joined at the bottom as well as the left-hand side, are also available. All can be obtained in a variety of colours which may be useful for "colour coding", according to subject, for example. Treasury tags and metal fastenings of various kinds may be used to secure the documents.

WALLET FOLDERS

When documents are too bulky for a folder they may be placed in an envelope or wallet folder made of card. The sides and bottom of the folder extend to approximately 25 mm but there is no means of securing the documents.

RING BINDERS

Ring binders are available in many different sizes. They normally have hard covers and two or more rings (attached to the inside of the spine) which open to allow the insertion and extraction of documents.

LEVER ARCH FILES

Lever arch files are hard covers which contain metal arches opened and closed by operating the lever. As each file can accommodate a large number of documents (up to 500 or so depending on the thickness of the paper) it is suitable for such documents as delivery notes, invoices and goods received notes. Its advantages are that papers can be kept in the order in which they are filed; papers can be referred to without removing them and filing of papers in sequence is quick and easy. By placing the file in a board cover or case the contents may be kept clean and dust-free.

BOX FILES

Box files have a lid, sometimes with a strap fastening, and may have a spring clip inside to hold the documents firmly in place. Box files are ideal for bulky documents such as catalogues, insurance policies or manuals.

CONCERTINA FILES

These files are made of card and contain a number of separate pockets, being flexible in capacity by reason of the concertina-like gussets at each side of the file. The file is usually bound with a strap, and is most useful either as a temporary filing system (for example, for letters awaiting filing), for the storage of such things as insurance policies, and for "diary" or "bring forward" filing.

It is worth looking at the types of file folders produced in continental countries, whose manufacturers seem to apply more imagination to this mundane product than their British counterparts. The higher cost of German, Italian and Swedish products is sometimes worth while for greater efficiency in use.

Suspension filing

For ease of storage and retrieval, suspension filing is ideal. Kraft file "pockets" with metal bars fitted across the top and protruding at the ends rest on a rectangular metal frame fitted into a standard filing cabinet drawer or in a lateral filing cupboard. The file pocket is thus suspended. The pockets may be individual or arranged in concertina file.

For vertical filing the pockets may be *flat topped*. The metal bars, which usually carry a transparent plastic strip under which the index slip is inserted, fasten over the top front of one file pocket and the top back of another pocket creating a "concertina" of interlocked pockets.

Alternatively tabbed pockets are available. Each pocket stands alone. The protruding metal tab clips on to the metal strip on the

[*Courtesy Roneo Vickers Ltd.*]

Fig. 100 *Suspension filing for computer printout (top rack).* Storage for magnetic tapes (second rack) and disks (third rack) is also provided in this cabinet.

pocket and can be moved to the position required. The filing clerk must ensure that a file really is placed inside a file pocket. If it is not it can slide down between the pockets and be "lost" until someone thinks to delve between the pockets.

For lateral filing the pockets are usually in concertina style with the index on the side of the pocket. Some types of plastic cover have a magnifying effect so that file identifications can be read more easily. Suspension box files are also available for use in rotary systems (*see* page 400).

Colour coding by means of coloured plastic index covers is easy and makes identification of files quicker. Documents may be placed directly in the file pocket and secured with a prong clip. The main disadvantage is that there can be no means of indicating that the file has been removed.

When interlocking suspension pockets are used it is usual to file the documents in folders which are placed in the appropriate pockets. When a file is removed it is easy to insert an OUT card in the pocket in its place.

The main disadvantages of suspension filing of documents are the amount of space required and the cost. However, the quicker retrieval of files may justify both.

Suspension filing equipment is also available for plans, drawings and computer printout (*see* Fig. 100). The documents are clipped into "hangers" which are easy to insert on and remove from specially designed rails.

Random-access files

Electronics have now been applied to filing in the form of random access. Cards—opaque, aperture, microfilm jackets or transparent envelopes containing microfiche—are edge punched to indicate a letter code. Combinations of letters can be devised *ad infinitem* to produce new codes. The codes are recorded and the punched cards placed at random in the trays. When a particular item of information is required the relevant code letter keys are depressed and all the cards containing that information are automatically ejected.

The system consists of trays (capacity 2,000 cards), a push-button console and a coder which is activated by the console to edge punch the cards. One console can be used to select from up to ten trays (i.e. 20,000 cards), which can be searched simultaneously in three seconds (*see* Fig. 101).

Random-access filing has many applications including hospital records, insurance records, intelligence, documentation, inventory control and personnel records.

[*Courtesy Herbert Zippel (U.K.) Ltd.*

Fig. 101 *Access System 60.* The cards are edge-punched by a coder. Any group of cards can be selected within three seconds from up to 20,000 cards in the storage trays.

Ancillary equipment

TRAYS

It is essential that documents awaiting filing should be temporarily stored in trays, which are available in wood, metal, plastic or wire mesh. Where large quantities of documents are constantly being received for filing, as in a central filing registry, several trays can be used to provide the first "rough" sorting into main filing sections.

SORTERS

To facilitate preliminary sorting prior to filing, there are special devices available. A rack of pigeon-holes marked with letters, numbers or dates is a cheap, simple and easy method. A "flap-sorter" is very useful because it requires less space. It consists of hinged flaps on which are indicated alphabetical, numerical and chronological divisions. Documents are placed under the appropriate flap as they are sorted.

TRANSFER FILES

There comes a time with every filing system when either the equipment will not accommodate any more folders, however tightly packed, and/or there is a vast amount of "dead" material which needs clearing out. As discussed in Chapter 33, certain documents must be available for reference for a minimum period even though they may be "non–active". They can be stored in cardboard or steel boxes known as transfer files to ensure that they are kept clean and in correct sequence.

FILING SHELF AND STOOL

Where a great volume of filing is involved, it can become a laborious job, especially when it comes to filing in the lower drawers of cabinets. There are two simple but useful adjuncts which can be used in this connection. The first is a filing shelf, which hooks on to the handle of a drawer, and speeds up filing by bringing material to be filed within easy reach. The shelf can be moved about from one cabinet to another in a matter of seconds, and has a paper bail to prevent papers from blowing away, and a groove in front to hold pen or pencil. Lateral filing shelves/cabinets can be provided with a pull-out tray at a suitable height. The second is a filing stool which reduces fatigue for bottom-drawer filing, and ensures more accurate filing.

Conclusion

The most suitable equipment for individual filing systems may be the most expensive, but it may be a worthwhile investment. On the other hand, the cheapest and simplest is often perfectly adequate. It is essential to determine the type or types of equipment required on the basis of present and future volume, types of records, operator expertise and availability and security requirements.

36. Microcopying

Microcopying or microfilming is simply a means of retaining information by photographing records to reproduce them as miniature films. The films are negative copies, and after developing are stored as a permanent record, often instead of the records themselves. To view documents which have been microfilmed, a machine called a "viewer" or "reader" is used, which projects the film on to a screen for reading. When a paper copy of the document is required the relevant film is processed by a "reader/printer". There is nothing very new in the idea, for there are records of miniature photography as long ago as 1853, and there is a story (printed in *The Times*) of microfilmed messages being taken by carrier pigeon to beleagured Paris in 1871!

Partly because of improvement in the techniques of microcopying, and partly because of the increased applicability to business management, this subject has attracted much more interest in recent years. It is important because it is a means of saving office space, office paper and overhead expenditure.

The film

Records are photographed by a camera, sometimes referred to as a "recorder". The International Conference on Documentation in 1938 resolved that the normal size cine film (35 mm) should be used, but 16 mm film is the most popular size used in industry (35 mm is more suitable for book and library work). The reduction in size of the original on film is about 30:1, and films may be 15, 30 or 60 m in length. The number of documents which can be recorded on a reel of film depends on the size and length of the film, the reduction ratio of the photography, and the arrangement of the microphotographs on the film. Figure 102 shows various types of microfilm—fiche, jacket, aperture card and roll on spool.

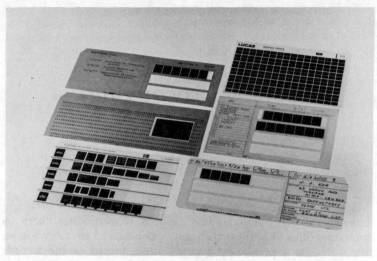

Fig. 102 *Microfilm.* (*a*) Unitised formats. *Left* (front to rear): a jacket, an aperture card and a Tab-Jac; *right* (front to rear): a translucent Tab-Jac an "Ektawrite" film folio and a microfiche.

[*Courtesy Kodak Ltd.*

Fig. 102 *Microfilm.* (*b*) Roll film formats. *Front left:* open spool 16 mm; *front right:* open spool 35 mm; *back left:* open spool 16 mm in "Ektamate" self-threading magazine; *back right:* open spool 16 mm in "Thread Easy" magazine; *centre:* 16 mm microfilm in magazine.

To give some idea of the possible capacity of a roll of film, 3,000 letter-sized documents, or 24,000 cheques (one side only) can be recorded on 100 ft (30 m) of 16 mm film. The film is fireproof, and there is no reason why, with good processing and proper treatment and storage, it should not last indefinitely.

Types of microcopy

Before deciding on microfilming, it is necessary to decide on the form of microfilm record most suited to the circumstances of the work. Thus, for high-volume, low-reference systems, an ordinary roll microfilm might be sufficient, but where there is a high degree of reference, then the microfilm jacket or microfiche might be preferable. The different styles of microfilm are as follows.

(1) *Roll*. All film is usually first made in a continuous roll, so this is the cheapest and easiest, but with a large number of frames to a 200-foot (61 m) roll of film, reference might be slow.

(2) *Cassette*. The roll of film is housed in a plastic box which is just clipped into the machine. It is slightly more expensive than single-spooled roll film, but gives better security against dust and is quicker to insert into the machine.

(3) *Jacket*. Small strips of film are slid into channels of a transparent folder, which offers a neat, easy way of keeping consecutive frames of a small series; it can be added to, from time to time (e.g. medical case histories, correspondence on particular subjects, etc.). Each jacket is thus equivalent to a folder with a variable number of frames. Up to seventy-five images of letter-sized documents can be stored in one jacket. Jackets are available in various sizes with channels arranged in different ways to cater for a wide range of documents.

(4) *Microfiche*. This is a rectangular sheet of microfilm with rows of images. A standard A6 fiche (105 × 148 mm) normally contains 60–98 images depending on reduction ratio, but can hold up to 3,000. This is the kind used extensively for parts lists in big store departments, aeroplane parts at airports, etc. A disadvantage of microfiche is that newly filmed microcopies cannot be inserted.

(5) *Aperture cards*. An individual microfilm (35 mm or 70 mm) is mounted in an aperture in a punched card, which can be punched and sorted for frames of, for example, individual contracts. This is widely used for engineering drawings, and proved invaluable for communicating between the U.K. and France the 300,000 drawings made in connection with the Concorde project. Quick retrieval is possible by using a punched card sorter.

Photography

Speed of microfilming depends on the type of machine used. On a manually operated machine, documents are fed into the throat of the machine where they are held against a rotating drum by rollers, and then photographed and automatically processed. Manual speeds vary between 1,000 and 4,000 documents an hour, depending on the type of document being microfilmed.

On a machine with automatic feed, the fronts and backs of forty cheques can be photographed simultaneously, side by side on 16 mm film, in five seconds, a speed of over 28,000 an hour.

Processing the film

A large installation might best be serviced by a processing unit which automatically develops, dries and spools 100 feet (30 m) of film every ten minutes. The machine is totally enclosed, and can therefore be used in broad daylight. Alternatively films can be returned to the manufacturers, who usually provide a 24-hour processing service at quite a nominal charge.

Reproduction

When the films have been dried and stored, reference to the records microfilmed may be either by obtaining prints from the film, or more usually by viewing through a reader (*see* Fig. 103). This machine consists of a box with a ground-glass screen and the film is projected from behind on to the screen, the enlargement being as large or larger than the original document. Portable readers make it possible for people to carry large quantities of reference material on microfilm when necessary.

The reader is usually very easy to operate, the winder handle being highly geared, so that one turn of the handle turns about 40 to 50 "frames", which are usually numbered. One machine uses a meter calibrated to tenths of a foot, and to facilitate reference, details of groups of documents photographed and meter readings are written on the carton in which the film is stored. Where prints are wanted, some readers allow facsimile copies (enlarged to original size) to be obtained by inserting photographic paper into the machine, followed of course by developing and printing processes.

Modern readers or reader/printers have now been fitted with motorised transport, so that at the press of a button, film is automatically wound from one spool to another.

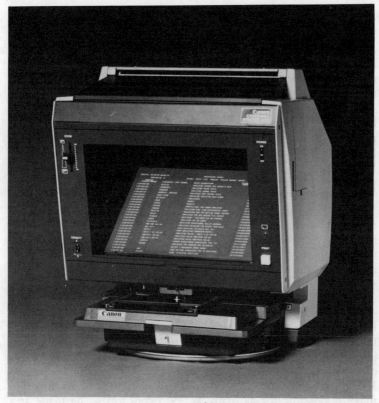

[*Courtesy Canon Business Machines U.K. Ltd.*

Fig. 103 *Microfilm reader/printer.*

Furthermore, by inserting different code numbers on each frame, it is possible to enter the code number on a control keyboard; when the film is moved, the code numbers are electronically scanned, and the film travel stops in seconds at the precise frame number required.

Although the film is developed film, which is obviously suitable for photographic enlargement and printing when prints are required, it is now possible to have an electrostatic printer attached to the reader, which prints clear copies (with 40 times enlargements) very quickly.

Methods of installation

There are three ways in which an organisation can use the process of microphotography: (i) by installing a camera, reader, and processing unit; (ii) by obtaining a camera and reader, and then sending films to the manufacturers for processing; (iii) by hiring a specialist firm to get the microfilming done (off the premises or *in situ*) and installing a reader only, for reference purposes. These are in descending order of cost, and while (ii) is the most popular method, (iii) would be suitable for a small concern wishing to avail itself of the advantages of microfilming.

Cost

The cost of microfilming will naturally vary with the type of machine purchased, and with the method adopted (*see* above), together with the extent to which the apparatus is used. For very occasional use, (iii) above would be recommended, but (i) or (ii) are more economical for larger concerns.

70 mm film

For very large originals (generally larger than 500 × 400 mm), a larger machine using 70 mm film can be used. This machine is an important feature in drawing office practice today. The negatives can be made singly or in rolls, and originals as big as 1,000 × 1,500 mm can be microfilmed. The rolls of 70 mm film make it possible for as many as 250 exposures to be made at a loading.

Advantages of microcopying

(1) Space is saved by replacing bulky files by compact cartons of film. A100-foot reel of 16 mm film recording 3,200 letters takes about 131 cm³ of space, compared with the equivalent 8,125 cm³ needed for 6½ reams of paper—a saving of 98 per cent.
(2) Time is saved by copying documents at great speed—as much as six or seven times faster than by any other method.
(3) Safety of original documents is ensured by substituting microfilm records for those in general use.
(4) Durability of records is increased, as film is more wear-resistant than paper.
(5) Business systems make use of microfilming by photographing current records instead of making carbon copies of them.

(6) Where constant reference to microfilmed records is required, thousands of microfilm records can be accommodated in a desk, thus saving the movement of staff to filing cabinets.

(7) C.O.M. (Computer Originated Microfilm) is a development by which computer output is recorded directly on microfilm (with no intermediate paper copy) in a fraction of the time required for printing out on paper. The microcopy can be on 16, 35 or 105 mm film.

(8) There is saving in filing equipment as well as floor space.

(9) Low cost distribution: if information has to be sent by expensive air-mail, microcopying can reduce postage costs substantially.

(10) There is fixed file continuity. This means that it is not possible to misplace or misfile any of the records on microfilm, as it would be with loose papers in a folder.

Disadvantages of microcopying

(1) If frequent reference is required, it may be relatively slow, because the film has to be viewed through the reader.

(2) On many microfilm readers, location of a particular frame may be difficult, causing further delay and frustration.

(3) While it may be an advantage that microfilm cannot be altered, thus preventing fraudulent alteration, it might also be a disadvantage because sometimes it is necessary to make corrections or make insertions to the stored information.

(4) Unless constant vigilance is exercised, the film may be unreadable; this is usually due to poor processing with stale chemicals.

(5) The labour involved in sorting papers, removing pins, etc. may make a microfilming project very expensive, and cheaper storage space would obviously be more advisable.

(6) Unless carefully chosen, the reduction ratio of some documents can be so extreme as to make it difficult to read on the reader.

(7) Records in coloured paper are sometimes difficult to reproduce.

Applications: an example

An example of a practical application of microcopying to a business operation is that of the conversion of an invoicing system to cycle billing, incorporating the abolition of ledger cards.

The sales, receipts and return vouchers are retained until the appropriate cycle date comes round, and the details from the vouchers are then entered on a statement, which is prepared in duplicate. The carbon copy of the statement is kept in the files to give the pick-up balance (if necessary) for the next month's statement.

The top copy of the statement together with the vouchers are then microfilmed, and as soon as the film is processed, the statement and vouchers are sent to the customer. The billing of an actual cycle (about 200 names), checking of balances, and microfilming of the documents can be accomplished with ease in a working day. Two days is the normal period between the closing of a cycle and the despatch of the statements. All the sales records are photographed in chronological and alphabetical order, and the locating of any one of them on a reader only takes a few moments, should it be necessary to refer to them.

The sales documents covering six months would occupy six shelves, each about 4 m in length. The microfilm records for a similar period would occupy ten boxes each some 100 mm square by about 20 mm thick.

PART SIX
DATA PROCESSING

37. Some Data-processing Systems

There are many data-processing systems for many purposes ranging from straightforward collection and payment of money to the provision of complicated information to management as a basis for forecasting and decision-making. The office manager is likely to be concerned with the systems which keep the organisation ticking over, viz. stock control, sales invoicing, purchasing and wages. From these four basic systems stem the more complicated systems which provide data for analysis, forecasting, etc.

Stock control

In the U.K. under the Companies Act 1948 every company must produce a profit and loss account and balance sheet annually. These documents must be audited and certified by the auditors as presenting a "true and fair view" of the company's financial position at a specified date. The valuation of stock held at that date is an important, and sometimes critical, factor in the figures presented. Stock valuation is the final stage of stock control, which includes the method of ordering, keeping and issuing stock items, keeping and monitoring stock records, and stock-taking.

Although stock control is closely connected with the production side of a business, stock records are probably as important as any of the books and records maintained by a business. It is possible for a company to declare dividends which have been earned not out of profits, but by the overvaluation of stocks—and the parties responsible would be liable to repay any such dividends distributed.

The systems of stock control depend very largely on the type and

415

size of business, although certain common, fundamental principles are usually followed.

RECEIPT OF GOODS

Each consignment of goods received in the stores must be checked and recorded. When goods are delivered the consignee is asked to sign a receipt which may be a copy delivery, despatch or consignment note, a receipt note or a consignment book. It is not usually possible to check the condition of the goods at the time of receipt and this should be indicated on the document. If packages or crates are obviously damaged in any way this should be noted on the document.

Goods received should be checked as soon as possible to ensure that they are (i) in good condition; and (ii) in accordance with the order. Goods can be checked either against a copy of the original order or "blind", i.e. the goods are listed as they are unpacked. The disadvantage of the former method is that careless checking may not bring to light shortages or inaccuracies. Blind checking is time-consuming if the list has to be handwritten but this can be overcome by stock clerks dictating the list, using a portable dictating machine. The list is then typed and checked by the appropriate section of the purchasing or accounts department.

When a consignment arrives it is common practice to complete a goods received note which is sent to the purchasing or accounts department. The format of goods received notes varies from one organisation to another but usually includes the date, supplier's name, quantity and description of goods, number of containers or packages, carriage paid or not paid and the signature of the receiving stores clerk.

STOCK (OR STORES) ISSUES

Stock should be issued only against written, numbered requisitions which have been signed by the person requiring the goods and, when appropriate, by the person authorising the requisition. The purpose for which the items are required should also be stated. In many organisations each job is given a number. A job card is kept so that all costs relating to that job can be charged to it. Stock issues for particular jobs must indicate the job number for this purpose.

There are many systems for issuing stock items but the success of the system depends very largely on the stores personnel, whose efficiency can be crucial to the successful operation of the production function of the organisation.

Every business has its own particular form of records, and its own system of entering them. The record can vary from a simple card containing "receipts, issues and balance" figures for each item to a computer file which provides numbers and financial values of receipts, issues and balances, job codings for issues, maximum, reorder and minimum levels for each item, values for major groups of items, and any other information required such as location of items by code references. In one business a record of quantities is adequate; in another a priced stock record is necessary. The stores record, whether a card, sheet or computer file, must be kept up to date with data from the goods received notes and stores requisitions.

STOCK RECORDS

The purpose of stock records is (i) to check on the issuing sytem; (ii) to ascertain the balance of any particular item at any time (and the value, if required); and (iii) to check with the physical stock-taking which every business carries out periodically. It is usually the duty of the storekeeper to maintain bin records of each item of stock and to record receipts and issues, which should agree with the office stock records. Where possible, stock records should be kept in a separate office, so that they constitute a check on the recorded actions of the storekeeper (by comparison with the bin cards). Whichever system is used, a machine will do the tedious job of posting much quicker than if carried out by hand and provide an automatic check on the accuracy of the postings (with pre-listings in a similar way to invoice posting). At the same time it will automatically give a new balance on each stock account.

STOCK-KEEPING

Goods must be easily located when required. It is common practice to use a coding system so that goods can be stored in sequence facilitating fast location. This function is now computerised in some large stores so that there is no physical "fetching and carrying". Coding overcomes the difficulty of an item of stock being called different names by different people. The coding system should be as simple as possible.

In a large stores the code may consist of a series of digits which identify the bays of racks, the racks, the shelves and the shelf divisions. Simplicity of system, coupled with economy in space and operation, are the desired requirements. Mobile racks which can be stored close together and moved on rails, either mechanically or electronically, when required save space. For small stock items, e.g. pharmaceuticals, automated rotary racks save a lot of space and time as the operator remains at one spot operating the control panel and retrieving the goods as they are brought into position.

STOCK-TAKING

To avoid dislocation of ordinary business at three-, six-, or twelve-monthly intervals, many organisations use the perpetual inventory system. A different section of stock is checked and compared with the stock ledger at frequent intervals throughout the year, so that when the end of the financial year is reached the book figures can be taken as "physical stock". Every item of stock must have been checked at least once during the course of the year.

If the perpetual inventory system is not possible, the inevitable rush and dislocation caused by the annual stock-taking is unavoidable. All arrangements should be made beforehand. The stocktaking must be under the control of one person who must have reliable assistants. The following decisions must be taken:

    (1) the timetable for the stock-taking (starting and finishing dates and interim progress check times/dates);

    (2) the order of checking items;

    (3) the method of checking the stock, depending on the degree of accuracy required (e.g. checking by individual count or by weighing);

    (4) any goods not to be included in the stock-taking;

    (5) deadlines after which invoiced goods should not be included (goods received but not invoiced should not be included);

    (6) method of recording issues during stock-taking (this is usually done on a special form so that the items issued before being physically counted can be included in the stock valuation).

All staff involved in stock-taking should be given precise instructions based on the decisions listed above, the method of completing stock-taking records (usually inventory forms), and the procedures to be followed when queries arise. Staff not physically involved in stock-taking should be informed of the dates and asked to co-operate by limiting requests for stores issues to a minimum.

VALUATION OF STOCK

The normal accounting method of valuation of stock-in-trade, and one which has been accepted by the Inland Revenue in the U.K., is the established principle of "cost or market value", whichever is the lower. Although the cost value seems a simple enough basis, there are several ways of arriving at what is considered to be a fair cost value for stores issues, as follows.

    (1) *Specific method.* Each item or batch of items is priced out at its

specific cost. This method is most suitable for bulk stocks and for very expensive items of stock.

(2) *"First in, first out" (F.I.F.O.).* This is the method which assumes that the goods which have been held the longest are the first issued. This ensures that remaining stocks are priced at the level of the more recent purchases, and unless cost of replacement is increasing rapidly, is quite suitable for many concerns.

(3) *"Last in, first out" (L.I.F.O.).* This is the name given to the method of pricing goods at the earlier purchase price, and in times of rapidly advancing prices eliminates stock profit which might be made under the F.I.F.O. method. The U.K. Inland Revenue authorities have not agreed to this method of stock valuation.

(4) *Average cost method.* This method aims at minimising the disadvantages of both F.I.F.O. and L.I.F.O. and consists of periodically averaging out the cost of stock and subsequent purchases at the beginning of the year. This system is quite extensively used, and is perhaps the most satisfactory system where prices fluctuate, although to be successful the averaging should be done at frequent intervals (often once a month).

(5) *Standard cost system.* This is a system used by manufacturing concerns, where manufactured goods have been budgeted at a predetermined or standard cost, based on values in a normal period.

When the stock-taking has been completed, the items priced out, and the total value of stocks ascertained, it is usual for the auditors of a company to require a stock certificate in a form similar to that shown in Fig. 104.

I hereby certify that the Stocks of the Company have been taken

at 31st March 1980, that the quantities are correct to the best of

my knowledge and belief, that the prices do not exceed cost or

market price whichever is the lower, and that the total value is

£140,500, as set out in the attached Schedule.

Signed

D. Bartlett

Director

Fig. 104 *A stock certificate.*

OTHER AREAS OF STOCK CONTROL
Stores control and stock-taking is a wide subject. Only a few of the
more important aspects have been covered. Coding of stores, audit
control, centralisation of stores and purchasing need closer study
by anyone involved in this area of office management.

Sales invoicing

As with stock control only a brief outline of sales invoicing can be
given in this chapter. The administrative side of sales consists of
receiving orders, credit control, checking availability of stock and
preparation of all documents including the invoice.

PURPOSE OF INVOICING
The main purpose of invoicing is to notify the customer of the price
of each item delivered to him and the total amount due including
such items as packing, postage or other delivery charge, and Value
Added Tax, less trade discount if any. The invoice should also
indicate terms and methods of payment, e.g. cash discount for
payment in full within a certain number of days.

SALES DOCUMENTS
There is a range of documents related to selling: not all of them are
likely to be used by any one company. The individual documents
and the number of copies of each depends on the type and size of
the organisation, the simplicity/complexity of the systems and the
geographical location of the departments involved. Table VI
indicates the type of document, for whom it is prepared and its
purpose.

PROCEDURES
Invoicing procedures vary with the type of business and products,
but commonly the basic steps are as follows:
   (1) check whether the goods ordered are in stock; if not, query
stock replacement;
   (2) check customer's credit situation;
   (3) acknowledge customer's order, advising him whether the
goods are being supplied, when and by what means they will be
despatched;
   (4) obtain goods and pack for delivery;
   (5) arrange for delivery;
   (6) price order and prepare invoice;
   (7) get goods and invoice despatched.
The sequence of these activities and the time-span between them

TABLE VI. TYPES OF SALES DOCUMENT

Document	Sent to	Purpose
Acknowledgment of order.	Customer	Notification that order is receiving attention.
Job card(s).	Factory	Instruction to produce goods.
Stores issue request.	Stores/ warehouse	Instruction to withdraw from stock.
Pro-forma invoice.	Customer	Notification cost of items.
Advice note.	Customer	Notification that goods are being despatched.
Despatch note.	Transport department	Instruction to deliver goods (deliveries have to be programmed in advance).
Packing note.	Customer (with goods)	Identification of individual contents.
Despatch/ consignment note.	Customer (usually with goods)	Identification of contents; number of packages.
Receipt note.	Customer	Signature acknowledging receipt of goods.
Invoice— original.	Customer	Notification of cost of individual items and total amount due.
copy	Accounts department	Amount to be charged to and collected from customer.
copy	Sales department	Analysis of sales.
copy	Sales representatives	Sales to customers.
copy	Stores/ warehouse	Part or call-off deliveries.

depend on many organisational factors. It is important that these details are carefully planned to ensure continuity of deliveries to customers and avoidance of bottle-necks in the paperwork procedures which may delay delivery of the orders.

METHODS OF PREPARATION
It is usual to prepare in one operation some or all of the documents used. This can be done by typewriter (no carbon required sets, one-time carbon sets, or continuous stationery sets), data word-processing machine, billing machine with adding registers, addressing machine, spirit duplicator, copying, electronic accounting machine, or computer. These processes are explained in the relevant chapters.

It must be stressed that the simpler the system, the more efficient it is likely to be. When sequential procedures are involved one copy of a document can be circulated so that the necessary action is taken at each circulation point before the document is passed on. This ensures that there is no duplication of procedures, but the efficiency of the system depends on fast transmission between action stations.

INVOICING CONTROLS

Whatever invoice system is used, controls are essential to ensure that:

(1) all orders are given attention, and without delay;

(2) no goods are despatched unless the customer's credit has been checked;

(3) no goods are despatched unless they are invoiced (on the grounds of speedy service, invoicing is sometimes delayed until after delivery, although many firms prefer to send invoices with the goods);

(4) invoices are not sent off to arrive before the goods are delivered to the customer;

(5) all invoices sent out are charged to the appropriate ledger accounts.

There are various methods of control including numbering of invoices, keeping an order register and credit control.

CREDIT CONTROL

The method of controlling credit depends on the type of goods sold, their value, and the geographical location of the sales units. Four methods are mentioned here.

(1) Coloured signals or tabs may be affixed on ledger accounts, so that when orders are sent for checking they can be marked accordingly. This ensures that the credit limit is kept in line with the state of the account, and gives the opportunity for altering the limit from time to time.

(2) A separate card index (preferably visible) may be maintained, on which the credit limit is indicated by a coloured signal.

(3) Sales staff may obtain credit authorisation quickly and confidentially from a central credit sanctions section by using a special telephone device. The sales assistant lifts the receiver on the telephone, dials the appropriate ledger section, states the name of the customer and the amount, and places the bill for certification in the base of the machine. The assistant can then leave the machine and continue serving customers, and as soon as the credit control

clerk has verified the limit he presses a button in the sanctions office which automatically stamps the date of sanction as well as a symbol which tells the assistant the credit limit.

(4) Customers may use credit cards which indicate the amount of credit allowed to the holder. Usually the sales assistant has to check with a central credit sanctions section for larger amounts to ensure that the customer is not overstepping his monthly credit limit.

CYCLE BILLING

From the use of control accounts for separate parts of the sales ledger (the usual procedure with mechanised accounts) it is quite a simple step to cycle billing. A letter of the alphabet is allotted to each working day of the month and statements of account are prepared and sent off to customers within that section of the ledger each day.

This spreading of the task of preparation of customers' statements:

(1) eliminates the usual month-end work peak;

(2) produces an even flow of payments throughout the month, instead of being concentrated in the first week or so;

(3) makes continuous use of staff and equipment, thereby saving money.

Purchase control

PURPOSE

The main purpose of the system devised to pay for goods purchased must be to ensure that, before payments are made, the goods have been received and the charges are in order.

PROCEDURES

The basic procedures for paying accounts are usually as follows:

(1) check invoices against the copy order, i.e. quantities, descriptions, prices, discounts, terms of payment;

(2) check invoices against Goods Received record;

(3) check accuracy of figures (see below);

(4) approve for payment.

The common method is to have every invoice rubber-stamped with the initials of the people completing the various stages listed above. It is an important principle that, as far as possible, invoice checking should be performed by a person other than the clerk responsible for making payments.

CHECKING

The checking of the order and of receipt of the goods must be performed manually, but calculating machines are invariably used for checking the figures on invoices. Wholesale checking of large numbers of purchase invoices may be uneconomic. Usually it is adequate to check invoices of, say, £100 and over, with spot checking or batch checking (*see* page 514) of invoices for smaller amounts.

SERVICE INVOICES

A problem in many businesses is how to deal with invoices for services supplied. Where this occurs very frequently there should be a standard procedure for dealing with it. A good system is to have a list of specified executives whose signature is sufficient certification of the invoice; all that is then necessary is to ascertain which services an officer is responsible for and submit invoices accordingly.

MAKING PAYMENT

Generally speaking, there are four ways of making payment:

(1) at the beginning of each month, as suppliers' statements are received, made up to the end of the previous month;

(2) at a specified date each month, regardless of whether statements have been received or not (the date is usually fixed to coincide with the holding of a finance committee meeting);

(3) weekly, to obtain special discounts for payment within (usually) seven days;

(4) daily or almost daily settlement of invoices, as they are received.

The last-mentioned method requires the organisation to be highly capitalised. It has the great advantage to the management that they know there are no contingent liabilities for purchases, and it saves accounting work as the accounts can be charged direct to the relative expense accounts, without maintaining creditors' accounts. It is usual to rubber-stamp the statement (or a form in lieu) to certify that the total shown thereon is passed for payment.

The drawing of cheques should preferably be performed by a person other than the one who checks invoices and makes up the statements. The question of safeguard against fraud is discussed in Chapter 48.

Wages systems

In the U.K., every employer has a statutory obligation to pay his employees in accordance with the terms agreed either on an individual basis or on the basis of negotiations with union representatives and agreed by the union members they represent. The amount of wage/salary and other fringe benefits must be stated in the letter of appointment which an employer has to give to every new employee, who works more than sixteen hours per week, within thirteen weeks of his starting work with the organisation. This obligation, and the obligation to issue a wage/salary statement when an employee is paid, were laid down in the Contracts of Employment Act 1972, and are now contained in the Employment Protection (Consolidation) Act 1978. Details given on the wage/salary statement must include gross pay, deductions and net pay.

Preparation of wages in a large organisation needs a large number of staff since there is a limited amount of time in which the job can be done.

Although there are common principles in the preparation of wages, the different systems used arise from the complications of costing requirements, of the different methods of remuneration, and of the geographical and organisational circumstances of the working units.

THE PURPOSE OF WAGES SYSTEMS

Some of the many purposes of a wages system are:

(1) to calculate and pay the employees the correct amounts to which they are entitled;

(2) to record the differences between gross and net pay, that is, to record all deductions from pay;

(3) to allocate these deductions to their respective funds or other purposes;

(4) to calculate individual and total pay according to a timetable, so that it can be paid out at the recognised times;

(5) to compile wages in such a way that the records can also be used for costing purposes (labour costs in costing should agree with the pay-roll).

INFORMATION REQUIRED

Having the objects clearly in mind, what information is required before the pay-roll can be produced? The following points include some of the usual information that is necessary, although it may be more or less than this according to the business concerned.

(1) *Attendance records.* Most organisations require evidence of each employee's attendance at work: this is usually done by automatic time-recorders (*see* Chapter 15), by the production of time cards, by the writing of time-sheets (endorsed by a foreman or supervisor), or by entries in a time book.

(2) *Work records* are required where manual workers have a bonus rate related to the work produced.

(3) *Occupations and gradings* of all workers are required, so that appropriate rates of pay can be entered, and occupations are often entered on the pay-roll. Schedules of rates of pay for each occupation should also be completed.

(4) *Regulations* of Wages Councils, Wages Boards, etc., and all the up-to-date variations in them.

(5) *Conditions of service* appropriate for each class of employee, and individual details of dates of joining or leaving, sickness and holiday pay entitlement, special leave, etc.

(6) *Compulsory deductions,* including National Insurance, P.A.Y.E. details (code number, and previous pay and tax of new employees), and pension contributions.

(7) *Voluntary deductions,* which may include savings, sports fund, benevolent fund, etc.

(8) *Union contributions,* which employers may agree to collect from union members on behalf of the union(s).

From this short list it can be seen that the information required is partly general (National Insurance), partly individual (number of hours worked), partly constant (P.A.Y.E. code number), and partly variable (piece-work pay). These considerations will influence the wages system used.

In the U.K., statutory obligations are laid down in detail under the Social Security Pensions Act 1975, the Payment of Wages Act 1960, the Employment Protection (Consolidation) Act 1978, the Shops Acts and the Truck Acts. The Truck Acts (1831 to 1940) prevented workers from being paid in kind and legalised certain deductions from wages. A concise summary is given in the *Memorandum on the Truck Acts,* published by H.M. Stationery Office in 1947. The Truck Acts (now repealed) were modified by the Payment of Wages Act 1960, mention of which is included at the end of the chapter.

THE PAY-ROLL

The pay-roll is the list of individual employees and is where wage calculations are usually made; the separate sheets are sometimes referred to as "wages sheets". Employees are listed against the pay numbers allocated to them (this facilitates identification and is helpful for both time and staff records). Gross wages, made up of basic pay plus overtime, are entered for each employee; all deductions (both compulsory and voluntary) are entered, totalled and subtracted from the gross pay; to this amount due are added any special allowances such as mileage. The employer's contributions towards National Insurance are entered in separate columns.

The total of the gross pay when added to the employer's National Insurance contributions will be the amount to charge in the firm's books of account; the total of the income tax column represents the tax collected, which must be paid to the Inland Revenue authority together with the National Insurance contributions from employer and employee (usually monthly); and the total of the net pay column will be the amount of cash to be withdrawn from the bank and paid out to the employees, or the total amount of cheques drawn or credit transfers.

In a large organisation with thousands of employees there will be a number of separate wages sheets which need to be summarised to ascertain the total pay-roll figures. This pay-roll summary can be compiled while the different sheets are being prepared, so that by the time the last wages sheet is calculated the summary can be completed and total figures ascertained.

Organisations which have a computer normally have the pay-roll prepared on it (*see* Chapter 40).

STEPS IN WAGES PREPARATION
The whole procedure of preparing and paying wages can be summarised as follows.

(1) Collect time and attendance records.

(2) Telephone the bank a few days before pay-day, to give some idea of the total amount of cash required.

(3) Obtain details of changes in the standard pay-roll. These will be mainly details of new employees, and of those leaving, as well as of staff sickness and holidays. Special forms are usually completed weekly by the personnel department to notify the wages department of these details.

(4) Calculate wages on the pay-roll.

(5) Prepare pay statements and pay envelopes.

(6) Prepare pay-roll summary, i.e. the summary of all the individual pay-roll sheets.

(7) Carry out a cash analysis, that is, calculate how many and what value of notes and different coins are required for paying out.

(8) Post National Insurance and income tax deductions to individual earnings records (Inland Revenue requirements).

(9) Put up cash. This is usually done by allocating different parts of the pay-roll to different clerks and giving them the exact amount to "make up" into pay packets. Known as the "exhaust method", it is the best way of guarding against mistakes. Alternatively, cheques may be prepared or a credit transfer list prepared for the bank (*see* page 544).

(10) Distribute wages (discussed later), cheques and/or pay statements.

(11) Prepare and submit income tax and National Insurance returns to Inland Revenue authority.

THE PAY-OUT

The pay office should be sited as centrally as possible and should be accessible to the workers; this expedites the paying-out process. It is important that wages should be given to the right persons named on the pay-roll. With a small staff it is easy to identify the workers who will be known individually to members of the staff. With larger concerns the most usual means of identification is for the worker to produce his time card (in some businesses the worker signs the card as a receipt for his wages). It is advisable to have two members of staff paying out the wages; this puts the employer in a stronger legal position should a dispute arise.

An essential safeguard is to devise a system for taking care of uncollected pay packets. Usually they are listed, returned to the cashier, and a receipt is obtained for them. Their total should, of course, agree with wages marked on the pay-roll as uncollected.

PAY AS YOU EARN (P.A.Y.E.)

"Pay As You Earn" is the name generally used for the system of tax collection whereby income tax is deducted by instalments from remuneration as the pay is earned. In the U.K. all employers are legally bound to deduct P.A.Y.E. tax on all Schedule E payments, i.e. "wages, salaries, fees, pensions, or profits accruing by reason of office or employment", and to account for it to the Inland Revenue authority.

Employees are given code numbers, which vary according to their personal allowances, and by reference to special tables the employer can (i) ascertain the tax-free pay for that code number; (ii) calculate the total tax payable on the balance of taxable pay; (iii) deduct the tax-due figure (i.e. tax already paid) up to the last week or month; to give (iv) the tax payable for the current week or month. The earnings record for each employee must include the following:

Gross pay for week or month
Cumulative pay to date
Cumulative free pay to date   } All for each week
Cumulative taxable pay to date   or month of the
Total tax due to date   income tax year
Tax deducted or refunded

The office work in connection with P.A.Y.E. can be summarised as follows.

(1) Obtaining P45 form from all new employees, or, if not supplied by them, notifying the local Collector of Taxes on form P46.

(2) In the meantime, deducting tax by reference to Week 1 or Month 1 and entering on a Deduction Card.

(3) Deducting tax each week or month by reference to the individual Tax Code Numbers supplied, and the Tax Tables.

(4) Maintaining running records of the cumulative pay, etc., and tax deducted on the appropriate P11 Tax Deduction Cards.

(5) Once a month sending a cheque for tax deducted (together with National Insurance contributions) to the local H.M. Collector of Taxes, together with the P30 Remittance Card.

(6) When an employee leaves, preparing a P45 form of pay, tax deducted, etc., and sending Part 1 to the local Inspector of Taxes, and handing Parts 2 and 3 to the employee.

(7) After the end of the income tax year, issuing to all employees a P60 statement of pay and tax deducted in the year.

(8) Making a return to the local Collector of Taxes, not later than 19th April, of all tax deducted in the income tax year, together with the Tax Deduction Cards maintained during the year, and a P35 Annual Declaration Certificate.

The most important forms used in connection with P.A.Y.E. are as follows.

P2   Notice of Coding (sent to employee).

P6   Notice of Amended Coding (sent to employer).

P11 Deduction Card (monthly and weekly).

P12 Simplified Deduction Card (where employees are paid at a fixed rate).

P30 Remittance Card.

P35 Yearly Summary and Certificate.

P45 Particulars of Employee Leaving.

P46 Notification to Tax Office of new employee without a Code Number.

P47 Employer's Application to Refund Tax in excess of £50.

P60 Employer's Certificate of Pay and Tax Deductions (given to employees at the end of the year).

By arrangement with the Inland Revenue authority, a company can use its own form of earnings record for incorporation with a mechanical wages system, but otherwise the standard P11 Tax Deduction Cards must be used.

Many ingenious devices have been introduced to lessen the work in connection with P.A.Y.E., and perhaps one of the most notable is the enlargement, on a board one or two metres square, of the free pay and of the tax equivalent to each code number in a particular week. This may be glanced at by the tax calculator, and saves a great deal of time which would otherwise be consumed in referring to separate tables.

Full information about P.A.Y.E. can be obtained from the *Employer's Guide to P.A.Y.E.*, published by the Board of Inland Revenue. One last point is that the amount shown in the books of account as P.A.Y.E. tax owing should be agreed at least quarterly with the amounts shown in the different pay-rolls, before payment is made to the local Collector of Taxes.

NATIONAL INSURANCE

Under the Social Security Pensions Act 1975 every employee and self-employed person must pay National Insurance contributions based on the wage/salary received or income earned. School-leavers obtain a National Insurance number from their local Careers Office. They receive a card quoting the number which is recorded at the Department of Health and Social Security at Newcastle-upon-Tyne. It should be quoted when making any enquiry or claiming any benefit, e.g. sickness or unemployment.

There are two levels of contribution, depending on whether the employer is "not-contracted-out" or "contracted-out". In the former case the full contribution is payable, as follows.

Employee: 6.5 per cent of gross earnings above £19.50 per week or £84.50 per month up to a maximum of £135 per week or £585 per month.

Employer: 13.5 per cent of the employee's gross earnings within the same limits.

Contracted-out employers have pension schemes approved by the Department of Health and Social Security. The National Insurance contributions are then as follows.

Employee: 6.5 per cent of gross earnings up to £19.50 per week or £84.50 per month and 4 per cent on the balance of gross earnings up to a maximum of £135 per week or £585 per month.

Employer: 9 per cent of the balance of gross earnings between the minimum and maximum amounts stated above.

The percentages and figures quoted are correct at September 1979.

DUMMY WAGES

The term "dummy wages" is applied to the payment of money to non-existent workers entered on the pay-roll with bogus names, and is a common method of embezzling from the firm's cash. The first and perhaps best method of prevention is to install a system of internal check (*see also* Chapter 48), by allocating the different jobs—preparation of pay-roll, drawing of cash from the bank, paying out—all to different members of the staff, or to different departments. Each member of the team should then check on what another has done. Even then, collusion between two members of the staff is possible, and other steps that should be taken include the following:

(1) regular agreement of the names on the pay-roll with the staff records, and the issue of all pay instructions regarding changes in personnel from the latter department to the wages department;

(2) internal audit check at irregular intervals, and preferably at the time of paying out;

(3) obtaining a signature for all wages paid out, or the production of a time card;

(4) foreman's certification that the time record is in order;

(5) preparation of time cards by the mangement only;

(6) checking with National Insurance cards;

(7) having good quality staff and adequate supervision.

Where casual labour is employed, particularly on contracts in out-of-the-way parts of the country, it is very difficult to check on the veracity of pay records, and circumstances will dictate the best method of checking on dummy wages. There are times when ultimately, whatever checks are in force, the integrity of the clerical staff is the only real safeguard against this form of dishonesty, and it pays to have well-paid and experienced staff in charge.

Finally, where applicable, instead of paying cash, the possibility of paying by cheque or credit transfer should be considered. The credit transfer system entails the completion of an individual slip for each employee endorsed with the name of his nominated bank and the amount of his pay, and this has to accompany a summary sheet which is sent to the firm's bank, who make a direct credit to the employee's bank account and debit the firm's account with the total of the pay-roll. It is essential to send a pay statement to the individual employee of the amount placed to his credit.

CENTRALISATION OF WAGES
Where there are a number of similar establishments in an organisation it may be advantageous to centralise the wages preparation, for this ensures the employment of experts, uniformity of record, and some control over dummy wages or irregular payments, and is generally more economical, particularly when the pay-roll is on computer.

Payment may be best handled by the individual establishments, the totals of each pay-roll being withdrawn from local banks. Wage packets are then prepared and paid out locally also, which assists in the identification of workers being paid. The suitability of a centralised system depends on individual circumstances, and the advantages and disadvantages of centralisation generally (*see* Chapter 3) should be borne in mind.

PAYMENT OF WAGES ACT 1960

This Act was introduced to avoid the difficulties presented by the Truck Acts in the payment of wages not in cash but by cheque or other means. It legalises the payment of an employee's wage in certain specified ways:

(1) if an employee requests in writing, and the employer does not refuse:

    (*a*) by payment into the employee's bank account;

    (*b*) by cheque (legalised from 1st March 1963);

    (*c*) by Postal Order.

(2) payment can be made without request, when employees are absent through sickness or injury, by Postal Order, but not by cheque.

The employer is not allowed to make any deduction for payment in any of the specified ways.

Regarding the methods mentioned in (1) above, either party may cancel the arrangement at any time by giving four weeks' notice in writing, or both parties can agree in writing between them to end it immediately or on any specified date.

The advantages of paying wages by cheque are that it achieves economy (particularly in the bagging up); it overcomes the risk of pay-roll bandits; and employees have the advantage of cheque facilities, i.e. if they open bank or giro accounts.

38. Data-processing Methods and Equipment: Non-computerised

The accounting function is based to a great extent on the analysis of income and expenditure. The information needed for forecasting and other areas of management decision-making has to be provided from an analysis of past performance, research, potential markets, etc. This analysis, or classification of data into homogeneous groups, is a major aspect of data processing. The collation and analysis of the mass of data contained on slips, cards and forms of every size and colour creates a sizeable problem too.

Hand-operated analysis systems

There are four well-known hand-operated analysis devices, viz. peg-boards, marginally (or edge) punched cards, slotted cards and feature cards.

PEG-BOARDS
A peg-board consists of a rectangular board with evenly spaced metal pegs along the top. Forms having evenly spaced punchings along their tops are then hung on these pegs, so that each form overlaps its neighbour, with one or more columns visible. By this means only the information required is revealed, and can be analysed by cross-casting the figures on the forms, either mentally or on an adding machine. A line-guide, or "cursor", running the full length of the forms can be moved up and down to enable the operator to cross-total quickly and accurately.

On the peg-board illustrated in Fig. 105, the forms are in fact fixed to a bar which is reversible and interchangeable, so that both sides of the forms can be used without rearrangement. A second bar can be loaded up and quickly changed with the first set of forms as soon as they have been analysed.

[*Courtesy Kalamazoo Ltd.*

Fig. 105 *A peg-board, showing forms arranged with cursor half-way up board.* The lower part of the illustration shows how the forms can be taken off and reversed, so that information on the backs of the forms can also be summarised.

A peg-board is a useful inexpensive device for small jobs. A baker with twenty roundsmen who wishes to analyse his sales into white bread, brown bread, cakes, etc., asks his roundsmen to complete analysis forms for their daily sales and the forms can then be analysed once daily, or on a weekly basis. Without a peg-board it would be necessary to enter all the figures from the forms into an analysis book for cross-casting, and then to check the entries and cross-cast them. With a peg-board, the possibility of error from the copying is completely eliminated.

MARGINALLY (OR EDGE) PUNCHED CARDS

This system uses cards with a series of punched holes along one or more edges. The numbers and positions of these holes are determined by the headings and subdivisions of the analysis required; each hole represents a number or value. After entries have been made in the body of the cards, the holes are slotted out to represent the details on the card. A small pair of ticket-clippers can be used for the slotting.

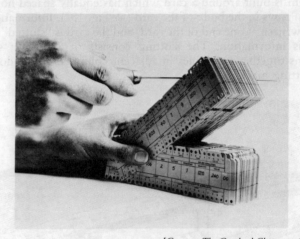

Fig. 106 *Sorting marginally (edge) punched cards.*

When any particular group of cards is needed a needle is passed through the appropriate hole and lifted so that the cards which have been slotted at that particular position fall out of the pack (*see* Fig. 106).

The system has great flexibility, as any size card can be used, although there is obviously a limit to the size for handling convenience. The cards have a corner cut away to assist initial sorting, that is to ensure that the cards are all facing the right way, and are the right way up.

Keysort system. Although this chapter is concerned with "hand-operated systems of analysis", mention should be made of a mechanised version of marginally punched cards known as the "keysort" method. The system uses hand or electric slotting machines; a special selector machine fitted with dropping platform (instead of merely a sorting needle); and an automatic tabulator. The tabulator acts in the same way as its counterpart in a mechanised punched-card system; it simultaneously accumulates and prints information slotted in the cards.

The keysort system possesses the advantage of having the data entered in the body of the card and slotting to record the information round the edges—similar to the simple marginal punched-card system.

SLOTTED CARDS

This system is built around a card which has equally spaced holes punched in rows in the body of the card (*see* Fig. 107). Information is usually written at one end of the card, and the card is "slotted" to record this information. The slotting consists of a straight slit which joins together two holes in adjacent columns, and is done with a slotting machine.

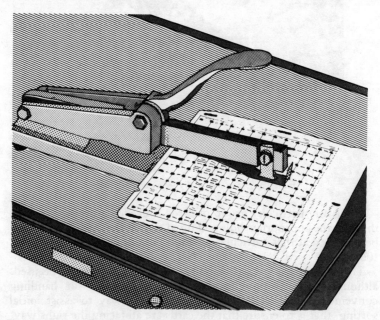

Fig. 107 *Slotting punch, showing how the adjacent holes are joined together to record data on the card.*

The different columns signify different details and are printed according to the requirements of the record.

When slotted, the cards are placed in a sorting "cradle", or selector, and rest on two rods which fit in notches cut from the lower edges of the cards. Metal rods are passed through marginal slots of the cards to prevent their falling out. To operate, other metal rods are placed through the front plate of the selector (*see* Fig. 108(*a*) and (*b*) at the desired positions, and the selector is then

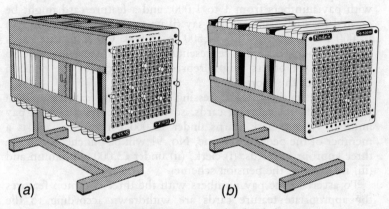

Fig. 108(*a*) *Sorter inverted; selected cards drop.*
Fig. 108(*b*) *Selected cards are offset when sorter is returned to correct position.*

swivelled over on its pivot. Cards which have two or more adjacent positions slotted out will then fall down about half an inch, when a locking rod is run through the bottom row of holes to prevent the cards falling back in position.

When the selector is turned upright again, the cards raised above the others can be counted or listed, or they may be raised by means of passing another rod through the holes provided at the tops of the cards.

Should it be necessary to select cards having three things in common, say details of sex, age and occupation in staff records cards, three rods can be inserted simultaneously, and the cards which drop down when the selector is inverted will be those with the three characteristics.

The amount of information which can be recorded on the cards depends on the ingenuity of the coding when the card is designed. The potential for analysis purposes can be gauged from the fact that with twenty available slotting positions and the use of three rods, as many as 1,140 combinations are possible.

FEATURE CARDS

A feature card has anything from 1,000 to 10,000 numbered positions, each denoting an item in a series. Each card represents one feature or characteristic of that series. If any item in that series has the feature index on the card, then the item numbered is punched out with a hole.

For personnel records, there might be, say, 1,000 employees with pay numbers from 1 to 1,000, and a feature card might be created for each salary range, say (i) up to £3,000 per annum, (ii) £3,000 to £4,500 and (iii) £4,500 to £6,000. Other feature cards might be indexed as sales representatives, clerks, storemen, and so on, while yet others might represent members of the pension scheme or of the sports club.

The items in the series possessing these separate features are then punched into the relevant cards, so that if an employee with pay number 91 is a clerk, earns under £3,000 per annum, and is a member of the pension scheme, No. 91 will be punched in all the three appropriate cards: (i) clerk, (ii) under £3,000 per annum and (iii) member of the pension scheme.

To ascertain the pay numbers with the three common features the appropriate feature cards are withdrawn according to the multiple analysis required, the cards are placed on top of one another, and, when the cards are held up to the light, it will be seen immediately which numbers have the common characteristics, for light will shine through them.

With feature cards, it is possible to select and compare items, and sets of items, at great speed. It is a fairly simple system, and it is quite economic, requiring only a hand punch and the printing of the feature cards.

Feature cards may be used for membership records, operational research, personnel records, medical research, market research and other fields of analysis.

Machines used with hand-operated analysis systems

ADDING MACHINES

Adding machines may be either manually or electrically operated, and either non-printing or printing. The printing machine incorporates a "tally roll" on which the amounts are printed, with symbols indicating figures not included in the calculation (e.g. account numbers), figures subtracted, sub-totals and totals:

64781 <	figure not included in calculation
48571 −	figure subtracted
72181 ◇	sub-total
76783 ★	total

The totals are printed in red on some machines when a bi-coloured ribbon is fitted. Machines which print are known as add-listing machines.

Most adding machines now have a full keyboard, i.e. keys for each figure from 0 to 9. Amounts are usually presented in decimal format to two decimal places. The number of digits which can be included in any amount is usually a minimum of 8, but frequently is more.

Some older adding machines (and calculating machines) had half keyboards, i.e. keys for figures from 0 to 5. For digits above 5 two keys have to be depressed, e.g. three would be depressed twice for 6, three and four would be depressed for 7. Multiplication can be achieved by repeated addition of the figure to be multiplied.

Uses of adding machines. An adding machine can be used for any kind of clerical work where adding or subtracting is required, and it is often worth purchasing as an accessory to a handwritten account-ing system, for example when an accounting machine is too expensive. Pre-listing of invoices is a standard technique for proving the postings made on accounting machines, and it can be used for other accounting purposes, such as when taking out a trial balance. Listing cheques received in the post is another use and an adding machine can be used for any similar operation such as adding up payments to the bank, cash receipts, checking of cash tills, etc. In conjunction with peg-boards, an adding machine can produce sales-analysis figures often as quickly as the more expen-sive accounting machines.

CALCULATING MACHINES

All calculating machines can perform the standard calculations, including multiplication, division, percentages and square roots.

As with adding machines, calculators may be printing or non-printing. Until the advent of the electronic calculator there were various types operated in different ways. Now there is a very wide range of machines available for every possible purpose, either battery and/or mains operated. The great advantage of electronic calculators is that there are no moving parts to wear out.

Calculators are now used universally, being available in sizes as small and slim as a credit card up to full size desk models. The small models, known as pocket calculators, have all the principal calcula-tion facilities, but are non-printing. The input figures and totals appear on a visible register, usually in green or red.

The desk models can range from straightforward calculators to machines which can be programmed, e.g. for automatic discount calculation for a pre-set percentage. A machine may have store and recall memories and dual-column independent calculations. These very sophisticated types of calculator are really miniature computers which will be dealt with in Chapters 39 and 40.

There are calculators for specialist functions, e.g. scientific, which have facilities for calculations such as logarithms, etc.

As with typewriters many printing calculators have a cartridge ribbon which greatly facilitates ribbon-changing.

Machine-operated analysis systems

All book-keeping takes the form, in one way or another, of detailed analysis of figures which are collated from the relevant invoices, job-cards, books of account, and vouchers. One example where analysis is most important is in the sales department of a business, where for control purposes sales figures must be analysed into departments or products, for commission purposes they must be analysed into sales areas, and for posting purposes they must be analysed into customers. The two main types of machine used are discussed below.

CASH-REGISTER TYPE MACHINES

A cash-register type machine is appropriate when a printed receipt is required simultaneously with a posting slip and a sales analysis. This prints every item on an audit record which is visible through a glass panel on top of the machine. Symbols are used which indicate analysis totals and identify totalling operations. This record is kept under lock and key and forms a complete unalterable record of the machine's operation. The machine can also print a unit docket which can be used for further analysis, as a posting medium. Automatic cash registers post the information as it is fed into the machine on to another input medium such as magnetic tape for subsequent processing by computer. There are also electronic cash registers used as terminals linked to a computer. This enables the stock position to be updated at each transaction.

ACCOUNTING MACHINES

Although many accounting operations are now computerised, electronic accounting machines are used in smaller organisations. They may be operated by keys or by some other form of input such as punched card or magnetic card.

An accounting machine is basically a calculator which can perform a wide variety of tasks including invoicing, pay-roll and stock records. In addition to standard calculations it normally calculates extensions, credit transactions and new balances, and can analyse data. Several documents can be completed in one operation, e.g. an invoice can be calculated and printed and the sales ledger card updated at the same time.

Most accounting machines produced today are, in fact, micro or minicomputers. They may be used individually or as terminals in a computer system. This will be explained in Chapter 39.

Punched-card systems

Punched cards are used as input for mechanical and electronic machines.

The basis of a punched-card system is the use of manilla cards of uniform size, each of which has predetermined punching positions. These positions are normally in columns of 0 to 9 and the cards are punched in appropriate columns to represent various data. After punching, the cards are mechanically sorted at great speed and a printed record is then obtained after the holes have been "sensed" by mechanical or electronic means. The printing may also incorporate the addition of information under the various analysis heads (printed along the top of the card).

PROCESSES IN A BASIC PUNCHED-CARD SYSTEM

A simple, fairly average installation will include the following processes: (i) preparation of punching documents; (ii) punching of the cards; (iii) verifying the punching; (iv) sorting; and (v) tabulating.

Before information can be recorded in punched-card form it is usually necessary to produce a "punching document" bearing the data in a simplified and tabulated form, and on which the data is translated into a numerical code ready for punching. When the information has been coded in this way, cards are punched in the appropriate columns by machines called key-punches, which may be manually or electrically operated. On the manual key-punch the keys actually punch holes in the cards, but with the second kind, the automatic key-punch, the operator sets up the figures on the keys and the card is then punched "in one" by electric operation. As information is set into one column the carriage on the machine automatically moves along to the next column in readiness for subsequent punching.

Once the card is punched, it can be used for any type of analysis desired (that is, for any of the analysis columns on the card), but it is essential that the whole punching should be accurate. The next stage is therefore "verification", or the checking of the punching process. There are two methods of verifying punched cards: (i) the "direct" method by the use of a special key-punch on which the operator repeats the punching operation—the carriage on the machine automatically locks itself should an error be found in a card; and (ii) by the use of an automatic verifier—this method involves the repeat punching of cards to make oval holes, after which the cards are fed into an automatic verifier which indicates errors in punching by inserting different coloured cards.

The cards are then sorted very rapidly. They are fed into a sorter and ejected at speed over a number of rotating rollers; the sorting takes place by the cards being trapped at each roller in accordance with the punching in the cards.

After sorting into the required analysis heads, the punched cards are fed into a tabulator which senses the punching and prints on a sheet of paper both the numerical and the alphabetical information contained in the cards. In addition to printing, the tabulator adds or subtracts figures, so that totals under different analysis heads can be obtained according to the sorting operation.

ALPHABETICAL PRINTING

Letters of the alphabet can be reproduced by an appropriate coding system. A specimen card showing how letters of the alphabet can be punched into a card is illustrated in Fig. 109, and it can be seen

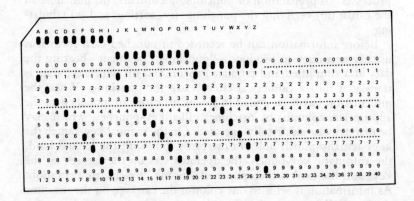

Fig. 109 *Specimen card showing how alphabetical data can be punched into a card.*

how each letter is represented by a two-hole system of coding. The method of coding is varied according to the size of the card used.

DUAL-PURPOSE CARDS

Although the standard punched cards have all the punching positions indicated by printing on the face of the card, to enable the users to "read" it, the machines would punch in the correct positions without the presence of this printing at all. Therefore, some different printing can be on the face of the card, for example the original data from which the punching is made (instead of a separate punching document). Such a card is known as a "dual-purpose card" and can be used for job tickets, pay statements, etc.

OTHER MACHINES

Many other auxiliary machines are obtainable, and which ones to use can only be decided when considering the system in which punched cards are to be used. The manufacturers advise on this. The following are some of the more important ones.

A *gang punch* is a machine which automatically punches a pattern of punching in a number of cards at the same time.

A *reproducing punch* is rather similar in effect and reproduces a pattern of punching from a specimen card into a number of blank cards.

A *collator* (or *interpolator*) automatically compares different sets of cards, and punches, interfiles or segregates cards as desired. It can be used for verifying a set of punched cards with another set and will automatically signal mistakes in the sequence of the cards.

Summary card punch. By attaching this machine to the tabulator, summary or balance cards can be automatically obtained without interrupting the speed of tabulating. Thus, for example, where punched cards are used for the preparation of invoices, summary or invoice totals can be automatically produced for posting to the appropriate ledger accounts.

Calculating punch. The tabulator adds or subtracts figures, but if it is wished to multiply or divide, an electronic calculating punch can be attached which, after performing the calculations required, will punch the results into new cards. A figure punched into a card can be multiplied by a factor in the same card or by a group multiplier punched in a single "master" card. This machine is also used in the preparation of invoices.

Mark-sensing. One type of electronic punch senses graphite pencil marks (that is, with metallic content) in appropriate positions on a punched card, and punches holes in the card accordingly. This saves the need for separate punching documents and, provided the cards are correctly marked, the machine can be relied on to punch the information accurately.

Interpreter. An interpreter can be used to "read" the punched holes and print the reading on the face of that card (or on another one). This machine may be used for preparing pay statements, for once a punched card is created the information from it can be interpreted and printed on to another blank card which constitutes the statement of pay. Modern punches do this automatically, however.

USES OF PUNCHED–CARD EQUIPMENT

The scope of the punched–card system is almost unlimited as it can be used whenever analysis of data is required. When used for the preparation of invoices, a sales analysis can be obtained at the same time; when used for wages preparation, a costing analysis can also be obtained. Stock control and production control, in fact all kinds of accounting work, can be performed by such means.

39. Electronic Data Processing

Electronic Data Processing (E.D.P.) is the method by which information and data of all kinds are processed by a computer. All large organisations either own, lease or rent a computer or use computer services. With the advent of mini and microcomputers it has become possible for many smaller businesses to have their own computer systems. The applications and ramifications of a computer system are now virtually infinite. It is essential for an office manager to understand the basic concept in order to assess the relevance of various systems to his own situation and foresee possible applications which will increase efficiency and minimise costs in his organisation.

A computer system

A computer system comprises a series of electronic devices for carrying out the receiving, recording, sorting, analysing, comparing, calculating, summarising, storing, retrieving, reproducing and transmitting of information and data. Certain of the devices in a system are linked by telephone network. This means that wherever there is a telephone network of the standard needed for data transmission it is possible to have communication between the various parts of a system and from one computer system to another over very long distances.

A computer can only do what it is instructed to do and cannot do anything that could not be done by a human being. Its advantage over the human brain is the speed at which it works. A calculation can be made in a nanosecond, i.e. one thousandth of one millionth of a second.

A computer consists of a *central processing unit*, or *mainframe*, which handles the actual processing of the data, and a number of *peripherals* (*see* Fig. 110(*a*)). The central processing unit (C.P.U.)

445

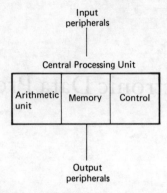

Fig. 110(*a*) *The central processing unit (C.P.U.) of a computer system.*

[*Courtesy International Computers Ltd.*

Fig. 110(*b*) *A typical computer room,* showing computer system with tapes, disks, printers, cardpunchers and readers.

comprises three units. These are the arithmetic unit which calculates data, the memory which holds the data it is working on, and the control unit which ensures that the data is processed in the sequence required. The C.P.U. has a predetermined capacity which dictates the amount of work it can handle at any one time. A typical computer room in which the C.P.U. is installed is illustrated in Fig. 110(*b*).

The peripherals are divided into two groups, viz. input peripherals for feeding data into the computer, and output peripherals for receiving information from the computer.

The critical aspect for anyone involved in computer processing is the input. A computer cannot make mistakes but human beings can and do. Therefore any mistakes made by the human being responsible for the input is processed by the central processing unit and reflected in the data output. GIGO is a term used "in the trade" meaning "Garbage In and Garbage Out". Mistakes are often blamed on a computer when in fact they originate with the input.

How a computer works

A computer has to be programmed, i.e. instructed, to carry out arithmetic calculations in sequence. Programming is a highly specialised operation which is discussed later in the chapter.

Our normal arithmetic method is called "denary", which is based on the figures 0 to 9 before combining in pairs (tens), threes (hundreds), etc. Computers work on a binary method using only two figures, 0 and 1. These two figures are combined to represent the figures 0 to 9 as follows:

Denary	Binary
1	1
2	10
3	11
4	100
5	101
6	110
7	111
8	1000
9	1001
10	1010

It will be noted that 2 = 10 (binary); × 2 (4) = 100; × 2 (8) = 1,000; × 2 (16) = 10,000, etc., so that to convert a binary number to denary it is only necessary to equate the position of the digits, thus:

$$1 \quad 1 \quad 0 \quad 1 \quad 0 \quad 1 \quad 1 \text{ Binary}$$
$$2^6 + 2^5 + 0 + 2^3 + 0 + 2 + 1 \text{ Denary}$$

Methods of input

One of the peripheral devices of a computer is a reader which can identify information presented in a certain form. There are a variety of ways in which information can be presented to the reader.

(1) *Punched cards*. The preparation and verification of punched cards has been dealt with in Chapter 38. It is possible to produce punched cards when processing material on a typewriter, accounting machine or cash register. This means that as an operation is being performed on one of these machines a punched card is being produced simultaneously which will be used for updating information held in the computer system.

There are two other methods of producing punched cards automatically. Mark-sense readers can convert writing on punched card into punch holes on the same card so that no manual punching of data is necessary. The small perforated tickets, called kimble tags, often found on goods in dress shops, etc. can be fed into an automatic converter which produces punched cards from the information contained in the kimble tag perforation.

(2) *Perforated paper tape* is usually produced on a typewriter or on a telex machine. The strip of paper is punched with a pattern of holes. This method is used mainly for transmission of telex messages.

(3) *Magnetic Ink Character Readers* (M.I.C.R.). The printed numbers on cheques (cheque number, account number, bank reference, etc.) are printed in a magnetic ink which can be read by the computer. The figures are printed in a special style.

(4) *Optical Character Readers* (O.C.R.) The characters, similar in style to the M.I.C.R. figures, are printed with ordinary ink. The computer recognises the characters by their shape.

(5) *Mark readers*. Marks on a paper form are recognised and read, similar to the mark sensing on punched cards. People are nowadays commonly asked to complete forms by writing in a series of squares. These forms are used as direct input to the computer.

(6) *Document readers*. In the same way that mark readers will accept and convert information written on paper forms, so the document readers will accept and convert information from documents produced on machines such as typewriters, adding machines, cash registers, high-speed printers, etc.

(7) *Remote input units*. Information can be fed into a computer from a remote area using a plastic badge or a pre-punched card.

(8) *Magnetic tape encoder*. This machine writes directly on to magnetic tape. The speed of input is very fast but the method is expensive.

(9) *On-line terminals*. On-line means that the terminal operator has access to the central processing unit at any time. The most common form of on-line terminal is video based. It consists of a visual display unit (V.D.U.) and keyboard, as shown in Fig. 111,

[*Courtesy I.B.M. (United Kingdom) Ltd.*

Fig. 111 *On-line terminal consisting of a visual display unit and keyboard.*

usually arranged in the same way as the typewriter keyboard, for "keying-in" information.

(10) *Key-to-disk★* systems provide a means of intermediate storage of information on magnetic disk from a number of terminals. The disk then provides the input to the computer for updating files. Disks may be individual "floppy disks" or in stacks in a cartridge.

★ "Disk" rather than "disc" is now the generally accepted spelling in computer terminology.

(11) *Light pens* are used to touch a particular spot on the front of a cathode ray tube to select an item from several displayed on the screen. (This is most likely to be applied to educational and research operations.)

(12) *Electronic writing pad.* Another kind of terminal allows input data to be handwritten with a pen or pencil on an electronic pad (*see* Fig. 112). The written characters are read by a mark–sensing device and converted into code and transmitted to the computer. The computer validation routine to detect errors can be programmed to indicate an error on the display register so that corrections can be made immediately by simply overwriting.

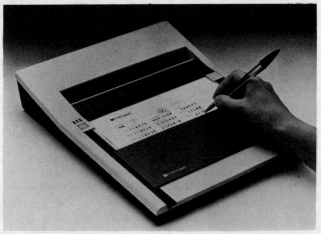

[*Courtesy Micropad Ltd.*

Fig. 112 *Micropad handprint data entry terminal.*

TEMPORARY STORAGE OF INPUT DATA

Information can be fed into a minicomputer, usually via an on-line terminal, and stored on tape or disk. The stored data can then be fed into the mainframe computer, usually overnight, to update the main "files" (*see* Fig. 113). On-line transmission is usually reserved for applications where instant or quick access to data is required during working hours (peak time), since the capacity of the C.P.U. is limited. This also ensures maximum use of the mainframe computer, which normally works twenty-four hours a day.

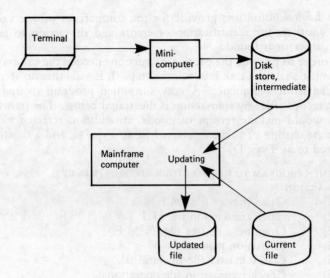

Fig. 113 *Input data can be put in temporary store for later updating of the main computer file.*

Programming

A computer will only process information in accordance with instructions. This means that the instructions have to be explicit and one hundred per cent accurate. There are standard instructions for routine procedures, e.g. starting a calculation, passing information to file storage, etc. For everything else a special program* must be written.

There are four types of instruction which a computer can carry out.

(1) *Input, output and file instructions.* An input instruction tells the computer to read the next input item, e.g. the next punched card or the next item on a magnetic tape or disk. The output instruction indicates that a line is to be printed on paper, a microfilm is to be produced or a line presented on the visual display unit. The file instruction tells the computer to include the information on the file storage device; for example, write to the magnetic tape or disk.

(2) *Internal transfer instructions* tell the computer to move data around from input information to file records, to withdraw information from the file record for updating, etc.

(3) *Arithmetic instructions* tell the computer to calculate.

---

* "Program" rather than "programme" is now the generally accepted spelling in computer terminology.

(4) *Logical instructions* provide for the comparison of one value with another, the identification of errors and the action to take when an error is found.

In order to provide the precise instructions needed the programmer must analyse a task into minute steps. It is vital that no step is omitted from a sequence. A very simplified program to update stock records files by transaction is illustrated below. The transactions would include receipt of goods; an addition referred to as Type A; change of balance referred to as Type C; and a deletion referred to as Type D.

SPECIMEN PROGRAM TO UPDATE STOCK RECORDS FILES BY TRANSACTION

(1)	Open master file (M.F.).
(2)	Open transaction file (T.P.).
(3)	Open new master file (N.M.F.).
(4)	Switch on printer.
(5)	Check master file operational.
(6)	Check transaction file operational.
(7)	Check new master file operational.
(8)	Check printer operational.
(9)	Read first stock code on T.F.
(10)	Read and identify first type on T.F.

IF TYPE A

(11)	Read first stock code on M.F.
(12)	Compare M.F. and T.F. stock codes.
(13A)	If M.F. stock code less than T.F. stock code, transfer all information under M.F. stock code to N.M.F.
(13B)	If M.F. stock code same as T.F. stock code, print error report: "stock code already exists".
(13C)	If M.F. stock code greater than T.F. stock code, transfer all information and T.F. stock code to N.M.F.

IF TYPE C

(11)	Read first stock code on M.F.
(12)	Compare M.F. and T.F. stock codes.
(13A)	If M.F. stock code less than T.F. stock code, transfer all information under M.F. stock code to N.M.F.
(13B)	If M.F. stock code same as T.F. stock code, update relevant information under M.F. stock code and transfer existing and updated information to N.M.F.
(13C)	If M.F. stock code greater than T.F. stock code, print error report: "no stock code exists".

IF TYPE D

(11)   Read first stock code on M.F.
(12)   Compare M.F. and T.F. stock codes.
(13A)   If M.F. stock code less than T.F. stock code, transfer all information under M.F. stock code to N.M.F.
(13B)   If M.F. stock code same as T.F. stock code, proceed to next T.F. stock code, step (14).
(13C)   If M.F. stock code greater than T.F. stock code, print error report: "no stock code exists".

IF ELSE

(11)   Print error report: transaction type not valid.

(14)   Read next stock code on T.F.
         Repeat steps (10) to (13) until all master and transaction file items have been compared.
(15A)   Process remaining transaction file items if any.

OR

(15B)   Transfer remaining M.F. codes (if any) to N.M.F.

END OF RUN

(16)   Remove error report from printer.
(17)   Copy new master file.
(18)   Run printout of master file.
(19)   Master file, new master file and transaction file to storage.
(20)   Printout for further processing/distribution.

LANGUAGES

Standard computers cannot understand normal written or spoken instructions. Therefore a medium had to be devised for presenting instructions to the computer. Thus programming languages were born.

There are three main categories of computer language, viz. machine languages, low-level languages, and high-level languages. *Machine languages* are rarely used except for special tasks which cannot be programmed by any other means. The machine language is a set of binary code instructions. Unfortunately this method is wide open to human error.

Low-level languages are really series of abbreviations which represent standard functions carried out on a computer. For example, a frequent operation is to retrieve information from the memory of the computer. A standard abbreviation enables the programmer to give the necessary instructions without having to identify the precise place in the memory.

High-level languages most nearly relate to plain English. There are a number of these languages, each one having been devised for a particular use. The most commonly used for commercial activities is COBOL (COmmon Business Oriented Language).

Languages used when mathematical formulae are involved are Fortran and Algol.

Methods of output

There are various ways in which the computer can produce information and data.

(1) PRINTOUT

The standard method of written output is known as printout which is produced on continuous stationery in O.C.R. style printing. High-speed printers produce at the rate of 1,500 lines per second.

Laser printers are being introduced to speed up the printing process. This type of printer can be incorporated in an information processor, or "intelligent copier" which can receive information direct from a computer and merge it with a standard letter reproduced from a storage medium. Up to thirty-six A4-size letters can be produced a minute, each one individually "typed".

(2) VISIBLE DISPLAY

Information is produced on the screens of on-line terminals (V.D.U.s) when requests are keyed in. The information may be obtainable from a data base, i.e. a store of information/data which is constantly updated from a central point for use by anyone allowed access to it. Alternatively the information may be updated via the terminal, e.g. airline reservations. When a reservation is keyed in, the number of seats available on that particular flight is automatically adjusted. Information can be obtained in diagrammatic and graphic form as well as textual form (*see* Fig. 111).

Access to information is obtained by keying in a code. Where security is involved each person entitled to access has a personal code which, when keyed in, allows the computer to release the information.

(3) COMPUTER OUTPUT MICROFILM (C.O.M.)

It may be desirable to have information available on microfilm for distribution or for archives. There are various methods of producing C.O.M. One method allows the direct production of microfilm from magnetic tape without printout (*see also* page 413).

(4) STORAGE MEDIA

It is essential to have "back-up" files because it is possible accidentally to destroy a tape or disk. Most organisations keep at least one set of back-up files. At least one security firm offers off-site security storage for computer back-up files.

Methods of storage

Information may be stored on punched card, punched tape, magnetic tape, floppy disk (single disk) or hard disk (a cartridge of disks in a stack).

Tapes and disks are usually stored in racks in code sequence.

Security

The security, i.e. confidentiality, of data stored on computer and in transmission between peripherals and the central processing unit is a matter of vital importance. Access to the rooms where the "files" are stored and where the switching equipment is installed should be strictly limited. The transmission of data is usually protected by an interceptor which "scrambles" and "descrambles" the information at the points of entry and exit to terminals and the C.P.U. This ensures that any unauthorised link into the telephone line will not be able to procure any comprehensible information.

The question of the integrity of the computer staff is an essential consideration. Careful recruitment is the obvious answer. References should be taken up and personality and character assessments should be scrutinised. There may well be a case for involving at least two, possibly more, senior people in addition to personnel staff and the computer manager, in the interviewing and assessing procedures.

A further point which has been a matter of concern to many people is the confidentiality of personal information. The possibility of enacting legislation to control national and international transmission of data related to individuals is under discussion.

Fire precautions are of paramount importance. The risk of fire is a good argument for securing back-up files off site.

As with all machinery, dust and dirt are arch enemies. Airconditioning is essential, both to minimise atmospheric dust and to ensure the even temperature necessary for the operation of electronic equipment. If this seems a costly luxury, consider the cost of a computer breakdown—disputes caused by non-payment of wages, orders not supplied because of non-payment of debts, decisions not taken because information is not available resulting in loss of business and ultimately profit!

Computer staff

When a computer is to be installed everyone whose work will be affected, no matter how slightly, must be brought into the consultations. Their co-operation in explaining precisely what they do manually is vital if the computer staff are to provide an efficient computer system. Training must be given to all staff concerned with input data, and to all staff who will receive output data.

The *systems analyst* is the person who investigates existing systems and draws up a system specification for each job which is to be computerised, e.g. pay-roll, stock records.

The *programmer* takes over the system specification and translates it into a set of detailed instructions which can be understood and acted upon by the computer (*see* page 452).

The *operations staff* are those who run the systems once they are installed and working satisfactorily. The operations manager is the main link between the D.P. department and the departments it serves.

Complex systems

Computer systems can range from simple microcomputers to a highly complex system interlinking mainframe computers and peripherals in various parts of the world.

Where communication is required between parts of the computer system it is necessary to use telephone lines, either private circuits or switched (public) circuits. It is necessary to have "modems", a word made up from two words—modulator and demodulator. Modems are necessary to encode input from a terminal into an acceptable form for the computer to handle (*see* Fig. 114). Similarly, output from the computer to the terminals must be decoded so that the operator can understand it.

It is usual to have several terminals linked to a computer by one telephone line. Since the speed of operation is rapid, access time is usually minimal even when another terminal is "on the line".

Glossary of computer terms

Access time. Technically access time is the lapse of time between

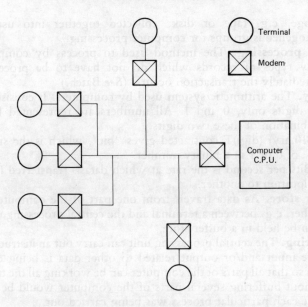

Fig. 114 *Modems are needed in a computer system to encode and decode data transmitted between terminals and the central processing unit.*

the moment of giving an instruction to obtain information from storage, or feed information into storage, and the moment when the actual transfer of data begins. In everyday usage access time is the term commonly used to refer to the lapse of time between keying in on a terminal a request for information and the presentation of the information on the terminal screen.

Address. Identification of a storage location, usually one or a sequence of data characters comprising a name or number.

Arithmetic unit. The part of the central processing unit of the computer which actually does the calculating.

Assembler. A computer program which converts statements written by a programmer in a language known as "assembly language" into a code which can be "read" by the computer.

Assembly language. A language consisting of symbols used by programmers.

Backing store device. Tapes or disks on which data are stored, *usually in large quantities*, either temporarily or permanently. Backing store data is usually off-line and therefore slow to access.

Batch. Records, in document form or on some form of magnetic storage, e.g. tape or disk, collected together into usually homogeneous groups for computer processing.

Batch processing. The method used to process by computer many types of records which do not have to be processed immediately the transaction occurs. (*See* Batch.)

Binary. The arithmetic system used by computers. It consists of two digits only, 0 and 1. All numbers are represented by a combination of these two digits.

Bit. BI(nary) (digi)T contracted gives "bit", which is the single value of 0 or 1 in a binary number.

Bps. Bits per second is the rate at which data is transferred from one location to another.

Buffer store. As data travels from one part of the computer to another, e.g. between a terminal and the central processing unit, it can be held in a buffer store.

Buffering. The central processing unit can carry out an instruction while input and/or output related to other data is being dealt with so that all parts of the computer can be working all the time. Without buffering several parts of the computer would be idle while each particular process was being carried out.

Byte. A group of consecutive binary digits, usually representing one alphanumeric character.

Central processing unit. The "core" of the computer comprising main information and program storage unit, arithmetic (calculation) unit and the control unit. The C.P.U. is commonly referred to as the "mainframe".

Character printer. A printer which prints character by character, as, for example, a typist has to do (also known as a serial or matrix printer).

Cluster. More than one terminal connected to a line or data channel at a single point are referred to as a cluster.

Communication link. The physical link, e.g. a telephone line, which connects one part of a computer system to another for the purpose of transmitting data, e.g. from a terminal to a storage unit.

Computer Output/Originated Microfilm (C.O.M.). Microfilm produced by a computer as output either in place of or as well as printout.

Console. The main control unit used by computer operators to monitor computer processing.

Console typewriter. The console typewriter is used by a computer operator to communicate directly with the computer.

Core. The part of the central processing unit which holds the data in store.

Data base. The data base, or data bank, is the information held on computer file readily accessible to users. A data base often comprises a number of small files rather than one very large one to give quicker access.

Datel services. British Telecom provides special data telephone lines for transmission of data between terminals and computer centres. There are various speeds of transmission.

Debugging. When a new computer program is prepared it must be thoroughly tested to ensure accuracy. The process of identifying and correcting mistakes is known as debugging.

Digital computer. A computer which handles data in numeric form as opposed to an analogue computer which handles data in specific magnitudes, e.g. voltages of electric current.

Digital data network. A communications network designed specifically for the transmission of data in digital form. Telephone networks are designed primarily for the transmission of information/data by other means, e.g. voice.

Direct access. The method by which a terminal operator can obtain information direct from storage upon request. The required data, which is usually stored on magnetic tape, disk or drum, is located by the operation of a storage key. Direct access is often referred to as random access because the data are not stored in logical sequence but by some form of arithmetic calculation.

Disks. A disk is a group of grooved "plates", stacked on a central spindle with a gap between each one. Each plate has "tracks" on both sides similar to the grooves on a gramophone record but invisible. Information is stored on each "face" or surface in the form of magnetised dots. Each face has its own read/write head for identifying and recording information.

Edit. Check data and amend as necessary to ensure accuracy.

Encode. Any process by which data are "translated" from one form into another form.

File. A collection of data organised and stored in a way that allows immediate retrieval.

Flag. A symbol which indicates that a particular record requires special attention.

Front-end processor. A computer which accepts and controls data communications before sending them to the mainframe computer for processing.

Hardware. The actual machinery of a computer system.

High-level language. A language, similar to English, which can be understood by the computer.

Indexed sequential. Data records are indexed to show where they are stored so that by consulting the index direct access to any item of information is possible.

Input. The data fed into the computer.

Instruction. A code which directs a computer to perform a particular operation.

Intelligent terminal. A terminal which can be programmed to process data sent to and received from the central processing unit, i.e. a self-contained computer.

K. A thousand. Computer storage is often expressed in *x* thousand bits to indicate the maximum amount of material that can be held in the central processing unit.

Key-in. Operate the keyboard (usually a standard QWERTY keyboard as used on British typewriters) of a computer terminal.

Leased network. A network of telephone or telegraph lines, usually leased from British Telecom, for the private use of the subscriber.

Limited distance modem. A modem (*see* below) which will operate for relatively short distances of up to about 55 kilometres. They are generally leased or privately owned wires.

Line printer. A peripheral to a computer which prints a whole line at a time as distinct from a character printer which prints character by character as on a typewriter.

Line switching. Any method by which access to a transmission line is gained for the period required, e.g. by dialling. The line is available to the user only for the period of his "call" which is charged by the time used.

Logging-in procedures. Many organisations have terminals linked to a mainframe computer owned by a bureau. To obtain access to the computer the user must follow a routine which ensures the security of the data, i.e. only the "owner" of the data can gain access to it.

Low-level language. A programming language comprising simple codes used by programmers to translate instructions to the computer into a form which it can "understand".

Magnetic disks. *See* Disks.

Magnetic drum. A storage device with a magnetised surface on which data are recorded as the drum rotates.

Magnetic Ink Character Recognition (M.I.C.R.). A form of "reading" by a computer peripheral device from characters written in magnetic ink, as on bank cheques.

Magnetic tape. Magnetised plastic tape on which data can be recorded, and subsequently retrieved when required, using a peripheral device called a magnetic tape drive.

Mainframe. *See* Central processing unit.

39. ELECTRONIC DATA PROCESSING 461

Memory. The storage section of the central processing unit of a computer.

Microsecond. A millionth of a second.

Millisecond. A thousandth of a second.

Modem. A contraction of the words "modulator" and "demodulator". A device for transforming data from a form which is suitable for data transmission to a form which is suitable for computer acceptance and vice versa.

Multipoint. A line or data channel which connects terminals at more than two points.

Multiprocessing. The operation of more than one program simultaneously in a computer system.

Nanosecond. One thousandth of one millionth of a second.

Off-line. A peripheral unit which is not connected to the central processing unit at the time of operation, meaning that data are processed by it at a later date.

On-line. A peripheral which is connected to the central processing unit at the time of operation on so that information can be transmitted and received to and from the CPU and the terminal.

Operating system. The basic computer program which is required to control all programs, i.e. the instructions to the computer to perform various standard processes which have to be performed in recording, retrieving and storing information.

Optical Character Recognition (O.C.R.). A form of "reading" by a computer peripheral device from characters written in a special fount, similar in shape to magnetic characters.

Output. The data provided by the computer after processing.

Parallel processing. Computers may have multiple arithmetic and control units which allow two or more sets of instructions to be carried out simultaneously.

Peripheral. Any piece of equipment within the computer system other than the central processing unit.

Program. A carefully structured set of instructions which "tell" the computer's central processing unit what to do.

Protocol. Regulations which control the flow of information in a communication system.

Random access. *See* Direct access.

Real time. Immediate processing of data when received by the central processing unit so that files are updated and information retrieved thereafter is accurate.

Record. A number of related items of information or data which are grouped together to form a record.

Redundancy checking. A means by which data additional to the basic data being processed can be transmitted to allow comparison which may indicate an error.

Remote Terminal System (R.T.S.). The term used to describe terminals which are situated physically far from the central processing unit.

Serial. Items on a serial file are physically adjacent to each other but there may be no relationship between the subjects of the items.

Software. The non-machine parts of the computer system, i.e. the programs.

Terminal. A peripheral device which can directly transmit data to and receive data from the central processing unit.

Time-sharing. When more than one terminal has access to a central processing unit transmission may be carried out by all simultaneously, though this may create a slight delay in gaining access to the C.P.U.

Visual Display Unit (V.D.U.). A television-type screen, usually attached to a keyboard terminal. Information keyed-in and received is displayed on the screen.

40. Computer Applications

It is possible to perform virtually any transaction or operation on computer and the number of applications is increasing rapidly. Organisations which have a computer system are constantly finding additional uses for it. As the physical size of computers decreases and their working and storage capacity increases, so it becomes more and more worth while to give them more work to do. Nevertheless it is not true to say that it is worth while computerising all operations indiscriminately. Careful consideration has to be given to the advantages of computerising a particular operation in terms of speed, cost and access, and also to the disadvantages. Even with computers there are times when staff have to accept some less efficient aspects of a system in order to achieve greater efficiency in critical areas.

In this chapter we shall consider a variety of applications in common use. It must be borne in mind, however, that every application must be tailored to the organisation it serves.

Standard applications

There are certain standard applications which are normally the first programs used when an organisation installs a computer or uses a computer service (*see* Computer Bureaux). These include:

(1) order processing;
(2) sales billing/invoicing;
(3) credit control;
(4) stock records and stock control;
(5) production control;
(6) pay-roll;
(7) ledgers—sales, purchases, nominal;
(8) pensions;
(9) personnel and training records.

More and more organisations are using standard software packages, i.e. programs purchased from computer manufacturers or firms specialising in the production of these materials. So long as no major modifications are needed to make the package fit the organisation it is usually considerably cheaper to buy a ready-made package than produce one within the organisation. These routine applications are well tried and debugged and do not usually involve any major changes in transaction procedures for the organisation changing over to computerised systems.

SPECIALIST TERMINALS

There are now certain specialist terminals for some standard applications. For example, building societies use terminals for entering on to their records cash received; retail stores use "point of sale" terminals which automatically adjust stock records when a sale is made; in machine shops and factories job progress can be recorded, updating progress charts which can be reviewed on terminals or produced on printout; automatic clocking-in by employees can be used for calculation of wages including overtime, deduction for lateness, etc.

Information is presented in either green or blue on most visual display units. Some systems have the facility for presenting certain information in another colour. For example, a list of customers can be shown with those who are overdue with outstanding accounts indicated in red. One possible application of this facility is credit control where the credit limit would also be indicated and an immediate decision could be made as to whether or not to pass an order from a customer. It would also enable credit controllers to be selective about sending out "follow-up" letters for unpaid accounts. In other words, this facility gives greater flexibility within the computer system.

SYSTEMS DOCUMENTATION

For any application there is a basic format of documentation. The system as a whole consists of:

(1) procedure narrative of the current (manual or machine) system and the proposed (computer) system;

(2) procedure charts;

(3) systems flow charts (illustrated in Fig. 115);

(4) run diagrams;

(5) program flow charts and coding sheets;

(6) program printout;

(7) operating instructions;

(8) testing routines;

(9)   error routines;   ⎫ All programs must incorporate
(10) program modifications; ⎬ checks and controls.
(11) computer log.   ⎭

Auditing computerised accounts

In many large organisations the accounts are now held on computer file. That is to say that the well-known tomes called ledgers have disappeared. This means that auditors cannot "check the books" in the old way. For some time this presented problems for auditors. Now they are specially trained to undertake a computer audit. There are special programs written specifically for the purpose of auditing accounts held on computer. One such program called "Auditfind" is produced by International Computers Limited.

Management applications

A major contribution that computers have made to management is the provision of a wider range of information, more quickly and more accurately than was possible before. There are many types of information which a manager or group may need in order to make a decision or series of decisions. Some examples of the kind of activity which can be aided by information produced by computer are:

(1) manpower planning;
(2) sales forecasting;
(3) discounted cash flow;
(4) analysis of data—sales, costs, etc.;
(5) network analysis;
(6) sensitivity analysis;
(7) operational research;
(8) mathematical models, which are means of setting up an experimental system without upsetting the on-going operational system, and testing it to make sure that it will do what is wanted before putting it into operation.

A data base or data bank (*see* page 459) can be built up to provide relevant information for decision-making. The type of information and the format in which it is required to be presented vary greatly from one organisation to another, and from one department to another. Some simple examples of information which might be readily available are specifications of any kind; training courses— their content, objectives, for whom intended; stock items; travel information; mailing lists of customers; statistics of all kinds; trends; and costs. It has to be stressed that the data base must be

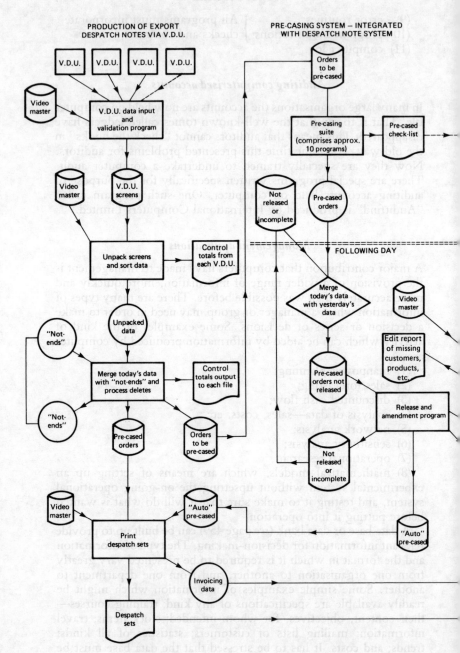

PRODUCTION OF EXPORT
DESPATCH NOTES VIA V.D.U.

PRE-CASING SYSTEM — INTEGRATED
WITH DESPATCH NOTE SYSTEM

V.D.U.   V.D.U.   V.D.U.   V.D.U.

Video
master

V.D.U. data input
and
validation program

Orders
to be
pre-cased

Pre-casing
suite
(comprises approx.
10 programs)

Pre-cased
check-list

Video
master

V.D.U.
screens

Not
released
or
incomplete

Pre-cased
orders

FOLLOWING DAY

Unpack screens
and sort data

Control
totals from
each V.D.U.

Merge
today's data
with yesterday's
data

Video
master

Unpacked
data

Edit report
of missing
customers,
products,
etc.

"Not-
ends"

Merge today's data
with "not-ends"
and process deletes

Control
totals output
to each file

Pre-cased
orders not
released

Release and
amendment program

"Not-
ends"

Pre-cased
orders

Orders
to be
pre-cased

Not
released
or
incomplete

Video
master

Print
despatch sets

"Auto"
pre-cased

"Auto"
pre-cased

Invoicing
data

Despatch
sets

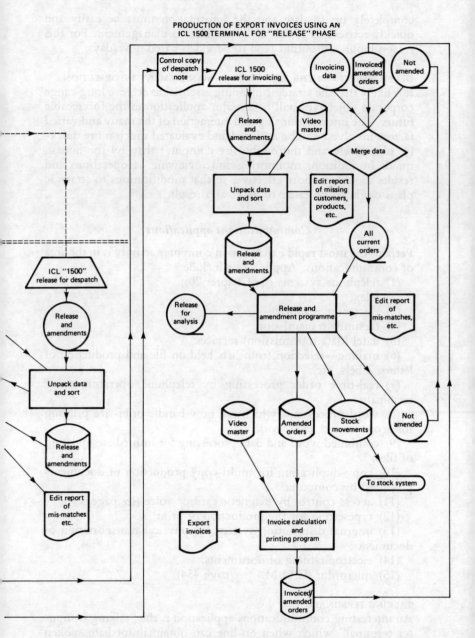

Fig. 115 *Flow chart of the production of export despatch notes and invoices via visual display units.*

completely up to date and the information must be easily and quickly retrievable if it is to be of value to management. For this reason input and output tend to be video based nowadays.

DEVELOPMENTS IN THE PROVISION OF MANAGEMENT INFORMATION
It is likely that the strategic planning essential to achieve long-range corporate objectives will be a major application in the foreseeable future. The interrelationship and interaction of the many and varied factors involved will be analysed and evaluated much more quickly, objectively and thoroughly by computer than by the human mind. In addition, monitoring and reviewing of operations and results should be more effective, so that modifications to strategic plans ought to be easier to make as a result.

Communications applications

Perhaps the most rapid expansion in computer activity is in the area of communications. Applications include:

(1) telephone systems (*see* Chapter 20);

(2) telex;

(3) electronic mailing;

(4) facsimile transmission;

(5) datel (data transmission) services;

(6) mailing—selection from lists held on file and production of letters, labels, etc.;

(7) real-time order processing by telephone operators using terminals;

(8) word processing, which can now handle brief-size printing for accounts and legal work;

(9) combined word and data processing for immediate updating of files;

(10) copy-duplicating for multi-copy production of documents produced by computer;

(11) access control by magnetic card or voice (*see* page 550);

(12) typesetting for the production of print;

(13) internal distribution system for physical transportation of documents;

(14) electronic filing of documents;

(15) microfilm (C.O.M.) (*see* page 454).

TALKING TERMINALS
An interesting communications application is the "talking computer terminal" which when on-line can obtain immediate spoken response from the computer. This system has been introduced into

the distributors of one large car manufacturing company in the U.K. When a customer requires a part the storeman can dial directly into the manufacturer's computer memory banks and key-in enquiries about the availability of that particular part. The pre-recorded spoken answer includes availability, changed part numbers and the latest price. The storeman can then place the order, the computer monitoring the information keyed in to ensure that no detail needed to execute the order is omitted. If there is an omission the computer indicates the requirement.

TRANSFER OF INFORMATION BY TAPE

Not perhaps strictly a communications application is the agreement of H.M. Customs & Excise to allow traders to submit export statistical data direct to the Statistical Office on magnetic tape. This information is required for statistical purposes only, not for auditing. This means that information that previously had to be produced on forms can be quickly reproduced on tape, which is mailed. A written declaration has to accompany each tape.

DEVELOPMENT OF VOICE COMPUTERS

Digital voice computers are being developed in the United States of America. They do exist and are in use but more research is needed. The speech is quite recognisable though intonation tends to be distorted as the speech is by syllables and in a monotone. Voice computers are probably most likely to be used for educational and research purposes. They are at present very expensive.

PAYMENT BY COMPUTER

An international application is the payment of money from certain countries (Japan is one) from the bank abroad to an international bank in Britain. The client abroad instructs his bank to make a payment to a supplier. The bank enters the transaction on its computer with appropriate instructions. The client's account is debited and within a short time, perhaps half an hour (depending on transmission availability) the transaction is recorded on the computer in Britain. The supplier is duly informed of the payment, thus eliminating the need for documentary credit to secure payment for goods supplied. On production of a bill of lading the supplier's account is credited, thus ensuring supply of the consignment to the customer.

Installing a computer

If it is decided that a computer may be necessary for certain applications and desirable for other applications within the organisation, a decision has to be made to install or not to install. A lot of preliminary work must be done to provide the information on which to base a decision.

Installing a computer can be a complicated affair lasting many years, and, as with any other office machine, the main factor to consider is work requirements. Business managers are apt to view a computer in terms of reducing paperwork (which it rarely does), or of saving staff (which it may not do; in fact often it means more staff). It is obviously necessary to examine very closely what advantages are likely to accrue from using a computer, and at the same time to face up to the possible disadvantages. Steps to be taken are set out below under three headings: feasibility, the machine, and installation.

FEASIBILITY

(1) Conduct a feasibility study (*see* below).

(2) If feasible, and a decision is made to install a computer, the appropriate machine has to be chosen.

THE MACHINE

(1) Establish the volume and types of work involved.

(2) Investigate all machines on the market.

(3) Decide whether to buy, rent or lease a machine—this may depend on finance available; tax considerations—and the intended rate of computerisation of systems (it is easier to change a rented machine than one purchased outright).

(4) Decide on the methods of input and output.

(5) Decide what speed of processing is needed for efficient work performance.

(6) Determine the present cost of the work and what it will cost using the computer.

INSTALLATION

(1) Make changes that are necessary in the organisation of the whole concern.

(2) Train *all* staff involved, however slightly.

(3) Make necessary changes in systems.

(4) Make necessary changes in stationery.

(5) Prepare premises for the computer and auxiliary equipment (including air-conditioning if it is not already installed).

(6) Prepare time schedule for actual installation, testing, running in parallel (manual and computer systems), and finally live operation.

FEASIBILITY STUDY

A most important part of the installation of a computer is the previous examination of office systems and data processing (perhaps previously performed by accounting machines), and the assessment of the possibility and the advisability of installing a computer.

A computer manufacturer will carry out this study as part of an advisory service to business, but as the sale of an expensive machine is involved the assessment of needs may not be wholly impartial. It is essential that those who know the business, the line of trade and the requirements of management are involved in the study.

While internal staff with many years of experience could produce a report on data processing requirements, they would not necessarily have computer expertise on the capabilities of machines, or the detailed requirements of programming, etc., and in fact many businesses do not even have experts in office systems. Anyone involved in the feasibility study who is not *au fait* with computers should attend a computer appreciation course as part of his or her involvement.

It is usual for a feasibility team to consist of representatives from the accounts department, line managers from the departments most affected by the proposed changeover and the O & M officer or equivalent if there is one. Representatives of, say, two computer manufacturers may be asked to join the team, which will jointly investigate the business information and data processing systems and make a report to management on the possibility and advisability of installing a computer. This can take anything up to six or even twelve months, and on its thoroughness depends a great deal of the ultimate success of a computer.

ADVANTAGES OF COMPUTERS

It is doubtful whether there can be any standard advantages reaped by all users of computers, since the needs of every organisation are peculiar to that organisation. The advantages suggested below are the most common.

(1) The provision of more information than was possible or at any rate feasible previously; this particularly applies to analysed statistical information about all aspects of the business.

(2) The provision of control information faster than previously. This may be a very big advantage in a large business where it is possible, for example, to obtain stock figures for several hundred branches inside a day or two instead of weeks as previously. (One international organisation receives statistics from its branches all over the world each day, analyses and collates them overnight, and

every branch managing director has a copy of the world-wide figures on his desk next morning.)

(3) The financial saving which may be effected indirectly, for example by having prompt stock valuations (leading to smaller stock-holdings), can in one year pay for the computer installation.

(4) Clerical staff are relieved of monotonous routine jobs such as ledger-posting and can be deployed more effectively.

(5) Extraordinary speed with complicated calculations. This advantage is apparent where a computer is used in connection with Operational Research, but it is doubtful whether a great proportion of office work consists of such calculations.

(6) Flexibility of operation, because any number of programs can be prepared for different business operations; and a computer is more flexible than accounting machines.

(7) A computer may save in staff and labour costs if there is sufficient work to keep the machine occupied. However, experience shows that this does not always happen and it is not unusual to find that there is no saving in staff.

(8) Better centralised management control—because the machine (in time) usually processes data for the whole business centrally.

(9) Greater accuracy; on the occasions when computers do produce wrong information, it is usually the fault of the input, not the machine.

PROBLEMS OF INSTALLATION

There are inevitably problems associated with such a major changeover as computerisation involves. Some of the problems which may have to be faced are suggested below.

(1) The installation of a computer often means as much as two or three years' preparatory work at great expense.

(2) It has an upsetting effect on all systems and on the organisation of the business.

(3) Not least is the effect on staff who fear they will be made redundant. These fears are often groundless, but there is also the management problem of retraining them in the new computer systems.

(4) A problem which reports from all sources continue to emphasise is the shortage of trained, experienced and capable computer programmers and systems analysts. Computer manufacturers will assist, and even provide, training, but this all means extra cost.

(5) Capital outlay is involved, either in buying a machine or in

making provision for the accommodation of a rented/leased machine.

(6) Maintenance and maintenance costs must be considered. If a business relies on a computer for the production of all its paper-work, what will happen if it breaks down for any length of time?

(7) It takes a year or so from the ordering of a computer until it is installed, and in the meantime the model ordered may become outdated. It is a field of constant technical development, so possible future developments must be discussed with the manufacturers and consideration must be given to the possible uses of the computer in the future.

(8) While centralisation of control can be viewed as an advantage to management, it can also be a disadvantage because it shifts the balance of power; some observers have commented on the extent to which other departments become beholden to the computer room.

(9) Business concerns often fail to realise the complexity of the problems involved—the size of the computer required is underestimated; salary costs are higher than was envisaged; equipment is chosen which is not suitable to the application of the computer; and the elimination of errors in the data files is found to be not as easy as was thought.

ON-LINE SYSTEMS

In considering on-line and off-line facilities it is worth mentioning that a major consideration of on-line systems is the cost.

The advantages of the system are that:

(1) errors can be "trapped" as soon as they occur;

(2) the user has virtually instant access to information; and

(3) information in store is updated immediately when new data is fed into the computer.

These advantages are well worth the cost involved in certain types of business, but it is essential to determine their value before being committed to the installation of on-line terminals.

CAUSES OF COMPUTER SYSTEM FAILURE

Computers are not a panacea for all evils. Indeed they can and do solve problems; equally they may not only fail to solve problems, they may add to those that already exist. It is worth studying the causes of computer project failure in other organisations so that they can be avoided in any new project. A few such causes are mentioned below.

(1) The company as a whole was not committed, i.e. the board and senior management had not been sufficiently interested and involved in the project, perhaps through inadequate briefing.

(2) The wrong system had been chosen for computerisation in the first place.

(3) Staff were inadequately trained—both the data processing staff and those who would be concerned with input and output.

(4) Management needs were not properly understood by the data processing staff.

(5) The project was not properly managed, i.e. planning, organisation and control were lacking or inadequate.

(6) The equipment—hardware and/or software—was not suitable for the job it was required to do.

(7) Input and user staff were not co-operative perhaps because they were not sufficiently involved from the beginning and so did not understand what was required of them.

(8) The procedure manual was badly written, causing operational problems.

(9) The manual systems were not continued in parallel with the new computer systems until debugging had been completed.

(10) When the project was obviously not successful no one would take a decision to terminate it, or re-evaluate, i.e. go back to the feasibility study stage and see where the mistakes had occurred.

Computer bureaux

There are many computer bureaux, some of them run by the computer manufacturers. Originally this service was used by the medium-sized companies who could not afford, or make cost-effective use of, a mainframe computer. This is no longer true and the advent of mini and microcomputers has made computerisation a viable proposition for even quite small companies. Some large organisations use a computer bureau for the routine applications—pay-roll, for example—retaining their own computer capacity for programs unique to their own organisations, e.g. the provision of specialist information to management. With the extension of useful management information applications this makes sense. Offloading routine programs to a bureau also allows for the extension of on-line and real-time operations.

Computer services are paid for by the hour and regular time can be reserved. The administration has then to ensure that the input data are available to the bureau by the agreed deadline.

Microcomputers

A great deal is heard about the microprocessor—the "chip" revolution. Certainly the advent of the "chip" has brought many innovations from the microwave oven to taxi meters to language translators. It is likely that future office technology will be based largely on the microprocessor. A few examples illustrate the diversity of these applications.

A language translator translates common words and phrases into French, Spanish, Italian, Japanese and German. It could, no doubt, be extended into virtually any language. Its use in the export trade could be of great value, particularly as the same machine can be used as a calculator and for metric conversion.

Intercommunication systems can frequently carry only one conversation at a time. Microprocessors make it possible for the system to carry two conversations simultaneously.

An addressing machine with either manual or automatic feed can have a microprocessor programmed to select from the mailing list only the names required for a particular mailing.

A "Mind Reader" enables individual executives to key in their appointments, thus building up a file for each day. Each day the appropriate information is displayed on the screen.

There is much speculation about the "takeover" of office jobs by microprocessors. It is said that about 20 per cent of office tasks could be performed by micros within ten years. This will inevitably mean a decrease in staff, although the increase in business which ought to be generated could offset this decrease to some extent.

Convergence

Convergence is the term used to indicate an integrated computer system which takes in various communications systems (telephone, telex, facsimile transmission, electronic mailing, word processing, etc.), together with on-line and/or off-line applications. There are problems associated with convergence, one of the most difficult being the compatibility of equipment. It is not always possible to buy all the satellite or peripheral systems from the computer manufacturer, because either his equipment does not give the facilities required by the user, or a particular piece of equipment is more expensive than the user needs or can afford, or the manufacturer does not make the equipment required.

There is also the question of intercommunication between computers, as in an international organisation where the mainframes of various branches around the world need to be in contact with the head office mainframe for collection and analysis of data, retrieval of information from files, etc. A very recent British invention has produced a machine called a *compiler* which overcomes the problem of incompatibility. The compiler consists of two disks which can convert the output/input of one computer into input/output for another computer. It is virtually a translation device using a high-level language called ATLAS, which contains 440 words, is 800 per cent larger than most other computer languages and can be read by both men and machines, thus giving it a big advantage over other computer languages.

Extending a computer system into communications areas, even if the central processing unit has the capacity, is not a simple operation. Even the addition of word processors can create problems. The preparation needed is almost as great as for the installation of the computer itself if the system is to operate successfully.

Conclusion

The uses and operation of computers is a wide subject, and only an outline is possible in a book of this nature. While computers are fundamentally office machines, they represent considerable problems, even today, and can be so expensive that they warrant special study. The lessons of the past have still not been learned in many organisations.

There is no doubt that computerisation will continue its advance but computers will not replace many of the machines used for routine operations, such as copying and accounting in small offices, nor the people who operate the machines and carry out the various functions.

Computer time and data transmission are costly and that fact alone will act as a brake on the drive towards the "paperless office". In any case, since business consists mainly of small organisations which will of financial necessity continue to use paper, it is difficult to see how the large organisations can avoid remaining, to some extent at least, involved in documentation.

PART SEVEN

OFFICE SYSTEMS CONTROL

41. Office Systems

Every office has its own systems. The procedures which make up the systems must be designed for maximum efficiency bearing in mind many factors including the type and size of business, the type and size of the individual units within it, the physical factors of location, logistics, equipment, etc., cost, calibre of staff and extent of control needed.

The requirements of different businesses vary tremendously. Standard systems for routine operations such as invoicing, wages, etc. exist but nearly always have to be modified or adapted to suit individual circumstances. Invoice systems and wages preparation were covered in Chapter 37, but it must be stressed that an invoicing system suitable for a hotel will differ from that for a business selling fertilisers, and from that for a department store. The differences will depend on the product or service, and on the invoice requirements. Speed will be a most important element in a hotel business; economy of operation in a mail-order business; and absolute accuracy in a stockbroker's.

Principles of office systems

Every system in the office should be devised with the following aims in mind:

(1) to have a good flow of work without bottle-necks;
(2) to avoid duplication of work and records;
(3) to keep the movements of staff to a minimum;
(4) to avoid unnecessary writing;
(5) to make the best use of specialisation;
(6) to keep the amount of paperwork to the absolute minimum;

(7) to use the principle of management by exception;

(8) to make as few exceptions to the procedure rules as possible;

(9) to avoid unnecessary checking;

(10) to make the best use of machines, but not to use them unnecessarily;

(11) to seek simplicity, for complicated systems usually mean mistakes.

Importance of office systems

Organisation and systems are both based on the work to be performed, and are interrelated. A good system cannot mitigate the faults of bad organisation, but a bad system can ruin the best organisation, invalidate the best efforts of first-class staff and create havoc in the area of public relations. Good systems are essential:

(1) to ensure the smooth running of the office, eliminating delays and bottle-necks in work;

(2) to ensure fast and accurate work;

(3) to help in the prevention of fraud by having in-built control procedures and internal checks;

(4) to save direct labour and overhead expenditure;

(5) to minimise paperwork in an organisation;

(6) to ensure co-ordination between sections or departments;

(7) to enable new and existing staff to be properly trained;

(8) to ensure maximum co-operation with service to clients/customers.

Procedures within systems

The term "office procedures" is used to describe the various operations which form a system. The amount of work involved in an operation varies greatly. "Balancing ledger accounts" is an operation which might take four hours to complete, while "selecting an index card" is also an operation but might only take twenty seconds. It is usual to analyse operations by means of "procedure records" (*see* Fig. 118 in Chapter 44) and by means of various kinds of charts which are discussed in Chapter 44.

Office forms used for recording and communicating information are an important part of many systems. The procedures for completion and transmission of the forms must be closely related to other procedures within a particular system. (For forms control and design, *see* Chapter 43.)

Written procedures

Some organisations have a written record of systems and procedures compiled into an "office manual". An office manual includes written instructions on what has to be done, how, when and where, and gives information on the organisation supporting the systems. It may be in book form but is better in loose-leaf form so that updating sheets for changes in existing procedures or the addition of new procedures may be inserted easily. Another advantage of the loose-leaf form is that the manual can be devised in such a way that only relevant sections are issued to staff, the complete record being kept by management only. This abridged version is sometimes referred to as "duty lists".

It is essential that procedure manuals should be very well presented if they are to inspire the respect, confidence and attention of the staff who are to use them.

Putting procedures into writing has some useful advantages, as follows.

(1) It enforces close attention to the systems, which may disclose inadequacies.

(2) Supervision is made easier.

(3) It provides a basis for the training of personnel.

(4) It provides a basis for defining the limits of each individual's authority and responsibility in the organisation.

(5) The interrelationship of procedures within a system can be identified and the effect of changes should be more easily recognised.

(6) Improvements to procedures are easier when steps have been identified.

There are also the following disadvantages.

(1) Office manuals can be expensive to prepare (they are particularly expensive of management time).

(2) They can be difficult to keep up to date.

(3) They may introduce inflexibility in the manner of work performance.

(4) If operations and procedures are not in accordance with the manual or if the manual is not kept up to date, it will be disregarded, and the position will be more chaotic than if there were no manual.

Establishing an office procedure

The first step in establishing a procedure is to look at the whole of the office "in the round". The manager has to establish (i) what the main objective of the office is; (ii) what work is involved in achieving the objective; (iii) who is doing the work—this entails listing all staff, and their present contributions to the work; (iv) the methods used to perform each operation; and (v) the quality of the work being done. Then it is necessary to make a full and detailed analysis of each operation.

Each step in the analysis must be examined closely (i) to check whether it is necessary, i.e. whether it achieves a specific purpose; (ii) to see whether and where bottle-necks are occurring (to maintain the flow of work, these must be eliminated); and (iii) to identify the interaction of the work involved with other sections/ departments of the organisation.

The bigger a system grows, the more chance there is of duplication of work and of records, and this must be guarded against. Unnecessary writing, movement or effort must be avoided, as should all needless checking. The procedures should be devised in such a way as to make exceptions unnecessary, or at least as few as possible. It is important to ensure that the cost of operating the procedure is effective in terms of increased efficiency, whether productivity or any other benefit.

Improving an office procedure

Before anything can be improved, it is necessary to examine what is being done, in order to identify and segregate the symptoms and the cause of the fault.

To improve office procedures there are some essential steps to be taken.

(1) Determine the purpose of the assignment (e.g. whether it is to reduce costs, reduce paperwork, increase output or eliminate errors).

(2) Examine existing methods and forms (by inspection, interviewing, self-recording diary, etc.).

(3) Write procedure records (i.e. descriptions of the steps involved).

(4) Depict the procedures on the appropriate chart or charts (see Chapter 44).

(5) Examine closely each procedure or set of procedures to identify the problem areas and the causes of inefficiency.

(6) Assess alternative methods of performance (bearing in mind costs, purpose of the procedure, purpose of the assignment, and control).

(7) Decide on the best possible methods and forms to use.

(8) Rechart procedure; designate new machines and redraft

forms if necessary.

(9) Introduce new procedure (ideally with "dummy" runs using draft forms for testing purposes).

(10) Prepare new job specifications for staff involved.

(11) Establish new or revised procedure, with new forms and new methods.

(12) Give instructions for reporting on problems that arise and in any case follow up after not too long an interval, to ensure that the procedure is working. Modify it if necessary.

The "exception principle"

It is an established rule of efficient working that much needless recording and checking can be avoided by the adoption of the "exception principle". This means that where regular procedures have been laid down and scheduled, and where the work is to a great extent routine, records are made only of exceptions from the norm, not of all transactions. For example, if three days is the maximum time for an order enquiry to be dealt with, a special note is made of any orders still outstanding after three days of being received. This system can be operated only if regular routine procedures and proper control have been established.

Control and review of procedures

Procedures can become outdated yet still be maintained because no one thinks to modify or eliminate them. An annual review of systems and procedures is as essential as an annual "spring clean" of the filing or an annual appraisal of staff competence and progress. It is rare for a system to be perfect, but the aim is to achieve optimum efficiency within the inevitable constraints of finance, staff, etc. On the other hand, constant "tinkering" with procedures is the biggest "morale-degenerator". Equally, change for the sake of change is frustrating for the staff and creates inefficiency.

42. Office Machines

The term "office machines" includes anything from a date stamp costing less than a pound to an integrated computer system costing millions of pounds. Machines of one kind or another are needed in all offices, whatever their size and type. The office manager must consider the advantages and disadvantages of using machines in various circumstances and must know the procedures to follow when buying, leasing or renting a machine.

Role of machines

All basic tasks in an office (writing, calculating, filing, sorting, analysing) can be performed by a machine, usually more quickly and accurately than they can be performed manually. This does not mean that purchasing a machine is automatically the right thing to do. Every machine used in an office requires some amount of human operation and supervision, and the task itself usually requires special preparation before it can be dealt with by the machine. When considering the advantages and disadvantages of machine methods versus manual methods it should be borne in mind that a machine changes the degree of manual operation but does not eliminate it entirely. In addition, the volume of work available for the machine is important. The use of machines does not necessarily solve all the problems of an office; indeed it may create some. Machinery is a part of the "means" aspect of office management, along with organisation, method, environment and personnel, all of which have an important bearing on efficiency in the office.

Possible advantages

An office manager has often to decide whether a machine would be an advantage or not. He should first ask himself the following questions.

(1) Does it save labour? This is the main reason for the installation of many machines, but it is not necessarily the most important one. By saving labour is meant an actual saving on the pay-roll, or an increased volume of work handled by the existing staff. It is of little use saving labour if the staff numbers are the same as previously, and if they merely have idle time as a result of the introduction of machinery. Until recently the usual long-term result of the use of machinery has been that the calibre of staff was lower than previously, although the numbers may have been the same or in some cases even more. With the introduction of more sophisticated machines, e.g. in word processing (*see* Chapter 28), it is now becoming necessary to employ staff with a high level of intelligence.

(2) Does it save time? If time is saved, what use is made of this? In some cases the saving of time is in itself sufficient justification for the installation of a machine. The use of machines is invaluable for jobs which have to be completed in a specified time (e.g. preparation of wages or dividend warrants).

(3) Does it give greater accuracy? Often the greatest advantage of using accounting machines is that the management can be sure of obtaining accurate figures from its books of account. The use of an addressing machine for invoice preparation ensures that the details printed are 100 per cent accurate, provided input (plates) is accurate and up to date. Human errors in operating the machines or omitting to update addressograph plates can still create problems.

(4) Does it relieve monotony? Machine operation can be monotonous but many machine applications actually relieve manual drudgery. The mechanisation of certain tasks often paves the way for the spread of more interesting tasks among the staff, i.e. job enlargement leading to job enrichment (*see* Chapter 16). To that extent machinery improves morale and increases the chance of recruiting staff for the work involved.

(5) Will it lessen the chance of fraud? Sometimes machines will not save time or labour, but their intrinsic value is in minimising the opportunity for fraud. A good example of such a machine is the cheque-writing machine (*see* page 545), which is often used even where the number of cheques is quite small.

(6) Can the facility be used by more than one department in the organisation? Very often an expensive machine becomes economically viable when the service it can provide is made available to the organisation as a whole rather than to a single department.

(7) Does it save money? What is the present cost of doing the

work? What capital outlay and running costs would be involved in installing a machine over one to five years?

In addition to these seven, there are other subsidiary advantages which can be added. The larger accounting machines perform two or more operations simultaneously—something beyond human capabilities. These machines write figures, add them up at the same time and then move the paper ready for the next entry. In addition, by the use of carbon devices, several documents can be written with identical information at the one posting. This can be done to some extent manually (*see* page 533), but some machines can create as many as twenty copies of a document simultaneously. Analysis can be obtained automatically at the time of entering in ledger accounts, stock records, etc.

Lastly, from the management point of view, greater control is possible and more information may be available than before, hence the greater use of machines should mean that office work is performed more efficiently.

Possible disadvantages

There are some disadvantages in using machines in the office, although most of them are concerned with their use rather than the machines themselves.

(1) An expensive machine which is bought for one department or section of a business, and is used only for a fraction of the working week, presents the problem of whether to have centralised or decentralised control. Central control increases the likelihood of machines being used cost-effectively. Not every machine needs to be used continuously to make it a worthwhile investment but a certain load factor may be necessary when a specially trained operator is required, or when capital outlay is very high.

(2) The use of a machine may require the mechanisation of systems causing some inflexibility. Where office work requires very great skill and the making of decisions on many things out of the routine, then human labour is generally better than a machine.

(3) Some machines quickly become obsolete. It may not be possible for machines purchased for specialised jobs to be adapted when it is necessary to introduce new systems. Office machines should be as universal in application as possible. Leasing (*see* page 485) or hiring may overcome the problem of obsolescence.

(4) Unless great care is taken, the machine will become more important than the work it produces. It has been known in more than one business concern for detailed weekly costing statements to

be distributed far and wide inside the firm, although much of the information was never used by anybody.

(5) Some machines require trained and experienced operators. The absence of an operator can cause an accumulation of work so two operators may have to be employed, even though there is only sufficient work for one.

(6) Machines may break down (particularly when electrically controlled).

(7) Capital outlay may be high and special stationery, servicing and so on increase expenditure, hence the necessity to ensure cost savings in time, manpower, accuracy, etc.

Choosing a machine

When deciding which particular type, make and model of machine to buy, the first step is to list the various functions the machine should be capable of performing. The required features should then be listed in order of priority. A chart should be prepared listing the features in priority order with vertical columns headed by the makes/models of various machines. The specifications in sales literature can be checked, demonstrations arranged in distributors' showrooms and tests carried out using the actual work material. Machines with alternative features should also be investigated because ideas can often be improved upon. The suitability of each machine can be fairly accurately determined from the chart. The next step is to check the most suitable machines—there may be more than one—for capacity, capital and running costs including special stationery, service facilities, degree of training required by the operator and normal output. The final questions may be: "Will the quality/quantity/control of the work be improved?" "If so, by how much?" "Would the purchase of the machine prove cost-effective?"

The question of machine operation is important. A machine is no better than its operator, and because an office procedure has been mechanised or automated, it does not mean that there is no chance of mistakes being made. Operators of any machines should be properly trained, and not "left to pick it up".

Leasing and hiring/renting

Many organisations now lease or rent machines rather than buy them because the capital outlay on copiers, computer hardware, telecommunications installations, etc. can be astronomical.

LEASING

Either the company selling the machine or special finance companies enter into leasing arrangements whereby the customer pays a monthly or quarterly rental for a stated period, e.g. two years. At the end of the period the customer sells the machine and pays the leasing company a percentage of the original new price. Any balance on the sale is retained by the customer.

Maintenance and service are the responsibility of the customer.

The great advantage of leasing is that large amounts of capital are not tied up, which obviates the need for borrowing at high rates of interest and leaves capital available for more productive investment. The leasing charge is allowable against tax.

HIRING OR RENTING

The customer pays a monthly or quarterly fee for the use of the machine which remains the property of the company which hires it out. Usually maintenance and service are included in the rental.

In some cases, a charge is made based on the amount of work done by the machine, e.g. the number of copies run off on a copier. All rental charges can be offset against tax.

LEASE PURCHASE

A fairly recent innovation is the lease purchase arrangement. The buyer pays the capital cost of the machine plus interest over a 3, 4 or 5-year period in equal monthly or quarterly instalments. The full amount of Value Added Tax (if applicable) and capital allowance against tax can be claimed when the first payment is made.

43. Organisation and Methods

Objectives of Organisation and Methods (O & M)

Everyone agrees that office work should be free of red tape, and that it should be made as effortless and as free from drudgery as possible. It is generally agreed that the simplest way is the best. To eliminate waste in every direction would be a fair description of the prime objective of O & M. To achieve this objective, work procedures are codified and made clear; the flow of work should also be improved.

In addition to eliminating waste, there is usually a desire to improve the existing work output at the same time, although increased output would not have to be at the expense of accuracy. Indeed, one of the objectives might well be to improve accuracy. Another objective is to improve the support service given by office staff. On occasions this may mean recommending the employment of additional staff. O & M is concerned with efficiency of service as well as efficiency in the manner of providing it.

Even if an O & M enquiry did not perform anything spectacular in achieving any one of the above objectives, a vital yet less generally recognised objective is that of making the staff "efficiency conscious", and of encouraging their active participation and interest in the office work.

"Work simplification", the American term for O & M, has been defined as "the organised use of common sense to find easier and better ways of doing work", and as "a scientific checking on the way work is done, to ensure that utmost efficiency is obtained". It is a very broad, comprehensive study and can be applied to organisation structures, systems, procedures, methods, forms, equipment and personnel.

An O & M assignment may be to check on one aspect of, say, an invoice system, or it may be concerned with the entire office

487

system of an organisation. A simple O & M assignment might be to consider the size and wording of an office form, how many copies are made, who receives each copy, and the use made of each copy, when and where. On the other hand, it could be to undertake a complete revision of a system such as central filing.

O & M personnel

All large organisations in both public and private sectors have at least one O & M (Organisation and Methods) officer and frequently a team of them. In many cases the "O & M man" is a member of the management services division alongside work study officers and systems analysts. Whatever his position in the organisation structure, the function of an O & M officer is normally advisory, and his services are available to all departments in the organisation. He may have to work closely with one or more systems analysts where data processing and/or computer systems are involved.

Most governments have a management services department which provides advice, usually on request, to all departments. This may include the public sector as well as the Civil Service. Local authorities and all large business concerns have their own management services personnel including O & M specialists. Small concerns can obtain the services of O & M consultants if necessary. The cost is usually recovered many times over from increased efficiency.

It is usual to have one person appointed as head of the O & M department. He is normally an O & M specialist. He needs qualities of patience, acumen and persuasion, and must have a good knowledge of clerical work management, i.e. clerical systems, procedures, etc., including mechanised and electronic methods. He must have a keen analytical mind and be capable of approaching people to obtain information, in such a way as to gain their co-operation.

Although any office manager should have a sound knowledge of O & M, there are many advantages in having an O & M survey by an independent person:

(1) he is free from routine work, and has the time to make the investigation;

(2) he is, by definition, independent, and need not worry about departmental feelings, nor think of his own position;

(3) being apart from any section of the office he can view the work objectively;

(4) he brings to the study the accumulated experience of previous investigations.

Method of operation

An O & M assignment usually falls into the following five broad sections.

(1) *Determining the objective of the assignment.* It must be clear from the outset what the real objective of the survey is. It is usual to have this defined in writing before work is commenced.

(2) *Planning the assignment.* The actual planning depends on what the assignment is, the size of the departments to be surveyed, their geographical dispersion and so on. This must be followed by a preparatory meeting (*see* page 490).

(3) *Collecting the facts.* This is time-consuming for the O & M officer and may be time-wasting for the office staff if preparation is inadequate. There is a danger either of collecting too many facts about procedures not concerned with the enquiry, or of not collecting enough relevant material.

There are several ways of collecting the facts, the main ones being study of existing records, personal observation, discussion with people doing the job and their supervisors and managers, and written questionnaires. Questionnaires are notoriously open to misinterpretation, and a suitable combination of the other methods is usually used.

(4) *Analysing the facts.* Every stage in the various office procedures has to be examined, which means the O & M officer has to ask many questions.

What is done, and what is the unit of work?

Why is it done? (This may give answers connected with other office routines.)

When is it done? The questions of timetables, frequency of operation and cycles of time have to be considered.

Where is it done? Is it necessary for it to be done where it is, or could it be done better elsewhere?

Who does it? This involves the study of the relationship between staff and the work.

How is it done, and how many are concerned in it? This involves a mastery of procedures, equipment, office machines and so on.

(5) *Submitting proposals.* After enquiries have been made, the facts analysed and improvements planned, the proposals must then be submitted for subsequent action. It is usual for the proposals to be shown to the managers of the departments concerned. This is not for approval or criticism, but so that they know what is recommended, and are prepared for whatever course of action the management decides on.

Difficulties of conducting an O & M survey

No objection can be validly raised to an O & M enquiry properly carried out, but its success depends so much on the personal qualities of the investigator, so much on his experience, training and knowledge, that disadvantages may arise from the method of using the O & M technique. The activities and the work are all concerned with human beings, and if great care is not taken it can easily degenerate into a coldly scientific enquiry which upsets the workers and appears like a "fault-finding commission". A measure of the success of the O & M investigator is the degree to which he can obtain staff co-operation.

O & M experts are employed in a consultative capacity only, and since their objectives are mainly to aid management, there is sometimes a tendency for them to identify themselves as a part of management. This may lead to a feeling of insecurity among office staff. They feel that they are subject to "snooping raids" by the representatives of the management, and this may have a lowering effect on morale.

Every O & M survey should be preceded by a meeting of all the people concerned from the head of the department to the newest junior, at which the purpose and methods of the survey are explained. Since O & M surveys frequently result in a need for less staff, reassurance must be given on the question of redundancies. Today there must be very few firms who would not achieve staff savings either by redeployment or by natural wastage.

There are always plenty of reasons given by staff as to why changes should not be made. Here is a random selection of forty reasons.

(1) Our company is different.
(2) It's too expensive.
(3) It isn't my job.
(4) There isn't enough time.
(5) We've done alright without it.
(6) Let's shelve it.
(7) Let's form a committee.
(8) It's years ahead of its time.
(9) It's not our problem.
(10) It's alright in theory.
(11) Why change it—it's working O.K.
(12) It won't work in this industry.
(13) The unions won't buy it.
(14) It's against company policy.
(15) It's not in the budget.

(16) Don't like the idea.
(17) Good idea—but impractical.
(18) It needs more thought.
(19) We tried it before.
(20) It's beyond our responsibility.
(21) Haven't got the time.
(22) Will make other equipment obsolete.
(23) Can't teach an old dog new tricks.
(24) The staff won't like it.
(25) We've never tried it before.
(26) We're not ready for it.
(27) What do our competitors do?
(28) Let's have it in writing.
(29) Not that again!
(30) We'll be a laughing stock.
(31) Supposing it doesn't work?
(32) We'd lose money in the long run.
(33) What's the use?
(34) We'll never get it approved.
(35) What you're really saying is . . .
(36) I agree with you, but . . .
(37) Leave it with me.
(38) We'd just be wasting our time.
(39) It's never been tried out.
(40) It won't work.

Forms control

Forms are the basic tools of all office work, and they assist in the fundamental functions of receiving, recording, arranging and giving information in the office. What is more, by reason of their close affinity to office systems, they have a bearing on the efficiency of office organisation. An office form may be defined as "a printed piece of paper or card, on which entries are made, usually against marked headings". It is a systematic means of communicating data. The term excludes plain envelopes, which are stationery, but includes all printed matter of any kind.

The importance of forms should be reflected in proper management control of them to ensure that they are efficient and economical in design and use. The design of forms is another important aspect, and is studied in another section of this chapter.

Government departments and other public authorities have in recent years given much attention to forms. In the Greater London Council, for example, a Forms Officer has been nominated in each

Department to control the issue of new forms and to assist in their design while the O & M staff act as clearing-house for the Forms Officer's ideas.

OBJECTIVES OF FORMS CONTROL

By means of forms control, the office manager seeks to:

(1) retain and use only those forms that are really necessary;

(2) ensure that the required forms are designed most efficiently, i.e. with the users in mind, and give the greatest aid at the lowest cost;

(3) produce forms by the most appropriate and economical method;

(4) distribute copies of forms only to those who have a justifiable reason for having them;

(5) determine whether a proposed new form or revised old form is necessary;

(6) review periodically all forms in use to keep them in line with the current system requirements of the office;

(7) evaluate forms design primarily on the basis of the amount of time required to use the forms.

INITIATING FORMS CONTROL

It may be useful to know how to start control of forms in an organisation where none has previously existed. It is first necessary to announce to all staff and departments that a forms control section is being established, and to define its function and its authority. All departments should be informed that all forms activity must be "frozen" and all printing requirements submitted to the new section for approval. At least two copies of every office form in use must be collated into a forms register, and an itemised list of all forms must be prepared.

Since forms control and design is closely connected with office procedures, a list of all office procedures (as far as practicable) should be obtained, after which the relevant forms should be classified, marked and numbered according to the procedure or department using them. All forms must then be investigated and analysed to see if any of them can be eliminated, combined with others, or improved.

Investigation will often reveal that instead of separate entries being made on a number of forms, the system can be reorganised so that basic information is typed or written on a set of forms and reproduced simultaneously on the others. Alternatively, one form can take the place of several identical copies, by the simple expedient of passing the form from one office worker to another, according to a timetable.

A final major step is standardisation if the forms situation is suitable for it. Even if it is not possible to standardise on forms content, it is often possible to standardise on size and colour, so as to facilitate filing and reference.

Systems and forms

It might be asked which is the most important, the office system or the forms that are used to operate the system? In other words, which comes first? Undoubtedly, the system must be considered first, for the form is only a reflection and a handmaiden of the system. Thus, in designing a form, the first essential is to look at the office procedures it is to serve.

The two stages of considering the office systems and of drafting the relevant forms are closely connected. It often happens that an office system is reconsidered only when the forms are due for reprinting. The principle remains that the system and procedures must be consulted before paying attention to the design of the form.

Forms design

Forms are essential tools in the office for recording and communicating information. When badly designed they seriously impede this function and can cause a vast amount of unnecessary expenditure, inaccuracy, frustration and even loss of business. Although a well-designed form cannot correct a faulty system, a badly designed form can ruin a good system.

PRINCIPLES OF FORMS DESIGN

When designing a form it should be structured to take into account the following principles.

(1) *Ease of entry of data.* The writing surface, the style of print, the proper sequence of information, and the method of entry are important to ensure easy and rapid completion of the form.

(2) *Use of data.* Extracting information from the form is related to proper sequence again, readability, etc.

(3) *Reduction of errors.* Horizontal and vertical alignment, number of copies, thickness of paper, method of copying, and static and variable data affect accuracy.

(4) *Economy.* The size, quality of paper, number of copies, and method of producing forms should be decided with costs in mind.

(5) *Identification (and handling).* The colour of the paper and

printing inks, numbering, titling and filing must take into account visual impact on the users.

THE BROAD APPROACH

Before examining all the questions which should be asked when designing a form, it is useful to look at the subject broadly. In the first place, it should be asked, *can the form be eliminated?* A great deal of paperwork is necessary in any office but there are offices which have a great deal too much of it. The simpler the system, the fewer pieces of paper, the greater speed and accuracy is likely to be achieved.

If the form cannot be eliminated, it may be possible to use some other existing form, or to combine one with some other form, suitably redesigned. In the latter case some temporary substitutes may have to be printed until stocks of the original form are exhausted.

Before starting to draft the form it is also necessary to establish who will provide the information to be recorded on the form, how the information will be provided, who will record the information, in what way the information will be recorded, and who will make use of the information on the completed form either in part or wholly.

Having established the necessity for the form and the people who are involved with it, other aspects to be considered include:

(1) purpose of the form;
(2) size and arrangement of the form;
(3) wording;
(4) number of copies;
(5) paper and printing.

These aspects are considered in detail below.

DETAILED EXAMINATION OF A FORM

Purpose of the form. It is necessary to consider whether routine or handling instructions need to be put on the form. Should it be designed to fit a window envelope? If this is already the case, is it satisfactory? (Sometimes a form is so designed, but window envelopes are never used with it!) Could the form be despatched as a postal folder to save envelopes completely? Is the volume sufficient to warrant the installation of a folding machine?

Size and arrangement. Forms should be designed on a suitable size from the I.P.S. (International Paper Size) range. These sizes are given in Chapter 47.

If a machine is used to record information on a form the size of paper must be suited to the machine. The majority of forms are A4 size though A5 is suitable when there is only a small amount of information to be recorded. There is now available a two-thirds A4 size, which is useful when an A5 is too small and A4 too large.

Other considerations regarding size and arrangement include the following.

(1) Is the size of the form the most convenient for handling, for filing, for any other purpose to which it is put?

(2) Is all the standing information printed, so that only variable information has to be inserted? (Much clerical work can be saved in this way.)

(3) Should a space be provided for a signature, or if it has one can it be eliminated?

(4) Are the entry spaces the correct length and correct width for whatever method is used for entering, e.g. typing or handwriting?

(5) Is the most important information in the most important place?

(6) Does the form look *neat, simple, easy to read and understand*? This is a primary criterion on which the success of a form is based.

There is now an internationally accepted format for trading documents. Systematic Export Documentation provides for the production of a master containing information needed on all export documents. From the master each document, including job cards and labels, can be reproduced with the relevant information only printed on it. This is achieved by masking or line selection (*see* Chapter 29). Advice on the format can be obtained from the Simplification of International Trade Procedures Board, 11/12 Waterloo Place, London SW1Y 4AU.

Similar standardisation is being prepared by the British Standards Institution for home trade documentation.

The documents are designed for maximum ease of completion by typewriting, having zones of suitable size for type pitch and line-spacing. An example of a master is shown in Fig. 116.

Wording. The words printed on the form can prejudice its success before it is issued if they are not adequate, clear in meaning and in logical sequence.

(1) Does the form clearly indicate its purpose, i.e. has it a title? With very few exceptions, every form should have a title, so that everyone identifies it in the same way.

(2) Is the name of the organisation on the form? If so, is it necessary or can it be eliminated? If not, ought it to be inserted?

(3) If the form is a revised form can it be clearly distinguished from its predecessor? If not, it is hardly to be wondered if an office system is upset by the sudden reversion to some old-type forms which have not been destroyed.

Number of copies. The objective of forms control, and therefore of

Start →

Enter Port Scale if Required ▼

MASTER DOCUMENT

Exporter	Vehicle Bkg. Ref.			Tariff Heading
SITPRO EXPORT LIMITED HIGH STREET BURTON ON TRENT STAFFS., DE15 1YZ, ENGLAND	0415 CAN 99999			4813

	Invoice No. and Date	Exporter's Reference	
	16418 1Nov 1976	364/B205/190	
	Buyer's Reference	F/Agent's Ref.	S.S. Co. Bkg. No.
	ED1814-97-10-3	IR76-4740	BU64

Consignee (If "Order" State Notify Party and Address)	Buyer (If not Consignee)
SITPRO IRAN LTD. Khiaban Takhte Shiraz IRAN	SITPRO IRAN LTD. Avenue Ferdowsi Tehran, IRAN

	Name of Shipping Line	Port Account No.
		12742

Forwarding Agent/Merchant	Coding for H.M. Customs ▶	Destination ICD	Container	Ro Ro (a) (b)	Flag	Port
Burton Forwarding Ltd. 210 Station St. Burton on Trent, Staffs., DE15 4ZY	IR			9	GB	LIV

	Country of Origin of Goods	Country of Final Destination
	United Kingdom	Iran

Receiving Date(s)	Dock, Container base Etc.	Terms of Delivery and Payment
4 - 9 Nov 76	SE3 Canada Dock	CIF Bushire. Payment against sight
Pre-Carriage By	Place of Receipt by Pre-Carrier	draft accompanied by documents through
Our vehicle		British International Bank, Tehran

Vessel/Aircraft Etc.	Port of Loading	EURI Remarks
Bebington	Liverpool	

Port of Discharge	Place of Delivery by On-Carrier	Insured Value (state Currency)	Name of Receiving Authority
Bushire	Shiraz	Stg £2660.00	British Line

Marks, Nos. and Container No.; No. and Kind of Packages; Description of Goods (specify Nature of Hazard if any)	Tariff/Trade Code Number	Gross Weight (Kg)	Cube (M³)
SITPRO ED1814A SHIRAZ VIA BUSHIRE Nos. 1-3	3 Cases: Refills for ballpoint pens (Cat. no. 43-746)		1) 186	0.126
		2) 213	0.369
SITPRO ED1814A SHIRAZ VIA BUSHIRE No. 4	1 Case: Electronic duplicator stencils (Cat. no. 42-648)	3) 26	0.042
		4) 67 kg	0.175

		Quantity 2	Net Weight	FOB Value (£)
SITPRO ED1814C SHIRAZ VIA BUSHIRE No. 5	1 Carton: Self-adhesive labels size 70mm x 50mm boxed in packs of 1000 (Cat. no. 40-070)		1) 154	
			2) 180	

		Quantity 3		
SITPRO ED1814D SHIRAX VIA BUSHIRE No. 6	1 Case: Self-inking hand operated rubber date stamps (Cat. no. 44-101)		3) 24	
			4) 50 kg	

X	Customs Free Status / Customs Pre-Entry	Special Stowage	AGI/ATRI/CT – attached to C273	AG1/ATR1/CT form not required	Invoice Total (State Currency)
			Form type .... lodged-Customs No		£ 2416.68

	Total Gross Wt. (Kg)	Total Cube (M³)
	492	0.712

We certify this invoice to be true and correct and in accordance with our books, also that the goods are of United Kingdom origin. We hereby certify that the prices stated in this invoice are the current export market prices for the merchandise described therein and we accept full responsibility for any inaccuracies or errors therein.

Cost of freight £62.40 Cost of insurance £17.55	Ocean Freight Payable at Liverpool	Signatory's Company and Telephone Number Sitpro Export Ltd/0283-41835
	Number of Bills of Lading 2 Original 4 Copy	Name of Authorised Signatory H J Helliar, Chief Clerk
		Place and Date of Issue Burton, 1 November 1976
		Signature H.J. Helliar

Fig. 116 *Master for a series of export forms.* Reproduced by courtesy of the Simplification of International Trade Procedures Board.

forms design, is to develop the most efficient system. While asking if all copies are necessary, it is equally important to ask whether additional copies are required. The information needed on the form should be examined to see whether it is all necessary. This means investigating the clerical systems very closely. It is essential to consult both the clerks who use the form and the head of the department(s) concerned.

The actual number of copies depends on who uses the information and for what purpose(s). The question arises as to whether the information really is needed by each individual for action purposes or merely for information. If it is simply a matter of keeping several people informed, perhaps one circulating copy is adequate. Cases are known of thirteen copies of a document being circulated and only two of them being even read, with only one of them actually used for action to be taken.

Paper and printing. It is essential to obtain the right type of paper consistent with the purpose and use of the form. Expensive heavy quality paper should only be used if the form is to be handled a great deal. From the points of view of cost and storage the thinner the paper the better. Types and qualities of paper are dealt with in Chapter 47. Methods of reproduction have been dealt with in Chapter 29.

The question of colour also has to be considered.

(1) Should the forms be of different colours to facilitate routeing and filing? This is particularly important when using a multi-part set.

(2) Can the same form be printed on different colours for coding purposes?

Other aspects which need to be examined are the requirements for punching, perforation, padding, folding, etc.

Common faults in forms

It is only when confronted with a form for completion that the faults become apparent. When designing a form the designer should complete one himself and also ask one or more intended users to complete one. The extraction of information from the form should also be tested. If practicable a "trial run" of forms reproduced by a cheap method such as spirit or ink duplicating enables the designer to eliminate faults. Many firms today send out forms which are almost incomprehensible to the recipients. Application forms are a particular example as many applicants for jobs know to their cost! The forms designer may find it useful to make a check-list of the faults found in forms used over a period. When a new form is designed it can be checked against the list to ensure that these faults are avoided. Some common faults are listed below.

(1) Insufficient horizontal space allowed for Christian names or forenames.

(2) Inadequate space for an address.

(3) No lines provided where forms are to be handwritten.

(4) Too much printed information such as "publicity blurb" printed on the form.

(5) Too many type founts used (two or three should be sufficient).

(6) Lack of distinction between forms, e.g. credit notes and invoices.

(7) Inadequate information on forms produced on some types of accounting machines. (Unless the balance agrees with the account in the buyer's ledger, it may be necessary to write for further details.)

(8) The space for a signature placed too near the bottom edge of the paper.

(9) The name of the organisation in small print at the foot of the form (it should be clearly placed at the top).

(10) Inadequate margins (at least 25 mm should be allowed at the left-hand side of the form for filing purposes, and a similar amount of space at the top and bottom for forms which are to be inserted into a typewriter).

(11) The various sections of the form not properly separated so that it is difficult and confusing to complete and extract information from it.

Figure 117 shows an example of a badly designed order form and the same form redesigned taking into consideration the various points listed above. The two forms should be compared, the redesigned example being checked against the principles and faults explained in this chapter.

Design of an invoice

An invoice is a form common to every business concern and it is useful to examine the guiding principles for its design. The form should be clearly labelled with its title, viz. INVOICE, and should be clearly distinguishable from any other form emanating from the same or any other organisation. It is advisable to number it. The information on the form should be reduced to a minimum, and the layout should be such that entries can be made as quickly as possible so as to reduce clerical error to a minimum. Headings and instructions should be clear and brief, and data to be used as a filing

Left form:

THE STERLING RUBBER COMPANY
(Sundries Dept.)
London S. W. 17

Purchase Order

Date _____
Order No. 4756
Req. No. _____
Date to send _____
via _____
Terms _____

To: Name _____
Address _____

Please send to _____

Quantity	Our Stock No.	Description	Price

(Please do not fail to acknowledge promptly)

CONDITIONS AND INSTRUCTIONS—READ
CAREFULLY
All invoices must show our stock number, etc. etc.

Sterling Rubber Co. _____

Right form:

ORDER   No. 4756

THE STERLING RUBBER COMPANY
(Sundries Dept.)
Tooting Broadway, London S.W.17

Please send to

⌐ ⌐

Please acknowledge
receipt of this
Order.

Date	Delivery by	via	Terms

Quantity	Our Stock No.	Description	Price

(For conditions of Ordering, please see overleaf.)

for STERLING RUBBER COMPANY

Fig. 117 *Redesign of an order form. Left:* before redesigning. *Right:* after modification. Compare with the list of common faults in the text.

reference should be prominently sited, for example in the top right-hand corner.

If entries on the invoice are to be made by machine, whether typewriter or accounting machine, as many items as possible should be entered on the same line to minimise the number of lines of typing; tabulator stops should be kept to a minimum; shift key operations should be minimised by typing in block capitals as much as possible. No printed horizontal lines are necessary.

44. Work Charts

Purpose of work charts

Various types of charts can be used to show visually the procedures, movements of documents and people, machine activity, etc. that form part of a system. Analysis from a visual presentation makes systems reviews and revisions easier and proposed changes can be assessed for practicability and interaction with related procedures.

Procedure analysis

When preparing a chart for the purpose of work simplification or fault rectification it is often helpful to prepare a written analysis of the procedure first. This is known as a procedure record. The beginning of such a record is shown in Fig. 118.

IN	*OPERATIONS*	*OUT*
Documents, and from whom		Documents, and to whom
Letters from public	*Inwards mail* (1) Receive mail from . . . (2) Open mail (3) Time and date-stamp letters (4) Sort letters into departments (5) Empty envelopes to junior clerk	 To messenger Envelopes to junior clerk

Fig. 118 *Procedure record.*

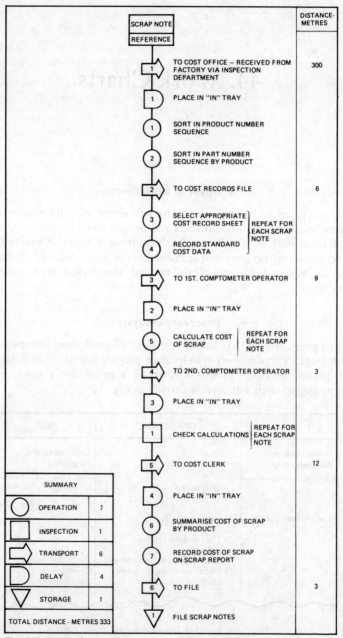

Fig. 119 *Process chart symbols*.   Fig. 120 *Flow process chart*.

Types of chart

From the information in the procedure record, a chart can be drawn up, the type of chart depending on the purpose for which it is needed. There are a number of different charts which can be used for the analysis of office work; the most useful ones are explained briefly below.

PROCEDURE ANALYSIS (OR PROCESS) CHART
A procedure analysis chart consists of a list of written descriptions of all the operations in a procedure, with a symbol at the side of each operation indicating its type. The standard B.S.S. work symbols shown in Fig. 119 are used. The descriptions on the chart are very brief. There may be an additional column indicating the forms used for each operation.

The purpose of a procedure chart is to aid the study and analysis of the procedure so that the steps involved and their sequence can be seen at a glance. After this comes the difficult task of analysis of faults and making improvements.

Figure 120 shows a type of chart (sometimes known as a diagnostic chart) in which the procedure is analysed in vertical columns for the purpose of diagnosing and assessing faults. In such a chart, the distance travelled by documents and the time taken are recorded by subsequent study.

MOVEMENT CHART (OR STRING DIAGRAM)
This chart involves drawing lines on a layout plan, to depict the movement of a piece of work. It shows the route of a paper through an office, and it is surprising how often the movement will "double back" on its course from desk to desk. When the flow of work has been improved, another chart is then drawn to show how the movements have been reduced and the route streamlined. An alternative to drawing lines on a diagram is to attach a string to pins which can be moved about until a satisfactory arrangement has been made.

Such a chart may be used for the movement of employees as well as of the papers they use.

PROCEDURE (OR FORMS) FLOW CHART
A procedure flow chart shows the flow of work from one workstation to another, or between different departments. It is very useful for presenting the movements of multiple copy forms. Figure 121 illustrates the sequence of operations in connection with the receipt of an order, and shows what happens to the various parts of the invoice, etc.

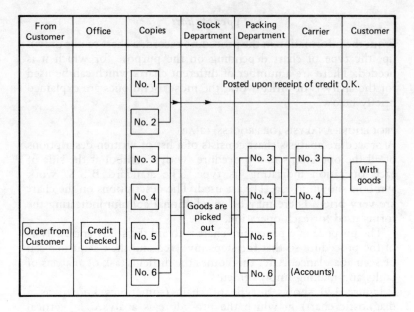

From Customer	Office	Copies	Stock Department	Packing Department	Carrier	Customer
		No. 1		Posted upon receipt of credit O.K.		
		No. 2				
		No. 3		No. 3	No. 3	With goods
		No. 4	Goods are picked out	No. 4	No. 4	
Order from Customer	Credit checked	No. 5		No. 5		
		No. 6		No. 6	(Accounts)	

Fig. 121 *Procedure flow chart, showing the history of a customer's order.*

WORK DISTRIBUTION CHART

To find out what jobs are done in an office, and who does them, a work distribution chart is used. It is based on observations made over a fixed period of a day or week and gives a brief indication of the type of work performed and how long is spent on it by each person in an office. It is a method of analysing the work content of a department, but not of the operation detail of each worker. Figure 122 shows the beginning of such a chart.

PRODUCTION STUDY CHART

Before developing a work analysis chart, it might be useful to compile individual production charts for all employees. Production charts (*see* Fig. 123) present an analysis of the exact way in which time is spent throughout the day. To obtain the information the investigator, often an Organisation and Methods officer, sits at the side of the worker throughout the day, or has a diary chart completed by each individual.

OPERATION CHART

An operation chart is used mainly when studying the work of an

Type of work	John Brown	Man Hours	Doreen Smith	Man Hours	Eric Green	Man Hours
Correspondence	Opens and reads letters	6	Takes shorthand Transcribes	15	Writes Post Book	9
Invoices	Drafts Invoices	3	Types Invoices	2		

Fig. 122 *Beginning of a work distribution chart.*

Time	Transcrip- tion	Filing	Telephone	Personal	Misc.	Remarks
9/9.20					20	Cleaning typewriter
9.50	30					
10.05			15			Business call
10.18	13					
10.25		7				
10.45					20	Coffee

Fig. 123 *Part of a production study chart.* The columns are totalled at the end of the day to obtain an analysis of how an employee spends his time.

individual, although it can be drawn up for a group of employees. Figure 124 shows how it can be used for comparing the operating time with the idle time of both a machine and its operator. This chart is appropriate for both factory and office work involving the use of machines.

From an operation chart the proportion of a person's time spent in typing, filing, answering the telephone, etc. can be assessed. It might reveal that a typist spends perhaps only 50 per cent of her time actually typing, and the remainder in performing junior duties, which might well be transferred to a junior clerk.

CONCLUSION

These are not the only kinds of work chart, but they are the main types used in connection with work simplification. Other types of patent wall charts used in connection with work control are dealt with in Chapter 45.

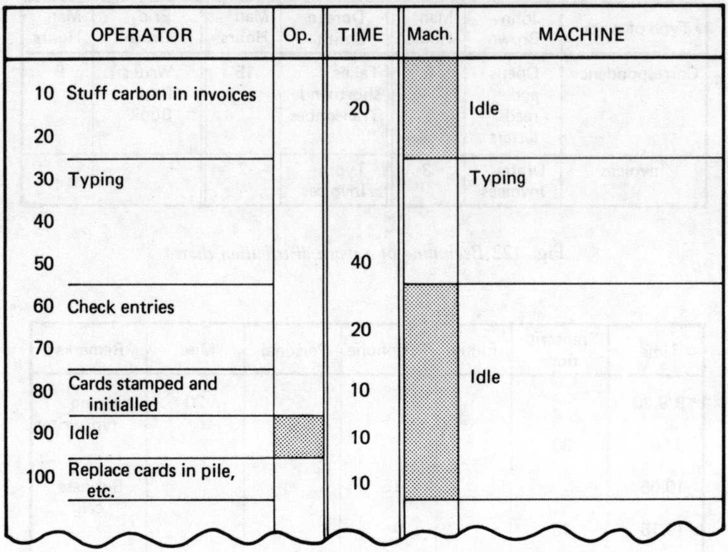

	OPERATOR	Op.	TIME	Mach.	MACHINE
10	Stuff carbon in invoices		20		Idle
20					
30	Typing				Typing
40					
50			40		
60	Check entries				
70			20		Idle
80	Cards stamped and initialled		10		
90	Idle		10		
100	Replace cards in pile, etc.		10		

Fig. 124 *Operation chart, useful for comparing the operating time and idle time of both machine and operator.*

45. Work Measurement and Control

Control means establishing standards, making regular comparisons of actual performance with these standards, and then taking action to correct deviations from the standards. There must be a system of reporting so that the comparison can be made and corrective action taken. Control of the work is as important as control of personnel, machines, methods and equipment.

There are three kinds of work control, viz. (i) over the quantity of work performed; (ii) over the way in which it is done, or "quality control"; and (iii) over the time element where the quantity of work is fixed. The last of these, time control, is known as "scheduling".

Quantity control

To control quantity, it is necessary to measure the work done. Ledger posting, preparation of statements, envelope addressing, envelope franking, filing and many other everyday tasks can be measured easily. When the work entails mental effort and is non-repetitive, it is more difficult to measure output, but it has been estimated that an average of up to two-thirds of all office work can be measured.

The selection of the unit of measurement is easier in some office jobs than in others. It is easy to determine the number of ledger postings performed in a day, but measuring the work of shorthand-typists is not so simple because of varied and complex factors involved, e.g. the speed and fluency of the dictation. In such a case it is necessary to take some unit which has a connection with the particular kind of work done. In the case of typists, to count the number of letters might be very misleading, as one letter can easily be twenty times longer than another. Typewritten work can be measured in several ways, such as the following.

(1) Number of lines of type.

(2) Square inches of typed material. A grid on a transparent overlay is used as a measure. This method is set out in *Typewriting Work Measurement* by W W. Burke and J. Maxim Watts (Pitman 1968).

(3) Treasury unit, used in the Civil Service. Again a transparent overlay is used, measurement being based on a curve designed to indicate the quantity of work at each point.

The simplest method is the number of lines. A measure in inches divided into sixths can be used to count the number of lines in the body of typing. Ten per cent should be added for addresses, etc. on a letter. The average amount of work expected of a competent typist is sixty lines an hour (elite type) or seventy-two lines an hour (pica type).

There are various factors which may affect typewriting productivity, including:

(1) the complexity and accuracy required, e.g. legal work;

(2) the amount of tabulation work;

(3) the number of copies required;

(4) the legibility (or otherwise!) of the draft;

(5) the standard of dictation;

(6) the number of times the typist has to refer to other sources for information;

(7) interruptions, e.g. telephone calls, originator of the material asking how the work is progressing;

(8) the technical nature of the material.

There is also the question of the amount of work given. A typist can only produce what she is asked to produce. If she has no other duties and her output is low, the question of input must be investigated. Perhaps she could work for more people.

Where there is a wide variety of work done in a department, it may be convenient to measure the total output of all the staff as a group. Where work done by an individual is variable, for example the writing of orders, some of which may take ten times as long as others to write, a "block measurement" can be used. A block of, say, 100 orders is very much the same as another block of 100 orders, and this can be taken as a measurement of output. Alternatively, where the work is variable between, say, three different types of operation, a weighted measurement can be used, which gives different values of time to the different items of work.

METHODS OF MEASUREMENT

Some of the different methods (varying from imprecise to very

precise) which can be used in measuring the quantity of office work
are:

(1) estimates by supervisors;
(2) estimates by subordinates;
(3) diary sheets (completed by staff);
(4) activity sampling;
(5) inspection and counting of records;
(6) personal observation repeated over a period of time;
(7) application of Predetermined Method Time System
(P.M.T.S.) standards;
(8) application of British Work-Measurement Data Foundation
standards;
(9) Management Action Data Computer Analysis Programme
(M.A.D.C.A.P.), a computer-assisted activity sampling technique,
developed by the Dickinson Robinson Group Limited.

Estimates by supervisors may be reasonable in the case of repetitive
work. However, when a subordinate's work is very varied the
supervisor is not likely to be aware of the full extent of the duties
and the time spent on each. In such a case an estimate made by a
supervisor without consultation with the subordinate concerned
could cause resentment and even negative reaction.

Estimates by subordinates may not be completely reliable since
subjective considerations are likely to have an influence, even
though subconsciously. On the other hand, each person should be
able to assess the implications of an individual task or series of tasks
and give a reliable estimate of the time it will take to complete. The
imponderables, such as interruptions by a senior, the telephone and
visitors, may make the estimated completion time completely
incorrect, though experience should be a guide. A supervisor who
consults a subordinate about a deadline for a piece of work or a
project ought to be able to expect a realistic decision.

Diary sheets are completed either daily or weekly by each individual
member of staff involved in the survey. Daily sheets are more
precise for recording purposes. The information can then be
collated and recorded on weekly sheets.

A daily diary sheet is illustrated in Fig. 125(*a*). The working day
is divided into five-minute intervals. The individual indicates the
time (to the nearest five minutes) when he begins and ends a task.
There may be overlapping, e.g. a telephone call received while
working on a larger task. Apart from fulfilling the objective of
measuring work, a diary sheet reveals imbalance in time spent on
different tasks. It frequently provides an "eye-opener" to the
individual as to where time is spent—and possibly wasted.

A Summary of Unmeasured Work Chart is illustrated in Fig.

DAILY LOG OF UNMEASURED WORK

Name: *Bertha*
Department: ....
Date: ....

Time Off: ....
Overtime: ....
Boss Away: ....

	A.M.	TOTAL
(1)	Taking Dictation (inc. walk to & from)	30
(2)	Unmeasured Typing	
(3)	Amendments to Stencils	
(4)	Check by Call-over with another typist	
(5)	Collating & Stapling Reports	
(6)		
(7)	Opening, Sorting & Despatching Mail	
(8)	Filing	10
(9)	Messages & Errands	
(10)	Work connected with Survey	
(11)	Sickness absence return	10
(12)	Telephone enquiries	25
(13)	Queries	20
(14)	Travelling expenses	
(15)	Despatching teleprinter message	
(16)	Checking film report	
(17)	Diary entries	5
(18)		
(19)		
(20)	Waiting Time (no work available)	40

No. of Envelopes typed ⊞ ⊞ ⊞ ⊞
No. of Phone calls ....
No. of Emidiscs loaded & unloaded ....
No. of Emidiscs loaded & unloaded ....

Notes: Horizontal lines should be drawn as work is done to show how time has been spent.

No lines of less than five minutes should be entered. All jobs should be rounded off to the nearest full five minutes.

Number of envelopes, phone calls, etc. to be recorded in five barred gate fashion against the appropriate description. (⊞)

Fig. 125(a) *Daily diary sheet for recording secretarial work which cannot be measured* (morning only).

SUMMARY OF UNMEASURED WORK

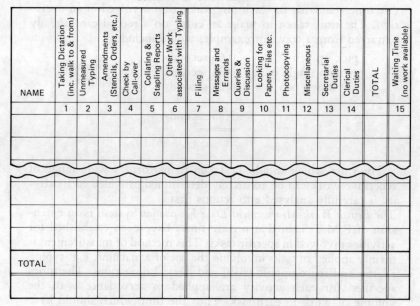

NAME	Taking Dictation (inc. walk to & from)	Unmeasured Typing	Amendments (Stencils, Orders, etc.)	Check by Call-over	Collating & Stapling Reports	Other Work associated with Typing	Filing	Messages and Errands	Queries & Discussion	Looking for Papers, Files etc.	Photocopying	Miscellaneous	Secretarial Duties	Clerical Duties	TOTAL	Waiting Time (no work available)
	1	2	3	4	5	6	7	8	9	10	11	12	13	14		15
TOTAL																

Fig. 125(b) *Specimen summary of unmeasured work chart.*

125(b). This could be used for either a daily or a weekly summary of the work of a group of secretarial staff.

Activity sampling involves repeated random inspections of work being done at different times of the day. From the records made the kinds of work being done by each member of staff can be identified and the volume of each kind of work can be estimated.

Inspection and counting of records is time-consuming and likely to cause antipathy between supervisor and subordinate. A check of work outstanding is a more positive approach, always provided the amount of work given was realistic.

Personal observation is similar to activity sampling but is applied to particular activities. The main disadvantage with any observation technique is that individual workers may react in one of two ways. Either they put on a special effort while being observed or they are inhibited and worried causing them to be less efficient than usual. If a quantitative standard is being set for a group of workers a good cross-section of individuals must be observed to ensure a fair decision of what is required.

Predetermined Method Time System (P.M.T.S.) comprises very precise time standards for each physical action involved in an operation. The time taken to make an entry on a record card already extracted from a tray, for example, would include:

pick up pen	0.65 seconds	
write a single digit	0.35 seconds	notional figures
put down pen	0.25 seconds	
	1.25 seconds	

The time which should be taken to perform a wide range of repetitive work can be accurately determined provided each activity is carefully analysed into actions first.

The British Work-Measurement Data Foundation system is an extension of P.M.T.S. in that precise times have been established for activities involved in specific tasks. This method of measurement is mainly applied to tasks involving the use of a machine, e.g. typing a letter and reprographic tasks, and clerical operations. The times specified for each activity are applied in accordance with the volume of work in each task. Thus the time which should have been taken to type a particular letter can be calculated according to its length and complexity. A Relaxation Allowance (R.A.) of 15 per cent is built into the times.

When a work measurement exercise is carried out, typists are asked to make an extra copy of every document they type. Machine operators are asked to record the work they do. At the end of each day the time which should have been taken to do the work is calculated. If work done does not add up to the time in a working day investigation is necessary. What difficulties did the worker have? Is there a lack of work? Are other non-measurable tasks being undertaken? In the latter case it is usual to combine the diary sheet system with the measurement system to obtain an accurate over-all return of work done.

MADCAP is the name given to a computer-assisted method of recording and analysing the behaviour of complex systems. It is primarily intended to provide a factual basis for the measurement of creative and managerial areas of administration. When applied to systems which cross departmental boundaries, e.g. sales, production control, buying, design, personnel or work study, it indicates behaviour patterns, problems and opportunities for improvement. It is now possible for non-computer staff to be trained to use this method of work measurement.

Time and motion study

Time study and motion study, or both combined, were once considered to be a technique of factory management only. They are now an integral part of Organisation and Methods study. The movements made by workers with machinery are analysed and the elements grouped. Each group of movement elements is timed to decimal places of a second and recorded. The results of these studies are then applied to the measurement and timing of future work, and payment is made accordingly.

Time and motion study can be applied to repetitive work which can be measured. It is usually, though not necessarily, mechanical work. Though clerical work is to some extent non-repetitive, there are many areas in which repetitive procedures are carried out, and are therefore suitable for time and motion study.

Motion study always precedes time study. Motion study principles can always be applied, either fully or partially, to office work. It is concerned with the way a job is done; the speed of operation; the availability of equipment; the right layout of machines or tools; whether the right kind of seating is supplied and so on. The remainder of the study concerns the movements of the operator— the actual stretch of the arms and the use of the right or left arm, etc.

Provided the work is standardised and mechanical it is possible to proceed with a time study so that a reasonable performance time can be decided for each unit of work.

Setting standards

Having devised a unit of measurement, it is a fairly simple task to chart what should be performed in comparison with what is actually done by individuals or by a whole department.

This setting of standards is the keystone of management control. Standards should be set with great care, for if they are too liberal little benefit will be gained by the control, and if they are too stringent, they will demoralise the staff and may even precipitate industrial action. Standards may be based on past experience, on carefully formed estimates, or on scientific assessments. Estimates are open to subjective judgment so a combination of past experience and assessment is probably the best.

A standard should not be static. In the interests of good management, departmental efficiency and individual satisfaction, the aim should be to raise the standards of all work as high as possible. This applies to quality as well as to quantity control.

Quality control

It is deplorable that the quality of work in many offices falls far below the standard expected. There are many reasons for this, arising from faults of both management and staff. Whatever the reasons for mistakes in office work, there must be control over the quality of the work performed.

A badly typed letter, a mistake in an invoice, a file put in the wrong cabinet, all cause waste. It has been known for some people to spend the whole of a day looking for an important file which has been mislaid. Where a hospital patient is to undergo a serious operation, it may make the difference between life and death if his case notes are not to hand. A figure 0 omitted from a million by a typist could result in a costly enquiry to find the missing £900,000.

METHODS OF CONTROL

There are three main methods of exercising control over errors in office work.

(1) *One hundred per cent checking.* This should not be done unless the work is very important (e.g. statistics for the Board of Directors, material being sent for printing, printer's proofs). Otherwise, complete checking amounts to doing the work twice over, which is wasteful and far too costly.

(2) *Random sampling* (or spot checking). The supervisor takes samples of the work at random but on regular occasions, to see if there are any faults. The frequency and percentage of random checking may vary with the experience of the staff and the importance of the work being done.

(3) *Partial checking.* Only the most important part of the work done, or the area of work in which most errors occur, is checked. For example, in posting accounts to the sales ledger, if posting to the wrong accounts is the most usual mistake, a check of the account numbers only may be sufficient.

When errors are made, the cause, as well as the effect, must be investigated. Systems of internal check (e.g. having control accounts in different ledgers) and internal audit are dealt with in Chapter 48.

CLERICAL ERRORS

Errors in any type of work are exasperating to management, to customers and to the staff themselves. Some errors may be unavoidable because they are caused by outside factors, but apart from these, errors should be analysed with a view to preventing their recurrence. Staff should not be automatically reprimanded when a mistake comes to light. It is wise to make a full enquiry because the mistake may arise from bad organisation, bad management and/or faulty office systems. It may be the result of ignorance on the part of the staff because of lack of training.

The following is a brief summary of the causes of errors.

(1) *Fault of the worker.* Too hasty work (causing, perhaps, transposition of figures); lack of method in working (because of bad training); lack of theoretical knowledge; inexperience; bad writing (schooling may be to blame); tiredness (perhaps for domestic reasons, or because of office conditions); gossiping (lack of supervision).

(2) *Fault of management.* Defective training (either initial or follow-up training); bad selection of staff; insufficient and vague instructions; no specialisation; lack of control; bad organisation (perhaps unsuitable for the purpose of the office); bad morale ("couldn't care less" attitude); system too complicated (work simplification needed); forms badly designed and worded.

(3) *Poor working conditions.* Bad lighting (especially where filing cabinets are housed); unsuitable colour of paper used for office forms; temperature not controlled, inadequate ventilation; too much noise so as to spoil concentration; unsuitable furniture which results in unnecessary fatigue; unsuitable decor.

It is difficult to obtain standards of error tolerance which can be applied in all circumstances. In America, it has been established by the big insurance companies that the job of sorting cards into alphabetical order has an error rate of anything up to 33 per cent, although the common standard elsewhere was about 1 per cent. In punching cards for a punched-card system, the number of items and the layout of the card have to be taken into account. In a large American oil company an error rate of 0.5 per cent for 45-column cards rose to 1 per cent for 80-column cards.

Some managements found that a bonus which reduces pro rata with the number of errors made is of great assistance. In proof of this, an American life assurance company found that an error rate of 0.65 per cent before the introduction of a bonus system was reduced to 0.22 per cent after it was introduced.

Scheduling

Scheduling may be defined as the determination of a work cycle so that the actual performance is compared with the predetermined starting and finishing dates. It is control over the *time* in which the work is done, not over the quanity or quality, though quality control is always essential.

Not all office operations can be scheduled, but it is possible for tasks such as preparation of the pay-roll, monthly statements, daily invoices, etc. It is usually essential for work which must be finished by a certain time. If the time limit for preparation of wages is 1600 hrs. on Thursday afternoon, the time required can be assessed by working backwards from that time, allowing the time needed for each operation that has to be completed.

The object of scheduling is to see that each operation is carried out strictly according to the timing of the schedule. Thus if all gross wages calculations have to be finished by Wednesday afternoon, that part of the job must be finished that day even if overtime working is necessary.

There are four common methods of scheduling.

(1) *Manual control* where a supervisor gives the work out in even-numbered batches (perhaps in folders), the whole of which must be completed by a certain time. This is suitable for such work as straightforward typing.

(2) *Visible card index* systems, incorporating coloured signals for control purposes. On opening the cards, the position of the signals shows immediately which work is in advance of or behind the scheduled times or dates (*see* Fig. 126).

(3) *Charts* which can be written up in a variety of ways. One example of this is the Gantt chart. The object of such a chart is to show the comparison of work planned and work accomplished in relation to time. Figure 127 shows a Gantt chart, with the work completed drawn in light lines, and the scheduled work in heavy lines.

(4) *Patent machine charts* which can either stand on the desk or be hung on the wall. These usually take the form of perforated wood or metal panels, on which a chart is constructed by affixing various coloured signals in the perforations. Alternatively, charting may be done by the sliding of coloured index strips in channels (*see* Fig. 128). A wide variety of charts is available. A network plan is shown in Fig. 129.

Work fluctuations

Office work is influenced by outside factors and is therefore liable to a great deal of fluctuation, which is sometimes extremely difficult to control. Where there is a rhythmic fluctuation, say at the end of each week or of each month, it is easy to make standing arrangements to meet the peak loads, but where it is haphazard other more flexible arrangements have to be made.

[Courtesy Twinlock U.K. Ltd.

Fig. 126 *Visible card index*. A visible card index system can be used for many kinds of records including stock. The strip which is visible at the bottom of each card when the tray is "closed" enables information to be retrieved without delay.

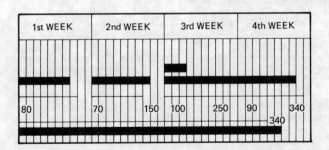

Fig. 127 *Gantt chart*.

Proper control of staff, of work and particularly of scheduling will assist in recognising the problem when it arises, and in dealing with it. It is then essential for the office manager to find out which machines are available, how many of them are required, how many

[Courtesy Modulex Systems Ltd.

Fig. 128 *Control Board*. Pocket board used to control the whereabouts and usage of tools. Different colours are used to indicate the tools in stock, tools in repair and tools in use.

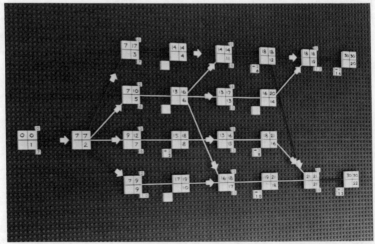

[Courtesy Modulex Systems Ltd.

Fig. 129 *Control board*. Network analysis (*see* p. 560)—the blocks are clipped on to a perforated board: event numbers are written on with a felt marker.

staff are needed and the most efficient ways of doing the work. For proper control of fluctuation in work, there must be full knowledge about everything which is subject to control, and about equipment which is available, and it is essential to see that such equipment is supplied when it is needed. The office manager should institute a regular routine of work-reporting, so that a "rush" period is not on top of the office before proper arrangements can be made to meet it. There are many ways of meeting this most common of all office problems, including the following.

(1) *Using part-time help*. This is not always a satisfactory solution as the use of untrained part-time staff may not be much help. It is generally advisable only for routine work.

(2) *Overtime*. This is the usual answer to the rush period, but here the question of fatigue should be taken into account, as well as the effect on the morale of workers. Some firms whose work is seasonal are known to require unpaid overtime, and to grant equivalent time off in the slack periods of the year. Clerical workers today expect overtime to be paid for at enhanced rates and this is an additional problem, particularly if they are underemployed in other periods.

(3) *Interchange of staff*. A system whereby staff can be readily moved from one department to another (this could be a part of their training) facilitates the organisation of office staff when extra help is required.

(4) *Flying squads*. Where an organisation is large enough special mobile squads can be employed, whose job it is to move about as required to meet any excessive workloads.

(5) *Office appliance firms*. Many of the office appliance firms will perform any set task out of the ordinary routine. Thus, one of the firms making addressing machines will perform the whole of the dividend warrant routine on being supplied with the relevant information. Secrecy is assured by them when doing so.

(6) *Rearrangement of the work*. Where possible, the work-load should be spread out, so that peak periods can be handled with ease. In most wages systems a fair amount of preparatory work of the actual calculation of wages can be done in advance. A modern example of the rearrangement of work is the use of a cycle-billing routine; this is explained more fully in Chapter 37.

Incentive payment schemes

In many offices workers are paid according to output. Some managers think that, the more office work becomes mechanised, the more should incentive schemes be applied.

The main advantages of such schemes are that they reward the hard workers, at the same time giving management greater output; they are often the fairest method of payment; they aid supervision; and they encourage a high speed of working while retaining accuracy.

The disadvantages include the difficulties in operating such schemes when the work is intermittent; the possibility of the scheme having an adverse effect on the quality of work; lower morale may cause friction between management and subordinates; and extra administrative duties may be necessary to keep records of work performed, as well as for checking its quality.

Any incentive bonus scheme must be carefully devised in consultation with all staff concerned, and must be implemented with precision. One large nationally known business which introduced such a scheme for its punched-card operators had a 90 per cent labour turnover in the course of eighteen months. The company thus lost all the training and experience gained by the operators.

It is a remarkable fact that, wheras many large *industrial* concerns have abandoned incentive schemes in the factory, at the same time such schemes seem to be extending in the office. It may be of interest that Philips Electronic and Associated Industries Ltd have started a Premium Pay Plan by which the *employee* sets the initial pace of working, thereby earning a minimum rate of pay, and, if the employee thinks she can increase her production, *she* requests to be placed on a higher rate according to her ability. This is interesting because it is claimed that it gives higher productivity without being unduly repressive on the employees.

46. Production Control

Interrelationship of production planning and production control

Production planning and production control are often treated as separate subjects, but the contents of both overlap to a considerable extent. Planning is concerned with forecasting and organising all the factors of production before anything is actually produced, whereas production control then ensures that the quality of goods produced is up to the standards required, and that volume of production is in accordance with quantity scheduled.

Office systems in this context are more concerned with production control than planning, but it should be recognised that planning is the foundation-stone of efficient production. There can be too much emphasis on control, and not enough on planning. The necessity for too much progress-chasing may indicate inadequate planning.

General principles of production control

Only general principles can be dealt with, for the actual methods used will depend on (i) the type of production; (ii) the size of the concern; and (iii) the policy of top management. The type of production in particular will greatly affect the systems and therefore the forms in use. One-off type of production, batch production and flow production each have their own special requirements.

Purchasing and sales routines, wages and stock control are all important in any business. In a manufacturing business production planning and control are probably more important still. The purposes of production control are to ensure that:

(1) delivery dates can be met;
(2) there is smooth production flow;
(3) manpower, materials and machines are used to the best advantage;

(4) bottle-necks in production are prevented.

The possible complexity of a production control system can be gauged from a detailed statement of its scope:

(1) to specify and communicate the nature of work to be done;

(2) to allocate movement of raw material, work-in-progress and finished goods;

(3) to allocate where and when different manufacturing processes should be done;

(4) to decide what personnel are needed;

(5) to fix standards of performance and the schedule of quantities to be made;

(6) to ensure that all goods produced are charted and compared with these standards; and

(7) to institute cost control through all stages of production.

Systems and forms

It is obvious that in all larger manufacturing concerns having a number of different products, the diversity of possible systems and forms is endless.

Broadly speaking, production control can be divided into five stages:

(1) scheduling, i.e. planning quantities and dates of production;

(2) loading, or the control of the machines available and their use from time to time;

(3) material control, involving the purchase, supply and movement of all materials required;

(4) despatch, or the actual issue of manufacturing instructions;

(5) progressing, or the continuous checking of the quantities manufactured with those scheduled.

This still excludes other aspects such as maintenance of machines, and inspection routines.

Table VII gives some idea of the possible procedures, forms and departments involved. Although titles in common use have been given to the forms in this table, in practice they have many other titles. The information listed is often combined on only one or two forms.

JOB CARD

For smaller quantities in a less complicated processing system, a job card is attached to each job. There are printed sections on the card for each operation. After completion of each operation the worker inserts his pay number and date. When the goods are finished the job cards are detached and passed to the production control

TABLE VII. PRODUCTION CONTROL PROCEDURES.

Information	Department	Form
(1) Product to be made	Sales Dept.	Works Order
(2) Delivery date	Sales Dept.	Works Order
(3) Quantity required	Sales Dept.	Works Order
(4) Manufacturing methods	Production Dept.	Route Card
(5) Timing and sequence of operations	Production Dept.	Route Card
(6) Materials required	Drawing Office	Materials List
(7) Materials available	Stores	Stock Record Card
(8) Materials availability	Purchasing Dept.	—
(9) Production capacity	Production Dept.	—
(10) Machine maintenance	Maintenance Dept.	Maintenance Schedule
(11) Inspection	Inspection Dept.	Inspection Ticket and Schedules
(12) Progress of manufacture	Progress Dept.	Work Tickets and Production Schedule

department to be processed in the same way as the work tickets.

Where manufacturing entails many complicated processes and perhaps assembly of parts, separate cards are issued for each operation. Thus there may be, say, seven copies of a ticket containing the same basic information, e.g. drawing specification number, order number, etc., which are distributed to the production control, despatch, inspection, stores and costing departments, and the tool room, plus a delivery copy (for part orders).

Production of the various documents recording the same information can be produced by addressing machines, copying processes and spirit duplicating. Where there is a long list of parts and only a selected few are required for different sub-assemblies, a line selector duplicator can be used, which will duplicate selected lines from a list of parts as required (*see* Chapter 29).

Example of production control

Since it is impossible in a book of this size to give more than a general outline of the office systems involved in production control, a specimen of a fairly simple one in operation is explained to illustrate the application of a system. The business concerned manufactures precision tools, some of which are stock items, while others are made to specification, and about a thousand orders a month (for 6,000 individual items) are placed with the factory.

Each morning, customers' orders are scrutinised and a triplicate works order set (*see* Fig. 130) is prepared for each item. One copy is

JOSEPH THOMPSON (SHEFFIELD) LTD.				

WORKS ORDER

	Copied	Checked

Customer's Order No.	Customer	Works Order No. 26999
Date		

Items	Quantity	Description	Date Due

Despatching Instructions

Fig. 130 *Works order: top copy of set.*

passed to the production department and the other two to the inspection and progress departments respectively. The works orders are filed in numerical sequence of works order number. The production department decides which goods can be supplied from stock, which need manufacture to replenish stock, and which need special manufacture.

For each stock item, a master order and despatch record is created (*see* Fig. 131), which shows (i) orders received for any particular item; and (ii) what instructions have been placed with the factory for stock manufacture. If existing stocks are sufficient, no job card is required, but if they are insufficient, one is prepared, i.e. for each product to be manufactured.

The job card (*see* Fig. 132) has four detachable tickets for the four key operations, viz. turning, milling, hardening, and grinding. The

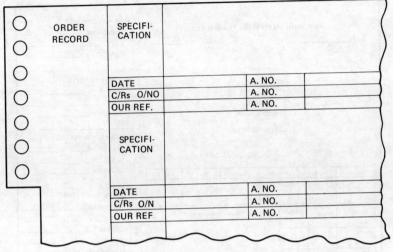

[*Courtesy Kalamazoo Ltd.*

Fig. 131 *Master order and despatch record.*

job card is put in a transparent envelope which accompanies the job through the factory, and at each stage the appropriate ticket is detached and, after signature by the operator and dating, is passed to the progress department.

The "awaiting despatch" ticket at the end of the job card is sent to the production department where details of the goods manufactured are entered on the right-hand side of the master order and despatch record.

Before the job card is passed to the factory, a progress control slip (in the form of a strip index) is prepared showing date of order and order number. As the different manufacturing operations are completed, the lower part of this form is date-stamped, so that progress can be compared with the promised delivery date also entered in the top corner of the slip. These progress control slips are filed in date order in loose-leaf binders, and when the "awaiting despatch" card is received, the slips are removed from the binder.

For special orders, works orders are also used to write up master order records which are kept in different colours for different categories of product. These are kept in loose-leaf binders, in alphabetical order of customers' names. This is a continuous record of all special orders and manufactures against them over a course of several years for each customer.

18% T. HIGH SPEED STEEL PLAIN MILLS

DATE _____   JOB REF. No. _____

LEFT HAND SPIRAL

STANDARD TYPE

Order No.	Quantity	Diameter	Width	Hole	Keyway

Operation	Operator's Number	Quantity	General Instructions
Blanking			
Boring			
Turning			
Milling			
Keywaving			
First Inspection			
Heat-Treating			
Hardness Testing			
Sand Blasting			
Holes Grinding			
Face Grinding			
Tooth Grinding			
Etching			
Final Inspection			
Packing			

DATE DUE _____

TURNING COMPLETED
JOB REF. No. _____
DATE _____
QUANTITY _____

MILLING COMPLETED
JOB REF. No. _____
DATE _____
QUANTITY _____

HARDENING COMPLETED
JOB REF. No. _____
DATE _____
QUANTITY _____

GRINDING COMPLETED
JOB REF. No. _____
DATE _____
QUANTITY _____

AWAITING DESPATCH INSTRS.
QUANTITY _____
JOB REF. No. _____

ALLOCATION

QTY.	REFERENCE No.

Fig. 132 *Job card with detachable ticket for key operations.*

This system gives emphasis to the scheduling, despatch and progressing functions. Materials handling and machine loading are not included, as they may be of less importance in a small manufacturing concern.

Production control by computer systems

In large organisations, production control may be a part of an over-all electronic data processing system. Orders are fed into the computer which then produces the necessary documentation, indicates stock items required to fulfil the order or job and makes the necessary calculations and adjustments to the stock record. There are many other ways in which production may be controlled by computer ranging from the simple to the highly sophisticated.

47. Control of Stationery, Equipment and Services

The purchase or hire, and storage and issue of stationery and equipment may be controlled by the office manager. He may also have to hire and control various office services such as cleaners. It is an area where costs and wastage can be very high. Therefore systems must be devised to minimise costs and control supplies.

Control of stationery

It is just as important to have the right kind of paper readily available when needed for a particular task as it is to have the most suitable machine and a trained operator. It has been estimated that the cost of ordering, issuing and storing stationery in the average office can be reduced by 25 per cent.

Some causes of waste are bad buying, over-stocking, poor systems of control over issue, inadequate reorder and minimum levels leading to running out of stock, inadequate and/or unsuitable storage space, and acceptance of unsuitable materials as substitutes for goods ordered.

The guide-lines below indicate the essential requirements for a good system of dealing with stationery.

(1) Maintain as little stock as possible, bearing in mind quantities for economic buying and constant supplies.

(2) Buy efficiently in the right quantities.

(3) Arrange stationery storage so as to prevent deterioration, and to save space, lighting and heating.

(4) Plan the issuing system to eliminate wasteful consumption as far as possible.

(5) Include the proper control over the use of stationery in the duties of office supervisors.

These points are discussed in more detail overleaf.

527

Stationery levels

Three levels of stock should be set, viz. *maximum*—to ensure that the amount ordered is likely to be used within the predetermined storage period; *reorder*—at which point tenders or quotations are called for and orders placed; *minimum*—to ensure that orders not yet received are chased. The two lower levels must be determined on the basis of usage and time taken to obtain supplies bearing in mind contingencies such as holiday periods, delayed deliveries, etc.

All levels should be entered on the stock cards. As issues are entered on the record and new balances calculated requisitions should be prepared for each item which has reached reorder level. As a double check to ensure that reorder and minimum levels are strictly adhered to it is advisable to place coloured tickets at the appropriate places near the bottom of each item. Two colours should be used—one for reorder level, the other for minimum level. This latter method is, of course, practicable only for piles of stationery such as forms, envelopes, etc.

Efficient buying

There are four main methods of buying which may be used individually or in combination.

Very large firms and local authorities use the system of buying by tender. The items of stationery and the quantities wanted for, say, a year are decided. Advertisements are inserted in the local and/or national press inviting stationery manufacturers to tender prices for the different lots. Delivery of the goods may then be taken altogether, or in instalments, as required throughout the year. This system saves a great deal of time in price discussion, and once the contract has been awarded it is easy to requisition the quantities needed. However, contract methods have their disadvantages; for example, the lowest tender is not always the best supplier.

The quotation system is a method of asking different firms to submit quotations, perhaps accompanied by specimens, every time a large quantity of any item is required. This gives many stationery firms the chance of supplying, and although it takes more staff time than the tender system it does ensure that the best market price is obtained for each item of goods required.

Many organisations buy from the same suppliers every time. This usually happens when a firm has found good quality and service which may justify constant ordering from the same supplier. However, where this has been done over a period of years, it may come as quite a shock when a low competitive quotation is obtained instead of placing a "blind order".

Lastly stationery supplies may be purchased through various sales representatives as they call on firms. They sometimes bring samples, and invariably seek to increase the quantities ordered. This is definitely not a recommended way of buying.

The stockroom

Stationery is often stored on open shelves or in dark and gloomy cupboards, and it may be badly arranged and difficult to find any item. Under these circumstances it is almost impossible to take stock when required.

Printed matter is particularly expensive today and should be stored in the best possible way. The minimum conditions required of the room allocated are that it should have good light, be within easy reach of all departments, be clean and dry, and have a good lock. The items should be spaced out on narrow adjustable steel shelving, which is both fire-resistant and adjustable to suit the height of the stationery.

The physical arrangement of the stock is a major factor in its preservation. Printed matter should be left in its wrapping paper and be clearly labelled on the end facing outwards (some printers do not even label their parcels), and the parcels should be stacked for ease of counting in, say, fives or tens. The shelves should be numbered consecutively, and a loose-leaf or card index, from which the relevant shelf number for any item can be obtained, should be kept up-to-date.

Issuing system

In a firm of any size, a system of requisitioning is necessary to make sure that goods and quantities required are officially approved. The system should be simple but well planned. For example, issues should only be made on written requisitions signed by authorised persons, who should be designated beforehand. Specific times should be set for stationery issues, e.g. one particular day a week, or between certain hours each day. There are always exceptions which have to be made to this rule. If work is not to be interrupted, staff must be supplied with the necessary tools and materials for the job whenever they are needed. Nevertheless staff should be encouraged to think of their stationery requirements ahead of time to avoid "panic" requisitioning.

As with any system of stock control, the efficiency of issuing will depend in the last resort on the personal capacity of the storekeeper. He should be aware of the size of departments and their usual requirements so that he can query abnormally large requisitions.

While a system of written requisitions is strongly recommended wherever possible, it must be complemented by a sensible system of collection/delivery. A great deal of time can be wasted by constant ordering of small quantities of items and regular visits to the stationery department to collect them.

Control of consumption

Various measures have to be taken to keep consumption down to a minimum. Responsibility for consumption of stationery must be placed on those who sign the requisitions. In addition, the cost of supplies to each department can be charged out, so that it is known which departments are consuming most. Small items such as paper-clips should be packaged in small envelopes. Nothing induces waste more than being over-liberal with individual issues.

Typewriter ribbons and carbon papers can be obtained in a wide range of qualities, thicknesses and colours. They should be chosen by reference to "wear-down" tests in accordance with the office use of them. Bi-chrome (two-colour) typewriter ribbons are not economical as the red half is used far less than the black half. Carbon or plastic ribbons are now used in many offices. As these give "one-time" use only typists should be encouraged to use fabric ribbons (nylon or silk) for internal work, such as memoranda, where typewriters with easily interchangeable facilities such as a dual ribbon device or a cartridge are used.

Stock should be inspected regularly to determine what is *not* being used. Obsolete office forms should be made up into scrap pads for use in the office. Where stock records are maintained there should be a regular physical stock-taking to check with the balances appearing on the stock records.

Paper

MANUFACTURE

Paper is made from wood pulp, rags, straw, esparto grass or other fibres. The strength and character of paper and board are determined by the length of the beaten fibre, and the type of fibre used. Many papers consist of a "furnish", which is a mixture of the various raw materials used in paper making.

The strongest paper is made of rag. Chemical wood paper is strong while esparto, though pleasant for writing purposes, lacks strength and is unsuitable for documents which are handled constantly.

Paper should be used on the "right" side, which is smoother than the "wrong" side. The most usual way of identifying the right side is to hold the sheet up to the light so that the watermark can be read. If it is the right way round the "right" side of the paper is facing you.

QUALITIES AND GENERAL USES

The quality of a paper depends on its weight and finish. Paper is measured in grams per square metre, abbreviated to g/m^2 and referred to as grammage. The most common uses of the various weights of paper are as follows:

$47 \ g/m^2$—copy, flimsy or manifold paper for carbon copies
$75 \ g/m^2$—general copying and forms, standard letterheads and envelopes
$80/100 \ g/m^2$—prestige letterheads and envelopes, contracts, etc.
$50 \ g/m^2$—airmail

Other types of paper include "Azure Laid" used for ledger work; "Cream Laid" used for good quality lined writing paper; "duplicating" paper, which is semi-absorbent and is used for running off ink stencils; and "Art Paper" which has a non-absorbent shiny surface and is used for running off spirit masters.

SIZES

Most offices now use the metric sizes established by the International Standards Organisation (I.S.O.). The chart below indicates the standard sizes and their uses.

Size	Measurements mm	mm	Most common uses
A0	841 ×	1,189	Posters of various kinds, wrapping paper.
A1	594 ×	841	
A2	420 ×	594	
A3	294 ×	420	Legal and accounts documents.
A4	210 ×	297	Letters, reports.
$\frac{2}{3}$ A4	140 ×	297	Letters, invoices.
A5	148 ×	210	Letters, business documents.
A6	105 ×	148	Postcards.
A7	74 ×	105	Invitation cards, compliments slips.
A8	52 ×	74	Business cards.

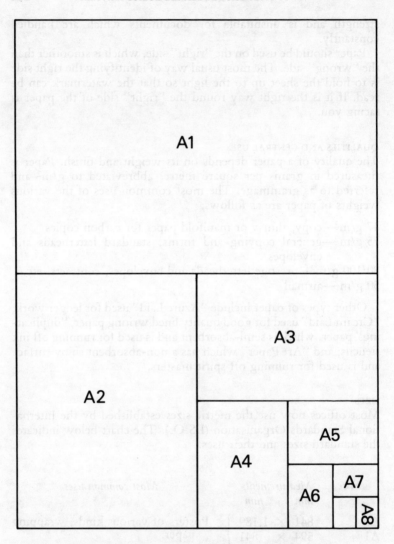

Fig. 133 *ISO paper sizes*. Each size is one half of a sheet folded in half with the two short edges brought together, e.g. A1 is half A0 (the whole sheet).

A4 is the most commonly used size as it is suitable for nearly all general office communications. Paper is normally supplied in quantities of 500 or 1,000 sheets. The standard ream is 500 sheets.

ENVELOPES

Envelopes are also made in various types and weights of paper including manilla (for general commercial use), cream laid and parchment (for prestige use). A4 size paper can be folded neatly to fit either a C6 or a DL envelope but as the DL size is more suitable when two or more sheets are to be inserted it is probably advisable to standardise on this size. The difference in cost between C6 and DL is minimal. Larger sizes correspond to the sizes of paper, e.g. a C5 envelope takes an A5 size sheet (or A4 folded in half).

Methods of copying

There are various methods of obtaining a number of copies at one typing.

ONE–TIME CARBON

This very thin, cheap carbon paper is usually interleaved into sets of forms or into continuous stationery (explained later in this chapter). It is used once only and thrown away. This apparent waste is more than offset by the time saved in collating carbon packs.

CARBON BACKING

The back of an otherwise ordinary sheet of paper has a carbon deposit on it so that when the paper is typed or written on, a carbon copy is reproduced on the copy paper underneath. This is sometimes known as "spot" or "zone" carboning, because it can be applied to certain areas of the paper only. It is quite an expensive process. The advantages of carbon backing are that it saves the insertion and removal of carbon paper, and the carbon can be applied to just the areas where the carbon impression is wanted on the various forms in a set so that only the information relevant to each particular document is reproduced on it.

CARBON POCKET

A carbon pocket is made up of heavy carbon papers sewn together at the sides but not at the bottom. It is used for typing one set of forms, after which the pocket is automatically moved back in the machine and is then ready for typing the next set. This type of copying is used on machines specially adapted for typing invoices in continuous stationery form. These machines, commonly known as "billing machines", are used for the production of bills or invoices.

NO CARBON REQUIRED

"No carbon required" (N.C.R.) paper has a chemical coating on the reverse side which produces carbon copy when the paper is written or typed on. No carbon paper is necessary. Best results are obtained when a hard backing is used. The number of copies which can be obtained depends upon the thickness and weight of the paper.

The advantages of using N.C.R. paper are that carbon paper handling is eliminated and the thickness of multicopy stationery sets is considerably reduced.

The disadvantages are that it is not possible to erase if a mistake is made, the paper must be handled very carefully because chemical coating is sensitive, and accidental pressure is likely to make marks on the copies.

There is now an improvement on the chemical coating. Micro-encapsulated ink crystals are embedded in the paper, so that writing or typing on the paper "explodes" the crystals and produces the carbon copy required.

CARBON PAPER

There are many weights and types of carbon paper. Film carbon, though expensive, has by far the longest life, is clean to handle, and gives good reproduction. Some film carbons have plastic backing which gives extra long life.

It is worth experimenting with different kinds of carbon for various types of work. Suppliers will normally provide samples for this purpose.

Storage of carbon paper is important. It should be kept in a cool, dry place, never placed on radiators or left in the sun. It should be kept flat in boxes. If long-life carbons are used they can be issued in small quantities in plastic folders.

Continuous stationery

Continuous stationery was first introduced in Britain in 1906. Sets of forms are joined together into a continuous strip, separated by perforations. Reproduction is usually by means of one-time carbons, carbon backing or no carbon required.

There are three basic types of continuous stationery as follows.

(1) *Roll stationery*. The forms are produced in a continuous roll, as used, for example, on a teleprinter. Two-, three-, or four-ply teleprinter rolls can be obtained. There are no perforations and the forms are torn off against a metal cutting edge when the message has been typed.

(2) *Interfold stationery*. Interfold is the name given to continuous stationery which is perforated, interleaved with one-time carbons and folded flat in "concertina" style. It is also known as "flat-pack".

(3) *Fanfold stationery*. The forms are joined together at the sides as well as top and bottom, and are divided from one another by perforations both horizontally and vertically. If a number of sets of fanfold stationery were pulled out they would open up in the form of a fan. This kind of continuous stationery is particularly useful when forms of different widths are incorporated in a set, and when pre-punching of filing holes prevents the use of sprocket feeding (*see* below).

SPROCKET FEEDING

When forms are fed through a typewriter or similar kind of machine they are held in place by the normal friction-feed rollers which grip the paper underneath the platen. This is not very satisfactory where several forms are interleaved with several carbon papers, as the forms easily get out of alignment; in the case of business documents such as invoices it could be serious to have figures in the wrong places.

To avoid this difficulty sprocket feeding is used for continuous stationery. Both sides of the paper are punched with evenly spaced holes and the forms are controlled on a special typewriter platen assembly which is fitted with sprockets (wheels with protruding pins). This device ensures that the stationery is held rigid and that perfect alignment is obtained.

DECOLLATING

Each set of documents may be torn off at the perforation after typing and the carbons removed (one-time carbon sets). A cut-away corner of the carbon sheets allows this to be done easily. Alternatively the typed roll or pack can be passed through a decollating machine which separates the sets at the perforations and removes the carbon sheets. The various copies are then arranged in stacks.

CONTINUOUS STATIONERY MACHINES

The interfold stationery can be most suitably contained in a rectangular machine, where the forms are drawn over a hard writing surface and the top copy or two detached while carbon copies (still joined together) are retained in the machine, folding themselves automatically into a flat pack at the other end of the "box". This is known as a manifold machine, or autographic

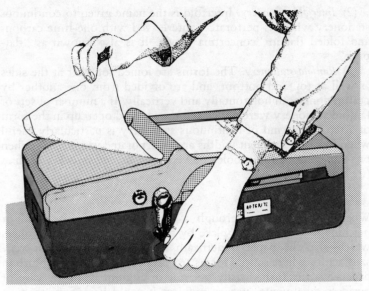

Fig. 134 *A crank-operated autographic register.*

register (*see* Fig. 134), where the movement of the forms is
performed by hand or by operating a crank which moves forward
the next set of forms ready for writing on.

The usual method of mounting the carbon paper in manifold
registers is in rolls, from which it traverses horizontally across the
forms; as the carbon impression becomes weak it is moved on as
required. Registers of this kind can be mounted on cash tills and are
constructed so that it is not possible to open the till drawer unless a
set of forms has been used and moved on.

Continuous stationery is also used in all types of book-keeping
machines, addressing machines, the tabulator of punched-card
installations, and for the printout of word-processing machines and
computers.

ADVANTAGES AND DISADVANTAGES

Assembling various copies of a form, interleaving with carbon
paper, feeding them into the machine, aligning them and decollating them afterwards are laborious and time-consuming tasks. The
main advantage of using continuous stationery is the saving in

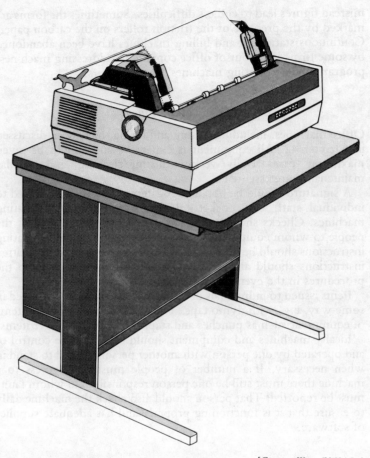

[Courtesy Wang (U.K.) Ltd.

Fig. 135 Continuous stationery being used for printout from a word processor.

time, which will obviously be related to the amount of typing on the forms (the more writing, the less proportionate time saved); and to the number of copies required (the greater number of copies, the more time saved).

The main disadvantage of using continuous stationery (see Fig. 135) is the difficulty of making alterations, particularly where a large number of forms are used in each set. This is particularly irksome when accurate typists are difficult to find. When used on some machine installations, the bottom copies are very faint and misread figures lead to endless difficulties. Sometimes the forms are marked by the pressure of the friction rollers on the carbon paper. Continuous stationery and billing machines have been abandoned by some firms in favour of office copying or addressing machines, programmed accounting machines, or computers.

Control of equipment

Office machines, including leasing and hiring, have been discussed in Chapter 42. All equipment is expensive and should be given maximum care. Daily/weekly dusting/cleaning and regular maintenance are essential.

A signature should be obtained for items of equipment issued to individual staff, e.g. pocket calculators and portable dictating machines. Checks should be made at intervals to ensure that the people to whom equipment has been issued still have it. Operating instructions should be given with each piece of equipment. Written instructions should also be given at the time of issue as to the procedures in the event of malfunction, loss or damage.

Items issued to individuals or to departments should be named in some way, e.g. with dymo tape. This should apply to small items of equipment such as punches and staplers as well as bigger items.

Ideally machines and equipment should be under the control of and operated by one person with another person trained to stand in when necessary. If a number of people must have access to a machine there must still be one person responsible, to whom faults must be reported. That person should also check the machine daily to ensure that it is functioning properly and has adequate supplies of software.

Office services

CLEANERS

An organisation may employ its own cleaning staff, usually on a part-time basis. Offices must be cleaned either before or after normal working hours. This can present a slight problem when office staff work flexi time because they may be working earlier or later than normal, thus "clashing" with cleaning staff.

Many organisations now use contract cleaning companies. A monthly, quarterly or annual charge is made by the cleaning company, which sends as many staff as necessary at an agreed time. For security reasons the time factor is important.

Contract cleaning staff may be less efficient than employees because the client organisation is not their own employer. Any complaint should be made to the cleaning company management, not to the cleaners themselves.

VENDING MACHINES

Tea ladies come expensive these days and many organisations now have vending machines installed at strategic points in the building. Staff may then obtain drinks when they wish either at a small cost or free. There is a wide variety of vending machines available, some of which dispense hot soups as well as hot and cold drinks of several types.

As with office machines, one person must be responsible for the vending machine(s). They have to be cleaned, refilled with cups and ingredients and switched on and off each day. Vending machines may be purchased, leased or hired.

LEASING

There are organisations which arrange leasing of any item from a mammoth computer or a Rolls-Royce to a desk copier. The advantages of leasing were discussed in Chapter 42. It is important to discuss the implications of leasing with the financial people in the organisation to ensure that it is worthwhile, but the possibility of leasing should always be considered along with purchasing and hiring when new equipment is being acquired.

PRESS CUTTINGS

It is vitally important that an organisation knows what is being reported about it. It may also be necessary to be informed of the latest developments in professional, technical or scientific fields. To ensure that all the latest information is acquired, to save time scanning every relevant journal and to save the expense of purchasing every journal even remotely connected with the field(s) of interest, a press cuttings service can be obtained from an agency. Relevant cuttings are usually sent to subscriber organisations weekly.

Before the cuttings are distributed to the staff concerned it is advisable to copy them so that should the distributed copy be lost or mislaid there is back-up material from which further copies can be made.

RESEARCH

There are agencies which undertake research for organisations. The agency must be given a clear specification as to the general purpose and objectives of the research so that only relevant information is obtained.

Consultants

No one person can be expert in everything. Each office manager almost certainly has some special expertise of his own or within his department, e.g. in Organisation and Methods, which he uses in running his department. There may, however, be some specialist knowledge needed occasionally which is not readily available among his own staff. Help must be sought, first from within the organisation. If the expertise needed is still not available, there are external consultants.

There are advantages and disadvantages to using external consultants. The main disadvantage is that someone from outside the organisation does not know the systems, staff, political situations, etc. On the other hand, the external consultant has no axe to grind and may be able to persuade people to accept changes and/or innovations more easily than people from within the organisation.

It is essential to use reputable consultants. A contract should be drawn up before the consultant starts work. The contract should state precisely what is to be done, how and when. Submission of reports should be included. Conditions should be clearly set out as should terms of payment and what charges are to be covered by the hiring organisation. Consultants are expensive so the client has the right to know precisely what he is paying for.

48. Prevention of Fraud

There are many ways in which an employee can defraud his
employer, from simply dipping a hand in the cash till to feeding
false information into a computer. Office organisations continue to
grow in size and complexity and inflation means that ever larger
amounts of money are involved in all transactions. The consequent
extension of mechanisation and the use of computers add to the
scope of the possibilities for fraud. It is therefore essential to design
systems which prevent or minimise fraud by incorporating checks
against it, and by setting up checking systems which quickly detect
inconsistencies.

Internal check

Prevention of fraud and the safeguarding of the firm's cash is an
essential feature of all office management. One of the best methods
of prevention is to institute systems of internal check. This should
not be confused with "internal audit" which applies to an audit of
books of account, vouchers, etc. by a separate department or
person of the firm. Basically an internal audit is the same as the
audit made by professional auditors, but is carried out by the
company's own staff. Internal check ensures that the duties to be
performed in an office or organisation as a whole are arranged so
that, as far as possible, the work of one member of the staff or
group of members is independently checked by some other member
or members of the staff.

Some examples of internal check systems are given below.

(1) The work is spread between several members of the staff, so
that the efforts of each one act as a check on the work of some other
member.

(2) The duties of each member of the staff are changed periodically, so that fraud or collusion can be more easily discovered.

(3) All persons are obliged to take their annual leave, so that any frauds to which they are party may be discovered in their absence.

(4) The cashier must not have control over the accounting side of the business, nor the accounts clerks any control over cash.

(5) Self-balancing ledgers are used, and "check figures" systems are instituted, so that an independent check is made of postings, etc.

These few examples of internal check methods do not make fraud impossible, but they do minimise the opportunity and, at the same time, reduce the possibility of genuine errors remaining undetected.

Wages system

The payment of wages provided at one time perhaps the commonest means of embezzlement, partly because until fairly recently wages and weekly salaries were paid in cash. Fictitious names on the pay-roll, non-removal of the names of dead men or leavers from the pay-roll, and inaccurate records of wages paid to employees were among the fraudulent methods used to obtain money (*see also* Chapter 37). Although many organisations pay wages and salaries directly to their employees' bank accounts nowadays, it is still necessary to have internal check systems built into the wages systems. The commonest method is to divide the work so that one man (or department) is responsible for the calculation of wages, another for the drawing of cash from the bank, and yet another for the paying out. This is so that collusion (e.g. for the payment of "dummy" wages) is made virtually impossible. The paying clerk can only pay out what is drawn from the bank, and the total drawn must agree with the pay-roll as calculated separately from the other operations. It is advisable to have surprise internal audits (particularly on pay day) and to have an occasional checking of the names on the pay-roll with the staff records at irregular intervals.

In many organisations the pay-roll is now on computer and employee recruitment and leaving procedures are normally dealt with by a personnel officer so that fraud is more difficult to accomplish. Smaller organisations may use machine wages systems or even one-time writing systems in which pay-roll, earnings records and pay statements are produced in one operation. By a repeat printing of the net wages (mechanised systems), the pay envelopes can also be entered with the certainty that the amounts on them will agree with the pay-roll.

Payment of wages by credit transfer (*see* page 544) eliminates the possibility of fraud and saves many hours of physical labour in "putting up" and paying out wages. The possibility of collusion between an employee in the wages department and a "gang" for a snatch when money is taken to or collected from the bank can be almost eliminated by using a security firm, such as Securicor, to carry the money. Alternatively, the precaution of having employees go to the bank in pairs acts both as a deterrent against fraud and as a safeguard against attack.

Cash receipts

Safeguards for handling money must be considered separately for receiving cash and for making payments. The latter is dealt with on page 544.

CASH COLLECTED OUTSIDE THE ORGANISATION

Where cash is received by salesmen and representatives who may travel all over the country, it is advisable to issue instructions that:

(1) such cash must be paid regularly, ideally daily, into a branch of the company's bank;

(2) official numbered receipts must be issued for all payments received;

(3) customers must be advised to insist on official receipts when paying money to the firm's representatives;

(4) a statement should be sent to head office of all amounts received (even if it is only a carbon copy of the issued receipts);

(5) customers' ledger accounts should be credited quickly with money received;

(6) monthly statements should be issued not more than a week (if possible) after the end of the accounting month; and

(7) customers should be asked to notify the firm immediately if payments made by them do not appear on the statements.

CASH COLLECTED ON PREMISES

Where cash is received on the company's premises it is advisable to install cash registers, which not only add up the sales as they are registered on the machine, but may issue a receipt ticket for the customer as well as printing a continuous record of money received, which should agree with the cash in the till.

CASH RECEIVED BY POST

An internal check system should be used when cash, cheques, etc. are received by post. The total of all such cash is recorded (and perhaps added on an adding machine) immediately the post is opened. The total is compared daily with the bank paying-in book and with the debit side of the cash book. Where an accounting machine is used, the receipts, cash book and paying-in list may all be prepared simultaneously, but the total cash should still be compared with the post-opening record.

Cash payments

Most businesses do not allow payments to be made in hard cash, other than for petty disbursements. For these payments a petty cash book maintained on an imprest system is best. There should be a rule that every payment, no matter how small, must be supported by a properly authenticated docket.

Even so it has been known for a firm to be defrauded of a large sum of money by the simple expedient of presenting vouchers purporting to be signed by the managing director, and stating that it was on his instructions that a sum of money was needed immediately. The criminal is usually a person occupying a position of trust, and it would be wise if a rule were made that, where payment of cash in this way is authorised, it should be restricted to a low limit unless payment is made to the executive in person.

Payment of wages in advance and cashing of cheques for employees are two ways which give opportunity for fraud. They should be discouraged, or better still, forbidden.

There are some simple rules to safeguard payments by cheque. All cheques should have printed crossings to prevent the possibility of their being used for withdrawal of cash from the bank. The firm's cheques should require two or three signatures. For example, for amounts under, say, £250 the signatures of an official and a director are required; up to, say, £2,000 two directors must sign; above £2,000 the chairman/managing director and a director must sign. If all payments cannot be made centrally requests for cheques should be made on an official cheque requisition which must be authorised by one or more specified people. All cheques remitted should be accompanied by a voucher of some kind, a copy of which is filed.

To avoid using cheques at all, for payment of either salaries or accounts, payment may be made by credit transfer. The payee informs the drawer of the branch and bank at which he holds an account, quoting the bank branch code number (shown in the top right-hand corner of the cheque) and his account number (usually the third set of digits at the bottom of the cheque). The drawer completes a credit transfer slip stating the name and account number of the payee, the bank branch code and the amount to be paid. The drawer sends the completed transfer to his bank which makes the required payments and debits his account. For wages a payment list covered by a credit transfer slip for the total amount may be sent to the bank (*see* Chapter 37). Where the pay-roll is on computer the payment list can be produced on computer printout. The total amount can either be debited by the bank to the drawer's account, or for accounting purposes, a cheque may be paid by the drawer to the bank.

Use of machines

The commonest machine used as a safeguard against fraud is the cash register, but the proprietors of chain stores will testify that they do not prevent the dishonest assistant from taking the firm's cash, although they do act as a deterrent.

Machines can be used for writing, crossing, and for signing cheques. Apart from speed and convenience these machines provide protection against fraud. Cheques are completed with carbon or indelible ink and are claimed to be 100 per cent safe against fraudulent alteration.

A cheque-signing machine can be used when large numbers of cheques have to be signed regularly. The signature(s) is printed by use of a metal plate which must be kept in a very safe place when not in use. Access must be by one or two specified people only.

Many firms have a practice of rubber-stamping the face of all cheques as soon as received, with the impression of a crossing, the firm's name, and the name of their bankers. This is a good precaution, and prevents any fraudulent endorsement or conversion.

Theft

The aspect of actual theft of the firm's cash must be considered. Safes which are positively proof against fire and theft hazards are available. Cash should be banked as often as possible and placed in the bank's night safe when large amounts of money are received after banking hours. It is sometimes unavoidable that large amounts of money have to be left in a safe so it is advisable to install a burglar alarm system. It has been known for the safe to be stolen!

Information on anti-theft devices is given in Chapter 49.

Insurance against fraud

It is possible to obtain insurance cover against fraud by employees and other risks where cash is involved. Types of cover include the following.

(1) *Fidelity guarantee* against theft or embezzlement of cash by an employee. People handling cash must be named on the insurance policy. In large organisations it is usual to name the chief accountant who is responsible for the systems which should prevent fraud.

(2) *Cash in transit* to and from the bank, usually subject to a maximum amount.

(3) *Cash in safe overnight* subject to approval by the insurer of the type of safe, and of a maximum amount.

The premiums for these types of cover are usually fairly expensive but the risk is also quite high.

Attitudes

As with minimising safety hazards and maximising cost-consciousness, prevention of fraud is largely an attitude of mind. The office manager who is responsible for any system involving finance or money should check to identify possible weaknesses which may allow fraud to occur. Weak links in a chain of procedures must be strengthened to prevent fraud of any kind, however trivial. The suggestions made in this chapter are but a few of the main ones to consider in an average organisation. Methods must be devised to suit the individual organisation, its type, size, business, location, range and type of staff, etc.

Ultimately the prevention of fraud must depend on the integrity of the staff. It is vitally important to ensure that there are the minimum of opportunities for fraud of any kind—some people simply cannot resist temptation.

49. Security

Importance of security

Industrial espionage, terrorist activities including bombs (scares or real) and kidnapping of senior executives, hijacking of goods-carrying vehicles and thieving of any type of vehicle are all things which happen. They happen not just somewhere on the Continent or in the U.S.A., or in places we have never heard of; they happen here, wherever "here" may be. Security ought to be top priority in every organisation, not only against the more dramatic risks but against everyday risks such as pilfering, by the public and by staff, against fire and safety hazards (*see* Chapter 7) and against carelessness generally.

The risks

In large organisations security is under the control of a senior executive, possibly ex-police, who has an "army" of security officers who cover the various security risks. In a smaller organisation the office manager may well find himself responsible for security as well as for the normal confidentiality requirements in any office. The various hazards which must be guarded against may include the following.

(1) Unauthorised visitors.

(2) Undesirable visitors.

(3) Leaving open doors and windows, including skylights, which should be closed and locked.

(4) Doors open which should be locked.

(5) Unguarded entrances and exits to the compound and to the premises.

(6) Access to confidential documents of all kinds including plans, drawings, policy documents, personnel information, project plans, etc,

(7) Copying of confidential documents by unauthorised people.

(8) Obscure places where packages can be left unattended and unnoticed.

(9) No checking of visitors' brief-cases, etc.

(10) Alarm systems not working.

(11) Access to cash and/or safes by too many people.

(12) Lack of control over keys: too many people having keys, especially master keys.

(13) Staff talking of confidential matters both inside and outside the organisation.

(14) Staff taking files/documents out of the offices.

(15) Staff whose private lives may be open to compromise.

(16) Cars and other vehicles left in places where they can be tampered with.

(17) Theft of printed stationery.

(18) Theft of office equipment and supplies (pilfering by staff).

(19) Theft of small, and not so small, parts in the factory.

(20) Staff newly recruited from competitor organisations and not vetted strictly enough.

(21) Too much cash kept on the premises.

Security policy

In far too many organisations security is not taken seriously. Everyone in an organisation should be security-conscious (as well as safety- and cost-conscious). This can only happen if there is a clearly defined policy approved and implemented at all levels, including the top. Every individual ought to know what security procedures have to be followed in all situations which they are likely to meet in the course of their work and as a part of normal daily activities such as entering the building.

Preventive systems

Every year companies lose millions of pounds by industrial espionage. The cost, in terms of loss of profits, or a shutdown because of a bomb scare can be highly damaging to a company's financial viability. The cost in terms of staff morale can be incalculable. The person in charge of security must therefore take every possible precaution to ensure that all the risks are reduced to the lowest possible minimum. Some of the ways in which this can be done are suggested in this chapter.

PREMISES

There are two main types of burglar alarms. One type sets a bell ringing when the circuit is broken by a door or window being opened. The bell may or may not be heard by any burglar and may or may not be reported to the police. The second type is connected to the telephone which automatically shows an alarm at the local police station in the event of a break-in. A pre-set recording attached to the burglar alarm circuit announces the name and address of the firm so that the police can take action immediately. The disadvantage of this system is that the alarm would not work if the telephone wire were cut before the premises were entered.

Regular patrols by security men or nightwatchmen is another method of making entry to the premises difficult. Most security officers would probably feel much more secure themselves if they had a properly trained patrol to accompany them on their rounds. It is important that the route and schedule of the rounds should be constantly changed to avoid the possibility of their movements being "charted".

Guard dogs, as distinct from trained patrol dogs, may be suitable for smaller premises.

VISITORS

The credentials of all visitors should be checked. No one should be allowed into an office unless he is known to the person he is to see or he can produce proof of identity, e.g. a card, preferably containing a photograph of the person, from the electricity or gas board. Of course, anyone can produce a fictitious business card so vigilance is needed to ensure that people calling themselves sales representatives see only junior staff until their credentials are assured, and that they are not left alone or allowed to go to places where they could leave packages which might contain a bomb.

Notices instructing all visitors to report to security or reception should be large and clear, and in a prominent position so that they are clearly seen by everyone entering the building. The security or reception point must be manned at all times. There should be access to the building by one entrance only unless each entrance can be covered by a security point. Every visitor should be provided with a pass in the form of a self-adhesive label which should be worn throughout his visit (see Fig. 136). It is essential that each visitor returns his pass to security when he leaves the building. All passes issued must be accounted for at the end of the day. Some visitors' passes have a validation date on them, which is a useful means of ensuring that visitors have been "checked in" on the day when the pass was issued.

Fig. 136 *Visitor's pass*. Ideally this should be produced in the form of a self-adhesive label to be worn by a visitor while in the organisation. It should be handed in to security when the visitor leaves.

Another means of screening visitors, frequently used in Embassies, is to have the outer doors locked and require each visitor to identify himself by speaking into an intercommunication panel affixed to the door. When the security officer is satisfied that the visitor is genuine he opens the door by remote control.

STAFF

As mentioned earlier in the chapter, all staff should be aware of security as a normal part of their everyday activities at work. The following suggestions are some of the measures which can be taken to ensure that everyone in the organisation is covered by security regulations.

(1) Every employee should have some form of identification, preferably an indestructible card with the photograph and signature of the individual (*see* Fig. 137). Different colours can be used for special security areas such as the computer room, file registry, etc. Anyone without the correct coloured identification card should not be allowed to enter the security areas without authorisation.

There are non-manual systems of controlling access to individual rooms and to premises. The card access system is one whereby certain people have a card with a magnetic strip. The card is inserted into a card reader which allows the door to be opened. A safeguard against theft of the card involves the person keying in a security code at the door in addition to the insertion of the card. Thus anyone finding the card could not gain access unless he knew the security code.

The card access system can be difficult for staff who have to carry

NAME

Mr. J. Brown,
Macdonald & Evans,
Publishers.

EXPIRY DATE

30th November 1980

SIGNATURE

John Brown

Fig. 137 *A typical identification card.*

equipment, etc. A magnetic token can be worn by authorised individuals. The token transmits electro–magnetic signals which release the door catch. The person steps on a pressure mat in front of the door, thus opening it.

Voice access is installed in some organisations. The person wishing to gain access speaks a code into a microphone outside the door. The microphone is in fact an input peripheral to a computer which recognises the voice (or not, as the case may be). Every individual person has a unique voice in the same way as he or she has unique finger prints. If the computer "recognises" the voice the door catch is released.

(2) Every employee, no matter how senior, should identify him/herself to the security officer on duty at each entrance of the building.

(3) If practicable each employee can be allocated a particular entrance to the building and anyone entering by a different entrance to that allocated should have to obtain authorisation.

(4) All staff should be instructed on the procedures to take in the event of finding an unidentifiable package in the same way that procedures are published for evacuation of the building in case of fire.

(5) The movement of high security risk staff, e.g. top level

management and computer staff, should be monitored so that their whereabouts can be established immediately if necessary. In particular it should be noted when they leave the building. If they remain late at night to work, a watch should be kept by the security staff to ensure that all is well. It should in any case be a regulation that all staff working in the offices outside office hours must notify security. It is in their own interest to do so.

(6) Reception staff should be trained in security procedures and precautions. Staff who expect visitors should notify the gatehouse staff and/or reception of the time and date at which each named visitor is expected.

COMMUNICATIONS

It is all too easy to forget that communications can present a security risk. Telephone tapping is not so difficult for people determined to find out the secrets of a rival manufacturer. The opening of mail is not impossible. Therefore all administrative systems should be designed with the security aspect in mind.

It is important that everyone who works alone has access to communication of one kind or another. It is difficult to cover every single section of a building. It would be possible for someone to have a heart attack in a cloakroom and not be found for hours if that particular cloakroom was not used by many people. Where telephones are installed in cloakrooms, it would also be useful to have a card giving telephone numbers to call in the event of illness, taps overflowing, or other such emergencies.

There should be clear instructions in all lifts, and at the side of lift entrances, as to the action which should be taken if a lift should stop between floors. Not all lifts have telephones installed.

There is an emergency altering system available in the form of a miniature pocket transmitter (see Fig. 138), which has a range of up to about 400 metres, depending on operating conditions. A 999 autodialler is incorporated in the transmitter. By pressing a button a pre-recorded message is transmitted to the emergency number. The transmitter operates a central radio receiver which can be used to operate a variety of other devices in addition to the emergency call. For example, the transmitter can be used to control machines and processes by remote control, or to switch on security lights or sound alarms, also by remote control.

Standard telephone instruments should have close at hand, preferably affixed to a wall or other clear surface, a clearly printed list of numbers to dial (internal or external) in case of emergency. The state of the card should be regularly inspected to ensure that it is always legible.

[*Courtesy Cass Electronics Ltd.*

Fig. 138 *A miniature pocket transmitter with a built-in 999 autodialler, which is operated by a button for instant communication.*

COMPUTERS

Security in relation to computers has been discussed in Chapter 39. It is stressed here that security of computer printout, disks, tapes, microfilm, etc. is of paramount importance. It is possible to glean useful information from routine documentation and this fact should not be overlooked in an organisation working in a competitive or vulnerable market.

VEHICLES

There is the question of vehicles being stolen. Drivers should be instructed always to lock all doors, the bonnet and the boot of a car when leaving it anywhere at any time. The steering lock should be operated on cars which have this device. There are a variety of alarm systems for cars, some more satisfactory than others. Some systems particularly recommended by the police are:

(1) a secret switch which cuts off the ignition;

(2) a "Selmar" car alarm which activates the car hooter when the vehicle is handled for a short time;

(3) the "Krooklok", which is a good safeguard because most car thieves rely on a quick getaway as soon as they have broken into the car.

Wherever possible vehicles should be parked overnight in a place safe from pilfering—wheels, batteries, windscreen wipers, etc. are not difficult to remove. Staff who have the use of company vehicles should be instructed on these security risks.

Goods-carrying vehicles are open to much greater risk. All the company's goods-carrying vehicles should have a rigorous security check when leaving the premises. All drivers should have to stop at the gatehouse and produce the weighbridge copy of the consignment note or notes. Drivers should actually pack or assist in packing their vans in drop sequence, i.e. in the order of delivery, or should devise the route and be responsible for checking their loads before leaving the premises so that if any individual consignment or part consignment has not been loaded, can be reported before the driver sets out. Routes should be varied frequently.

There should be strict security procedures for long-distance drivers of goods vehicles. These procedures should be complied with whenever the vehicle is left for even a few seconds. There was a period when hijacking loaded long-distance lorries was almost a routine occurrence. Though not so prevalent now it could quite easily become so if security were lax.

SECURITY SERVICES

Very large organisations employ their own security staff. For smaller organisations which do not wish to employ or are unable to recruit trained security staff there are security companies which can provide the whole range of security services and facilities which may be required. These services include, for example, a night security officer who will be on the premises from the time the staff leave in the evening until they return in the morning. An armoured van and armed guard can be provided for moving large amounts of cash. Security patrol staff with patrol dogs are also available.

There is a scheme whereby watchmen of various firms in a small police area telephone each other at predetermined intervals during the night. Any break in the chain, i.e. if a call is not received at the appointed time, is reported to the local police who can investigate by car immediately.

Terrorist activities

The most usual terrorist activities are the placing of bombs in buildings, sending bombs through the post in small packets, and kidnapping senior executives. Each country has its own particular known "public enemies" who are likely to indulge in these activities, but there are also gangs who wish to draw attention to their "grievances" and who are not particular where they do so. It should be constantly borne in mind that every public building, i.e. a building where members of the general public work, shop, eat, visit, etc., is a potential target.

"It would be the easiest thing in the world to slip a bomb in there" is a comment frequently heard. If the uninitiated think a place is vulnerable, how much easier would it be for the experts in terrorism to carry out their nefarious activities!

Again vigilance is the watchword. It is better to be too "fussy" and have nothing happen than to be neglectful and pay dearly for it, possibly with loss of life. It is not a bad thing for the office manager responsible for security, even within his own department, to say to himself "Could this happen in this building/department?" If there is any possibility that a breach of security is possible something should be done about it with the full co-operation of staff. If staff are involved in security, as in any other activity, there is a much greater chance of effective implementation.

Collaboration with the police

It is the purpose and aim of the police force to protect life and property—in that order. The police have highly efficient expertise in security and it is almost certainly true to say that any senior police officer would be only too happy to be called upon for advice which, when carried out, would minimise the vulnerability of an organisation to any form of security hazard. At every divisional police station there is an appointed Crime Prevention Officer, usually a sergeant, who has experience of many types of security systems and safeguards.

Perhaps even more important, if one has suspicions of any security risk, be it a place or a person, the police are the people to deal with it. They are not indiscreet in this area and their intervention may well benefit the company to a far greater degree than the cost involved in the occurrence of a risk. Fot example, if the plans of a new project are stolen, not only may it mean that the company will lose its market and profits in that area, it may also lose its image and its entire future viability with consequent loss of jobs. The ramifications are endless.

There are many methods of ensuring security which should not be disclosed to anyone except the person in charge of security. This is the person who should be in contact with the police for advice and guidance.

Insurance cover

In general it is not easy, and sometimes it is impossible, to insure against security risks. It would no doubt be possible to insure the chief executive of an international organisation against kidnapping but the premium might well be extortionate. In other words, it is virtually true to say that an organisation is "on its own" as far as covering against security risks is concerned.

Cost

Security is expensive. Nevertheless it is a great deal more expensive if the risks happen. Expenditure on security is, in fact, a form of insurance. Since the stakes are usually high the premium is also high. On the other hand common sense, constant alertness on the part of staff, and firm discipline in the application of security regulations cost nothing and are very effective measures.

50. Office Management Performance

The manager has to appraise his own performance from time to time in order to assess himself as a leader, and to review his achievements. He cannot do this unless he has first determined the objectives of his department and set targets for himself and his staff, foreseeing problems which may arise in implementing the targets. He has then to identify problems and solve them when they occur. Two fundamental rules for avoiding problems as far as possible are cost control and work planning, which may not eliminate problems completely but will certainly make their identification and solution a great deal less onerous.

It is essential that the four basic steps in management, viz. planning, organising, directing and controlling, are followed. Inevitably they overlap.

Determining objectives

In Chapter 1 we defined the role and functions of an office. The objectives of an office manager must be determined in relation to the services required in the organisation as a whole and in each department of the organisation. Depending on the sphere in which the office manager is working, the objectives must be determined by analysing the services his section/department is required to provide, to whom, at what time, in what place, by what methods and for what reasons. The achievement of these requirements in such a way as to provide maximum support to the people on the receiving end is the prime objective.

Setting targets

Organisations are living entities and as such are constantly changing and developing. Within the predetermined objectives the office

557

manager must set and review targets at regular intervals to ensure not only that new systems and procedures are introduced according to schedule as required, but that existing systems and procedures are maintained at a high standard and, if possible, improved.

A target should be specific. It must be measurable in some way and it must have a date for interim and/or final achievement. For example, if a new filing system is to be introduced a time schedule must be established. Within that time schedule there should be individual targets for each major section of the task. In this way it is possible to check progress and revise the time schedule if necessary. Targets are often related to productivity, improved accuracy, reduction in costs, or some other area in which improvement is desirable.

An office manager might set as his own target an improvement in communications with other managers. This in itself is not measurable though it is necessary to identify specific weaknesses and set individual targets to overcome them. The achievement of such targets might be implemented in conjunction with a diary sheet which would indicate the number of times communications had been ineffective. Improvement would be measured by the decrease in the events or activities which were a direct result of ineffective communication.

Similarly an inaccurate typist could be encouraged to mark a chart every time she made a mistake. A lessening number of errors would provide the motivation for even greater efforts. However, this kind of target must be accompanied by appropriate training.

Foreseeing problems

In the organisation stage of management the most critical aspect is foreseeing problems. A manager must consciously try to identify the implications, repercussions and ramifications of the various courses of action he proposes to take to achieve his aims. The problems may involve time scales, people, both inside and outside the organisation, machines, legislation, etc. For example, a major report of 150 pages is being prepared. A time schedule has been drawn up in consultation with the authors and the printing department manager. It needs only one critical activity to be delayed and the report would not be ready for distribution on the date publicised. It is therefore essential to scrutinise each critical activity and the people involved very thoroughly in order to identify likely delays and take action to avoid them *before* they occur.

Identifying problems

However carefully one tries to foresee problems, there are inevitably some which occur without warning. There are also times when having foreseen the possibility of a problem one must take a calculated risk and hope that it will not occur. The important thing is to have a method of identifying problems as soon as they occur, which means a strict monitoring system.

The principle of management by exception is one of the best ways of both giving staff adequate responsibility and ensuring that you are concerned with only those difficulties that no one else can deal with. As long as everything is going according to plan you are not informed. When anything out of the ordinary occurs you are informed immediately and told what action, if any, has been taken. This presupposes adequate consultation and training of all staff in the process of delegation. It also presupposes adequate, well thought-out feedback procedures from which difficulties can be identified.

Solving problems

The solving of problems is not as easy as sometimes appears because the real problem may not be the abnormal situation identified. That abnormal situation may be the effect of a quite different root cause, which could be in an entirely different area of a system, department or organisation.

It may be necessary to take quick action to remedy the immediate cause for concern, but that is not adequate if it is likely to recur as a result of some primary cause. Tracking down the primary cause may involve a full scale O & M exercise, better communications, consultation within the department and/or with other departments, or improvements in systems or procedures in related areas—there are endless possibilities.

One thing is certain. It is worth the effort to identify the true cause of problems and apply the remedy there.

Work planning

Apart from planning the work of the section/department, every individual member of staff must plan his or her work to a greater or lesser extent. Only in this way is it possible to ensure that priority tasks are identified and completed by the deadline, that all tasks are allocated a realistic deadline and that there is sufficient flexibility to cope with the inevitable emergencies which arise in even the best run offices.

Work planning must take into account routine work and non-routine work. It is easy to underestimate the time required for routine tasks when special tasks arise. A prerequisite of effective work planning is the ability to assess with reasonable accuracy the time needed to complete a particular task or project. From the management point of view this means knowing the capabilities of each individual member of staff—some may be able to achieve better results on certain types of work than others.

From the individual point of view your own capabilities and limitations must be realised. The principle of delegating anything which anyone else can do is a sound basis to work on provided the subordinate staff would not be overloaded with work as a result. In other words, your own work planning has to be considered in relation to the work-load of the department as a whole.

There are many methods of work planning and it is up to each individual to undertake this essential activity in the way which suits him or her best. The principle is always the same: start with the largest unit of time, e.g. a year, and work backwards to the smallest unit of time, normally a day. The yearly tasks are analysed into activities which may be spread over several months or weeks, or may involve one single activity which must take place at a specific time. These yearly activities must be considered in conjunction with the monthly and weekly activities. This gives an over-all view which enables the individual to spread the work-load to avoid violent peaks and troughs. Every activity should have a deadline and when deciding the week's and the day's activities they should be allocated into "must do", "should do" and "could do".

If major projects involving numerous activities arise, activity scheduling on a year plan chart is a useful means of both planning and monitoring. A check-list is a sound basis on which to work. The activities are numbered and the numbers only entered on the chart. It is then necessary merely to refer to the key (the check-list) to identify which activities must be carried out each day.

NETWORK ANALYSIS

One method of determining the minimum length of time needed to achieve a target is network analysis, also referred to as Critical Path Analysis (C.P.A.). This type of planning provides identification of critical activities, i.e. those activities which must be kept on schedule to ensure that the completion date is met. It also provides the basis for monitoring the progress of the activities involved in a project.

There are six basic steps involved in the first phase of a network analysis as follows.

(1) *Analyse the task/project into individual activities.* To take a very simple example, the activities involved in the task of direct mailing of circulars might be as follows.

(1) Compose letter and agree with colleagues/superior.
(2) Prepare mailing list.
(3) Type letter.
(4) Reproduce letter.
(5) Insert variable details on letters.
(6) Fold letters, insert in window envelopes and seal.
(7) Frank and despatch.

(2) *Determine the sequence of the activities* including those activities which can be carried out simultaneously. Plot the activities into a network format. Using the analysis above, the network would appear as follows.

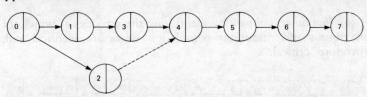

NOTE: Each arrow represents an activity; each circle represents a completed activity or "event". There is no activity between activities 2 and 4 but activity 2 must be completed before activity 5 can be started.

(3) *Establish the time needed to complete each activity.* Enter on network.

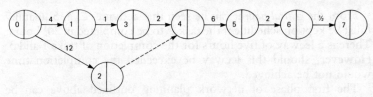

NOTE: Time in hours.

(4) *Calculate the cumulative time needed to reach each activity.*

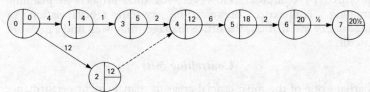

NOTE: The time required to complete activity 4 reflects the time required to complete activity 2 (12 hours) which must be completed before activity 5 can be started.

(5) *Calculate the minimum time required to complete each activity*, working backwards from the time required to complete the final activity.

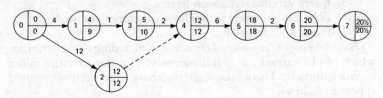

(6) *Plot the critical path* by identifying the activities at which the maximum and minimum completion times are identical and, therefore, critical.

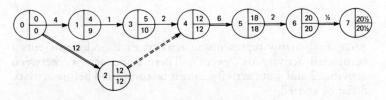

NOTE: Double line indicates the critical path.

From the *critical path* it can be seen that activities 2, 4, 5, 6 and 7 must be kept on schedule if the task is to be completed in 20½ hours. There is a leeway of five hours for the completion of tasks 1 and 3. However, should this leeway be exceeded the completion time would not be achieved.

The first phase of network planning outlined above can be followed by further phases using the first phase as a basis for the allocation of resources—staff and machines.

As was explained in Chapter 40, very sophisticated networks are prepared by computer. However, for such projects as planning training, conference organisation, system reorganisation or machinery installation, the office manager may well find a network useful.

Controlling costs

Perhaps one of the most crucial areas of management performance

Code	Item	Month 1				Month 2				Month 3			
		Budget	Actual	Variance	Variance to date	Budget	Actual	Variance	Variance to date	Budget	Actual	Variance	Variance to date
1.01	Staff salaries	1,200	1,180	+ 20	+ 20	1,200	1,295	− 95	− 75	1,200	1,230	− 30	− 105
1.02	National insurance	120	118	+ 2	+ 2	120	129	− 9	− 7	120	123	− 3	− 10
1.03	Pensions	120	98	+ 22	+ 22	130	115	+ 15	+ 37	120	115	+ 5	+ 42
1.04	Luncheon vouchers	45	44	+ 1	+ 1	60	63	− 3	− 2	52	49	+ 3	+ 1
1.05	Temporary staff	—	—	—	—	600	900	− 300	− 300	300	240	+ 60	− 240
2.01	Telephone	500	385	+ 115	+ 115	500	568	− 68	+ 47	500	467	+ 33	+ 80
2.02	Rentand rates	500	500	—	—	500	500	—	—	500	500	—	—
2.03	Electricity	100	79	+ 21	+ 21	100	115	− 15	+ 6	120	115	+ 5	+ 11
3.01	Travel and subsistence	—	18	− 18	− 18	200	165	+ 35	+ 17	100	113	− 13	+ 4
4.01	Training	500	—	+ 500	+ 500	500	780	− 280	+ 220	500	512	− 12	+ 208
5.01	Stationery	600	895	− 295	− 295	750	675	+ 75	− 220	600	560	+ 40	− 180
5.02	Ancillary equipment	50	30	+ 20	+ 20	50	32	+ 18	+ 38	50	48	+ 2	+ 40
5.03	Machine maintenance	—	—	—	—	—	16	− 16	− 16	148	148	—	− 16
5.04	Machine repairs	70	68	+ 2	+ 2	70	68	+ 2	+ 4	120	114	+ 6	+ 10
	Total	3,805	3,415	+ 390	+ 390	4,780	5,421	− 641	− 251	4,430	4,334	+ 96	− 155

Fig. 139 Budgetary control sheet showing monthly and cumulative variances.

is that of costs. It is essential to keep expenditure within the approved budget. Again a system of constant monitoring is essential to ensure that any over-expenditure is revealed immediately. Most large organisations have a system of producing budgetary control sheets showing budget variances each month so that managers can take action to reduce expenditure on any items which are above the limit. (A budgetary control sheet is illustrated in Fig. 139.) Where large items of expenditure are being considered it may be advisable to check with the finance department to ensure that it will be within the budget.

All staff should be cost conscious and should be encouraged to economise in any way which is not to the detriment of the work. Some suggestions are given below.

(1) Use telex instead of the telephone.

(2) Staff travelling for a conference, training course or other purpose should share transport when practicable.

(3) Buy stationery in bulk with part delivery or call-off delivery.

(4) Set reasonable maximum rates for hotel meals and accommodation for staff when travelling.

(5) Reduce the distribution of copies by circulating one copy to people who need only see it for information as distinct from taking action on it.

(6) Run off copies on two sides of the paper when practicable.

(7) Ensure that correct copy is sent to a printer to avoid corrections at proof stage.

(8) Ensure that everyone who uses a piece of equipment or a machine is trained to do so.

(9) Establish a system for reporting all faults on equipment and machines.

(10) Obtain quotations for equipment maintenance contracts.

(11) Make telephone calls after 1 p.m. whenever possible.

(12) Prepare telephone calls before dialling.

(13) Restrict private calls, perhaps by "busying" for S.T.D. calls on extensions where long-distance calls are not required for business purposes.

(14) Have small items of equipment, e.g. calculators, indelibly marked "stolen from (name of company)" so that people will hesitate to remove them from the premises.

(15) Use old forms and unused non-confidential copies for scrap pads.

There are many other ways of economising and the office manager should be constantly on the alert to identify them.

Assessing performance standards

However efficient, well liked and successful a manager may be, there is invariably room for some improvement. It is not easy to be objective in assessing oneself and one's own job performance, but it is a useful exercise. With the advent of staff appraisal this has become a more generally accepted part of career progress. There are three major questions to ask.

(1) What do I not do as well as it should or could be done?

(2) Why is my performance of that activity, or in that area, below standard?

(3) What action is necessary to bring my performance of that activity, or in that area, up to standard?

It may be that other people are involved and it may be that you must expect less than the best for reasons outside your own control. It may be that consultation with a superior, subordinates and/or colleagues is indicated. You may feel inadequate through lack of training in one particular aspect of your work. Identify the reason for your deficiency and take action. If you recognise your weaknesses and limitations you are halfway to curing them.

At the same time it is important to recognise your strengths. Perhaps one of the greatest strengths a manager can possess is the ability to recognise the strengths of individual subordinate staff. If the individual strength of yourself and your staff can be harnessed into a composite departmental effort the success of the department is your success.

Appendix I
Questions, Projects and Case Studies

Part 1 Questions

The questions have been grouped by main areas of office management rather than by the individual chapters in the book because most meaningful questions relate to more than one aspect of a topic. It is important to think in terms of the inter-relationship and integration of activities. Chapter references are indicated as a general guide, but the questions usually cover a wider range than that covered by a single chapter.

Some of the questions require the student to undertake research: often the answers may vary from one student to another depending on their experience and the organisation(s) with which they are familiar. Basic principles are fundamental but the student should elaborate these principles with real-life examples. Some of the questions may well be used for group discussion. At the beginning of each section are those questions from the fourth edition that have been retained. These are followed by questions from recent past examination papers of individual professional institutes. Permission to reproduce these is gratefully acknowledged. The institutes concerned are:

Association of Cost and Executive Accountants
The Institute of Administrative Accounting and Data Processing
The Institute of Administrative Management
The Institute of Chartered Secretaries and Administrators
The Institute of Cost and Management Accountants
The Institute of Health Service Administrators
The Institute of Marketing

SECTION I THE OFFICE MANAGEMENT FUNCTION (Chptrs. 1 and 2)
1. Analyse the purpose of an office giving examples of activities involved in fulfilling that purpose. (Ch. 1)
2. Consider the relationship of the office function to those of production and selling in a manufacturing business. Suggest some services the office can give them. (*IAM*) (Ch. 1)
3. Tabulate the basic clerical operations and indicate as comprehensively as possible the various means by which each can be performed. (Ch. 1)

4. Define the role of the office manager. (Ch. 2)
5. "As a result of technological development in the office the role of the office manager has changed and will continue to change." Discuss this statement giving your views for and/or against its truth. (Ch. 2)
6. Today office management is considered to be a specialist function. Discuss this statement and give your views as to how it compares with any other specialisation. (Ch. 2)
7. Prepare job descriptions for an office manager and an office supervisor indicating as clearly as you can the difference in duties and levels of responsibility. (Ch. 2)

Institute of Administrative Management
Approach to Office Administration I
8. How would you define work? Relate your answer particularly to the kinds of work found in an office. (1978) (Ch. 1)
9. "Office management has undergone and will continue to undergo drastic change." (P. W. Betts.) Discuss this statement indicating some of the more important changes that have taken place in the last 10 years and suggest some that might take place in the next 10 years. (1979) (Ch. 1)
10. What part should the Office Supervisor play in the translation of policy into action? (1979) (Ch. 1)

Approach to Organisation and Methods I
11. The managing director of an expanding firm is finding that the administrative aspects are taking up too much of his, and his technical staff's time and he is considering the appointment of an office manager as a solution. Describe the job of an office manager and the factors to be borne in mind when setting up such a position. (1979) (Ch. 2)

Institute of Chartered Secretaries and Administrators
Office Administration
12. It has been said that the first step in the application of systematic control over office routine is the analysis of that routine into its primary functions and subsequent analysis of these functions into individual tasks and groups of tasks. Discuss this statement and describe four primary functions which you would expect to find in the administration of an organisation. (1977) (Ch. 1)

Institute of Health Service Administrators
Principles of Organisation and Management I
13. "Surely the ultimate answer must be that there are certain essential features common to all managers' jobs and that there are also uniquenesses that distinguish every type of managerial job." (H. Mintzberg.) Do you agree? (1978) (Ch. 2)
14. What role can an administrator play as a member of the senior executive team of an organisation? (1979) (Ch. 2)
15. In order effectively to fulfil his or her duties, what management skills does an administrator need? (1979) (Ch. 2)

SECTION II   OFFICE ORGANISATION (Chptrs. 3–7)

1. Discuss the advantages and disadvantages of the centralisation of clerical work, giving examples from your own experience if possible. (Ch. 3)

2. Write brief notes on: (a) line organisation; (b) staff relationship; (c) lateral relationship; (d) functional responsibility; (e) span of control; (f) line of communication; (g) accountability; (h) division of responsibility.

3. When planning an office system, specialisation must be taken into account for a number of reasons. What are these reasons? (IHSA) (Ch. 3)

4. You have been appointed manager of an office employing 100 clerks responsible for accounts, wages and general clerical services. Assuming that you are familiar with the concern to which the office is attached, but not the office itself, summarise the steps you would take to get the measure of your responsibilities. (Ch. 3)

5. What are the major principles which contribute towards making an office organisation effective? (ICMA) (Ch. 3)

6. A small department is staffed by ten consultant engineers, each of whom has the assistance of one clerk/typist. The consultant engineers spend roughly half their time out of their offices but the demand they make on their assistants varies considerably. It is proposed to place the clerk/typists under the control of a senior clerk who would be responsible for providing a clerical and typing service to the consultant engineers. Comment on this proposal. (ICMA) (Ch. 3)

7. Comment on the following statement: "The real problem is to achieve that fine balance which on the one hand allows staff to exercise discretionary authority and initiative and on the other exercises a sufficient degree of control to ensure compliance with the company's long-term objectives". (ICMA) (Ch. 3)

8. Prepare a chart to illustrate a pattern of organisation for a large office which is based on a functional relationship. In what respects does this type of chart differ from one based upon "line relationships". (IAM) (Ch. 4)

9. Draw up an organisation chart for any office with which you are familiar. Comment on the effectiveness—or otherwise—of the organisation and suggest improvements (giving reasons) if appropriate. (Ch. 4)

10. The headquarters of a large organisation, comprising 800 staff, aim to move to new office accommodation on a ground floor and five other floors. The departments and approximate numbers of staff in each are: secretarial, including purchasing (180); accounting (80); operations (220); construction (230); personnel (70); research and development (20). The accounting department uses a digital computer and the construction department includes a large drawing office, a training section, and a print room; there will also be a canteen, several committee rooms, and a board room. Explain how you would prepare an outline allocation of departments and sections in the new building. (ICSA) (Ch. 5)

11. Your company is finding its present accommodation inadequate and it proposes to draw up a list of premises to which its office staff could be transferred. State the factors which could influence your ultimate choice. (ICMA) (Ch. 5)

12. Discuss individual working areas and the arrangements of desks in relation to different kinds of office work. (*IHSA*) (Ch. 6)

13. The posture assumed by a clerk at his desk can affect his standard of efficiency. Comment on this statement, mentioning the common faults in seating arrangements and how they can be remedied. (*IHSA*) (Ch. 6)

14. Functional design of desks and tables is of great importance and can make a valuable contribution to increased efficiency in the office. Describe the sections of the office to which this will apply and state the factors you would take into consideration before changing to functional and purpose designed office furniture. (*ICSA*) (Ch. 6)

15. Write notes on the following (inter alia): Office lighting, heating and ventilation. (*ICSA* Final.) (Ch. 7)

16. Explain the importance of physical surroundings in relation to concentrated mental work. (*IHSA*) (Ch. 7)

17. Discuss noise in relation to clerical work, and the ways in which noise can be reduced. (*IHSA*) (Ch. 7)

18. What are the factors to be taken into account when choosing the floor-covering for an office? Do you think the purchase of carpets or rugs can be justified? (*IHSA*) (Ch. 7)

19. To what extent do you consider the office manager should be concerned with safeguarding the health of members of his staff? (*IHSA*) (Ch. 7)

20. Give five common sources of distraction preventing concentration in offices. Suggest steps to reduce distraction arising from two of them. (*Inst. M.*) (Ch. 7)

21. Planning is necessary for the speedy and efficient handling of possible sudden sickness, faints, fits and accidents amongst office staff. Describe the various points you would provide for in the plan. (*AIA*) (Ch. 7) (Ch. 7)

Institute of Administrative Management papers (Ch. 7)
Approach to Office Administration I (Ch. 7)

22. What are the advantages and disadvantages of progressing a project by committee? (1977) (Ch. 3)

23. What is meant by line organisation? Discuss the advantages and disadvantages of having a line organisation. (1978) (Ch. 3)

Approach to Organisation and Methods I

24. The following terms are often used in discussing organisation. Explain how they are connected with each other. (*a*) Authority. (*b*) Responsibility. (*c*) Delegation. (*d*) Span of control. (1977) (Ch. 3)

25. Explain the essential differences between the "formal organisation" and "informal organisation". Using examples, from your own experience where possible, describe what significance informal organisation has for an O & M officer. (1977) (Ch. 3)

26. Your O & M unit is expanding, and a new manager has recently been appointed. It is an opportune time to reconsider the structure within the unit and also its position in the organisation. You are asked to provide the manager with some proposals, with a supporting theory, as to how the

unit should be structured and how it should relate to the rest of the organisation. (1978) (Ch. 3)

27. The design of organisation structures is an important aspect of O & M work. What guidelines should be borne in mind when designing a structure, and why are they important? (1978) (Ch. 3)

28. Describe and illustrate what is meant by a "line and staff" structure. Explain why it is found so frequently and say what problems might exist with such a structure. (1979) (Ch. 3)

29. Some organisations are structured on a "matrix" basis. Give your understanding of the main features of such a structure and the reasons for its adoption in certain circumstances. (1979) (Ch. 3)

30. What are the purposes of an organisation chart? Describe the facts that it can show. What are its limitations? Are these limitations sufficient to warrant their limited use in organisations? (1977) (Ch. 4)

People and Organisations I

31. What do you consider are the advantages and disadvantages for the individual of belonging to a group, and what might be the practical implications in the work situations? (1977) (Ch. 3)

32. Assess the contribution made by the "informal organisation" towards the achievement of organisational goals. (1979) (Ch. 3)

33. An organisation chart only shows one view of how an organisation works. Estimate the contribution of informal organisation towards achieving company objectives. (1977) (Ch. 4)

34. A manufacturing company has decided to rehouse its administrative staff of approximately 80 employees. You have been asked to design the new offices. Describe, and give reasons for, the type of layout you would choose and indicate the problems that might arise in the changeover. (1977) (Ch. 5)

35. Describe the main characteristics of an "open plan" office. Giving detailed practical examples, discuss how far your think the inherent conflict between the need for privacy and for communal facilities can be solved. (1978) (Ch. 5)

36. A company in South East England which manufactures micro-electronic components is thinking of setting up its head office in London. The site would house mainly research and development, marketing, legal and administrative functions, including centralised typing facilities. What factors would you need to consider when making such a decision? Describe the type of layout you might recommend, giving reasons for your choice. (1979) (Ch. 5)

37. Outline the statutory provisions and environmental factors which need to be considered when planning the layout of new office premises. (1979) (Ch. 5)

People, Organisation and Change II

38. Modern management thinking emphasises the importance of the individual at work. What organisational policies do you consider essential to ensure an individual's dignity of labour? (1979) (Ch. 3)

39. What are the fundamental principles governing organisation structures and how do they facilitate the achievement of organisational objectives? (1979) (Ch. 3)

40. What basic features should an organisation possess in order to fulfil its function as a mechanism for planning and controlling work? (1977) (Ch. 3)

Institute of Chartered Secretaries and Administrators
Office Administration

41. Distinguish between and give examples of: (*a*) vertical organisation; (*b*) horizontal organisation. Discuss the relative merits of each. (1978) (Ch. 3).

42. Office work can be analysed into a number of basic operations. Describe these operations and consider the advantages and disadvantages of specialisation in clerical work. (1978) (Ch. 3)

43. Due to the expansion of your administration it has been necessary to take over additional office space in a new building which follows the open-plan system. Many of the staff who moved there have reacted unfavourably about this situation and complain of excessive noise, various distractions and in some cases lack of privacy. Set out your recommendations on what should be done to overcome the difficulties without abandoning the open-plan system. (1977) (Ch. 5)

44. The existing accommodation of the purchasing department which has expanded over the past few years consists of a number of varying size rooms formed by movable partitioning. It has now become necessary to review and replan the available space for this department. Set out in detail the main points which must be considered in the replanning of this office. (1979) (Ch. 5)

45. You have been asked by the senior administrative officer of a commercial organisation to submit proposals for the re-arrangement of the lay-out of the General Office in which 25 staff are employed. Describe fully how you would proceed with this assignment. (1978) (Ch. 5)

46. It is considered that the existing office space in your organisation is not being used efficiently and effectively. Explain the important aspects to be considered in re-planning the office space available, and state the relevant legislation with which you should comply. (1978) (Ch. 5)

47. In planning accommodation for administration staff it is necessary to comply with the requirements of the Offices, Shops and Railway Premises Act. Explain the main provisions of this Act with which you must comply. (1979) (Ch. 5)

48. Discuss what you consider to be the most common defects in the physical accommodation provided for clerical staff and explain how these defects may be minimised. (1977) (Ch. 7)

49. "Most people probably regard office cleaning as a necessary evil. It is after all very costly . . . the cleaning and maintenance of a building over 15 to 20 years can equate to its construction cost". (*Professional Administration*, January 1978.) As office manager set out the main factors to be considered when deciding upon an office cleaning service and state how you would exercise control over its operation and cost. (1978) (Ch. 7)

Personnel: Principles and Policy
50. Organisations are sometimes compared with football teams: united by their desire to attain the common objective. Is this a realistic and appropriate analogy? (1977) (Ch. 3)
51. Discuss the contribution you think a personnel manger could make to the review and redesign of a corporate organisational structure. (1977) (Ch. 3).
52. It is known that the existence of work group norms can complicate management decision making. Why do such norms come into existence and what continuing functions do they serve? How far can or should management influence these norms? (1978) (Ch. 3)

Institute of Health Service Administrators
Principles of Organisation and Management
53. What factors determine the appropriateness of a centralised form of administration, and how do they apply to the health service? (1978) (Ch. 3)
54. ". . . throughout any administrative structure there should be a clear definition and allocation of responsibilities." Do you think this is (a) possible, (b) desirable? (1978) (Ch. 3)
55. Do you think that a matrix form of organisation structure could help resolve line and staff coordination difficulties in the health service? (1978) (Ch. 3)
56. What advice would you offer to an administrator involved in the planning of a major organisational change? Can the principles of scientific management be usefully applied in an organisation today? (1978) (Ch. 3)
57. Why are there often problems in the relationship between line and staff managers? (1978) (Ch. 3)
58. Is there an ideal size for an organisation? (1978) (Ch. 3)
59. Can committees be effective in decision making ? (1978) (Ch. 3)
60. What are the advantages of decentralisation? (1979) (Ch. 3)
61. What is a matrix organisation? (1979) (Ch. 3)
62. "Authority, status, and power are necessary for executive action." Are they necessary for effective administration? (1979) (Ch. 3)
63. What are the advantages of committees? (1979) (Ch. 3)
64. How would you define a decentralised organisation? (1979) (Ch. 3)
65. When is it worth while forming a committee? (1979) (Ch. 3)
66. What do you consider to be the key deficiencies of an organisation chart? (1978) (Ch. 4)
67. Do you consider organisation charts to be of any practical value? (1979) (Ch. 4)

SECTION III STAFF MANAGEMENT (Chptrs. 8–17)
1. What do you consider to be the essential personal qualities of an office manager? (Ch. 8)
2. Outline the duties of an office supervisor in charge of about thirty clerks (IAM) (Ch. 8)
3. Prepare a job description for the head of the mail department in a large organisation. The department is responsible for the collection, despatch,

etc., of incoming, internal and outgoing mail. (*ICSA*) (Ch. 8)

4. What steps can an office manager take to ensure that an equitable salary policy is applied in his office? (*IAM*) (Ch. 9)

5. The following additional staff is required for an expanding concern organised on modern lines: (*a*) accounts department manager to control a staff of five; (*b*) personal secretary/stenographer for managing director; (*c*) commissionaire; (*d*) clerk for general office duties. State the qualities you would look for in selecting personnel for these vacancies. (*ICSA* Inter) (Ch. 10)

6. In submitting an application for a new post, X gives the name of Y, his present employer, for reference purposes. Is Y under any legal obligation to give a reference as to X's character and ability? Would it make any difference if he gave only an oral reference? (*ICSA* Final) (Ch. 10)

7. You are required to interview candidates for an advertised vacancy on your staff. In order to save time, and to ensure that all essential questions are asked and answered, draft a form of application to be filled in by applicants for the appointment. (*ICMA*) (Ch. 10)

8. What are your views on the value of "previous experience" and "references" of candidates when selecting new staff? (*IHSA*) (Ch. 10)

9. How would an applicant for clerical work distinguish between a good and a bad interview with an office manager? How would the manager distinguish between a good and a bad applicant? (*IAM*) (Ch. 10)

10. Explain the purpose of quality rating systems. In your opinion, what degree of importance should be attached to qualify rating reports? (*IHSA*) (Ch. 10)

11. As secretary of a limited company, what policy would you adopt in connection with application for testimonials or character references from members of your clerical staff, either during their continuing service or on leaving? (*AIA*) (Ch. 10)

12. As a part of a recruitment policy, it is important that the applicants for jobs should know what the employer has to offer. State what information you, as an engagement officer, would feel it necessary to give to applicants. (*Inst.M.*) (Ch. 10)

13. Describe the practice of certain large companies which retain firms of "appointment selection consultants" to select candidates for executive appointments, and consider its merits and/or demerits (*a*) for the company concerned, and (*b*) for those seeking employment. (*ICSA*) (Ch. 10)

14. The main board of directors of your company have decided that a small division located fifty miles from the parent company, and which to date has been administered from head office, should now be administered locally. As senior administrator designate of the division, indicate the possible sources from which you would expect to recruit the office staff required. State also the arrangements you would make for the interview of prospective office staffs and the manner in which you would conduct such interviewing. (*ICSA*) (Ch. 10)

15. Compare the problems of recruitment, training and retention of: (*a*) office machine operators; (*b*) general clerical workers. (*ICMA*) (Ch. 10)

16. The rate of clerical staff turnover in your organisation has reached

alarming proportions, even though salaries and conditions compare quite favourably with those of other similar organisations in the area. It appears that the primary cause is that of "square pegs in round holes". You are asked to carry out an investigation and make recommendations for better recruitment aimed at reducing turnover to an acceptable level. State how you would carry out your investigation, what weaknesses in recruitment procedures you would look for, and what recommendations might be appropriate. (Ch. 10)

17. Draft a form suitable for keeping records relating to employees. In a large-scale undertaking, what method would you use to ensure quick reference to such records? (*ICSA* Inter.) (Ch. 10)

18. Do you consider staff promotions should be by ability or seniority? Give your reasons. (*IHSA*) (Ch. 12)

19. As office manager in charge of an office of some 200 clerks, prepare for the guidance of your subordinate supervisors a statement of policy and a programme for the progress of clerks. (*IAM*) (Ch. 12)

20. Factors of unpunctuality of attendance, sickness and other absenteeism, often enter into consideration in incremental and promotion prospects for clerical staff. How would you record this? (*AIA*) (Ch. 12)

21. A company which has successfully pursued a policy of promotion from within is now about to expand rapidly. Examine the case for continuing this policy. (*ICMA*) (Ch. 12)

22. State the factors likely to make a policy of promotion from within successful and the circumstances in which there is a danger of this policy failing. (*ICMA*) (Ch. 12)

23. Explain the steps you would take to ensure that the capabilities and merits of each officer receive full consideration when opportunities of promotion occur. (*IHSA*) (Ch. 12)

24. What methods of training are undertaken by employers? In what situations is each type of training appropriate? (Ch. 13)

25. There is no Industrial Training Board specifically for clerical training. What do you consider to be the advantages and disadvantages of having clerical employees under the umbrella of the ITB related to the organisation's type of industry? (Ch. 13)

26. In your opinion, what simple routine tasks should all members of the office staff be capable of performing satisfactorily though not necessarily with equal efficiency? Give reasons for your answer. (*IHSA*) (Ch. 13)

27. Define the fundamentals of effective training for clerical work. How would you prepare a training programme? (*IHSA*) (Ch. 13)

28. Imagine you are a section supervisor. No clerk on your section has had less than two years' service on the section. Explain how training is an important point of your normal duties. (*IAM*) (Ch. 13)

29. Set out the important stages in a training programme for office personnel. What precautions ought to be taken in preparing and implementing such a programme? (*ICSA*) (Ch. 13)

30. Write brief notes on the purpose and nature of the following: (*a*) induction training, (*b*) job rotation, (*c*) training for promotion. (*IAM*) (Ch. 13)

31. It is often said that the training of office staff presents problems which are not normally encountered with the training of factory operatives. Discuss this statement and outline what these problems are likely to be and how they should be overcome. (*ICSA*) (Ch. 13)

32. On appointment as head of the personnel department in a medium sized organisation, you consider that the training of administrative staff, particularly to prepare them for more senior positions, is inadequate. Prepare a memorandum for consideration by the board setting out your ideas on training programmes for such staff. Also show the benefits likely to accrue to both staff and management if your policy is adopted. (*ICSA*) (Ch. 13)

33. Following a series of thefts from the inward mail there are reasonable grounds for assuming that John Smith, an old and trusted employee, is responsible, but there is no definite proof. The Office Services Supervisor, who is responsible to you, wants to have Smith dismissed. How would you deal with the situation? (Ch. 14)

34. As a result of proposed reorganisation within your company it appears that a number of clerical posts are likely to become redundant within the next six months. State what steps you would take in this situation. (Ch. 14)

35. Draw up a set of conditions of employment for clerks covering such matters as working hours, overtime, meal breaks, holidays, sick pay and long-service privileges. (*IAM*) (Ch. 15)

36. Your employers are seriously concerned about the number of hours lost to production through bad time-keeping, and have requested you to see what can be done to improve time-keeping. In your capacity of secretary, prepare a report for your board, setting out the results of your inquiries and any recommendations you may wish to make. (*ICSA*) (Ch. 15)

37. State how you would organise and control rest periods and breaks for tea, coffee or the like within an office, indicating the benefits and disadvantages of such breaks, and what you regard as suitable lengths of time to be set aside for such purposes. (*ICSA*) (Ch. 15)

38. Certain members of your staff have put to you a proposal that there should be granted some freedom of choice in times of commencing and finishing work and breaks to be taken within the working day, whilst still maintaining the present total weekly working hours. The proposal is to be considered at the next meeting of the staff committee, and you are to prepare a memorandum setting out the management's views on the regulation of such a scheme and the restrictions which must be imposed in order to maintain the continuing efficient operation of the Office. (*ICSA*) (Ch. 15)

39. Your Managing Director is considering an incentive scheme for his senior administrative staff. In connection with such a scheme state: (*a*) the benefits which could be obtained, (*b*) the problems which need to be solved for its successful operation. (*ICSA*) (Ch. 16)

40. "A high salary is not necessarily an incentive to put forth the best effort". Comment on this statement. (*IHSA*) (Ch. 16)

41. Suggest eight factors which you consider would tend to reduce staff turnover in an organisation, placing them in what you consider their order

QUESTIONS, PROJECTS AND CASE STUDIES 577

of importance and giving your reasons for selecting this order. (*ICSA*) (Ch. 16)

42. One of the office staff is leaving and gives as the reason that he is not happy in his job. Prepare a list showing what should be reviewed regularly in order to avoid such a situation. (*IAM*) (Ch. 16)

43. What is meant by "job design"? Do you think it has any relevance for clerical jobs? Give reasons for your answer. (Ch. 16)

44. The Advisory, Conciliation and Arbitration Service (ACAS) has a number of functions. State what these functions are, giving brief explanations. (Ch. 17)

45. The Advisory Conciliation and Arbitration Service (ACAS) has published Codes of Practice. Name the Codes of Practice and outline the main provisions of each Code. (Ch. 17)

Institute of Administrative Management
Approach to Office Administration I

46. You have been asked to consider the appointment of a firm of office cleaners to service your firm's offices which consist of 20 rooms on 3 floors. Write a letter setting out their tasks as you see them. (1977) (Ch. 8)

47. As the person responsible for office administration of a group of companies, you are required to interview shortlisted applicants for the position of Office Manager for a member company of the Group. Prepare a checklist for use at the interview of: (*a*) information you would seek to obtain from applicants (include that which would appear on an application form); (*b*) information you would expect to be asked for by the applicants. (1977) (Ch. 10)

48. Provide an outline description, illustrated by examples from your own experience, of TWO accepted methods of assessing the work performance of an individual. (1977) (Ch. 11)

49. What, in your opinion, is the effect in the field of administration of legislation concerned with training? Ensure that you cover both the employee's and the employer's point of view. (1979) (Ch. 13)

50. Work, in the context of office administration, is often defined in terms of jobs, tasks, operations and elements. What do you understand by these terms? (1979) (Ch. 13)

51. What part should an office supervisor play in training his own staff? (1979) (Ch. 13)

52. Discuss the additional requirements which a manager responsible for employing personnel will have to take into account as a result of recent legislation in the field of redundancy. (1977) (Ch. 14)

53. Policy formation is principally the concern of senior management. In what ways might this process be supported and influenced by report and comment from the lower levels of staff in the organisation. (1978) (Ch. 16)

54. What might be the effect of an incentive scheme upon the quality and the output of office work? (1978) (Ch. 16)

55. How would you attempt to use a member of staff, who shows a

considerable degree of flair and initiative, in the work of a department which has mostly standardised procedures? (1977) (Ch. 16/17)

56. Set out the common law obligations of both employers and employees. (1977) (Ch. 17)

57. It is becoming more and more difficult for the administrative manager to keep abreast of all legislation affecting his area of responsibility. In this situation, how would you attempt to solve his problem? (1978) (Ch. 17)

58. Provide a broad outline of the rights acquired by employees under the Employment Protection Act 1975 and indicate any areas which may cause particular concern to an employer. (1978) (Ch. 17)

59. Assess the effects legislation on equal pay and sex discrimination has had upon the employment situation in the office. (1979) (Ch. 17)

60. The most economical aid to administration is the human being. Discuss this statement in relation to the clerical function. (1979) (Ch. 17)

61. Analyse some of the ineffective ways of dealing with people that you have observed and suggest how these methods might be made effective. (1979) (Ch. 17)

Approach to Organisation and Methods I

62. Design of the way in which work should be carried out is an important aspect of the O & M task. State, with reasons, what you believe to be the features of a job that encourage productivity and satisfaction in those doing the work. (1979) (Ch. 16)

63. In seeking to improve effectiveness it is important to consider the needs of both the people and the organisation. Describe what you see to be the needs of the people and the ways in which O & M activity can help both sets of needs to be met or can sometimes highlight the conflict with organisational needs. (1977) (Ch. 17)

Business Communication

64. Discuss the benefits of the programmed instruction method of training office staff. Highlight difficulties likely to be encountered if this method is employed. (1977) (Ch. 13)

65. Construct a chart which contains four different job categories of entrants to an organisation showing educational and work experience selection criteria and an appropriate planned training programme for each category. (1978) (Ch. 13)

66. (a) Two terms used in training are "learning curve" and "learning plateau". Sketch a graph to illustrate each of these and describe what each term means. (b) What do such curves and plateaux represent, and how can such information assist the development and assessment of training programmes? (1978) (Ch. 13)

67. As training officer for a medium sized organisation you have to develop a series of training programmes for clerical and manual workers. What basic factors have to be borne in mind when selecting appropriate training techniques? Describe briefly your teaching methods which may be eventually chosen. (1979) (Ch. 13)

68. A manager colleague, newly appointed to your organisation and seeking guidance from you, complains that his boss has counselled him to get more work done through his own work team and do less of it himself. Describe the advice you would offer your colleague to help him understand his boss's comment and thereby achieve more effective results. (1978) (Ch. 17)

People and Organisation I

69. Draw up a job description for ONE of the following: (a) a stock records clerk; (b) a forms controller. (1977) (Ch. 8)

70. What is a job description? How would you produce one and for what purposes might it be used? (1978) (Ch. 8)

71. In what way can recent government legislation and controls affect company pay structures? (1977) (Ch. 9)

72. Taking any one clerical job of your choice, describe the stages involved in carrying out a Job Analysis and explain how the information gained can be used. (1977) (Ch. 9)

73. Which do you consider is fairer—a pay structure based on management appraisal of performance or one based on age and length of service? How can the two viewpoints be reconciled into a single pay structure? (1977) (Ch. 9)

74. Choosing any one *analytical* method of job evaluation, describe the stage involved. (1977)

75. Describe The Institute of Administrative Management Job Grading Scheme. What do you consider are its main advantages? (1977) (Ch. 9)

76. In what ways should a salary structure reflect market factors? (1977) (Ch. 9)

77. What should be the main objectives of an organisation's salary policy? Outline the type of salary structure which you think best achieves these objectives. (1978) (Ch. 9)

78. What do you understand by: (a) job evaluation; and (b) merit rating? (1978) (Ch. 9)

79. The greatest problem personnel managers may now have to grapple with is that of employees, confronted with a definite limitation of monetary reward, seeking to establish a differential via fringe and non-monetary regards. Discuss. (1979) (Ch. 9)

80. Select an organisation and describe in detail the job evaluation system which you consider would be most applicable, giving reasons for your choice. (1979) (Ch. 9)

81. Formulate a salary structure which you would consider suitable for clerical staff of 20 years old and under. How would you incorporate it into the main salary structure of the organisation and what problems might arise? (1979) (Ch. 9)

82. Give a detailed description of any one merit rating scheme of your choice, commenting on its advantages and disadvantages, and discussing the basic principles of its administration. (1978) (Ch. 11)

83. How would you develop the potential of a supervisor in relation to the training and development of his subordinates? (1977) You are preparing for

a training session with some Clerical Supervisors, the title of the session being: "Effective ways of dealing with people". Outline a case history you might use to illustrate your talk. (1977) (Ch. 13)

84. Plan an induction programme for junior clerical employees and evaluate its contribution both to the company and to the employee. (1977) (Ch. 13)

85. The supervisor may discharge the training responsibility in a variety of ways. Describe THREE methods of training clerical staff. (1977) (Ch. 13)

86. How would you present a three-day training course on Human Relations for ten office supervisors, and what information would you expect to impart? (1978) (Ch. 13)

87. You have been appointed Head Office Training Officer to an engineering organisation employing approximately 200 Head Office staff. How would you define their training needs and how would you try to ensure that the training programmes you produce answer those needs? (1978) (Ch. 13)

88. Assess the role of the supervisor in the training and development of subordinates. (1979) (Ch. 13)

89. What principles of learning should be incorporated into an instruction programme? Mention any specific problems of learning you might encounter when retraining older workers and describe how you would try to deal with them. (1979) (Ch. 13)

90. The evaluation of training is a difficult but essential task. How can a training department determine the effectiveness of its services? (1979) (Ch. 13)

91. Comment on the concept of flexible working hours, and describe its main advantages and disadvantages to both employees and employers. If you were considering the introduction of flexible working hours into your organisation, what do you think would be the main factors which would need to be discussed? (1978) (Ch. 15)

92. What basic factors influence the formation of attitudes and to what extent can established attitudes be changed? (1977) (Ch. 16)

93. "The problem of motivating a work force whose primary needs have been met is a major task to-day". How best can this task be approached? (1977) (Ch. 16)

94. Why do people go to work? (1978) (Ch. 16)

95. The introduction of a financial incentive scheme for fifteen staff selling by telephone has been suggested in your organisation. What factors would you need to take into account when considering the suitability of such a proposal? (1978) (Ch. 16)

96. What do you consider to be the place of the supervisor in the management team? Justify your view, illustrating your answer with examples. (1977) (Ch. 17)

97. The responsibility of *all* employees for safety in the work place is now generally accepted in principle. How can such a comprehensive responsibility be ensured in practice? (1977) (Ch. 17)

98. Organisations are becoming more aware of their responsibility to retiring employees. What problems might such employees face and how

can they be helped in overcoming them by their employers? (1978) (Ch. 17)
99. "Responsibility for safety should be regarded as a normal management function". How does the Health and Safety at Work Act try to ensure this? (1978) (Ch. 17)
100. The responsibility for preventing industrial hazards and sickness should be pinned squarely on those who create them. What provisions in the Health and Safety at Work Act attempt to accomplish this? (1979) (Ch. 17)
101. Discuss the policies and practices which you think are most likely to satisfy the needs of an individual at work. (1979) (Ch. 17)

People, Organisation and Change II
102. The interview can often be an inaccurate selection technique. How can its accuracy be increased, both by the improvement of the interview itself and by the use of additional techniques? (1977) (Ch. 10)
103. You have been asked to recruit six additional technical clerks within the next two months. Describe the main stages of the recruitment process and indicate the problems most likely to arise and how they might be overcome. (1979) (Ch. 10)
104. "Staff appraisal is a time consuming administrative chore." How would you attempt to convince company middle management of the true value of a suitable appraisal scheme? (1977) (Ch. 11)
105. Staff appraisal has many different purposes. Specify the main purposes and describe ONE method of staff appraisal which you think most likely to achieve those purposes. Compare and contrast the underlying philosophy and methods of operation of traditional and objective-setting appraisal systems. (1978) (Ch. 11)
106. What is the best way to plan for internal career progression? (1977) (Ch. 12)
107. Discuss the relative advantages and disadvantages of promoting from within, and indicate the main problems involved in establishing a management training system based on internal promotion. (1977) (Ch. 12)
108. Despite the continuing emphasis on the need for equal opportunities for all, in practice problems still exist in the planning of a realistic career structure for women. Comment on these problems indicating, where possible, ways of overcoming them. (1979) (Ch. 12)
109. How would you design and run a training course in communication skills for middle managers? (1978) (Ch. 13)
110. How would you try to ensure management succession in an organisation? (1978) (Ch. 13)
111. You are the Training Manager of an engineering company employing approximately 700 personnel. Produce for presentation to the management board a training and development programme for the supervisors and managers of the company. (1979) (Ch. 13)
112. Identify the main functions of the Manpower Services Commission in relation to training and state what you believe have been the main achievements and problems so far. (1979) (Ch. 13)
113. Design an Induction Programme for professional staff, indicating the timing, duration and contents of the programme. Comment on the

benefits you would expect to gain for both employer and employee. (1979) (Ch. 13)

114. One result of technology has been to increase the number of boring jobs. What factors would you consider essential when looking at job design? (1977) (Ch. 16)

115. Describe in detail *two* approaches to man-management through which you would attempt to integrate personal goals with company objectives. (1977) (Ch. 16)

116. Why do individuals resist change at work and how best can such resistance be overcome? (1977) (Ch. 16)

117. What considerations underlie a successful approach to teambuilding? (1977) (Ch. 16)

118. "Decisions which come as a surprise tend to be an unpleasant surprise". How can employees be involved in decision making? (1977) (Ch. 16)

119. "Constructive forces for change often spring from below". How would such a view affect an organisation's structure? (1978) (Ch. 16)

120. Examine the position of the "loner", that is—a person who does not readily integrate into the team. Using your knowledge of motivation and communication, how would you react as a supervisor of a "loner" in this context? (1978) (Ch. 16)

121. There is an opportunity for redesigning some jobs in your organisation. What factors would you consider before attempting such a task and what benefits would you hope to achieve? (1978) (Ch. 16)

122. How would you attempt to measure the level of morale in your organisation and how accurate do you think your measurement would be? (1978) (Ch. 16)

123. How can the concept of staff participation in decision making be applied in an administrative department of twelve people? (1979) (Ch. 16)

124. Describe the main phases involved in carrying out a company manpower plan for a five year period. (1977) (Ch. 17)

125. "Management in future must be by consent, not by authority". Discuss this statement. (1977) (Ch. 17)

126. Outline TWO contrasting management styles and describe practical examples where each has been adopted successfully. (1978) (Ch. 17)

127. In what ways might the current theories on motivation be practically implemented in an organisation of your choice? (1978) (Ch. 17)

128. Describe the main purposes and characteristics of a management by objectives scheme. Are there shortcomings to this scheme? (1978) (Ch. 17)

129. You have recently been made supervisor of a group of eight audio typists. What management style would you adopt to ensure an efficient and happy work team? (1978) (Ch. 17)

130. Estimate the value of manpower planning to an organisation in today's environment. (1978) (Ch. 17)

131. Describe the type of data you would normally collect when formulating an organisational manpower plan, and assess the value and limitations that such a plan might have. (1979) (Ch. 17)

132. "All managers must delegate". How would you determine what to

delegate? What problems might you encounter and what benefits would you expect to gain? (1979) (Ch. 17)

Institute of Chartered Secretaries and Administrators
Communication
133. Draft a short talk which, as personnel officer, you would give to a small group of new junior employees on time-keeping. (1977) (Ch. 13)
134. Give two main aims of a firm's suggestion scheme. Give the main points you would incorporate in a scheme you were asked to devise. (1977) (Ch. 16)

Office Administration
135. Explain the objects and nature of a job grading scheme for administrative staff. (1977) (Ch. 9)
136. Your organisation has taken over several small companies, and has decided to centralise the main administration departments in a group office. It is found that there are now many anomalies in the administration of the wages and salaries structure and it is suggested that a new structure be introduced based on job evaluation and merit rating. You are required to prepare a memorandum explaining the concept of job evaluation and merit rating and state how you think the staff and the company might benefit from the introduction of such a scheme. (1978) (Ch. 9)
137. The supervisor of the typing pool is resigning from your organisation and as office manager you are to advertise for a replacement. Draft the advertisement as you wish it to appear in the press and state the qualities your interviewing panel should be looking for in the successful applicant. (1979) (Ch. 10)
138. It is proposed to issue a staff handbook to each new employee joining your organisation. Relating your answer to a specific type of organisation of your choice, describe the form the staff handbook might take and indicate the information it is likely to contain. (1977) (Ch. 10)
139. It has been decided to engage six additional trainee administrative managers from 1st September and it has been agreed that a suitable induction course should be prepared for them. Outline the main items which should be included in such an induction programme and state what benefits are likely to accrue to the new members of staff. (1979) (Ch. 13)
140. In an article on flexible working hours in *Professional Administration*, May 1976 the author expressed surprise at the small percentage of the working population who had adopted this system of working. He stated that from the employer's point of view there are many disadvantages. Explain fully what these disadvantages are and suggest what may be done to overcome them. (1977) (Ch. 15)
141. In your role as office manager state the advice you would give your section heads on the subject of delegation. (Ch. 17)

Personnel: Principles and Policy
142. What are the strengths and weaknesses of job evaluation? (1977) (Ch. 9)

143. What are the economic and other arguments in favour of "payment by results" wage systems? Why are the supposed benefits of such systems rarely achieved in practice? (1977) (Ch. 9)

144. What are the advantages and limitations of job evaluation as a way of settling problems of wage differentials? (1979) (Ch. 9)

145. Comment on the usefulness of the seven point plan for the classification of people and as a guide in the selection process. (1977) (Ch. 10)

146. Discuss the elements of what you would consider to be a good recruitment (as distinct from selection) policy. (1978) (Ch. 10)

147. "The reliability and validity of the interview is usually so low as to render it practically useless as a selection technique." To what extent is this true? (1978) (Ch. 10)

148. What steps would you take to meet the major criticisms of the interview as a selection procedure? (1979) (Ch. 10)

149. Review the arguments for and against the use of tests in a selection procedure. (1977) (Ch. 10)

150. What are the components of an effective appraisal scheme? (1977) (Ch. 11)

151. Assess the validity of the reasons usually advanced in favour of a formal, systematic appraisal scheme. Why is an effective appraisal scheme so difficult to achieve in practice? (1978) (Ch. 11)

152. Clarify what you would consider to be appropriate objectives for a performance appraisal system, and indicate the criteria which should be met if such a system is to be successful in attaining its objectives. (1979) (Ch. 11)

153. What is "leadership"? To what extent can the ability to lead be developed in people by means of training? (1977) (Ch. 13)

154. Discuss the importance of an analysis of training needs as a foundation for effective training within an organisation. (1977) (Ch. 13)

155. What is the difference between "training" and "development" when these terms are incorporated in such phrases as "management training" and "management development"? (1978) (Ch. 13)

156. Indicate the practical problems which a personnel manager might have to overcome in dealing with a major collective (i.e. not purely individual) redundancy. (1977) (Ch. 14)

157. Examine and assess the problems you see for the personnel manager in devising, implementing and controlling a dismissals procedure. (1978) (Ch. 14)

158. Write a guide, as if addressed to a newly-promoted manager, on all relevant aspects of the conduct of a disciplinary interview. (1978) (Ch. 16)

159. What are the arguments for employee participation in management decisions? How can such an aim be implemented? (1977) (Ch. 16)

160. Discuss the problems involved in measuring and assessing the causes of labour turnover in an organisation. (1977) (Ch. 16)

161. What do you predict will be the major trends in employee attitudes to work over the next decade, and how best can personnel managers prepare themselves to meet these trends? (1977) (Ch. 16)

162. What do you understand by "employee welfare"? What place has

there been for it, what place has it now, and what place do you envisage for it in the future. (1977) (Ch. 16)

163. Prepare an assessment of the advantages and disadvantages of an employee suggestion scheme (incorporating financial or other rewards) and show how such a scheme might be administered. (1978) (Ch. 16)

164. What is "morale"? What is the precise relationship, if any, between productivity, morale, and other indices of employee behaviour? (1978) (Ch. 16)

165. What is the evidence for the assertion that, in general, manual and non-manual workers hold different attitudes towards their work? What could or should be done about such a state of affairs? (1978) (Ch. 16)

166. "When unemployment is high, workers are more concerned with job security than with job satisfaction". What evidence is there to support or refute this contention? (1978) (Ch. 16)

167. Discuss the place of financial incentive schemes in what you would consider to be a sound wages and salary policy. Where possible, illustrate your answer with examples. (1978) (Ch. 16)

168. "There is little or no evidence to support the hypothesis that man has needs or that these needs are arranged in a hierarchy." Evaluate this view, and discuss its implications for an analysis of the behaviour of people at work. (1979) (Ch. 16)

169. It is increasingly held that status differences (in terms of working conditions, hours of work, payment systems, etc.) between different groups of employees are undesirable and should be removed. Indicate the arguments for and against such a change. (1979) (Ch. 16)

170. Discuss the possible meanings of the term "participation" when used in an industrial/commercial context. How far do you believe that "participation" holds any promise of improving industrial relations? (1979) (Ch. 16)

171. Can you give the concept of "job satisfaction" any precise meaning? What, if anything, can and should the personnel manager do about it in his own organisation? (1979) (Ch. 16)

172. What *skills* (as opposed to knowledge) does the personnel manager need if he is to perform effectively? (1977) (Ch. 17)

173. "The trouble with human relations is that it creates the very problems it is designed to solve. It encourages people to pick at the scabs of their psychic wounds." (Professor Malcolm McNair, *Harvard Business Review*.) Is this a justifiable charge? (1977) (Ch. 17)

174. Outline the precise relationship between the formulation of organisational objectives and the effective execution of manpower planning. Illustrate your answer, where appropriate, with practical examples. (1977) (Ch. 17)

175. Evaluate the role of law in industrial relations. (1977) (Ch. 17)

176. "Manpower planning is just another name for personnel management." Discuss. (1977) (Ch. 17)

177. How would you go about the formulation of a written personnel policy for an organisation? (1978) (Ch. 17)

178. From a management point of view, are trade unions desirable or not?

Justify your views. (1978) (Ch. 17)
179. Discuss the argument that the effective personnel manager nowadays requires specialist training in the behavioural sciences. (1978) (Ch. 17)
180. Outline the role which you think the personnel manager should play in the formulation and administration of an effective safety policy in an organisation. (1978) (Ch. 17)
181. "Manpower planning is now the central aspect of the personnel function." Discuss and account for the growing emphasis on manpower planning. (1978) (Ch. 17)
182. "Management always gets the shop stewards it deserves." To what extent do you regard this as an adequate analysis of the industrial relations climate in an organisation? (1978) (Ch. 17)
183. Discuss with appropriate examples the changing impact of the law on the personnel function. (1979) (Ch. 17)
184. Discuss the extent to which, in your view, it is possible to regard the elimination of industrial conflict as an attainable objective. (1979) (Ch. 17)
185. What are the necessary ingredients of an organisation's safety policy? How should it be evaluated, implemented and maintained? (1979) (Ch. 17)

Institute of Health Service Administrators
Principles of Organisation and Management I
186. What have motivational theorists to offer the practising administrator in the health service? (1978) (Ch. 16)
187. Is job enrichment merely a method of extracting more work from the same number of staff? (1978) (Ch. 16)
188. Can a manager learn to be a good leader? (1978) (Ch. 16)
189. What is "human asset accounting"? (1978) (Ch. 16)
190. ". . . for most men working does not simply function as a means of earning a livelihood" (Morse and Weiss). Do you agree? (1978) (Ch. 16)
191. What is "job satisfaction", and can it be measured? (1979) (Ch. 16)
192. Which of the various theories of motivation to work do you consider of most practical value? (1979) (Ch. 16)
193. What is job enlargement? (1979) (Ch. 16)
194. In 1977 Abrahamson published *Bureaucracy or Participation*. Can there be participation within a bureaucracy? (1979) (Ch. 16)
195. What advice should be offered to a manager concerning delegation? (1978) (Ch. 17)
196. Describe how one author you have read has assisted your understanding of management? (1978) (Ch. 17)
197. "Bureaucratic organisations tend to have rigid job definitions, poor communications, long decision time, and poor ability to react to changes in their environment." Do you agree? (1978) (Ch. 17)
198. "Administrators could not be experts in personnel management; they must have personnel managers. What they were responsible for was the style of management" (Lady McCarthy). How do you interpret this statement? (1979) (Ch. 17)
199. "A manager gets things done through other people" (Rosemary

Stewart). In practice how is this achieved? (1979) (Ch. 17)

200. What is the best way to ensure efficient decision-making within an organisation? (1979) (Ch. 17)

201. Is it possible to learn to be a leader? (1979) (Ch. 17)

Personnel and Labour Relations II

202. What are the principal methods of remuneration in British industry and what factors would you take into account in choosing an appropriate method for a particular group of employees? (1978) (Ch. 9)

203. In what ways are job description and personnel specification documents important in selection procedures? (1979) (Ch. 10)

204. Comment on the value of (a) assessors and (b) references in selection procedures for senior staff. (1979) (Ch. 10)

205. "Since the proportion of married women in the working population continues to rise, their employment can no longer be regarded simply as a necessary expedient in times of labour shortage. A much more positive attitude is required." Discuss the practical implications of this quotation. (1979) (Ch. 12)

206. "Health authorities cannot develop administrators; they must be expected to develop themselves." Discuss this statement in the light of current training policies. (1978) (Ch. 13)

207. Describe the methods which should be used to assess staff training needs and to evaluate the effectiveness of the training subsequently provided. (1979) (Ch. 13)

208. Outline a satisfactory procedure for dealing with the staffing problems which arise from the decision to close a hospital. (1978) (Ch. 14)

209. Outline and justify a model discipline and dismissal procedure for an Area Health Authority (in Scotland, a Health Board) indicating briefly the separate stages and the responsibilities and roles performed at each stage. (1978) (Ch. 14)

210. What are the main techniques of participative management? What evidence is there that they are practised in the NHS? (1979) (Ch. 14)

211. What difficulties are involved in measuring labour turnover, and what use can the personnel manager make of such measurements? (1978) (Ch. 16)

212. "One of the main objectives of manpower planning is to ensure that the right staff are in the right place at the right time." What are the main factors which have to be taken into account if this objective is to be achieved by a Health Authority? What external pressures may inhibit its own attempts to formulate an effective manpower plan? (1978) (Ch. 17)

213. Analyse the distinction between the roles of the specialist personnel manager and the line managers who are responsible for staff working in their departments. (1978) (Ch. 17)

214. Distinguish between the terms consultation, negotiation and participation. What factors will influence their existence and development within an organisation? (1978) (Ch. 17)

215. The portering department in a hospital which you administer is causing great anxiety. Staffing has recently fallen well below establish-

ment, labour turnover and absenteeism have suddenly increased to an alarming rate, and there have been several complaints about lack of concern being shown to patients and of insolence towards professional members of staff. Whenever approached about these matters the Head Porter simply protests that he cannot recruit suitable staff, and yesterday he burst out that "the porters resent the stuck-up attitudes of doctors and nurses and there will be trouble if things go on like this." What action would you take immediately to prevent any further deterioration in this situation, and in the long term to try to improve matters? (1979) (Ch. 17)
216. What information should an area personnel department have available in order to carry out meaningful manpower planning in its area? (1979) (Ch. 17)

SECTION IV COMMUNICATION SYSTEMS (Chptrs. 18 to 28)

1. You have been asked to report upon telephone systems suitable for internal and external purposes. In particular your report has to deal with (a) a small office in which ten personnel are located at three different floor levels, and (b) an office in which 200 personnel are located in one open-plan building. In the latter case, it is frequently necessary to communicate with a warehouse located twenty miles away. (ICSA) (Ch. 20)
2. It has been decided by the undertaking which employs you as office manager to install an internal telephone system to serve twenty offices. Prepare a report to your chief executive explaining the various systems which could be installed and the one you would recommend, giving reasons for your choice. (ICSA Final) (Ch. 20)
3. Give brief descriptions of three different "staff location" systems. (IHSA) (Ch. 20)
4. What personal qualities would you look for when engaging a telephone operator? Which do you consider the most important, and why? (IAM) (Ch. 21)
5. You are employed by a corporate body and you are asked to investigate its expenditure on telephone services. What steps would you take and how would you control such expenditure? (IHSA) (Ch. 21)
6. Propose a system for use by the receptionist or telephone operator for ensuring that calls, inquiries and messages for company officers (who are not immediately available) are handled efficiently. (AIA) (Ch. 21)
7. Describe the following communication systems, giving details of how each can be used: (a) telex; (b) direct-facsimile transmission equipment; (c) PAX, PBX, and PABX. (ICMA) (Ch. 22)
8. Explain the Post Office services available (a) to give faster delivery than ordinary mail; (b) to provide security for the contents of letters and packages. Explain the Datel and Datapost services. (Ch. 23)
9. Draft a staff circular on the subject of absence due to sickness. (ICSA Inter) (Ch. 24)
10. Draft a letter of appointment to a new employee after thirteen weeks, bearing in mind the statutory requirements of such a letter. (Ch. 24)

11. As office manager, you have to submit a memorandum to the secretary of your organisation about the uses and efficiency of three machines coming under your control. Prepare the memorandum. (*ICSA*) (Ch. 24)
12. Much time can be saved by the use of standardised replies in answering routine correspondence. Enumerate the other advantages and disadvantages of such standardisation and state your recommendations. (*ICMA*) (Ch. 24)
13. The cost of business letters to an organisation can be considerable. What are the constituents of their cost, and how might this be reduced? (*ICMA*) (Ch. 24)
14. In what circumstances might the use of "blitz" replies be acceptable? (Ch. 24)
15. Write a report recommending the introduction of certain staff amenities, stating the cost involved and the advantages which may accrue to the employer. (*ICSA* Inter) (Ch. 25)
16. Draft a report for your manager on a member of your staff who is to be considered for promotion to a higher grade. (Marks will be awarded for clarity, layout and the use of headings.) (*IAM*) (Ch. 25)
17. "Information placed before management in the form of special reports is of little value unless it assists the formation of judgement and decisions being taken." State what you consider to be the most important points in preparing special reports. (*Inst. M*) (Ch. 25)
18. "Management must be made aware of the increasing importance of maintaining good communications, both internal and external". Why are good communications so important, and what oral, written and visual methods of communication are available to those responsible for management? (*ICSA*) (Ch. 26)
19. Discuss the various types of dictation recording machines and the features which make some types more suitable than others for particular tasks. (*IHSA*) (Ch. 27)
20. What are the advantages and disadvantages (if any) of audio-typing pools from the point of the dictaters and of the transcribers. (Ch. 27)
21. There are various means of communicating information; list as many methods as you can, giving the advantages and disadvantages of each. (*IAM*) (Ch. 27)
22. "An efficient communication service is one in which the means selected in any particular case are adequate, taking into account all relevant factors, including cost". State the major factors to be considered when arriving at a decision as to the means of communication to be used. (*Inst.M*) (Ch. 27)
23. "The electric typewriter has ousted the manual typewriter; the day is coming when the word processor will oust the electric typewriter." Comment on this statement.
24. You are administrative manager in a manufacturing organisation employing 3,000. A deputation of the senior managers' secretaries comes to you asking that the company should look into the possibility of installing word processors. Assuming that you agreed to their request, what action would you take?
25. What factors have to be taken into consideration when deciding

whether or not to install word processing? If a decision is taken to install, what factors are important when deciding which machine to have?

Institute of Administrative Accounting and Data Processing
Business Communications

26. What, in your view, are the main advantages of the spoken word over all other forms of business communication? (1978) (Ch. 18)

27. What is a cliche? Give ten examples of cliches in all too common use. (1978) (Ch. 18)

28. What types of redundancy are common in written communications? (1978) (Ch. 18)

29. On which important points would you give advice to anyone drawing up a company's press releases? (1979) (Ch. 18)

30. Much, though not all, of the responsibility for the effectiveness of a board or committee meeting can depend on the chairman. What can an individual member do to help make a meeting as effective as possible? (1977) (Ch. 19)

31. It is very important for a speaker to maintain contact with his audience. How do you suggest this be achieved? (1978) (Ch. 19)

32. If you were given the opportunity to check a reproduction of your speaking voice on tape to what points would you pay particular attention? (1978) (Ch. 19)

33. What do you consider to be a good platform manner for the public speaker? (1978) (Ch. 19)

34. What are the four principal methods of delivering an oral presentation and which do you recommend speakers to use? Give reasons. (1979) (Ch. 19)

35. In communicating there are certain advantages in what are known as "face-to-face exchanges". Enumerate those known to you. (1977) (Ch. 19)

36. Explain the initial steps that might be taken in dealing with the inward mail of a large business organisation. (1979) (Business Knowledge paper) (Ch. 23)

37. Write a letter to a customer of yours asking for payment of a debt which you feel has been outstanding for an unreasonable period. (1977) (Ch. 24)

38. Write a letter on behalf of your junior accounting colleagues enquiring about courses being run at your local college. (1978) (Ch. 23)

39. What is the purpose of the memorandum in business communications and to what particular points would you pay attention when writing a memorandum? (1978) (Ch. 23)

40. Why is it generally felt that concise writing is important in business communications? (1979) (Ch. 23)

41. Why is it important for an organisation to ensure it sends out sound business letters? (1979) (Ch. 23)

42. Assume that the training division of your company has conducted a weekend seminar for its employees studying for professional examinations. As one of the delegates write a report on the seminar for the company's chief accountant. (1977) (Ch. 25)

43. Write a report to your Chief Accountant on the current state of credit control in your organisation. Note: marks will be allotted for *form* as well as *content*. (1978) (Ch. 25)

44. List at least six different reports which are produced from time to time in most business organisations. (1978) (Ch. 25)

45. A "bibliography" and/or an "appendix" often appear in written reports. What is the difference between them? (1979) (Ch. 25)

46. Outline the circumstances where graphic forms of presentation are to be preferred in the communicating process. (1977) (Ch. 26)

47. The turnover of a particular company for the months of 1975 and 1976 was as follows:

	1975 £'000	1976 £'000		1975 £'000	1976 £'000
January	70	75	July	320	347
February	80	83	August	250	297
March	86	95	September	187	204
April	98	107	October	123	135
May	108	125	November	104	127
June	276	300	December	55	57

You are required to illustrate the situation throughout 1976 by means of a "Z" chart. (1977) (Ch. 26)

48. A company's sales over a five year period were as follows:

1971	£100,000
1972	£120,000
1973	£130,000
1974	£150,000
1975	£140,000

Over the same period its costs were made up as follows:

	1971	1972	1973	1974	1975
Material	£20,000	£22,000	£23,000	£25,000	£26,000
Labour	18,000	25,000	27,000	33,000	37,000
Works expenses	17,000	19,000	20,000	22,000	22,000
Admin. expenses	10,000	12,000	14,000	16,000	17,000
Sales expenses	8,000	10,000	13,000	15,000	16,000

Illustrate these figures and include the element of profit made, for inclusion in the Directors' Report by means of a natural band chart. (1977) (Ch. 26)

49. "One picture is worth a thousand words." How, in your view, should this statement be applied by those who are actively engaged in business communications? (1977) (Ch. 26)

50. Suggest a suitable type of chart or diagram to show the following: (a) progress of work being made in the completion of a plan; (b) the circulation of *The English News* in each county in the UK; (c) the division of a product's total costs into seven main categories. (1978) (Ch. 26)

51. List four visual aids (in addition to textual and tabular infirmation)

which you would expect to find in the report of a public company. Write notes briefly on any two of these aids. (1978) (Ch. 26)

52. Summarise the utility of bar graphs in the presentation of management information. (1979) (Ch. 26)

53. Illustrate the difference between simple bar charts, compound bar charts and component bar charts. (1978) (Ch. 26)

54. If you were asked to give a lecture to employees of your company on the work done in its accounting department which visual aids would be useful to you in your task? (1979) (Ch. 26)

55. What do you understand by the term "Gantt chart" and in which business function is it normally used? (1979) (Ch. 26)

56. Indicate six different types of charts and graphs which can be used in conjunction with either a flip-chart or blackboard. (1979) (Ch. 26)

57. Discuss the circumstances in which you feel a graph may be considered superior to other forms of communication. (1979) (Ch. 26)

58. The managing director of your company is considering the purchase of a dictating machine and seeks your advice. Submit a report to your managing director, clearly stating the advantages and disadvantages as to the use of such a machine. (1979) (Business Knowledge paper) (Ch. 27)

Institute of Administrative Management
Approach to Office Administration

59. It is said that different management styles demand different communication processes. Do you agree with this statement? Give reasons for your views and use examples to support your argument. (1977) (Ch. 18)

60. You have recently been appointed as a manager in an organisation. (Name your own choice.) The time is opportune to review the communication processes. To do this you have decided to brief your subordinates on what you expect from them and to learn from them what they expect from you. Describe the potential benefits you hope to gain for the communication process by adopting this "expectations approach". (1977) (Ch. 18)

61. You are to address a group of newly appointed office supervisors on the subject of: "The place of the supervisor in the pattern of communication." What are the main points that would be covered in your talk and why are they important? (1977) (Ch. 18)

Approach to Organisation and Methods

62. What are the main difficulties in curbing the ever-increasing amount of paper work circulating in and among organisations? What developments do you think could help reverse this trend? (1978) (Ch. 18)

63. You have been asked to assist the manager of a large department by designing a revised information system. Describe how you would tackle such an assignment and give details of the facts you would require. (1978) (Ch. 18)

64. Describe your approach to fact-finding interviewing and elaborate on any differences that would arise when interviewing a middle manager as opposed to clerical staff. (1978) (Ch. 19)

65. "The quality of the O & M report is the key to achieving implementation of recommendations." Discuss this statement. (1979) (Ch. 25)

66. What are "terms of reference"? Why are they important and what should be done, both before and after formulating them, to ensure that they are of most benefit? (1979) (Ch. 25)

67. Discuss the benefits and disadvantages which can result from the centralisation of typing services. (1977) (Ch. 28)

68. A senior manager in your organisation has read of the benefits to be gained from the acquisition of word processing systems and has asked for advice from the O & M branch. Write a note advising this manager of the nature of such systems and also of the considerations you think he ought to take into account should he decide to establish word processing. (1978) (Ch. 28)

Business Communications

69. As a line manager indicate what you would take in your daily work to ensure that your skills in communication and your consideration for good human relations at work are complementary to each other. (1977) (Ch. 18)

70. Recent government legislation places heavy demands upon managers who are required not only to keep up-to-date with legislation but also to apply those practices in which they are concerned. As administrative manager of a company, show how you would ensure that all its managers are provided with the information they require. Show how you would ensure the managers were equipped to implement the changes needed to be made in existing and new practices. State how you would ensure their responsibilities were being adequately met. (1977) (Ch. 18)

71. (a) List TEN means by which organisations may communicate information to employees; and (b) Discuss briefly the advantages and shortcomings of any TWO of the methods you have listed which encourage feedback. (1978) (Ch. 18)

72. There is a widespread acceptance that organisations will benefit by increasing employee participation. What communication channels need to be developed by management to encourage participation? (1978) (Ch. 18)

73. You are supervisor in an office. The company for whom you work has recently taken over another company in the same line of business; in fact they barely avoided the attentions of the Monopolies Commission. Your department can just cope with the flow of work, and you know that this is soon to be increased. Accordingly you know that the departmental staff will probably have to be increased by about 50 per cent. At this stage you hear from a reliable source that there are rumours of impending redundancies. What are the dangers involved in taking no action? What do you think should be done at this stage? (1979) (Ch. 18)

74. With regard to the following, state what channels of communication you would use:

(a) publicising a suggestion scheme; (b) a reprimand on a minor matter; (c) details of increased output by the company; (d) notice of an informal meeting. (1979) (Ch. 18)

75. Despite the fact that your management is receiving large volumes of information it is felt that their efficiency as managers is declining. What facts are likely to emerge from an investigation into this problem? Suggest possible solutions. (1979) (Ch. 18)

76. A new administration building is being planned for your organisation. As communications manager you have been invited to participate in the preliminary design and planning operations. What basic factors will have to be defined which will eventually affect your responsibility area? (1979) (Ch. 18)

77. An organisation is having problems in communicating with members of its staff who spend only a small part of the day in their offices. Certain key personnel driving company cars may also have to visit customers during the course of their duties. Describe the modern systems of communications which may be used to solve the problems of this organisation. (Ch. 18)

78. Suggest four possible methods of despatching information from one location to another, and discuss how far modern developments are likely to supersede the conventional postal method. (1979) (Ch. 19)

79. Describe the significant stages in preparing for and delivering a formal presentation to a large group of managers in an organisation of your choice. (1977) (Ch. 19)

80. Interviews take place for different purposes (selection, disciplinary, grievance, appraisal etc.). Notwithstanding the purpose, what general attributes should all interviews possess? (1978) (Ch. 19)

81. What are the advantages and disadvantages of informal lecturing and discussion techniques when used with a group of people who need the information to do their jobs? (1979) (Ch. 19)

82. Describe administrative practices necessary for controlling capital and revenue expenditures associated with telecommunications services in large organisations employing a variety of media. (1977) (Ch. 20)

83. What main purposes are served by a telephone switchboard in large organisations? What telephone services/facilities are available which will economically augment an orthodox but overloaded switchboard? Briefly justify your recommendations. (1977) (Ch. 20)

84. It has been said that telephone system planning is concerned with something much more than the physical installation of telephones. What, in your view, comprises the "something much more" which must be considered when planning a telephone system? (1978) (Ch. 20)

85. Describe types of telephone instruments and facilities (or sub systems of the main system/s) for the following areas in an organisation.
(a) Sales office. (b) Factory floor. (c) Senior executives area. (d) General office. (1978) (Ch. 20)

86. Your managing director has read about modern equipment for logging and analysing company telephone calls. Prepare a report for him outlining the benefits your company might expect to get from installing such equipment. (1978) (Ch. 20)

87. What facilities are available on a PABX system in addition to those which could be obtained on a manual exchange? Write notes on four of these. (1979) (Ch. 20)

88. Define the role of a telecommunications manager. Describe and contrast his administrative and managerial responsibilities. How may his performance be measured? (1978) (Ch. 20)

89. Organisations are now acquiring costly computer controlled telecommunications systems. What might be the justification for such expenditures? What services and facilities can this sort of equipment offer over and above more conventional and less expensive equipment? (1978) (Ch. 20–21)

90. A firm employs drivers and sales representatives who need to communicate with headquarters even when they are working in other parts of the country. Describe the telephone services which may be used to provide the necessary contact between the firm and its employees. (Ch. 21)

91. As office manager, you are concerned about the shortcomings in the range of telecommunication services available in your organisation. Write a report to your superior outlining these shortcomings, and include a summary of the benefits to be obtained from using telex. (1977) (Ch. 22)

92. Describe the type of organisation where a private telegraph network is likely to be used in addition to telex facilities. Identify the main components of a typical private network and summarise the potential benefits it is likely to afford. (1977) (Ch. 22)

93. Facsimile and telex have co-existed for a number of years. Describe the principal differences between these two modes of communication. State why telex system growth has been greater than that of facsimile. (1978) (Ch. 20–22)

94. Your firm has a system of processing the incoming mail involving the use of clerical staff in charge of an office supervisor who, as a team, report for this special duty at 8.30 a.m. each day. Prepare a procedure which should control the security of incoming cash and cheques as well as documents and letters of a confidential nature. (1977) (Ch. 23)

95. The once common practice of employing postal messengers/clerks to undertake a variety of duties is fast diminishing in contemporary administration. Why is this so? What tasks are associated with such jobs and by what alternative means might they be accomplished? (1977) (Ch. 23)

96. State the importance of the Post Office postal coding system to the Post Office and service users. Indicate what occurs when the postal code is omitted from an address. Describe the extent to which the system is used and what the limitations are that constrain expansion. (1977) (Ch. 23)

97. Describe any FOUR of the following Post Office Services: recorded postal delivery; registered post FAX; business reply service; confravision; P.O Box numbers. (1977) (Ch. 23)

98. Describe THREE of the following Post Office services; datapost; freepost; viewdata; closed circuit television. (1978) (Ch. 23)

99. As a firm increases in size so the demand for service from a post room increases too. Describe with reasons the progression through the various levels of mechanisation. (1979) (Ch. 23)

100. Describe briefly the kinds of communications services, both internal and external, that could be used by an industrial undertaking with a factory and head office in the Scottish lowlands, and sales and after-sales service depots in four main U.K. towns and an overseas centre. (1979) (Ch. 23)

101. How can you ensure that cheques and cash are correctly handled within your organisation? (1979) (Ch. 23)

102. The Post Office offers a wide range of postal services. Describe in details the systems available for satisfying the following types of commercial need. (*a*) Large volumes of low value standard packages. (*b*) Returning valuable watches and cameras to customers after repair. (*c*) Final reminders sent to debtors threatening legal action. (*d*) Persuading potential customers to respond to an advertising campaign promoted in a national magazine. (1979) (Ch. 23)

103. Suggest various ways by which you might reduce the cost of correspondence conducted by your office. (1979) (Ch. 24)

104. Define a "report". Describe two types of report and their applications. Discuss the qualities of a good report and outline a typical structure for one of the report types you identify. (1978) (Ch. 25)

105. You have been requested by management to investigate the possibility of your organisation taking an exhibition stand at a forthcoming international trade fair. Write a formal and detailed report to the Marketing Director evaluating the suggestion. Choose your own product or service. (1979) (Ch. 25)

People, Organisations and Change II

106. "The grapevine is one of the fastest means of communication and its capacity for distortion is limitless." What measures would you take to ensure that this medium of communication becomes an effective and accurate channel? (1977) (Ch. 18)

107. "A major task of any organisation is to motivate its members to communicate effectively." Discuss the various methods which might be used to improve organisational communication. (1978) (Ch. 18)

108. You wish to hold a meeting of five supervisors to discuss the effects of recent changes in work allocation. How would you arrange for, and conduct the meeting in order to ensure maximum communication effectiveness? (1979) (Ch. 25)

Institute of Chartered Secretaries and Administrators
Communication

109. What are the main channels of communication that can be used in a large organisation to give information to employees? (1977) (Ch. 18)

110. Write an obituary notice of 300 words about your late company secretary for the firm's newsletter. Give some details of his education, career and outside activities. Mention his personal qualities. (1978) (Ch. 18)

111. "The best system of communication is that achieved with the least paperwork." Say how far you agreed with this statement and explain the advantages of (*a*) oral, (*b*) written communication in business. (1979) (Ch. 18)

112. What do you understand by the term "readability"? How would you assess the readability of a lengthy printed document intended for unskilled workers? (1979) (Ch. 18)

113. Give briefly the meaning and the purpose of the following: (a) a computer, (b) telex, (c) microfilm, (d) card index, (e) the mass media. (1979) (Ch. 18)

114. What is meant by the term "the grapevine"? Explain the reasons for its existence in large organisations, the drawbacks of this form of communication and the best ways of forestalling them. (1978) (Ch. 18)

115. "A committee is a body of people who individually do nothing and collectively decide that nothing can be done." How far do you agree? What guidelines would you observe in order to make best use of a committee meeting. (1978) (Ch. 18)

116. "What matters at an interview is not what is said, but how it is heard." How far do you think this is true? (1977) (Ch. 19)

117. Explain how you would use a tape recorder in a training session for telephone operators. Which aspects of the job would you emphasise as important? (1977) (Ch. 19)

118. As office manager write a circular to members of your staff to suggest ways in which the telephone should and should not be used. (1978) (Ch. 24)

119. As secretary of your firm's sports club write (a) a formal letter of resignation to the chairman of the club (b) an informal and private letter to the chairman, a friend of yours, explaining in more detail why you wish to resign. (1977) (Ch. 24)

120. State the main features of a good business letter. Enumerate some undesirable features the writer of a business letter should avoid. (1978) (Ch. 24)

121. (a) Write a letter to your employer asking for an immediate increase in salary, giving reasons for your request. (b) Write the employer's reply explaining why it is not possible to grant the request. (1978) (Ch. 24)

122. (a) As secretary of a firm write a letter to a successful applicant for a job as senior clerk, setting down the terms of service. (b) As the successful applicant write a letter accepting the appointment. (1978) (Ch. 24)

123. A group of colleagues have decided that a Sports Club is badly needed within the firm. As hon. secretary of the informal group you have been asked to write to the managing director to explain the situation and to seek his support. Give an outline of your main proposals. (1978) (Ch. 24)

124. (a) As principal of a college write a letter to the Personnel Officer of a large firm inviting him to address a group of students who hope to join his organisation. (b) As the personnel officer write a reply accepting the invitation. Outline the main points you will include in your talk. (1979) (Ch. 24)

125. The chairman has asked for a review of the committees operating within your organisation. Write a report on the advantages and drawbacks of these committees and make suggestions for changes you would like to introduce. (1977) (Ch. 25)

126. Write a profile of some 400 words, real or imaginary, of a company secretary or senior administrator. Explain what qualities he possesses and the handicaps he has had to overcome in the course of his career. (1977) (Ch. 25)

127. As a safety officer write a report to your chief executive of an accident that has occurred in your firm because of a breach of safety regulations. Make recommendations which should prevent the recurrence of such an accident. (1977) (Ch. 25)

128. Write a report to the secretary of your local student society for the benefit of other candidates on how you have prepared yourself for this examination. (1978) (Ch. 25)

129. What sort of diagrams, charts or tables would you suggest for inclusion in the annual report of an organisation of your choice. (1977) (Ch. 25)

130. You receive a telephone call from a colleague in another office two miles away asking you to direct him to your office through a town. Imagine he wishes to visit you (a) at once, (b) in two days' time. You are required: (i) for (a) above, to set out your immediate telephone instructions in writing; (ii) for (b) above, to draw a sketch map showing the route, which you will send him by post; (iii) to explain the advantages and disadvantages of these two methods of communication. (1977) (Ch. 26)

131. Write notes on each of the following: charts; diagrams; graphs; tables; as an aid to effective communication. (1978) (Ch. 26)

132. Write a memorandum to the manager of your organisation to suggest ways of economising in the use of office supplies. (1978) (Ch. 26)

Office Administration

133. Over the past few months the time schedules for the production of information have not been met by some sections and the reason given by section leaders is "insufficient time to complete all the tasks". You feel that a great deal of section leaders time is being wasted. Explain where and how this time is wasted and what steps should be taken to improve the situation. (1977) (Ch. 18)

134. It is asserted that unless there is effective communication in business it is unlikely that administrative management will achieve a high level of efficiency. Elaborate on this statement and show how you would ensure that the communication process in your organisation is effective. (1978) (Ch. 18)

135. "The astronomical cost of telecommunications has created a new priority with businesses of all sizes: how to cut the cost of it without damaging vital communication services. The most essential piece of communication equipment and the one that romps away with the money is the telephone." (*Professional Administration*, November 1977.) Discuss this statement and outline some of the options available to an organisation which will help to reduce the cost of the telephone account and enable it to use the service more efficiently. (1978) (Ch. 21)

136. Good reporting is the basis of effective communication between the various levels of management within an organisation. Elaborate on this statement and set out the main points which should be borne in mind in the preparation of reports. (1977) (Ch. 21)

137. "With the average letter in Europe costing £6 to produce and typists' output being a mere quarter of the theoretically possible, new techniques

and equipment are likely to gain considerable acceptance as business attempts to exercise greater control over costs and operational efficiency in offices." (*Professional Administration,* June 1977.) Discuss this statement and show how the inefficiencies implied in the statement may be overcome by the introduction of new techniques and equipment. (1978) (Ch. 28)

138. In the capacity of office manager draft an advertisement for a supervisor of the typing pool to replace the existing supervisor on her retirement. Also state who should comprise the interview panel and state the advice you would give to the panel regarding the qualities you are looking for in the successful applicant of this post. (1978) (Ch. 28)

Institute of Health Service Administrators
Principles of Organisation and Management

136. Provide an example of a "communication problem" in an organisation, and describe how you would provide a successful solution. (1978) (Ch. 18)

137. Can the manner in which an information system is used affect management performance? (1978) (Ch. 18)

138. In what manner is communication important to an administrator? (1978) (Ch. 18)

139. Every organisation has within it an informal structure and an informal communication network. Why is an understanding of these necessary for an administrator? (1979) (Ch. 18)

140. Write a brief for senior staff on the techniques of interviewing for (i) appointment to an information officer post; (ii) investigating a complaint; (iii) collection of research data. (Specimen) (Ch. 19)

141. Discuss the value of using standard questionnaires to collect information on one aspect of hospital management directly affecting patients e.g. catering, or waiting times, over a number of different hospitals. (Specimen) (Ch. 19)

SECTION V   REPRODUCTION, STORAGE AND RETRIEVAL OF DOCUMENTS (Chptrs. 29 to 36)

1. You have been asked to decide between the purchase of a spirit hectograph or a stencil duplicator. Write a report on their relative merits. (*Inst. M*) (Ch. 29)

2. You are asked to make recommendations on the different pieces of equipment which might be installed in a department to be set up for the reproduction of documents. State the information you would require before making your report. (*ICMA*) (Ch. 29)

3. What method of duplicating or copying would you select for the following jobs? Give your reasons. (a) 3,000 copies of a price list; (b) 12 copies of a multi-coloured chart; (c) 4 copies of a schedule in a foreign language; (d) 30 copies of a report. (*IAM*) (Ch. 29)

4. Explain how office systems and methods can be adapted to take advantage of copying processes. (*IAM*) Ch. 30)

5. When contemplating the purchase of a document-copying machine, what considerations should be borne in mind? (*ICMA*) (Ch. 30)

6. Storage space presents a problem in your organisation. Prepare instructions regarding the period for which six different types of records or documents should be retained before they can be destroyed. (*ICSA* Inter) (Ch. 33)

7. In every organisation, business records of all kinds accumulate very rapidly. What procedure would you suggest for dealing with these old records? For how long would you retain the various classes of records? (*ICMA*) (Ch. 33)

8. Describe a system for filing and recording details of insurance relating to a business with which you are familiar. Specify the type of organisation you have in mind. (*ICSA* Inter) (Ch. 33)

9. What are the advantages and disadvantages of a central filing department? If such a department is in existence, which records, if any, should be retained by other departments? (*ICMA*) (Ch. 33)

10. Along what lines would you proceed to draw up a system of classification and coding of accounts and what advantages would you expect to derive from such a system? (*ICMA*) (Ch. 33)

11. Submit your recommendations for a filing system (or systems) embracing all vouchers and correspondence which you would expect to meet within a medium-sized manufacturing business. (*ICMA*) (Ch. 33)

12. What are the essentials of a good system of indexing? Describe any modern form of indexing with which you are familiar and suggest specific uses for such a system. (*ICSA* Inter) (Ch. 34)

13. State the most important advantages of visible recording systems. Explain the means you would adopt of utilising them fully in connection with: (*a*) sales ledger control; (*b*) stores control. (*ICMA*) (Ch. 34)

14. Describe four types of manual filing equipment stating the advantages and disadvantages of each. Suggest the types of document which might be stored in each type of equipment you mention. (Ch. 35)

15. Explain what is meant by automated filing. In what circumstances would you consider installing this type of equipment? (Ch. 35)

16. You are asked to advise on the problem of finding space for storing patients' notes. In your opinion, would microfilming be the answer? What are the advantages and disadvantages? (*IHSA*) (Ch. 36)

17. State what you know about the following: thermofax, microfilm, photostat, dye-line, reflex, offset-litho, stencil, hectograph. (*IAM*) (Ch. 36)

18. Devise a system for use in a wholesale business to provide rapid reference to prices of over 1,000 different types of merchandise. Provision should be made for price variations to be communicated to, and recorded by, the sales staff at three branch offices in England. (*ICSA* Inter) (Ch. 36)

19. You are asked to examine and report on the filing and indexing systems in your organisation. Prepare the report, including your recommendations for improvements. (*ICSA* Inter) (Ch. 36)

20. To avoid correspondence being overlooked, a good filing system must provide for a "follow-up". Discuss this statement and describe any such system you would recommend. (*IHSA*) (Ch. 36)

Institute of Administrative Accounting and Data Processing
Business Knowledge
21. Describe fully, TWO methods of office duplicating. (1978) (Ch. 29)
22. List and discuss the possible uses that might be made of a photocopying machine within a business organisation. (1979) (Ch. 30)
23. A business operates a departmental filing system. List the advantages that might accrue by installing a central filing department. (1977) (Ch. 34)

Institute of Administrative Management
Office Systems and Mechanisation
24. What factors would you take into account in advising the administrative manager regarding the equipment needed to provide an effective copying and duplicating service for a large modern organisation? (1978) (Ch. 29–30)
25. Outline the manner in which you would attempt to cost and control the copying and duplicating service in a large administrative headquarters. (1978) (Ch. 29–30)
26. What resources would you require to provide an efficient copying and duplicating service within an organisation? (1979) (Ch. 29–30)
27. Discuss both the benefits and disadvantages of introducing a high speed unlimited access copying and duplicating service to your organisation. (1979) (Ch. 30)
28. How would you deal with the situation arising from the inclination of some staff members to retain unnecessary documents and files and to clutter the working areas with papers and other impedimenta? (1979) (Office Administration paper) (Ch. 33)
29. If you were called upon to review information storage and retrieval methods within your organisation how would you carry out this task? (1979) (Ch. 33)
30. You have been asked to review and comment on the efficiency of a filing system. What points would you examine at each stage of the filing procedures, and what sort of overall control would you consider suitable? (1977) (Ch. 35)
31. Outline the benefits which might be derived from modern microfilm techniques and summarise filming, storage, and retrieval devices currently available. (1977) (Ch. 36)
32. Select THREE of the following tasks and describe for each the microfilm media and equipment you might use: (a) Storage and retrieval of engineering drawings; (b) Long term storage of infrequently accessed documents; (c) Organisation of information on cases dealt with by a Social Services Department; (d) Distribution of technical articles and data sheets to service stations of an international airline. (1979) (Ch. 36)

Institute of Chartered Secretaries and Administrators
Office Administration
33. State what you consider to be the most suitable methods for producing (a) 10 copies of a report from branch office to head office; (b) 100 copies of a

price list; (c) 500 copies of a high-class circular on the firm's letter heading; (d) 2 or 3 copies of an incoming letter. (1977) (Ch. 29)

34. Management have asked to be advised of the procedures adopted in your organisation to ensure the security of documents and confidential files. Outline the procedures which you consider are essential and should be followed in order that security is maintained. (1979) (Ch. 33)

35. The efficiency of a filing system depends very largely upon the care taken in selecting the headings under which documents are classified. Detail the main classifications which may be adopted and suggest which documents may suitably be filed under each classification. (1977) (Ch. 33)

36. You are considering engaging the services of a company which specialises in the filing and storing of documents and papers on their premises, for other organisations. Set out in the form of a report to the senior administrative officer the types of papers and documents which could be dealt with in this way and state the main points you would wish to settle with the company before you implemented such a scheme. (1977) (Ch. 33)

37. Your management is concerned with the cost and space involved in the storage of documents, letters, reports and schedules. Set out in the form of a memorandum to the senior administrator, your recommendations on how the problem can be overcome. (1977) (Ch. 33)

38. Discuss the advantages and disadvantages of microfilming as an alternative to filing copies of letters and documents. (1978) (Ch. 36)

39. "The twentieth century has experienced an exponential increase of information, and storage facilities in the modern company must adapt to cope with the voluminous information and records which need to be kept and made available for reference." (*Professional Administration,* December 1978). Elaborate on this statement and discuss the benefits which could arise if microfilming is introduced to cope with the problem. (1979) (Ch. 36)

SECTION VI   DATA PROCESSING (Chptrs. 37–40)

1. The financial year of a large concern ends on 31st March. Draw up a set of stocktaking instructions. (*ICMA*) (Ch. 37)

2. Write a brief outline of one manual and one mechanised method of keeping stock records. (*IAM*) (Ch. 37)

3. Describe the organisation of a full physical inventory in a manufacturing business so that the operation will be carried through in the most efficient manner. (*ACA*) (Ch. 37)

4. In the case of a manufacturing company, what methods would you suggest for the recording and otherwise dealing with orders received by, and placed by the company? Write out a directive to the accounts department with regard to checking the receipt of all goods invoiced to the company. (*ICSA* Inter) (Ch. 37)

5. On your appointment as secretary of a body with several thousand customers, you find that no effective system exists for dealing with debtors

whose accounts are overdue. Prepare a memorandum relative to a system you recommend should be adopted in future by the accounts department. (*ICSA* Final) (Ch. 37)

6. As the person in charge of the credit control department of your firm, describe the procedures you would adopt before passing on for execution an order from: (*a*) an existing customer, (*b*) a new customer. (*ICMA*) (Ch. 37)

7. (*a*) What is the purpose of sales accounting? (*b*) For what purpose can invoices be used other than for notifying customers of their indebtedness? (*Inst.M*) (Ch. 37)

8. Describe any system of sales invoicing from the point at which the customer's order is received up to the point of executing the order and despatching the goods. (*Inst.M*) (Ch. 37)

9. Give the names of four forms commonly used in connection with the sale, despatch, and payment of goods. Describe their uses. (*Inst.M*) (Ch. 37)

10. Describe a wages system, an invoicing system, or a stock control system with which you are familiar, and give the advantages of using that particular system over others which might have been used. (*IAM*) (Ch. 37)

11. Describe a procedure of control and the forms likely to be used for the purchasing, storing and ultimate payment for goods, from the time a purchase requisition is received by the chief buyer to the time a cheque is despatched to the supplier. (*ICSA*) (Ch. 37)

12. A manufacturing company has approximately 500 employees whose wages are based on various hourly rates. Describe a system for compiling the weekly pay-roll which has to provide for the normal income tax and national insurance and fixed weekly contributions to a pension fund. Give details of the staff required to operate your scheme and state the cost of any special equipment you may recommend. (*ICSA* Inter) (Ch. 37)

13. For the guidance of your staff draft a circular explaining how the PAYE system of taxation works. (*ICSA* Final) (Ch. 37)

14. A manufacturing firm has twelve works in various parts of the country making more or less the same type of product, the number of operatives at each works varying between 25 and 400. What are the advantages and disadvantages of each works having its own staff to deal with wages, and compared with a central wages department at head office? (*ICMA*) (Ch. 37)

15. Outline an effective system for the compilation, control and payment of weekly wages payable to the staff of a large hospital or other organisation. Show a specimen of at least one form used in this system. (*IHSA*) (Ch. 37)

16. In connection with the payment of salaries and/or wages, certain deductions are sometimes made. Give four examples of such deductions, at least two of these examples being non-statutory deductions. In the case of each of the four examples, state the way in which the sums deducted are transferred to the recipients, and in the case of the non-statutory examples specify the form of authority required to make the deductions.

17. In relation to Income Tax deducted from employees' earnings, what

are the employer's responsibilities and rights relative to: (a) the employees, and (b) the tax authority? (*ICSA*) (Ch. 37)

18. Outline some of the recent developments in computers for business purposes and illustrate your answer by reference to some recently announced applications. (*ACA*) (Ch. 39)

19. A company is considering installing a computer to replace its mechanised accounting department, which can no longer maintain up-to-date records. What enquiries should the company make before it finally decides to purchase a computer? (*ACA*) (Ch. 39)

20. How are punched cards used in connection with electronic computers? Describe also an alternative to punched cards, directing attention to the comparative advantages and disadvantages. (*ICSA*) (Ch. 39)

21. Indicate how the following difficulties which are liable to arise when a computer is installed may be overcome: (a) access to detailed records of intermediate clerical processes; and (b) the ability rapidly and effectively to deal with non-standard queries. (*ICSA*) (Ch. 40)

22. What type of controls do you consider necessary to ensure accuracy in the preparation of commercial data, when a computer is used? (*ACA*) (Ch. 40)

23. Give details of the techniques and equipment available for input into a computer. (*ICMA*) (Ch. 40)

24. What is meant by vetting of input data? What are the main problems associated with it? How can these be overcome? (*ICMA*) (Ch. 40)

25. Write short notes on: (a) computer typesetting; (b) convergence; (c) intelligent terminals; (d) buffer store; (e) real-time operation; (f) software; (g) hardware; (h) protocol; (i) flow-chart; (j) modem.(Ch. 40)

26. Explain briefly five communications applications of a computer system. State the advantages, and disadvantages (if any) of computerised communication systems. (Ch. 40)

Association of Cost & Executive Accountants
Management Information Systems and Data Processing
27. What are the advantages and disadvantages of using electro-mechanical accounting machines, as compared with manual methods of accounting? (1977) (Ch. 38)

28. What are the elements of a computer system? Show these in a diagram and explain clearly the function of each element you have shown. (1977) (Ch. 39)

29. Describe the types of software and service which you would expect a computer manufacturer to provide with his hardware (a) initially and (b) subsequently, and explain what purpose each serves. (1977) (Ch. 39)

30. A number of companies are using models to simulate corporate activities for which computer packages have been developed. Explain what is meant by "model" and describe computer package. (1977) (Ch. 40)

31. "The quality of management information is directly related to its timing". Discuss. (1977) (Ch. 40)

32. An engineering company operating in a dozen different places in the UK is considering the use of a computer bureau for its payroll. Write a

report to the chairman explaining the control features to be incorporated into the new system. (1977) (Ch. 40)

33. The quality of management information is directly related to its timing. (*a*) Discuss the statement, with particular reference to: (i) the different purposes for which the information may be required; and (ii) the relative merits of speed versus accuracy in each case. (*b*) Explain in what ways the timing of information flows should be taken into account when designing information systems. (1978) (Ch. 40)

Institute of Administrative Accounting and Data Processing
Business Knowledge
34. Describe the procedures that might be carried out in preparing a typical wages system. (1979) (Ch. 37)

35. What do you understand by the term "credit control"? Discuss the advantages that might accrue in a business by installing a credit control system. (1979) (Ch. 37)

36. What are the principal purposes for the use of stock control in a business organisation? (1979) (Ch. 37)

37. What are the main advantages of keyboard accounting machines over the manual method? (1977) (Ch. 38)

Institute of Administrative Management
Office Systems and Mechanisation
38. In a typical material control system we find the variables of "re-order level", "safety stock", "re-order quantity" and "lead time". Draw a diagram linking these factors and say how you would calculate the level of each of them. (1977) (Ch. 37)

39. Describe a typical payroll system in a large manufacturing concern. (1977) (Ch. 37)

40. How would you attempt to ensure that the stock records maintained in an organisation always provide an accurate reflection of the stock available? (1978) (Ch. 37)

41. Outline a purchasing system suitable for an agency supplying a number of laboratories with experimental equipment on a non-repetitive purchasing basis. The agency is not responsible for "consumables", deals with about 4 requests per day, and spends about £250,000 per annum. (1979) (Ch. 37)

42. Checking and calculating are two important office functions. How may these be assisted by machines? (1978) (Ch. 38)

43. "Mechanisation is more flexible than automation and, therefore, more useful." Using examples discuss this assertion in relation to office work. (1979) (Ch. 38)

44. Write short notes on any FOUR of the following: (*a*) high level languages; (*b*) operating systems; (*c*) magnetic or floppy disks; (*d*) multiprogramming; (*e*) check digits. (1977) (Ch. 39)

45. Describe briefly the various methods of input available with modern computers and comment on the suitability of each for particular systems applications. (1977) (Ch. 39)

46. Draw up a diagram of a modern computer showing major functional areas (e.g. "output" devices). Briefly describe each functional area defining those which are indispensable and those optional for particular applications. (1977) (Ch. 39)

47. How would you set about the acquisition and installation of a mini-computer in a small retail business? List suitable applications in such an enterprise. (1977) (Ch. 39)

48. Outline the typical stages of a purchasing system and briefly describe the likely contents of each document within it. (1978) (Ch. 39)

49. What is meant by data preparation in relation to commercial computing? Discuss the various methods of data preparation available and the suitability of each for different types of data. (1978) (Ch. 39)

50. Outline the typical stages of a project intended to convert a basic clerical system to a computer system. (1978) (Ch. 39)

51. Describe any THREE devices currently used with present-day computers for on-line backing storage. (1978) (Ch. 39)

52. Your organisation is considering the use of a remote computer location which can accept input data by any established method. Describe and evaluate TWO methods which utilise special British Telecom services. (1978) (Business Communication) (Ch. 39)

53. Security and safety are important components of any administrative manager's daily work. What extra problems are imposed upon him by computers and how may he set about solving such problems? (1979) (Ch. 39)

54. Four facilities available with modern computers are: multi-programming, remote terminals, high-level programming and data bases. Briefly describe each of these and show how they may assist administration. (1979) (Ch. 39)

55. What are the main factors you would bear in mind when choosing computer input media for administrative systems? (1979) (Ch. 39)

56. The respective technologies of data processing and telecommunication have converged and reached a stage of integration in several systems applications. Comment on this statement; give THREE examples and discuss ONE of them in detail. (1977) (Business Communication) (Ch. 40)

57. Describe some typical processes which might be carried out with the use of a computer terminal. (1978) (Ch. 40)

58. What are the various ways in which you might carry out the wages preparation in an organisation employing in excess of 10,000 people? (1978) (Ch. 40)

59. With the advent of progressive miniaturisation and particularly with reference to microprocessors how do you see the future of main-frame computers in administration? (1979) (Ch. 40)

60. How can a computer assist with the integration of the basic commercial functions of sales, purchasing and stock control? (1979) (Ch. 40)

61. "The increased provision of computerised management information can have effects on all levels of management." State why this should be so and explain what sort of effects could be expected. (1979) (Office Administration) (Ch. 40)

SECTION VII   OFFICE SYSTEMS CONTROL (Chptrs. 41–50)

1. Outline a technique for the review and design of a clerical procedure. (*IAM*) (Ch. 41)

2. Enumerate and briefly describe those aims which must be kept in mind when designing an office system. (*ICMA*) (Ch. 41)

3. Describe any labour-saving machines you would install in a busy and expanding accounts department, and give brief reasons for your choice. (*IHSA*) (Ch. 42)

4. "Unless full use is made of office machinery, its purchase is not justified." Comment on this statement. (*IHSA*) (Ch. 42)

5. "Most offices have more machinery than they actually need and it is very doubtful if each such office has the right kind of machine in the right place." Comment on this statement. (*IHSA*) (Ch. 42)

6. Discuss the case for replacing maintenance contracts for office machinery by a policy of servicing machines only as and when required. In what circumstances and for what types of machine would the latter policy be more suitable? (*ICMA*) (Ch. 42)

7. Write a short report recommending the purchase of one of the following machines for work not at present mechanised: (*a*) key-driven calculator, (*b*) addressing equipment, (*c*) a dictating machine, (*d*) an automatic typewriter, (*e*) an accounting machine. (*Inst.M*) (Ch. 42)

8. How would you ensure that all forms in use are serving a necessary purpose in the carrying out of business routines? (*ICMA*) (Ch. 43)

9. State the procedure you would follow in order to inform yourself whether all the forms in your organisation are being fully utilised. (*ICMA*) (Ch. 43)

10. "Forms are the foundations of clerical systems." Comment on this statement. (*IHSA*) (Ch. 43)

11. What is the purpose of a printed form? What conditions must be satisfied before an additional form is essential and brought into use? (*IHSA*) (Ch. 43)

12. Forms control has been referred to as "one of the greatest tools of management". State what you understand by forms control; describe how you would initiate such a system of control in any organisation with which you are familiar, and enumerate the benefits you would expect your management to derive. (*ICSA* Final) (Ch. 43)

13. The head of the statistics department is concerned about the volume of statistical reports, both *ad hoc* and routine, which his department produces, because at present he does not know how many of these reports justify the cost of producing them. Indicate (*a*) what steps you would recommend him to take to eliminate unnecessary and unrewarding statistics; (*b*) what suggestions you would make for simplifying the production of existing statistical reports? (*ICMA*) (Ch. 43)

14. If you were explaining to a trainee the difference between a badly-designed form and a well-designed form, what points would you bring to his attention? (*IAM*) (Ch. 43)

15. Design a form suitable for completion by 25 sales representatives which will show customers by classification, orders received, complaints made,

APPENDIXES

and any other details which you consider relevant. One form should be completed for each customer and then sent to the sales office for a daily analysis to be extracted for use by the sales manager. (ICMA) (Ch. 43)

16. It has been decided to hold "exit interviews" for all personnel leaving your organisation and to record appropriate information on a form. Design such a form. (*ICSA*) (Ch. 43)

17. What difficulties would you expect to find in trying to set time standards for work in an office? (*ACEA* 1976) (Ch. 45)

18. Describe an ideal store in which to keep stocks of stationery and the procedure you recommend for issuing stationery. (*IHSA*) (Ch. 47)

19. Outline a system for organising the ordering, custody, and issue of stationery requisites in your office, to reduce waste, pilfering, etc. (*AIA*) (Ch. 47)

20. An organisation issues 2,000 cheques four times a year, and at present these are signed personally by two executives. Explain two alternative methods by which the time spent signing cheques could be reduced or eliminated, giving details of the procedure involved and of any safeguards that should be introduced. (*ICSA* Inter) (Ch. 48)

21. Set out and explain the rules that you consider should be in force in a large commercial office to prevent or bring to light irregularities in cash handling, fraudulent or unintentional. (*ACA*) (Ch. 48)

22. How can the fraudulent drawing or alteration of cheques be prevented? (*ICMA*) (Ch. 48)

23. The auditors have commented adversely on the method in use in the general office of emptying telephone call boxes in the hospital and of checking and recovering the money collected. Describe a system which you would consider offered the maximum safeguards against fraud and error. (*IHSA*) (Ch. 50)

24. Draw a network diagram of the steps you would have to take to prepare and produce for distribution to all employees (1,000) in your organisation a booklet on telephone techniques. (Ch. 50)

Institute of Administrative Accounting and Data Processing
Business Communications

25. What questions do you feel it is necessary to consider when you are called upon to design a form? (1977) (Ch. 43)

26. Practically all business organisations use purchase order forms. Design one appropriate to a wholesaler's use when ordering from the manufacturer. (1978) (Ch. 43)

Business Knowledge

27. What are the main differences between an office manual and a policy manual? (1977) (Ch. 41)

28. What machines and equipment might be used, and for what purposes, so as to help create an efficient system in the preparation and payment of wages? (1978) (Ch. 42)

29. "Office stationery can be an excessive overhead cost if it is not controlled efficiently." In respect of this statement, discuss fully what you consider to be the essentials of control of office stationery. (1978) (Ch. 47)

Institute of Administrative Management
Approach to Office Administration
30. "When it comes to the office procedure manual and what to include in it, there is always the question of whether you cover all possible exceptions and obscure the main procedures, or leave out the exceptions and deal with these on an *ad hoc* basis." In the light of this statement, give your own account of what should be included in a procedure manual and state your reasons. (1978) (Ch. 41)
31. Having experienced a period of growing inefficiency in the office, you have been able to set up a series of procedures which have greatly improved the situation. How will you ensure that the situation does not start to deteriorate again? (1978) (Ch. 41)
32. Describe an administrative control system known to you and then indicate what sort of information the system should provide for management. (1979) (Ch. 41)
33. On the completion of an O & M assignment based on a particular department, describe the part that you think should be played by the O & M specialist and the department manager in supervising the recommended changes. (1978) (Ch. 43)
34. "The help of the O & M department should perhaps be enlisted to evaluate alternatives and help to implement any change." (B. H. Walley) Consider this statement and give your comments under the two headings: (a) evaluation of alternatives, and (b) implementation of change. (1978) (Ch. 43)
35. There appears to be a growing incidence of error in the invoices produced in your company. How would you diagnose the cause of the increase? (1977) (Ch. 45)
36. Indicate the kind of office work which appears suitable for measurement by group performance rather than by individual performance and suggest a method of assessment. (1977) (Ch. 45)
37. "Ideally, the work of the office should be planned to flow evenly at all times." State the factors which, in your opinion, govern the situation. (1978) (Ch. 45)
38. "In controlling the quality of work produced by the office, it is essential to set the correct standards." How would you set these standards in relation to three different types of work in the office? (1978) (Ch. 45)
39. When the incidence of error increases, it is important to diagnose the causes and take preventive action. Select an area of administrative work which you consider to be prone to error and state how you would proceed to diagnosis and prevention. (1979) (Ch. 45)
40. It is reasonably straightforward to control quality and output where regular procedures are concerned but what controls can be utilised where special jobs are concerned? (1979) (Ch. 45)
41. You are asked to negotiate a contract to cover office machine maintenance. List the points that would most concern you and say why. (1977) (Ch. 47)
42. Outline a system of control which might be applied to the procedure for purchasing office furniture. (1977) (Ch. 47)

43. Outline a simple but effective stock control system to be used for the issue and re-ordering of office stationery. (1978) (Ch. 47)

44. As administrative manager, you are responsible for supplies of stationery throughout the organisation. You are about to set up a section to be responsible for the replenishment of supplies. Design a procedure to cover the work of this section. (1978) (Ch. 47)

45. Some writers on "office administration" consider that the function of internal audit should go much further than checking the accuracy of financial data and security of assets. What do you consider should be included in this wider concept of the internal auditor's function? (1977) (Ch. 48)

46. There are different views on what is meant by "internal audit". Give your own views on the internal audit function, placing emphasis on the problems of achieving an effective internal audit. (1979) (Ch. 48)

47. In your opinion, is budgetary control an effective way of controlling expenditure? Support your argument with evidence from your own experience, if possible, or from your studies. (1978) (Ch. 50)

48. "In the office, overhead costs appear to increase each year, and it seems difficult to control them." Do you agree with this statement? If so, state why control is difficult. If you disagree, suggest some methods of controlling overheads. (1978) (Ch. 50)

49. You have been asked to investigate the effectiveness of the use of "budgetary control" in your organisation. Set out and discuss the problem areas you would expect to find. (1979) (Ch. 50)

50. Discuss the advantages and problems of introducing a scheme of departmental charging in the allocation of costs. (1979) (Ch. 50)

51. Discuss some of the problems involved in applying a budgetary control system in the administrative areas. (1979) (Ch. 50)

Approach to Organisation and Methods

52. You are about to play a major part in an assignment designed to improve the effectiveness of office work in your organisation. Outline your general approach to such an assignment and describe the aspects you would examine in seeking ideas for improvement. (1977) (Ch. 43)

53. Discuss the advantages and disadvantages of encouraging managers to do their own O & M rather than to rely on a central O & M unit, indicating where you think the balance of advantage lies. (1977) (Ch. 43)

54. Give your views, with reasons, as to the purpose and importance of a formal report in an O & M assignment, and describe the features that you would expect to see in a good report. (1977) (Ch. 43)

55. Describe methods of collecting data for an O & M assignment, and explain the advantages and disadvantages associated with each one. (1977) (Ch. 43)

56. O & M work usually brings about change. Explain why this can lead to reaction from those affected by the change, and how the O & M officer can contribute to effecting the change. (1977) (Ch. 43)

57. Describe and explain the purpose and situation (in terms of position and relationship) of the O & M unit within an organisation. (1977) (Ch. 43)

58. Briefly explain the benefits of communicating with the staff concerned at various stages during an assignment, and provide the guidelines an O & M officer should follow when interviewing clerical staff. (1977) (Ch. 43)

59. Describe the main stages of an O & M assignment, elaborating on the preliminary steps you would take before commencing work in the assignment area. (1977) (Ch. 43)

60. When new methods of work are introduced operating staff must become familiar with them quickly. Give your views on the benefits of the O & M officer being involved in this training process and explain and illustrate the form of instruction for operating a new procedure which you prefer. (1977) (Ch. 43)

61. As manager of an O & M unit you are concerned that it should be successful. Discuss the criteria you would use in judging the success of the unit, explaining also the ways in which you would measure those criteria. (1978) (Ch. 43)

62. "A form is a window through which you may look inside a business organisation." Explain how an O & M man can learn about an organisation by studying its forms. (1978) (Ch. 43)

63. It has been suggested that management in those areas of an organisation most needing the attention of O & M will tend to be the last ones to ask for it and the O & M unit should, therefore, have authority to investigate any part of the organisation rather than reply upon invitation. Give your views on this suggestion and the consequences of implementing it. (1978) (Ch. 43)

64. The increase in the strength and activity of "white collar" unions is one of the major changes of recent years. Describe when and how you would expect the union to be involved, if at all, in an O & M assignment. How would you present the role of O & M to a group of union representatives? (1978) (Ch. 43)

65. Drawing on your own experiences where possible, illustrate the ways in which O & M assignments arise. If there is a choice, what criteria would you use to decide priorities between assignments? (1978) (Ch. 43)

66. List and explain the advantages and disadvantages of employing on an O & M assignment: (a) consultants from outside the organisation; (b) O & M personnel who are part of the organisation (c) a combination of (a) and (b). (1978) (Ch. 43)

67. Why do you think many people resist change? What can the organisation and methods officer do to minimise such resistance? (1979) (Ch. 43)

68. Describe the methods you might use in the fact-finding phase of an O & M assignment. For each method comment on how accurate the results are likely to be. How would you improve the quality of the fact-finding? (1979) (Ch. 43)

69. It is expensive for an organisation to run an internal organisation and methods unit. How would you justify the cost of maintaining such a unit in your own organisation? (1979) (Ch. 43)

70. Explain the purposes of a preliminary survey in an O & M assignment, and describe fully the tasks involved in carrying out such a survey. (1979) (Ch. 43)

71. Describe in what ways, if any, O & M staff should be involved in an

assignment after their recommendations have been presented to management. Give reasons for your views and guidance for success in the activities
you have suggested. (1979) (Ch. 43)

72. Describe FOUR ways in which the office of the future might differ
from today's office, and assess the long-term implications for the O & M
practitioner. (1979) (Ch. 43)

73. There are many benefits to be gained from employing O & M staff, yet
there are often cases of under-utilisation of the O & M unit or resistance on
the part of managers and staff to implementing the recommendations.
What might be the causes of this happening? (1979) (Ch. 43)

74. The O & M unit in you organisation is about to recruit some
assignment officers. To aid that recruitment you are asked to provide a job
description and an analysis, with appropriate explanation, of the qualifications and qualities applicants should possess. (1979) (Ch. 43)

75. Explain the form of each of the following and describe their different
uses: (a) a string diagram; (b) a flow process chart. Illustrate the flow
process chart and provide a key to the symbols used. (1977) (Ch. 44)

76 Charts are used in O & M work to record or present information. What
advantages do they have over narrative reports, and what stages are
involved in making and using a chart? (1978) (Ch. 44)

77. Describe THREE different types of charts (other than organisation
charts) an O & M officer might employ on assignments, and state in what
circumstances each would be used. (1978) (Ch. 44)

78. Draw up a fully annotated flow process chart for an office procedure
with which you are familiar, and state the purposes for which such a chart
could be used. (1979) (Ch. 44)

79. Suggest and describe ways in which the number of inspections or
checks of clerical work can be reduced in an office. What fears might a
manager have about such a reduction, and how would you allay them?
(1978) (Ch. 45)

80. Problem-solving is a major aspect of O & M assignment work.
Describe this process fully. (1978) (Ch. 50)

Business Communication
81. Forms control is sometimes regarded as being mundane, unglamorous
and irksome—especially by those users of forms who prefer to get their
jobs done in their own way unhindered by the influence of formal
procedures. Nevertheless, formal procedures are often necessary to ensure
efficient administration. (a) As an administrative manager in a large
organisation, how would you seek to persuade your superiors and peers of
the need for such a control function? (b) What elements should be
contained in a plan to establish a central forms control function? (c) How
would you implement the plan whilst recognising the need to avoid stifling
flexibility and initiative within the organisation? (1978) (Ch. 43)

82. Describe in detail FOUR systems of designing and printing forms
which lead to speed, accuracy and economy in the use of forms. Give
examples of the systems in which they may be used. (1979) (Ch. 43)

83. Outline typical systems which can be used for any two of the following

administrative functions: (a) the collection of rates in a local authority; (b) addressing of envelopes; (c) the purchasing of capital items; (d) share records and registration, and dividend payments; (e) the maintenance of medical records, for example in a group practice, or a hospital, or a company, etc. (1979) (Ch. 41)

84. How may mechanisation affect the work and the jobs of the clerical worker and the supervisor? What steps could be taken to minimise the disadvantages and maximise the advantages of mechanisation? (1977) (Ch. 42)

85. What effects may mechanisation have on office cash systems? (1977) (Ch. 42)

86. Distinguish between mechanisation and automation and consider their varying effects on people and on people and on systems. (1978) (Ch. 42)

87. "Efficiency is not something which can be bought in the market place". Discuss this statement in relation to office mechanisation. (1979) (Ch. 42)

88. As an administrative manager you are responsible for the introduction of major new office machines. Outline likely sources of advice and assistance, and explain how these would be integrated into the process of selection of machines and during implementation. (1979) (Ch. 42)

89. Describe, and show in diagrammatic form, the flow of documents in a typical purchasing system. What management and control information would be required at each stage of the system? (1977) (Ch. 44)

90. How would you control the flow of work, the quality, and the collection and distribution of data in a large organisation? (Your answer need not be based on the use of a computer.) (1977) (Ch. 45)

91. How would you design and install a system of planned/preventive maintenance for the office equipment within your organisation? (1977) (Ch. 47)

92. How would you attempt to control the use of consumables in a large office? What particular problems might your control system encounter? (1978) (Ch. 47)

93. Slackness in cash handling is an invitation to theft. What steps would you take to obviate the risk of such theft? (1978) (Ch. 49)

94. You are the administrative manager in a small firm producing plastic components on a sub-contracting basis. Current growth has led you and other senior members of the firm to recognise a need for closer cost control. What could be the components of such control and what responsibility should you have in it?

People and Organisations
95. What benefits would you expect to gain from the introduction of work measurement in the office context? (1977) (Ch. 45)

96. "The success or failure of a clerical work measurement system is in the hands of the supervisor." Taking any one standard system of your choice, identify the role of the supervisor throughout its introduction and operation. (1978) (Ch. 45)

97. "Clerical work cannot be measured effectively." Discuss this statement

in the light of the clerical work measurement techniques available. (1979) (Ch. 45)

98. How would you expect the introduction of a clerical work measurement programme to improve the efficiency of your organisation? (1979) (Ch. 45)

Institute of Chartered Secretaries and Administrators
Office Administration

99. Efficiency in office administration can be improved through the intelligent replacement of existing office machines and equipment with more modern equipment. State what investigations you would make before replacing machines and equipment and show how you think such replacement would improve efficiency. (1979) (Ch. 42)

100. Describe the main stages of an organisation and methods investigation and implementation, and also state how you would evaluate the results. Relate your answer to *one* of the following: (a) mechanisation of office processes; (b) reprographic services. (1977) (Ch. 43)

101. An O & M unit is about to be set up in your organisation but it has yet to be decided to whom it should be responsible. Discuss the relative advantages and disadvantages of making the unit responsible to: (a) the chief administrative officer; (b) the chief accountant; or (c) some other officer. (1978) (Ch. 43)

102. Show by means of a "control chart" the processing of the work through a purchasing department in a light manufacturing organisation, stating precisely how control is effected. (1978) (Ch. 44)

103. Because of the seasonal nature of the products of your organisation there are periodical acute variations in the volume of work in some administrative departments. Set out the steps you recommend are taken to overcome the uneven flow of work problem without increasing the number of administrative staff currently employed. (1977) (Ch. 45)

104. State how you would organise the work of compiling the annual administrative budget for any organisation with which you are familiar. (1978) (Ch. 45)

105. Various measures are normally taken in a business to prevent serious loss through the default or misdeeds of employees. State the internal security measures you would recommend are taken in order to reduce the possibility of losses within your organisation. (1977) (Ch. 48)

106. Your organisation has a number of small branches which deal in cash sales and the receipt of monthly cash payments from hire purchase customers. Describe the internal check system you would establish to control the cash received in each of the above circumstances. (1977) (Ch. 49)

107. Set out the main features which you would expect to find in a good cash control system in an office. (1978) (Ch. 49)

108. Describe in detail the duties and responsibilities of an internal auditor and show their relationship to those of the external auditor. (1979) (Ch. 49)

109. Explain four techniques a risk manager may employ as an alternative to insurance. (1977) (Ch. 49)

110. In most articles written about company insurance emphasis is placed upon "loss prevention measures". In this context explain the important measures which organisations can take to minimise or prevent loss of assets. (1978) (Ch. 49)

111. "All businesses need insurance to a greater or lesser degree' The art is to be able to assess the degree". (*Professional Administration*, April 1978.) Discuss this statement and state how you would go about assessing the need for insurance in your organisation. (1978) (Ch. 49)

112. Explain how "control" may be achieved through the setting and use of administration department budgets. (1977) (Ch. 50)

113. Explain what is meant by budgetary control. Show how the figures are coordinated in an administrative budget and how control of expenditure can be exercised through the budgeting process. (1979) (Ch. 50)

Part 2   Case Studies and Projects

Individual project and group discussion

1. The corporate image of an organisation is manifested by the company livery, letterhead, letter presentation and telephone contact. Add to this list as many more manifestations as you can. Draw a pie chart indicating what you consider to be the proportionate impact of each item on the corporate image as a whole. In groups of not less than four/not more than six compare and discuss the information shown in the group members' pie charts.

Group project

2. You have to organise the removal of an office of 50 people to new premises. There are:

4 section managers; 35 clerical staff (5 use computer terminals); 6 secretaries providing a full secretarial service for 15 senior managers (who work elsewhere on the floor); and 5 word processor operators.

It has been decided that the office shall be landscaped. The building is at the stage where you, the tenant, can state what systems of heating, lighting, etc. you would like. All furniture and equipment is to be new. There is no daylight. The area is 250 square metres and is 10 metres wide by 25 metres long. Divide into three groups, each group to undertake one of the following activities:

(*a*) Decide what type of lighting, heating, and ventilation should be installed.

(*b*) Prepare a plan of the electric wiring to provide adequate power points and lighting outlets.

(*c*) Decide the furniture and equipment (excluding electronic and telecommunications) to be purchased.

(*d*) Design the layout of the office.

(*e*) Decide the electronic and telecommunications equipment required.

(*f*) Prepare a plan to show the electric and telecommunications outlets required.

Use catalogues and visit showrooms to obtain details and prices. Each group will have to consult and liaise with the other groups. It is suggested

APPENDIXES

that each group should appoint one or two 'liaison officers' for the purpose. Each group should prepare a detailed cost schedule with the specification of requirements.

Practical exercises

3. A "task" has a definable beginning and end. Bearing this in mind, choose any task undertaken by a clerical or secretarial worker and prepare a task analysis. Use any method or methods and any sources of information available to you. (This assignment is best undertaken by two people working together. A larger group can divide into pairs, each pair undertaking the analysis of a different task.)

4. Collect examples of advertisements for staff from six different newspapers and/or journals. Determine the readership and then establish the merits and demerits of each advertisement. Redraft any advertisements which you consider could be improved.

5. Obtain a job description for any office worker. Prepare a job specification and a personnel specification. Draft an advertisement for inclusion in a suitable newspaper/journal. (This assignment may be undertaken by two people working together, each pair having a different job description.)

Group discussion

6. You dictated a letter to a prospective customer quoting a figure of £10,000. You signed the letter hurriedly at the end of the day to catch the post. The customer replies by telex accepting your offer "at the cost stated in your letter". The order is fulfilled. An invoice for £10,000 is raised. The customer returns the invoice saying that there is an error: the amount should be £1,000. He refers to his acceptance by telex of your offer. The copy of the letter containing the offer is checked: it contains the figure £1,000.

(*a*) Who is to blame for the error?

(*b*) Should disciplinary action be taken? If so, what action, against whom?

(*c*) What action should be taken with regard to the customer? Reasons must be established for all suggestions made.

7. Select any office or section of an office of not less than ten and not more than twenty staff. Obtain the information about the staff and their work which you need to undertake a manpower planning exercise. Imagine yourself in charge of the office you have chosen and prepare a plan indicating training needs and possible recruitment over the next five years. The aim is to ensure the maximum level of efficiency at all times.

Case study

8. Mr. Croft, a supervising officer, has received a complaint from a member of the public about his secretary, Elaine Green. The member of the public, Mr. Waters, has said that when he telephoned Elaine was most unhelpful—could not say where Mr. Croft was, when he would be

available or answer any straightforward questions about the processing of his application. Mr. Croft tackled Elaine by saying "Elaine, if you can't do better than this you will have to go or be transferred to a department where you won't be in contact with the public. This sort of complaint is so bad for our reputation".

Elaine felt very resentful. She secretly agreed with the client but felt that it was not her fault because Mr. Croft never told her where he was going, when he would be back, nor anything about the progress of work in the department. She says nothing and considers the situation. She decides to give in her notice and tells Personnel she doesn't care for the work she is doing.

Personnel inform Mr. Croft that Elaine has given in her notice. His reaction is "just because I told her off—still it's probably a good thing. She's hopeless on the 'phone."

Elaine is an excellent typist, careful and accurate. She enjoys the kind of work she is doing and is keen to progress. She is very shy and never discusses her thoughts or feelings with people.

Comment on this situation and decide what contribution Mr. Croft and Elaine could each have made towards avoiding it.

Practical exercise

9. Prepare a set of extension users' procedures for an electronic telephone system. Start by drawing up a list of facilities. Consider the situations which can arise when an extension user receives a call and prepare procedures to cover all likely situations.

Case study

10. The Big Sell Company is part of a large retail marketing group of companies with sales, administration and production functions. Their telephone call costs and equipment charges have recently risen sharply and management have called for measures to reduce the expenditure on telephones. An analysis of the distribution of charges indicates the following: (a) telephone equipment rentals are 35 per cent; (b) telephone call charges are $57\frac{1}{2}$ per cent; and (c) telephone changes and removals are $7\frac{1}{2}$ per cent. Call charges are the highest single cost and the obvious area for savings. By cutting out telephones and simplifying systems considerable rental savings are also possible. Some reductions are also possible by minimising moves and changes. Further scrutiny in these areas reveals the following.

(a) *Telephone equipment rentals.* The company is serviced by a private automatic branch exchange with three operators. There is an extension for every person, a considerable number of additional facilities i.e. Manager/Secretary Plan 107, loud-speaking telephones for executives, auto-dialling aids for sales staff, several secretarial concentrator units, and key and lamp positions for enquiry and sales groups.

(b) *Telephone call charges.* There is heavy morning traffic; every extension has free out-dialling access to the STD network (level "9"); many calls are to company long-distance locations; call durations are excessive; at lunch-time there is a surprisingly heavy amount of traffic; all calls are made by STD. No details exist of who makes the calls, to where or how much each department is costing for the telephone service it uses.

(c) *Telephone changes and removals.* There are frequent moves of personnel and offices requiring both normal and week-end work; British Telecom are often called to move telephones and re-locate the lines; there is an increasing demand by executives and other working groups for more sophisticated facilities which cost considerably more.

(d) *Staff attitude and awareness.* There seems to be little evidence of staff and management being aware of the high costs, of exercising constraint in the excessive use of the telephone. No training or guidance is given to newcomers or the importance of good manners and brevity developed in existing staff.

From these basic facts, list areas and methods whereby reductions in telephone costs can be achieved. (*By courtesy of Brian D. Simmons.*)

Project
11. The Modern Enterprises Co. Ltd. has until now sent all its printing work to an outside printer. The only facilities available in-house are a plain paper copier on each of three floors, available for use by any member of the staff, and an ink duplicator, rarely used. It has been decided to investigate the possibility of establishing an in-house printing department. Current expenditure on printing is some £50,000 per year. The work includes brochures, user instruction leaflets, letters for mailing shots, forms and stationery (letterheads etc.)

You are asked to: (a) decide the equipment and space required to cope with the work; (b) determine the capital cost; (c) estimate running costs (excluding materials).

Bearing in mind the advantages and disadvantages (if any) of in-house printing and taking into consideration your costs decide whether or not you would recommend setting up a printing department.

Group discussions
12. Some companies make their computer facilities available to all departments free of charge. Other companies charge out computer time to the user departments. Working in groups discuss methods of charging for computer time used internally. Co-ordinate the group suggestions and discuss in plenary session the factors involved in deciding whether or not to charge departments for computer time used on their behalf.

13. The Super Manufacturing Co. Ltd. has fully computerised standard systems including sales invoicing, purchasing, stock control, credit control, payroll. Terminals in the stores are on line so that the stock position is right up-to-date. The telephone and telex systems are linked in to the computer systems. There is also a network of word processors at remote locations which are used for up-dating information held in the computer store as well as for production of documents. There is the possibility of a strike by the computer operations staff. Discuss the implications for:

(*a*) the various groups of staff—clerical, managerial, manufacturing operatives; and (*b*) the organisation.

Group project

14. Working in groups of three (or four), prepare a network analysis and determine the critical path for the activities involved in the following assignments.

(*a*) Removal of a department of 100 people from its existing accommodation to new accommodation one mile away. All furniture and equipment has to be moved.

(*b*) Implementation of a board decision to install word processing. A preliminary investigation to establish the need has been carried out. No word processor suppliers have been approached as yet.

(*c*) Implementation of a decision to computerise the payroll.

(*d*) The publication of an organisation's first house journal. The idea has been approved by the Board but no action has yet been taken.

(*e*) The planning and organisation of a conference in the U.K. for 60 senior managers from the company's 14 overseas branches. There are no adequate facilities for such a conference at the head office.

Case study

15. A Computer Services Department has recently installed a new computer and is currently transferring work to it from the existing but more limited computer. As the existing systems need to be adapted for the new machine the opportunity has been taken to review them and incorporate improvements in the information provided. Those systems which have been transferred are not operating without constant amendments to correct faults in the output of information. These faults are found to be caused by poor system design and programming and are in no way related to the new machine. As a result of the problems arising operational schedules are not being maintained with, for example, monthly accounts and costing statistics being 6 weeks overdue. This has serious implications for the accountants and line managers who need accurate and up-to-date information for effective decision-making.

The General Manager, a recent appointment, discusses the situation with the Computer Services Manager and it is decided, subject to agreement with the staff representatives, to adopt the following strategy:

(*a*) in the short term to stop the transfer of any further work from the old to the new computer and to concentrate computer development staff resources on rectifying those systems which have been transferred and to deal with any other problems preventing operational schedules being met; and

(*b*) for the medium/longer term to call in consultants to review the overall operation of the department including the systems development section and the computer operations unit and to make recommendations for improving it.

The staff representatives concur fully with the approach proposed on the understanding that they will have an opportunity to study and comment on the consultants' report. This is agreed.

The consultants' review takes place and in the meantime the short term measures outlined in (a) above achieve only marginal improvements. In due course the consultants' report is received and made available to the staff. The observations of the staff on the report reflect general agreement with the organisational and technical proposals but further comments indicate significant dissatisfaction with the way the Department is being run. This dissatisfaction is expressed in comments set out below.

Explain how the General Manager might tackle the problem of improving the performance of the Computer Services Department following the consultants' report and the observations of the staff.

Staff observations

"There is no sense of urgency if things go wrong."

"It worries me that after only 15 months I find myself engulfed by the apathy that surrounds me."

"If we were reprimanded for important errors rather than petty matters . . . ."

"Management does not keep us informed on the direction of the department as a whole."

"I believe the main cause (of the problems) is the management of the division; to be precise, the management style of the Computer Services Manager."

"Management style, attitude and achievement has been distant, impersonal and infrequently able to portray achievement—this has led to an apathetic, uncaring, lazy style of work—lack of control, lack of purpose, lack of urgency, lack of achievement."

"The reason for failure is not in the organisation structure but in the management of the organisation."

"We do not know what is expected of us."

"Thank goodness I was well trained before I came here but even so I cannot see how my skills are going to be fully utilised."

Appendix II
B.S.I. Standards

Office standards

STATIONERY

B.S. 1808: 1970 (Part 1), 1967 (Part 2) Sizes and recommended layout of commercial forms—letterheads, purchase orders, advice notes, invoices and statements.

B.S. 3203: 1964 Glossary of paper, stationery and allied terms—various classes of paper and board, technical terms.

B.S. 4000: 1968 Sizes of papers and boards.

B.S. 4264: 1976 Envelopes for commercial, official and professional use (terms and sizes).

FILING

B.S. 1467: 1972 Dimensions of folders and films for correspondence filing—folders, letter files, arch files, box files and transfer cases.

B.S. 1749: 1969 Alphabetical arrangement—guide on alphabetical classification.

B.S. 3700: 1976 Preparation of indexes for books, periodicals and other publications, hazards of storage, use of microfilms.

B.S. 1371: 1973 Microfilm, readers and reels—dimensions and features of readers and microfilm; guidance on arrangement of images, sequence of pages, etc.

B.S. 1153: 1975 Recommendations for the storage of microfilm.

MACHINES AND FURNITURE

B.S. 3738: 1964 Specification for dictating machines (all types).

B.S. 2481: 1975 Specifications for typewriters—layout of keyboard for ease of typing.

B.S. 3044: 1958 Anthropometric design of chairs and tables.

B.S. 3079: 1959 Anthropometric design of chairs and tables.

B.S. 3404: 1961 Office chairs for machine operators.

B.S. 3893: 1965 Office desks, tables and seats—includes most of recommendations in previous three B.S.s.

B.S. 3861: 1965 Electrical safety of office machines:
    Part 1: 1965—General requirements and tests for earthed equipment;
    Part 2: 1968—Requirements for machines presenting special hazards;

Part 3: 1970—General requirements and tests for double insulated and all insulated equipment.

B.S. 5459: 1977 Specifications for performance requirements and tests for office furniture:

Part 1—Desks and tables;

Part 2—Adjustable chairs.

DATA PROCESSING

B.S. 4636: 1971 (Part 3), B.S. 4730: 1974 Specification for alpha-numerical punching (cards).

B.S. 3880: 1971 (Part 3), B.S. 4730: 1974 Specification for alpha-numerical punching (tape).

B.S. 3880: 1971 (Part 3) Representation on one-inch punched tape of 6 and 7 bit coded character sets for data interchange.

MISCELLANEOUS

B.S. 3138: 1969 Work study. (1979 revision due.)

B.S. 3723: 1973 Specification for dividend, and interest warrants and related tax vouchers—layout, content, dimensions and requirements.

Documentation standards

B.S. 1000C: 1963 Guide to the Universal Decimal Classification (U.D.C.).

B.S. 1153: 1975 Recommendations for the storage of microfilm.

B.S. 1219: 1958 Recommendations for preparation of *mathematical* copy and correction of mathematical proofs.

B.S. 2489: 1971 Sequence of measurements for printed matter.

B.S. 3700: 1976 Preparation of indexes for books, periodicals and other publications.

B.S. 4187: Microfiche:

(Part 1): 1973—60 frame format;

(Part 2): 1973—98 frame format;

(Part 3): 1978—Formats of 208, 270, 325 and 420 frames (except COM).

B.S. 4191: 1976 Essential characteristics of 35 mm microfilm reading apparatus.

B.S. 4940: 1973 Recommendations for the presentation of technical information about products and services in the construction industry.

B.S. 5261: Copy preparation and proof corrections:

(Part 1): 1975—Recommendations for preparation of typescript copy for printing;

(Part 2): 1976—Specification for typographic requirements, marks for copy; preparation and proof correction, proofing procedure.

NOTE: There are many British and International Standards relating to computers. These are listed in the Sectional List of British Standards SL43 (August 1978).

The above list of British Standards is supplied by permission of the British Standards Institution. Copies of any of the standards are obtainable from their Sales Branch at 101 Pentonville Road, London N1 9ND, telephone 01 837 8801.

Appendix III
Further Reading

Section II Office organisation

Organisation Charts, Mason, IAM
Better Offices, Institute of Directors
Office Design: a study of environment, Manning, Liverpool University Press
Office Landscaping, Duffy and Wankum, Anbar
Open Landscaped Offices, Management Checklist No. 10, BIM
The War on Paper Bureaucracy (Occasional Paper No. 4), Rayner, IAM

Section III Staff management

The clerk in industry, Dale, Liverpool University Press
Clerical job grading and merit rating, IAM
Job evaluation, BIM
Filling a Vacancy, (Management Checklist No. 8), BIM
Selecting Staff, (Management Checklist No. 9), BIM
Office Staff—Selection, Supervision and Training, Pepperell, Industrial
  Society
Secretarial Management—a Guide to the Effective Use of Staff, Shaw,
  Macdonald & Evans
Induction (Management Checklist No. 7), BIM
*Analysis of Standard Clerical and Secretarial Tasks for the Development of
  Occupational Skills and Competence*, International Labour Office
Manpower Planning (Management Checklist No. 6), BIM
Labour Turnover (Management Checklist No. 20), BIM
Personnel Management, Armstrong, Kogan Page
Success in Management: Personnel, Hackett, John Murray
Are you Delegating? (Management Checklist No. 62), BIM
Decision making (Management Checklist No. 19), BIM
Keeping Yourself Up-to-date (Management Checklist No. 17), BIM
The Employee Handbook (Management Checklist No. 25), BIM

Section IV Communications

Effective Communications (Management Checklist No. 76), BIM

Planning a Meeting (Management Checklist No. 13), BIM
Arranging Meetings: Some Practical Questions (Management Checklist No. 40), BIM
Giving a Talk (Management Checklist No. 50), BIM
A Guide to Telephone System Planning (Occasional Paper No. 9) Lawson, IAM
A Guide to Telex (Occasional Paper No. 8), Lawson, IAM
A Guide to the Writing of Business Letters, BACIE
Report writing, Trott, Heinemann
Report writing, BACIE
Report Writing (Management Checklist No. 2), BIM
Hours into Minutes, Perry, BACIE
How to take Minutes, Graham-Helwig, Pitman
Mail handling, RIPA
Using Visual Aids Effectively (Management Checklist No. 61), BIM
House Journals (Management Checklist No. 32), BIM

Section V   Reproduction, storage and retrieval of documents

Filing, Standingford, IAM

Section VI   Data processing

Sales accounting methods, Matley, IAM
Invoicing methods, IAM
Stock control and Storekeeping, BIM
Business Systems, Anderson, Macdonald & Evans
Introduction to Computers, London, Faber and Faber
Errors in Computer Input Data (Occasional Paper No. 3), IAM
Management and Computer Control, Thompson, Gee
The Administrator's Role in Computer Projects (Occasional Paper No. 11), Sterndale-Bennett, IAM

Section VII   Office systems control

Procedure Charts for Administrative Work, IAM
How to cut office costs, Longman, Anbar
Work Study in the Office, Cemach, Maclaren & Sons
Clerical work Measurement, Harmer, HMSO
Work Measurement in Typewriting, Burke and Watts, Pitman
Improving Office Efficiency (Management Checklist No. 26), BIM
The Practice of O & M HMSO
The Design of Forms in Government Departments 3rd Edn, HMSO, 1972
Effective Use of Executive Time (Management Checklist No. 1), BIM
Managing Your Own Time (Guidelines for the Smaller Business No. 13), BIM
The Working Day of a Manager in Local Government (Management Information Sheet No. 53), BIM

Fraud: Internal Security Checklist (Management Checklist No. 67), BIM
Safeguarding the Office (Occasional Paper No. 6), IAM
The Civil Servant as Manager and Administrator (Occasional Paper No. 10),
Allen, IAM

Journals

Administrative Management (monthly). The Institute of Administrative
Management, 205 High Street, Beckenham, Kent BR3 1BA
Business Equipment Digest (monthly). Bridge House, Restmor Way,
Wallington, Surrey SM6 7BZ
Datarama (bi-monthly). International Computers Limited,
International Division Headquarters,
Bridge House South, Putney Bridge,
London SW6 3JX
Industrial and Commercial Training (monthly). Wellens Publishing,
Guilsborough, Northampton NN6 8PY
Management Today (monthly). Haymarket Publishing Limited,
Craven House, 34 Foubert's Place,
London W1
Office Equipment INDEX (monthly). Maclaren Publishers Limited,
P.O. Box 109, Croydon CR9 1QH
Office Skills (monthly). Pitman Publications Limited,
41 Parker Street, Kingsway,
London WC2B 5PB
Personnel Management (monthly). Business Publications Limited,
109–119 Waterloo Road,
London SE1 8UL
The Director (monthly). Institute of Directors,
116 Pall Mall, London SW1Y 5ED

Index

199, 556
lateness (unpunctuality), 124, 154, 163
misconduct, 150, 153, 154
procedures, 113
time-keeping, 162, 177
Discounted cash flow, 465
Discussion, 94, 171, 181, 184, 197, 198,
199, 203, 226, 248, 489
Dismissal, 120, 149-54
compensation, 151, 152
grounds for, 150-1
instant, 149, 153, 161
medical grounds, 153-4
procedures, 154
unfair, 151-2
warning, 120, 154
Disputes, 164
Document reader, 448
Drafting 279
Drill,
Drinking water, 58
Duplicating
advantages, disadvantages, 351, 352-5
addressing, 368-72
collating unit, 349
colour reproduction, 343, 344, 346,
351
costs, 349, 351
electronic scanner, 344, 346
line selection, 343-4, 495, 523
masking, 343-4, 495
masters, 342, 344, 345, 346, 350, 351,
352-5, 361, 362, 369, 400
offset, 348-9, 354
operator, 345, 348
paper, 341, 342, 344
running off, 342, 345, 531, 564
spirit, 343-4, 352, 361, 421, 497, 523
stencil/ink, 344-6, 348, 352, 497
uses, 352-5
Duties, 8, 9, 15, 18, 20, 31, 78, 79, 80,
81, 82, 99, 107, 541
Dvorak keyboard, 322

Edge/marginally punched card, 435-6
Education, 90, 97, 100, 101, 106, 130,
169
Electronic
mailing, 468, 475
machines, 3, 439, 440, 441
scanner, 344, 346
writing pad, 450
Emergency alerting systems, 552
Employee shareholdings, 169
Employment

bureau, 102
law, 308
Employment Agencies Act 1973, 102
Employment and Training Act 1973, 133
Employment Appeal Tribunal, 152
Employment Protection Act 1975, 57,
114, 149, 150, 152, 154
Employment Protection (Consolidation)
Act 1978, 113, 149, 153, 425, 426
Employers' associations, 188
Envelopes, 262, 270, 283, 335, 491, 501,
530, 531, 533
aperture, 262
sizes, 533
window, 262, 494
Environment, 7, 12, 57, 69, 75, 172,
197, 204, 482
Equipment (see also Machines), 7, 8, 9,
44, 51, 53, 54, 65, 73, 77, 114, 165,
187, 194, 423, 477, 487, 491, 507,
513, 527, 548, 564
control, 538
faults, 564
maintenance, 194, 363, 473, 564
Ergonomics, 52
Errors, clerical 514
Error tolerance, 515
Examinations
internal, 131
professional, 130
public, 108
Exception principle, 481
Experience, 17, 24, 90, 97, 100, 101,
103, 106, 108, 129, 130, 141, 490. 515
Export documents, 495, 496

Facsimile transmission, 468, 475
Factories Acts, 57, 114
Factory inspectors, 59
Fatigue, 52, 56, 57, 59, 89, 156, 329,
334, 515, 519
Feature cards, 437-8
Fidelity guarantee, 546
File, 54, 65, 194, 382, 386, 389, 514, 547
binders, 400, 402,
box, 400, 402, 404
concertina, 402-3
folders, 401-3
lever arch, 400, 402
loose-leaf, 525
movements, 381, 382, 388
reference, 282, 493, 500
transfer, 405
Filing, 51, 86, 380, 481, 489, 493, 494,
495, 496, 497, 498, 505, 507